TABLE II Present Value Interest Factors, PVIF, Discounted at k Percent for n Periods:

$$PVIF_{k,n} = \frac{1}{(1+k)^n}$$

Discount Rate, k

Number of Periods, n	0%	1%	2%	3%	4%	5%	6%	7%	8%	9%	10%	12%	14%	16%	18%	20%	25%	30%	35%	40%	45%	50%
0	1.0000	1.0000	1.0000	1.0000	1.0000	1.0000	1.0000	1.0000	1.0000	1.0000	1.0000	1.0000	1.0000	1.0000	1.0000	1.0000	1.0000	1.0000	1.0000	1.0000	1.0000	1.0000
1	1.0000	0.9901	0.9804	0.9709	0.9615	0.9524	0.9434	0.9346	0.9259	0.9174	0.9091	0.8929	0.8772	0.8621	0.8475	0.8333	0.8000	0.7692	0.7407	0.7143	0.6897	0.6667
2	1.0000	0.9803	0.9612	0.9426	0.9246	0.9070	0.8900	0.8734	0.8573	0.8417	0.8264	0.7972	0.7695	0.7432	0.7182	0.6944	0.6400	0.5917	0.5487	0.5102	0.4756	0.4444
3	1.0000	0.9706	0.9423	0.9151	0.8890	0.8638	0.8396	0.8163	0.7938	0.7722	0.7513	0.7118	0.6750	0.6407	0.6086	0.5787	0.5120	0.4552	0.4064	0.3644	0.3280	0.2963
4	1.0000	0.9610	0.9238	0.8885	0.8548	0.8227	0.7921	0.7629	0.7350	0.7084	0.6830	0.6355	0.5921	0.5523	0.5158	0.4823	0.4096	0.3501	0.3011	0.2603	0.2262	0.1975
5	1.0000	0.9515	0.9057	0.8626	0.8219	0.7835	0.7473	0.7130	0.6806	0.6499	0.6209	0.5674	0.5194	0.4761	0.4371	0.4019	0.3277	0.2693	0.2230	0.1859	0.1560	0.1317
6	1.0000	0.9420	0.8880	0.8375	0.7903	0.7462	0.7050	0.6663	0.6302	0.5963	0.5645	0.5066	0.4556	0.4104	0.3704	0.3349	0.2621	0.2072	0.1652	0.1328	0.1076	0.0878
7	1.0000	0.9327	0.8706	0.8131	0.7599	0.7107	0.6651	0.6227	0.5835	0.5470	0.5132	0.4523	0.3996	0.3538	0.3139	0.2791	0.2097	0.1594	0.1224	0.0949	0.0742	0.0585
8	1.0000	0.9235	0.8535	0.7894	0.7307	0.6768	0.6274	0.5820	0.5403	0.5019	0.4665	0.4039	0.3506	0.3050	0.2660	0.2326	0.1678	0.1226	0.0906	0.0678	0.0512	0.0390
9	1.0000	0.9143	0.8368	0.7664	0.7026	0.6446	0.5919	0.5439	0.5002	0.4604	0.4241	0.3606	0.3075	0.2630	0.2255	0.1938	0.1342	0.0943	0.0671	0.0484	0.0353	0.0260
10	1.0000	0.9053	0.8203	0.7441	0.6756	0.6139	0.5584	0.5083	0.4632	0.4224	0.3855	0.3220	0.2697	0.2267	0.1911	0.1615	0.1074	0.0725	0.0497	0.0346	0.0243	0.0173
11	1.0000	0.8963	0.8043	0.7224	0.6496	0.5847	0.5268	0.4751	0.4289	0.3875	0.3505	0.2875	0.2366	0.1954	0.1619	0.1346	0.0859	0.0558	0.0368	0.0247	0.0168	0.0116
12	1.0000	0.8874	0.7885	0.7014	0.6246	0.5568	0.4970	0.4440	0.3971	0.3555	0.3186	0.2567	0.2076	0.1685	0.1372	0.1122	0.0687	0.0429	0.0273	0.0176	0.0116	0.0077
13	1.0000	0.8787	0.7730	0.6810	0.6006	0.5303	0.4688	0.4150	0.3677	0.3262	0.2897	0.2292	0.1821	0.1452	0.1163	0.0935	0.0550	0.0330	0.0202	0.0126	0.0080	0.0051
14	1.0000	0.8700	0.7579	0.6611	0.5775	0.5051	0.4423	0.3878	0.3405	0.2992	0.2633	0.2046	0.1597	0.1252	0.0985	0.0779	0.0440	0.0254	0.0150	0.0090	0.0055	0.0034
15	1.0000	0.8613	0.7430	0.6419	0.5553	0.4810	0.4173	0.3624	0.3152	0.2745	0.2394	0.1827	0.1401	0.1079	0.0835	0.0649	0.0352	0.0195	0.0111	0.0064	0.0038	0.0023
16	1.0000	0.8528	0.7284	0.6232	0.5339	0.4581	0.3936	0.3387	0.2919	0.2519	0.2176	0.1631	0.1229	0.0930	0.0708	0.0541	0.0281	0.0150	0.0082	0.0046	0.0026	
17	1.0000	0.8444	0.7142	0.6050	0.5134	0.4363	0.3714	0.3166	0.2703	0.2311	0.1978	0.1456	0.1078	0.0802	0.0600	0.0451	0.0225	0.0116	0.0061	0.0033	0.0018	
18	1.0000	0.8360	0.7002	0.5874	0.4936	0.4155	0.3503	0.2959	0.2502	0.2120	0.1799	0.1300	0.0946	0.0691	0.0508	0.0376	0.0180	0.0089	0.0045	0.0023	0.0011	
19	1.0000	0.8277	0.6864	0.5703	0.4746	0.3957	0.3305	0.2765	0.2317	0.1945	0.1635	0.1161	0.0829	0.0596	0.0431	0.0313	0.0144	0.0068	0.0033	0.0017	0.00	
20	1.0000	0.8195	0.6730	0.5537	0.4564	0.3769	0.3118	0.2584	0.2145	0.1784	0.1486	0.1037	0.0728	0.0514	0.0365	0.0261	0.0115	0.0053	0.0025	0.0012	0.00	
25	1.0000	0.7798	0.6095	0.4776	0.3751	0.2953	0.2330	0.1842	0.1460	0.1160	0.0923	0.0588	0.0378	0.0245	0.0160	0.0105	0.0038	0.0014	0.0006	0.0002		0.0000
30	1.0000	0.7419	0.5521	0.4120	0.3083	0.2314	0.1741	0.1314	0.0994	0.0754	0.0573	0.0334	0.0196	0.0116	0.0070	0.0042	0.0012	0.0004	0.0001	0.0000		0.0000
35	1.0000	0.7059	0.5000	0.3554	0.2534	0.1813	0.1301	0.0937	0.0676	0.0490	0.0356	0.0189	0.0102	0.0055	0.0030	0.0017	0.0004	0.0001	0.0000	0.0000		0.0000
40	1.0000	0.6717	0.4529	0.3066	0.2083	0.1420	0.0972	0.0668	0.0460	0.0318	0.0221	0.0107	0.0053	0.0026	0.0013	0.0007	0.0001	0.0000	0.0000	0.0000		0.0000
45	1.0000	0.6391	0.4102	0.2644	0.1712	0.1113	0.0727	0.0476	0.0313	0.0207	0.0137	0.0061	0.0027	0.0013	0.0006	0.0003	0.0000	0.0000	0.0000	0.0000		0.0000
50	1.0000	0.6080	0.3715	0.2281	0.1407	0.0872	0.0543	0.0339	0.0213	0.0134	0.0085	0.0035	0.0014	0.0006	0.0003	0.0001	0.0000	0.0000	0.0000	0.0000		0.0000

TEXAS INSTRUMENTS

BAII PLUS Rebate Terms and Conditions

This offer is valid only for BAII PLUS purchases between December 1, 1996 and October 31, 1998. All claims must be postmarked by November 15, 1998. Allow 8 to 10 weeks for processing. All purchases must be made in the U.S. or Canada. Rebates will be sent only to addresses in the U.S. and Canada and paid in U.S. dollars. Not redeemable at any store. Send this completed form along with the cash register receipt (original or copy) and the UPC bar code to the address indicated. This original mail-in certificate must accompany your request and may not be duplicated or reproduced. Offer valid only as stated on this form. Offer void where prohibited, taxed, licensed, or restricted. Limit one rebate per household or address. Texas Instruments reserves the right to discontinue this program at any time and without notice.

IH151996

Yes! I Want $5 Back On My Purchase of the BAII PLUS.

FINANCIAL
MANAGEMENT

PRINCIPLES
AND
PRACTICE

FINANCIAL MANAGEMENT

PRINCIPLES AND PRACTICE

TIMOTHY J. GALLAGHER
PROFESSOR OF FINANCE, COLORADO STATE UNIVERSITY

JOSEPH D. ANDREW, JR.
CHIEF FINANCIAL OFFICER, X-CHANGE SOFTWARE, INC.

Prentice Hall
Upper Saddle River, New Jersey 07458

Acquisitions Editor: Paul Donnelly
Development Editor: Charlotte R. Morrissey
Assistant Editor: Gladys Soto
Editorial Assistant: MaryBeth Sanok
Editor-in-Chief: James Boyd
Director of Development: Stephen Deitmer
Marketing Manager: Sandra Steiner
Managing Editor, Production: Carol Burgett
Production Coordinator: Renee Pelletier
Manufacturing Supervisor: Arnold Vila
Manufacturing Manager: Vincent Scelta
Senior Designer: Ann France
Design Director: Patricia Wosczyk
Interior Design and Illustrations: A Good Thing, Inc.
Cover Design: Lorraine Castellano
Cover Art/Photo: John Lund/Tony Stone Images
Composition: Clarinda Prepress Services
Project Management: Shepherd, Inc.

©1997 by Prentice-Hall, Inc.
A Simon & Schuster Company
Upper Saddle River, New Jersey 07458

Library of Congress Cataloging–in–Publication Data
Gallagher, Timothy James
    Financial management : principles and practice / Timothy J. Gallagher, Joseph D. Andrew, Jr.
        p.   cm.
    Includes bibliographical references and index.
    ISBN 0–02–340271–7
    1. Corporations—Finance.   I. Andrew, Joseph D.   II. Title.
HG4026.G348   1996
658.15—dc20   96–34125
                                                                        CIP

Prentice-Hall International (UK) Limited, London
Prentice-Hall of Australia Pty. Limited, Sydney
Prentice-Hall Canada, Inc., Toronto
Prentice-Hall Hispanoamericana, S.A., Mexico
Prentice-Hall of India Private Limited, New Delhi
Prentice-Hall of Japan, Inc., Tokyo
Simon & Schuster Asia Pte. Ltd., Singapore
Editora Prentice-Hall do Brasil, Ltda., Rio de Janeiro

Printed in the United States of America

10   9   8   7   6   5   4   3   2

Photo Credits

Page 1:	Bob Daemmrich/The Image Works
Page 9:	Courtesy of Melanie Rosen
Page 18:	Courtesy of Shiva Corporation
Page 38:	Courtesy of First Union Bank of Florida
Page 57:	Sandra Baker/Gamma-Liaison, Inc.
Page 79:	Chris Corsmeier Photography
Page 94:	Courtesy of Lee Anne Schuster
Page 111:	Peter Hirth/Sovfoto/Eastfoto
Page 136:	Courtesy of Ford Motor Company
Page 167:	Shonna Valeska
Page 203:	Jeffery Titcomb/Gamma-Liaison, Inc.
Page 230:	Courtesy of NASA Headquarters
Page 246:	Courtesy of Jim Bruner
Page 268:	Courtesy of Cragar Industries, Inc.
Page 288:	Focus on Sports
Page 300:	Courtesy of Fred Higgins
Page 316:	M. Antman/The Image Works
Page 343:	Dick Frank/The Stock Market
Page 367:	SuperStock, Inc.
Page 369:	Frank LaBua/Simon & Schuster/PH College
Page 371:	Courtesy of Chris Heller
Page 391:	Teri Stratford
Page 410:	H. Dratch/The Image Works
Page 420:	Courtesy of Michael Coleman
Page 428:	Richard Pasley/Stock Boston
Page 433:	Courtesy of Karen Noble
Page 451:	Courtesy of Philip R. Theibert
Page 472:	Courtesy of Joann Jones
Page 482:	Roy Morsch/The Stock Market
Page 503:	Robert Dyer
Page 515:	Courtesy of Don Burton

To Susan and Em
—*T.J.G.*

To Emily
—*J.D.A.*

Brief Contents

Contents

PART TWO
ESSENTIAL CONCEPTS IN FINANCE

Chapter 4: Review of Accounting   57

Chapter 5: Analysis of Financial Statements   79

Chapter 6: Forecasting for Financial Planning   111

Chapter 7: Risk and Return   136

Chapter 8: The Time Value of Money   167

Chapter 9: Bond and Stock Valuation   203

PART THREE
LONG-TERM FINANCIAL MANAGEMENT DECISIONS

Chapter 10: Capital Budgeting Decision Methods   230

Chapter 11: Estimating Incremental Cash Flows   268

Chapter 12: The Cost of Capital   288

Preface

The Challenge

Finance professors often start the first day of class behind the eight ball. Many students sign up for a class in financial management because they must, not because they want to. Or, students sign up because they believe the course will teach them all they need to know to succeed on Wall Street. Once students learn the course focus is managing a firm's finances, their attention wanes.

How do we convince students that the concepts and tools they will learn in corporate finance are key to their business success? Each professor, we suspect, has a different strategy to grab students' attention so that the learning can begin. No matter what your strategy, we know that our text will bolster your efforts. How? We help students make the most of their time, and we make finance fun, real, and relevant to their lives.

Helping You Meet the Needs of Today's Finance Students

This book is intended for business students, and many other majors required to take this course. What a broad audience that is! Today's students are a patchwork of all ages, sexes, and cultural backgrounds. Perhaps more importantly, unlike the days when most students attended college full-time and held no jobs, most students now juggle much more than their bookbags. They have jobs, families, and other concerns that compete for their attention.

Helping Students Make Better Use of Their Time

No book can give students more time. However, our text helps them make better use of their time. We know that students have neither the time nor inclination to sort through pages of detail that seem irrelevant to their careers. First, with the help of countless students and reviewers, we streamlined our text to focus on only essential topics in finance, rather than special topics that are rarely covered in this first finance course. Second, our comprehensive learning system helps students master the material more quickly. We present chapter objectives that are directly linked to the chapter summary and to the end-of-chapter problems. We also include student tips in the margin that offer ideas for learning, additional clarification, or links to related topics.

Helping Students Have More Fun Learning

We know that finance can be fun. In *Financial Management: Principles and Practice,* we cover the basics of business financial management in a clear, conversational tone that engages students. We also use vivid, real-life examples. These range from high-profile examples, such as Magic Johnson's venture with Sony to bring a movie theater to southern Los Angeles, to inspirational examples of lesser-known businesses, such as Thunder Sports, Inc., a business formed by two University of Nebraska students to bring indoor soccer to fans. The purpose of the examples is twofold: to heighten interest and to show students how to apply the concepts so they can, in turn, use them outside the classroom walls.

To add even more fun, we use movie character names in many end-of-chapter problems and some in-text examples that students may enjoy trying to identify. We also rely on cartoons to add humor and (sometimes) to make a financial point.

Helping Students Become Business Leaders

Business students want to learn skills that they will use in the workplace. What are those skills and how can this text help students develop them? The **American Assembly of Collegiate Schools of Business (AACSB)** surveyed employers nationwide about the competencies business students should have to succeed in the world of work. We list four of the most highly rated competencies next and show you how our text helps students develop these skills.

- *Analytic Thinking* and *Judgment:* Fifteen chapters in our text require students to use analytic skills and judgment. Beginning with chapter 4, "Analyzing Financial Statements," students learn how to analyze financial statements critically so that they can read and understand the basic "report cards" of business. They then move to forecasting, risk and return, the time value of money, valuation, capital budgeting techniques, estimating cash flows, and short-term budgeting techniques. For every concept, we provide an application to show students how to use analytic tools in the workplace. End-of-chapter problems also reinforce and test students' judgment. For instance, we include challenge problems that disguise the subject of the problem, so students must decide what concept to apply to find the answer. In addition, we have complex comprehensive problems that require students to ferret out relevant information to problem solve and to apply more than one concept. Finally, our boxed features pose questions that often do not have a "right" or "wrong" answer.
- *Achievement Drive:* We recognize that we can't teach students to achieve. However, we can give students opportunities to excel and apply their knowledge in many ways. We provide research tools and communication activities that not only help students master content, they teach students how to learn continuously. At the end of every chapter we offer two Build Your Communication Skills exercises that require students to conduct library research, interview community leaders, debate issues with their peers, or make a classroom presentation. Also, we offer a free Prentice Hall *New York Times* Dodger, a collection of recent news articles on finance. The Dodger encourages students to read the newspaper to educate themselves about the role of finance around the globe. Finally, we offer PHLIP, an Internet access site that students and professors may visit to gather financial information. These tools teach students how to gather information to build new knowledge and skills.
- *Integrity:* This book integrates social and professional responsibility topics in the chapter text and in boxed features in an approachable way. For instance, in chapter 4, we present a box on the ethics of movie studios using "net profits" to compensate the authors whose books provide the basis for mega-hit movies. Our aim is to expose students to the main ethical issues in finance so they will be better prepared to make ethical business decisions.
- *Teamwork Skills:* Our text is the only finance text to offer exercises that promote teamwork and networking skills. Over half of the Build Your Communication Skills exercises at the end of each chapter focus on teams or networking.

Quality Guarantee

One of the greatest hurdles a first-edition finance text faces is the concern that the text will have errors that a tried-and-true text may not. To meet this concern head-on, hundreds of students across the nation tested the text at every stage of manuscript development. The class tests not only helped to eliminate quantitative errors, they helped us shape the text into one that reached a broader audience. We are proud to report that the reaction to the final version from students and faculty has been overwhelmingly positive.

But we didn't stop in the classroom. Aside from the many talented reviewers of the text, we had four additional quality checks. Vickie Bajtelsmit and Susan Singer reviewed the text material, figures, charts, in-text examples, and problem materials for technical accuracy. We also had Sibnath Mitra and Sue Hine check and recheck the problems and solutions to all in-text examples and end-of-chapter problems. Many thanks to our quality checkers for their painstaking efforts.

Our Approach

First, we take a valuation, rather than a balance-sheet approach. That is, market values are emphasized over book values wherever possible. We stress marginal analysis, cashflows, and the creation of value. The risk and return coverage focuses on creating value for the firm's owners, subject to legal, regulatory, and ethical constraints.

Second, we balance financial theory with skill development. More specifically, we show students how to use theory to solve real-world problems. The end result? Students will learn not only *how* to solve a financial problem, but *why* the solution works.

Third, the focus of the text is not exclusively on large corporations. Most students plan to work for small-to-medium sized businesses, so we balance examples of small, medium, and large businesses throughout the book. We also selected many entrepreneurial examples to make the financial principles presented seem more useful to the students taking this course.

Fourth, we supplement the financial management material with essential background information on financial markets and institutions. This coverage helps students better understand the environment in which a firm operates so that they can become more effective financial decision makers.

Streamlined Coverage

We know time is a precious commodity, so we offer 21 chapters instead of the more typical 25. The annotated table of contents that follows provides a quick glance at the main themes of each chapter.

ANNOTATED TABLE OF CONTENTS

Chapter 11. Estimating Incremental Cash Flows	Through the chapter explanation and examples, students learn which cash flows are relevant to a capital budgeting project and how to estimate those cash flows.
Chapter 12. The Cost of Capital	Here, we investigate the cost of different types of capital, how to estimate a firm's cost of capital, and how those costs affect a firm's financing and investment decisions.
Chapter 13. Capital Structure Basics	This chapter examines the effects of capital structure on a firm's value. Specifically, it presents the concepts of leverage and the associated risks with each type of leverage. It also covers the risks and return possibilities of a leveraged buyout.
Chapter 14. Corporate Bonds, Preferred Stock, and Leasing	We discuss the features and uses of corporate bonds, preferred stock, and leases. We also compare and contrast a genuine lease and a disguised purchase contract, examine the accounting treatment of leases, and explore the lease-or-buy decision.
Chapter 15. Common Stock	We explain common stock basics and look at why firms may or may not want to use equity financing. We also describe how firms issue common stock and describe the risk and return features of rights and warrants.
Chapter 16. Dividend Policy	Students learn in this chapter the how and why of a firm's dividend policy, how a firm pays dividends, and alternatives to paying cash dividends.

Part 4—Short-Term Financial Management Decisions—presents the concepts of working capital policy, cash and marketable securities, accounts receivable and inventory, and short-term financing.

Chapter 17. Working Capital Policy	This chapter examines the importance of managing a firm's current assets, how firms manage their working capital, why they accumulate it, and how they determine their working capital policies.
Chapter 18. Managing Cash	Presented here are the factors that affect the level of a firm's cash assets, how to target an optimal cash balance, how to prepare a cash budget, and how to manage cash flows to maximize value.
Chapter 19. Accounts Receivable and Inventory	In this chapter students will learn what accounts receivable and inventory are and methods for managing them and for determining their optimal level. We show students how to take a value-added approach to accounts receivable and inventory management. We also cover alternative inventory management approaches, and show how firms make credit decisions and create collection policies.
Chapter 20. Short-Term Financing	Here, we look at the advantages and disadvantages of short-term financing, sources of that financing, and methods for calculating the cost of each source. We also investigate loan terms and sources of short-term loan collateral.

Part 5—Finance in the Global Economy—covers international finance topics, in addition to the international coverage woven throughout the book.

| **Chapter 21. International Finance** | This chapter presents the global environment in which firms operate and explains the basics of international finance, such as exchange rate risks and theories, and major international trade agreements. |

Book Features

Our text contains innovative features that will help you meet AACSB objectives and help students prepare for their careers. We offer *real world opening vignettes, performance-based learning objectives, chapter summaries that link directly to the objectives, self-test questions with fully worked-out solutions, review questions,* and *student-tested problem material.* In addition, we have the following features that set us apart from other texts:

- **Take Note** features, located in the margins of the text pages, are student annotations. No other book has these helpful notes. They contain learning tips, offer additional examples, or show how the material links to business practice.
- **Concept Connections** are cross-references to related topics. This simple but innovative feature, placed in the text margins, identifies the page and chapter number for topics related to the one being discussed. Students who use the cross-references not only reinforce their understanding with a topic review, they will see connections between concepts more effectively.
- **Ethical Connections boxes** highlight an actual ethical dilemma that relates to the chapter concepts. Closing questions challenge students to think critically about the issue. The boxes, in addition to the in-text ethics coverage, comply with the AACSB requirement of ethics integration.
- **Financial Management and You boxes** take financial management concepts and show students how to apply them to personal finance decisions. Unique to our text, these features make the concepts more relevant to students— especially to those students who expected an investments course.
- **Finance At Work** interview boxes are in direct response to an AACSB standard that urges schools to teach students how each functional area relates to other areas of business. This innovative feature shows how finance affects decision makers in other business areas, such as management, marketing, and production.
- **Financial Calculator Solutions** to all general time value of money and specific security valuation problems are included. This material is presented with the TIBAII+ calculator in mind, but a conversion card allows students to use a variety of financial calculators with clear instruction.
- **Build Your Communication Skills,** another feature unique to our text, are two end-of-chapter exercises designed to build a student's written and oral communication skills. Many of the exercises involve teamwork or networking, two skills employees need to succeed in the 21st century.
- **Challenge Problems** and **Comprehensive Problems:** Like many texts, we identify the subject of all non-comprehensive problems. However, we are the only text to include one *challenge problem* per chapter that does not have an identifier, so that students develop issue-spotting skills. The *comprehensive problems* build on earlier concepts and often include irrelevant information so that students must select and use relevant information to problem solve. This type of problem better replicates what students will face on the job.

Instructor and Student Resources

As with our text, we tried to offer the most useful, relevant, and interesting support package on the market. The following list describes key support materials for both professors and students.

Instructor Resources

1. The **Instructor's Resource Manual** contains over 400 pages of course preparation materials. This handy lecture tool provides chapter reviews, an in-depth analysis of critical chapter concepts and objectives, lecture outlines, lecture tips and suggestions, in-class examples, discussion starters, and additional problem material.

2. A **Computerized Test Item File** based on powerful testing technology developed by Engineering Software Associates, Inc., gives instructors the ability to create and tailor exams to their own needs, administer them traditionally or online, then automatically transfer the data for evaluation. The program, available in Windows or DOS, uses *algorithmic technologies* so that an infinite number of select test items can be generated. The test bank includes multiple choice, problem, and essay questions.

3. The **Problems/Solutions Manual** contains worked-out solutions to all problems contained in the text.

4. **Spreadsheet Software** containing problem-solving templates is available for instructors and students on disk or through the Internet.

5. The **Transparency Acetates** and **PowerPoint Slides** are for classroom presentation of text material and teaching visual aids. We offer a package of over 150 color acetates of art from the text and over 800 PowerPoint full-color electronic presentation screens.

6. **Internet Faculty Support through the PHLIP** (Prentice Hall's Learning through the Internet Partnership—*http://www.finance.fac.marist.edu/phlip*) allows adopting faculty to sign in with their *user name* and *password* and download lecture aids, including lecture notes, PowerPoint presentations, problem and case solutions, and chapter outlines and updates. Services such as "PHLIPping through the News" tie current events and news stories directly to text chapters and pages to enhance currency of faculty lectures.

Source: CALVIN AND HOBBES © 1992, 1993 Watterson. Dist. by UNIVERSAL PRESS SYNDICATE. Reprinted with permission. All rights reserved.

Student Resources

1. Our **Study Guide** is designed to reinforce concepts and skills and to aid understanding and application. This resource contains chapter summaries and outlines, helpful hints, study tips, self-tests, and practice problems (with solutions) requiring both mathematical and verbal ability.

2. **FinCoach Software** (The Financial Management Math Practice Program, Version B) includes over 7 million practice problems and self-tests in mathematical areas of corporate financial management, from valuation of single cash flows to CAPM and firm valuation.

3. **Career Paths in Finance,** the ultimate job-search tool, teaches students how to position themselves competitively in the field of finance. Instead of wasting valuable time scouring the library for multiple references, students find all key information pulled together on one hybrid CD-ROM (ISBN: 0-13-531336-8).

4. **PHLIP** (Prentice Hall's Learning through the Internet Partnership–http://www.finance.fac.marist.edu/phlip) gives students access to news stories and to additional finance resources, academic and government resources, search engines and indexes. Students may also download from this site spreadsheet files for use with problems in the text identified with a computer logo.

Acknowledgments

The authors gratefully acknowledge the help of the following assistants, editors, reviewers, colleagues, students, friends, relatives, and others without whom the production of this book would not have been possible. First, we would like to thank the folks at Prentice Hall who worked so hard on this book: Paul Donnelly, Senior Acquisitions Editor; Jim Boyd, Editor in Chief, Business; Charlotte Morrissey, Senior Development Editor; Steve Deitmer, Editor in Chief, Development; Carol Burgett, Managing Editor; Patricia Wosczyk, Design Director; Sandy Steiner, Marketing Director; Patti Arneson and Susan McLaughlin, Marketing Managers; Teresa Cohan and Gladys Soto, Assistant Editors; and MaryBeth Sanok, Editorial Assistant. We would also like to thank Jill Leckta and Roz Sackoff at Macmillan, who were there for us at the project's inception.

For those colleagues who listened, reviewed, and offered hours of input, special thanks go to Heather Addison, Dianne Furr, Hank Leaper, Dana Perry, Steve Quentmeyer, Gayle Reising, Jim Schubert, Bradley-Alison Smith, Phil Theibert, and David Vermillion.

For those whose hard work and vision helped create the support package, our warmest kudos go to Joe Brocato, Vickie Bajtelsmit, Dan Cooper, Lise Graham, and Sue Hine.

A special thanks to Sibnath Mitra who worked tirelessly on many aspects of the book, including computer software development, end-of-chapter problem assistance, and manuscript review. His industry experience, as an engineer and financial manager holding an MBA-Finance degree, proved very beneficial to this project.

For the academics and professionals who offered their invaluable feedback, we thank all of you. In particular, we would like to thank:

Stephen L. Avard, East Texas State University

Joseph M. Brocato, Tarleton State University

Robert E. Chatfield, University of Nevada, Las Vegas

Louis T. W. Cheng, Murray State University

Anthony A. Cioffi, Lorain County Community College

Anand S. Desai, Kansas State University

Dean Drenk, Montana State University

David R. Durst, University of Akron

Donald R. Escarraz, University of North Dakota

James Frew, Willamette University

Alan E. Grunewald, Michigan State University

Delvin D. Hawley, University of Mississippi

Thomas K. Y. Kam, Hawaii Pacific University

Robert T. Kleiman, Oakland University

Claudia S. Kocher, University of Michigan - Dearborn

Iqbal A. Memon, Fort Lewis College

Dianne R. Morrison, University of Wisconsin - LaCrosse

Richard M. Osborne, American University

Charles R. Rayhorn, Northern Michigan University

Rajiv Sant, Mankato State University

Atul K. Saxena, Mercer University - Macon

D. Sue Singer, Western Maryland College

Timothy R. Smaby, Pennsylvania State University - Erie

Srinivasan Sundaram, Ball State University

Amir Tavakkol, Kansas State University

Oscar Varela, University of New Orleans

Joe Walker, University of Alabama - Birmingham

Allen L. Webster, Bradley University

Mike M. Williams, Bethune-Cookman College

Steve B. Wyatt, University of Cincinnati

Timothy J. Gallagher

Joseph D. Andrew, Jr.

About the Authors

Timothy J. Gallagher is professor of finance at Colorado State University. Tim received his Ph.D. in finance in 1978 from the University of Illinois at Urbana - Champaign.

Professor Gallagher has taught undergraduate and graduate finance courses for twenty years, including courses in financial management, markets and institutions, and investments. He has taught traditional and nontraditional students at all levels, including executive MBAs, and in all types of classroom settings—large lecture, small seminar, and distance learning.

Tim has published in journals such as *The Journal of Money, Credit, and Banking; The Journal of Portfolio Management; Financial Management;* and *The Financial Review;* among others.

Joseph D. Andrew, Jr. is the chief financial officer of X-Change Software, Inc., a software development company in Oakton, Virginia. As CFO he has management responsibility for corporate investment policy, cash flow planning, purchasing, forecasting and analysis, and external financing.

In addition to his CFO responsibilities, Joe teaches finance for Webster University of St. Louis, Missouri, dividing his time between the university's Washington, D.C., campus and its international campus in Hamilton, Bermuda. Joe's past experience includes teaching for National-Louis University in McLean, Virginia; Webster University, the University of Southern Colorado, and Chapman University in Colorado Springs; and McMurry College in Abilene, Texas. Joe also served 23 years as a Missile Maintenance Specialist in the U.S. Air Force, retiring at the rank of Chief Master Sergeant in 1982.

Tim and Joe's partnership in this book's creation represents a unique opportunity for readers to experience the best of both worlds—Tim's development of the theory and logic of financial principles and Joe's real-world financial orientation. Their combined experience with students ensures that readers will learn theory and practice in an innovative, up-to-date, accurate manner.

FINANCIAL MANAGEMENT

PRINCIPLES
AND
PRACTICE

chapter 1

Finance and the Firm

The race is not always to the swift, nor the battle to the strong, but that is the way to bet.

Rudyard Kipling

Finance Grabs the Business Headlines

Headlines from the front page of some recent *Wall Street Journal* editions:

- First Interstate agreed to merge with First Bank System in a pact valued at $9.8 billion . . .
- Lucent posted strong quarterly revenue growth . . .
- Several major Mexican companies may join the government to form a $5 billion fund in an effort to support the peso . . .
- Time Warner struck a deal with the FTC that would let it buy Turner for $6.7 billion . . .
- Major League Baseball negotiated a strong TV package

expected to bring the league $1.7 billion over five years . . .

What do all these stories have in common? They deal with finance. Companies buying other companies, companies selling other companies, governments propping up their currencies, sports leagues negotiating contracts—these are just a sampling of business stories involving finance that appear every day in the press.

The amount of money involved in business financial issues is staggering. In our one-day sample, nearly $20 billion changed hands. Imagine the amount of money that flows through businesses and governments around the world in a year!

Finance is at the heart of business management. No business firm—or government, for that matter—can exist for long without following at least the basic principles of financial management.

This book is designed to introduce you to basic financial management principles and skills. Some of these concepts and skills are surprisingly straightforward; others are quite challenging. All, however, will help you in the business world, no matter what career you choose. ❊

Chapter Overview

In this chapter we will introduce financial management basics that provide a foundation for the rest of the course. First, we will describe the field of finance and examine the role of financial management within a business organization. Then we will investigate the financial goal of a business firm, and the legal and ethical challenges financial managers face. We will end with a description of the three forms of business in the U.S. economy: sole proprietorship, partnership, and corporation.

The Field of Finance

In business, financial guidelines determine how money is raised and spent. Although raising and spending money may sound simple, financial decisions affect every aspect of a business—from how many people a manager can hire, to what products a company can produce, to what investments a company can make.

For example, when IBM needed software development expertise, it decided to acquire Lotus, a company well-known for its spreadsheet software. IBM executives knew that Lotus was valuable because of its talented software engineers, who created and developed products such as *Lotus Notes,* a successful groupware product. To recruit these skilled employees, IBM worked out complex financial packages that included retirement and benefits options. IBM succeeded—at a cost of $3.5 billion—in purchasing Lotus and retaining the top Lotus software engineers.[1]

Money continually flows through businesses. It may flow in from banks, from the government, from the sale of stocks, and so on, and it may flow out for a variety of reasons—to invest in bonds, to buy new equipment, or to hire topnotch employees. Businesses must pay constant attention to ensure that the right amount of money is available at the right time for the right use.

In large firms it may take a whole team of financial experts to track the firm's cash flows and to develop financial strategies. For instance, when the Walt Disney Company acquired Capital Cities/ABC in 1996, teams of financial analysts worked on every detail of the $19 billion decision to determine how Disney could raise the money to buy the other company.[2]

---

[1]Judith H. Dobrzynski, "The Art of the Hostile Deal," *The New York Times* (June 22, 1995), D1, D2.
[2]Steve McClellan, "Shareholders Approve Disney/CapCities Merger," *Broadcasting & Cable,* 126, iss. 2 (January 8, 1996), 17.

TABLE 1-1

Careers in the Field of Finance

Financial management	Manage the finances of a business firm. Analyze, forecast, and plan a firm's finances; assess risk; evaluate and select investments; decide where and when to find money sources, and how much money to raise; and determine how much money to return to investors in the business.
Financial markets and institutions	Handle the flow of money in financial markets and institutions, and focus on the impact of interest rates on the flow of that money.
Investments	Locate, select, and manage money-producing assets for individuals and groups.

Finance Career Paths

Finance has three main career paths: financial management, financial markets and institutions, and investments. Financial management, the focus of this text, involves managing the finances of a business. Financial managers—people who manage a business firm's finances—perform a number of tasks. They analyze and forecast a firm's finances; assess risk, evaluate investment opportunities, decide when and where to find money sources and how much money to raise, and decide how much money to return to the firm's investors.

Bankers, stockbrokers, and others who work in financial markets and institutions focus on the flow of money through financial institutions and the markets in which financial assets are exchanged. They track the impact of interest rates on the flow of that money. People who work in the field of investments locate, select, and manage income-producing assets. For instance, security analysts and mutual fund managers both operate in the investment field.

Table 1-1 summarizes the three main finance career paths.

Financial Management

Financial management is essentially a combination of accounting and economics. First, financial managers use accounting information—balance sheets, income statements, and so on—to analyze, plan, and allocate financial resources for business firms. Second, financial managers use economic principles to guide them in making financial decisions that are in the best interest of the firm. In other words, finance is an applied area of economics that relies on accounting for input.

Because finance looks closely at the question of what adds value to a business, financial managers are central to most businesses. Let's take a look at what financial managers do.

The Role of the Financial Manager

Financial managers measure the firm's performance, determine what the financial consequences will be if the firm maintains its present course or changes it, and recommend how the firm should use its assets. Financial managers also locate external financing sources and recommend the most beneficial mix of financing sources, and they determine the financial expectations of the firm's owners.

All financial managers must be able to communicate, analyze, and make decisions based on information from many sources. To do this, they need to be able to analyze financial statements, forecast and plan, and determine the effect of size, risk, and timing of cash flows. We'll cover all of these skills in this text.

Finance in the Organization of the Firm   Financial managers work closely with other types of managers. For instance, they rely on accountants for raw financial data and on marketing managers for information about products and sales. Financial managers coordinate with technology experts to determine how to communicate financial information to others in the firm. Financial managers also provide advice and recommendations to top management.

Figure 1-1 shows how finance fits into a typical business firm's organization.

The Organization of the Finance Team   In most medium-to-large businesses, a chief financial officer (CFO) supervises a team of employees who manage the financial activities of the firm. One common way to organize a finance team in a medium-to-large business is shown in Figure 1-2.

In Figure 1-2, we see that the **chief financial officer** (CFO) directs and coordinates the financial activities of the firm. The CFO supervises a Treasurer and a Controller. The **treasurer** generally is responsible for cash management, credit management, and financial planning activities, while the **controller** is responsible for cost accounting, financial accounting, and information system activities. The treasurer and the controller of a large corporation are both likely to have a group of junior financial managers reporting to them.

At a small firm, one or two people may perform all the duties of the treasurer and of the controller. In very small firms, one person may perform all functions, including finance.

Figure 1-1   **The Organization of a Typical Corporation**

Figure 1-1 shows how finance fits into a typical business organization. The vice president for finance, or chief financial officer, operates with the vice presidents of the other business teams.

Figure 1-2   An Example of How to Organize a Finance Team

This chart shows how to organize a finance team in a medium-to-large business. Most teams include both a finance function (on the left) and an accounting function (on the right). The chief financial officer usually reports to the CEO as shown in Figure 1-1.

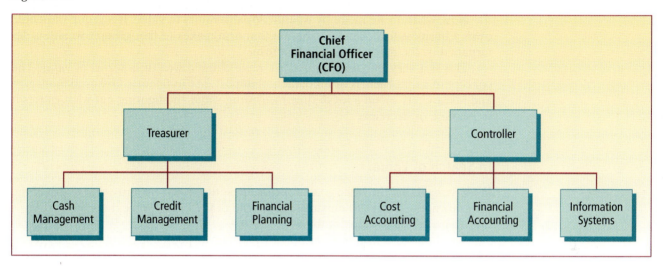

The Basic Financial Goal of the Firm

The financial manager's basic job is to make decisions that add value to the firm. When asked what the basic goal of a firm is, many people will answer, "To make a lot of money" or "To maximize profits." While no one would argue that profits aren't important, the single-minded pursuit of profits is not necessarily good for the firm and its owners. We will explain why this is so in the sections that follow. For now, let's say that a better way to express the primary financial goal of a business firm is to "maximize the wealth of the firm's owners." This is an extremely important, even crucial, point, so we will say it again: *The primary financial goal of the business firm is to maximize the wealth of the firm's owners.*

Everything the financial manager does—indeed, all the actions of everyone in the firm—should be directed toward this goal, subject to legal and ethical considerations that we will discuss in this chapter and throughout the book.

Now, what do we mean by wealth? **Wealth** refers to value. If a group of people owns a business firm, the contribution that firm makes to that group's wealth is determined by the market value of that firm.

This is a very important point: We have defined wealth in terms of *value*. The concept of value, then, is of fundamental importance in finance. Financial managers and researchers spend a lot of time measuring value and figuring out what causes it to increase or decrease.

In Search of Value

We have said that the basic goal of the business firm is to maximize the wealth of the firm's owners—that is, to maximize the value of the firm. The next question, then, is how to measure the value of the firm.

The value of a firm is determined by whatever people are willing to pay for it. The more valuable people think a firm is, the more they will pay to own it. Then the existing owners can sell it to investors for more than their original purchase price, thereby increasing current stockholder wealth. The financial manager's job is to make decisions that will cause people to think more favorably about the firm and, in turn, to be willing to pay more to purchase the business.

For companies that sell stock to the general public, stock price can indicate the value of a business because *stockholders*—people who purchase corporate shares of stock—become part owners of the corporation.[3] (We will discuss stock in greater detail in chapter 2.) People will pay a higher price for stock—that is, part ownership of a business—if they believe the company will perform well in the future. For instance, Netscape, a developer of Internet access software, originally sold its stock for $28 per share. (A share is one unit of ownership.) Because of the potential of its Internet software, Netscape stock sold for $116.25 per share three months later—for a total stock market value of more than $5 billion.[4] The increase in Netscape's stock price increased the value of the stockholders' holdings, thereby increasing their wealth.

For businesses that sell stock publicly, then, the financial manager's basic role is to help make the firm's stock more valuable. Although some businesses do not sell stock to the general public, we will focus on stock price as a measure of the value of the firm. Keep in mind, however, that investing in one share (one unit) of stock means the investor only owns one small piece of a firm. Many firms sell hundreds of thousands or millions of shares of stock, so the total value of the firm is the equivalent of the sum of all the stock shares.

---

[3] Actually, as we will see later in the text, the wealth of the stockholder owners is determined by both stock price changes and the receipt of company dividends. Stock price is by far the largest indicator of stockholder wealth, however, so we will ignore the dividend issue for now.
[4] Interview with James Clark, "Striking It Rich on the Net," *U.S. News and World Report* (January 15, 1996): 51; Floyd Norris, "Hot Internet Stocks Soar. Are 'Shorts' in Squeeze?" *The New York Times* (November 21, 1995): D1, D8.

Next, let's look closely at three factors that affect the value of a firm's stock price: cash flow, timing, and risk.

The Importance of Cash Flow   In business, cash is what pays the bills. It is also what the firm receives in exchange for its products and services. Cash is therefore of ultimate importance, and the expectation that the firm will generate cash in the future is one of the factors that gives the firm its value.

We use the term *cash flow* to describe cash moving through a business. Financial managers concentrate on increasing cash *in*flows—cash that flows into a business—and decreasing cash *out*flows—cash that flows away from a business. Cash outflows will be approved if they result in cash inflows of sufficient magnitude and if those inflows have acceptable timing and risk.

It is important to realize that sales are not the same as cash inflows. Businesses often sell goods and services on credit, so no cash changes hands at the time of the sale. If the cash from the sale is never collected, the sale cannot add any value to the firm. Owners care about actual cash collections from sales—that is, cash inflows.

Likewise, businesses may buy goods and services to keep the firm running, but may make the purchase on credit—so no cash changes hands at that time. However, bills always come due sooner or later, so owners care about cash expenditures for purchases—cash outflows. For any business firm (assuming other factors remain constant), the higher the expected cash inflows and the lower the expected cash outflows, the higher the firm's stock price will be.

The Effect of Timing on Cash Flows   The timing of cash flows also affects a firm's value. To illustrate, consider this: Would you rather receive $100 cash today and $0 one year from now, or would you rather receive $0 cash today and $100 one year from now? The two alternatives follow:

	TODAY	ONE YEAR FROM NOW
Alternative A	+ $100	$0
Alternative B	$0	+ $100

Both alternatives promise the same total amount of cash, but most people would choose Alternative A because they realize they could invest the $100 received today and earn interest on it during the year. By doing so they would end up with more money than $100 at the end of the year. For this reason we say that—all other factors being equal—cash received sooner is better than cash received later.

Owners and potential investors look at when firms can expect to receive cash and when they can expect to pay out cash. All other factors being equal, the sooner companies expect to receive cash and the later they expect to pay out cash, the more valuable the firm and the higher its stock price will be.

The Influence of Risk   We have seen that the size of a firm's expected cash inflows and outflows and the timing of those cash flows influence the value of the firm and its stock price. Now let us consider how risk affects the firm's value and its stock price.

�◀ **Take Note**

The point about cash received sooner being better than cash received later works in reverse, too: It is better to pay out cash later rather than sooner. (All other factors being equal, of course).

TABLE 1-2

Accomplishing the Primary Financial Goal of the Firm

The Goal: Maximize the wealth of the firm's owners Measure of the Goal: Value of the firm (Measured by the price of the stock on the open market for corporations)	
FACTOR	**EFFECT ON STOCK PRICE**
Size of expected future cash flows	Larger future cash inflows raise the stock price. Larger cash outflows lower the stock price. Smaller future cash inflows lower the stock price. Smaller future cash outflows raise the stock price.
Timing of future cash flows	Cash inflows expected sooner result in a higher stock price. Cash inflows expected later result in a lower stock price. (The opposite effect occurs for future cash outflows.)
Riskiness of future cash flows	When the degree of risk associated with future cash flows goes down, stock price goes up. When the degree of risk associated with future cash flows goes up, stock price goes down.

Risk affects value because the less certain owners and investors are about a firm's expected future cash flows, the lower they will value the company. The more certain owners and investors are about a firm's expected future cash flows, the higher they will value the company. In short, companies whose expected future cash flows are doubtful will have lower values than companies whose expected future cash flows are virtually certain.

What isn't nearly as clear as the *way* risk affects value is *how much* it affects it. For example, if one company's cash flows are twice as risky as another company's cash flows, is its stock worth half as much? We can't say. In fact, we have a tough time quantifying just how risky the companies are in the first place.

We will examine the issue of risk in some detail in chapter 7. For now, it is sufficient to remember that risk affects stock price—as risk increases, stock price goes down; and conversely, as risk decreases, stock price goes up.

Table 1-2 summarizes the influences of cash flow size, timing, and risk on stock prices.

Profits versus Cash Flow   Earlier in the chapter we said that the single-minded pursuit of profits is not necessarily good for the firm's owners. Indeed, the firm's owners view stock value, not profit, as the appropriate measure of wealth. Stock value depends on future cash flows, their timing, and their riskiness. Profit calculations do not consider these three factors. Profit, as defined in accounting, is simply the difference between sales revenue and expenses. If all we were interested in were profits, we could simply start using high-pressure sales techniques, cut all expenses to the bone, and then point proudly to the resulting increase in profits. For the moment, anyway. In all probability, managers practicing such techniques would find their firm out of business later, when the quality of the firm's products, services, and work force dropped, eventually leading to declining sales and market share.

It is true that more profits are generally better than less profits. But when the pursuit of short-term profits adversely affects the size of future cash flows, their timing, or their riskiness, then these profit maximization efforts are detrimental to the firm. Concentrating on stock value, not profits, is a better measure of financial success.

Melanie Rosen, Electronic Media, *The New York Times*

Melanie Rosen

Melanie Rosen is the Director of Electronic Media for The New York Times Informational Services Group. She runs a new company within *The New York Times* that will produce educational products for schools. One product is called *Live from the Past. Live from The Past* takes historical articles from *The New York Times* and converts them to digital format so that the articles and videotapes from actual events can be used in the classroom online, from a CD, or in any other electronic format. Melanie is a natural for this type of endeavor because she was a communication/graphics major in college, and then earned an M.B.A.

Q. *What are some of your daily responsibilities?*

Two main aspects of my business are production and finance. Production involves figuring out how to combine many types of media to create the best product possible. To create such a product, though, I have to know the financial impact of what I invest in—will the company benefit from my production decisions?

Q. *In effect, you are starting a new company within* The New York Times. *How would you describe what you do?*

I function as a general manager, financial manager, product manager, and sales manager, all under one hat. About 50 percent to 60 percent of my time is devoted to financial management. That is, I constantly evaluate the finances of the product line. I try to assess how much money it will cost to design and produce a product, how much it will cost to market it, how much of the product we will produce, what our risks are, and what our revenues will be.

I budget and monitor my group's performance against its budgeted, or forecasted, performance. I'm also responsible for keeping management informed about how much money our group has invested so far, how much more we expect to invest, how much money we expect to generate, and when.

Q. *How supportive is* The New York Times *of your "new company"?*

When a product like *Live from the Past* is in start-up mode, the company is always supportive. Management tries to provide the opportunity to make as much money as possible. But there are constraints. Most corporations like to see new businesses become profitable in the third year. In fact, many corporations try to push for a two-year time frame. That's because companies are concerned about cash flowing into investments without seeing an accompanying return from the investment.

Q. *What basic financial "tools" would you suggest future business people should master?*

I'd recommend students should understand some basic financial concepts when they leave college. Business people need to be able to read and understand financial statements, including the statement of cash flows. Only then will they understand how much money the business has before and after taxes, where the money is going, and what the timing is of those cash flows. Too many businesses fail because of poor cash flow.

Source: Interview with Melanie Rosen, November 5, 1995.

Legal and Ethical Challenges in Financial Management

Several legal and ethical challenges influence financial managers as they pursue the goal of wealth maximization for the firm's owners. Examples of legal considerations include environmental statutes mandating pollution control equipment, workplace safety standards that must be met, civil rights laws that must be obeyed, and intellectual property laws that regulate the use of others' ideas.

Ethical concerns include fair treatment of employees, customers, the community, and society as a whole. Indeed, many businesses have written ethics codes that articulate the ethical values of the business organization.[5]

Three legal and ethical influences of special note include the agency problem, the interests of non-owner stakeholders, and the interests of society as a whole. We will turn to these issues next.

Agency Issues

The financial manager, and the other managers of a business firm, are agents for the owners of the firm. An **agent** is a person who has the implied or actual authority to act on behalf of another. The owners whom the agents represent are the **principals.** For example, the board of directors and senior management of IBM are agents for the IBM stockholders, the principals. Agents have a legal and ethical responsibility to make decisions that further the interests of the principals.

The interests of the principals are supposed to be paramount when agents make decisions, but this is often easier said than done. For example, the managing director of a corporation might like the convenience of a private jet on call twenty-four hours a day, but do the common stockholder owners of the corporation receive enough value to justify the cost of a jet? It looks like the interests of the managing director (the agent) and the interests of the common stockholder owners (the principals) of the corporation are in conflict in this case.

The Agency Problem   When the interests of the agents and principals conflict, an **agency problem** results. In our jet example, an agency problem occurs if the managing director buys the jet, even though he knows the benefits to the stockholders do not justify the cost.

Another example of an agency problem occurs when managers must decide whether to undertake a project with a high potential payoff but high risk. Even if the project is more likely to be successful than not, managers may not want to take a risk that owners would be willing to take. Why? An unsuccessful project may result in such significant financial loss that the managers who approved the project lose their jobs—and all the income from their paycheck. The stockholder owners, however, may have a much smaller risk because their investment in company stock represents only a small fraction of their financial investment package. Because the risk is so much larger to the manager as compared to the stockholder, a promising but somewhat risky project may be rejected even though it was likely to benefit the firm's owners.

The agency problem can be lessened by tying the managers' compensation to the performance of the company and its stock price. This tie brings the interests of the managers and those of the firm's owners closer together. That is why companies often make shares of stock a part of the compensation package offered to managers, especially top executives. If managers are also stockholders, then the agency problem should be reduced.

Agency Costs   Sometimes firms spend time and money to monitor and reduce agency problems. These outlays of time and money are **agency costs.** One common

---

[5]Betsy Stevens, "Using the Competing Values Framework to Assess Corporate Ethical Codes," *The Journal of Business Communication* 33, no. 1 (January 1996): 71.

example of an agency cost is an accounting audit of a corporation's financial statements. If a business is owned and operated by the same person, the owner would not need an audit—she could trust herself to report her finances accurately. Most companies of any size, however, have agency costs because managers, not owners, report the finances. Owners audit the company financial statements to see whether the agents have acted in the owners' interests by reporting finances accurately.

The Interests of Other Groups

Stockholders and managers are not the only groups that have a stake in a business firm. There are also non-manager workers, creditors, suppliers, customers, and members of the community where the business is located. These groups are also **stakeholders**—people who have a "stake" in the business. Although the primary financial goal of the firm is to maximize the wealth of the owners, the interests of these other stakeholders can influence business decisions.

One example of outside stakeholder influence is pressure from political lobbyists or consumer groups. For instance, Magic Johnson, basketball star of the Los Angeles Lakers, partnered with Sony to assist a neighborhood in Los Angeles that had been severely damaged in the events following the original Rodney King beating trial. No company was willing to run the risk of operating a movie theater in the area because the risk of property damage was so high.[6] So—despite the risk of monetary loss—Magic Johnson and Sony built a clean, safe movie theater in the neighborhood, offering job opportunities as well as first-run films.

It was such a successful venture, both for the L.A. neighborhood and its founders, that Magic and Sony plan to build similar theaters in the inner cities of Atlanta, New York, Chicago, Washington, and Houston.[7]

The Interests of Society as a Whole

Sometimes the interests of a business firm's owners are not the same as the interests of society. For instance, the cost of properly disposing of toxic waste can be so high that companies may be tempted to simply dump their waste in nearby rivers. In so doing, the companies can keep costs low and profits high, and drive their stock prices higher (if they are not caught). However, many people suffer from the polluted environment. This is why we have environmental and other similar laws: So that society's best interests take precedence over the interests of individual company owners.

When businesses take a long-term view, the interests of the owners and society often (but not always) coincide. When companies encourage recycling, sponsor programs for disadvantaged young people, run media campaigns promoting the responsible use of alcohol, and contribute money to worthwhile civic causes, the goodwill generated as a result of these activities causes long-term increases in the firm's sales and cash flows, which translate into additional wealth for the firm's owners.

---

[6]Interview with Taylor Braugh, Public Relations Director of Magic Johnson Enterprises, Inc., January 10, 1996; Kenneth Noble, "Magic Johnson Finding Success in a New Forum, *The New York Times* (January 8, 1996): 8.
[7]Noble, "Magic Johnson: 8."

Figure 1-3 **Influences on Financial Managers**

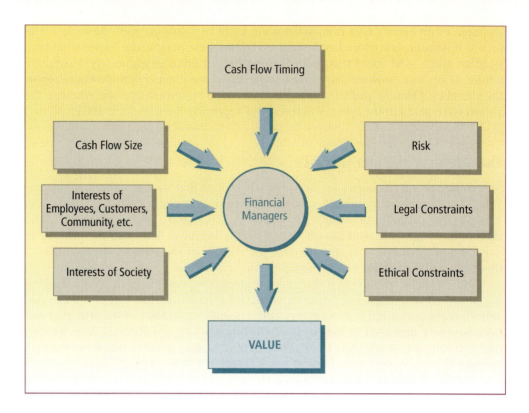

Although the traditional primary economic goal of the firm is to maximize shareholder wealth, the unbridled pursuit of value is too simplistic a view of this goal. Firms often take into account ethical factors, the interests of other stakeholders, and the long-term interests of society.[8]

Figure 1-3 summarizes the various influences that financial managers may consider in their pursuit of value.

FORMS OF BUSINESS ORGANIZATION

Businesses can be organized in a variety of ways. The three most common types of organization are proprietorships, partnerships, and corporations. The distinguishing characteristics give each form its own advantages and disadvantages.

The Proprietorship

The simplest way to organize a business is to form a **proprietorship,** a business owned by one person. An individual raises some money, finds a location from which to operate, and starts selling a product or service. The profits or losses generated are reported on a form called Schedule C of the individual's form 1040 income tax re-

---

[8]Not everyone agrees with this approach. Milton Friedman, Nobel laureate in economics, claims that any action taken by a manager that is not legally mandated, and that reduces the value available to the owners, is theft.

turn. The sole proprietor is responsible for any tax liability generated by the business, and the tax rates are those that apply to an individual.

The sole proprietor has *unlimited liability* for matters relating to the business. This means that the sole proprietor is responsible for all the obligations of the business, even if those obligations exceed the amount the proprietor has invested in the business. If a customer is injured on the company premises and sues for $1 million, the sole proprietor must pay that amount if the court awards that amount to the plaintiff customer. This is true even if the total amount invested by the sole proprietor in the business is only $10,000.

Although unlimited liability is a major disadvantage of a proprietorship, liability insurance is often available to reduce the risk of losing business and nonbusiness assets. However, the risk always remains that the business will be unsuccessful and that the losses incurred will exceed the amount of the proprietor's money invested. The other assets owned by the proprietor will then be at risk.

The Partnership

Two or more people may join together to form a business as a **partnership.** This can be done on an informal basis without a written partnership agreement, or a contract can spell out the rights and responsibilities of each partner. This written contract is called the *articles of partnership* and is strongly recommended so as to lessen the likelihood of disputes between partners.

The articles of partnership contract generally spells out how much money each partner will contribute, what the ownership share of each partner will be, how profits and losses will be allocated among partners, who will perform what work for the business, and other matters of concern to the partners. The percent of ownership for each partner does not have to be the same as the percent each partner invests in the partnership.

Each partner in a partnership is usually liable for the activities of the partnership as a whole.[9] This is an important point. Even if there are a hundred partners, each one is technically responsible for all the debts of the partnership. If ninety-nine partners declare personal bankruptcy, the hundredth partner still is responsible for all the partnership's debts.

Some partnerships contain two different classes of partners, *general partners* and *limited partners*. General partners are almost always active participants in the management of the business, while limited partners are not. As a result, general partners usually contract for a more favorable allocation of ownership, profits, and losses compared to limited partners. General partners have unlimited liability for the partnership's activities. Limited partners are only liable for the amount they invest in the partnership. If you are a limited partner who invests $5,000 in the business, then $5,000 is the most you could lose. For this reason, every partnership must have at least one general partner (a partnership could have all general partners, but it could not have all limited partners).

A partner's profits and losses are reported on Schedule K-1, which is attached to each partner's individual form 1040 income tax return. The partners pay any taxes owed. The partnership itself is not taxed because the income merely passes through the partnership to the partners, where it is taxed.

---

[9]But see the discussion that follows on general and limited partners.

The Corporation

The third major form of business organization is the **corporation.** Unlike proprietorships and partnerships, corporations are legal entities separate from their owners. To form a corporation, the owners specify the governing rules for the running of the business in a contract known as the *articles of incorporation.* They submit the articles to the government of the state in which the corporation is formed, and the state issues a charter that creates the separate legal entity.

Corporations are taxed as separate legal entities. That is, corporations must pay their own income tax just as if they were individuals.[10] This is where the often-discussed "double taxation" of corporate profits comes into play. First a corporation pays income tax on the revenue it receives. Then the corporation may distribute to the owners the profits that are left after paying taxes. These distributions, called dividends, count as ordinary income for the owners and are taxed on the individual owners' income tax returns. Thus the IRS collects taxes twice on the same income.

Double taxation of dividends is bad news for the owners of corporations, but there is good news as well. Stockholders, the corporation's owners, have limited liability for the corporation's activities. They cannot lose more than the amount they paid to buy the stock. This makes the corporate form of organization very attractive for owners who desire to shelter their personal assets from creditors of the business.

Corporations have other benefits too. For example, because they exist separately from their owners, they can "live" beyond the death of their original owners. Another benefit of the corporate form of business is that corporations generally have a professional management team and board of directors, elected by the owners. It is the board's job to look out for the interests of the owners (the stockholders). Stockholders, especially in the case of large corporations, usually do not take an active role in the management of the business, so it is the board of directors' job to represent them.

Subchapter S Corporations   In a special type of corporation called a **Subchapter S corporation,** the owners are taxed as if they were members of a partnership—thereby avoiding the double-taxation problem faced by the owners of other corporations. Subchapter S corporations are generally very small; in fact, this form of business ownership was created to relieve small businesses, as specified in the federal tax code, from some of the rules that large Subchapter C corporations have to follow. The stockholders of Subchapter S corporations also have limited liability.

Table 1-3 summarizes the advantages and disadvantages of the various forms of business ownership.

Whatʼs Next

In this book we will look at how firms raise and allocate funds, and how firms invest in assets that generate returns at a reasonable risk. In part 1 of the text, we discuss the environment in which financial managers make decisions. In chapter 2 we will examine how funds are raised in the financial marketplace. In chapter 3 we'll explore how financial institutions and interest rates affect financial decisions.

---

[10]Corporations file their income tax returns using Form 1041.

TABLE 1-3

Characteristics of Business Ownership Forms

	PROPRIETORSHIP	PARTNERSHIP	CORPORATION
Ease of formation	Very easy	Relatively easy	More difficult
Owners' liability	Unlimited	Unlimited for general partners	Limited
Life of firm	Dies with owner, unless heirs continue operating or sell the business	Surviving partners must deal with the deceased partner's heirs	Can live beyond owners' lifetimes
Separate legal entity?	No	No	Yes
Degree of control by owners	Complete	May be limited for individual partner	May be very limited for individual stockholder

Summary

1. Describe the field of finance.

Finance is important to business people. Financial decisions about how to raise, spend, and allocate money can affect every aspect of a business—from personnel to products. Finance also offers career opportunities in three main areas: financial management, financial markets and institutions, and investments. Financial management focuses on managing the finances of a business.

2. Discuss the duties of financial managers.

Financial managers use accounting information and economic principles to guide their financial decisions. They measure the firm's financial condition, forecast, budget, raise funds, and determine the financial goals of the firm's owners. They also work closely with other managers to further the firm's goals.

At medium and large firms, more than one person usually handles the financial management duties. In some firms a chief financial officer (CFO) supervises the financial activities, including cash and credit management, financial planning, and accounting.

3. Identify the basic goal of a business firm.

The basic goal of the business firm is to maximize the wealth of the firm's owners by adding value; it is not to maximize profits. The value of a firm is measured by the price investors are willing to pay to own the firm. For businesses that sell stock to the general public, stock price indicates the firm's value because shares of stock are units of ownership. So the basic financial goal of such firms is to maximize the price of the firm's stock.

4. List factors that affect the value of a firm.

The value of a firm is affected by the size of future cash flows, their timing, and their riskiness.

- Cash inflows increase a firm's value while cash outflows decrease it.
- The sooner cash flows are expected to be received, the greater the value. The later those cash flows are expected, the less the value.
- The less risk associated with future cash flows, the higher the value. The more risk, the lower the value.

5. Discuss the legal and ethical challenges financial managers face.

Legal and ethical considerations include the agency problem, the interests of other stakeholders, and the interests of society as a whole.

- The agency problem exists when the interests of a firm's managers (the agents) are in conflict with those of the firm's owners (the principals).
- Other stakeholders whose interests are often considered in financial decisions include employees, customers, and members of the communities in which the firm's plants are located.
- Concerns of society as a whole—such as environmental or health problems—often influence business financial decisions.

6. Identify the three different forms of business organization.

The three most common forms of business organization are the proprietorship, the partnership, and the corporation.

- Proprietorships are businesses owned by one person. The owner is exposed to unlimited liability for the firm's debts.
- Partnerships are businesses owned by two or more people, each of whom is responsible for the firm's debts. The exception is a limited partner, a partner who contracts for limited liability.
- Corporations are separate legal entities. They are owned by stockholders who are responsible for the firm's debts only to the extent of their investment.

Self-Test

ST-1. What are the three main areas of career opportunities in finance?

ST-2. What are the primary responsibilities of a person holding the title of treasurer at a large corporation?

ST-3. Who is a "principal" in an agent–principal relationship?

ST-4. What legal and ethical factors may influence a firm's financial decisions?

ST-5. What is a Subchapter S corporation?

Review Questions

1. How is finance related to the disciplines of accounting and economics?
2. List and describe the three career opportunities in the field of finance.
3. Describe the duties of the financial manager in a business firm.
4. What is the basic goal of a business?
5. List and explain the three financial factors that influence the value of a business.
6. Explain why accounting profits and cash flows are not the same thing.
7. What is an agent? What are the responsibilities of an agent?
8. Describe how society's interests can influence financial managers.
9. Briefly define the terms proprietorship, partnership, and corporation.
10. Compare and contrast the potential liability of owners of proprietorships, partnerships (general partners), and corporations.

Build Your Communication Skills

CS-1. Divide into small groups. Each small group should then divide in half. The first group should defend the idea that managers of a firm should consider only the interests of stockholders, subject to legal constraints. The other group should argue that businesses should consider the interests of other stakeholders of the firm and society at large.

CS-2. Assume you work for WealthMax Corporation in New York City. You've noticed that managers who work late charge the corporation for their dinners and transportation home. You've also noticed that almost all employees from these managers' departments take office supplies, ranging from pens to computer software, for personal use at home. You estimate the costs of this pilfering at a shocking $150,000 a year. Your boss, the chief financial officer for WealthMax, asks you to write a memo to the offending managers describing why their actions and those of their employees violate their duties and conflict with the goal of the firm. Write this memo.

Answers to Self-Test

ST-1. Financial management, financial markets and institutions, and investments.

ST-2. The treasurer of a large corporation is responsible for cash management, credit management, and financial planning.

ST-3. A principal in an agent–principal relationship is the person who hires the agent to act on the principal's behalf. The principal is the person to whom the agent owes a duty.

ST-4. Legal and ethical factors influence businesses. Examples of legal constraints include environmental, safety, and civil rights laws. Examples of ethical considerations include fair treatment of workers, environmental sensitivity, and support for the community.

ST-5. A Subchapter S corporation is a small corporation that is taxed as if it were a partnership. As a result, the owners of a Subchapter S corporation avoid double taxation of corporate income paid to stockholders.

chapter 2

Financial Markets and Interest Rates

Chapter Objectives

After reading this chapter, you should be able to:

1. Describe how the U.S. financial system works.

2. Define financial securities.

3. Explain the function of financial intermediaries.

4. Identify the different financial marketplaces.

5. Describe the securities traded in the money and capital markets.

6. Identify the determinants of the nominal interest rate.

7. Construct and analyze a yield curve.

It is better to give than to lend, and it costs about the same.

Philip Gibbs

Stomach-Churning Investment Bankers and Other Delights

"I was ready to throw up," said Frank Ingari, the chief executive of Shiva Software, as the company sold shares of stock to the public for the first time in what is known as an initial public offering (IPO).

Ingari knew that you just don't waltz down to Wall Street and sell your company's stock. He sought out Goldman Sachs, the famous investment banking house, to help sell shares of his company's stock to the public. Lawton W. Fitt, one of the partners who runs IPOs for Goldman Sachs, let Ingari know that it wasn't going to be easy to line up investors. Eight investment bankers were put on the project, more than 200 sales people were involved, armies of lawyers, accountants, and bankers geared up, and Ingari had to register Shiva with the Securities and Exchange Commission. Altogether Ingari spent $900,000 on audits and other expenses.

Frank Ingari

As a part of the IPO, Ingari and Daniel Schwinn, a company founder, spent two grueling weeks visiting sixteen cities. At each stop, they made an impassioned plea to large institutional investors such as Fidelity Investments, Wellington Management, Janus, and Alliance Capital.

"We felt like door-to-door salesmen," Ingari said.

But they were successful door-to-door salespeople. When the road show ended, orders for the stock exceeded the 2 million or so shares offered by a factor of 30.

Ingari and Schwinn became instant millionaires when the stock hit the market. The shares of Shiva Software sold in the offering brought $28 each to the company's coffers—about $56 million. Goldman Sachs made $3 million, or 7 percent of the total offering. ✵

Sources: Glenn Rifkin, "Anatomy of a Highflying I.P.O., Nosebleeds and All," *The New York Times* (February 19, 1995): 7; "Shiva Corporation," *Wall Street Journal* (October 5, 1995): B3.

Chapter Overview

The Shiva Software stock sale illustrates the importance of financial markets to business firms. Most businesses do not make millions each time they go to the financial markets, but they certainly would face difficulties if markets were not available for raising funds and investing.

One of the central duties of a financial manager is to acquire capital—that is, to raise funds. Few companies are able to fund all their activities solely with funds from internal sources. Most find it necessary at times to seek funding from outside sources. For this reason, all business people need to know about financial markets.

As we see in this chapter, there are a number of financial markets, and each offers a different kind of financial product. In this chapter we discuss the relationship between firms and the financial markets, and briefly explain how the financial system works, including the role of *financial intermediaries*—investment bankers, brokers, and dealers. Next, we explore the markets themselves and describe financial products, ranging from government bonds to corporate stocks. Finally, we examine interest rates.

The Financial System

Take Note

In the U.S. economy, several types of individuals or entities generate and spend money. We call these *economic units*. The main types of economic units include governments, businesses, and households (households may be one person or more than one person). Some economic units generate more income than they spend, and have funds left over. These are called **surplus economic units.** Other economic units generate less income than they spend, and need to acquire additional funds in order to sustain their operations. These are called **deficit economic units.**

The purpose of the financial system is to bring the two groups—surplus economic units and deficit economic units—together for their mutual benefit.

The financial system also makes it possible for participants to adjust their holdings of financial assets as their needs change. This is the *liquidity function* of the financial system—that is, the system allows funds to flow with ease.

To enable funds to move through the financial system, funds are exchanged for financial products called *securities*. A clear understanding of securities is essential to

The words "surplus" and "deficit" do not imply something good or bad, they simply mean that some economic units need funds, and others have funds available. If Disney needs $2 billion to build a theme park in a year when its income is "only" $1.5 billion, Disney is a deficit economic unit that year. Likewise, if a family earns $40,000 in a year but spends only $36,000, it is a surplus economic unit for that year.

understanding the financial system. So before we go further, let's examine what securities are and how they are used.

Securities

Securities are documents that represent the right to receive funds in the future. The person or organization that holds a security is called a **bearer.** A security certifies that the bearer has a *claim* to future funds. For example, if you lend $100 to someone and the person gives you an IOU, you have a security. The IOU represents your claim on the $100 you are owed. The IOU may also state *when* you are to be paid, which is referred to as the **maturity date** of the security. When the date of payment occurs, we say the security matures.

Securities have value because the bearer has the right to be paid the amount specified. So a bearer who wanted some money right away could sell the security to someone else for cash. Of course, the new bearer could sell the security to someone else too, and so on down the line. When a security is sold to someone else, the security is being *traded.*

Business firms, as well as local, state, and national governments, sell securities to the public to raise money. After the initial sale, investors may sell the securities to other investors. As you might suspect, this can get to be a complicated business. That's why organizations called *financial intermediaries* exist to help the initial sellers and markets are available for the subsequent traders to execute their transactions.

Financial Intermediaries

Financial intermediaries act as the grease that enables the machinery of the financial system to work smoothly. They specialize in certain services that would be difficult for individual participants to perform, such as matching buyers and sellers of securities. Three types of financial intermediaries are investment bankers, brokers, and dealers.

Investment Bankers Institutions called **investment banking firms** exist to help businesses and state and local governments sell their securities to the public. For example, when Shiva Software wanted to sell 2 million shares of stock to the public, the investment banking firm of Goldman Sachs handled the arrangements.

Investment bankers arrange securities sales on either an *underwriting basis* or a *best efforts basis.* The term **underwriting** refers to the process by which an investment banker (usually in cooperation with other investment banking firms) purchases all the new securities from the issuing company and then resells them to the public.

Investment bankers who underwrite securities face some risk because occasionally an issue is overpriced and can't be sold to the public for the price anticipated by the investment banker. The investment banker has already paid the issuing company or municipality its money up front, and so must absorb the difference between what it paid the issuer and what the security actually sold for. To alleviate this risk, investment bankers sometimes sell securities on a **best efforts basis.** This means the investment banker will try its best to sell the securities for the desired price, but there are no guarantees. If the securities must be sold for a lower price, the issuer collects less money.

Brokers Brokers—often account representatives for an investment banking firm—handle orders to buy or sell securities. **Brokers** are agents who work on behalf of an investor. When investors call with an order, brokers work on their behalf to find someone to take the other side of the proposed trade. If investors want to buy, brokers find sellers. If investors want to sell, brokers find buyers. Brokers are compensated for their services when the person whom they represent—the investor—pays them a commission on the sale or purchase of securities.

Dealers   **Dealers** make their living buying securities and reselling them to others. They operate just like car dealers who buy cars from manufacturers for resale to others. Dealers make money by buying securities for one price, called the *bid price,* and selling them for a higher price, called the *ask (or offer) price.* The difference, or *spread,* between the bid price and the ask price represents the dealer's fee.

Financial Markets

As we have pointed out, the financial system allows surplus economic units to trade with deficit economic units. The trades are carried out in the *financial markets.*

Financial markets are categorized according to the characteristics of the participants and the securities involved. In the *primary market,* for instance, deficit economic units sell new securities directly to surplus economic units and to financial institutions. For instance, Shiva Software sold its newly issued stock shares to buyers in the primary market. In the *secondary market,* investors trade securities among themselves. Primary and secondary markets can be further categorized as to the maturity of the securities traded. Short-term securities—securities with a maturity of one year or less—are traded in the *money market;* and long-term securities—securities with a maturity of more than one year[1]—are traded in the *capital market.* A number of other financial markets exist, but we are mainly concerned with these four. In the following sections, we examine each of these markets in turn.

Do not confuse financial markets with financial institutions. A financial market is a forum in which financial securities are traded (it may or may not have a physical location). A financial institution is an organization that takes in funds from some economic units and makes them available to others.

The Primary Market

When a security is created and sold for the first time in the financial marketplace, this transaction takes place in the **primary market.** Thus, when Shiva Software went to Goldman Sachs and arranged to sell its 2 million shares of stock to the public, the stock sale took place in the primary market. In this market the issuing business or entity sells its securities to investors (the investment banker simply assists with the transaction).

The Secondary Market

Once a security has been issued, it may be traded from one investor to another. Many of the investors who originally bought Shiva's stock, for example, have since traded their shares to other investors. The **secondary market** is where previously issued securities—or "used" securities—are traded among investors. Suppose you called your stockbroker to request that she buy 100 shares of stock for you. The shares would usually be purchased from another investor in the secondary market. Secondary market transactions occur thousands of times daily as investors trade securities among themselves.

---

[1] The dividing line between "short-term" and "long-term" is arbitrarily set at one year.

The Money Market

We discuss these securities later in the chapter on pages 23–34.)

Short-term securities (a maturity of one year or less) are traded in the **money market.** Networks of dealers operate in this market. They use phones and computers to make trades rapidly among themselves and with the issuing organizations. The specific securities traded in the money market include Treasury bills, negotiable certificates of deposit, commercial paper, and other short-term debt instruments.

The Capital Market

Bonds are discussed on pages 25–28. Stocks are discussed on pages 28–29.

Long-term securities (maturities over one year) trade in the **capital market.** Federal, state, and local governments, as well as large corporations, raise long-term funds in the capital market. Firms usually invest proceeds from capital market securities sales in long-term assets like buildings, production equipment, and so on. Initial offerings of securities in the capital market are usually large deals put together by investment bankers, although after the original issue, the securities may be traded quickly and easily among investors. The two most widely recognized securities in the capital market, bonds and stocks, will be discussed later in the chapter.

Security Exchanges

Security exchanges, such as the New York Stock Exchange (NYSE), are organizations that facilitate trading of stocks and bonds among investors. Corporations arrange for their stock or bonds to be *listed* on an exchange so that investors may trade the company's stocks and bonds at an organized trading location. Corporations list their securities on exchanges because they believe that having their securities traded at such a location will make them easier to trade and therefore boost the price. Exchanges accept listings because they earn a fee for their services.

Each exchange-listed stock is traded at a specified location on the trading floor called *the post*. The trading is supervised by specialists who act either as brokers (bringing together buyers and sellers) or as dealers (buying or selling the stock themselves).

Prominent international securities exchanges include the New York Stock Exchange (NYSE), the American Stock Exchange (AMEX), and major exchanges in Tokyo, London, Amsterdam, Frankfurt, Paris, Hong Kong, and Mexico.

The Over-the-Counter (OTC) Market

In contrast to the organized exchanges, which have physical locations, the **over-the-counter market** has no fixed location—or, more correctly, it is everywhere. The over-the-counter market, or OTC, is a network of dealers around the world who maintain inventories of securities for sale. Say you wanted to buy a security that is traded OTC. You would call your broker, who would then shop among competing dealers who have the security in their inventory. After locating the dealer with the best price, your broker would buy the security on your behalf.

Some dealers in the OTC market are connected through a computer network called NASDAQ (the National Association of Securities Dealers Automated Quote system). But many others, especially those dealing in securities issued by very small companies, simply buy and sell over the telephone.

Market Efficiency

The term **market efficiency** refers to the ease, speed, and cost of trading securities. In an efficient market, securities can be traded easily, quickly, and at low cost. Markets lacking these qualities are considered inefficient.

The major stock markets are generally efficient because investors can trade thousands of dollars worth of shares in minutes simply by making a phone call and paying a relatively small commission. In contrast, the real estate market is relatively inefficient because it might take you months to sell a house and you would probably have to pay a real estate agent a large commission to handle the deal.

The more efficient the market, the easier it is for excess funds in the hands of surplus economic units to make their way into the hands of deficit economic units. In an inefficient market, surplus economic units may end up with excess funds that are idle. When this happens, economic activity and job creation will be lower than it could be, and deficit economic units may not be able to achieve their goals because they could not obtain needed funds.

Financial markets help firms and individual investors buy and sell securities efficiently. So far, we have discussed the various markets in which securities are traded. Now let's turn to the securities themselves.

SECURITIES IN THE FINANCIAL MARKETPLACE

Securities are traded in both the money and capital markets. Money market securities include Treasury bills, negotiable certificates of deposit, commercial paper, Eurodollars, and banker's acceptances. Capital market securities include bonds and stock. We describe each of these securities briefly in the following discussion.

Securities in the Money Market

Governments, corporations, and financial institutions that want to raise money for a short time issue money market securities. Buyers of money market securities include governments, corporations, and financial institutions that want to park surplus cash for a short time, and other investors who want the ability to alter or cash in their investments quickly.

Money market securities are very liquid, that is, they mature quickly and can be sold for cash quickly and easily. Money market securities also have a low degree of risk because purchasers will only buy them from large, reputable issuers (investors don't want to spend a long time checking the issuers' credit for an investment that may only last a few days). These two characteristics, liquidity and low risk, make money market securities the ideal parking place for temporary excess cash.

Let's take a closer look at the main money market securities.

Treasury Bills Every week the United States Treasury issues billions of dollars of **Treasury bills** (T-bills). These money market securities are issued to finance the federal budget deficit and to refinance the billions of dollars of previously issued government securities that come due each week. After the T-bills are initially sold by the U.S. government, they are traded actively in the secondary market. At maturity, the government pays the face value of the T-bill.

Treasury bills are considered the benchmark of safety because they have essentially no risk. This is because obligations of the U.S. government are payable in U.S.

The Dog Ate My Investment

When you play around in the financial marketplace, you can expect to be burned every now and then. But if you get burned, who should you blame? It seems there is a growing trend among America's business leaders to blame everyone but themselves.

For example, Gibson Greetings Inc. of Cincinnati and Orange County, California, recently lost millions of dollars on derivatives, complex financial dealings that some people complain even Einstein couldn't understand. When Gibson lost millions, its financial officers argued that it had been swindled by slick New York sophisticates who never should have let the company engage in such risky deals.

Robert L. Citron, who served for more than two decades as Orange County's treasurer and was in charge of its investments, argued the same thing. "I was an inexperienced investor" who relied on "financial professionals," Citron said.

But Paul Critchlow, a spokesman for Merrill Lynch, said in response that Citron's statement rang "hollow when he claims he didn't know what he was doing," and that he "chose to ignore repeated warnings" that his $20 billion investment fund was "vulnerable to large losses as interest rates grew."

When investors don't get paid, investment funds are also ready with excuses. A missing minus sign is the reason Fidelity Investments gave for a $2 billion-plus mistake in calculating Magellan Fund shareholders' payments, saying an accountant omitted the minus sign from a spreadsheet and no one noticed.

It seems that excuse making has become so prevalent in financial markets that it has even spawned consultants who tell corporations why they shouldn't make excuses. One such consultant is Edward P. Wolfram, Jr., who served ten years in prison for embezzling $47 million from Bell & Beckwith, a brokerage firm in Toledo. His embezzlement put the firm out of business.

When it comes to excuses, Wolfram says he has heard them all. "Look, some things are illegal and inexcusable," he said, "like embezzlement, although I admit that at first I tried to blame anyone but myself for what I did. But we're talking about excuses becoming a way of life for folks who make bad judgments and don't want to take responsibility for their mess."

There may be a fine madness behind the recent outbreak of excuse making. If you admit that your company was at fault, you may be facing a lawsuit from angry stockholders. To the extent that lawyers, the Securities and Exchange Commission, or others say they'll scrutinize a company when things go badly and go after its managers with a class-action or regulatory club, the market for excuses will grow, explains Clifford W. Smith, Jr., a professor at the University of Rochester's Simon School of Business Administration.

Meanwhile, if you invest in financial markets and you lose a bundle, look on the bright side. There must be someone around that you can blame it on.

Questions to Consider

▶ Why do you think excuse making surges when a financial crisis occurs? What can a business do to avoid excuse making?

▶ If you invest in a financial market on the advice of a broker, is it your broker's fault when you lose money? Explain.

▶ In what circumstances would it benefit a firm to accept responsibility for a financial problem that was not the firm's fault?

Source: Margot Slade, *We Forgot to Write a Headline. But It's Not Our Fault, The New York Times* (February 19, 1995): F5.

---

dollars—and, theoretically, the U.S. government could print up all the dollars it needs to pay off its obligations.

Negotiable Certificates of Deposit   You may already be familiar with the certificates of deposit (CDs) that you can purchase from your local bank. They are simply pieces of paper that certify that you have deposited a certain amount of money in the bank, to be paid back on a certain date with interest. Small-denomination consumer CDs are very safe investments and they tend to have low interest rates.

Large-denomination CDs (of $100,000 to $1 million or more), with maturities of two weeks to a year, are **negotiable CDs** because they can be traded in the secondary market after they are initially issued by a financial institution. Large corporations and other institutions buy negotiable CDs when they have cash they wish to invest for a short period of time; they sell negotiable CDs when they want to raise cash quickly.

Commercial Paper   **Commercial paper** is a type of short-term promissory note— similar to an IOU—issued by large corporations with strong credit ratings. Commercial paper is *unsecured,* meaning that the issuing corporation does not provide any property as collateral that the lender (the one who buys the commercial paper note) can take instead of a payment if the issuing corporation defaults on the note. That is why commercial paper is only issued by financially strong, reliable firms.

Commercial paper is considered to be a safe place to put money for a short period of time. The notes themselves are issued and traded through a network of commercial paper dealers. Most of the buyers are large institutions.

Eurodollars   **Eurodollars** are interest-paying deposits denominated in U.S. dollars but located in banks outside the United States. Although Eurodollars originated in Europe—thus the name—Eurodollars now can be housed in banks throughout the world, from Asia to South America, although "Euro" is still in the name.

Eurodollars are deposited and borrowed by large institutions with good credit ratings. Because of the solid credit standing of the players, and because foreign bank regulations are usually less strict than U.S. bank regulations, Eurodollars often generate a higher rate of return and may be borrowed at often lower interest rates than dollar-denominated deposits in U.S. banks.

Banker's Acceptances   A **banker's acceptance** is a short-term debt instrument that is guaranteed for payment by a commercial bank (the bank "accepts" the responsibility to pay). Banker's acceptances thus allow businesses to avoid problems associated with collecting payment from reluctant debtors. They are often used when firms are doing business internationally because they eliminate the worry that the lender will have to travel to a foreign country to collect on a debt.

Securities in the Capital Market

When governments, corporations, and financial institutions want to raise money for a long period of time, they issue capital market securities. In contrast to money market securities, capital market securities may not be very liquid or safe. They are not generally suitable for short-term investments.

The two most prominent capital market securities are bonds and stocks. We'll examine these two securities in some depth now.

Bonds   **Bonds** are essentially IOUs that promise to pay their owner a certain amount of money on some specified date in the future—and in most cases, interest payments at regular intervals until maturity. When companies want to borrow money (usually a fairly large amount for a long period of time), they arrange for their investment bankers to print up the IOUs and sell them to the public at whatever price they can get. In essence, a firm that issues a bond is borrowing the amount that the bond sells for on the open market.

Bond Terminology and Types.   Although many types of bonds exist, most bonds have three special features: face value, maturity date, and coupon interest.

- *Face value:* The amount that the bond promises to pay its owner at some date in the future is called the bond's **face value,** or **par value,** or **principal.** Bond face values range in multiples of $1,000 all the way up to more than $1 million. Unless otherwise noted, assume that all bonds we discuss from this point forward have a face value of $1,000.
- *Maturity date:* The date on which the issuer is obligated to pay the bondholder the bond's face value.
- *Coupon interest:* The interest payments made to the bond owner during the life of the bond.[2] Some bonds pay coupon interest once a year; others pay it twice a year. Some bonds don't pay any interest at all. These bonds are called **zero-coupon bonds.**

The percentage of face value that the coupon interest payment represents is called the *coupon interest rate.* For example, assuming the face value of the bond was $1,000, a bond owner who received $80 interest payments each year would own a bond paying an 8 percent coupon interest rate:

$$\$80 \ / \ \$1,000 = .08, \text{ or } 8\%$$

The major types of bonds include Treasury bonds and notes, issued by the federal government; municipal bonds, issued by state and local governments; and corporate bonds, issued by corporations. The significant differences among these types of bonds are described in the following sections.

Treasury Notes and Bonds.   When the federal government wants to borrow money for periods of more than a year, it issues Treasury notes or Treasury bonds (T-notes and T-bonds for short). T-notes and T-bonds are identical except for their maturities. T-notes have maturities from one to ten years, and T-bonds have maturities greater than ten years. Both T-notes and T-bonds pay interest semi-annually, in addition to the principal, which is paid at maturity.

T-notes and T-bonds are auctioned by the Treasury every three months to pay off old maturing securities and to raise additional funds to finance the federal government's new deficit spending.

Although Treasury securities, such as T-notes and T-bonds, are extremely low-risk, they are not risk-free. Without the congressional authority to print money, the U.S. Treasury cannot legally pay its obligations, including the interest and principal on Treasury securities. In late 1995 and early 1996, Congress refused to raise the legal ceiling on outstanding Treasury debt unless President Clinton agreed to sign a seven-year balanced budget bill that restructured and eliminated many federal programs. President Clinton vetoed several budget bills because he opposed some of the budget measures.[3] The confrontation between the executive and congressional branches ended before the Treasury defaulted on its debts, but such a confrontation could feasibly result in default.

---

[2]The name originated decades ago when bondholders would actually tear off coupons from their bond certificates and mail them to the bond issuer to get their interest payments. Hence the name *coupon* interest.

[3]Adam Clymer, "Treasury Takes Retirement Funds to Avert Default," *The New York Times* (November 16, 1995): A1.

In May of 1996 the US Treasury announced that it would begin selling treasury bonds that are inflation-indexed. Interest rates adjust and are pegged to the inflation rate. This protects the investor from erosion of the purchasing power of the dollars they receive from this investment.

Municipal Bonds.   The bonds issued by state and local governments are known as **municipal bonds** or "munis." Many investors like municipal bonds because their coupon interest payments are free of federal income tax.

Municipal bonds come in two types: general obligation bonds (GOs) and revenue bonds. They differ in where the money is expected to come from to pay them off. General obligation bonds are supposed to be paid off with money raised by the issuer from a variety of different tax revenue sources. Revenue bonds are supposed to be paid off with money generated by the project the bonds were issued to finance—such as using toll bridge fees to pay off the bonds to finance the toll bridge.

Figure 2-1 shows a general obligation bond issued by the State of Illinois.

Figure 2-1   **A General Obligation Bond Issued by the State of Illinois**

This is a picture of a general obligation bond from The State of Illinois. The face value of the bond is $5,000, it promises to pay the face value to the bearer, and it matures on August 1, 2003. The bond was purchased on November 7, 1989, for $1,943.60. (Bond provided courtesy of The First National Bank Of Chicago.)

FINANCIAL MANAGEMENT AND YOU

How to Buy Treasury Securities without Using a Broker

Most people use a broker to buy Treasury securities, even though purchasing them is not difficult. If you are interested in investing in treasury securities, follow these four simple steps:

1. Contact your regional Federal Reserve Bank or its branch and request a Tender Application Form.
2. Fill out the form, indicating that you wish to submit a noncompetitive tender, and the particular security you wish to buy. Treasury bills come in minimum denominations of $10,000; Treasury notes of two- and three-year maturities come in minimum denominations of $5,000; Treasury notes of five- and ten-year maturities and Treasury bonds having a thirty-year maturity come in minimum denominations of $1,000.

3. Send the form back, along with your check for the amount of the face value of the securities you selected. A cashier's check must be sent for Treasury bills, while a personal check is accepted for Treasury notes and bonds. Your investment in Treasury notes, bills, or bonds will be in book-entry form on the computers of the U.S. Treasury. You will receive a confirmation receipt verifying your investment.
4. In the case of Treasury bills, you will receive a check within a few weeks for the amount of the face value minus the price determined at the auction. At maturity all bills, notes, and bonds will pay the face value. Notes and bonds will also pay semi-annual interest until the maturity date.

Corporate Bonds.   Corporate bonds are similar to T-bonds and T-notes except they are issued by corporations. Like T-bonds and T-notes, they pay their owner interest during the life of the bond and repay principal at maturity. Unlike T-bonds and T-notes, however, corporate bonds sometimes carry substantial risk of default. As a last resort, the U.S. government can print money to pay off its Treasury bill, note, and bond obligations; but when private corporations run into trouble, they have no such latitude. Corporations' creditors may get paid late or not at all.

Relatively safe bonds are called *investment-grade bonds*. Many financial institutions and money management firms are required to invest only in those corporate bonds that are investment grade. Relatively risky bonds are called *junk bonds*.[4] Junk bonds are generally issued by troubled companies, but may be issued by financially strong companies that later run into trouble.

This completes our introduction to bonds. Now let's turn our attention to the other major security in the capital market, corporate stock.

Corporate Stock   Rather than borrowing money by issuing bonds, a corporation may choose to raise money by selling shares of ownership interest in the company. Those shares of ownership are **stock.** Investors who buy stock are called stockholders.

---

[4]The term junk bond is a slang term that is now widely accepted. Firms trying to sell junk bonds hate the term, of course. They would prefer to call such bonds "high-yield."

As a source of funds, stock has an advantage over bonds: The money raised from the sale of stock doesn't ever have to be paid back, and the company doesn't have to make interest payments to the stockholders.

A corporation may issue two types of corporate stock, *common stock* and *preferred stock*. Let's look at their characteristics.

Common Stock. Common stock is so called because there is nothing special about it. The holders of a company's common stock are simply the owners of the company. Their ownership entitles them to the firm's earnings that remain after all other groups having a claim on the firm (such as bondholders) have been paid.

Each common stockholder owns a portion of the company represented by the fraction of the whole that the stockholder's shares represent. Thus, if a company issued 1 million shares of common stock, a person who holds one share owns one-millionth of the company.

Common stockholders receive a return on their investment in the form of common stock **dividends,** distributed from the firm's profits, and from **capital gains,** realized upon the sale of the shares.[5]

Preferred Stock. **Preferred stock** is so called because if dividends are declared by the board of directors of a business, they are paid to preferred stockholders first. If any funds are left over, they may be paid to the common stockholders. So why would anyone buy common stock? First, preferred stockholders normally don't get to vote on how the firm is run. Second, common stock normally provides a slightly higher expected return because it is a more risky investment—that is, dividends are not guaranteed. However, common stockholders—as owners—are entitled to all the residual income of the firm, and there is no upper limit on how great the residual income of the firm might be.

INTEREST

No one lends money for free. When people lend money to other people, a number of things could happen that might prevent them from getting all their money back. Whenever people agree to take risk, compensation is required before they will voluntarily enter into an agreement. In financial activities, we refer to this compensation as interest. **Interest** represents the return, or compensation, a lender demands before agreeing to loan money.

Determinants of Interest Rates

The prevailing rate of interest in any situation is called the **nominal interest rate.** In the Take Note, for example, the nominal interest rate for the one year $100 loan is 10 percent.

The nominal interest rate is actually the total of a number of separate components, as shown in Figure 2-2. We will explore each of these components in the following sections.

Take Note

When we refer to interest, we normally express it in percentage terms, called the interest rate. Thus, if you lend a person $100 for one year, and the return you require for doing so is $10, we would say that the interest rate you are charging for the loan is $10/$100 = .10, or 10 percent.

---

[5]Of course there is no guarantee that a common stockholder's stock will increase in price. If the price goes down, the stockholder will experience a capital loss.

Figure 2-2 Components of the Nominal Interest Rate

The nominal interest rate is composed of the real interest rate plus a number of premiums. The nominal risk-free interest rate is the real rate plus an inflation premium. When risk premiums are added, the result is the total nominal interest rate.

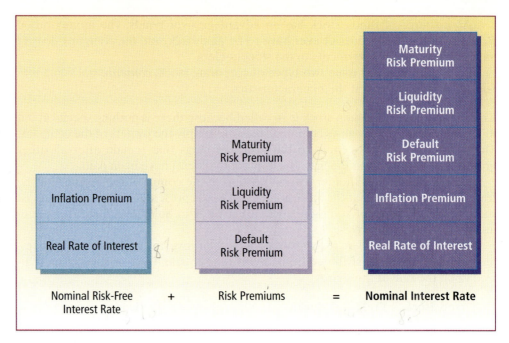

	Maturity Risk Premium
	Liquidity Risk Premium
	Default Risk Premium
Maturity Risk Premium	Inflation Premium
Liquidity Risk Premium	Real Rate of Interest
Inflation Premium	Default Risk Premium
Real Rate of Interest	

Nominal Risk-Free Interest Rate + Risk Premiums = **Nominal Interest Rate**

The Real Rate of Interest Lenders of money must postpone spending during the time the money is loaned. Lenders, then, lose the opportunity to invest their money for that period of time. To compensate for the cost of losing investment opportunities while they postpone their spending, lenders demand, and borrowers pay, a basic rate of return—the **real rate of interest.** The real rate of interest does not include adjustments for any other factors, such as the risk of not getting paid back. We'll describe this in a moment.

Let's continue with the example in the Take Note on page 29, in which you lent a person $100. The total interest rate that you charged was 10 percent (the nominal interest rate). The portion of the total nominal rate that represents the return you demand for forgoing the opportunity to spend your money now is the real rate of interest. In our example, assume the real rate of interest is 2 percent.

Source: FRANK & ERNEST © 1996 United Feature Syndicate, Inc. Reprinted by Permission.

Additions to the real rate of interest are called *premiums*. The major premiums are the inflation premium, the default risk premium, the liquidity risk premium, and the maturity risk premium.

The Inflation Premium   Inflation erodes the purchasing power of money. If inflation is present, the dollars that lenders get when their loans are repaid may not buy as much as the dollars that they lent to start with. Therefore lenders who anticipate inflation during the term of a loan will demand additional interest to compensate for it. This additional required interest is the **inflation premium.**

If, when you lent $100, you thought that the rate of inflation was going to be 4 percent during the life of the loan, you would add 4 percent to the 2 percent real rate of interest you charged for postponing your spending. The total interest rate charge—so far— would be 6 percent.

The Nominal Risk-Free Rate   The interest rate that we have built so far, containing the real rate of interest and a premium to cover expected inflation, is often called the **nominal risk-free rate of interest,** as shown earlier in Figure 2-2. It is called this because it does not include any premiums for the uncertainties associated with borrowing or lending. The yield on short-term U.S. Treasury bills is often used as a proxy for the risk-free rate, since the degree of uncertainty associated with these securities is very small.

▶ Take Note

You can find the yield on U.S. Treasury bills very easily just by looking in The Wall Street Journal *on page C-1. Yields on T-bills and a number of other securities are published there every business day.*

Risk Premiums   The remaining determinants of the nominal interest rate represent extra charges to compensate lenders for taking risk. Risks in lending come in a number of forms. The most common are default risk, liquidity risk, and maturity risk.

The Default Risk Premium.   A *default* occurs when a borrower fails to pay the interest and principal on a loan on time. If a borrower has a questionable reputation or is having financial difficulties, the lender faces the risk that the borrower will default. The **default risk premium** is the extra compensation lenders demand for assuming the risk of default.

In our $100 loan example, if you weren't completely sure that the person to whom you had lent $100 would pay it back, you would demand extra compensation—let's say, 2 percentage points—to compensate for that risk. The total interest rate demanded so far would be 2 percent real rate of interest + 4 percent inflation premium + 2 percent default risk premium = 8 percent.

The Liquidity Risk Premium.   Sometimes lenders sell loans to others after making them. (This happens often in the mortgage business, where investors trade mortgages among themselves.) Some loans are easily sold to other parties and others are not. Those that are easily sold are *liquid,* and those that aren't sold easily are considered *illiquid.* Illiquid loans have a higher interest rate to compensate the lender for the inconvenience of being stuck with the loan until it matures. The extra interest that lenders demand to compensate for the lack of liquidity is the **liquidity risk premium.**

You will probably not be able to sell your $100 loan to anyone else, and will have to hold it until maturity. Therefore you require another 1 percent to compensate for the lack of liquidity. The total interest rate demanded so far is 2 percent real rate of interest + 4 percent inflation premium + 2 percent default risk premium + 1 percent liquidity risk premium = 9 percent.

The Maturity Risk Premium. If interest rates rise, lenders may find themselves stuck with loans paying the original rate prevailing at the time the loans were made, while other lenders are able to make new loans at higher rates. However, if interest rates go down, the same lenders will be happy to receive higher interest rates than the rate at which other lenders must make new loans.

If lenders think interest rates might rise in the future, they will *increase* the rate they charge now to compensate for this risk. Conversely, if lenders think interest rates might fall in the future, they will *decrease* the rate they charge now to encourage borrowers to come in and lock in the current rate. The up or down adjustment that lenders make to their current interest rates to compensate for the uncertainty as to the change in rates is the **maturity risk premium.** The maturity risk premium can be either positive or negative.

In our example, if you thought interest rates would probably rise before you were repaid the $100 you loaned, you might demand an extra percentage point to compensate for the risk that you would be unable to take advantage of the new higher rates. The total rate demanded is now 10 percent. (2 percent real rate of interest + 4 percent inflation premium + 2 percent default risk premium + 1 percent liquidity risk premium + 1 percent maturity risk premium = 10 percent, the nominal interest rate.)

The total of the real rate of interest, the inflation premium, and the risk premiums (the default, liquidity, and maturity risk premiums) is the nominal interest rate the compensation lenders demand from those who want to borrow money.

Next, we will consider the *yield* curve—a graph of a security's interest rates, depending on the time to maturity.

The Yield Curve

A yield curve is a graphical depiction of interest rates for securities that differ only in the time remaining until their maturity. Yield curves are drawn by plotting the interest rates of one kind of security but with various maturity dates. The curve depicts the interest rates of these securities at a given point in time.

Yield curves of U.S. Treasury securities are most common because with Treasury securities it is easiest to hold constant the factors other than maturity. All Treasury securities have essentially the same default risk (almost none) and about the same degree of liquidity (excellent). Any differences in interest rates observed in the yield curve, then, can be attributed to the maturity differences among the securities, since other factors have essentially been held constant.

Figure 2-3 shows a Treasury securities yield curve. The yield curve in Figure 2-3 is upward sloping and would be called a "normal" yield curve. Although less common, yield curves may also be downward sloping, or "inverted."

Making Use of the Yield Curve The shape of the yield curve gives borrowers and lenders useful information for financial decisions. Borrowers, for example, tend to look for the low point of the curve, which indicates the least expensive loan maturity. Lenders tend to look for the highest point on the curve, which indicates the most expensive loan maturity.

Finding the most advantageous maturity is not quite as simple as it sounds because it depends on more factors than cost. For instance, the least expensive matu-

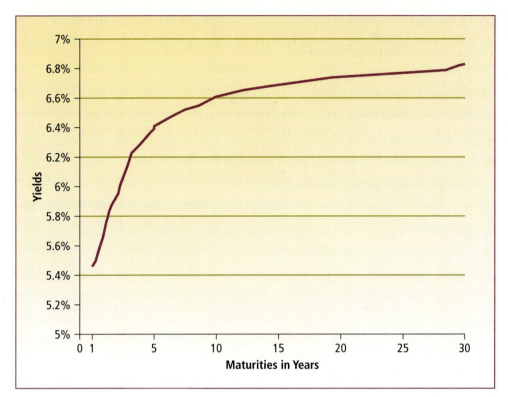

Figure 2-3 **Treasury Yield Curve**

This yield curve shows interest rates on April 24, 1996, for treasury securities having maturities from one to thirty years.

Source: *The Wall St. Journal* (April 25, 1996): C18.

rity is not always the most advantageous for borrowers. If a firm borrows short-term, for example, it may obtain the lowest interest rate, but the loan may mature in a short time and have to be renewed at a higher rate if interest rates have risen in the interim. Borrowing for a longer term may cost a borrower more at the outset but less in the long-run because the interest rate is locked in.

Lenders face the opposite situation. Granting long-term loans at relatively high interest rates may look attractive now; but if short-term rates rise, the lenders may miss profitable opportunities because their funds have already been invested. Both borrowers and lenders must balance their desire for return with their tolerance for risk.

WHAT'S NEXT

In this chapter we investigated financial markets, securities, and interest rates. In the next chapter, we will look at another part of the financial environment, financial institutions.

Summary

1. Describe how the U.S. financial system works.

The financial system is made up of surplus economic units, entities and individuals that have excess funds, and deficit economic units, entities and individuals that need to acquire additional funds. The financial system provides the network that brings these two groups together so that funds flow from the surplus economic units to the deficit economic units.

2. Define financial securities.

Securities are documents that represent a person's right to receive funds in the future. Firms issue securities in exchange for funds they need now, and investors trade securities among themselves.

3. Explain the function of financial intermediaries.

Financial intermediaries act to put those in need of funds in contact with those who have funds available. Investment banking firms help businesses acquire funds from the public by issuing securities in the financial marketplace. Brokers help members of the public trade securities with each other. Dealers buy and sell securities themselves.

4. Identify the different financial markets.

Financial markets are forums in the financial system that allow surplus economic units to transact with deficit economic units and for portfolio adjustments to be made. Securities change hands in financial markets. The financial markets include the primary market, where new securities are issued for the first time; the secondary market, where previously issued securities are traded among investors; the money market, in which securities with maturities of less than one year are traded; and the capital market, in which securities with maturities longer than one year are traded. Some securities are traded on organized exchanges, like the New York Stock Exchange, and others are traded over-the-counter (OTC) by a network of securities dealers.

5. List and define the securities traded in the money and capital markets.

Securities traded in the money market include:

- *Treasury bills:* short-term debt instruments issued by the U.S. Treasury that are sold at a discount and pay face value at maturity.
- *Negotiable certificates of deposit (CDs):* certificates that can be traded in financial markets and represent amounts deposited at banks that will be repaid at maturity with a specified rate of interest.
- *Eurodollars:* U.S. dollar-denominated deposits in banks outside the United States.
- *Bankers acceptances:* documents that signify that a bank has guaranteed payment of a certain amount at a future date if the original promisor doesn't pay.

The two major securities traded in the capital market include:

- *Bonds:* long-term securities that represent a promise to pay a fixed amount at a future date, usually with interest payments made at regular intervals. Treasury bonds are issued by the U.S. government, corporate bonds by firms, and municipal bonds by state and local governments.
- *Stocks:* shares of ownership interest in corporations. Preferred stockholders have a promised dividend, but usually no voting rights. Common stockholders may receive dividends paid at the discretion of the board, but do have voting rights.

6. Identify the determinants of the nominal interest rate.

The nominal interest rate has three main determinants:

- *The real rate of interest:* the basic rate lenders require to compensate for forgoing the opportunity to spend money during the term of the loan.
- *An inflation premium:* a premium that compensates for the expected erosion of purchasing power due to inflation over the life of the loan.
- *Risk premiums:* premiums that compensate for the risks of default (the risk that the lender won't be paid back), liquidity (the risk that the lender won't be able to sell the security in a reasonable time at a fair price), and maturity (the risk that interest rates may change adversely during the life of the security).

7. *Construct and analyze a yield curve.*

A yield curve is a graphical depiction of interest rates on securities that differ only in the time remaining until their maturity. Lenders and borrowers may use a yield curve to determine the most advantageous loan maturity.

Self-Test

ST-1. To minimize risk, why don't most firms simply finance their growth from the profits they earn?

ST-2. What market would a firm go to if it needed cash for ninety days? If it needed cash for ten years?

ST-3. If your company's stock was not listed on the New York Stock Exchange or the American Stock Exchange, how could investors purchase the shares?

ST-4. What alternatives does General Motors, a very large and secure firm, have for obtaining $3 million for sixty days?

ST-5. Assume Treasury security yields for today are as follows:

> One-year T-notes 5.75%
> Two-year T-notes 5.5%
> Three-year T-bonds 5.25%
> Five-year T-bonds 5.0%
> Ten-year T-bonds 4.75%
> Twenty-year T-bonds 4%
> Thirty-year T-bonds 3.25%

Draw a yield curve based on this data.

Review Questions

1. What are financial markets? Why do they exist?
2. What is a security?
3. What are the characteristics of an efficient market?
4. How are financial trades made on an organized exchange?
5. How are financial trades made in an over-the-counter market? Discuss the role of a dealer in the OTC market.
6. What is the role of a broker in security transactions? How are brokers compensated?
7. What is a Treasury bill? How risky is it?
8. Would there be positive interest rates on bonds in a world with absolutely no risk (no default risk, maturity risk, and so on)? Why would a lender demand, and a borrower be willing to pay, a positive interest rate in such a no-risk world?

Build Your Communication Skills

CS-1. Imagine the following scenario:

Your firm has decided to build a new plant in South America this year. The plant will cost $10 million and all the money must be paid up front. Your boss has asked you to brief the board of directors on the options the firm has for raising the $10 million.

Prepare a memo for the board members outlining the pros and cons of the various financing options open to the firm. Divide into small groups. Each group member should spend 5 minutes presenting his or her financing option suggestions to the rest of the group members, who should act as the board members.

CS-2. Prepare an IOU, or "note," that promises to pay $100 one year from today to the holder of the note.

a. Auction this note off to someone else in the class, having the buyer pay for it with a piece of scratch-paper play money.
b. Compute the note-buyer's percent rate of return if he or she holds the note for a year and cashes it in.
c. Ask the new owner of the note to auction it off to someone else. Note the new buyer's rate of return based on his or her purchase price.
d. Discuss the operation of the market the class has created. Note the similarities between it and the bond market in the real world.

Problems

2-1. If the real rate of interest is 2 percent, inflation is expected to be 3 percent during the coming year, and the default risk premium, liquidity risk premium, and maturity risk premium for the Bonds-R-Us corporation are all 1 percent each, what would be the yield on a Bonds-R-Us bond?

2-2. Assume Treasury security yields for today are as follows:

Three-month T-bills 6.5%
Six-month T-bills 6.0%
One-year T-notes 5.75%
Two-year T-notes 5.5%
Three-year T-bonds 5.25%
Five-year T-bonds 5.0%
Ten-year T-bonds 4.75%
Thirty-year T-bonds 4.5%

Draw a yield curve based on this data. Discuss the implications if you are:

a. a borrower
b. a lender

Answers to Self-Test

ST-1. In most cases, profits are insufficient to provide the funds needed, especially with large projects. Financial markets provide access to external sources of funds.

ST-2. To obtain cash for ninety days, a business firm would go to the money market where it would sell a ninety-day security. To obtain cash for ten years, a firm would sell a security in the capital market.

ST-3. Investors would simply purchase the shares over-the-counter from a dealer.

ST-4. General Motors could:

- obtain a sixty-day loan from a financial institution
- delay payments to its suppliers
- sell commercial paper notes in the money market

ST-5. The yield curve follows:

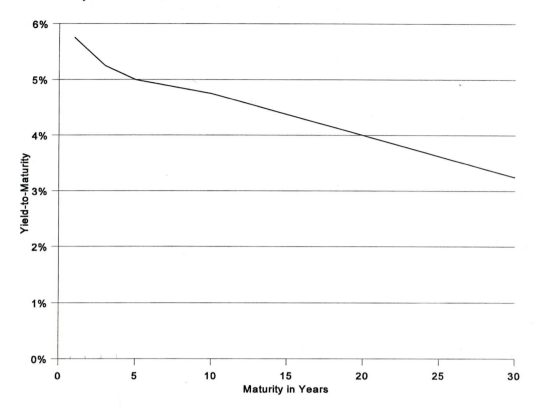

chapter 3

Financial Institutions

A banker is a fellow who lends his umbrella when the sun is shining and wants it back the minute it begins to rain.

Mark Twain

The Miami Dolphins versus Microsoft: A Whole New Ball Game

South Florida can put its money where its team spirit is—in the Dolphins' Banking Club, a checking account offered by First Union National Bank of Florida. Customers who join the club receive specially designed Miami Dolphins logo checks, a free checkbook cover sporting the Dolphins logo, and a free Dolphins baseball-style hat.

Sports fans are likely to see more "sports banking clubs" spring up around the country. The reason? Your local bank is facing tough competition to keep you as a customer. This competition comes from many sources, including Microsoft.

Microsoft may soon offer an Internet service called E-cash that will transform the way we transact our financial business. What is E-cash? It's digital money. With E-cash, you will no longer need a wad of bills. Instead, you'll carry a credit-card-size piece of plastic that allows you to make purchases online, replacing cash and checks for everyday purchases.

There may be big money in E-cash products and services. That's why Microsoft CEO Bill Gates has dozens of programmers designing a sweeping system, where people can bypass their local bank, use Microsoft's E-cash, and do business worldwide.

In short, when E-cash becomes a reality, a competitive free-for-all will result. Because the Internet knows no boundaries, any company that offers E-cash services can gain direct access to millions of consumers and businesses—no matter what country they're in. "The retail banking market will collapse and give way to global competition," says Eric Huges, president of Open Financial Networks.

To keep your checking account, your local bank must move fast to keep up. Ronald A. Braco, head of electronic banking at Chemical Bank, estimates that banks have less than five years to come up with viable E-cash products and services. Meanwhile, your local bank will try to keep you loyal by offering special accounts such as the Miami Dolphins Account.

But like the Miami Dolphins, your local bank also knows the competition is tough out there. ✳

Sources: Elizabeth Bliss, PR Newswire (November 15, 1995); Kelley Holland and Amy Cortese, "The Future of Money," *Business Week* (June 12, 1995).

Chapter Overview

In the last chapter we discussed how the financial system makes it possible for deficit and surplus economic units to come together, exchanging funds for securities to their mutual benefit. In this chapter we will examine how financial institutions help channel available funds to those who need it. We will also see the important role the Federal Reserve plays in regulating the financial system, protecting both deficit and surplus economic units.

Financial Intermediation

The financial system makes it possible for surplus and deficit economic units to come together, exchanging funds for securities, to their mutual benefit. When funds flow from surplus economic units to a financial institution to a deficit economic unit, the process is known as **intermediation.** The financial institution acts as an intermediary between the two economic units.

Surplus economic units can channel their funds into financial institutions by purchasing savings accounts, checking accounts, life insurance policies, casualty insurance policies, or claims on a pension fund. The financial institutions can then pool the funds received and use them to purchase claims issued by deficit economic units, such as Treasury, municipal, or corporate bonds; and common or preferred stock. (The institutions may purchase real assets too, such as real estate or gold.)

At first glance it might seem that intermediation complicates things unnecessarily. Why do the surplus and deficit economic units need a middle person? The answer is that financial institutions can do things for both that they often can't do for themselves. Here are some examples of the services that financial institutions provide.

Denomination Matching

Members of the household sector (net surplus economic units) often have only a small amount of funds available to invest in securities. Although, as a group, they are net suppliers of funds and have a large amount of funds available, this is often not the case for individuals or families. Businesses and government entities (net deficit economic units) usually need large amounts of funds. Thus it is often difficult for these surplus and deficit economic units to come together on their own to arrange a mutually beneficial exchange of funds for securities. The surplus economic units typically want to supply a small amount of funds, while the deficit economic units typically want to obtain a large amount of funds.

A financial institution can step in and save the day. A bank, savings and loan, or insurance company can take in small amounts of funds from many individuals, form a large pool of funds, and then use that large pool to purchase securities from individual businesses and governments. This pooling of funds is depicted in Figure 3-1.

The typical surplus economic unit likes to make funds available to others for a short period of time. Most people, for example, would like to get their money back on short notice if the need were to arise. They would prefer to buy securities that have a short maturity. Most businesses and government entities, on the other hand, want to make use of funds for a long period of time. The new plants, roads, airports, and the like that businesses and governments buy and build are long-term projects that often require long-term financing. They would prefer to sell securities that have a long maturity.

Here's the problem: How can exchanges agreeable to both sides be arranged when the surplus economic units want the right to get their funds back quickly and the deficit economic units want to keep the funds for a long time? Remember, a financial institution has many different surplus economic units buying its securities (savings accounts, checking accounts, insurance policies, and so on). The number that will want their funds back on any given day is likely to be small, and they will probably withdraw only a very small percentage of the total funds held in the financial institution. So a large percentage of the funds held by the financial institution

 Maturity Matching

Figure 3-1 shows how small amounts of funds from many small surplus economic units (SEUs) can be pooled and channelled into the hands of a relatively small number of deficit economic units (DEUs). The financial institution provides each what it needs.

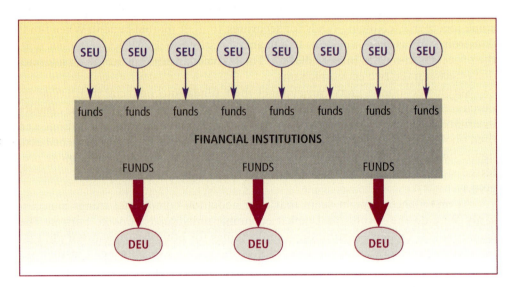

can be invested in the long-term securities of deficit economic units, with little danger of running out of funds.

Absorbing Credit Risk

Credit risk is the risk that the issuer of a security may fail to make promised payments to the investor at the times specified. When surplus and deficit economic units try to arrange for a direct transfer of funds for securities, this problem is often a large one. Surplus economic units do not usually have the expertise to determine whether deficit economic units can and will make good on their obligations, so it is difficult for them to predict when a would-be deficit economic unit will fail to pay what it owes. Such a failure is likely to be devastating to a surplus economic unit that has lent a proportionately large amount of money. In contrast, a financial institution is in a better position to predict who will pay and who won't. It is also in a better position, having greater financial resources, to occasionally absorb a loss when someone fails to pay.

Now let us turn to the various types of financial institutions. We'll start with commercial banks, which are regulated by various government entities. We'll also discuss the Federal Reserve System, which plays a major role in bank regulation and in overseeing the financial system.

COMMERCIAL BANKS

Commercial banks are financial institutions that exist primarily to lend money to businesses. Banks also lend to individuals, governments, and other entities, but the bulk of their profits typically come from business loans. Commercial banks make money by charging a higher interest rate on the money they lend than the rate they pay on money lent to them in the form of deposits. This difference between the rate charged to borrowers and the rate paid to depositors is known as the **interest rate spread.**

Banking is different from many other types of business in that it must have a "charter" before it can open its doors. A bank charter—much more difficult to ob-

Source: FRANK & ERNEST © 1996 United Feature Syndicate, Inc. Reprinted by Permission.

tain than a city license needed to open another type of business—is an authorization from the government granting permission to operate. Commercial bank charters are issued by the federal government or the government of the state where the bank is located. You can't just rent some office space, buy a vault and some office furniture, put up a sign that says "Joe's Bank," and begin taking in deposits and making loans.

Banks can't operate without a charter because banking is a business intimately involved in the payment system and money supply of the economy. To protect individual economic units and the economy as a whole, the government has decided to control entry into this business and to regulate it, too.

Bank Regulation

After a bank has been granted a charter, government entities continue to scrutinize it. To begin with, all banks with federal charters must be members of the Federal Reserve System (commonly known as "the Fed"). State-chartered banks may apply for membership in the Federal Reserve System but are not required to do so. All members of the Federal Reserve System must also belong to the Federal Deposit Insurance Corporation (FDIC), which insures customer deposits at participating institutions for up to $100,000. Nonmember banks, along with other types of financial institutions, may belong to the FDIC also. Almost all banks—whether federally or state chartered, members of the Fed or not—have FDIC insurance for their depositors.

So many agencies regulate banks that it can be difficult to sort them out. To lessen the potentially extensive overlap of authority, bank regulating entities have worked out an agreement. The Office of the Comptroller of the Currency (OCC) has primary responsibility for examining national banks, ensuring that they meet accepted standards. The Fed has primary responsibility for examining state-chartered member banks. The FDIC assumes primary responsibility for examining state nonmember banks having FDIC insurance. State banking authorities have primary examining authority over state nonmember banks with no FDIC coverage for their depositors. Figure 3-2 shows the main examination authority structure for commercial banks.

Commercial Bank Operations

Commercial banks operate with more government oversight than most businesses, but they are managed just like other companies. Commercial banks have stockholders, employees, managers, equipment, and facilities, and the primary financial goal of such banks is to maximize value for their stockholders. The banks do most of their business by receiving funds from depositors and lending the funds to those who need them. Commercial banks also occasionally issue long-term bonds to raise funds, borrow from the Federal Reserve, or borrow deposits kept by other financial institutions in Federal Reserve banks in what is known as the *federal funds market.*

Commercial Bank Reserves   Commercial banks are not allowed to lend all the funds they get from depositors. The Federal Reserve requires all commercial banks to keep a minimum amount of reserves on hand. *Reserves* are cash assets, vault cash, and deposits at the Fed that are available to a bank to meet the withdrawal demands of its depositors and to pay other obligations as they come due. Actually, the reserve requirement is set more with monetary policy in mind than to ensure that banks meet their depositors' withdrawal requests.

Figure 3-2   The Commercial Bank Examination System

Figure 3-2 shows the primary and potential examining authorities for different kinds of banks.

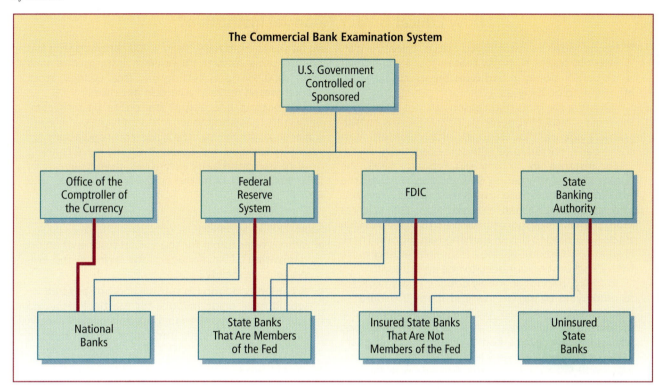

The required level of reserves a bank must hold is determined by applying a certain percentage to the average weekly deposits held by the bank. The exact percentage of deposits a bank must hold in reserve, called the **required reserve ratio,** depends on the type of deposit and the size of the bank. It varies from time to time as determined by the Federal Reserve, subject to certain statutory limits (see Table 3-1).

Table 3-1 shows the amount of reserves financial institutions are required to keep, depending on the amount of different kinds of deposits. Vault cash and deposits in the bank's account at the Fed are used to satisfy these reserve requirements; they are called **primary reserves.** These primary reserves are non-interest-earning assets held by financial institutions.

In addition to primary reserves, commercial banks generally hold some **secondary reserves**—assets that can be quickly and easily sold and converted into cash.

0 percent on first $4.3 million of transaction deposits
3 percent on transaction accounts greater than $4.3 million, up to $52.0 million
10 percent on transaction accounts above $52.0 million
0 percent on nonpersonal time deposits
0 percent on Eurocurrency liabilities
Source: *Federal Reserve Bulletin* (April 1996, A9).

TABLE 3-1

Reserve Requirements as of April 1996

How Ethical Is Your Financial Institution?

The financial world cringed when twenty-eight-year-old trader Nicholas Leeson lost $1 billion of his bank's money in bad investments, causing Barings Bank to go belly-up.

Yet there are hints that Leeson was not working in the most ethical environment. In fact, there is considerable evidence that Barings, Britain's oldest merchant bank, skirted rules with some regularity.

For instance, in January and February 1995, the bank routed a staggering $890 million to cover the costs of maintaining the futures and options contracts into which Leeson had entered. That sum was far more than Barings should have used to cover the contracts according to British banking regulations. Those regulations forbade Barings from committing more than 25 percent of its money to one investment.

In Japan, Barings allegedly dodged salary taxes for its employees by paying many of them "offshore"—that is, outside of Japan. For example, large portions of Barings's employees' income, often including bonuses, were earmarked for employees but set aside until the employees left Japan. That way, employees didn't have to pay full income tax in Japan.

Plus, Barings engaged in other questionable practices, such as giving commission "rebates" to valuable customers. Certain valued customers were charged negotiated commissions and then received part of the money back as a rebate. The commission fees, then, depended on the customer.

In fact, the collapse of Barings may have occurred because bank officials violated a banking rule that no bank can hold more than 1,000 contracts that bet on the same market movement. Barings had well over 1,000 contracts betting that the Japanese stock market would move in a certain direction.

The bottom line is that the entire Barings company culture seemed to wink at employees who were clever enough to skirt the rules and regulations set down by England and Japan. It should have come as no surprise to top bank executives, then, that one of their employees bent the rules, bet the bank, and lost.

Questions to Consider

▶ Who is responsible for the ethical culture of an organization? The managers, the owners, the employees, or society?

▶ If Leeson had won his futures and options bet, he would have made millions for the bank. How do you think the bank managers and owners would have viewed Leeson's infractions of the rules in that instance?

▶ What ethical message do you think Barings' managers sent its employees? How can a business do a better job communicating its code of ethics? Why should owners be interested in corporate ethics?

Source: Marcus W. Brauchili, "Many Who Knew Barings PLC Suggest Firm Wasn't Model Corporate Citizen," *The Wall Street Journal* (March 8, 1995): A16.

Secondary reserves consist of short-term securities such as Treasury bills or commercial paper. They serve as a buffer between the very liquid primary reserves and the rest of the bank's assets (mostly loans), which are generally less liquid.

THE FEDERAL RESERVE SYSTEM

The **Federal Reserve System** serves as the central bank of the United States. It regulates the nation's money supply, makes loans to member banks and other financial institutions, and regulates the financial system, as described in the previous section.

Open-market purchases of government securities, making loans to financial institutions, and decreasing reserve requirements all lead to an increase in the money supply. Open-market sales of government securities, receiving payments on loans made to financial institutions, and increasing reserve requirements all lead to a decrease in the money supply.

Organization of the Fed

The Fed is made up of twelve district Federal Reserve banks spread throughout the country, as shown in Figure 3-3, along with a seven-member Board of Governors and a Federal Open Market Committee (FOMC) that has twelve voting members. Both the Board of Governors and the Federal Open Market Committee are located in Washington, D.C. They hold most of the power of the Fed.

The seven members of the Board of Governors are appointed by the president of the United States, subject to confirmation by the United States Senate. The governors serve staggered fourteen-year terms, partly to insulate them from political influences. It would be naive to believe that these members are not subject to some political influences, but a president would normally have to be well into a second (and final) term before successfully replacing a majority of the Fed members.

Figure 3-3   **The 12 Fed Districts in the U.S.**

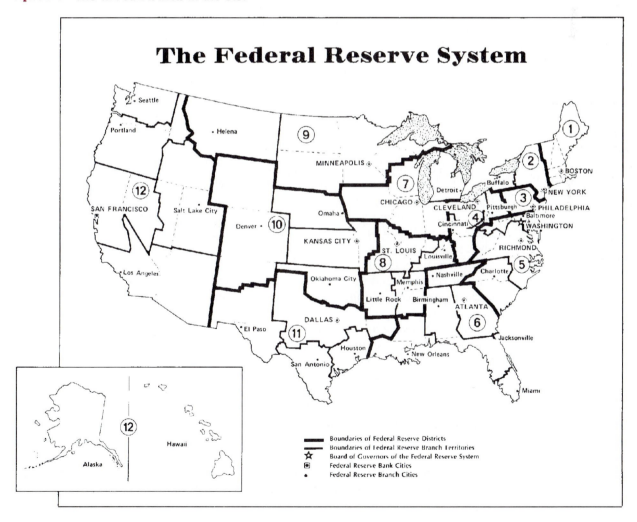

The twelve voting members of the Federal Open Market Committee (FOMC) are the seven members of the Board of Governors plus five of the twelve presidents of the district Federal Reserve banks. The district bank presidents take turns serving as voting members of the FOMC, although the president of the Federal Reserve Bank of New York is always one of the five. The nonvoting presidents of the district Federal Reserve Banks usually attend the FOMC meetings and participate in discussions.

Controlling the Money Supply

The main focus of the FOMC is to recommend **open-market operations** that the Fed should implement to increase or decrease the money supply. Open-market operations are purchases and sales of government securities and foreign currencies conducted in the Federal Reserve Bank of New York at a trading desk that exists for this purpose.

When the Fed *buys* government securities or currencies, it increases bank reserves and the money supply. When the Fed *sells* government securities or currencies, it decreases bank reserves and the money supply.

When the Fed wishes to increase the money supply, it instructs its traders at the Federal Reserve Bank of New York to buy government securities (primarily T-bills) on the open market. The traders contact government securities dealers (who are mostly commercial banks) around the country and buy the required amount of securities. These dealers have accounts at the Fed. When the Fed buys government securities from a dealer, it credits that dealer's account at the Fed. This action increases the amount of funds held by the dealer banks and enables them to make additional loans and investments. When the additional loans and investments are made, the supply of money in circulation increases, thus accomplishing the Fed's objective.

The exact opposite occurs when the Fed wishes to decrease the money supply. The Fed calls its traders at the Federal Reserve Bank of New York and instructs them to sell government securities on the open market. The traders contact government securities dealers around the country and sell the required amount of securities to them. When the dealers receive their securities, their accounts are debited and the amount of funds held by these banks decreases. The amount of loans and investments, then, that these banks can support also decreases. Some maturing loans are not renewed and some marketable security investments are not replaced because of the loss of funds. The result is a decrease in the supply of money in circulation.

Why, you might ask, would the Fed want to increase or decrease the money supply? The answer is simple: to influence economic activity. When the members of the FOMC feel that the economy is growing too slowly, the Fed increases the money supply, thus increasing liquidity in the economy and stimulating growth. When the economy is growing too fast and inflation seems imminent, the Fed decreases the money supply (or slows down its growth). This causes the economy to "cool off," since liquidity has decreased.

Although the government securities and currency markets are very large and efficient, the Fed is like a large elephant: people notice when it enters the market. It buys and sells in huge amounts; so when the Fed buys or sells securities, its actions can't help but affect prices (and interest rates) across the whole market.

The Discount Window

The twelve district Federal Reserve Banks lend money to financial institutions at the *discount window.* Originally, only member banks in a Federal Reserve Bank's district came to the discount window for loans. Since 1980, however, the district Federal Reserve banks have extended loans to nonmember banks and to nonbank financial institutions, too.

The district Federal Reserve banks also provide clearing services—collecting and paying for checks written on and deposited in banks. The Fed charges fees for the services it provides. The fees collected, interest earned on government securities held, and other sources of income provide the funds the Fed needs to operate. The Fed does not require appropriations from Congress. In fact, if excess profits are left over, as is usually the case, they are turned over to the U.S. Treasury. There are not many federal government entities that turn money over *to* the Treasury.

SAVINGS AND LOAN ASSOCIATIONS

Like commercial banks, **savings and loan associations (S&Ls)** are in business to take in deposits and lend money, primarily in the form of mortgage loans. *Mortgage loans* are loans that are secured by real property such as real estate. If a borrower defaults on a mortgage loan, the lender can take legal possession of the property. The property can then be sold and the lender keeps the proceeds from the sale up to the amount owed. S&Ls make a profit by charging a higher interest rate on the money they lend than the rate paid on deposits they take in.

Like banks, S&Ls can borrow from the Federal Reserve and from other financial institutions. S&Ls can also borrow from one of the twelve Federal Home Loan banks to meet some of their funding needs. The Office of Thrift Supervision is the primary regulator of federally chartered S&Ls.

Legislation Affecting S&Ls

The Depository Institutions Deregulation and Monetary Control Act of 1980 (MCA)[1] took the cap off interest rates that S&Ls may pay to depositors. It also brought S&Ls under the control of the Fed with regard to reserve requirements. The MCA authorized S&Ls to raise funds from new sources such as negotiable orders of withdrawal (NOW accounts).

The 1982 Garn–St. Germain Act authorized S&Ls to offer money market accounts. It also expanded the lending and investing powers of S&Ls. The S&L crisis in the latter years of the 1980s demonstrated that these new powers were not always exercised wisely. Probably the most widely known S&L failure was that of Charles Keating's Lincoln Savings and Loan of California. That one failure cost the federal government about $2 billion.

In 1989 Congress passed the Financial Institutions Reform, Recovery, and Enforcement Act (FIRRE Act) to clean up the mess made when hundreds of S&Ls failed. Bad loans, bad investments, a recession, and fraud were among some of the reasons S&Ls failed during the 1980s. The FIRRE Act created the Resolution Trust

---

[1]This mouthful is also referred to simply as the Monetary Control Act (MCA).

Corporation (RTC) to preserve the remaining value of failed S&Ls, liquidate those that were hopelessly insolvent, and sell some failed S&Ls to other institutions where possible. The RTC often purchased poor quality assets itself to allow a healthy institution to merge with a failing S&L.

It is often said that Congress, having created the RTC, bailed out the failed S&Ls. This is not true. The owners of these failed S&Ls lost most or all their investments. It was the *depositors* who were protected. If Congress had not authorized the $200 billion or so needed to keep S&L depositors from taking losses, thousands of individuals, including many of modest means, would have lost substantial savings.

Regulation of S&Ls

Like commercial banks, savings and loan associations must apply for either a federal or a state charter that authorizes them to operate. All federally chartered S&Ls are regulated by the Office of Thrift Supervision (OTS), and almost all S&Ls have their deposits insured by the Savings Association Insurance Fund (SAIF), which is part of the FDIC.

Savings and loan associations also have to keep reserves based on their size and the amount and type of deposit. The OTS dictates the reserve requirement for S&Ls insured by the FDIC–SAIF.

Mutual Companies versus Stockholder Owned Companies

Some savings and loan associations are owned by stockholders, just as commercial banks and other corporations are owned by their stockholders. Other S&Ls, called **mutuals,** are owned by their depositors. In other words, when a person deposits money in an account at a mutual S&L, that person becomes a part owner of the firm. The mutual S&L's profits (if any) are put into a special reserve account from which dividends are paid from time to time to the owner/depositors.

On the one hand, mutual S&L owner/depositors do not face as much risk as regular stockholder owners: If the mutual S&L loses money, the loss isn't taken out of the owner/depositors' accounts. (Regular stockholder owners, of course, may well see the value of their holdings decline in bad times.) On the other hand, mutual S&L owner/depositors do not enjoy as much reward potential as regular stockholder owners. For example, unlike regular stockholders, who might be able to sell their stock for a profit, mutual S&L owner/depositors can't sell their deposits to other investors at all.

The Problem of Matching Loan and Deposit Maturities

Most of the mortgage loans made by S&Ls have very long maturities (the thirty-year mortgage is most common, although fifteen-year mortgages are becoming increasingly popular). However, most of the deposits that provide the money for these loans have zero or short maturities (passbook savings accounts have zero maturity because the depositor can withdraw at any time; CDs come in maturities of up to five years). This gap between the fifteen- to thirty-year maturity of the S&Ls' major assets and the zero- to five-year maturity of their deposits creates a problem if market interest rates rise. Consider the following example.

TABLE 3-2

First-Year Profit for an
S&L with a 7% Loan
Financed by a 3% CD

Interest received from the loan:	$100,000 × .07 = $7,000
Interest paid out to the CD holder:	$100,000 × .03 = $3,000
	Net income: $4,000

Note: For simplicity in this example, we assume the loan's terms allow the borrower to make only interest payments each year, deferring payment of the principal until the end of the loan's term.

TABLE 3-3

Second-Year Loss for an
S&L with a 7% Loan
Financed by a 9% CD

Interest received from the loan:	$100,000 × .07 = $7,000
Interest paid out to the CD holder:	$100,000 × .09 = $9,000
	Net income: ($2,000)

Suppose an S&L wanted to make a thirty-year fixed-rate mortgage loan for $100,000 at 7 percent interest. To raise cash for the loan, the S&L sells a one-year $100,000 CD at 3 percent interest. This creates a favorable spread (7% − 3% = +4%) as long as interest rates stay where they are. Table 3-2 shows the S&L's profit during the first year of the loan.

At the end of the first year, the CD matures and the S&L must pay the CD holder $100,000 plus 3 percent interest ($3,000). So the S&L sells another one-year CD for $100,000, giving the proceeds to the first CD holder. Then it uses $3,000 of its interest income from the loan to pay the interest due on the first CD. At the end of the second year and thereafter, the cycle repeats itself with the S&L selling a new one-year CD each year and using the profits from the loan to pay the interest due on the old CDs. You can see that as long as each new CD is issued for 3 percent interest, the S&L will net a yearly profit of $4,000 ($7,000 income from the loan minus $3,000 paid to the CD holder).

What happens, however, if interest rates rise during the first year, such that at the end of the year the S&L must pay 9 percent to get anyone to buy a new one-year CD? Now the S&L is in trouble. It has to sell a new CD to pay the $100,000 owed to the holder of the first CD, but it can only do so by offering an interest rate two points higher than its mortgage loan is paying. So at the end of the second year, when the S&L must pay the interest to the CD holder, it must pay $9,000 instead of $3,000 and suffers a $2,000 loss for the year. Table 3-3 summarizes the situation.

Of course, market interest rates can go down too, creating extra profits for the S&L, but S&Ls face a risk of loss when market interest rates move against them.

S&Ls' Real Assets

S&Ls also own buildings and equipment that are needed to conduct business. These assets, which do not earn an explicit rate of return, are supposed to be kept to a low level subject to the needs of the institution. As the fraud of the 1980s showed, however, that has not always been the case. Many S&L executives spent much of their companies' money on private business jets, luxurious offices, and even vacation retreats—a clear example of the agency problem discussed in chapter 1.

We discussed the agency problem on pages 10–11.

CREDIT UNIONS

Credit unions are member-owned financial institutions. They pay interest on shares bought by, and collect interest on loans made to, the members. Members are individuals rather than businesses or government units.

Credit unions are able to make relatively low interest loans to their members because they are cooperative organizations. They don't have to charge extra to make a profit and they don't pay federal income taxes. Also, they make loans *only* to members, who are presumed to be somewhat better credit risks than the general population.

The Common Bond Requirement

To help ensure that credit union members actually are better credit risks than the general population, credit union members must have a *common bond* with one another. This could mean that all members work for the same company, belong to the same labor union, or perhaps just live in the same town as the other members. The theory is that people who all belong to the same group, sharing common values, will be less likely to default on loans supported by money from their fellow group members.

Members as Shareholders

Credit unions are owned by their members. So when credit union members put money in their credit union, they are not technically "depositing" the money. Instead, they are purchasing *shares* of the credit union.

Like owners of other businesses, credit union members are entitled to any income the credit union has after debts and expenses have been paid. This residual income may be distributed in the form of extra dividends paid on the members' shares, or by a rebate on interest paid on loans.

Credit Unions Compared to Banks

Traditionally, credit unions were small institutions that did not compete much with banks. However, they have grown rapidly in recent years and now provide most of the same services as do commercial banks. Since banks now see credit unions as more of a threat, the banking lobby is pressuring Congress to begin taxing credit unions.

Credit Union Regulation

Credit unions must have charters giving them authority to operate, just like banks and S&Ls. They obtain these charters either from the state where they are located or from the federal government. The federal chartering and regulatory body for credit unions is the National Credit Union Administration (NCUA). The NCUA also oversees the National Credit Union Share Insurance Fund (NCUSIF). This fund insures share accounts up to $100,000. All federally chartered credit unions have NCUSIF insurance. State chartered credit unions may also apply for NCUSIF insurance for the share accounts of their members.

If credit unions have emergency borrowing needs, they can turn to the Central Liquidity Facility (CLF), which was created by Congress in 1978 and is administered by the National Credit Union Administration. Credit unions can also turn to the Federal Reserve Bank in the district where the credit union is located.

FINANCE COMPANIES, INSURANCE COMPANIES, AND PENSION FUNDS

Finance companies are nonbank firms that make short-term and medium-term loans to consumers and businesses. They often serve those customers who don't qualify for loans at other financial institutions.

Like banks and S&Ls, finance companies operate by taking in money and lending it out to their customers at a higher interest rate. A major difference between finance companies and other financial institutions, however, lies in the source of finance company funds. Banks and S&Ls receive most of their funds from individuals and businesses that deposit money in accounts at the institutions. Finance companies generally get their funds by borrowing from banks, or by selling commercial paper.

Types of Finance Companies

There are three main types of finance companies: consumer, commercial, and sales. In the following sections, we will explain the characteristics and functions of each type.

Consumer Finance Companies   Consumer finance companies, sometimes known as small-loan companies, make small loans to consumers for car purchases, recreational vehicles, medical expenses, vacations, and the like. Consumer finance companies often make loans to customers with less than perfect credit. Because the customers are a higher risk, the interest rates charged on loans are usually a little higher to compensate for the greater risk.

Commercial Finance Companies   These firms concentrate on providing credit to other business firms. A special type of commercial finance company is called a *factor.* Factoring is the buying of a business firm's accounts receivable, thus supplying needed funds to the selling firm. Commercial finance companies also make loans to businesses, usually with accounts receivable or inventory pledged as collateral. This type of financing will be examined in detail in chapter 20.

Sales Finance Companies   The mission of sales finance companies is to help the sales of some corporation (indeed, many are subsidiaries of the corporation whose sales they are promoting). In the automotive industry, for example, customers are more likely to buy cars from dealers that offer financing on the spot than from dealers who have no financing programs.

A finance company generally gives its retail dealers a supply of loan contract forms, which the dealers fill out at the time of sale. The contract is immediately sold to the finance company (at a slightly reduced price, of course, to allow for the finance company's profit). General Motors Acceptance Corporation (GMAC) and the Ford Motor Credit Company are prominent examples of sales finance companies.

Insurance Companies

Insurance companies are firms that, for a fee, will assume risks for their customers. They collect fees, called premiums, from a large number of customers. Then they draw on the pool of funds collected to pay those customers who suffer damages from the perils they have insured against.

There are two main types of insurance companies: life insurance companies, and property and casualty insurance companies.

Life Insurance Companies
Life insurance companies sell policies that pay the beneficiaries of the insured when the insured person dies. You might ask how life insurance companies make any money, because *everybody* dies sooner or later. If the risk life insurance companies were taking in return for the premium received were the risk of their customers dying, it is true that none of them would make any money. The real risk they are taking, however, is that the insured person will die *sooner than expected.*

To help assess this risk, insurance companies employ **actuaries.** Actuaries help calculate the premium for a life insurance policy for a person of a given age, gender, and state of health, so that the insurance company can pay the insurance benefit, cover expenses, and make a profit. Actuaries cannot tell specifically *who* is going to die when; but they can predict, with a high degree of accuracy, *how many* in a group of 100,000 healthy forty-year-old males will die during the coming year.

Life insurance companies function as financial intermediaries essentially the same way commercial banks or savings and loan associations do. They take money in from surplus economic units in the form of policy premiums and channel it to deficit economic units in the form of investments in common stock, corporate bonds, mortgages, and real estate. Their pay-out can be predicted with a high degree of accuracy, so they need only a small amount of liquid assets.

Property and Casualty Insurance Companies
Property and casualty insurance companies insure against a wide range of hazards associated with person and property. These include theft, weather damage from hurricanes, tornadoes and floods, fire, and earthquakes. Two close relatives of property and casualty companies are health insurance companies, which insure people against injuries and illnesses, and disability insurance companies, which insure people against loss of income from being unable to work.

One special hazard that these companies insure against is a policyholder's own negligence. This kind of insurance is called **liability insurance.** Most people are familiar with automobile liability insurance; but liability coverage can also be purchased for such things as medical malpractice, dog bites, and falls by visitors on your property.

The risks protected against by property and casualty companies are much less predictable than are the risks insured by life insurance companies. Hurricanes, fires, floods, and trial judgments are all much more difficult to predict than the number of sixty-year-old females who will die this year among a large number in this risk class. This means that property and casualty insurance companies must keep more liquid assets than do life insurance companies.

Pension Funds
Pension funds are set up by companies, governments, and unions to pay retirement benefits for their employees. They are essentially savings plans. Employees generally contribute money to the funds now in order to draw it out later, on retirement. Employers usually contribute money on behalf of the employ-

FINANCIAL MANAGEMENT AND YOU

ees, too. All the money is pooled and invested, and the investment returns are added to the pot. It is always possible, of course, that the sponsor (the company, government, or union) will not be able to pay promised benefits. If this happens the pension fund is said to have *failed,* and the worker may not collect all the promised benefits.

Pension funds invest so much money that they are the country's greatest source of long-term capital. They have *trillions* of dollars invested in a wide range of securities and other assets, such as real estate. Pension fund officials often hire money management firms just to manage the fund's investments. Bank trust departments and insurance companies also manage pension fund money.

Pension funds generally use one of two types of procedures for determining benefits for retired workers: a defined benefit plan and a defined contribution plan. In a defined benefit plan, retirement benefits are determined by a formula that usually considers the worker's age, salary, and years of service. The employee and/or the firm contribute the amounts necessary to reach the goal. In a defined contribution plan, the contributions to be made by the employee and/or employer are spelled out, but retirement benefits depend on the total accumulation in the individual's account at the retirement date.

Annuities   An *annuity* is a series of equal payments that are made at regular time intervals, such as monthly, for a specified period of time. Pension fund benefits are often paid out in the form of annuities. Sometimes the sponsor of a pension fund will use the funds accumulated during the retiring person's working years to purchase an annuity from an insurance company. This provides the retired person's benefits. Insurance companies also sell annuities to investors. In return for the amount paid to the insurance company, the investor receives payments (usually monthly) for the remainder of his or her life. A person who receives annuity payments is called an

annuitant. The size of the payments depends on how much money is paid to the insurance company at the time of the employee's retirement, along with factors such as the age, gender (if allowed by law), and state of health of the annuitant. If the pension fund investments made on behalf of a given employee earned a high return, a large amount of money will be available to purchase a large annuity. If the defined contribution pension fund investments performed poorly, the retired employee will be able to purchase only a small annuity.

Sometimes the investments made in an employee's behalf will be paid out in a lump sum at retirement. It is then up to the retired employee to invest this money wisely so as to generate the needed income during retirement.

What's Next

In this chapter we have seen how financial institutions help to bring together suppliers and users of funds to the benefit of both and to the economy. Commercial banks, savings and loan associations, credit unions, finance companies, insurance companies, and pension funds do this in different ways, and have different constituents, but all assist in this efficient flow of funds.

In the following two chapters we will review financial statements and learn how to analyze them from the perspective of a financial manager.

Summary

1. Explain financial intermediation and the role of financial institutions.

Financial institutions act as intermediaries between surplus and deficit economic units. They coordinate the flow of funds, absorbing differences between the amount of funds offered and the amount of funds needed, between the length of time funds are offered and needed, and between the degree of risk that surplus economic units are willing to bear and that inherent in the securities offered by the deficit economic units.

2. Define commercial banks and explain how reserve requirements influence their operations.

Commercial banks are financial institutions that are owned by stockholders, that take in deposits, and that make loans (primarily to businesses). Reserve requirements force banks to maintain minimum levels of reserves (vault cash and deposits at the Fed) based on the level and type of deposits they have. Reserves are nonearning assets, so although they provide liquidity for the bank, they limit its ability to make a profit.

3. Describe how the Federal Reserve regulates financial institutions.

The Federal Reserve is the central bank of the United States. It has seven members on its Board of Governors and a twelve voting-member Federal Open Market Committee. The twelve district Federal Reserve Banks make loans to financial institutions and perform other functions to assist member banks and other financial institutions. The Federal Reserve sets reserve requirements and influences the money supply through its open-market purchases and sales of government securities and foreign currencies. The Fed regulates financial institutions and uses its powers to try to maintain stability in the financial system.

4. Explain how savings and loan associations differ from commercial banks.

Savings and loan associations (S&Ls) are financial institutions that take in deposits and make primarily mortgage loans. The Office of Thrift Supervision is the primary authority for overseeing S&Ls.

5. Describe how credit unions operate.

Credit unions are financial institutions that take in funds by selling shares to members and make loans to those members. People are eligible for membership in a credit union if they meet the requirement of having a common bond with the other members. This might be working for a given company, belonging to a certain union, or living in a specified area.

6. Compare and contrast finance companies, insurance companies, and pension funds.

Finance companies take in funds primarily by selling commercial paper and make personal loans. Insurance companies sell policies, collecting premiums and paying beneficiaries if the insured-against event the insurance covers occurs. Pension funds take in funds, usually contributed by both the employer and employee, and invest those funds for future payment to the worker when he or she retires. This retirement benefit may be determined by a formula (a defined benefit plan), or by how much is in the investment fund at the time of retirement (a defined contribution plan).

Self-Test

ST-1. Why is intermediation sometimes needed to bring together surplus and deficit economic units?

ST-2. Is it better to be a surplus economic unit or a deficit economic unit? Explain.

ST-3. Define secondary reserves that are held by a bank?

ST-4. What is the difference, if any, between the way commercial banks and credit unions are taxed?

ST-5. What is the common bond requirement that credit union members must have to be eligible for membership?

ST-6. What is a Federal Reserve discount window loan?

ST-7. What are Federal Reserve open-market operations?

Review Questions

1. Define "intermediation."
2. What can a financial institution often do for a surplus economic unit that it would have difficulty doing for itself if the surplus economic unit (SEU) were to deal directly with a deficit economic unit (DEU)?
3. What can a financial institution often do for a deficit economic unit (DEU)that it would have difficulty doing for itself if the DEU were to deal directly with an SEU?
4. What are a bank's "primary reserves"? When the Fed sets reserve requirements, what is its primary goal?
5. Compare and contrast mutual and stockholder-owned savings and loan associations.
6. Who owns a credit union? Explain.
7. Which type of insurance company generally takes on the greater risks: a life insurance company or a property and casualty insurance company?
8. Compare and contrast a "defined benefit" and a "defined contribution" pension plan.

Build Your Communication Skills

CS-1. Women live longer than men, on average, but some insurance regulators are forcing insurance companies to ignore this fact when setting rates. Do you think it is ethical to charge women and men, who are otherwise similar in age and other risk factors, different amounts for life insurance? Have two groups of students debate this issue.

CS-2. Read three articles about the Federal Reserve's current monetary policy. Use sources such as *The Wall Street Journal, Fortune* magazine, the *Federal Reserve Bulletin,* or sources available on the Internet or CD databases. Write a brief report (two or three pages) summarizing the Fed's current monetary policy. What issues seem to be influencing the Fed's actions the most? What actions are being taken by the Fed to achieve the goals it has defined for itself?

Answers to Self-Test

ST-1. Intermediation is sometimes needed when surplus and deficit economic units cannot agree as to the denomination, maturity, and risk of the security offered and bought. Financial intermediaries can often give each side what it needs by stepping into the middle of the exchange of funds for securities.

ST-2. There is nothing inherently good or bad in the classification of either surplus economic unit or deficit economic unit.

ST-3. Secondary reserves are short-term liquid securities that a bank can sell quickly and easily to obtain cash that can be used to satisfy primary reserve requirements.

ST-4. Commercial banks pay federal income taxes on their profits while credit unions do not.

ST-5. Credit union members are required to have some common bond with the other members before the request for membership is approved. Examples of common bonds required by various credit unions include working for a given company, belonging to a certain union, or living in a certain area.

ST-6. A Federal Reserve discount window loan is a loan made by one of the twelve district Federal Reserve banks to a financial institution from that district.

ST-7. Federal Reserve open-market operations are the purchasing and selling of U.S. government securities and foreign currencies by the Federal Reserve. This is done to affect the amount of reserves in the banking system.

chapter 4

Review of Accounting

Anyone who isn't confused here doesn't really understand what is going on.
Anonymous

There's No Accounting for Europe

Americans have a tough time playing Chinese baseball because the rules are very different. In Chinese baseball, after the player hits the ball, the other team can stack the bases, hide them in the outfield, basically do anything they want with them. Trying to adapt to Chinese baseball is easier, though, than trying to adapt to accounting systems in Europe. The rules change from country to country.

Many were enthused when the European nations combined into one common market, known as the European Union. Yet this enthusiasm has dimmed as U.S. firms entering the common market realize that it doesn't have a common accounting system.

Because of this lack of common accounting standards, it can be

tough to figure out how a European company is really doing. In fact, many European companies try to report as low a profit as possible. Why? The higher the profit, the more tax they must pay. Because of this, many European companies do not even account for their assets.

You want an open audit of a European company? Good luck. In Germany, Austria, and Switzerland, any audit is strictly confidential,

Chapter Objectives

After reading this chapter, you should be able to:

1. Explain how financial managers use the three basic accounting financial statements: the income statement, the balance sheet, and the statement of cash flows.

2. Discuss how depreciation affects cash flow and compute depreciation expense.

3. Explain how taxes affect a firm's value and calculate marginal and average tax rates.

available only to the supervisory board and not the shareholders.

Are you carrying any inventory? Okay, write off the overhead associated with it. No, not if you're in Germany. Writing off overhead associated with inventory is disallowed.

Do you have a retirement plan for your workers? What is that costing your company? Forget it. German and Austrian companies do not have to account for retirement benefits that were in place before January 1, 1987.

The point is, the European Union is struggling toward a common accounting system. And they may arrive at one,

well, maybe. The accounting standard they're striving for allows many countries to make accounting choices "by local guidance," and the standards will not apply to non-European Union countries in Europe. Plus, officials admit there are still gaps in their regulations, such as the lack of common rules over audit procedures.

If you think all this is confusing, count your blessings. At least you're not an accountant in the United States, trying to determine the value of a European company. If you were, you might give up and go play a game of Chinese baseball. It would be easier. ❋

Source: Mark I. Merryweather, "There's No Accounting for Europe," *The Journal of European Business* (May/June 1994): 12; Terry Lockhart and Joseph Nellis, "Assessing Financial Services in the European Union," *Journal of Retail Banking* 16, no. 3 (Fall 1994): 19–25.

CHAPTER OVERVIEW

Accounting plays an important role in a firm's financial success. Accountants prepare financial statements that financial managers use to analyze the condition of a firm and to plan for its future. Financial managers must understand, then, how to analyze and interpret financial statements as they make decisions. The financial manager who knows how to use financial statements can help create value for the firm's owners.

In this chapter we will review the three major financial statements: the income statement, the balance sheet, and the statement of cash flows. We will also study how depreciation and taxes affect a firm's cash flows.

REVIEW OF ACCOUNTING FUNDAMENTALS

All public corporations in the United States must follow certain accounting guidelines known as Generally Accepted Accounting Principles (GAAP), which require that public corporations prepare financial statements that comply with GAAP rules. The Financial Accounting Standards Board (abbreviated FASB and pronounced Fahz-bee), a private, professional accounting body, publishes these rules governing how public corporations must account for their business activities.

The Securities and Exchange Commission (SEC) requires all public corporations to file financial statements, and make them available to the public, on 10-K and 10-Q reports. The **10-K reports** are audited financial statements submitted annually to the SEC for distribution to the public. The **10-Q reports** are unaudited financial statements submitted quarterly, also for public distribution.

The following basic accounting equation is central to understanding the financial condition of a firm:

$$\text{Assets} = \text{Liabilities} + \text{Equity}$$

Assets are the items of value a business owns. *Liabilities* are claims on the business by nonowners, and equity is the owners' claim on the business. The sum of the liabilities and equity is the total **capital** contributed to the business. Capital contributions come from three main sources: creditors (including bondholders and banks), preferred stockholders, and common stockholders.

Basic Accounting Financial Statements

You can get a good picture of how a firm is doing by looking at its financial statements. The three basic financial statements are the *income statement*, the *balance sheet*, and the *statement of cash flows*. Each of these statements gives a slightly different view of the firm. Let's look at these financial statements and how they interrelate.

The Income Statement

We can compare the **income statement** to a video: It measures a firm's profitability over a period of time. The firm can choose the length of the reporting time period. It can be a month, a quarter, or a year. (By law, a publicly traded corporation must report its activities at least quarterly, but may report more frequently.)

THE FAR SIDE By GARY LARSON

© 1992 FarWorks, Inc./Dist. by Universal Press Syndicate

Cossaccountants

Source: THE FAR SIDE © 1995, 1992 FARWORKS, INC. Dist. by UNIVERSAL PRESS SYNDICATE. Reprinted with permission. All rights reserved.

The income statement shows *revenues, expenses,* and *income.* Revenues represent gross income the firm earned during a particular period of time (usually from sales). Expenses represent the cost of providing goods and services during a given period of time. Net income is what is left after expenses are subtracted from revenues.

Figure 4-1 shows an income statement for Acme Company, a firm that manufactures birdseed, anvils, rockets, explosives, and giant springs. Acme Company is primarily a mail order company with many customers in the southwestern United States. The income statement is for the year ended December 31, 1996. This income statement describes sales, expenses, and net income for Acme Company from the beginning of the business day on January 1, 1996, until the end of the business day on December 31, 1996.

Revenues   As Figure 4-1 shows, Acme earned sales of $10 million during 1996. Generally, the income statement does not distinguish between cash and credit sales. As a result, we are not sure how much actual *cash* came into the firm from the $10 million in reported sales.

Expenses   Expenses include costs incurred while conducting the operations of the firm and financial expenses, such as interest on debt and taxes owed. These items are matched to the revenues that were generated as the expenses were incurred.

Cost of Goods Sold.   The first expense subtracted from sales is *cost of goods sold,* which consists of the labor, materials, and overhead expenses allocated to those goods and services sold during the year.

Subtracting cost of goods sold of $4 million from sales of $10 million gives Acme's *gross profit,* which equals $6 million.

Selling and Administrative Expenses.   From gross profit, we next subtract Acme's *selling and administrative expenses* ($800,000). Selling expenses include marketing and salespeoples' salaries. Administrative expenses are for expenses that are difficult to associate directly with sales for a specified time period. These would include office support, insurance, and security.

Take Note

Notice that **cost of goods sold** *is not called* **cost of goods produced.** *Only costs of goods sold are reported on this year's income statement. Goods produced but not sold are considered inventory.*

Figure 4-1   **ACME Corporation Income Statement for the Year ended December 31, 1996**

Sales	$10,000,000
Cost of Goods Sold	− 4,000,000
Gross Profit	= 6,000,000
Selling & Administrative Expenses	− 800,000
Depreciation Expense	− 2,000,000
Earnings Before Interest and Taxes (EBIT, or Operating Income)	= 3,200,000
Interest Expense	− 1,350,000
Earnings Before Taxes (EBT)	= 1,850,000
Taxes (40%)	− 740,000
Net Income (NI)	= 1,110,000
Preferred Stock Dividends Paid	− 110,000
Earnings Available to Common Stockholders	= 1,000,000
Earnings per Share (EPS) (1,000,000 shares)	= $1.00
Common Stock Dividends Paid	− 400,000
Addition to Retained Earnings	= 600,000

Depreciation Expense. *Depreciation expense* is subtracted next—$2 million for Acme in 1996. Depreciation expense is the year's allocation of the cost of plant and equipment that have been purchased this year and in previous years. Because assets provide their benefits to the firm over several years, accountants subtract the cost of long-lived assets a little at a time over a number of years. The allocated cost of a firm's assets for the income statement's period of time is the depreciation expense.[1]

Operating Income and Interest Expense. When we subtract selling and administrative expenses and depreciation expense from gross profit, we are left with Acme's *earnings before interest and taxes (EBIT),* also known as operating income. This figure is $3,200,000.

Gross Profit	=6,000,000
Selling & Administrative Expenses	− 800,000
Depreciation Expense	−2,000,000
Earnings Before Interest and Taxes (EBIT, or Operating Income)	=3,200,000

EBIT is the profit that the firm receives from its business operations before subtracting any financing expenses. From EBIT, we then subtract *interest expense* associated with any debts of the company to arrive at Acme's *earnings before taxes (EBT).* Acme has $1,350,000 in interest expense. When we subtract this figure from the $3,200,000 EBIT figure, we find Acme had earnings before taxes (EBT) of $1,850,000.

All the expenses subtracted so far are tax deductible. In other words, the Internal Revenue Service (IRS) allows firms to subtract these expenses from their gross income before computing the tax they owe. We will discuss income taxes later in the chapter.

Net Income Finally, after we subtract all operating expenses, financing expenses, and taxes from revenues, we arrive at the firm's *net income* (NI). For Acme, net income in 1996 was $1,110,000. This is the firm's accounting net profit for the year.

Earnings per Share (EPS). Acme's stockholders are very interested in their individual share of the corporation's earnings. Therefore, under the entry *earnings per share* (EPS), the income statement shows total earnings available to common stockholders divided by the number of shares of common stock outstanding. The earnings available to common stockholders figure comes straight from the income statement.

Net Income (NI)	=1,110,000
Preferred Stock Dividends Paid	− 110,000
Earnings Available to Common Stockholders	=1,000,000
Earnings per Share (EPS) (1,000,000 shares)	= $1.00

The number of shares outstanding comes from the balance sheet. Acme has 1 million shares of common stock outstanding.

---

[1] We will discuss the role of depreciation, and depreciation rules, later in this chapter.

Box Office Hits—Who Profits?

Imagine you wrote a bestselling book that was made into a hit movie that grossed over $657 million. If you were Winston Groom, author of *Forrest Gump,* you would be licking your chops in anticipation of a big check. But it wasn't to be.

In fact, according to Hollywood accounting practices, the movie has yet to show a net profit. Paramount Pictures' accountants claim that the movie has lost $62 million. These types of accounting practices would even make a country boy like Forrest a bit suspicious.

Warner Pictures, a division of Time Warner, Inc., also claims that it does not owe any money to the estate of Jim Garrison, author of the book *On the Trail of the Assassin.* Garrison's book was the basis for Oliver Stone's 1991 movie *J.F.K.* That movie grossed more than $150 million. But again, the studio claims *J.F.K.* did not make a net profit.

Many experts have long cast suspicious glances at Hollywood accounting practices, which usually ensure that even the most successful movies don't report a net profit. Net profits in Hollywood are typically defined as the studio's share of the receipts of the film after subtracting production costs, distribution fees, prints, advertising, overhead, and promotion costs. Because a studio can take anywhere from 30 percent to 60 percent in distribution fees alone, it is a well-known maxim in Hollywood that a share of net profits is often worthless.

In contrast to authors, actors and directors can walk away from a successful film as millionaires. For instance, *Forrest Gump* star Tom Hanks and it's director, Robert Zemeckis, earned over $30 million apiece from the movie because they receive a percentage of the film company's share of the box office receipts.

When all is said and done, movie accounting is like a box of chocolates. When you open it, you never know what you might find.

Questions to Consider

▶ Is it ethical for actors to get more money than the author of the book on which a movie is based?

▶ Is it ethical for any business to cook the books, so that expenses outweigh the revenue? Or is this just a smart way to avoid paying taxes?

▶ Should a firm have to disclose how its accounting practices may affect the people it hires to provide services? Could disclosure of its practices conflict with the primary goal of a firm? Explain.

Sources: "Jim Garrison's Estate Sues Film Studios on Accounting," *The New York Times* (November 20, 1995): D2; John Lippman, "Author of 'Gump,' Paramount in Talks Over Net Profits," *Wall Street Journal* (Thursday, May 25, 1995): B6.

To calculate EPS, divide earnings available to common stockholders by the number of outstanding common stock shares. For Acme, we calculate EPS as follows:

$$\text{EPS} = \frac{\text{Earnings Available to Common Stockholders}}{\text{Number of Shares of Common Stock Outstanding}}$$

$$= \frac{\$1,000,000}{1,000,000}$$

$$= \$1.00$$

Acme's EPS, then, is $1.00, as shown on the income statement in Figure 4-1.

Dividends and Retained Earnings Dividends are not expenses. Dividends are cash payments made to preferred and common stockholders in exchange for their capital contributions to the firm. In the following sections, we will discuss preferred and common stock dividends, as well as retained earnings.

Preferred Stock Dividends.   After the net income entry, the income statement shows dividends the corporation paid to its preferred stockholders in 1996. Acme's preferred stock dividends amount to $110,000. After we subtract this amount from the $1,110,000 in net income, we're left with $1 million for the common stockholders.

Common Stock Dividends and Retained Earnings.   A company has two options as to what to do with earnings available to common stockholders. It can pay stockholder dividends, or it can retain the earnings. Retaining the earnings will likely lead to greater future growth in sales and net income as new assets are purchased or existing liabilities are paid. In 1996 Acme has chosen to pay $400,000 (40 percent of its available earnings) in dividends to its common stockholders. The remaining $600,000 is an *addition to retained earnings* of the firm. As shown in Figure 4-1, this amount is added to the earnings retained from past years.

In addition to the income statement, many firms prepare a short **statement of retained earnings,** as shown in Figure 4-2, that records dividend and retained earnings information. Assuming that Acme's end of 1995 retained earnings were $4,400,000, Acme's accountants add the 1996 earnings available to common stockholders less the 1996 dividends paid to those stockholders ($1,000,000 − $400,000 = $600,000) to the end of 1995 retained earnings. The result is $5 million ($4,400,000 + $600,000 = $5,000,000).

◀ Take Note

If the amount remaining after paying dividends had been **negative,** *then we would have* **subtracted** *our number from retained earnings instead of adding to it. For Acme, there is a positive number to add to retained earnings—$600,000.*

The Balance Sheet

If the income statement is like a video, a balance sheet is like a still photograph. The **balance sheet** shows the firm's assets, liabilities, and equity at a given point in time. This snapshot of a company's financial position tells us nothing about the firm's financial position before or after that point in time. Let's examine the end-of-1996 balance sheet for Acme. Figure 4-3 (page 64) shows the balance sheet for Acme as of the end of the business day, December 31, 1996.

On the balance sheet, the firm's assets are listed in order of their liquidity. As we learned in chapter 1, liquidity is the ease with which you can convert an asset to cash. This means that cash and near-cash assets called **current assets** are listed first. Assets that are difficult to convert to cash are listed later. On the other side of the balance sheet, the liabilities that are due earliest, **current liabilities,** are listed first. Current liabilities are almost always due within one year. The liabilities due later, such as long-term debt, are listed later on the balance sheet.

The equity section lists the claims of the owners (Acme's common stockholders). The owners' claims include both the amount the owners contributed when the common stock was first issued, as well as the total earnings retained by the firm at the time of the balance sheet.

The Asset Accounts   Acme has both current and fixed assets. Current assets provide short-term benefits, while fixed assets provide long-term benefits to the firm.

Retained Earnings, December 31, 1995	$4,400,000
+ 1996 Earnings Available to Common Stockholders	+ 1,000,000
− 1996 Dividends Paid to Common Stockholders	− 400,000
Retained Earnings, December 31, 1996	$5,000,000

Figure 4-2 ACME Corporation Statement of Retained Earnings for the Year Ended December 31, 1996

Figure 4-3 ACME
Corporation Balance
Sheet December 31, 1996

ASSETS			
Current Assets:			
Cash		$9,000,000	
Marketable Securities		8,000,000	
Accounts Receivable (Gross)	$1,200,000		
Less Allowance for Bad Debts	200,000		
Accounts Receivable (Net)		1,000,000	
Inventory		20,000,000	
Prepaid Expenses		1,000,000	
Total Current Assets			$39,000,000
Fixed Assets:			
Plant & Equipment (Gross)	20,000,000		
Less Accumulated Depreciation	9,000,000		
Plant & Equipment (Net)		11,000,000	
Total Fixed Assets			11,000,000
TOTAL ASSETS			$50,000,000
LIABILITIES & EQUITY			
Current Liabilities:			
Accounts Payable	$12,000,000		
Notes Payable	5,000,000		
Accrued Expenses	3,000,000		
Total Current Liabilities		$20,000,000	
Long-Term Debt:			
Bonds Payable (5%, due 2015)	20,000,000		
Total Long-Term Debt		20,000,000	
Total Liabilities			$40,000,000
Equity:			
Preferred Stock		1,000,000	
Common Stock			
(1 million shares, $1 par)		1,000,000	
Capital in Excess of Par		3,000,000	
Retained Earnings		5,000,000	
Total Equity			10,000,000
TOTAL LIABILITIES & EQUITY			$50,000,000

Current Assets. Acme has $9 million in *cash* at the end of 1996. Customers owe the company $1.2 million, the amount of *accounts receivable*. Acme provided a $200,000 allowance to cover the likelihood that it will not be able to collect some accounts receivable due to customer defaults. This leaves net accounts receivable of $1 million. *Marketable securities*—securities that can quickly and easily be converted to extra cash—are listed next. Acme has $8 million in these securities.

The company has $20 million of *inventory* and $1 million in *prepaid expenses*. The inventory figure reflects the amount of goods produced, but not yet sold to customers. The prepaid expense figure represents future expenses expected, but that have been paid in advance. An example of a prepaid expense is the premium paid on an insurance policy. You pay the premium in advance, so the insurance coverage is "owed" to you until the term of coverage expires. Since prepaid expenses, such as insurance premiums, have been paid for but not yet received, they are owed to the company and are considered assets.

Working capital is the sum of all current assets, including cash, marketable securities, net accounts receivable, inventory, and prepaid expenses. For Acme, this figure is $39 million.

Fixed Assets. Next to be listed are the fixed assets of the firm. **Fixed assets** are assets that are expected to provide a benefit to the firm for more than one year. These assets are generally less liquid than the current assets. Acme has $20 million of gross plant and equipment, which is listed at the original cost of these assets. The *accumulated depreciation* figure is the sum of all the depreciation expenses ever taken on the firm's income statements, for the assets still carried on the books. Acme's accumulated depreciation figure is $9 million. To find the net plant and equipment figure—or net fixed assets—subtract the amount of accumulated depreciation from gross equipment ($20 million minus $9 million). The result is $11 million.

The $39 million in current assets plus the $11 million in net fixed assets are the total assets of the firm. At the end of 1996, Acme's total assets were $50 million.

The Liabilities and Equity Accounts The liability and equity section of the balance sheet shows how the company's assets were financed. The funds come from those who have liability (debt) claims against the firm or from those who have equity (ownership) claims against the firm.

Liabilities. In the liability section of the balance sheet, current liabilities are listed first. Acme has accounts payable at the end of 1996 of $12 million. *Accounts payable* represent money a business owes to suppliers that have sold the firm materials on account.

Notes payable are $5 million for this company. Notes payable are legal IOUs that represents the debt of the borrower (Acme) and the claim the lender has against that borrower. Acme also has accrued expenses of $3 million. Accrued expenses are business expenses that have not been paid yet. For example, universities often make professors work for a full month before being paid. The universities accrue "wages payable" for the month before the payroll checks are finally issued. Acme's accounts payable, notes payable, and accrued expenses add up to $20 million in current liabilities.

Net working capital is current assets minus current liabilities. For Acme, this would be $19 million ($39 million current assets − $20 million current liabilities).

Next, long-term liabilities are listed. Long-term liabilities are liabilities that are not due for more than one year. Acme has $20 million in long-term bonds payable that mature in the year 2015. The $20 million figure listed on the balance sheet refers only to the principal on these bonds.

Preferred Stock, Common Stock, and Retained Earnings. The equity section of the balance sheet shows that Acme has preferred stock of $1 million. The common stock equity section of the balance sheet contains three items: common stock, capital in excess of par, and retained earnings. The common stock entry shows that Acme's common stock is $1 million, reflecting the 1 million shares issued to investors, each with a $1 par value. **Par value** is the stated value printed on the stock certificate. This figure is almost always very low, sometimes even zero.

The next common stock equity entry is *capital in excess of par.* Capital in excess of par is the original market price per share value of the stock sold minus that stock's par value times the number of shares issued. If Acme originally sold 1 million shares of common stock to the public for $4 each, and the par value of each share was $1, then the price of the stock was $3 in excess of par. Multiplying 1 million shares times $3 gives Acme's $3 million figure for capital in excess of par. You can see that the common stock and the capital in excess of par values together represent the equity capital raised when new common stock was sold.

The last entry in the common stock equity section is retained earnings. The *retained earnings* figure represents the sum of all the earnings available to common stockholders of a business during its entire history, minus the sum of all the common stock dividends which it has ever paid.[2] Those earnings that were not paid out were, by definition, retained. The retained earnings figure for Acme at the end of 1996 is $5 million.

The Statement of Cash Flows

The third major financial statement required of all publicly traded corporations by the Financial Accounting Standards Board (FASB) is the *statement of cash flows.* This statement, like the income statement, can be compared to a video: It shows how cash flows into and out of a company over a given period of time.

We construct the statement of cash flows by adjusting the income statement to distinguish between *income* and *cash flow,* and by comparing balance sheets at the beginning and at the end of the relevant time period. The statement of cash flows shows cash flows in operating, investing, and financing activities, as well as the overall net increase or decrease in cash flow for the firm. You can see Acme's statement of cash flows for the year 1996 in Figure 4-4.

Operating Activities   Operating activities on the statement of cash flows shows that Acme had $1,110,000 in net income for the year 1996. This number represents what was left after Acme paid all the firm's expenses for that year. We adjust that number to determine the operating cash flows for 1996.

Adjustment for Depreciation Expense   Although depreciation expense is a legitimate reduction of income for accounting purposes, it is not a cash outlay. In other words, firms record depreciation expense on financial statements but do not write checks to pay it. We must add the $2 million in depreciation expense because net income was reduced by this amount—even though depreciation is a noncash expense. Changes in marketable securities, accounts payable, accounts receivable (net), and inventory are shown in the operations section of Figure 4-4.

Changes in Balance Sheet Accounts   Changes in asset accounts on the balance sheet indicate changes in the company's cash flow. Because firms must pay cash to accumulate new assets, any increase in an asset account between the time one balance sheet is published and the time the next balance sheet is published indicates a cash outflow. Likewise, because firms sell assets to raise cash, any decrease in an asset account indicates a cash inflow.

---

[2]There are exceptions. If a company pays a dividend in the form of new common stock instead of cash, then there could be a transfer from retained earnings to the other common stock equity accounts. We will skip this exception for now. The use of stock dividends instead of cash dividends, and the resulting accounting treatment, will be examined in chapter 16.

Operations	Net Income		$1,110,000	
	Plus:			
	Depreciation Expense		2,000,000	
	Decrease in Marketable Securities		1,000,000	
	Increase in Accounts Payable		4,900,000	
	Minus:			
	Increase in Accounts Receivable, net		300,000	
	Increase in Inventory		2,200,000	
	Total Operating Cash Flow			+$6,510,000
Investments	*Minus:*			
	Increase in Plant & Equipment, gross	$5,000,000		
	Total Cash Flow from Investments			−$5,000,000
Financing	*Minus:*			
	Decrease in Preferred Stock		1,000,000	
	Preferred Stock Dividends		110,000	
	Common Stock Dividends		400,000	
	Total Financing Cash Flow			−$1,510,000
Net Cash Flow = $6,510,000−5,000,000−1,510,000 =				$0

Figure 4-4 ACME Corporation Statement of Cash Flows for the Year Ended December 31, 1996

Changes in the liability and equity section of the balance sheet signal cash flow changes. Because firms must pay cash to pay off obligations, any decrease in liability, preferred stock, or common stock equity accounts between the time one balance sheet is published and the time the next balance sheet is published indicates a cash outflow during those time periods. To raise additional cash, firms can incur debt or equity obligations; so any increase in liability, preferred stock, or common stock items indicate a cash flow.

Figure 4-5 shows two balance sheets for Acme side by side. We can compare them and note the cash inflows and outflows on the statement of cash flows.

In the asset section of the balance sheet, we see that net accounts receivable rose from $700,000 to $1 million, a $300,000 increase. This means Acme had a cash outflow of $300,000. Likewise, inventory increased from $17.8 million to $20 million, which indicates another cash outflow of $2.2 million. Marketable securities, however, decreased by $1 million, signaling that Acme sold some marketable securities to generate a cash inflow of $1 million.

In the liabilities and preferred stock section of the balance sheet, accounts payable increased $4.9 million. This represents a cash inflow. Acme's cash inflow shows that the firm received more financing from suppliers.

Investments Activities   The investments section of the statement of cash flows shows investing activities in long-term securities or plant and equipment. Increasing investments shows a cash outflow, and decreasing investments signals a cash inflow. For instance, Acme's plant and equipment increased to $20 million in 1996, up from $15 million in 1995. This $5 million increase reflects a cash outlay used to buy additional assets.

Financing Activities   The financing section of the statement of cash flows shows financing activities related to the sales and retirement of bonds, preferred and com-

> **Take Note**
>
> *Note that we do not mention the change in accumulated depreciation in the Statement of Cash Flows. The additional accumulated depreciation of $2 million is already included in the depreciation expense figure on the income statement. We don't want to count this twice.*

Figure 4-5 **ACME Corporation Balance Sheets**

	12/31/95	12/31/96	CHANGE
ASSETS			
Cash	$ 9,000,000	$ 9,000,000	0
Accounts Receivable (gross)	800,000	1,200,000	
– Allowance for Bad Debts	–100,000	–200,000	
Accounts Receivable (net)	700,000	1,000,000	+300,000
Inventory	17,800,000	20,000,000	+2,200,000
Marketable Securities	9,000,000	8,000,000	–1,000,000
Prepaid Expenses	1,000,000	1,000,000	0
Plant & Equipment (gross)	15,000,000	20,000,000	+5,000,000
– Accumulated Depreciation	–7,000,000	–9,000,000	–2,000,000
Plant & Equipment (net)	8,000,000	11,000,000	
Total Assets	$45,500,000	$50,000,000	
Total Change in Assets			+4,500,000
LIABILITIES & PREFERRED STOCK			
Accounts Payable	$ 7,100,000	$12,000,000	+4,900,000
Notes Payable	5,000,000	5,000,000	0
Accrued Expenses	3,000,000	3,000,000	0
Bonds Payable, 5%, due 2015	20,000,000	20,000,000	0
Preferred Stock	2,000,000	1,000,000	–1,000,000
COMMON STOCK EQUITY			
Common Stock	1,000,000	1,000,000	0
Capital in Excess of Par	3,000,000	3,000,000	0
Retained Earnings	4,400,000	5,000,000	+600,000
Total Liabilities & Equity	$45,500,000	$50,000,000	
Total Change in Liabilities, Preferred Stock, and Common Stock			+4,500,000

mon stock, and other corporate securities. The retirement of previously issued securities signals a cash outflow. The issuing of securities is a cash inflow. On the Acme balance sheet, for example, preferred stock decreased from $2 million to $1 million. The decrease shows that the firm spent $1 million to retire the outstanding preferred stock.

In the common stock equity section of the balance sheet, we see that retained earnings increased from $4.4 million to $5 million. Although this $600,000 increase in retained earnings represents a cash inflow to the firm, it is not recorded on the statement of cash flows. Why? Because the cash inflow it represents was recorded on the statement of cash flows as net income ($1,110,000) less preferred stock dividends ($110,000) less common stock dividends ($400,000). To include the increase in retained earnings again would result in double counting.

Net Cash Flow during the Period   We have now completed the adjustments necessary to convert Acme's net income for 1996 into actual cash flows. Figure 4-4 shows that the cash inflows exactly offset the cash outflows, resulting in a net cash outflow of zero for Acme in 1996. (Notice in Figure 4-5 that Acme's cash balance of $9 million on December 31, 1996 is unchanged from December 31, 1995.)

DEPRECIATION

Depreciation is important to financial managers because it directly affects a firm's tax liabilities—which, in turn, affect cash flows. Here's how: Taxes paid are negative cash flows. Tax savings realized by deducting expenses generates more cash for the firm—the equivalent of a cash inflow.

Accounting depreciation is the allocation of an asset's initial cost over time. Let's look at why it is important to depreciate fixed assets over time. Suppose Acme bought a piece of equipment in 1995 that was expected to last ten years. If Acme paid $1 million cash for the asset, and the entire cost were charged as an expense in 1995, the transaction would wipe out all but $850,000 of Acme's earnings before taxes for the year ($1,850,000 earnings before taxes − $1,000,000 fixed asset cost). Nothing would show that Acme had acquired an asset worth $1 million. Then, for the next nine years, Acme's income statements would show increases in profits generated by the asset—but there would be no corresponding accounting for the cost of that asset. In effect, it would look like Acme spent a lot of money in 1995, got nothing for it, and increased its profits for no reason over the next nine years. This would clearly be misleading.

To get around the problem, accountants apply the *matching principle:* Expenses should be matched to the revenues they help to generate. In other words, if you buy an asset, and the asset is expected to last for ten years, then you should recognize the cost of the asset over the entire ten-year period. The cost is *amortized,* or spread out, over the ten-year period. In that way, the value of the asset will be properly shown on the financial statements in proportion to its contribution to profits.

Accounting depreciation is very different from economic depreciation. The latter attempts to measure the change in the value of an asset. Because this involves making value estimates that may turn out to be wrong, accountants use an established set of rules to determine the amount of depreciation to allocate over a certain time period.

Calculating the Amount of Depreciation Expense

Depreciation expense for a given period is determined by calculating the total amount to be depreciated (the *depreciation basis*), and then calculating the percentage of that total to be allocated to a given time period (the *depreciation* rules).

The total amount to be depreciated over the accounting life of the asset is known as the **depreciation basis.** It is equal to the cost of the asset, plus any setup or delivery costs that may be incurred.[3]

Depreciation Methods   The cost of an asset can be allocated over time by using any of several sets of depreciation rules. These two most common depreciation rules used in tax reporting are *straight-line depreciation* and *MACRS.*

Straight-Line Depreciation.   The simplest method of depreciation is the *straight-line depreciation (SL)* method. To use the **straight-line depreciation** method, you divide the cost of the asset by the number of years of life for the asset according to

---

[3]Although in financial statements prepared by public corporations for reporting purposes, salvage value—the value of the asset if sold for salvage—may be subtracted in arriving at the depreciation basis. It is not considered part of the depreciation basis for tax reporting purposes.

Asset Class	3-Year Research Equipment & Special Tools	5-Year Computers, Copiers, Cars, & Similar Assets	7-Year Furniture, Fixtures, & Most Manufacturing Equipment	10-Year Equipment for Tobacco, Food, & Petroleum Production
Year	Depreciation Percentages			
1	33.3%	20%	14.3%	10%
2	44.5%	32%	24.5%	18%
3	14.8%	19.2%	17.5%	14.4%
4	7.4%	11.5%	12.5%	11.5%
5		11.5%	8.9%	9.2%
6		5.8%	8.9%	7.4%
7			8.9%	6.6%
8			4.5%	6.6%
9				6.5%
10				6.5%
11				3.3%

Table 4-1 lists MACRS asset class depreciation percentages for three-year to ten-year assets, and examples of assets in each class.

classification rules, and charge the result off as depreciation expense each year. For instance, if the managers at Acme bought a $1 million piece of equipment that belonged to the seven-year-asset class, then straight-line depreciation for the asset would be computed as follows:

> Asset's initial cost: $1,000,000
> Divided by length of service: 7 years
> Equals depreciation expense each year: $142,857[4]

The Modified Accelerated Cost Recovery System (MACRS). Since the Tax Reform Act of 1986, Congress has allowed firms to use the modified accelerated cost recovery system, or **MACRS** (pronounced "makers") to compute depreciation expense for tax purposes. MACRS specifies that some percent of the cost of assets will be charged each year as depreciation expense during the asset's life. Table 4-1 shows the 1996 MACRS percentages for various classes of personal property assets.[5]

---

[4]To be more correct, we would use what is known as the *half-year convention* in determining the annual depreciation. One-half a year's depreciation would be taken the year the asset was put into service and one-half in the final year. For example, for the above asset with a stated seven-year life, depreciation would in fact be spread over eight years. In this case, $71,429 in years one and eight, and $142,857 in years two through seven.

[5]The half-year convention is built into the MACRS depreciation percentages shown in Table 4-1.

So, under the MACRS, Acme's $1 million, seven-year asset would be depreciated 14.3 percent during its first year of life, 24.5 percent during the second year, and so on. Note that a seven-year asset is depreciated over eight years because of the half-year convention built into the table. Note also that MACRS is an accelerated depreciation method—greater percentages of the depreciation basis are subtracted from income in the early years, compared to the percentage applied in the later years. The acceleration is important because the more quickly firms can write off the cost of an asset, the sooner they save taxes from the tax deductible expenses.

INCOME TAXES

Tax rates are set by Congress. The Internal Revenue Service (IRS), determines the amount of federal income tax a firm owes. Federal tax rules dictate that different rates apply to different blocks of income. For instance, the first $50,000 of taxable income are taxed at a 15 percent rate, while the next $25,000 of taxable income are taxed at a 25 percent rate.

The tax rate that applies to the next dollar of taxable income earned, the **marginal tax rate,** changes as the level of taxable income changes. This pattern—tax rate increases as taxable income increases—reflects the **progressive tax rate structure** imposed by the federal government.[6]

Table 4-2 (page 72) shows the marginal tax rates for corporations in effect for tax year 1996.

Acme's EBT is $1,850,000, so its marginal tax bracket is 34 percent. Its next dollar of taxable income would be taxed at 34 percent. The federal income tax bill in 1996 would be:

$$
\begin{aligned}
& \$50,000 \times .15 && = && \$7,500 \\
+\ & \$25,000 \times .25 && = && \$6,250 \\
+\ & \$25,000 \times .34 && = && \$8,500 \\
+\ & \$235,000 \times .39 && = && \$91,650 \\
+\ & \underline{\$1,515,000 \times .34} && && = \underline{\$515,100} \\
\end{aligned}
$$

Taxable Income = $1,850,000 \qquad Taxes = $629,000

Financial managers use marginal tax rates to estimate the future after-tax cash flow from investments. Often, managers want to know how dollars generated by a new investment will affect its tax rates. If a new investment results in a huge jump in the company's tax rate, the project will be less desirable.

Average Tax Rates.   Financial managers use effective, or **average tax rates,** to determine what percentage of the firm's total before-tax income is owed to the government. Average tax rates are calculated by dividing tax dollars paid by earnings before taxes, or EBT. Acme's effective, or federal average tax rate, for 1996 is:

$$
\frac{\$629,000 \text{ (taxes paid)}}{\$1,850,000 \text{ (EBT)}} = .34, \text{ or } 34\%
$$

---

[6]The federal corporate tax rate schedule is not strictly progressive for every tax bracket, as shown in Table 4-2. Generally speaking, as a corporation's taxable income increases, its marginal tax rate increases. The exceptions, seen in the 1996 rates, usually apply to firms in upper-income tax brackets.

TABLE 4-2

Corporate Marginal Tax Rates Tax Year 1996

EARNINGS BEFORE TAXES (EBT)	TAX RATE
$0–$50,000	15%
$50,001–$75,000	25%
$75,001–$100,000	34%
$100,001–$335,000	39%
$335,001–$10,000,000	34%
$10,000,001–$15,000,000	35%
$15,000,001–$18,333,333	38%
over $18,333,333	35%

Table 4-2 shows 1996 marginal tax rates for corporations. The marginal tax rates do not increase continuously for higher brackets because Congress has established rates that take away certain tax benefits for higher-income corporations.

Take Note

*In the income statement shown in Figure 4-1, Acme Corporation's effective tax rate is shown as 40 percent, resulting in taxes of $740,000 on before-tax income of $1,850,000. The figure represents **both** Acme's federal and state tax obligations.*

Generally, the marginal tax rate will be greater than the average tax rate. It is unusual to have the marginal and average tax rates the same, as is the case for Acme. This occurred because the marginal tax rate changed from 34 percent to 39 percent and dropped to 34 percent again when Acme's tax bill was calculated.

Taxes are paid with cash. Since cash flow affects the value of a business, taxes are an important financial consideration. Financial managers need to understand marginal tax rates to see the marginal impact of taxes on cash flows.

FINANCIAL MANAGEMENT AND YOU

Your Personal Tax Rates

If you filed a federal income tax return, you can calculate your own personal average tax rate and marginal tax rate for last year.

1. Review your federal income tax return from last year. Determine the total amount of tax that you owed and divide by the amount of your taxable income (income after deductions). The answer is your average tax rate.

2. Now look up the amount of taxable income in the tax table that applied to you. It will be labeled Single, Married filing a joint return, Married filing a separate return, or Head of Household. (The

Head of Household is the classification for a single person with a child claimed as a dependent on the taxpayer's return.) You will note that there are different percentages that apply to different blocks of income. The percentages increase, in steps, as your taxable income increases.

3. Determine the percentage that would have applied to the next dollar of taxable income you would have earned. This is your marginal tax rate for that year.

4. How do your average and marginal tax rates compare?

What's Next

In this chapter we reviewed basic accounting principles and explained how financial managers use accounting information to create value for the firm. In chapter 5 we will discuss how to analyze financial statements.

Summary

1. **Explain how financial managers use the three basic accounting financial statements: the income statement, balance sheet, and statement of cash flows.**

Financial managers need to understand the key elements of financial statements to analyze a firm's finances and plan for its future.

- The income statement shows the amount of revenues, expenses, and income a firm has over a specified period of time.
- The balance sheet describes the assets, liabilities, and equity values for a company at a specific point in time.
- The statement of cash flows describes a firm's cash inflows and outflows over a period of time.

2. **Discuss how depreciation affects cash flow and compute depreciation expense.**

Depreciation is a noncash, tax-deductible expense. Since depreciation is tax deductible, it affects cash flow—the greater a firm's depreciation, the greater its cash flow is. Cash flow, in turn, affects the value of the firm. The more cash a firm has, the greater its value.

To allocate the cost of an asset over time, accountants use different depreciation methods, such as straight-line depreciation or the modified accelerated cost recovery system (MACRS). Whatever method is used, accountants must first find the depreciation basis—the total cost of the asset plus setup and delivery costs. Then they calculate the percentage of that total allocated for the time period at issue, as determined by either the straight-line depreciation method or MACRS.

3. **Explain how taxes affect a firm's cash flow and calculate marginal and average tax rates.**

The marginal tax rate—the rate that would apply to the next dollar of taxable income—aids financial decisions because financial managers use it to assess the impact that a new investment will have on cash flow. If the new investment results in such a big jump in taxes that cash flow is affected negatively. The amount of taxes owed is computed by multiplying each bracket of income by the corresponding tax rate set by Congress and adding the totals for each income bracket.

The average tax rate is calculated by dividing the amount of taxes paid by earnings before taxes.

Self-Test

ST-1. Brother Mel's Bar-B-Q Restaurant has $80,000 in assets and $20,000 in liabilities. What is the equity of this firm?

ST-2. Cantwell Corporation has sales revenue of $2 million. Cost of goods sold is $1,500,000. What is Cantwell Corporation's gross profit?

ST-3. Adams Computer Store had accumulated depreciation of $75,000 at the end of 1996, and at the end of 1995 this figure was $60,000. Earnings before interest and taxes for the year 1996 were $850,000. Assuming that no assets were sold in 1996, what was the amount of depreciation expense for 1996?

ST-4. Shattuck Corporation had net income of $2,500,000 in 1996, depreciation expense of $500,000, and dividends paid of $400,000. What is Shattuck's operating cash flow for 1996?

ST-5. Bubba's Sporting Goods Company had retained earnings of $3 million at the end of 1995. During 1996, the company had earnings available to common stockholders of $500,000 and of this paid out $100,000 in dividends. What is the retained earnings figure for the end of 1996?

ST-6. Ron's In-Line Skating Corporation had retained earnings at the end of 1996 of $120,000. At the end of 1995 this figure was $90,000. If the company paid $5,000 in dividends to common stockholders during 1996, what was the amount of earnings available to common stockholders?

ST-7. Hayes Company recently bought a new computer system. The total cost, including set-up, was $8,000. If this is five-year asset class equipment, what would be the amount of depreciation taken on this system in year two using MACRS rules?

ST-8. If Burns Corporation has taxable income of $800,000, how much federal income taxes are owed?

ST-9. If Badeusz Quarry Corporation has taxable income of $4 million what is the average tax rate for this company?

ST-10. If Parmenter Corporation has taxable income of $20 million, what is the marginal tax rate for this company?

Review Questions

1. Why do total assets equal the sum of total liabilities and equity? Explain.
2. What are the time dimensions of the income statement, the balance sheet, and the statement of cash flows? Hint: Are they videos or still pictures? Explain.
3. Define depreciation expense as it appears on an income statement. How does depreciation affect cash flow?
4. What are retained earnings? Why are they important?
5. Explain how earnings available to common stockholders and common stock dividends paid from the current income statement affect the balance sheet item retained earnings.
6. What is "accumulated depreciation"?
7. What are the three major sections of the statement of cash flows?
8. How do financial managers calculate the average tax rate?
9. Why do financial managers calculate the marginal tax rate?

Build Your Communication Skills

CS-1. Interview a manager or owner of an accounting firm. Ask that person what kinds of oral communication skills he or she needs to communicate financial information. Also ask what kinds of writing skills are required. What kinds of communications skills does this accounting firm executive look for when hiring a new person to do accounting or finance work for the firm? Report your findings to the class.

CS-2. Write a report that describes the best sources of financial information about publicly traded corporations. Discuss where you can find the basic financial statements for a corporation, which sources are the easiest to use, and what information sources—the library, the corporation, a brokerage firm, or the Internet—were most useful.

Problems

4-1. Identify whether the following items belong on the income statement or the balance sheet.

Classifying Financial Statement Items

a. Interest Expense
b. Preferred Stock Dividends Paid
c. Plant and Equipment
d. Sales
e. Notes Payable
f. Common Stock
g. Accounts Receivable
h. Accrued Expenses
i. Cost of Goods Sold
j. Preferred Stock

k. Cash
l. Capital in Excess of Par
m. Operating Income
n. Depreciation Expense
o. Marketable Securities
p. Accounts Payable
q. Prepaid Expenses
r. Inventory
s. Net Income
t. Retained Earnings

4-2. For all the items in problem 4-1 that are found on the balance sheet, indicate to which section they belong (current assets, fixed assets, current liabilities, long-term liabilities, or equity).

Balance Sheet Categories

4-3. You are interviewing for an entry-level financial analyst position with Zeppelin Associates. Monte Rutledge, the senior partner, wants to be sure all the people he hires are very familiar with basic accounting principles. He gives you the following data and asks you to fill in the missing information. Each column is an independent case.

Financial Statement Connections

	Case A	Case B
Revenues	200,000	_____
Expenses	_____	70,000
Net Income	_____	_____
Retained Earnings, Jan 1	300,000	100,000
Dividends Paid	70,000	30,000
Retained Earnings, Dec 31	270,000	_____
Current Assets, Dec 31	80,000	_____
Non-current Assets, Dec 31	_____	180,000
Total Assets, Dec 31	_____	410,000
Current Liabilities, Dec 31	40,000	60,000
Non-current Liabilities, Dec 31	_____	_____
Total Liabilities, Dec 31	140,000	_____
CS and Capital in Excess of Par, Dec 31	520,000	100,000
Total Stockholders Equity, Dec 31	_____	210,000

4-4. Fill in the following missing income statement values. The cases are independent.

Financial Statement Connections

	Case A	Case B
Sales	_____	250,000
COGS	200,000	_____
Gross Profit	_____	150,000
Operating Expenses	60,000	60,000
Operating Income (EBIT)	_____	_____
Interest Expense	10,000	_____
Income Before Taxes (EBT)	_____	80,000
Tax Expense (40%)	92,000	_____
Net Income	_____	_____

4-5. Lightning, Inc. has earnings before taxes of $48,000.

    a. Using the progressive tax rate schedule from Table 4-2, calculate the tax obligation for Lightning, Inc.

    b. What is Lightning's average (effective) tax rate?

4-6. Thunder, Inc. has earnings before taxes of $150,000.

    a. Using the progressive tax rate schedule from Table 4-2, calculate the tax obligation for Thunder, Inc.

    b. What is Thunder's average (effective) tax rate?

4-7. Below is a portion of Hitchcock Haven, Inc.'s balance sheet.

Common Stock ($1 par; 400,000 shares authorized; 200,000 shares issued)	$200,000
Capital in Excess of Par	$400,000
Retained Earnings	$100,000

What was the market price per share of the stock when it was originally sold?

4-8. A portion of Hitchcock Haven, Inc.'s comparative balance sheet is shown below. What is the amount of depreciation expense you would expect to see on the 1997 income statement? No assets that were on the books at the end of 1996 were sold or otherwise disposed of in 1997.

HITCHCOCK HAVEN, INC.
Balance Sheet as of December 31

	1996	1997
Plant, and Equipment	$200,000	$250,000
Less: Accumulated Depreciation	$60,000	$70,000
Net Plant and Equipment	$140,000	$180,000

4-9. The following financial data corresponds to Callahan Corporation's 1996 operations.

Cost of Goods Sold	$200,000
Selling and Administrative Expenses	40,000
Depreciation Expense	85,000
Sales	440,000
Interest Expense	40,000
Applicable Income Tax Rate	40%

Calculate the following income statement items.

    a. Gross Profit

    b. Operating Income (EBIT)

    c. Earning Before Taxes (EBT)

    d. Income Taxes

    e. Net Income

4-10. Wet Dog Perfume Company, a profit making company, purchased a process line for $131,000 and spent another $12,000 on its installation. The line was commissioned in January 1996 and it falls into MACRS seven-year class life. Applicable income tax rate for ABC is 40 percent and there is no investment tax credit. Calculate the following:

    a. 1996 depreciation expense for this process line

    b. Amount of tax savings due to this investment.

4-11. In 1996, Goodwill Construction Company purchased $130,000 worth of construction equipment. Goodwill's taxable income for 1996 without considering the new construction equipment would have been $400,000. The new equipment falls into the MACRS five-year class. Assume the applicable income tax rate is 34 percent. Taxes

    a. What is the company's 1996 taxable income?
    b. How much income tax will Goodwill pay?

4-12. Last year Johnson Flow Measurement Systems, Inc. had an operating profit of $600,000, paid $50,000 in interest expenses and $63,000 in preferred stock dividends. The applicable income tax rate for the year was 34 percent. The company had 100,000 shares of common stock outstanding at the end of last year. Income Statement

    a. What was the amount of Johnson's earnings per share last year?
    b. If the company paid $1.00 per share to its common stockholders, what was the addition to retained earning last year?

Use the comparative figures of Pinewood Company and Subsidiaries to answer questions 4-13 through 4-18 below.

PINEWOOD COMPANY AND SUBSIDIARIES
As of December 31

	1996	1997
Assets:		
Cash	$ 5,534	$ 9,037
Accounts Receivable (gross)	14,956	16,110
Less: Allowance for Bad Debts	211	167
Accounts Receivable (net)	14,745	15,943
Inventory	10,733	11,574
Marketable Securities	952	1,801
Prepaid Expenses	3,234	2,357
Plant and Equipment (gross)	57,340	60,374
Less: Accumulated Depreciation	29,080	32,478
Plant and Equipment (net)	28,260	27,896
Land	1,010	1,007
Long Term Investments	2,503	4,743
Liabilities:		
Accounts Payable	3,253	2,450
Notes Payable	—	—
Accrued Expenses	6,821	7,330
Bonds Payable	2,389	2,112
Stockholders' Equity:		
Common Stock	8,549	10,879
Retained Earnings	45,959	51,587

4-13. Compute the following totals for the end of 1996 and 1997. Balance Sheet

    a. Current Assets
    b. Total Assets
    c. Current Liabilities
    d. Total Liabilities
    e. Total Stockholders' Equity

4-14. Show whether or not the basic accounting equation is satisfied in problem 4-13. Basic Accounting Equation

4-15. Calculate the cash flows from the changes in the following from the end of 1996 to the end of 1997. Indicate inflow or outflow.

a. Accumulated Depreciation	**g.** Plant and Equipment
b. Accounts Receivable	**h.** Marketable Securities
c. Inventories	**i.** Land
d. Prepaid Expenses	**j.** Long Term Investments
e. Accounts Payable	**k.** Common Stock
f. Accrued Expenses	**l.** Bonds Payable

4-16. Prepare a statement of cash flows in proper form using the inflows and outflows from question 4-15. Assume net income (earnings after taxes) from the 1997 income statement was $10,628 and $5,000 in common stock dividends were paid. Ignore the income tax effect on the change in depreciation.

4-17. Show whether or not your net cash flow matches the change in cash between the end of 1996 and end of 1997 balance sheets.

4-18. Show whether or not the retained earnings equation balances.

Answers to Self-Test

ST-1. $80,000 assets − $20,000 liabilities = $60,000 equity

ST-2. Cost of goods sold = $1,500,000
Gross profit = $2,000,000 sales revenue − $1,500,000 cost of goods sold = $500,000

ST-3. $75,000 end of 1996 accumulated depreciation − $60,000 end of 1995 accumulated depreciation = $15,000 1996 depreciation expense

ST-4. $2,500,000 net income + $500,000 = $3,000,000 cash flow from operations (Dividends payments are not operating cash flows, they are financial cash flows.)

ST-5. $3,000,000 end of 1995 retained earnings + $500,000 earnings available to common stockholders − $100,000 dividends paid = $3,400,000 end of 1996 retained earnings

ST-6. $120,000 end of 1996 retained earnings − $90,000 end of 1995 retained earnings = $30,000 1996 change in retained earnings

1996 net income − $5,000 1996 dividends to common stockholders = $30,000 change in retained earnings from end of 1995 to end of 1996

ST-7. $8,000 depreciation basis × .32 (second year MACRS depreciation % for a 5-year class asset) = $2,500 year two depreciation expense

ST-8. ($50,000 × .15) + ($25,000 × .25) + ($25,000 × .34) + ($235,000 × .39) + ($465,000 × .34) = $272,000 federal income taxes owed

Note: $50,000 + $25,000 + $25,000 + $235,000 + $465,000 = $800,000 taxable income

ST-9. ($50,000 × .15) + ($25,000 × .25) + ($25,000 × .34) + ($235,000 × .39) + ($3,665,000 × .34) = $1,360,000 taxes owed; $1,360,000 ÷ $4 million = .34 = 34% average tax rate

Note: $50,000 + $25,000 + $25,000 + $235,000 + $3,665,000 = $4 million taxable income

ST-10. Taxable income over $18,333,333 is taxed at a 35% rate ∴ the marginal tax rate at $20 million in taxable income is 35%

chapter 5

Analysis of Financial Statements

When you can measure what you are speaking about, and express it in numbers, you know something about it.

William Thomson, Lord Kelvin

You Can't Analyze a Book by Its Cover

David Schwartz, President of Harry W. Schwartz Bookstores, heads six local bookstores in the Milwaukee, Wisconsin, area. He decided to meet and beat the competition of the big retailers in his area. When Waldenbooks and B. Dalton took the radical step of discounting bestsellers by 30 percent, Schwartz did the same. When they opened one or two stores in every new mall, Schwartz mustered the courage and the capital to open a mall store.

Yet, in one area, his company was terrible: analyzing financial statements to measure the health of

his business. When the bank evaluated the financial condition of his bookstores, it roundly criticized him for his store's anemic turnover of inventory, out-of-control salary expenses, and feeble advertising.

The failure to analyze financial statements to track his stores' progress was slowly killing Schwartz's business. "The way the company was operating, if there had been an overrun in payroll or an unexpected capital expense, there would have been no way to pay for it," Alvin Dominitz, Schwartz's business partner, explained.

The truth was, without maintaining and analyzing financial statements, the two partners were operating in the statistical dark. So they started to review line-by-line accountings of which items were moving and how fast. Store managers were ordered to run their stores adhering to basic financial principles. The managers had to know what they were spending on payroll, how much inventory they were turning over, and what their cash flow was.

The analysis of their financial records quickly showed them that they had to change the way they ordered books.

"I was the macho buyer who bought for the life of the book," says Schwartz. If he thought he could sell ten copies of a book, he would order ten copies up front and carry them until they sold out. But keeping that much inventory hurt cash flow. Now a new computerized inventory system and collective buying with other bookstores lets managers order in small batches, track the numbers, and only order what they need.

When Schwartz needed to raise capital for future expansion and pay past bills, he was able to line up a major investor. Why? With sales revenues of over $5 million per year, low inventory, low costs, and ample cash flow, he had a financial package of information that investors and creditors could review as positively as any bestseller. ❉

Sources: Tom Ehrenfeld, "New and Improved American Small Business," *Inc* Magazine (January 1995): 34–45; "IBC Signs Three New Stores, Welcomes More," (February 9, 1995): Retrieved from the Internet at http://www.ambook.org/bookweb/gtw/100295/art1.htm/

Chapter Overview

In chapter 4 we reviewed the major financial statements, the primary sources of financial information about a business. In this chapter we will learn how to interpret these financial statements in greater detail.

Schwartz and his partner needed to understand the financial condition of their bookstores to raise capital. In the same way, all business owners, investors, and creditors use financial statements and ratio analysis to investigate the financial health of a firm. We will see how financial managers calculate ratios that measure profitability, liquidity, debt, asset activity, and market performance of a firm. We will then explore how financial experts use ratios to compare the firm's performance to manager's goals, the firm's past and present performance, and the firm's performance to similar firms in the industry. We will also discuss sources of financial information.

Assessing Financial Health

Medical doctors assess the health of people. Financial managers assess the health of businesses. When you visit a doctor for an examination, the doctor may check your blood pressure, heart rate, cholesterol, and blood sugar levels. The results of each test should fall within a range of numbers considered "normal" for your age, weight, gender, and height. If they don't, the doctor will probably run additional tests to see what, if anything, is wrong.

Like doctors, financial managers check the health of businesses by running basic tests—such as a financial ratio analysis—to see whether the firm's performance is within the normal range for a company of that type. If it is not, the financial manager runs more tests to see what, if anything, is wrong.

Misleading Numbers

Both medical doctors and financial managers must interpret the information they have and decide what additional information they need to complete an analysis. For instance, suppose a doctor examines a six-foot, 230-pound, twenty-two-year-old male named Dirk. The doctor's chart shows that a healthy male of that age and height should normally weigh between 160 and 180 pounds. Since excess weight is a health risk, the numbers don't look positive.

Before the doctor prescribes a diet and exercise program for Dirk, she asks follow-up questions and runs more tests. She learns that Dirk, a starting fullback for his college football team, has only 6 percent body fat, can bench press 380 pounds, runs a 40-yard dash in 4.5 seconds, has a blood pressure rate of 110/65, and a resting heart rate of 52 beats per minute. This additional information changes the doctor's initial health assessment. Relying on incomplete information would have lead to an inaccurate diagnosis.

Like doctors, financial managers need to analyze many factors to determine the health of a company. Indeed, for some firms the financial statements do not provide the entire picture.

For instance, in 1995 Dow Corning, a leading manufacturer of silicon breast implants, reported record profits just before filing a Chapter 11 bankruptcy petition. Dow Corning faced a large number of pending product liability lawsuits that claimed Dow's silicone breast implants were faulty.[1] Because the outcome of the pending lawsuits was uncertain, the (potential) liabilities did not appear on the balance sheet. Financial analysis based only on the financial statements, then, gave a faulty impression of the company's health.

As the Dow Corning example demonstrates, accounting conventions may prevent factors affecting a firm's finances from appearing on financial statements. Just as Dirk's doctor looked beyond the obvious, financial managers using ratio analysis must always seek complete information before completing an analysis. In the sections that follow, we discuss ratios based on financial statements, ratios that use market information, and outside information sources.

FINANCIAL RATIOS

Financial managers use ratio analysis to interpret the raw numbers on financial statements. A **financial ratio** is a number that expresses the value of one financial variable relative to another. Put more simply, a financial ratio is the result you get when you divide one financial number by another. Calculating an individual ratio is simple, but each ratio must be analyzed carefully to effectively measure a firm's performance.

---

[1]Joseph Nocera, "Dow Corning Succumbs: How Product Liability Lawsuits Over Silicone Breast Implants Caused Company to Fail. Failed Litigation Part II," *Fortune* (October 30, 1995): 137.

Source: DILBERT © 1996 United Feature Syndicate, Inc. Reprinted by Permission.

Ratios are comparative measures. Because the ratios show relative value, they allow financial analysts to compare information that could not be compared in its raw form.[2] Ratios may be used to compare:

- one ratio to a related ratio
- the firm's performance to management's goals
- the firm's past and present performance
- the firm's performance to similar firms

For instance, say a company reaped huge revenues from one investment, but the cost of the investment was high. A financial manager could use a ratio to compare that investment to another that did not generate such high revenues but had low cost. Take Steven Spielberg's *Jurassic Park*. That blockbuster movie grossed more than $869 million—the number-one grossing movie for 1993. Compare *Jurassic Park's* total revenues to the $23.6 million revenues that Ang Lee's *The Wedding Banquet* generated.[3] Looking only at the total revenue figures, *Jurassic Park* looks like a better investment than the *The Wedding Banquet.*

However, analysts in the movie industry use a revenue-to-cost ratio (total revenues divided by total cost) to find a movie's net return per $1 invested. Using that ratio we see that *Jurassic Park*, at a cost of $63 million, had a return-on-cost ratio of 13.8 ($869,000,000 ÷ $63,000,000 = 13.8). *The Wedding Banquet,* at a cost of $1 million, had a return on cost ratio of 23.6 ($23,600,000 ÷ $1,000,000 = 23.6). Although *Jurassic Park* made more total revenue, *The Wedding Banquet* made more money relative to its cost than did *Jurassic Park*.

Financial managers, other business managers, creditors, and stockholders all use financial ratio analysis. Specifically, creditors may use ratios to see whether a business will have the cash flow to repay its debt and interest. Stockholders may use ratios to see what the long-term value of their stock will be. For example, in 1995 Euro Disney reported a yearly profit, its first ever since the Paris Disney theme park

---

[2]Financial managers that analyze the financial condition of the firms they work for act as financial analysts. The term *financial analyst,* however, also includes financial experts who analyze a variety of firms.
[3]*Colorado Springs Gazette-Telegraph* (January 15, 1994): A2

opened in 1992. However, analysts predicted that compared to its total costs—costs that included average interest payments of $30 million per year—the revenues were too low to guarantee Euro Disney's future financial success. Despite the reported profits, stock price dropped by 14 percent.[4]

The Basic Financial Ratios

Financial ratios are generally divided into five categories: profitability, liquidity, debt, asset activity, and market value. The ratios in each group give us insights into different aspects of a firm's financial health.

- *Profitability ratios* measure how much company revenue is eaten up by expenses, how much a company earns relative to sales generated, and the amount earned relative to the value of the firm's assets and equity.
- *Liquidity ratios* indicate how quickly and easily a company can obtain cash for its needs.
- *Debt ratios* measure how much a company owes to others.
- *Asset activity ratios* measure how efficiently a company uses its assets.
- *Market value ratios* measure how the market value of the company's stock compares to its accounting values.

Calculating the Ratios

We will use the financial statements for the Acme Corporation presented in chapter 4 as the basis for our ratio analysis. Figure 5-1 shows Acme Corporation's income statement for 1996, and Figure 5-2 shows its December 31, 1996, balance sheet.

---

[4]"Euro Disney Reports Profit for '95, but the Future Remains Cloudy," *The New York Times* (November 16, 1995): D7.

Sales	$10,000,000
Cost of Goods Sold	− 4,000,000
Gross Profit	= 6,000,000
Selling & Administrative Expenses	− 800,000
Depreciation Expense	− 2,000,000
Earnings Before Interest and Taxes (EBIT, or Operating Income)	= 3,200,000
Interest Expense	− 1,350,000
Earnings Before Taxes (EBT)	= 1,850,000
Taxes (40%)	− 740,000
Net Income (NI)	= 1,110,000
Preferred Stock Dividends Paid	− 110,000
Earnings Available to Common Stockholders	= 1,000,000
Common Stock Dividends Paid	− 400,000
Addition to Retained Earnings	= 600,000

Figure 5-1 Acme Corporation Income Statement for the Year 1996

Figure 5-2   Acme Corporation Balance Sheet as of December 31, 1996

ASSETS		LIABILITIES & EQUITY	
Current Assets		**Current Liabilities**	
Cash	$ 9,000,000	Accounts Payable	$12,000,000
Accounts Receivable (net)	1,000,000	Notes Payable	5,000,000
Inventory	20,000,000	Accrued Expenses	3,000,000
Marketable Securities	8,000,000	Total Current Liabilities	20,000,000
Prepaid Expenses	1,000,000	**Long Term Liabilities & Preferred Stock**	
Total Current Assets	39,000,000	Bonds Payable	20,000,000
Fixed Assets		(5%, due 2015)	
Plant & Equipment (net)	11,000,000	Preferred Stock	1,000,000
Total Assets	50,000,000	Total Long Term Debt & PS	21,000,000
		Common Stock Equity	
		Common Stock	1,000,000
		(1 million shares, $1 par)	
		Capital in Excess of Par	3,000,000
		Retained Earnings	5,000,000
		Total Common Stock Equity	9,000,000
		Total Liabilities, PS, & CS Equity	50,000,000

Now let's analyze Acme Corporation's financial health by calculating its profitability, liquidity, debt, asset utilization, and market value ratios.

Profitability Ratios   Profitability ratios measure how the firm's returns compare to its sales, asset investments, and equity. Stockholders have a special interest in the profitability ratios because profit ultimately leads to cash flow, a primary source of value for a firm. Managers, acting on behalf of stockholders, also pay close attention to profitability ratios to ensure that the managers preserve the firm's value.

We will discuss six profitability ratios. We discuss: gross profit margin, operating profit margin, net profit margin, return on assets, and return on equity. Some of the profitability ratios use figures from two different financial statements.

Gross Profit Margin.   The *gross profit margin* measures how much profit remains out of each sales dollar after the cost of the goods sold is subtracted. The ratio formula follows:

$$\text{Gross Profit Margin} = \frac{\text{Gross Profit}}{\text{Sales}}$$

This ratio shows how well a firm generates revenue compared to its costs of goods sold. The higher the ratio, the better the cost controls compared to the sales revenues.

To find the gross profit margin ratio for Acme, look at Figure 5-1, Acme's income statement. We see that Acme's gross profit for the year was $6 million and its sales revenue was $10 million. Dividing $6 million by $10 million yields Acme Corporation's gross profit margin of .6 or 60 percent. That ratio shows that Acme's cost of products and services sold was 40 percent of sales revenue, leaving the company with 60 percent of sales revenues to use for other purposes.

Operating Profit Margin.   The *operating profit margin ratio* measures the cost of goods sold, as reflected in the gross profit margin ratio, as well as all other operating expenses. This ratio is calculated by dividing earnings before interest and taxes (EBIT or operating income) by sales revenue.

$$\text{Operating Profit Margin} = \frac{\text{Earnings Before Interest and Taxes}}{\text{Sales}}$$

Acme's EBIT, as shown on its income statement (see Figure 5-1), is $3,200,000. Dividing $3.2 million by its sales revenue of $10 million gives an operating profit margin of 32 percent (3,200,000 ÷ 10,000,000 = .32 or 32%). Acme's operating profit margin indicates that 32 percent of its sales revenues remain after subtracting all operating expenses.

Net Profit Margin.   The *net profit margin* measures how much profit out of each sales dollar is left after *all* expenses are subtracted—that is, after all operating, interest, and tax expenses are subtracted. It is computed by dividing net income by sales revenue. Acme's net income for the year was $1.11 million. Dividing $1.11 million by $10 million in sales yields an 11.1 percent net profit margin. Here's the computation:

$$\text{Net Profit Margin} = \frac{\text{Net Income}}{\text{Sales}} = \frac{1,110,000}{10,000,000} = .111 \text{ or } 11.1\%$$

Net income, and the net profit margin ratio, are often referred to as "bottom-line" measures. The net profit margin includes adjustments for nonoperating expenses, such as interest and taxes, and operating expenses. We see that in 1996 Acme Corporation had 11.1 percent of each sales dollar remaining after all expenses were paid.

Return on Assets.   The *return on assets* (ROA) ratio indicates how much income each dollar of assets produces on average. It shows whether the business is investing in its assets effectively. The ROA ratio is calculated by dividing net income by the total assets of the firm. For Acme Corporation, we calculate this ratio by dividing $1.11 million in net income (see Figure 5-1, Acme income statement) by $50 million of total assets (see Figure 5-2, Acme balance sheet), for a return on assets (ROA) of 2.2 percent. Here's the calculation:

$$\text{Return on Assets} = \frac{\text{Net Income}}{\text{Total Assets}} = \frac{\$1,110,000}{\$50,000,000} = .022 \text{ or } 2.2\%$$

In 1996 each dollar of Acme Corporation's assets produced, on average, income of $.022. Although this return on assets figure may seem low, it is not unusual for certain types of companies, such as commercial banks.

Return on Equity.   The *return on equity* (ROE) ratio measures the average return on the firm's capital contributions from its owners (for a corporation, that means the contributions of stockholders). It indicates how many dollars of income were produced for each dollar invested by the common stockholders.

ROE is calculated by dividing net income by stockholders' equity. Because we are using common stockholders' equity to define this ratio, preferred stock will be treated as debt. Although accountants place preferred stock in the equity section of the balance sheet, as we did in chapter 4, from an economic point of view preferred stock is more like debt than like equity. Preferred stockholders have no claim on the residual income of the firm and are not owners. To calculate ROE for Acme Corporation, divide $1.11 million in net income by $9 million in total common stockholders' equity (see Figure 5-2, Acme balance statement). Acme's ROE is 12.3 percent, shown as follows:

$$\text{Return on Equity} = \frac{\text{Net Income}}{\text{Common Equity}} = \frac{1,110,000}{9,000,000} = .123 \text{ or } 12.3\%$$

Take Note

Do not confuse the ROE ratio with the return earned by the individual common stockholders on their common stock investment. The changes in the market price of the stock and dividends received determine the total return on an individual's common stock investment.

The ROE figure shows that Acme Corporation returned, on average, 12.3 percent for every dollar that common stockholders invested in the firm.

Mixing Numbers from Income Statements and Balance Sheets. When financial managers calculate the gross profit margin, operating profit margin, and net profit margin ratios they use only income statement variables. In contrast, analysts use both income statement and balance sheet variables to find the return on assets and return on equity ratios. A **mixed ratio** is a ratio that uses both income statement and balance sheet variables as inputs.

Because income statement variables show values over a period of time and balance sheet variables show values for one moment in time, using mixed ratios poses the question of how to deal with the different time dimensions. For example, should the analyst select balance sheet variable values from the beginning of the year, the end of the year, or the midpoint of the year? If there was a large change in the balance sheet account during the year, the choice could make a big difference. Consider the situation below:

Total Assets Jan 1, 1996	$1,000,000
Total Assets Dec 31, 1996	2,000,000
Net Income in 1996	100,000

Return on Assets based on Jan 1 balance sheet:

100,000/1,000,000 = .10, or 10%

Return on Assets based on Dec 31 balance sheet:

100,000/2,000,000 = .05, or 5%

Which figure is correct? There is no black-and-white answer to this problem. Some analysts add the beginning of the year balance sheet figure to the end of the year figure and divide by two to get an average figure.

Logic and common sense suggest that analysts should pick figures that best match the returns to the assets or to the equity. Say that Acme purchased a large amount of assets early in the year. The middle or end of year balance sheet figures would probably match the returns to the assets more effectively than beginning of the year figures because assets can only affect profit if they have been used. For simplicity, we used end of year balance sheet figures to calculate Acme's mixed profitability ratios.

Liquidity Ratios Liquidity ratios measure the ability of a firm to meet its short-term obligations. These ratios are important because failure to pay such obligations can lead to bankruptcy. Bankers and other lenders use liquidity ratios to see whether to extend short-term credit to a firm. Generally, the higher the liquidity ratio, the more able a firm is to pay its short-term obligations. Stockholders, however, use liquidity ratios to see how the firm has invested in assets. Too much investment in current—as compared to long-term—assets indicates inefficiency.

The two main liquidity ratios are the current ratio and the quick ratio.

The Current Ratio. The *current ratio* compares all the current assets of the firm (cash and other assets that can be easily converted to cash) to all the company's current liabilities (liabilities that must be paid with cash soon). At the end of 1996, Acme Corporation's current assets were $39 million and its current liabilities were $20 million. Dividing Acme's current assets by its current liabilities, as follows, we see that:

$$\text{Current Ratio} = \frac{\text{Current Assets}}{\text{Current Liabilities}} = \frac{\$39,000,000}{\$20,000,000} = 1.95$$

Acme's current ratio value, then, is 1.95. The ratio result shows that Acme has $1.95 of current assets for every dollar of current liabilities, indicating that Acme could pay all its short-term debts by liquidating about half its current assets.

The Quick Ratio. The *quick ratio* is similar to the current ratio, but is a more rigorous measure of liquidity because it excludes inventory from current assets. To calculate the quick ratio, then, divide current assets less inventory by current liabilities.

$$\text{Quick Ratio} = \frac{\text{Current Assets Less Inventory}}{\text{Current Liabilities}}$$

This conservative measure of a firm's liquidity may be useful for some businesses. To illustrate, suppose a computer retail store had a large inventory of personal computers with out-of-date Intel® 286 microprocessors. The computer store would have a tough time selling its inventory for much money.

At the end of 1996, the balance sheet figures show that Acme Corporation's current assets less inventory are worth $19 million ($39,000,000 − $20,000,000). Its current liabilities are $20 million. Dividing $19 million by $20 million, we see that its quick ratio is .95. A quick ratio of .95 means that Acme could pay off 95 percent of its current liabilities by liquidating its current assets, excluding inventory.

The remaining 5 percent of liabilities can be paid off if the inventory has some value. Only if the current inventory is valueless will Acme have to sell assets that may have poor liquidity, borrow money, or issue common stock and use the proceeds to pay off its short-term debts.

We will assume that Acme Corporation's inventory is hard to liquidate, making the quick ratio important. If the company being analyzed had very liquid inventory, such as a government securities dealer, the quick ratio would not be a useful analysis tool compared to the current ratio.

Debt Ratios   The financial analyst uses debt ratios to assess the relative size of a firm's debt load and the firm's ability pay off the debt. The three primary debt ratios are the debt to total assets, debt to equity, and times interest earned ratios.

Current and potential lenders of long-term funds, such as banks and bondholders, are interested in debt ratios. When a business's debt ratios increase significantly, bondholder and lender risk increases because more creditors compete for that firm's resources if the company runs into financial trouble. Stockholders are also concerned with the amount of debt a business has because bondholders are paid before stockholders.

The optimal debt ratio depends on many factors, including the type of business and the amount of risk lenders and stockholders will tolerate. Generally, a profitable firm in a stable business can handle more debt—and a higher debt ratio—than a growth firm in a volatile business.

Debt to Total Assets. The *debt to total assets* ratio measures the percentage of the firm's assets that are financed with debt. Acme Corporation's total debt at the end of 1996 was $41 million. This includes the $1 million in preferred stock we've classified as debt rather than equity. Its total assets were $50 million. The calculations for the debt-to-total-assets ratio follow:

$$\text{Debt to Total Assets} = \frac{\text{Total Debt}}{\text{Total Assets}} = \frac{\$41,000,000}{\$50,000,000} = .82 \text{ or } 82\%$$

Acme's debt to total assets ratio value is 82 percent, indicating that the other 18 percent of financing came from equity investors (the stockholders).

Debt to Equity. The *debt to equity ratio* is the percentage of debt relative to the amount of equity of the firm. At the end of 1996, Acme's amount of total debt was $41 million and the amount of equity was $9 million. Here is the calculation of Acme's debt to equity ratio:

$$\text{Debt to Equity} = \frac{\text{Total Debt}}{\text{Equity}} = \frac{\$41,000,000}{\$ 9,000,000} = 4.56$$

Acme's debt-to-equity ratio of 4.56 shows that the firm had 4.56 times as much debt as it had equity, indicating that Acme relies much more heavily on creditor-supplied funds than on owner-supplied funds.

Times Interest Earned. The times interest earned ratio is often used to assess a company's ability to service the interest on its debt with operating income from the current period. The *times interest earned* ratio is equal to earnings before interest and taxes (EBIT) divided by interest expense. Acme Corporation has EBIT of $3.2 million and interest expense of $1.35 million for 1996. Acme's times interest earned ratio is as follows:

$$\text{Times Interest Earned} = \frac{\text{EBIT}}{\text{Interest Expense}} = \frac{\$3,200,000}{\$1,350,000} = 2.37$$

Acme's times interest earned ratio value of 2.37 means that the company earned $2.37 of operating income (EBIT) for each $1 of interest expense incurred during that year.

A high times interest earned ratio suggests that the company will have ample operating income to cover its interest expense. A low ratio signals that the company may have insufficient operating income to pay interest as it becomes due. If so, the business might need to liquidate assets, or raise new debt or equity funds to pay the interest due. Recall, however, that operating income is not the same as cash flow. Operating income figures do not show the amount of *cash* available to pay interest. Because interest payments are made with cash, the times interest earned ratio is only a rough measure of a firm's ability to pay interest with current funds.

Asset Activity Ratios Financial analysts use asset activity ratios to measure how efficiently a firm uses its assets. They analyze specific assets and classes of assets. The three asset activity ratios we'll examine here are the average collection period (for accounts receivable), the inventory turnover, and the total asset turnover ratios.

Average Collection Period. The *average collection period* ratio measures how many days, on average, the company's credit customers take to pay their accounts. Managers, especially credit managers, use this ratio to decide who the firm should extend credit to. Slow payers are not welcome customers.

To calculate the average collection period, divide accounts receivable by the company's average credit sales per day. (This, in turn, is the company's annual credit sales divided by the number of days in a year, 365.)

$$\text{Average Collection Period} = \frac{\text{Accounts Receivable}}{\text{Average Daily Credit Sales}}$$

Acme Corporation had $1 million in accounts receivable and average daily credit sales of $27,397.26. (That is, $10 million total credit sales divided by 365 days in one year.) Dividing $1 million by $27,397.26 gives a value of 36.5. The ratio shows that in 1996 Acme Corporation's credit customers took an average of 36.5 days to pay their account balances.

Notice that, in calculating the ratio, we used Acme Corporation's total sales figure for 1996 in the denominator, assuming that all of Acme's sales for the year were made on credit. We made no attempt to break down Acme's sales into cash sales and credit sales. Financial analysts usually calculate this ratio using the total sales figure when they do not have the credit sales only figure.

Inventory Turnover. The *inventory turnover* ratio tells us how efficiently the firm converts inventory to sales. If the company has inventory that sells well, the ratio value will be high. If the inventory does not sell well due to lack of demand or if there is excess inventory, the ratio value will be low.

The inventory turnover formula follows:

$$\text{Inventory Turnover} = \frac{\text{Sales}}{\text{Inventory}}$$

Acme Corporation had sales of $10 million and inventory of $20 million in 1996. Dividing $10 million by $20 million, we see that the inventory turnover value is .5. This number means that in 1996 Acme "turned" its inventory into sales .5 times[5] during the year.

Total Asset Turnover. The *total asset turnover* ratio measures how efficiently a firm utilizes its assets. Stockholders, bondholders, and managers know that the more efficiently the firm operates, the better the returns.

If a company has many assets that do not help generate sales (such as fancy offices and corporate jets for senior management), then the total asset turnover ratio will be relatively low. A company that has a high asset utilization ratio suggests that its assets help promote sales revenue.

To calculate the asset turnover ratio for Acme, divide sales by total assets as follows:

$$\text{Total Asset Turnover} = \frac{\text{Sales}}{\text{Total Assets}}$$

---

[5]Many financial analysts define the inventory turnover ratio using *cost of goods sold* instead of *sales* in the numerator. They use cost of goods sold because sales is defined in terms of *sales price* and inventory is defined in terms of *cost*. We will use *sales* in the numerator of the inventory turnover ratio to be consistent with the other *turnover* ratios.

The 1996 total asset turnover ratio for Acme Corporation is its sales of $10 million divided by its total assets of $50 million. The result is .20, indicating that Acme's sales were .20 of its assets. Put another way, the dollar amount of sales was one-fifth the dollar amount of assets.

Market Value Ratios   The ratios examined so far rely on financial statement figures. But market value ratios mainly rely on financial marketplace data, such as the market price of a company's common stock. Market value ratios measure the market's perception of the future earning power of a company, as reflected in the stock share price. The two market value ratios we discuss are the price-to-earnings ratio and the market-to-book-value ratio.

Price-to-Earnings Ratio.   *The price to earnings* (P/E) ratio is defined as:

$$P/E = \frac{\text{Market Price per Share of Common Stock}}{\text{Earnings per Share}}$$

To calculate earnings per share (EPS), we divide earnings available to common stockholders by the number of shares of common stock outstanding.

Investors and managers use the P/E ratio to gauge the future prospects of a company. The ratio measures how much investors are willing to pay for claim to one dollar of the earnings per share of the firm. The more investors are willing to pay over the value of EPS for the stock, the more confidence they are displaying about the firm's future growth—that is, the higher the P/E ratio, the higher are investors' growth expectations. Consider the following marketplace data for Acme:

Current market price of Acme Corporation's stock:	$20.00
1996 EPS:	$1.00

$$P/E \text{ Ratio} = \frac{\text{Market Price per Share}}{\text{Earnings per Share}} = \frac{\$20}{\$1.00} = 20$$

We see that the $20 per share market price of Acme Corporation's common stock is 20 times the level of its 1996 earnings per share ($1.00 EPS). The 20 result indicates that stock traders predict that Acme has strong future earnings potential. It would take twenty years, at Acme's 1996 earnings rate, for the company to earn net profits of $20 per share, the amount an investor would pay today to buy this stock.

Market to Book Value.   *The market to book value* (M/B) ratio is the market price per share of a company's common stock divided by the accounting book-value-per-share (BPS) ratio. The book-value-per-share ratio is the amount of common stock equity on the firm's balance sheet divided by the number of common shares outstanding.

The book value per share is a proxy for the amount remaining per share after selling the firm's assets for their balance sheet values, and paying the debt owed to all creditors and preferred stockholders. We calculate Acme's BPS ratio, assuming the following information:

Total common stock equity at year-end 1996:	$9,000,000
Number of Common Shares Outstanding:	1,000,000

$$BPS = \frac{\text{Common Stock Equity}}{\text{Number of Common Shares Outstanding}} = \frac{9,000,000}{1,000,000} = \$9.00$$

Now that we know the book value per share of Acme's stock is $9, we can find the market to book value ratio as follows:

$$\text{Market to Book Value Ratio} = \frac{\text{Market Price per Share}}{\text{Book Value per Share}} = \frac{\$20}{\$9.00} = 2.22$$

We see that Acme's M/B ratio is 2.22. That value indicates that the market price of Acme common stock ($20) is 2.22 times its book value per share ($9).

When the market price per share of stock is greater than the book value per share, analysts often conclude that the market believes the company's future earnings are worth more than the firm's liquidation value. In our case the market seems to believe that the value of Acme's future earnings is more than twice its liquidation value. The difference between the firm's future earnings and liquidation value is the **going concern value** of the firm. The higher the M/B ratio, the greater the going concern value of the company seems to be.

Companies that have a market to book value of less than 1 are sometimes considered to be "worth more dead than alive." Such an M/B ratio suggests that if the company liquidated and paid off all creditors and preferred stockholders, it would have more left over for the common stockholders than what the common stock could be sold for in the marketplace.

The M/B ratio is useful, but it is only a rough approximation of how liquidation and going concern values compare. This is because the M/B ratio uses an accounting-based book value. The actual liquidation value of a firm is likely to be different than the book value. For instance, the assets of the firm may be worth more or less than the value at which they are currently carried on the company's balance sheet. In addition, the current market price of the company's bonds and preferred stock may also differ from the accounting value of these claims.

In this section we examined the key profitability, liquidity, debt, asset activity, and market value ratios. The value of each ratio tells part of the story about the financial health of the firm. Next, we explore relationships among ratios.

Relationships Among Ratios: The Du Pont System   As we discussed earlier, ratios may be used to compare one ratio to another related ratio. Financial analysts compare related ratios to see what specific activities add to or detract from a firm's performance.

The Du Pont System of ratio analysis is named for the company whose managers developed the general system. It first examines the relationships between total revenues relative to sales, and sales relative to total assets. The product of the net profit margin and the total asset turnover is the return on assets (or ROA). This equation, known as the Du Pont equation, follows:

$$\text{Du Pont Equation}$$
$$\text{Return on Assets} = \text{Net Profit Margin} \times \text{Total Asset Turnover} \qquad (5\text{-}1)$$
$$\frac{\text{Net Income}}{\text{Total Assets}} = \frac{\text{Net Income}}{\text{Sales}} \times \frac{\text{Sales}}{\text{Total Assets}}$$

Sales, on the right side of the equation, appears in the denominator of the net profit margin and in the numerator of the total asset turnover. These two equal sales figures would cancel each other out if the equation were simplified, leaving net income over total assets on the right. This, of course, equals net income over total assets, which is on the left side of the equal sign, indicating that the equation is valid.

This version of the Du Pont equation helps us analyze factors that contribute to a firm's return on assets. For example, we already know from our basic ratio analysis that Acme Corporation's return on assets for 1996 was 2.22 percent. Now suppose you wanted to know how much of that 2.22 percent was the result of Acme's net profit margin for 1996, and how much was the result of the activity of Acme's assets in 1996. Equation 5-1, the Du Pont equation, provides the following answer:

$$\text{Return on Assets} = \text{Net Profit Margin} \times \text{Total Asset Turnover}$$
$$\text{Return on Assets} = \frac{\text{Net Income}}{\text{Sales}} \times \frac{\text{Sales}}{\text{Total Assets}}$$

For Acme Corporation:

$$.0222, \text{ or } 2.22\% = \frac{\$1,110,000}{\$10,000,000} \times \frac{\$10,000,000}{\$50,000,000}$$
$$.0222 = .111 \times .200$$
$$\text{or}$$
$$2.22\% = 11.1\% \times 20\%$$

Acme Corporation, we see, has a fairly healthy net profit margin, 11.1 percent, but its total asset turnover is only 20 percent—or one-fifth— its sales. The 20 percent total asset turnover has the effect of dividing the 11.1 percent net profit margin by five, such that ROA is only 2.22 percent.

We might see a low total asset turnover and high net profit margin in a jewelry store, where few items are sold each day but high profit is made on each item sold. A grocery store, however, would have a low net profit margin and a high total asset turnover because many items are sold each day but little profit is made on each dollar of sales.

Another version of the Du Pont equation, called the Modified Du Pont Equation, measures how the return on equity (ROE) is affected by net profit margin, asset activity, and debt financing. As shown in Equation 5-2, in the modified Du Pont equation, ROE is the product of net profit margin, total asset turnover, and the **equity multiplier** (the ratio of total assets to common equity).

$$\text{ROE} = \begin{matrix}\text{Net}\\\text{Profit}\\\text{Margin}\end{matrix} \times \begin{matrix}\text{Total}\\\text{Asset}\\\text{Turnover}\end{matrix} \times \begin{matrix}\text{Equity}\\\text{Multiplier}\end{matrix} \qquad (5\text{-}2)$$

$$\frac{\text{Net Income}}{\text{Equity}} = \frac{\text{Net Income}}{\text{Sales}} \times \frac{\text{Sales}}{\text{Total Assets}} \times \frac{\text{Total Assets}}{\text{Equity}}$$

for Acme Corporation:

$$.1233, \text{ or } 12.33\% = \frac{1,110,000}{10,000,000} \times \frac{10,000,000}{50,000,000} \times \frac{50,000,000}{9,000,000}$$

$$.1234 = .111 \times .20 \times 5.56$$
$$\text{or}$$
$$12.34\% = 11.1\% \times 20\% \times 5.56$$

By examining the previous equation, we see that Acme's net profit margin of 11.1 percent accounts for nearly all of its 12.34 percent ROE. However, Acme's low productivity of assets ($.20 in sales for every dollar of assets employed) reduces the effect of the profit margin—11.1% x 20% = 2.222%. If no other factors were present, Acme's ROE would be 2.22 percent.

Now the equity multiplier comes into play. The equity multiplier indicates the amount of "financial leverage" a firm has. A firm that uses only equity to finance its assets should have an equity multiplier that equals 1.0. To arrive at this conclusion, recall the basic accounting formula—total assets = liabilities + equity. If a firm had no debt on its balance sheet, its liabilities would equal zero, so equity would equal total assets. If equity equals total assets, then the equity multiplier would be 1. Multiplying 1 times any other number has no effect, so in such a situation ROE would depend solely on net profit margin and total asset turnover.

If a firm does have debt on its balance sheet (as Acme does), it will have greater assets than equity and the equity multiplier will be greater than 1. This produces a multiplier effect that drives ROE higher (assuming net income is positive) than can otherwise be accounted for by net profit margin and asset turnover.[7]

Acme's equity multiplier of 5.56 indicates that Acme has assets that are 5.56 times its equity. This has the effect (called the **leverage effect**) of boosting Acme's return on equity from 2.22 percent to 12.34 percent. The leverage effect, caused by debt of $41 million shown on Acme's balance sheet, significantly alters Acme's ROE.

In this section we reviewed basic ratios, and analyzed relationships of one ratio to another to assess the firm's financial condition. Next, we will investigate how ratio analysis can be used to compare trends in a firm's performance, and to compare the firm's performance to other firms in the same industry.

---

[6]Notice that sales and total assets appear in both a numerator and a denominator in the right side of the equation and would cancel out if the equation were simplified, leaving net income over equity on both the right and the left of the equal sign.

$$\frac{\text{Net Income}}{\text{Equity}} = \frac{\text{Net Income}}{\cancel{\text{Sales}}} \times \frac{\cancel{\text{Sales}}}{\ } \times \frac{\cancel{\text{Total Assets}}}{\text{Equity}}$$

$$\frac{\text{Net Income}}{\text{Equity}} = \frac{\text{Net Income}}{\text{Equity}}$$

[7]We'll discuss leverage in more detail in chapter 13.

Lee Anne Schuster, Kitchell Contractors, Marketing

Lee Anne Schuster

Lee Anne Schuster is not rich, but she owns part of a major construction company. She is an employee–owner of Kitchell Contractors, one of the largest building contractors in the West. Lee Anne is not a financial expert, as she is the first to admit. But in her job as Marketing Coordinator for Kitchell, she must have a firm grasp of financial concepts because when Lee Anne submits a proposal for a new building project to a customer, they want to see Kitchell's financial position. Plus, as an employee–owner, Lee Anne carefully reads the financial statements to understand her company's financial health.

Q. *When you look at your company's financial statements, what do you look at?*

As an employee–owner, I have a strong interest in working smarter, to improve our company's bottom line. I always start with the profitability ratios. Those ratios combine many factors and reveal the bottom line. By looking at the net profit margin—what's left of revenues after all expenses and taxes have been taken out—I can get a quick snapshot of how the company is doing.

I also check to see our company's debt load. If we have too high a debt-to-equity ratio, we may have a hard time raising cash and staying ahead of our interest payments later. I prepare many reports for banks as part of my job duties, so I've learned that creditors also look at our debt ratios carefully, especially the debt-to-equity ratio.

Q. *What else do your creditors look at?*

They look at our current assets versus our current liabilities, the current ratio. They want to see how liquid the company is before they extend credit to us. For instance, say that the company hits a bad stretch. Lenders want to know that we can pay off our liabilities and still survive. If the current ratio is 1:1, the company's chances do not appear secure. If the ratio is higher, say it is two times the current assets compared to current liabilities, then creditors view Kitchell as a safer business to lend to in the event that we have a downturn.

Q. *Kitchell is not a publicly traded company. How do you value your stock?*

Because our stock is not traded publicly, it is tough to assign a value to it. Our stock is based on the value of the company, so after I review the profitability and debt ratios, I examine the asset activity ratios. The value of our assets creates value for the business. I try to find out how well the assets are performing over time to see if we're investing in assets wisely. The more our assets help generate sales, the brighter our future will be.

Q. *How else has reading financial statements helped you?*

I analyze the financial statements of my customers to see how well they are doing. If a customer has poor profitability or liquidity, debt ratios that are too high, or assets that are underperforming, our firm pays attention to those red flags before we agree to work with that customer. As an employee–owner, I appreciate that we don't sign up every customer that walks through our door. The risk of not getting paid may simply be too great.

Source: Interview with Lee Anne Schuster.

TREND ANALYSIS AND INDUSTRY COMPARISONS

Ratios are used to compare a firm's past and present performance and its industry performance. In this section we will examine trend analysis and industry comparison. Comparing a ratio for one year with the same ratio for other years is known as

trend analysis. Comparing a ratio for one company with the same ratio for other companies in the same industry is **industry comparison.**

Trend Analysis

Trend analysis helps financial managers and analysts see whether a company's current financial situation is improving or deteriorating. To prepare a trend analysis, compute the ratio values for several time periods (usually years) and compare them. Table 5-1 shows a five-year trend for Acme Corporation's ROA.

As Table 5-1 shows, Acme Corporation's ROA has risen steadily over this five-year period, with the largest growth occurring between 1993 and 1994. Overall, the trend analysis indicates that Acme's 1996 ROA of 2.22 percent is positive, compared to earlier years.

Usually, analysts plot ratio value trends on a graph to provide a picture of the results. Figure 5-3 is a graph of Acme's 1992–1996 ROA ratios.

The five-year upward trend in ROA, depicted in Figure 5-3, indicates that Acme Corporation increased the amount of profit it generated from its assets.

Trend analysis is an invaluable part of ratio analysis. It helps management spot a deteriorating condition and take corrective action, or identify the company's strengths. By assessing the firm's strengths and weaknesses, and the pace of change in a strength or weakness, management can plan effectively for the future.

	1992	1993	1994	1995	1996
ROA	−2.8%	−1.4%	0.5%	1.5%	2.22%

TABLE 5-1

Acme Corporation 5-Year Return on Assets (ROA) Trend Analysis

Figure 5-3 **Acme Corporation Five-Year Trend in ROA**

This figure shows the trend in the return on assets ratio from 1992 to 1996 for Acme Corporation

TABLE 5-2

Acme Corporation Cross-Sectional Analysis of ROA 1996

Company	ROA
Acme Corporation	2.22%
Company A	1.03%
Company B	4.35%
Company C	0.96%
Industry Average	2.14%
(Acme + A + B + C) ÷ 4 = 2.14	

Industry Comparisons

Another way to judge whether a firm's ratio is too high or too low is to compare it to the ratios of other firms in the industry (this is sometimes called **cross-sectional analysis**). This type of comparison pinpoints deviations from the norm that may indicate problems.

Table 5-2 shows a comparison between Acme Corporation's ROA ratio and the average ROA in Acme Corporation's industry for 1996.

Table 5-2 shows that, compared to other firms in Acme's industry, Acme achieved an above-average ROA in 1996. Only Company B managed to do better than Acme.

Cross-sectional analysis allows analysts to put the value of a firm's ratio in the context of its industry. For example, Acme's ROA of 2.22 percent is higher than average for its industry, and thus Acme would be looked upon favorably. In another industry, however, the average ROA might be 10 percent, causing Acme's 2.22 percent to appear much too low. Whether a ratio value is good or bad depends on the characteristics of the industry. By putting the ratio in context, analysts compare apples to apples and not apples to oranges.

SUMMARY ANALYSIS: TREND AND INDUSTRY COMPARISONS TOGETHER

A complete ratio analysis of a company combines both trend analysis and industry comparisons. Table 5-3 shows all the ratios presented in this chapter for Acme Corporation for the years 1992 through 1996 along with the industry averages for those ratios. (The industry averages are labeled IND in the table.)

First, let's review Acme's profitability ratios compared to the industry average for 1992–1996. In 1992 and 1993, Acme Corporation had negative net income. This gave a negative value to the net profit margin, return on assets, and return on equity for each of these years (since net income is the numerator for each ratio). There was steady improvement, however, in the profit ratios from 1992 to 1996.

Acme Corporation had lower gross profit, operating profit, and net profit margins than the industry norm for that five-year time period. With the exception of 1996, Acme also had a lower return on assets ratio than the industry average. As the summary analysis shows, the 1996 ROA is the result of a higher 1996 asset turnover ratio.

The return on equity figures paint a telling story over this five-year period. From 1992 to 1994, Acme Corporation had a much lower return on equity than did the average firm in its industry. In the years 1992 and 1993, these figures had significant negative values, while the industry norm was positive. In 1995 and 1996, however,

TABLE 5-3   Five-Year Ratio Analysis for Acme Corporation

RATIOS		1992	1993	1994	1995	1996
Profitability Ratios						
Gross Profit Margin	ACME	36.2%	38.9%	42.8%	58.9%	60.0%
(Gross Profit ÷ Sales)	IND	55.7%	58.9%	62.2%	66.0%	68.0%
Operating Profit Margin	ACME	14.3%	16.5%	18.6%	28.9%	32.0%
(EBIT ÷ Sales)	IND	34.2%	35.1%	37.5%	40.0%	42.0%
Net Profit Margin	ACME	−8.5%	−5.8%	3.4%	7.8%	11.1%
(Net Income ÷ Sales)	IND	4.3%	6.4%	10.2%	11.5%	13.4%
Return on Assets	ACME	−2.8%	−1.4%	.5%	1.5%	2.2%
(Net Income ÷ Total Assets)	IND	1.2%	1.8%	2.2%	2.5%	2.1%
Return on Equity	ACME	−14.6%	−7.5%	2.8%	8.3%	12.3%
(Net Income ÷ Equity)	IND	3.9%	4.4%	5.1%	5.6%	7.8%
Liquidity Ratios						
Current Ratio	ACME	2.15	2.22	2.30	2.48	1.95
(Current Assets ÷ Current Liabilities)	IND	1.98	2.00	2.10	2.15	2.20
Quick Ratio	ACME	.98	1.22	1.30	1.30	.95
(Current Assets Less Inventory ÷ Current Liabilities)	IND	1.10	1.00	1.10	1.12	1.15
Debt Ratios						
Debt to Total Assets	ACME	81%	81%	82%	81.5%	82%
(Total Debt ÷ Total Assets)	IND	62%	59%	57%	58%	60%
Debt to Equity	ACME	426%	426%	456%	442%	456%
(Total Debt ÷ Equity)	IND	163%	144%	133%	138%	150%
Times Interest Earned	ACME	1.10	1.20	1.20	1.37	2.37
(EBIT ÷ Interest Expense)	IND	3.70	3.80	4.00	4.20	4.25
Asset Activity Ratios						
Average Collection Period (Days)	ACME	33.80	31.50	30.10	28.40	36.50
(Accounts Receivable ÷ Average Daily Credit Sales)	IND	40.20	39.80	38.40	37.30	40.00
Inventory Turnover	ACME	.38	.49	.80	.51	.50
(Sales ÷ Inventory)	IND	.62	.66	.68	.72	.70
Total Asset Turnover	ACME	.33	.24	.15	.19	.20
(Sales ÷ Total Assets)	IND	.22	.20	.12	.15	.16
Market Value Ratios						
P/E Ratio	ACME	—	—	80.0	36.0	18.0
(Market Price per Share ÷ EPS)	IND	15.0	17.0	19.0	15.0	16.0
Market to Book Value	ACME	1.3	1.6	1.8	2.0	2.2
(Market Price ÷ Book Value)	IND	2.1	2.2	1.9	2.0	2.0

Acme Corporation had a much higher return on equity than the average firm in its industry.

If we examine the debt ratios in the summary analysis, we see the reason for the wildly fluctuating return on equity ratio values—Acme's high debt load. Look at the debt to asset and debt to equity ratio values. The debt to total asset ratio is consistently above 80 percent, while the industry norm for this ratio is 62 percent or less. A high debt load magnifies the changes in the return on equity ratio values. The negative values are more negative and the positive values more positive than they would otherwise be. This is because when times are bad, companies must still pay bondholders, bankers, and other creditors.

The times interest earned ratio shows that Acme Corporation barely covered its interest expense with its operating income. The value of this ratio was slightly more than 1 except for 1996, when it jumped to 2.37.

Next, we examine the liquidity ratios: the current and quick ratios. The current ratio has been consistently above 2 each year except for 1996, when it was slightly below that value. Having twice the amount of current assets as current liabilities is a good target for most companies. Since the industry norm for the current ratio was below the value Acme Corporation had until 1996, Acme had a comparatively good liquidity position. Given the 1996 change in its liquidity position management should watch the current ratio closely in 1997.

The quick ratio stayed near the industry norm throughout this period. This means that when inventory is subtracted from total current assets, Acme Corporation's liquidity looked steady. Again, however, 1996's below-average ratio value (.95 for Acme versus 1.15 for the industry norm) suggests that management watch liquidity in 1997.

Now let's look at the asset activity ratios: average collection period, inventory turnover, and asset turnover. The average collection period was significantly lower for Acme than for the average firm in its industry. It appears that Acme did a better than average job of collecting their accounts receivable.

The inventory turnover ratio was erratic over this 5 year period. The fluctuations suggest that Acme did not match its inventory to its demand for products. The numbers suggest that Acme's managers should have studied its inventory control policies to look for ways to match demand and inventory more closely. More about this in chapter 19.

The total asset turnover ratio was consistently higher than the industry norm. This helped the return on assets ratio during the years when net income was positive as described earlier.

Finally, we turn to the market value ratios. Acme had no meaningful P/E ratios for 1992 and 1993 because net income, and, therefore, EPS, were negative. The P/E ratio of 80 in 1994 shows investors had high expectations about Acme's future growth, but these expectations moderated in the next two years as the company matured. The market-to-book value ratio shows an upward trend over the five-year period showing that investors increasingly value Acme's future earnings potential above the company's asset liquidation value.

We have just finished a complete ratio analysis of Acme Corporation, including examinations of the company's profitability, liquidity, debt management, asset activity, and market value ratios. To conduct the analysis, we combined trend and industry analysis so that we could see how Acme performed over time and how it performed relative to its industry. Managers inside the company can use the results of the analysis to support proposed changes in operations or organization; and creditors and investors outside the company can use the results to support decisions about lending money to the company or buying its stock.

Locating Information about Financial Ratios

Ratio analysis involves a fair amount of research. Before analysts can calculate all the ratios, they must locate the underlying, raw financial data. Analysts can gather

TABLE 5-4   Sources of Financial Information

INFORMATION	MEDIUM	SOURCE
Business news, articles, market data, stock, bond, mutual fund price quotes	Newspapers	*Wall Street Journal* *Barron's* *USA Today*
Business news, articles	Magazines	*Forbes* *Fortune* *Business Week* *Money Magazine*
Data on the economy, industries; many financial statistics (interest rates, inflation, etc.)	Bound publications	*US Industrial Outlook* *Standard & Poor's Statistical Surveys* *Standard & Poor's Industry Surveys* *Federal Reserve Bulletin* *World Almanac* *Statistical Abstract of the United States* *Business Conditions Digest* (contains leading, lagging, and coincident indicators of the economy) *Economic Report of the President*
Summary data about industries, companies; advice on industries, stocks; analysis & forecasts	Investment advisory publications	*Value-Line Investment Survey* (each company report appears on one page) *Standard & Poor's Outlook*
Data on companies and industries	Computer databases	*Compustat PC Plus CD-ROM* *Value Screen*
Company performance; corporate financial data		Annual reports from the company (can often be obtained by phone from the company) *Standard & Poor's Stock Reports* (versions for the NYSE, AMEX, and OTC markets) *Standard & Poor's Corporation Records* (contains in-depth reports about companies, including financial statement data) *Moody's Handbook of Common Stocks* (similar to the S&P Stock Reports) *Moody's Industrial Manual, Moody's Bank & Finance Manual, Moody's OTC Manual, Moody's Public Utility Manual, Moody's Transportation Manual, Moody's International Manual* (all these Moody's Manuals contain in-depth reports on companies)
Information about bonds	Bound publications	*Moody's Bond Record* *Moody's Bond Survey*
Information about mutual funds	Bound publications	*Morningstar Mutual Funds* (similar to *Value-Line* but for mutual funds) *Weisenberger's Management Results* *Weisenberger's Current Performance & Dividend Record* (similar to *Moody's Manuals* but covers mutual funds)

information about publicly traded corporations at most libraries, on CD–ROM databases, and on the Internet.

A number of organizations publish financial data about companies and industries. Many publications contain ratios that are already calculated. Table 5-4 (page 99) contains a list of publications that financial analysts find useful when they are researching companies and industries. Many of them are available at local libraries.

What's Next

In this chapter we learned how to calculate and apply financial ratios to analyze the financial condition of the firm. In chapter 6 we will see how to use analyses to forecast and plan for the company's future.

Summary

1. Explain how financial ratio analysis helps assess the health of a company.

Just as doctors assess a patient's health, financial analysts assess the financial health of a firm. One of the most powerful assessment tools is financial ratio analysis. Financial ratios are comparative measures that allow analysts to interpret raw accounting data, and identify strengths and weaknesses of the firm.

2. Compute profitability, liquidity, debt, asset activity, and market value ratios.

Profitability, liquidity, debt, asset activity, and market value ratios show different aspects of a firm's financial performance. Profitability, liquidity, debt, and asset activity ratios use information from a firm's income statement or balance sheet to compute the ratios. Market value ratios use market and financial statement information.

Profitability ratios measure how the firm's returns compare to its sales, asset investments, and equity. Liquidity ratios measure the ability of a firm to meet its short-term obligations. Debt ratios measure the firm's debt financing and its ability pay off its debt. Asset activity ratios measure how efficiently a firm uses its assets. Finally, market value ratios measure the market's perception about the future earning power of a business.

The Du Pont system analyzes the sources of ROA and ROE. Two versions of the Du Pont equation were covered in this chapter. The first analyzes the contributions of net profit margin and total asset turnover to ROA. The second version analyzes how the influences of net profit margin, total asset turnover, and leverage affect ROE.

3. Compare financial information over time and among companies.

Trend analysis compares the past and present financial ratios to see how a firm has performed over time. Industry analysis compares a firm's ratios with the ratios of companies in the same industry. Summary analysis, one of the most useful financial analysis tools, combines trend and industry analysis to measure how a company performed over time in the context of the industry.

4. Locate ratio value data for specific companies and industries.

A number of organizations publish financial data about companies and industries. Many publications contain ratios that are already calculated. Table 5-4 contains a list of publications that financial analysts find useful when they are researching companies and industries.

Equations Introduced in This Chapter

Profitability Ratios:

$$\text{Gross Profit Margin} = \frac{\text{Gross Profit}}{\text{Sales}}$$

$$\text{Operating Profit Margin} = \frac{\text{Earnings Before Interest and Taxes}}{\text{Sales}}$$

$$\text{Net Profit Margin} = \frac{\text{Net Income}}{\text{Sales}}$$

$$\text{Return on Assets} = \frac{\text{Net Income}}{\text{Total Assets}}$$

$$\text{Return on Equity} = \frac{\text{Net Income}}{\text{Common Equity}}$$

Liquidity Ratios:

$$\text{Current Ratio} = \frac{\text{Current Assets}}{\text{Current Liabilities}}$$

$$\text{Quick Ratio} = \frac{\text{Current Assets less Inventory}}{\text{Current Liabilities}}$$

Debt Ratios:

$$\text{Debt to Total Assets Ratio} = \frac{\text{Total Debt}}{\text{Total Assets}}$$

$$\text{Debt to Equity} = \frac{\text{Total Debt}}{\text{Equity}}$$

$$\text{Times Interest Earned} = \frac{\text{Earnings Before Interest and Taxes}}{\text{Interest Expense}}$$

Asset Activity Ratios:

$$\text{Average Collection Period} = \frac{\text{Accounts Receivable}}{\text{Average Daily Credit Sales}}$$

$$\text{Inventory Turnover} = \frac{\text{Sales}}{\text{Inventory}}$$

$$\text{Total Asset Turnover} = \frac{\text{Sales}}{\text{Total Assets}}$$

Market Value Ratios:

$$\text{P/E Ratio} = \frac{\text{Market Price per Share}}{\text{Earnings per Share}}$$

$$\text{Market to Book Ratio} = \frac{\text{Market Price per Share}}{\text{Book Value per Share}}$$

Equation 5-1. The Du Pont Formula:

$$\text{Return on Assets} = \text{Net Profit Margin} \times \text{Total Asset Turnover}$$

$$\frac{\text{Net Income}}{\text{Total Assets}} = \frac{\text{Net Income}}{\text{Sales}} \times \frac{\text{Sales}}{\text{Total Assets}}$$

Equation 5-2. The Modified Du Pont Formula:

$$ROE = \begin{array}{c} Net \\ Profit \\ Margin \end{array} \times \begin{array}{c} Total \\ Asset \\ Turnover \end{array} \times \begin{array}{c} Equity \\ Multiplier \end{array}$$

$$\frac{Net\ Income}{Equity} = \frac{Net\ Income}{Sales} \times \frac{Sales}{Total\ Assets} \times \frac{Total\ Assets}{Equity}$$

Self-Test

ST-1. De Marco Corporation has total assets of $5 million and an asset turnover ratio of 4. If net income is $2 million, what is the value of the net profit margin?

ST-2. Francisco Company has current assets of $50,000. Total assets are $200,000; and long-term liabilities, preferred stock, and common stock collectively total $180,000. What is the value of the current ratio?

ST-3. If one-half the current assets in ST-2 consist of inventory, what is the value of the quick ratio?

ST-4. Sheth Corporation has a return on assets ratio of 6 percent. If the asset turnover ratio is .5, what is the firm's return on equity?

ST-5. Mitra Company has a quick ratio value of 1.5. It has total current assets of $100,000 and total current liabilities of $25,000. If sales are $200,000, what is the value of the inventory turnover ratio?

ST-6. Yates Corporation has total assets of $500,000. Its equity is $200,000. What is the company's debt-to-total-asset ratio?

ST-7. Pendell Company has total sales of $4 million. One-fourth of these are credit sales. The amount of accounts receivable is $100,000. What is the average collection period for the company? Use a 365-day year.

Review Questions

1. What is a financial ratio?
2. Why do analysts calculate financial ratios?
3. Which ratios would a banker be most interested in when considering whether to approve an application for a short-term business loan? Explain.
4. Which ratios would a potential long-term bond investor be most interested in? Explain.
5. Under what circumstances would market to book value ratios be misleading? Explain.
6. Why would an analyst use the Modified Du Pont system to calculate ROE when ROE may be calculated more simply? Explain.
7. Why are trend analysis and industry comparison important to financial ratio analysis?

Build Your Communication Skills

CS-1. Research a publicly traded company that has a presence in your community. Assess the financial health of this company in the areas of profitability, liquidity, debt, and asset activity. Write a report of your findings. Include in your report a discusssion of the strengths and weaknesses of the company, key trends, and how the company's ratios compare to other companies in its industry.

CS-2. You have just been given a job as a loan officer. It is your job to evaluate business loan applications. Your boss would like you to prepare a new set of guidelines to be used by the bank to evaluate loan requests, leading to the approval or denial decision.

Prepare a loan application packet. Include the specific quantitative and qualitative information you would want an applicant for a loan to provide to you. Explain in a brief report, oral or written, how you would use the requested information to decide whether a loan should be approved.

Problems

Problems 5-1 to 5-5 refer to the Consolidated Income Statement and Consolidated Balance Sheet of Pinewood Company and Subsidiaries shown below:

Pinewood Company and Subsidiaries Income Statement for the Year 1996 ('000 dollars)

Sales	$94,001
Cost of Goods Sold	46,623
Gross Profit	47,378
Selling and Administrative Expenses	28,685
Depreciation and R & D Expense (both tax deductible)	5,752
EBIT or Operating Income	12,941
Interest Expense	48
Interest Income	427
Earning Before Taxes (EBT)	13,320
Income Taxes	4,700
Net Income (NI)	8,620
Preferred Stock Dividends	—
Earnings available to Common Stockholders	8,620
Earnings per Share	.76

Pinewood Company and Subsidiaries Balance Sheet as of End of the Year 1996

	1996
Assets:	
Cash	$ 5,534
Accounts Receivable (gross)	14,956
Less: Allowance for Bad Debts	211
Accounts Receivable (net)	14,745
Inventory	10,733
Marketable Securities	952
Prepaid Expenses	3,234
Plant and Equipment (gross)	57,340
Less: Accumulated Depreciation	29,080
Plant and Equipment (net)	28,260
Land	1,010
Long Term Investments	2,503
Total Assets	66,971
Liabilities:	
Accounts Payable	3,253
Notes Payable	—
Accrued Expenses	6,821
Bonds Payable	2,389
Stockholders' Equity:	
Common Stock	8,549
Retained Earnings	45,959
Total Liabilities and Equity	66,971

5-1. Calculate the following profitability ratios for 1996.

    a. Gross profit margin
    b. Operating profit margin
    c. Net profit margin
    d. Return on assets
    e. Return on equity

Comment on net profit margin and return on assets ratios if the industry average for these two ratios are 5 percent and 14 percent respectively.

5-2. Calculate the following liquidity ratios for the end of 1996.

    a. Current ratio
    b. Quick ratio

Comment on the company's ability to pay off short-term debts.

5-3. Calculate the following debt ratios for the end of 1996.

    a. Debt to total assets
    b. Times interest earned

Would a banker like to extend a loan to Pinewood? Explain.

5-4. Calculate the following asset activity ratios for the end of 1996.

    a. Average collection period
    b. Inventory turnover
    c. Total asset turnover

Comment on Pinewood's asset utilization.

5-5. Construct and solve Pinewood's Modified Du Pont equation for 1996. Use the end of 1996 asset figures. Comment on the company's sources of ROE.

5-6. The following financial data relate to ABC Textile Company's business in 1996.

Sales	= $1,000,000
Net Income	= 80,000
Total Assets	= 500,000
Debt to Total Assets Ratio	= 0.5 or 50%

    a. Construct and solve the Du Pont and Modified Du Pont equations for ABC.
    b. What would be the value of the ROE ratio if the debt to total asset ratio were 70 percent?
    c. What would be the value of the ROE ratio if the debt to total asset ratio were 90 percent?
    d. What would be the value of the ROE ratio if the debt to total asset ratio were 10 percent?

5-7. From the values of the different ratios given below, calculate the missing balance sheet items and complete the balance sheet.

Sales	$100,000
Average Collection Period	55 days
Inventory Turnover	15
Debt to Assets Ratio	.4 or 40%
Current Ratio	3
Total Asset Turnover	1.6
Fixed Asset Turnover	2.9

Assets		Liabilities + Equity	
Cash	$6,000	Accounts Payable	6,000
Accounts Receivable	――――	Notes Payable	――――
Inventory	――――	Accrued Expenses	600
Prepaid Expenses	――――	Total Current Liabilities	――――
Total Current Assets	――――	Bonds Payable	――――
Fixed Assets	――――	Common Stock	16,000
		Retained Earnings	――――
Total Assets	――――	Total Liability + Equity	――――

5-8. Given the partial financial statement information from La Strada Corporation, a circus equipment supplier, calculate the return on equity ratio.   *Financial Relationships*

Total Assets:	$10,000
Total Liabilities:	6,000
Total Sales:	5,000
Net Profit Margin:	10%

5-9. What is the current ratio of Ah, Wilderness! Corporation, given the following information from their end of 1997 Balance Sheet?   *Liquidity Ratios*

Current Assets:	$ 5,000
Long Term Liabilities:	18,000
Total Liabilities:	20,000
Total Equity:	30,000

5-10. Rocinante, Inc. manufactures windmills. What is Rocinante's total asset turnover if their return on assets is 12 percent and their net profit margin is 4 percent?   *Du Pont Equation*

Use the following information to answer questions 11-17.

In 1997 Iron Jay opened a small sporting goods retail store called Iron Jay's Sports Stuff (IJSS). It immediately became very popular and growth was only limited by the amount of capital Jay could generate through profits and loans. Jay's financial manager advised him to incorporate. His manager said that by selling stock, Jay would have the necessary capital to expand his business at an accelerated pace. Answer the following questions relating to Iron Jay's Sports Stuff.

5-11. The management team at IJSS is looking toward the future. They want to maintain a gross profit margin of 50 percent. If the estimate for net sales in 1998 is $5,000,000, how much gross profit will be necessary in 1998 to maintain this ratio?   *Profitability Ratios*

5-12. If the management team estimated $200,000 in selling and administration expenses and $50,000 in depreciation expenses for 1998, with net sales of $5 million, what operating profit margin can they expect?   *Profitability Ratios*

5-13. What must net income be in 1998 if IJSS also wants to maintain a net profit margin of 20 percent on net sales of $5 million?   *Profitability Ratios*

5-14. What will IJSS's return on assets be if their total assets at the end of 1998 are estimated to be $20 million? Net sales are $5 million and the net profit margin is 20 percent in that year.   *Financial Relationships*

5-15. IJSS management knows the astute owners of IJSS stock will sell their stock if the return on stockholders' equity investment (return on equity ratio) drops below 10 percent. Total stockholders' equity for the end of 1998 is estimated to be $15 million. How much net income will IJSS need in 1998 to fulfill the stockholders' expectation of the return on equity ratio of 10 percent?   *Profitability Ratios*

5-16. Of the $20 million in total assets estimated for the end of 1998, only $2 million will be classified as noncurrent assets. If current liabilities are $4 million, what will IJSS's current ratio be?

5-17. Inventory on the balance sheet for the end of 1998 is expected to be $3 million. With total assets of $20 million, noncurrent assets of $2 million, and current liabilities of $4 million, what will be the value of IJSS's quick ratio?

5-18. Given the $20 million in total assets, $15 million in total stockholders' equity, and a debt-to-total-asset ratio of 30 percent for Folson Corporation, what will be the debt to equity ratio?

5-19. If total assets are $20 million, noncurrent assets are $2 million, inventory is $3 million, and sales are $5 million for Toronto Brewing Company, what is the inventory turnover ratio?

5-20. If the net profit margin of Dobie's Dog Hotel is maintained at 20 percent and total asset turnover ratio is .25, calculate return on assets.

5-21. The following data is from Saratoga Farms, Inc. 1996 financial statements.

Sales:	$2,000,000
Net Income:	200,000
Total Assets:	1,000,000
Debt to Total Asset Ratio:	60%

a. Construct and solve the Du Pont and Modified Du Pont equations for Saratoga Farms.
b. What will be the impact on ROE if the debt to total asset ratio were 80 percent?
c. What will be the impact on ROE if the debt to total asset ratio were 20 percent?

5-22. The following financial information is from two successful retail operations in Niagara Falls. Rose and George Loomis own Notoriously Niagara, a lavish jewelry store that caters to the "personal jet-set" crowd. The other store, Niagara's Notions, is a big hit with the typical tourist. Polly and Ray Cutler, the owners, specialize in inexpensive souvenirs such as postcards, mugs, and T-shirts.

Notoriously Niagara		Niagara's Notions	
Sales	$ 500,000	Sales	500,000
Net Income	100,000	Net Income	10,000
Assets	5,000,000	Assets	500,000

a. Calculate the net profit margin for each store.
b. Calculate the total asset turnover for each store.
c. Combine the equations used above to calculate the return on assets for each store.
d. Why would you expect Notoriously Niagara's net profit margin to be higher than Niagara's Notions considering both stores had annual sales of $500,000 and the same figure for return on assets?

5-23. Thunder Alley Corporation supplies parts for Indianapolis-type race cars. Current market price per share of Thunder Alley's common stock is $40. The latest annual report showed Net Income of $2,250,000 and total common stock equity of $15 million. The report also listed 1,750,000 shares of common stock outstanding. No common stock dividends are paid.

a. Calculate Thunder Alley's earnings per share (EPS).
b. Calculate Thunder Alley's price to earnings (P/E) ratio.
c. Calculate Thunder Alley's book value per share.
d. What is Thunder Alley's market to book ratio?
e. Based on this information, does the market believe that the future earning power of Thunder Alley justifies a higher value than could be obtained by liquidating the firm? Why or why not?

5-24. Carrie White, the new financial analyst of Golden Products, Inc. has been given the Industry Comparisions task of reviewing the performance of her company over three recent years against the industry information as shown below (figures in $000):

Year	Net Income	Current Assets	Current Liab.	Total Assets	Total Liab.	Sales
1994	$400	$500	$530	$3800	$2600	$4000
1995	425	520	510	3900	2500	4500
1996	440	550	510	4000	2400	4700

The Industry averages are:

NI/Sales	Current Ratio	Total Assets Turnover
9.42%	1.13	2.00

Should Carrie be critical of her company's performance?

5-25. Johnny Hooker, another financial analyst of Golden Products, Inc. is working with the Industry Comparisons same yearly figures shown in 5-24, but is trying to compare the performance trend using another set of industry averages:

The industry averages are:

Fixed Asset Turnover	Return on Assets	Debt to Equity Ratio	Return on Equity
1.33	11.00%	1.8	26%

Should Johnny be appreciative of his company's performance?

5-26. Vernon Pinkby , the financial analyst reporting to the chief financial officer of Alufab Profitability Ratios Aluminum Company, is comparing the performance of the company's four separate divisions based on profit margin and return on assets. The relevant figures are given below (figures in $000):

	Mining	Smelting	Rolling	Extrusion
Net Income	$ 500	$ 2600	$ 7000	$ 2500
Sales	15000	30000	60000	25000
Total Assets	12000	25000	39000	18000

a. Compare profit margin ratios of the four divisions.
b. Compare return on assets ratios of the four divisions.
c. Compute profit margin of the entire company.
d. Compute return on assets of the entire company.

5-27. George Hanson, the financial analyst reporting to the chief financial officer of FabAl Challenge Problem Aluminum Company is comparing the performance of the company's three separate divisions based on profit margin and return on assets. The relevant figures are given below (figures in $000):

	Mining	Smelting	Rolling
Net Income	$ 600	$ 3120	$ 8400
Sales	18000	36000	72000
Total Assets	14400	30000	46800

a. Assuming that it is possible to sell the division with the lowest return on assets at its book value and invest the proceeds in the division with the highest return on assets without changing its value, what will be the return on assets of the entire company?

b. Compute the profit margin of the entire company before and after the proposed sale and transfer of assets assuming that the additional assets will generate additional sales in the same proportion.

Challenge Problem **5-28.** From the values of the different ratios given, calculate the missing balance sheet and income statement items of National Glass Company (round up the figures to nearest tens).

Average Collection Period	48.67 days
Inventory Turnover	9×
Debt to Asset Ratio	.4 or 40%
Current Ratio	1.6250
Total Asset Turnover	1.5
Fixed Asset Turnover	2.647
Return on Equity	0.1933 or 19.33%
Return on Assets	0.116 or 11.6%
Operating Profit Margin	13.33%
Gross Profit Margin	48.89%

National Glass Company
Income Statement
for the Year 1996 (000 dollars)

Sales	$45000
Cost of Goods Sold	____
Gross Profit	____
Selling and Administrative Expenses	____
Depreciation	3000
EBIT or Operating Income	____
Interest Expense	____
Earning Before Taxes (EBT)	____
Income Taxes (@T = 40%)	2320
Net Income (NI)	____
Preferred Stock Dividends	0
Earning Available to Common Stock Holders	____

National Glass Company
Balance Sheet
as of End of the Year 1996

	1996
Assets:	$
Cash	____
Accounts Receivable (gross)	____
Inventory	____
Plant and Equipment (net)	____
Land	1000
Liabilities:	
Accounts Payable	2000
Notes Payable	____
Accrued Expenses	3000
Bonds Payable	____
Stockholders' Equity:	
Common Stock	4000
Retained Earnings	____

5-29. The King Tools Company (KTC) manufactures various types of high quality punching and deep-drawing press tools for kitchen appliance manufacturers. Homer Smith, the finance manager of KTC, has submitted a justification to support the application for a short-term loan from the Queensville Interstate Bank (QIB) to finance increased sales from 1996 to 1997. The Consolidated Income Statement and Balance Sheet of KTC, submitted with the justification to QIB, are shown below:

Comprehensive Problem

Kingston Tools Company
Income Statement for the Years 1996 and 1997 (000 dollars)

	1996	1997
Sales	$40,909	$45,000
Cost of Goods Sold	20,909	23,000
Gross Profit	20,000	22,000
Selling and Administrative Expenses	11,818	13,000
Depreciation	2,000	3,000
EBIT or Operating Income	6,182	6,000
Interest Expense	400	412
Earning Before Taxes (EBT)	5,782	5,588
Income Taxes (@40%)	2,313	2,235
Net Income (NI)	3,469	3,353
Preferred Stock Dividends	—	—
Earning available to Common Stock Holders	3,469	3,353
Dividends Paid (@21.86%)	758	733

Kingston Tools Company
Balance Sheet
as of End of the Year 1996 and 1997 (000 dollars)

	1996	1997
Assets:		
Cash	$ 2,000	$ 1,800
Accounts Receivable (gross)	6,000	7,600
Inventory	5,000	5,220
Plant and Equipment (gross)	26,000	31,000
Less: Accumulated Depreciation	10,000	13,000
Plant and Equipment (net)	16,000	18,000
Land	1,000	1,000
Liabilities:		
Accounts Payable	2,000	2,600
Notes Payable	3,000	3,300
Accrued Expenses	3,000	3,100
Bonds Payable	4,000	4,000
Stockholders' Equity:		
Common Stock	4,000	4,000
Retained Earnings	14,000	16,620

You are the loan officer at QIB responsible for determining whether KTC's business is strong enough to be able to repay the loan. To have a thorough analysis done,

a. Calculate the following ratios for 1996, compare with the industry averages shown in the parenthesis, and indicate if the company is doing better or worse than the industry and whether the performance is improving or deteriorating in 1997 as compared to 1996.
   (i) Gross profit margin (50%)
   (ii) Operating profit margin (15%)

   (iii) Net profit margin (8%)
   (iv) Return on assets (10%)
   (v) Return on equity (20%)
   (vi) Current ratio (1.5)
   (vii) Quick ratio (1.0)
   (viii) Debt to total asset (0.5)
   (ix) Times interest earned (25)
   (x) Average collection period (45 days)
   (xi) Inventory turnover (8)
   (xii) Total asset turnover (1.6)
 b. Discuss the financial strengths and weaknesses of KTC.
 c. Determine the sources and uses of funds and prepare a statement of cash flows for 1997.
 d. Compare and comment on the financial condition as evident from the ratio analysis and the cash flow statement.
 e. Which ratios should you analyze more critically before recommending granting of the loan and what is your recommendation?

Answers to Self-Test

ST-1. Sales $\div$ \$5,000,000 = 4 $\therefore$ sales = \$20,000,000
\$2,000,000 net income $\div$ \$20,000,000 sales = .1 = 10% net profit margin

ST-2. Current liabilities = \$200,000 total assets − \$180,000 LTD, PS, & CS = \$20,000
\$50,000 current assets $\div$ \$20,000 current liabilities = 2.5 current ratio

ST-3. Current assets − inventory = \$50,000 − (.5 × \$50,000) = \$25,000
\$25,000 $\div$ \$20,000 current liabilities = 1.25 quick ratio

ST-4. Sales $\div$ assets = .5 $\therefore$ assets $\div$ sales = 1 $\div$ .5 = 2
$$\text{ROE} = \text{ROA} \times (\text{A/S})$$
$$= .06 \times 2$$
$$= .12 = 12\%$$

ST-5. (\$100,000 current assets − inventory) $\div$ \$25,000 = 1.5 quick ratio $\therefore$ inventory = \$62,500
\$200,000 sales $\div$ \$62,500 inventory = 3.2 inventory turnover ratio

ST-6. Debt = \$500,000 assets − \$200,000 equity = \$300,000
\$300,000 debt $\div$ \$500,000 assets = .6 = 60% debt to total asset ratio

ST-7. Credit sales = \$4,000,000 $\div$ 4 = \$1,000,000
Average collection period = Accounts Receivable $\div$ average daily credit sales = \$100,000 accounts receivable $\div$ (\$1,000,000 annual credit sales $\div$ 365 days per year) = 36.5 days

chapter 6

Forecasting for Financial Planning

"Cheshire-Puss . . . would you tell me, please, which way I ought to go from here?" [said Alice]
"That depends a good deal on where you want to get to," said the Cat.
"I don't much care where—" said Alice.
"Then it doesn't matter which way you go," said the Cat.
From *Alice's Adventures in Wonderland* by Lewis Carroll

Chapter Objectives

After reading this chapter, you should be able to:

1. Explain why forecasting is vital to business success.

2. Describe the financial statement forecasting process.

3. Prepare pro forma (projected) financial statements.

4. Explain the importance of analyzing forecasts.

At Gdansk, the Forecast Was for Rough Seas Ahead . . .

If you're a manager in an American business, you should have some notions of forecasting. You can predict your sales, how much return you'll make on your investments, how many products to make, and how many people you should hire.

But imagine if your company never cared if it made or lost money. Imagine if your company had no idea or willingness to forecast anything. When Hans Szyc took over the Gdansk shipyard in Poland, he didn't fore-

cast or want to forecast. He figured the Communists would always subsidize his operations, pay his way, no matter what happened.

If someone had asked him for *pro forma* financial statements—that is, projected financial statements—an assessment of the competition, or a projected net profit margin, he would have stared blankly. These tools, all useful for planning, were simply techniques the Polish shipyard didn't need under Communist rule.

Then reality came knocking on the door. In 1990 the shipyard's primary client, the disintegrating Soviet Union, canceled all orders for new ships, forcing the shipyard to abandon three nearly completed vessels. However, Szyc didn't understand that losing his main customer would mean that he would have to forecast exactly what the shipyard could and could not afford. He would have to lay off workers or sell assets to reduce costs.

Instead of planning for the future, Szyc increased the workforce from 9,000 to 15,000, confident that the government would not let the business fail. Szyc also refused to dispose of nonessential assets, such as vacation resorts for employees and chauffeured limousines. The result? Losses mounted and bankers denied the shipyard additional credit. Szyc, discouraged, quit to pursue a career in politics. Hopefully, it wasn't in forecasting the future.

Crippled by debts of $120 million, low productivity, weak management, and poor investment, the Gdansk shipyard now faces closure unless the Polish government or a foreign investor steps in to provide cash and some badly needed forecasting lessons.

Source: Simon Johnson, David T. Kotchen, Gary Loveman, "Meanwhile in Gdansk," *Harvard Business Review* 73, No. 6 (November–December 1995): 55; Robin Knight, "A Sinking Shipyard," *U.S. News & World Report* (May 13, 1996).

Chapter Overview

A business owner who wants to run a successful business must be able to answer many questions about the future, including the following:

- How much profit will your business make?
- How much demand will there be for your product or service?
- How much will it cost to produce your product or offer your service?
- How much money will you need to borrow, when, and how will you pay it back?

Business people must estimate the future all the time. The task of estimating future business events is daunting and darn near impossible, but in business it is necessary. As the Gdansk shipyard example shows, without some idea of what is going to happen in the future, it is impossible to plan and to succeed in business.

We will look first at the forecasting task, discuss why it is important, and explain what forecasting approaches business people use. Then, step-by-step, we will build a set of projected financial statements. We will conclude with a discussion of how to analyze forecasts to plan for the financial success of the company.

Why Forecasting Is Important

Every day you make decisions based on forecasts. When you go shopping, for example, you decide how much money to spend based on your forecast of how much money you need for other reasons. When you plan trips, you decide how much money to take along based on your forecast of the trip's expenses. You choose what to wear in the morning based on the weather forecaster's prediction of the good or bad weather.

The situation is similar in business—particularly in finance. Financial decisions are based on forecasts of situations a business expects to confront in the future. Businesses develop new products, set production quotas, and select financing sources based on forecasts about the future economic environment and the firm's condition. If economists predict interest rates will be relatively high, for example, a firm may plan to limit borrowing and defer expansion plans.

Forecasting in business is especially important because failing to anticipate future trends can be devastating. The following business examples show why:

- The Sony Corporation's devotion to beta-formatted videotapes caused the firm to miss out on millions of dollars in sales of VCRs formatted for VHS.
- The Cray Computer Corporation's underestimate of the time and cost to develop new supercomputers, coupled with a drop in demand for such machines, caused the company to go bankrupt in 1995.
- The Coca-Cola corporation's introduction of "New Coke" in 1985 cost millions of dollars and failed miserably. Coca-Cola suffered another marketing flop in 1988 with the development of BreakMate, a small microwave oven-sized device designed to replace soda vending machines in small offices.[1]

Undoubtedly, each of these firms wishes that their forecasts had been more accurate.

Firms often spend a large amount of time, effort, and money to obtain accurate forecasts. Let's take a look at some of the ways forecasters approach the forecasting task.

FORECASTING APPROACHES

Forecasting simply means making projections about what we think will happen in the future. To make these projections, forecasters use different approaches depending on the situation. Financial managers concentrate on three general approaches: *experience, probability,* and *correlation.*

Experience   Sometimes we think things will happen a certain way in the future because they happened that way in the past. For instance, if it has always taken you fifteen minutes to drive to the grocery store, then you will probably assume that it will take you about fifteen minutes the next time you drive to the store. Similarly, financial managers often assume sales, expenses, or earnings will grow at certain rates in the future because that is how the rates grew in the past.

Probability   Sometimes we think things will happen a certain way in the future because the laws of probability indicate that it will be so. For example, let's say insurance company statisticians calculate that male drivers under twenty-five years of age during a one-year period will have a .25 probability of having an accident. That com-

[1]Michael A. Cusamo, et. al., "Strategic Maneuvering and Mass-Market Dynamics: The Triumph of VHS over Beta," *Business History Review* 66, No. 1 (Spring 1992): 51-94; "How the Numbers Crunched Cray Computer," *Business Week* (April 10, 1995): retrieved from Internet; Pat Selig, "All Over the Map," *Sales & Marketing Management* 141, No. 4 (March 1989): 58-64.

Source: FRANK & ERNEST © 1996 United Feature Syndicate, Inc. Reprinted by Permission.

pany insures 10,000 male drivers under twenty-five, so the company's financial manager—based on probability figures—would forecast that 2,500 of the firm's under-twenty-five male policyholders (.25 × 10,000 = 2,500) would have an accident during the coming year. Financial managers use probabilities to forecast the number of customers who won't pay their bills, the number of rejects in a production process, and so on.

Correlation   Sometimes we think things will happen a certain way in the future because there is a high correlation between the behavior of one item and the behavior of another item that we know more about. For example, if you know that most people buy new cars right after they graduate from college, you could forecast new car sales to graduates fairly accurately. You would base your plans on the amount of correlation between the number of people graduating and new car sales. In a similar manner, financial managers forecast more sales for tire chains in the winter and more sales of lawn mowers in the summer.

Why Forecasts Are Sometimes Wrong

In general, forecasting the future is based on what has happened in the past (either past experience, past probability, or past correlation). However, just because something has occurred in the past does not *ensure* that it will happen the same way in the future, which is why forecasts are sometimes spectacularly wrong. No one can forecast the future with absolute precision.

To illustrate, in 1987, Dr. Ravi Batra wrote in *The Great Depression of 1990,* that "at the end of 1989 or in the first half of 1990, the stock market will crash and will be followed by an abysmal decline in business activity and a sharply higher rate of unemployment." He added, "We can actually pinpoint 1990 as the year of the world's greatest depression."[2] Fortunately, Dr. Batra's forecast did not come true. In fact, the Dow Jones Industrial Average nearly doubled between 1990 and 1995.

---

[2]Dr. Ravi Batra, *The Great Depression of 1990* (Simon & Schuster, New York, 1987): 133, 140.

The approaches to forecasting range from being quite simple to complex and sophisticated, depending on what is being forecast and how much the business needs to rely on an accurate forecast. In the sections that follow, we will examine some of the approaches that business people use to predict future sales, and the way that finance people predict their firms' future.

FORECASTING SALES

Producing a sales forecast is not purely a financial task. Estimates of future sales depend on the demand for the firm's products, and the strength of the competition. Sales and marketing personnel usually provide assessments of demand and the competition. Production personnel usually provide estimates of manufacturing capacity and other production constraints. Top management will make strategic decisions affecting the firm as a whole. Sales forecasting, then, is a group effort. Financial managers coordinate, collect, and analyze the sales forecasting information. Figure 6-1 shows a diagram of the process.

Figure 6-1 **The Sales Forecasting Process**

This chart shows how a company's sales forecast is developed from many different sources. Marketing data, company goals, production capabilities, and accounting data are analyzed, weighed, and combined to produce the final sales estimate.

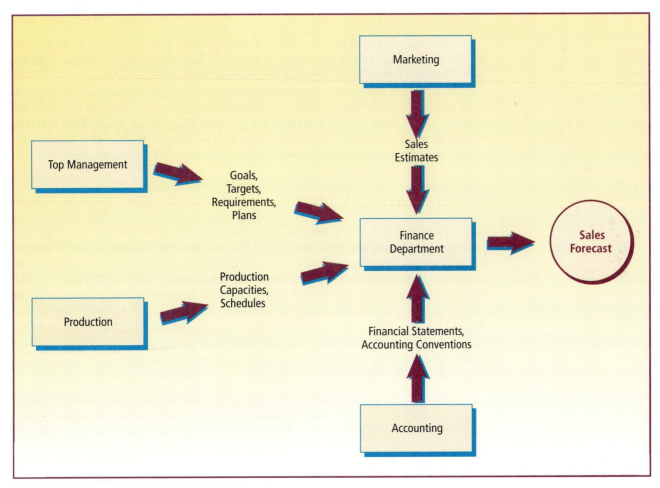

Figure 6-2 **Sales Record, Esoteric Enterprises**

This chart shows the sales record for Esoteric Enterprises, Inc., during 1991–96. Sales growth has been fairly constant during the five-year period. By extending the sales trend, an analyst might estimate Esoteric's sales in 1997 to be about $222,000.

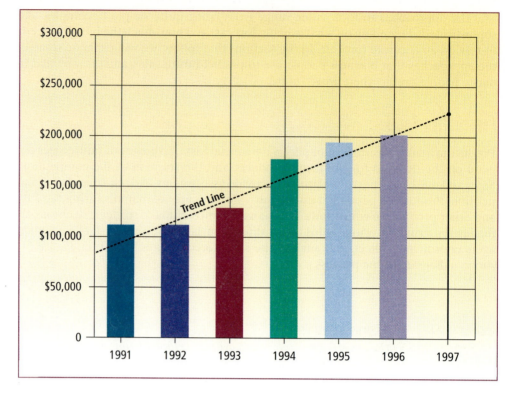

Sometimes financial analysts make a quick estimate of a company's future sales by extending the trend of past sales. Figure 6-2 illustrates this technique, with the sales record of Esoteric Enterprises, Inc., for the years 1991 to 1996.

The graph in Figure 6-2 shows that Esoteric's sales have been somewhat constant during the five-year period. A forecaster, by extending the past trend, would estimate that Esoteric's sales in the next year are likely to be about $222,000. The technique of extending a past trend works well when the past trend is discernable and no outside factors, such as new competition, act to change the trend.

FORECASTING FINANCIAL STATEMENTS

After the sales forecast is complete, financial managers determine whether the firm can support the sales forecast financially. They do this by extending the firm's financial statements into future time periods. These forecasted financial statements are commonly referred to as ***pro forma* financial statements.**[3] *Pro forma* financial statements show what the firm will look like if the sales forecasts are indeed realized and management's plans carried out. By analyzing the projected financial statements, managers can tell if funds needed to make purchases will be available, if the firm will be able to make loan payments on schedule, if external financing will be required, what return on investment the stockholders can expect, and so on.

---

[3]*Pro forma* is a Latin term meaning "as a matter of form." *Pro forma* financial statements show what the business will look like (its form) if expected events take place.

Budgets

Financial managers use a variety of budgets to help produce *pro forma* financial statements. Budgets contain estimates of future receipts and expenditures for various activities. Financial managers produce *pro forma* statements that assume the budget figures will, in fact, occur.

Two budgets are particularly important to forecasters. These are the *cash budget* and the *capital budget*. The **cash budget** shows the projected flow of cash in and out of the firm for specified time periods. The **capital budget** shows planned expenditures for major asset acquisitions. In the sections that follow, we will see how forecasters incorporate data from these budgets into *pro forma* financial statements.

Take Note

Developing a cash budget and a capital budget are complex matters. We discuss cash budgets in chapter 18, and capital budgets in chapters 10–11.

Producing *Pro Forma* Financial Statements

Now that we have reviewed the sales forecast and the budgets from which data are drawn to produce *pro forma* financial statements, we can discuss how to produce *pro forma* financial statements. In the following sections, we explore the step-by-step process of creating both a *pro forma* income statement and a *pro forma* balance sheet for Esoteric Enterprises, Inc.

Esoteric Enterprises makes one product: a rechargeable lithium battery used in industrial facilities throughout the United States to power emergency lights. The company's income statement and balance sheet for the year 1996 are shown in the first column of Figures 6-3a and 6-3b. We will create a *pro forma* income statement and balance sheet for 1997 by filling in the blanks in the second column of Figures 6-3a and 6-3b.

For convenience, assume that we are preparing this forecast on January 1, 1997. (Being dedicated, we have come in on New Year's Day to do this.)

	1996	FORECAST FOR 1997
Net Sales	$201,734	_____
Cost of Goods Sold	107,280	_____
Gross Profit	94,454	_____
Operating Expenses:		
Selling and Marketing Expenses	32,392	_____
General & Administrative Expense	10,837	_____
Depreciation	4,500	_____
Operating Income	46,725	_____
Interest Expense	2,971	_____
Before-Tax Income	43,754	_____
Income Taxes (tax rate = 40%)	17,502	_____
Net Income	$26,252	_____
Dividends Paid	$23,627	_____
Addition to Retained Earnings	$2,625	_____

Figure 6-3a Esoteric Enterprises Income Statements

The first column in this figure shows Esoteric Enterprises' income statement for 1996. The pro forma *forecast for 1997 will be inserted in the second column.*

Figure 6-3b **Esoteric Enterprises Balance Sheets**

The first column in this figure shows Esoteric Enterprises' balance sheet as of December 31, 1996. The pro forma *forecast for December 31, 1997, will be inserted in the second column.*

	ACTUAL DEC. 31 1996	FORECAST FOR DEC. 31 1997
ASSETS:		
Current Assets:		
Cash & Marketable Securities	$ 65,313	_____
Accounts Receivable	13,035	_____
Inventory	21,453	_____
Total Current Assets	99,801	_____
Property, Plant & Equipment (gross)	133,369	_____
Less Accumulated Depreciation	(40,386)	_____
Property, Plant & Equipment (net)	92,983	_____
Total Assets	$192,784	_____
LIABILITIES & EQUITY:		
Current Liabilities:		
Accounts Payable	$ 4,733	_____
Notes Payable	302	_____
Total Current Liabilities	5,035	_____
Long-Term Debt	37,142	_____
Total Liabilities	42,177	_____
Common Stock		
(35 mil. shares, $1.00 par value)	35,000	_____
Capital in Excess of Par	32,100	_____
Retained Earnings	83,507	_____
Total Stockholders' Equity	150,607	_____
Total Liabilities & Equity	$192,784	_____

Choosing the Forecasting Basis   Before we make *pro forma* forecasts of each income statement and balance sheet line item, let's consider our procedure. Unfortunately, no universal procedure applies to all line items on *pro forma* financial statements because forecasters choose values for a variety of reasons. The three main reasons are: (1) Management specifies a target goal, (2) the value is taken from either the cash or capital budgets, or (3) the value is an extension of a past trend. If management does not specify a target value, and if no value from a budget is available, then forecasters must evaluate how the item has behaved in the past and estimate a future value based on experience, probability, or correlation, as discussed earlier in the chapter.

As we consider each financial statement item on Esoteric's *pro forma* statements, we will determine its value by seeing whether management has a target goal, and whether a budget sets the value for the item. If not, we will extend the trend based on experience, probability, and correlation.

Let's begin with Esoteric Industries' *pro forma* income statement for 1997.

The *Pro Forma* Income Statement   To prepare the *pro forma* income statement, we project the values of the following items: sales, costs and expenses associated with sales, general and administrative expenses, depreciation, interest, taxes, dividends paid, and addition to retained earnings. We will examine how to project each value next.

The Sales Projection.   At the top of our *pro forma* income statement for 1997 (shown in Figure 6-3a), we need a figure for sales. Assume that our analysis of marketing, production, finance, and management information results in a sales forecast of $221,907. Enter this figure in the "Forecast for 1997" column of Figure 6-3a, as shown:

	FORECAST FOR 1997
Net Sales	$221,907

Cost of Goods Sold (COGS) and Selling and Marketing Expenses.   After sales, the next two items are cost of goods sold (COGS) and selling and marketing expenses. We do not have a management target or budget figure for these expenses, so we will forecast them based on past experience. For Esoteric Enterprises, experience suggests that over time both these items have remained a constant percentage of sales. That is, over the years, COGS has been about 53 percent of sales and selling and marketing expenses have been about 16 percent of sales. So we conclude that in 1997 these items will be 53 percent and 16 percent of sales, respectively, shown as follows:

	FORECAST FOR 1997
Cost of Goods Sold	$221,907 \times .53 = $117,611
Selling and Marketing Expenses	$221,907 \times .16 = $35,505

General and Administrative Expenses.   General and administrative expenses are closely related to the size of Esoteric's manufacturing plant. For our 1997 forecast, we assume that Esoteric's property, plant, and equipment will not change for 1997. This means that our projected value for general and administrative expenses is $10,837, the same value as in the previous year:

	FORECAST FOR 1997
General and Administrative Expenses	$10,837

Take Note

For simplicity we use the straight-line depreciation method instead of MACRS to determine depreciation expense for 1997. As a result, we obtain a constant depreciation expense value as long as no equipment is replaced.

Depreciation Expense.   For our depreciation expenses forecast, let us say that Esoteric Enterprises' capital budget does not include the purchase of any additional property, plant, or equipment, and that no equipment is near the end of its projected useful life. The projected depreciation expense, then, will be $4,500, the same value as it was for 1996:

	FORECAST FOR 1997
Depreciation Expense	$4,500

Figure 6-4   Esoteric
Enterprises *Pro Forma*
Income Statement for
1997

*This figure shows Eso-
teric Enterprises' anticipated 1997 values for
each income statement
line item. Each forecast
value was calculated sep-
arately, according to the
forecasting assumptions
given.*

	FORECAST FOR 1997
Net Sales	$221,907
Cost of Goods Sold	117,611
Gross Profit	104,296
Operating Expenses:	
Selling and Marketing Expenses	35,505
General & Administrative Expense	10,837
Depreciation	4,500
Operating Income	53,454
Interest Expense	2,971
Before-Tax Income	50,483
Income Taxes (tax rate = 40%)	20,193
Net Income	$30,290
Dividends Paid	$27,261
Addition to Retained Earnings	3,029

Interest Expense.   The amount of interest to be paid in 1997 depends on the amount of debt outstanding in that year. That hasn't been determined yet because it is part of the balance sheet forecast. At this point we have no information indicating new debt will be obtained or old debt paid off, so we will project that interest expense in 1997 will be $2,971, its 1996 value.

	FORECAST FOR 1997
Interest Expense	$2,971

As we see in Figure 6-4, Esoteric's before-tax income is expected to be $50,483.

Income Taxes.   Esoteric's effective 1996 tax rate, shown in Figure 6-3a, is 40 percent.[4] We assume no changes in the tax law for 1997, so to obtain income tax expense for 1997, multiply the 1997 before-tax income by 40 percent, as follows:

	FORECAST FOR 1997
Income Tax Expense	$50,483 × .40 = $20,193

---

[4]We assume that Esoteric pays 36 percent of its income to the federal government and 4 percent to the state. Caution: When you are forecasting, be sure to check the latest tax rate schedule set by Congress.

Dividends Paid and Additions to Retained Earnings. Esoteric's management plans to continue the current dividend policy of paying 90 percent of net income in dividends and retaining 10 percent in 1997. We forecast net income in 1997 as $30,290 (see Figure 6-4), so dividends paid and the addition to retained earnings will be as follows:

	FORECAST FOR 1997
Dividends Paid	$30,290 \times .90 = $27,261
Addition to Retained Earnings	$30,290 \times .10 = $3,029

This completes our *pro forma* income statement. The results are summarized in Figure 6-4. Now let's turn to the *pro forma* balance sheet.

The *Pro Forma* Balance Sheet   Now we will create the *pro forma* balance sheet for 1997 (December 31) by examining each individual line-item account. If no target value is specified by management, and if no value from a budget is available, then we will evaluate the item's past performance and estimate its future value based on experience, probability, or correlation.

Cash and Marketable Securities. The forecast value for cash and marketable securities is normally drawn from the company's *cash budget,* as discussed earlier. Let's assume that financial managers at Esoteric have prepared a cash budget that predicts the amount of cash on hand at the end of 1997 will be $71,853.

Accounts Receivable and Inventory. Experience has shown that the accounts receivable and inventory accounts tend to remain the same percentage of sales, similar to the cost of goods sold and selling and marketing expenses on the income statement. In the past, accounts receivable has been 6 percent of sales and inventory has been 11 percent of sales. Therefore we will assume that these items will be 6 percent and 11 percent of 1997 sales, respectively, at the end of 1997:

	FORECAST FOR 1997
Accounts Receivable	$221,907 \times .06 = $13,314
Inventory	$221,907 \times .11 = $24,410

Property, Plant, and Equipment. Esoteric's capital budget does not include any provision for purchasing production equipment, buildings, or land. In our income statement forecast, we assumed that in 1997 Esoteric Enterprises will not need any additional equipment, no equipment will be disposed of, and no equipment will reach the end of its useful life. Property, plant and equipment gross at the end of 1997, then, will be the same as its end of 1996 value of $133,369. Property, plant and equipment net will be the 1996 gross value less the additional depreciation expense ($4,500) accumulated during 1997. Here are the calculations:

	FORECAST FOR 1997	
	12/31/97	
Property, Plant & Equipment (gross)	(Same as 12/31/96)	$133,369
Less	—	
Accumulated Depreciation	$40,386 + $4,500 = $44,886	
[end of 1996 accumulated depreciation ($40,386) plus 1997 depreciation expense ($4,500)]		
Property, Plant & Equipment (net)		$88,483

Accounts Payable. Experience has shown that, like accounts receivable and inventory, accounts payable tends to remain the same percentage of sales. In the past accounts payable has been 2 percent of sales. Therefore we will assume that accounts payable at the end of 1997 will be 2 percent of 1997 sales. Here are the calculations:

FORECAST FOR 1997
12/31/97
Accounts Payable	$221,907 × .02 = $4,438

Notes Payable. We assume based on experience and management policy that any notes outstanding at the end of a year will be paid off by the end of the following year, resulting in a zero balance in the notes payable account. Accordingly, Esoteric's notes payable value for the end of 1997 will be $0, shown as follows:

FORECAST FOR 1997
12/31/97
Notes Payable	$0

Long-Term Debt. We will assume that no principal payments on Esoteric's long-term debt are due in 1997, and no new debt financing arrangements have been made yet. Therefore the long-term debt value at the end of 1997 will be the same as the end of 1996 value, $37,142.

	FORECAST FOR 1997
	12/31/97
Long-Term Debt (Same as 1996 value)	$37,142

Common Stock and Capital in Excess of Par.   Esoteric's management has no plans to issue or to buy back stock in 1997. The common stock and capital in excess of par values, then, will remain the same at the end of 1997 as they were at the end of 1996, $35,000 and $32,100, respectively. The forecast follows:

	FORECAST FOR 1997
	12/31/97
Common Stock (Same as 1996 value)	$35,000
Capital in Excess of Par (Same as 1996 value)	$32,100

Retained Earnings.   As discussed in chapter 4, the retained earnings account represents sum of all net income not paid out in the form of dividends to stockholders.[5]

At the end of 1997, the retained earnings value will be the total of the end of 1996 figure ($83,507) plus the 1997 addition to retained earnings ($3,209), as shown on the income statement forecast.

We discussed retained earnings in chapter 4, on pages 65–66.

	FORECAST FOR 1997
	12/31/97
Retained Earnings	$83,507 + $3,209 = $86,716

This completes our *pro forma* balance sheet. Figure 6-5 summarizes the results.

Now both our *pro forma* financial statements for Esoteric Enterprises are complete. Figures 6-6a and 6-6b contain the complete 1997 forecast, including source notes explaining the reasons for each forecasted item's value.

Additional Funds Needed   When the *pro forma* balance sheet is completed, total assets and total liabilities and equity will rarely match. Our forecast in Figure 6-6b—in which total assets are forecast to be $198,060, but total liabilities and equity are forecast to be only $195,396—is typical. The discrepancy between forecasted assets and forecasted liabilities and equity ($2,664 in our example) results when either too little or too much financing is projected for the amount of asset growth expected. The discrepancy is called **additional funds needed** (AFN) when forecast assets exceed forecast liabilities and equity. It is called **excess financing** when forecast liabilities and equity exceed forecast assets. Our forecast indicates that $2,664 of additional funds are needed to support Esoteric's needed asset growth.

The determination of additional funds needed is one of the most important reasons for producing *pro forma* financial statements. Armed with the knowledge of how much additional external funding is needed, financial managers can make the necessary financing arrangements in the financial markets before a crisis occurs. Esoteric only needs a small amount, $2,664; so the company would probably obtain

Raising funds in the financial marketplace is covered in chapters 2 and 3 on pages 21–29 and 41–54, respectively.

---

[5]Esoteric has no preferred stock, and therefore no preferred stock dividends paid. This means that its net income is the same as its earnings available to common stockholders discussed in chapters 4 and 5.

	FORECAST FOR DEC. 31, 1997
ASSETS:	
Current Assets:	
Cash & Marketable Securities	$ 71,853
Accounts Receivable	13,314
Inventory	24,410
Total Current Assets	109,577
Property, Plant & Equipment (gross)	133,369
Less Accumulated Depreciation	(44,886)
Property, Plant & Equipment (net)	88,483
Total Assets	$198,060
LIABILITIES & EQUITY:	
Current Liabilities:	
Accounts Payable	$ 4,438
Notes Payable	0
Total Current Liabilities	4,438
Long-Term Debt	37,142
Total Liabilities	$ 41,580
Common Stock	35,000
Capital in Excess of Par	32,100
Retained Earnings	86,716
Total Stockholders' Equity	153,816
Total Liabilities and Equity	$195,396

Figure 6-6a **Esoteric Enterprises Income Statements**

The first column in this figure shows Esoteric Enterprises' income statement for 1996. The second column shows the pro forma forecast for 1997. The last column contains notes on where each line-item value was obtained.

	1996	FORECAST FOR 1997	SOURCE NOTES
Net Sales	$201,734	$221,907	Sales Forecast
Cost of Goods Sold	107,280	117,611	53% of sales
Gross Profit	94,454	104,296	
Operating Expenses:			
Selling and Marketing Expenses	32,392	35,505	16% of sales
General & Administrative Expenses	10,837	10,837	Keep same
Depreciation	4,500	4,500	Keep same
Operating Income	46,725	53,454	
Interest Expense	2,971	2,971	Keep same
Before-Tax Income	43,754	50,483	
Income Taxes (tax rate = 40%)	17,502	20,193	Same tax rate
Net Income	$26,252	$30,290	
Dividends Paid	$23,627	$27,261	Same payout policy (90%)
Addition to Retained Earnings	$2,625	$3,029	Net income—dividends paid

Figure 6-6b Esoteric Enterprises Balance Sheets

	ACTUAL 12/31/96	FORECAST 12/31/97	SOURCE NOTES
Assets			
Current Assets:			
Cash & Marketable Securities	$ 65,313	$ 71,853	Cash budget
Accounts Receivable	13,035	13,314	6.5% of sales
Inventory	21,453	24,410	11% of sales
Total Current Assets	99,801	109,577	
Property, Plant & Equipment (gross)	133,369	133,369	Capital budget (keep same)
Less Accumulated Depreciation	(40,386)	(44,886)	1996 plus 1997 depreciation expense
Property, Plant & Equipment (net)	92,983	88,483	
Total Assets	$192,784	$198,060	
Liabilities & Equity			
Current Liabilities:			
Accounts Payable	$ 4,733	$ 4,438	2% of sales
Notes Payable	302	0	Pay off
Total Current Liabilities	5,035	4,438	
Long-Term Debt	37,142	37,142	Keep same
Total Liabilities	42,177	41,580	
Common Stock			
(35 mil. shares, $1.00 par value)	35,000	35,000	Keep same
Additional Paid-In Capital	32,100	32,100	Keep same
Retained Earnings	83,507	86,716	1996 + 1997 addition to retained earnings
Total Stockholders' Equity	150,607	153,816	
Total Liabilities & Equity	$192,784	$195,396	1997 AFN = $2,664

The first column in this figure shows Esoteric Enterprises' balance sheet for December 31, 1996. The second column shows the pro forma forecast for December 31, 1997. The last column contains notes on where each line-item value was obtained.

the funds from a line of credit with their bank. When large amounts are required, other funding sources include a new bond or stock issue.

A Note on Interest Expense.   According to Esoteric's *pro forma* financial statements, the company needs $2,664 of new external financing in 1997. If they borrow the money (as we implied they would), then Esoteric will incur new interest charges that were not included in the original *pro forma* income statement. To be accurate, forecasters should revise the *pro forma* income statement to include the new interest. However, if they make the revision, it will reduce 1997's net income—which, in turn, will reduce 1997's retained earnings on the balance sheet forecast. This will change the total liabilities and equity figure for 1997, throwing the balance sheet out of balance again and changing the amount of additional funds needed!

In forecasting circles, this is known as *the balancing problem*. If the forecast is done on an electronic spreadsheet, it is not difficult to recast the financial statements several times over until the additional amount of interest expense becomes negligible. In this chapter, however, to avoid repeating the forecast over and over, we will simply stay with our original interest expense figure.

Keith Ender, Customer Service Representative, James River Paper Company

Keith Ender is Customer Service Manager for the James River Paper Company, manufacturer of Brawny paper towels, Northern bathroom tissue, Dixie paper cups, and a variety of other products. Keith helps customers who buy in large quantities. For example, if a big grocery chain orders a huge amount of Brawny paper towels, Keith's department handles every aspect of the sale, from the initial order to the final payment.

According to Keith, forecasting is vital to the success of James River. He points out, however, that it is an inexact science. Internal and external factors can throw off even the best forecast.

Q. *Just how important is forecasting to your business?*

Our success is tied to accurate forecasts. Each department, including my own, makes assumptions about what will happen in the future by forecasting its needs and how it will perform. To help the company produce accurate financial forecasts, though, we must start with accurate sales forecasts. My department, for instance, may forecast how much product it will sell if given the resources to move the maximum amount of product.

To help with the sales forecast, we could eyeball sales trends and say, "We're going to sell this amount of Brawny paper towels, and this number of Dixie cups." Now, let's say that half-way through the year we realize that our sales team will sell fewer paper towels and more Dixie cups than forecasted. A chain reaction starts. Production will be affected because they planned, based on our sales forecast, to make more paper towels and less cups than we need. Production may not have the capacity, money, or materials to adjust to the need for more cups immediately. If we can't meet consumer demand, or have too much inventory, our projected revenues are affected. We lose sales revenue and so do our customers. In fact, a customer might withhold payments they owe us, claiming we caused them to lose business because they didn't have enough cups to meet their customers' demand.

In short, there are a lot of negative repercussions to the forecast if our sales projections are not on track.

Q. *What kind of things can throw off your forecast?*

Sometimes special promotions can affect our forecasts. We must always try to accurately cover the cost of sales and make the best net profit margin possible. But that doesn't always happen. Say we decide to push Brawny paper towels. To help, marketing offers customers a special promotion fee to sell the towels. Sometimes the promotion works too well, and we end up selling more towels than forecasted at that special promotion price. Now, we may be selling like mad, but our profitability is dropping, because we're basically selling the towels for a lower price. If we hadn't offered the promotion, more towels might have been sold for a higher profit to other customers.

Another thing that can throw off forecasts is the price of raw materials. These prices can fluctuate wildly. For example, the cost of paper, which we are totally dependent on, recently climbed to record highs that we didn't expect. As a result, our cost of goods sold will be much higher than our forecasted cost. The increased cost will reduce our profitability significantly.

Q. *How can competition affect your forecasting?*

Sometimes it's tough to forecast revenues accurately because we don't know what our competitors are going to do. They could decide to increase their promotional spending and take a short-term decrease in revenues if, in the long run, they will benefit. Say that a large, diversified competitor wants to increase its market share of the paper towel market, so it runs special promotions on its paper towels. Because it is such a large company, it may lose money for a while, but it will be worth it if its paper towels gains market share. And again, because the company is large and diversified, it can make up for the paper towel promotion if the profit it makes selling soap or other products can cover the cost.

The point is, if their promotion works, they may take away some of our market share. Once market share is lost, it is tough to regain. To maintain our market share, we often have to react quickly by lowering the price of our paper towels to compete—but that lower price shoots the heck out of our profit forecast.

Q. *How important is understanding finance to your career?*

Very important. Although I don't have a finance background—I was a journalism major in college—I have many financial job responsibilities. I budget for our department, I handle incoming cash, and I help with sales forecasts. I review my department's financial numbers all the time.

Q. *Do you have any advice for business students?*

Learn as much about finance as you can, no matter what field you choose. In college, I was always intimi-

dated by any course that dealt with numbers. I wish I hadn't been so intimidated because as I progressed in my work career, I learned I couldn't avoid numbers. The more I progressed, the more familiar I had to be with finance because finance is the language of business.

Source: Interview with Keith Ender, November 12, 1995.

Analyzing Forecasts for Financial Planning

The most important forecasting task begins after the *pro forma* financial statements are complete. At that time, financial managers must analyze the forecast to determine:

1. What current trends suggest what will happen to the firm in the future
2. What effect management's current plans and budgets will have on the firm
3. What actions to take to avoid problems revealed in the *pro forma* statements

When analyzing the *pro forma* statements, financial managers often see signs of emerging positive or negative conditions. If forecasters discover positive indicators, they will recommend that management continue its current plans. If forecasters see negative indicators, they will recommend corrective action.

To illustrate, let's see how Esoteric Enterprises' financial managers would analyze the company's *pro forma* financial statements and plan for the future.

Scanning the first column in Figure 6-6a, we calculate Esoteric Enterprises' 1996 net profit margin (net income divided by sales) as follows:

Current Net Profit Margin = $26,252 / $201,734 = .1301, or 13.01%

Using the figures from the *pro forma* forecast (see Figure 6-6a, column two), Esoteric's forcasted net profit margin is as follows:

Forecasted Net Profit Margin = $30,290 / $221,907 = .1365, or 13.65%

The expected increase in the net profit margin from 13.01 percent to 13.65 percent is a desirable trend, so Esoteric's financial managers will recommend that the business maintain its current course of action.

However, if the analysis had shown a projected decline in the net profit margin to 11 percent, the financial managers would try to determine the cause of this decline (perhaps administrative expenses are too high or asset productivity is too low). Once the financial managers find the cause, they would recommend appropriate corrective action. Once the company adjusts its plans to correct the problem, the financial managers would prepare a new set of *pro forma* financial statements that reflect the changes.

We presented a brief example to illustrate the process of analyzing *pro forma* financial statements. A complete analysis would involve calculating profitability ratios, asset productivity ratios, liquidity ratios, and debt management ratios, as described in chapter 5.

WHAT'S NEXT

In this chapter we described forecasting and prepared *pro forma* statements. In chapter 7 we turn to the risk/return relationship, one of the key concepts of finance.

Summary

1. Explain the need for forecasting.

Business planning is based on forecasts of the company's future financial performance. Without forecasting, a business cannot succeed. Incorrect forecasts can be costly—so costly, in some cases, that the mistakes lead to failure.

2. Describe the financial statement forecasting process.

Forecasting means making assumptions about what will happen in the future. The three main approaches to making these assumptions are:

- *Experience.* We assume things will happen a certain way in the future because they have happened that way in the past.
- *Probability.* We assume things will happen a certain way in the future because the laws of probability indicate that it will be so.
- *Correlation.* We assume things will happen a certain way in the future because of a high *correlation* between the thing we are interested in and another thing we know more about.

Financial managers use the sales forecast, a variety of budgets, and past trend information to produce financial statements for periods in the future. These projected financial statements are pro forma financial statements. Pro forma financial statements show what assets, liabilities, and equity a firm is expected to have in the future.

3. Producing **pro forma** *financial statements.*

Pro forma financial statements are based on a company's current financial statements. The forecasted value of each current financial statement line item is determined by a target specified by management, a value extracted from a budget, or an extension of a past trend. In *pro forma* financial statement preparation, no general rule can be applied universally to all line items. Instead, each item must be examined individually. If no target value is specified by management, and if no value from a budget is available, then forecasters must evaluate the past performance of the account and estimate a future value based on experience, probability, or correlation.

On the *pro forma* balance sheet the forecasted values for total assets and total liabilities and equity rarely match. When forecasted assets exceed forecasted liabilities and equity, the difference is called additional funds needed (AFN). When forecasted liabilities and equity exceed forecasted assets, the difference is called excess financing. Additional funds needed is the additional external financing required to support projected asset growth. Excess financing means that too much funding has been set aside for expected asset growth.

4. Explain the importance of analyzing forecasts.

Once the *pro forma* financial statements are complete, financial managers must analyze them to determine if the company should continue with its current plans (as in the case of *pro forma* statements that show a growth in revenues), or if plans need to be modified to avoid problems in the future. Financial managers analyze the *pro forma* statements by using the ratio analysis techniques described in chapter 5.

Self-Test

ST-1. For the last five years, cost of goods sold (COGS) for the Heaven's Gate Corporation has averaged 60 percent of Sales. This trend is expected to continue for the foreseeable future. If sales for 1998 are expected to be $2.5 million, what would be the forecast 1998 value for COGS?

ST-2. In 1997 the Ishtar Corporation had $180,000 in retained earnings. During 1998 the company expects net income to be $750,000. What will the value of retained earnings be on the company's *pro forma* balance sheet for December 31, 1998, if the company continues its policy of paying 50 percent of net income in dividends?

ST-3. The Far and Away Irish Import Company's *pro forma* balance sheet for December 31, 1998, indicates that total assets will be $8,420,000, but total liabilities and equity will be only $7,685,000. What should Far and Away do to resolve the discrepancy between assets and liabilities?

ST-4. Refer to the *pro forma* financial statements for Esoteric Enterprises, Figures 6-6a and 6-6b. Calculate Esoteric's return on equity (ROE) ratio for 1996 and 1997. Comment on the results.

Review Questions

1. Why do businesses spend time, effort, and money to produce forecasts?
2. What is the primary assumption behind the "experience" approach to forecasting?
3. Describe the sales forecasting process.
4. Explain how the cash budget and the capital budget relate to *pro forma* financial statement preparation.
5. Explain how management goals are integrated into *pro forma* financial statements.
6. Explain the significance of the term "additional funds needed."
7. What do financial managers look for when they analyze *pro forma* financial statements?
8. What action(s) should be taken if analysis of *pro forma* financial statements reveals positive trends? Negative trends?

Build Your Communication Skills

CS-1. Refer to the current and *pro forma* financial statements for Esoteric Enterprises in Figures 6-6a and 6-6b. Analyze the financial statements using the techniques in chapter 5 and prepare a report of Esoteric's strengths and weaknesses.

CS-2. Form small groups of four to six. Based on each group member's assessment of Esoteric's strengths and weaknesses, discuss whether Esoteric should change its business plans and how. Once the group has prepared a strategy, select a spokesperson to report the group's conclusions to the class.

Problems

6-1. Miniver Corporation grows flowers and sells them to major U.S. retail flower shops. Mrs. Miniver has asked you to prepare a forecast of expected future sales. The chart on page 130 shows the Miniver Corporation's sales record for the last six years. Make an estimate of 1997 sales by extending the trend. Justify your estimate to Mrs. Miniver.

Sales Forecasts

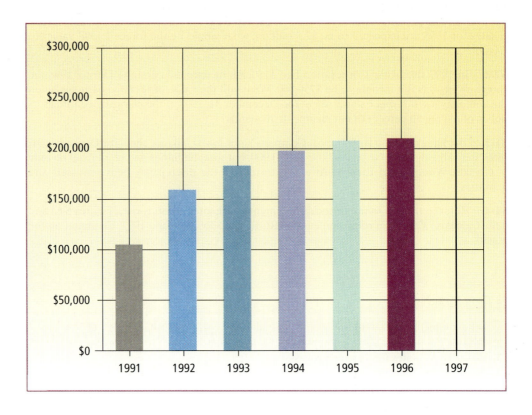

Additional Funds Needed

6-2. Complete the following *pro forma* financial statements. Use the forecasting assumptions in the far right-hand column.

	This Year	Next Year	Forecasting Assumption
Sales	100	_____	Sales will grow 20%
− Variable Costs	50	_____	Constant % of sales
− Fixed Costs	40	_____	Remains same
= Net Income	10	_____	
Dividends	5	_____	Keep 50% payout ratio
Current Assets	60	_____	Constant % of sales
Fixed Assets	100	_____	Remains same
Total Assets	160	_____	
Current Liabilities	20	_____	Constant % of sales
Long-Term Debt	20	_____	Remains same
Common Stock	20	_____	Remains same
Retained Earnings	100	_____	
Total Liabilities & Equity	160	_____	
		AFN = _____	

Additional Funds Needed

6-3. Jolly Joe's Pizza has just come out with a new pizza that Joe is sure will cause sales to double between 1996 and 1997. Using the following worksheet, complete Joe's *pro forma* financial forecast and answer the related questions.

You may assume that COGS, current assets, and current liabilities will maintain the same percentage of sales as in 1996. Further, you may assume that no new fixed assets will be needed in 1997, and the current dividend policy will be continued in 1997.

Jolly Joe's Pizza, Inc.
Financial Status and Forecast

	1996	Estimate for 1997
Sales	$10,000	20,000
COGS	4,000	9,000
Gross Profit	6,000	12,000
Fixed Expenses	3,000	3,000
Before-Tax Profit	3,000	9,000
Tax @ 33.33%	1,000	3,000
Net Profit	$2,000	6,000
Dividends	$0	0
Current Assets	$25,000	50,000
Net Fixed Assets	15,000	15,000
Total Assets	$40,000	65,000
Current Liabilities	$17,000	34,000
Long-Term Debt	3,000	3,000
Common Stock	7,000	7,000
Retained Earnings	13,000	19,000
Total Liabilities & Equity	$40,000	

Will Joe be able to get by without any additional funds needed in 1997? If not, how much will he need?

6-4. Jose Tine owns Sugar Cane Alley, a small candy shop in Aspen, Colorado. He would like to expand his business and open a second store in Vail. Mr. Tine does not have the capital to undertake this project and would like to borrow the money from the local bank. He knows the banker will need projected income statement data for his current store when considering his loan application. Net sales for 1996 were $90,000. Considering previous growth rates in his business and the anticipated increase in tourism, projected net sales for 1997 is $110,000. Answer the questions based on the following assumptions. Cost of goods sold and selling and marketing ex-penses will remain the same percent of sales as in 1996. General and administration expenses will remain the same value as 1996 at $5,000. Mr. Tine uses the straight-line method of depreciation, so last year's depreciation expense figure of $2000 can also be applied to 1997.

Pro Forma Income Statement

a. 1996 cost of goods sold was $48,000. What is the forecasted value of cost of goods sold for 1997?
b. What is the forecasted gross profit for 1997?
c. Selling and marketing expenses for 1996 were $13,000. What is the forecasted value for 1997?
d. Calculate the forecasted operating income for 1997.
e. Assume the interest expense for 1997 will be $800 and the tax rate is 30 percent. Calculate earnings before interest and taxes (EBIT) and net income expected for 1997 to the nearest dollar.
f. If $10,000 is distributed in dividends in 1997, what will be 1997's addition to retained earnings?

6-5. After completing the *pro forma* income statement in problem 6-4, Mr. Tine now realizes he should also complete a *pro forma* balance sheet. Net sales in 1996 were $90,000 and his forecasted sales for 1997 is $110,000. All of Sugar Cane Alley's current assets will remain the same percent of sales as they were in 1996. Mr. Tine does not plan to buy or sell any equipment, so his gross property and equipment amount will remain the same as 1996. In the liabilities and equity section, only accounts payable will remain the same percent of sales as in 1996. Except for retained earnings, the other accounts are expected to remain the same as 1996. The following balances were taken from Sugar Cane Alley's end of 1996 Balance Sheet:

Cash	$10,000
Accounts Receivable	2,220
Inventory	8,000
Property and Equipment (gross)	25,000
Accumulated Depreciation	4,000
Property and Equipment (net)	21,000
Accounts Payable	1,380
Long-Term Notes Payable	8,000
Retained Earnings	5,000
Common Stock	26,840

a. Calculate the forecasted end of 1997 values for each of the current asset accounts.
b. Depreciation expense for 1997 is estimated to be $2,000. Calculate the estimated total assets for the end of 1997.
c. Forecast the accounts payable for the end of 1997.
d. What will total liabilities be at the end of 1997?
e. Assuming the forecasted net income for 1997 is $19,351 and cash dividends paid equals $10,000, what total will be forecasted for the end of 1997 total liabilities and equity?
f. Based on these calculations of the *pro forma balance sheet,* are additional funds needed?
g. Net income for 1996 was $14,840. What was Sugar Cane Alley's net profit margin for 1996? The forecasted net income for 1997 is $19,357. What is Sugar Cane Alley's forecasted 1997 net profit margin?

6-6. The balance sheet of Free Enterprises, Inc., at the end of 1996, is given below:

Free Enterprises, Inc.
Balance Sheet, December 31, 1996
(Thousands of Dollars)

Assets		Liabilities + Equity	
Cash	$ 4,000	Accounts Payable	$ 4,400
Accounts Receivable	10,000	Notes Payable	4,000
Inventory	13,000	Accrued Expenses	5,000
Prepaid Expenses	400	Total Current Liabilities	13,400
Total Current Assets	27,400	Bonds Payable	6,000
Fixed Assets	11,000	Common Equity	19,000
Total Assets	$38,400	Total Liabilities & Equity	$38,400

Net sales for 1996 was $85,000,000. The average annual sales growth rate is expected to be 10 percent every year for the next three years. Over the past several years the earnings before taxes (EBT) was 11 percent of net sales and is expected to remain the same over the next three years. The company's tax rate is 40 percent and it plans to maintain the dividend payout ratio (dividends paid/net income) at 60 percent.

Prepare a *pro forma* balance sheet for Free Enterprises, Inc., for December 31, 1997. Assume the accounts that are not a function of sales (fixed assets and bonds payable) remain the same as they were in 1996. Current assets and current liabilities will remain the same percentage of sales as in 1996. Assume the only change to common equity is for the addition to retained earnings.

6-7. Consider the current and *pro forma* financial statements below.

Forecasting Ratio Values

	1996	1997
Sales	200	220
− Variable Costs	100	110
− Fixed Costs	80	80
= Net Income	20	30
Dividends	10	22
Current Assets	120	132
Fixed Assets	200	200
Total Assets	320	332
Current Liabilities.	40	44
Long-Term Debt	40	40
Common Stock	40	40
Retained Earnings	200	208
Total Liabilities & Equity	320	332
		AFN = 0

Compute the following ratios for 1996 and 1997:

	1996	1997
Current Ratio	_____	_____
Debt to Assets Ratio	_____	_____
Sales to Assets Ratio	_____	_____
Net Profit Margin	_____	_____
Return on Assets	_____	_____
Return on Equity	_____	_____

Comment on any trends revealed by your ratio analysis.

6-8.

Challenge Problem

1. Develop a pro forma income statement and balance sheet for the Bright Future Corporation. The company's 1996 financial statements are shown as follows. Base your forecast on the financial statements and the following assumptions:

- Sales growth is predicted to be 20 percent in 1997.
- Cost of goods sold, selling and administrative expense, all current assets, accounts payable, and accrued expenses will remain the same percent of sales they were in 1996.
- Depreciation expense, interest expense, gross plant and equipment, notes payable, long-term debt, and equity accounts *other than retained earnings* in 1997 will be the same as in 1996.
- The company's tax rate in 1997 will be 40 percent.
- The same dollar amount of dividends will be paid to the preferred and common stockholders in 1997 as was paid in 1996.
- Bad debt allowance in 1997 will be the same percentage of *accounts receivable* (not sales) as it was in 1996.

Bright Future Corporation
Income Statement for the Year Ended 1996

Sales	$10,000,000
Cost of Goods Sold	− 4,000,000
Gross Profit	= 6,000,000
Selling & Administrative Expenses	− 800,000
Depreciation Expense	− 2,000,000
Earnings Before Interest and Taxes (EBIT, or Operating Income)	= 3,200,000
Interest Expense	− 1,350,000
Earnings Before Taxes (EBT)	= 1,850,000
Taxes (40 %)	− 740,000
Net Income (NI)	= 1,110,000
Preferred Stock Dividends Paid	− 110,000
Earnings Available to Common Stockholders	= 1,000,000
Earnings per Share (EPS) (1,000,000 shares) = $100	
Common Stock Dividends Paid	− 400,000
Addition to Retained Earnings	= 600,000

Bright Future Corporation
Balance Sheet December 31, 1996

ASSETS:

Current Assets:			
Cash		$ 9,000,000	
Marketable Securities		8,000,000	
Accounts Receivable (Gross)	$1,200,000		
Less Allowance for Bad Debts	200,000		
Accounts Receivable (Net)		1,000,000	
Inventory		20,000,000	
Prepaid Expenses		1,000,000	
Total Current Assets			$39,000,000
Fixed Assets:			
Plant & Equipment (Gross)	20,000,000		
Less Accumulated Depreciation	9,000,000		
Plant & Equipment (Net)		11,000,000	
Total Fixed Assets			11,000,000
TOTAL ASSETS			$50,000,000
LIABILITIES & EQUITY:			
Current Liabilities:			
Accounts Payable	$12,000,000		
Notes Payable	5,000,000		
Accrued Expenses	3,000,000		
Total Current Liabilities		$20,000,000	
Long-Term Debt:			
Bonds Payable (5%, due 2015)	20,000,000		
Total Long-Term Debt		20,000,000	
Total Liabilities			$40,000,000
Equity:			
Preferred Stock		1,000,000	
Common Stock			
(1 million shares, $1 par)		1,000,000	
Capital in Excess of Par		3,000,000	
Retained Earnings		5,000,000	
Total Equity			10,000,000
TOTAL LIABILITIES & EQUITY			$50,000,000

2. **a.** Calculate Bright Future's additional funds needed, or excess financing. If additional funds are needed, add them to long-term debt to bring the balance sheet into balance. If excess financing is available, increase common stock dividends paid (and therefore decrease 1997 retained earnings) until the balance sheet is in balance.
    b. Calculate Bright Future's current ratio and total debt to total assets ratio for the end of 1996 and 1997.
    c. Calculate Bright Future's total asset turnover and inventory turnover ratios for 1997.
    d. Calculate Bright Future's total debt to total assets ratio for 1996 and 1997.
    e. Calculate Bright Future's net profit margin, return on assets, and return on equity ratios for 1996 and 1997.

3. Comment on Bright Future's liquidity, asset productivity, debt management, and profitability based on the results of your ratio analysis in b(2) through b(5), above.
4. What recommendations would you provide to management based on your forecast and analysis?

Answers to Self-Test

ST-1. If COGS is expected to remain 60 percent of sales, then in 1997 COGS will be 60 percent of 1997's Sales:

$$.60 \times \$2,500,000 = \$1,500,000$$

ST-2. If Ishtar earns $750,000 in 1997 and pays 50 percent of it to stockholders as dividends, then the other 50 percent, or $375,000 will be retained and added to the existing retained earnings account. Therefore retained earnings on Ishtar's December 31, 1997, *pro forma* balance sheet will be:

$$\$180,000 + \$375,000 = \$555,000$$

ST-3. Far and Away's total liabilities and equity are forecast to be $735,000 less than total assets. This means Far and Away must arrange for $735,000 in additional financing to support expected asset growth. Possible sources of this financing include bank loans, a bond issue, a stock issue, or perhaps lowering the 1997 dividend (if any).

ST-4.

$$ROE = \frac{Net\ Income}{Total\ Equity}$$

For Esoteric in 1996 (from the 1996 financial statements):

$$ROE = \frac{\$26,252}{\$150,607} = .1743,\ or\ 17.43\%$$

For Esoteric in 1997 (from the 1997 *pro forma* financial statements):

$$ROE = \frac{\$30,290}{\$153,816} = .1969,\ or\ 19.69\%$$

Take Note

Note that this is a favorable forecast. The over two-percentage-point gain in an already respectable ROE value should be particularly pleasing to the stockholders. Esoteric's financial managers should recommend that the company continue with its current plans, assuming that the increase in ROE does not signal an excessive increase in risk.

Remember that risk and return go hand in hand. The financial managers at Esoteric Enterprises must evaluate the risk associated with the ROE figures before concluding that current plans will lead to desirable results.

chapter 7

Risk and Return

Believe me! The secret of reaping the greatest fruitfulness and the greatest enjoyment from life is to live dangerously!

Friedrich Wilhelm Nietzsche

Will Ford Motor Company's Risky Reorganization Pay Off?

Alex Trotman, CEO of the Ford Motor Company, set out to integrate Ford's scattered operations around the world. He proposed consolidating Ford's national and international operations, creating a unified company that can serve distant India as handily as Indiana.

The massive effort is known as Ford 2000. It is one of the biggest reorganizations in the company's history, but it is also extremely risky. David Lewis, a business historian at the University of Michigan, likens the effort to Columbus setting off on his voyage to India—"He found North America, but he might have fallen off the edge."

The reorganization, according to Ford representatives, can save more than $4 billion a year from volume purchases and reduced duplication of effort. If so, that would more than double the $3.8 billion profit Ford's automotive operations made in 1994.

To succeed, however, the company must create cars and trucks that can simultaneously excite Argentines and Austrians, Chinese and Czechs, and Alabamans and Arizonans. At the same time, Ford must introduce its new models on time. Lee Sage, an

Alex Trotman

industry consultant for Ernst & Young says, "This is like changing the engines on a 747 while it is in the air, and keeping it a secret from the passengers." ❆

Source: Taylor Alexander, "Ford's really BIG leap at the future: It's risky, it's worth it, and it MAY NOT WORK," *Fortune* (September 18, 1995): 134.

CHAPTER OVERVIEW

Business firms face risk in nearly everything they do. The Ford 2000 plan may pay off well, but there is a risk that it may not pay off at all—leaving Ford in a much worse financial position.

Assessing risk is one of the most important tasks financial managers perform. In this chapter we will discuss *risk, risk aversion,* and the *risk–return relationship.* We will measure risk, using *standard deviation* and the *coefficient of variation.* We will identify types of risk and examine ways to reduce risk exposure or compensate for risk. Finally, we will see how the Capital Asset Pricing Model (CAPM) explains the risk–return relationship.

RISK

The world is a risky place. For instance, if you get out of bed in the morning and go to class, you run the risk of getting hit by a bus. If you stay in bed to minimize the chance of getting run over by a bus, you run the risk of getting coronary artery disease because of a lack of exercise. In everything we do—or don't do—there is a chance that something will happen that we didn't expect. **Risk** is the potential for unexpected events to occur.

Risk Aversion

Most people try to avoid risks if possible. Risk aversion doesn't mean that some people don't enjoy risky activities, such as skydiving, rock climbing, or automobile racing. In a financial setting, however, evidence shows that most people avoid risk where possible. Faced with financial alternatives that are equal except for their degree of risk, most people will choose the less risky alternative.

Risk aversion is the tendency to avoid additional risk. Risk-averse people will avoid risk if they can, unless they receive additional compensation for assuming that risk—such as a $1 million reward for jumping out of an airplane. In finance, the added compensation is a higher expected rate of return.

The Risk–Return Relationship

The relationship between risk and required rate of return is known as the **risk–return relationship.** It is a positive relationship because the more risk assumed, the higher the required rate of return most people will demand. It takes compensation to convince people to suffer.

Suppose, for instance, that you were offered a job in the Sahara Desert, working long hours for a boss everyone describes as a tyrant. You would surely be averse to the idea of taking such a job. But think about it: Is there any way you would take this job? What if you were told that your salary would be $1 million per year? This compensation might cause you to sign up immediately. Even though there is a high probability you would hate the job, you'd take that risk because of the high compensation.[1]

Not everyone is risk averse; and among those who are, not all are equally risk averse. Some people would demand $2 million before taking the job in the Sahara Desert, while others would do it for a more modest salary.

People sometimes engage in risky financial activities, such as buying lottery tickets or gambling in casinos. This suggests that they like risk and will pay to experience it. Most people, however, view these activities as entertainment rather than financial investing. The entertainment value may be the excitement of being in a casino with all sorts of people, or being able to fantasize about spending the multimillion-dollar lotto jackpot. But in the financial markets, where people invest for the future, they almost always seek to avoid risk unless they are adequately compensated.

Risk aversion explains the positive risk–return relationship. It explains why risky junk bonds carry a higher market interest rate than essentially risk-free U.S. Treasury bonds. Hardly anyone would invest $5,000 in a risky junk bond if the interest rate on the bond were lower than that of a U.S. Treasury bond having the same maturity.

MEASURING RISK

We can never avoid risk entirely. That's why businesses must make sure that the anticipated return is sufficient to justify the degree of risk assumed. To do that, however, firms must first determine how much risk is present in a given financial situation. In other words, they must be able to answer the question, "How risky is it?"

Measuring risk quantitatively is a rather tall order. We all know when something feels risky, but we don't often quantify it. In business, risk measurement focuses on the degree of **uncertainty** present in a situation—the chance, or probability, of an unexpected outcome. The greater the probability of an unexpected outcome, the greater the degree of risk.

Using Standard Deviation to Measure Risk

In statistics, *distributions* are used to describe the many values variables may have. A company's sales in future years, for example, is a variable with many possible values. So the sales forecast may be described by a distribution of the possible sales values with different probabilities attached to each value. If this distribution is symmetric, its mean—the average of a set of values—would be the expected sales value. Similarly, possible returns on any investment can be described by a *probability distribution*— usually a graph, table, or formula that specifies the probability associated with each possible return the investment may generate. The mean of the distribution is the most likely, or expected, rate of return.

---

[1]We do not wish to suggest that people can be coaxed into doing anything they are averse to doing, merely by offering them a sufficient amount of compensation. If people are asked to do something that offends their values, there may be no amount of compensation that could entice them.

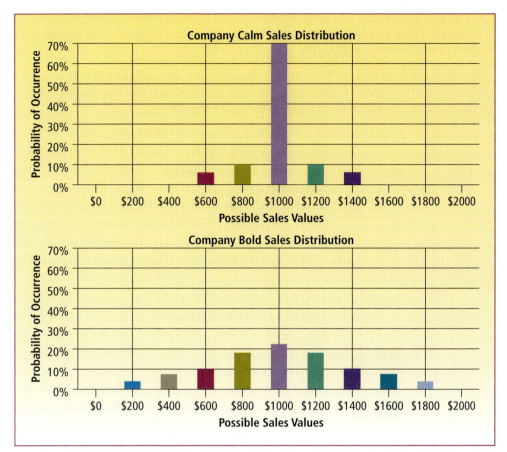

Figure 7-1 Sales Forecast Distributions for Companies Calm and Bold

Possible future sales distributions for two companies. Calm has a relatively "tight" distribution and Bold has a relatively "wide" distribution. Note that sales for Company Bold may have many more possible values than sales for Company Calm.[2]

The graph in Figure 7-1 shows the distributions of forecast sales for two companies, Company Calm and Company Bold. Note how the distribution for Company Calm's possible sales values is clustered closely to the mean, and how the distribution of Company Bold's possible sales values is spread far above and far below the mean.

The narrowness or wideness of a distribution reflects the degree of uncertainty about the expected value of the variable in question (sales, in our example). The distributions in Figure 7-1 show, for instance, that while the most probable value of sales for both companies is $1,000, sales for Company Calm could vary between $600 and $1,400, while sales for Company Bold could vary between $200 and $1,800. Company Bold's relatively wide variations show that there is more uncertainty about its sales forecast than about Company Calm's sales forecast.

One way to measure risk is to compute the standard deviation of a variable's distribution of possible values. The **standard deviation** is a numerical indicator of how widely dispersed the possible values are around a mean. The more widely dispersed a distribution is, the larger the standard deviation, and the greater the probability that the value of a variable will be greatly different than the expected value. The standard deviation, then, indicates the likelihood that an outcome different than what is expected will occur.

---

[2]These two distributions are *discrete*. If sales could take on any value within a given range, the distribution would be *continuous* and would be depicted by a curved line.

Let's calculate the standard deviations of the sales forecast distributions for Companies Calm and Bold to illustrate how the standard deviation can measure the degree of uncertainty, or risk, that is present.

Calculating the Standard Deviation To calculate the standard deviation of the distribution of Company Calm's possible sales, we must first find the expected value, or mean, of the distribution using the following formula:

Formula for Expected Value, or Mean (μ)

$$\mu = \Sigma\,(V \times P) \tag{7-1}$$

where: μ = the expected value, or mean
Σ = the sum of
V = the possible value for some variable
P = the probability of the value V occurring

Applying Equation 7-1, we can calculate the expected value, or mean, of Company Calm's forecasted sales. The following values for V and P are taken from Figure 7-1:

Calculating the Mean (μ) of Company Calm's Possible
Future Sales Distribution

POSSIBLE SALES VALUE (V)	PROBABILITY OF OCCURRENCE (P)	V × P
$600	.05	30
$800	.10	80
$1,000	.70	700
$1,200	.10	120
$1,400	.05	70
	$\Sigma = \overline{1.00}$	$\Sigma = \overline{1,000} = \mu$

Each possible sales value is multiplied by its respective probability. The probability values, taken from Figure 7-1, may be based on trends, industry ratios, experience, or other information sources. We add together the products of each value times its probability to find the mean of the possible sales distribution.

We now know that the mean of Company Calm's sales forecast distribution is $1,000. We are ready to calculate the standard deviation of the distribution using the following formula:

The Standard Deviation (σ) Formula

$$\sigma = \sqrt{\Sigma\,P(V - \mu)^2} \tag{7-2}$$

where: σ = the standard deviation
Σ = the sum of
P = the probability of the value V occurring
V = the possible value for a variable
μ = the expected value

To calculate the standard deviation of Company Calm's sales distribution, we subtract the mean from each possible sales value, square that difference, and then multiply by the probability of that sales outcome. These differences squared, times their respective probabilities, are then added together, and the square root of this number is taken. The result is the standard deviation of the distribution of possible sales values.

Calculating the Standard Deviation (σ) of Company Calm's
Possible Future Sales Distribution

POSSIBLE SALES VALUE (V)	PROBABILITY OF OCCURRENCE (P)	$V - \mu$	$(V - \mu)^2$	$P(V - \mu)^2$
$600	.05	−400	160,000	8,000
$800	.10	−200	40,000	4,000
$1,000	.70	0	0	0
$1,200	.10	200	40,000	4,000
$1,400	.05	400	160,000	8,000
				$\Sigma = 24,000$
				$\sqrt{24,000} = 155 = \sigma$

This standard deviation result, 155, serves as the measure of the degree of risk present in Company Calm's sales forecast distribution.

Let's calculate the standard deviation of Company Bold's sales forecast distribution.

Mean (μ) and Standard Deviation (σ)
of Company Bold's Sales Possible Future Sales Distribution

POSSIBLE SALES VALUE (V)	PROBABILITY OF OCCURRENCE (P)	MEAN CALCULATION $V \times P$	$V - \mu$	$(V - \mu)^2$	$P(V - \mu)^2$
$200	.04	8	−800	640,000	25,600
$400	.07	28	−600	360,000	25,200
$600	.10	60	−400	160,000	16,000
$800	.18	144	−200	40,000	7,200
$1,000	.22	220	0	0	0
$1,200	.18	216	200	40,000	7,200
$1,400	.10	140	400	160,000	16,000
$1,600	.07	112	600	360,000	25,200
$1,800	.04	72	800	640,000	25,600
		$\sum = 1,000 = \mu$			$\sum = 148,000$
					$\sqrt{148,000} = 385 = \sigma$

Take Note

In the following procedure, we combine two steps: (1) finding the mean of the distribution with Equation 7-1; and (2) calculating the standard deviation with Equation 7-2.

As you can see, Company Bold's standard deviation of 385 is over twice that of Company Calm. This reflects the greater degree of risk in Company Bold's sales forecast.

Interpreting the Standard Deviation   Estimates of a company's possible sales, or a proposed project's future possible cash flows, can generally be thought of in terms of a *normal* probability distribution. The normal distribution is a special type of distribution. It allows us to make statements about how likely it is that the variable in question will be within in a certain range of the distribution.

Figure 7-2 **Normal Distribution**

This normal probability distribution of possible returns has a mean, the expected rate of return, of 15%.

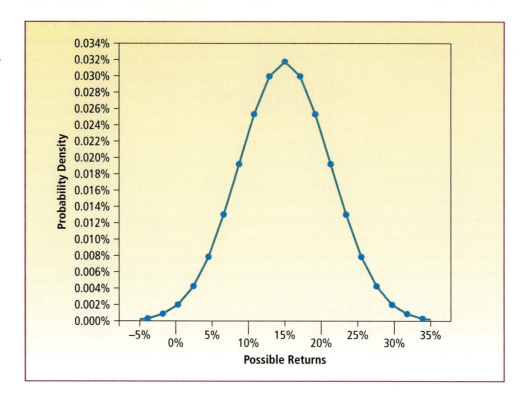

Figure 7-2 shows a normal distribution of possible returns on an asset. The vertical axis measures probability density for this continuous distribution so that the area under the curve always sums to one. Statistics tells us that when a distribution is normal, there is about a 67 percent chance that the observed value will be within one standard deviation of the mean. In the case of Company Calm, that means that there is a 67 percent probability that the actual sales will be $1,000 plus or minus $155 (between $845 and $1,155). For Company Bold it means there is a 67 percent probability that sales will be $1,000 plus or minus $385 (between $615 and $1,385).

Another characteristic of the normal distribution is that approximately 95 percent of the time, values observed will be within two standard deviations of the mean. For Company Calm this means that there is a 95 percent probability that sales will be $1,000 plus or minus $155 × 2, or $310 (between $690 and $1,310). For Company Bold it means that sales will be $1,000 plus or minus $385 × 2, or $770 (between $230 and $1,770). These relationships are shown graphically in Figure 7-3.

The greater the standard deviation value, the greater the uncertainty as to what the actual value of the variable in question will be. The greater the value of the standard deviation, the greater the possible deviations from the mean.

Using the Coefficient of Variation to Measure Risk

Whenever we want to compare the risk of investments that have different means, we use the *coefficient of variation*. We were safe in using the standard deviation to

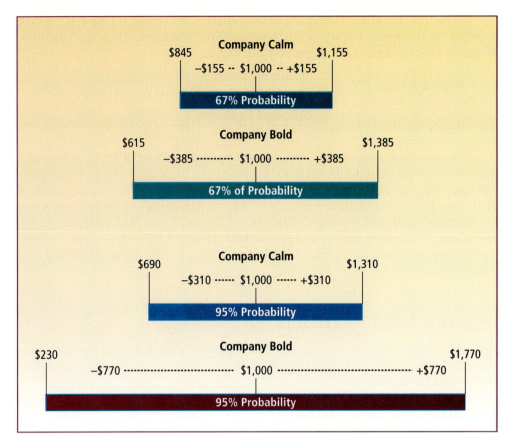

The standard deviation shows there is much more risk present in Co. Bold's sales probability distribution than in Co. Calm's. If the distributions are normal, then there is a 67% probability that Co. Calm's sales will be between $845 and $1,155, and a 95% probability sales will be between $690 and $1,310. For Co. Bold there is a 67% probability that sales will be between $615 and $1,385, and a 95% probability that sales will be between $230 and $1,770.

compare the riskiness of Company Calm's possible future sales distribution with that of Company Bold because the mean of the two distributions was the same ($1,000). Imagine, however, that Company Calm's sales were ten times that of Company Bold. If that were the case and all other factors remained the same, then the standard deviation of Company Calm's possible future sales distribution would increase by a factor of 10, to $1,550. Company Calm's sales would appear to be much more risky than Company Bold's, whose standard deviation was only $385.

To compare the degree of risk among distributions of different sizes, we should use a statistic that measures *relative* riskiness. The **coefficient of variation** (CV) measures relative risk by relating the standard deviation to the mean. The formula follows:

$$\text{Coefficient of Variation (CV)}$$
$$CV = \frac{\text{Standard Deviation}}{\text{Mean}} \tag{7-3}$$

The coefficient of variation represents the standard deviation's percentage of the mean. It provides a standardized measure of the degree of risk that can be used to compare alternatives.

To illustrate the use of the coefficient of variation, let's compare the relative risk depicted in Company Calm's and Company Bold's possible sales distributions. When we plug the figures into Equation 7-3, we see:

$$\text{Company Calm CV}_{\text{sales}} = \frac{\text{Standard Deviation}}{\text{Mean}} = \frac{155}{1{,}000} = .155, \text{ or } 15.5\%$$

$$\text{Company Bold CV}_{\text{sales}} = \frac{\text{Standard Deviation}}{\text{Mean}} = \frac{385}{1{,}000} = .385, \text{ or } 38.5\%$$

Company Bold's coefficient of variation of possible sales (38.5%) is more than twice that of Company Calm (15.5%). Furthermore, even if Company Calm were ten times the size of Company Bold—with a mean of its possible future sales of $10,000 and with a standard deviation of $1,550—it would not change the coefficient of variation. This would remain 1,550/10,000 = .155, or 15.5%. That's why we use the coefficient of variation instead of the standard deviation to *compare* distributions that have means with different values: because the CV adjusts for the difference, while the standard deviation does not.

The Types of Risks Firms Encounter

Risk refers to uncertainty—the chance that what you expect to happen *won't* happen. The forms of risk that businesses most often encounter are *business risk, financial risk,* and *portfolio risk.*

Business Risk

Business risk refers to the uncertainty a company has with regard to its operating income (also known as earnings before interest and taxes or EBIT). The more uncertainty about a company's expected operating income, the more business risk the company has. For example, if we assume that grocery prices remain constant, the only grocery store in a small town probably has little business risk—the store owners can reliably predict how much their customers will buy each month. In contrast, a gold mining firm in Wyoming has a lot of business risk. Because the owners have no idea when, where, or how much gold they will strike, they can't predict how much they will earn in any period with any degree of certainty.

Measuring Business Risk   The degree of uncertainty about operating income (and therefore the degree of business risk in the firm) depends on the volatility of operating income. If operating income is relatively constant, as in the grocery store example, then there is relatively little uncertainty associated with it. If operating income can take on many different values, as is the case with the gold mining firm, then there is a lot of uncertainty about it.

We can measure the variability of a company's operating income by calculating the standard deviation of the operating income forecast. A small standard deviation indicates little variability, and therefore little uncertainty. A large standard deviation indicates a lot of variability, and great uncertainty.

Some companies are large and others small. So to make comparisons among different firms, we must measure the risk by calculating the coefficient of variation of possible operating income values. The higher the coefficient of variation of possible operating income values, the greater the business risk of the firm.

TABLE 7-1

Expected Value (μ),
Standard Deviation (σ),
and Coefficient of
Variation (CV) of
Possible Operating
Income Values for
Companies Calm and
Bold, Assuming All
Expenses Are Variable.

COMPANY CALM

	Probability of Occurrence				
	5%	10%	70%	10%	5%
Sales	$600	$800	$1,000	$1,200	$1,400
Variable Expenses	516	688	860	1,032	1,204
Operating Income	84	112	140	168	196

μ of Possible Operating Income Values per Equation 7-1: $140
σ of Possible Operating Income Values per Equation 7-2: $21.69
CV of Possible Operating Income Values per Equation 7-3: 15.5%

COMPANY BOLD

	Probability of Occurrence								
	4%	7%	10%	18%	22%	18%	10%	7%	4%
Sales	$200	$400	$600	$800	$1,000	$1,200	$1,400	$1,600	$1,800
Var. Exps.	172	344	516	688	860	1,032	1,204	1,376	1,548
Oper. Inc.	28	56	84	112	140	168	196	224	252

μ of Possible Operating Income Values per Equation 7-1: $140
σ of Possible Operating Income Values per Equation 7-2: $53.86
CV of Possible Operating Income Values per Equation 7-3: 38.5%

This table shows the comparison of the standard deviation and coefficient of variation of possible operating income values for Company Calm (top) and Company Bold (bottom) **when all expenses are variable.** *The table indicates Company Bold's operating income is more than twice as volatile as the operating income of Company Calm.*

Table 7-1 shows the expected value (μ), standard deviation (σ), and coefficient of variation (CV) of operating income for Company Calm and Company Bold, assuming that the expenses of both companies vary directly with sales (that is, neither company has any fixed expenses).

The Influence of Sales Volatility   Sales volatility affects business risk—the more volatile a company's sales, the more business risk the firm has. Indeed, when no fixed costs are present—as in the case of Company Calm and Company Bold—sales volatility is equivalent to operating income volatility. Table 7-1 shows that the coefficients of variation of Company Calm's and Company Bold's operating income are 15.5 percent and 38.5 percent, respectively. Note that these coefficient numbers are exactly the same numbers as the two companies' coefficients of variation of expected sales.

The Influence of Fixed Operating Costs   In Table 7-1 we assumed that all of Company Calm's and Company Bold's expenses varied proportionately with sales. We did this to illustrate how sales volatility affects operating income volatility. In the real world, of course, most companies have some fixed expenses as well, such as rent, insurance premiums, and the like. It turns out that fixed expenses magnify the effect of sales volatility on operating income volatility. In effect, fixed expenses intensify business risk. The tendency of fixed expenses to magnify business risk is called **operating leverage.** To see how this works, refer to Table 7-2, in which we assume that all of Company Calm's and Company Bold's expenses are fixed.

As Table 7-2 shows, the effect of replacing each company's variable expenses with fixed expenses increased the volatility of operating income considerably. The coefficient of variation of Company Calm's operating income jumped from 15.7 per-

TABLE 7-2

Expected Value (μ), Standard Deviation (σ), and Coefficient of Variation (CV) of Possible Operating Income Values for Companies Calm and Bold, Assuming All Expenses Are Fixed.

COMPANY CALM

	Probability of Occurrence				
	5%	10%	70%	10%	5%
Sales	$600	$800	$1,000	$1,200	$1,400
Fixed Expenses	860	860	860	860	860
Operating Income	(260)	(60)	140	340	540

μ of Possible Operating Income Values per Equation 7-1: $140
σ of Possible Operating Income Values per Equation 7-2: $155
CV of Possible Operating Income Values per Equation 7-3: 110.7%

COMPANY BOLD

	Probability of Occurrence								
	4%	7%	10%	18%	22%	18%	10%	7%	4%
Sales	$200	$400	$600	$800	$1,000	$1,200	$1,400	$1,600	$1,800
Fixed Exp.	860	860	860	860	860	860	860	860	860
Oper. Inc.	(660)	(460)	(260)	(60)	140	340	540	740	940

μ of Possible Operating Income Values per Equation 7-1: $140
σ of Possible Operating Income Values per Equation 7-2: $385
CV of Possible Operating Income Values per Equation 7-3: 275.0%

Table 7-2 shows the comparison of the standard deviation and coefficient of variation of possible operating income values for Company Calm (top) and Company Bold (bottom) when all expenses are fixed. The table indicates that the volatility of both firms, operating income is increased by the presence of fixed expenses.

cent when all expenses were variable, to over 110 percent when all expenses were fixed. When all expenses are fixed, a 15.7 percent variation in sales is magnified to a 110.7 percent variation in operating income. A similar situation exists for Company Bold.

The greater the fixed expenses, the greater the change in operating income for a given change in sales. Capital-intensive companies, such as electric generating firms, have high fixed expenses. Service companies, such as consulting firms, often have relatively low fixed expenses.

Financial Risk

When companies borrow money, they incur interest charges that appear as fixed expenses on their income statements. (For business loans, the entire amount borrowed normally remains outstanding until the end of the term of the loan. Interest on the unpaid balance, then, is a fixed amount that is paid each year until the loan matures.) Fixed interest charges act on a firm's net income in the same way that fixed operating expenses acted on operating income—they increase volatility. The additional volatility of a firm's net income caused by the fixed interest expense is called **financial risk,** or **financial leverage.**

Measuring Financial Risk   Financial risk is the additional volatility of net income caused by the presence of interest expense. So we measure financial risk by noting the difference between the volatility of net income when there is no interest expense and the volatility of net income when there is interest expense. To measure financial risk, we subtract the coefficient of variation of net income without interest expense from the coefficient of variation of net income with interest expense. The coefficient of variation of net income is the same as the coefficient of variation of operating income when no interest expense is present. Table 7-3 shows the calculation for Company Calm and Company Bold assuming: (1) all variable operating expenses, and (2) $40 in interest expense.

Financial risk, which comes from borrowing money, compounds the effect of business risk and intensifies the volatility of net income. Fixed operating expenses increase the volatility of operating income and magnify business risk. In the same way, fixed financial expenses (such as interest on debt or a noncancellable lease expense) increase the volatility of net income and magnify financial risk.

Take Note

For simplicity, Table 7-3 assumes that neither firm pays any income taxes. Income tax is not a fixed expense, so its presence would not change the volatility of net income.

TABLE 7-3

Expected Value (μ), Standard Deviation (σ), and Coefficient of Variation (CV) of Possible Net Income Values for Companies Calm and Bold

COMPANY CALM

	Probability of Occurrence				
	5%	10%	70%	10%	5%
Sales	$600	$800	$1,000	$1,200	$1,400
Variable Expenses	516	688	860	1,032	1,204
Operating Income	84	112	140	168	196
Interest Expense	40	40	40	40	40
Net Income	44	72	100	128	156

μ of Possible Net Income Values per Equation 7-1: $100
σ of Possible Net Income Values per Equation 7-2: $22
CV of Possible Net Income Values per Equation 7-3: 22.0%

Summary:
CV of Possible Net Income Values When Interest Expense is Present: 22.0%
CV of Operating Income When Interest Expense Is *Not* Present
(from Table 7-1):   15.7%
Difference (financial risk): 6.3%

COMPANY BOLD

	Probability of Occurrence								
	4%	7%	10%	18%	22%	18%	10%	7%	4%
Sales	$200	$400	$600	$800	$1,000	$1,200	$1,400	$1,600	$1,800
Var. Exps.	172	344	516	688	860	1,032	1,204	1,376	1,548
Oper. Inc.	28	56	84	112	140	168	196	224	252
Int. Exp	40	40	40	40	40	40	40	40	40
Net Inc.	(12)	16	44	72	100	128	156	184	212

μ of Possible Net Income Values per Equation 7-1: $100
σ of Possible Net Income Values per Equation 7-2: $54
CV of Possible Net Income Values per Equation 7-3: 54.0%

Summary:
CV of Possible Net Income Values When Interest Expense is Present: 54.0%
CV of Operating Income When Interest Expense Is *Not* Present
(from Table 7-1):   38.6%
Difference (financial risk): 15.4%

*Table 7-3 illustrates the effect of financial risk. Compare the CVs of Possible Net Income Values in this table to those of Operating Income in Table 7-1. Note Company Calm's CV is increased by 6.3 percentage points and Company Bold's CV is increased by 15.4 percentage points as a result of the **presence of fixed interest expense**.*

Firms that have only equity financing have no financial risk because they have no debt on which to make fixed interest payments. Conversely, firms that operate primarily on borrowed money are exposed to a high degree of financial risk.

Portfolio Risk

A **portfolio** is any collection of assets managed as a group. Most large firms employ their assets in a number of different investments. Together, these make up the firm's portfolio of assets. Individual investors also have portfolios containing many different stocks or other investments.

Firms (and individuals for that matter) are interested in portfolio returns and the uncertainty associated with them. Investors want to know how much they can expect to get back from their portfolio compared to how much they invest (the portfolio's expected return) and what the chances are that they won't get that return (the portfolio's risk).

Investors who are dealing with an existing portfolio can usually estimate the expected return, or mean of the probability distribution of possible returns of the portfolio, and its standard deviation and coefficient of variation (as we did earlier in the chapter for the sales forecast distributions of Company Calm and Company Bold). Firms want to know whether adding another asset (or another portfolio) to an existing portfolio will change the overall risk of the firm.[3] To find the riskiness of the new combined portfolio, we must find the expected return and standard deviation of possible returns for the new portfolio. For example, suppose Company Calm merged with Company Bold to form a new firm called Company Cool. We can easily find the expected return of the new Company Cool portfolio, but calculating the standard deviation of the portfolio's possible return is a little more difficult.

For example, suppose the expected returns and standard deviations of possible returns of Company Calm's and Company Bold's asset portfolios are as follows[4]:

	COMPANY CALM	COMPANY BOLD
Expected Return E(R)	10%	12%
Standard Deviation σ	2%	4%

Also assume the new combined Company Cool is made up of 50 percent old Company Calm and 50 percent old Company Bold.

Finding the expected return of the combined Company Cool portfolio is easy. We simply calculate the weighted average expected return, $E(R_p)$ of the two asset portfolio using the following formula:

Expected Rate of Return of a Portfolio, $E(R_p)$,
Comprised of Two Assets, a and b

$$E(R_p) = (w_a \times E(R_a)) + (w_b \times E(R_b)) \quad (7\text{-}4)$$

---

[3]This assumes that management is concerned with firm specific risk and not stockholder risk.
[4]The mean (μ) of the probability distribution of possible returns is the expected value, $E(V)$ of this distribution. Since we are referring to possible returns here, it is the expected return, $E(R)$.

where: $E(R_p)$ = the expected rate of return of the portfolio composed of Asset a
and Asset b
w_a = the weight of Asset a in the portfolio
$E(R_a)$ = the expected rate of return of Asset a
w_b = the weight of Asset b in the portfolio
$E(R_b)$ = the expected rate of return of Asset b

Let's call Company Calm "Asset a" and Company Bold "Asset b." Then, according to Equation 7-4, the expected rate of return of a portfolio containing 50 percent Company Calm and 50 percent Company Bold is:

$$E(R_p) = (.50 \times .10) + (.50 \times .12)$$
$$= (.05 + .06)$$
$$= .11, \text{ or } 11\%$$

Now let's turn to the standard deviation of possible returns of the new combined Company Cool portfolio. Determining the standard deviation of a portfolio requires special procedures. Why? Because gains from one asset in the portfolio may offset losses from another, lessening the overall degree of risk in the portfolio. Figure 7-4 shows how this works.

Figure 7-4 shows that even though the returns of each company vary, the timing of the variations is such that when one company's returns increase, the other's decrease. Therefore the net change in the new combined Company Cool portfolio returns is very small—nearly zero. The weighted average of the standard deviations of returns of the two individual assets, then, does not result in the standard deviation of the portfolio containing both firms. The reduction in the fluctuations of the returns of Company Cool (the combination of Company Bold and Company Calm) is called the **diversification effect.**

Correlation How successfully diversification reduces risk depends on the degree of correlation between the two variables in question. **Correlation** indicates the degree to which one variable is linearly related to another. Correlation is measured by

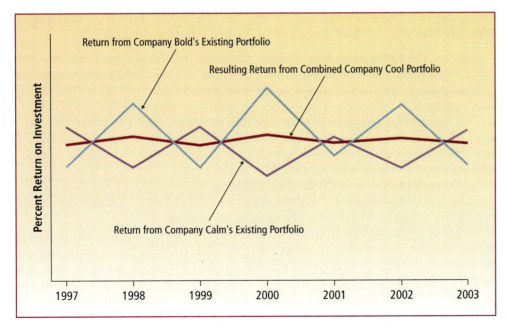

Figure 7-4 **The Variation in Returns Over Time for Company Calm, Company Bold, and the Combined Company Cool**

Figure 7-4 shows how the returns of the portfolios of Companies Calm and Bold might vary over time. Notice that the fluctuations of each curve are such that gains in one almost completely offset losses in the other. The risk of the combined Company Cool portfolio is small due to the offsetting effects.

Source: *DILBERT © 1996 United Feature Syndicate, Inc. Reprinted by Permission.*

the **correlation coefficient,** represented by the letter r. The correlation coefficient can take on values between +1.0 (perfect positive correlation) to −1.0 (perfect negative correlation). If two variables are perfectly positively correlated, it means they move together—that is, they change values proportionately in the same direction at the same time. If two variables are perfectly negatively correlated, it means that every positive change in one value is matched by a proportionate corresponding negative change in the other. In the case of Companies Calm and Bold in Figure 7-4, the assets are negatively correlated.

The closer r is to +1.0, the more the two variables will tend to move with each other at the same time. The closer r is to −1.0, the more the two variables will tend to move opposite each other at the same time. An r value of zero indicates that the variables' values aren't related at all. This is known as *statistical independence.*

In Figure 7-4 Company Calm and Company Bold had perfect negative correlation (r = −1.0). So the risk associated with each asset was nearly eliminated by combining the two assets into one portfolio. The risk would have been completely eliminated had the standard deviations of the two assets been equal.

Calculating the Correlation Coefficient. Determining the precise value of r between two variables can be extremely difficult. The process requires estimating the possible values that each variable could take, and their respective probabilities, simultaneously.

We can make a rough estimate of the degree of correlation between two variables by examining the nature of the assets involved. If one asset is, for instance, a firm's existing portfolio, and the other asset is a replacement piece of equipment, then the correlation between the returns of the two assets is probably close to + 1.0. Why? Because there is no influence that would cause the returns of one asset to vary any differently than those of the other. A Coca-Cola® Bottling company expanding its capacity would be an example of a correlation of about +1.0.

What if a company planned to introduce a completely new product in a new market? In that case we might suspect that the correlation between the returns of the existing portfolio and the new product would be something significantly less than +1.0. Why? Because the cash flows of each asset would be due to different, and probably unrelated, factors. An example would be Disney buying the Anaheim Mighty Ducks National Hockey League team.

> **Take Note**
>
> *Anytime the correlation coefficient of the returns of two assets is less than + 1.0, then the standard deviation of the portfolio consisting of those assets will be less than the weighted average of the individual assets' standard deviations.*

Calculating the Standard Deviation of a Two-Asset Portfolio   To calculate the standard deviation of a portfolio, we must use a special formula that takes the diversification effect into account. Here is the formula for a portfolio containing two assets.[5] For convenience, they are labeled Asset a and Asset b:

Standard Deviation of the Returns of a Two-Asset Portfolio

$$\sigma_p = \sqrt{w_a^2\sigma_a^2 + w_b^2\sigma_b^2 + 2w_aw_br_{a,b}\sigma_a\sigma_b} \qquad (7\text{-}5)$$

where: σ_p = the standard deviation of the returns of the combined portfolio containing Asset a and Asset b
w_a = the weight of Asset a in the two-asset portfolio
σ_a = the standard deviation of the returns of Asset a
w_b = the weight of Asset b in the two-asset portfolio
σ_b = the standard deviation of the returns of Asset b
$r_{a,b}$ = the correlation coefficient of the returns of Asset a and Asset b

The formula may look scary, but don't panic. Once we know the values for each factor, we can solve the formula rather easily with a calculator. Let's use the formula to find the standard deviation of a portfolio composed of equal amounts invested in Company Calm and Company Bold (that is, Company Cool).

To calculate the standard deviation of expected returns of the portfolio of Company Cool, we need to know that Company Cool's portfolio is composed of 50 percent Company Calm assets (w_a = .5) and 50 percent Company Bold Assets (w_b = .5). The standard deviation of Company Calm's expected returns is 2% (σ_a = .02) and the standard deviation of Company Bold's expected returns is 4% (σ_b = .04). To begin, assume the correlation coefficient (r) is −1.0, as shown in Figure 7-4.

Now we're ready to use Equation 7-5 to calculate the standard deviation of Company Cool's returns. For the purpose of the formula, assume Asset a is Company Calm and Asset b is Company Bold:

$$
\begin{aligned}
\sigma_p &= \sqrt{w_a^2\sigma_a^2 + w_b^2\sigma_b^2 + 2w_aw_br_{ab}\sigma_a\sigma_b} \\
&= \sqrt{(.50^2)(0.02^2) + (.50^2)(0.04^2) + (2)(.50)(.50)(-1.0)(.02)(.04)} \\
&= \sqrt{(.25)(.0004) + (.25)(.0016) - .0004} \\
&= \sqrt{.0001 + .0004 - .0004} \\
&= \sqrt{.0001} \\
&= .01, \text{ or } 1\%
\end{aligned}
$$

The diversification effect results in risk reduction. Why? Because we are combining two assets, Companies Calm and Bold, that have returns that are negatively correlated (r = −1.0). The standard deviation of the combined portfolio is much lower than that of either of the two individual companies (1 percent for Company Cool compared to 2 percent for Company Calm and 4 percent for Company Bold).

Nondiversifiable Risk   Unless the returns of one-half the assets in a portfolio are perfectly negatively correlated with the other half—which is extremely unlikely—some risk will remain after assets are combined into a portfolio. The degree of risk

---

[5]You can adapt the formula to calculate the standard deviations of the returns of portfolios containing more than two assets, but doing so is complicated and usually unnecessary. Most of the time, you can view a firm's existing portfolio as one asset and a proposed addition to the portfolio as the second asset.

that remains is **nondiversifiable risk,** the part of a portfolio's total risk that can't be eliminated by diversifying.

Nondiversifiable risk is one of the characteristics of market risk because it is produced by factors that are shared, to a greater or lesser degree, by most assets in the market. These factors might include inflation and real gross domestic product changes. Figure 7-5 illustrates nondiversifiable risk.

In Figure 7-5 we assumed that the portfolio begins with one asset with possible returns having a probability distribution with a standard deviation of 10 percent. However, if the portfolio is divided equally between two assets, each with possible returns having a probability distribution with a standard deviation of 10 percent, and the correlation of the returns of the two assets is, say +.25, then the standard deviation of the returns or the portfolio drops to about 8 percent. If the portfolio is divided among greater numbers of stocks, the standard deviation of the portfolio will continue to fall—as long as the newly added stocks have returns that are less than perfectly positively correlated with those of the existing portfolio.

Note in Figure 7-5, however, that after about twenty assets have been included in the portfolio, adding more has little effect on the portfolio's standard deviation. Almost all the risk that can be eliminated by diversifying is gone. The remainder, about 5 percent in this example, represents the portfolio's nondiversifiable risk.

Measuring Nondiversifiable Risk. Nondiversifiable risk is measured by a term called **beta** (β). The ultimate group of diversified assets, the market, has a beta of 1.0. The betas of portfolios, and individual assets, relate their returns to those of the

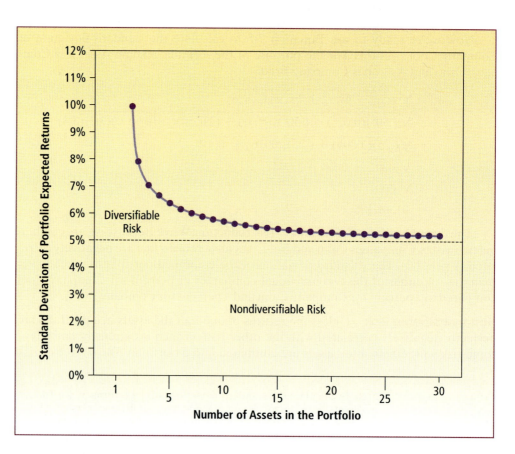

Figure 7-5 **The Relationship between the Number of Assets in a Portfolio and the Riskiness of the Portfolio**

The graph shows that as each new asset is added to a portfolio, the diversification effect causes the standard deviation of the portfolio to decrease. After about twenty assets have been added, however, the effect of adding further assets is slight. The remaining degree of risk is nondiversifiable risk.

overall stock market. Portfolios with betas higher than 1.0 are relatively more risky than the market. Portfolios with betas less than 1.0 are relatively less risky than the market. (Risk-free portfolios have a beta of zero.) The more the return of the portfolio in question fluctuates relative to the return of the overall market, the higher the beta, as shown graphically in Figure 7-6.

Figure 7-6 shows that returns of the overall market fluctuated between about 8 percent and 12 percent during the ten periods that were measured. By definition, the market's beta is 1.0. The returns of the average-risk portfolio fluctuated exactly the same amount, so the beta of the average-risk portfolio is also 1.0. Returns of the low-risk portfolio fluctuated between 6 percent and 8 percent, half as much as the market. So the low-risk portfolio's beta is 0.5, only half that of the market. In contrast, returns of the high-risk portfolio fluctuated between 10 percent and 16 percent, one and a half times as much as the market. As a result, the high-risk portfolio's beta is 1.5, half again as high as the market.

Companies in low-risk stable industries like public utilities will typically have low beta values because returns of their stock tend to be relatively stable. (When the economy goes into a recession, people generally continue to turn on their lights and use their refrigerators; and when the economy is booming, people do not splurge on additional electricity consumption.) Recreational boat companies, on the other hand, tend to have high beta values. That's because demand for recreational boats is volatile. (When times are tough, people postpone the purchase of recreational boats. During good economic times, when people have extra cash in their pockets, sales of these boats take off.)

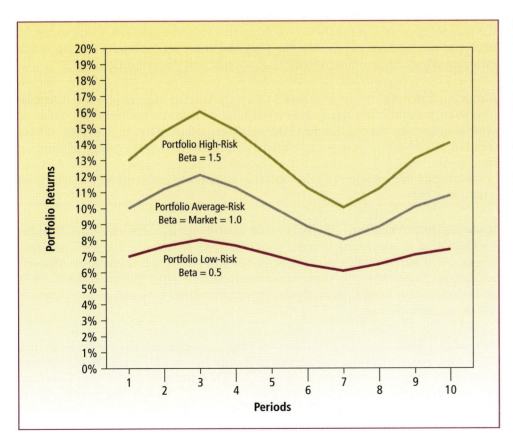

Figure 7-6 **Portfolio Fluctuations and Beta**

The relative fluctuation in returns for portfolios of different betas. The higher the beta, the more the portfolio's returns fluctuate relative to the returns of the overall market. The market itself has a beta of 1.0.

DEALING WITH RISK

Once companies determine the degree of risk present, what do they do about it? Suppose, for example, Ford evaluated the riskiness of the Ford 2000 plan (discussed at the beginning of this chapter) and found that if the project were adopted, the standard deviation of possible returns of the firm's portfolio of assets would double. So what? How should a firm deal with the situation?

There are two broad classes of alternatives for dealing with risk. First, you might take some action to reduce the degree of risk present in the situation. Second (if the degree of risk can't be reduced), you may compensate for the degree of risk you are about to assume. We'll discuss these two classes of alternatives in the following sections.

Risk-Reduction Methods

One way companies can avoid risk, is simply to avoid risky situations entirely. The Ford Motor Company, for instance, could simply reject Ford 2000 and thereby avoid the project's risk.

Most of the time, however, refusing to get involved is an unsatisfactory business decision. Carried to its logical conclusion, this would mean that everyone would invest in risk-free assets only, and no products or services would be produced. Bill Gates, founder and CEO of Microsoft, didn't get rich by avoiding risks. To succeed, businesses must take risks.

If we assume that firms (and individuals) are willing to take some risk to achieve the higher expected returns that accompany that risk, then the task is to reduce the degree of risk as much as possible. The following three methods help to reduce risk: reducing sales volatility and fixed costs, insurance, and diversification.

Reducing Sales Volatility and Fixed Costs   Earlier in the chapter, we discussed how sales volatility and fixed costs contribute to a firm's business risk. Firms in volatile industries whose sales fluctuate widely are exposed to a high degree of business risk. That business risk is intensified even further if they have large amounts of fixed costs.

Reducing the volatility of sales, and the amount of fixed costs a firm pays, then, will reduce risk.

Reducing Sales Volatility.   If a firm could smooth out its sales over time, then the fluctuation of its operating income (business risk) would also be reduced. Businesses try to stabilize sales in many ways. For example, retail ski equipment stores sell tennis equipment in the summer, summer vacation resorts offer winter specials, and movie theaters offer reduced prices for early shows to encourage more patronage during slow periods.

Insurance   Insurance is a time-honored way to spread risk among many participants and thus reduce the degree of risk borne by any one participant. Business firms insure themselves against many risks, such as flood, fire, and liability. However, one important risk—the risk that an investment might fail—is uninsurable. To reduce the risk of losing everything in one investment, firms turn to another risk-reduction technique, diversification.

Diversification   Review Figure 7-4 and the discussion following the figure. We showed in that discussion how the standard deviation of returns of Company Calm (2 percent) and Company Bold (4 percent) could be reduced to 1 percent by combining the two firms into one portfolio. The diversification effect occurred because the returns of the two firms were not perfectly positively correlated. Any time firms invest in ventures whose returns are not perfectly positively correlated with the returns of their existing portfolios, they will experience diversification benefits.

Compensating for the Presence of Risk

In most cases it's not possible to avoid risk completely. Some risk usually remains even after firms use risk-reduction techniques. When firms assume risk to achieve an objective, they also take measures to receive compensation for assuming that risk. In the sections that follow, we discuss these compensation measures.

Adjusting the Required Rate of Return   Most owners and financial managers are generally risk averse. So for a given expected rate of return, less risky investment projects are more desirable than more risky investment projects. The higher the expected rate of return, the more desirable the risky venture will appear. As we noted earlier in the chapter, the risk–return relationship is positive. That is, because of risk aversion, people demand a higher rate of return for taking on a higher-risk project.

Although we know that the risk–return relationship is positive, an especially difficult question remains: How much return is appropriate for a given degree of risk? Say, for example, that a firm has all assets invested in a chain of convenience stores

Take Note

*Diversification is a hotly debated issue among financial theorists. Specifically, theorists question whether a firm provides value to its stockholders if it diversifies its asset portfolio to stabilize the firm's income. Many claim that individual stockholders can achieve diversification benefits more easily and cheaply than a firm, so firms that diversify actually do a **disservice** to their stockholders. What do you think?*

Take Note

In capital budgeting a rate of return to reflect risk is called a risk-adjusted discount rate. See chapter 10.

FINANCIAL MANAGEMENT AND YOU

Mutual Funds and Risk

Most people don't put all their eggs in one basket. Instead, they diversify to protect against risk.

Many investors achieve diversification benefits by buying shares in mutual funds. Mutual funds are companies that invest money on behalf of shareholders in many different securities. Mutual fund investors, therefore, achieve instant diversification with very little effort. Investing in too many funds, however, may lead to superfluous diversification.

To investigate the risks of a mutual fund, consider the following tips:

1. *Determine what type of fund it is.* Is the fund a growth, income, or growth and income fund? A growth fund will be more volatile, whereas a growth and income less so. An income fund will

have steady income from dividends or bond interest to cushion the fund should stock prices fall. The type of fund you select often depends on your risk tolerance and how long you plan to invest your money.

2. *Learn whether the fund specializes.* If the fund invests in one industry only, you may want to invest in several funds to diversify or avoid that fund altogether.

3. *Check risk-rating services.* Mutual fund rating services—such as Morningstar Inc. of Chicago, Illinois—rate mutual funds according to risk. Mutual fund ratings are available in print or on-line.

Source: Timothy Middleton, "Trouble Ahead? Seven Funds Take Few Chances in the Long Run," *The New York Times* (November 12, 1995): F5.

that provides a stable return on investment of about 6 percent a year. How much more return should the firm require for investing some assets in a baseball team that may not provide steady returns[6]—8 percent? 10 percent? 25 percent? Unfortunately, no one knows for sure, but financial experts have researched the subject extensively.

One well-known model used to calculate the required rate of return of an investment is the **Capital Asset Pricing Model (CAPM).** We discuss CAPM next.

Relating Return and Risk: The Capital Asset Pricing Model

Financial theorists William F. Sharpe, John Lintner, and Jan Mossin worked on the risk–return relationship and developed the Capital Asset Pricing Model, or CAPM. We can use this model to calculate the appropriate required rate of return for an investment project given its degree of risk as measured by beta (β).[7] The formula for CAPM is presented in Equation 7-6.

CAPM Formula

$$k_p = k_{RF} + (k_M - k_{RF}) \times \beta \tag{7-6}$$

where: k_p = the required rate of return appropriate for the investment project
k_{RF} = the risk free rate of return
k_M = the required rate of return on the overall market
β = the project's beta

The three components of the CAPM include the risk-free rate of return (k_{RF}), the market risk premium ($k_M - k_{RF}$), and the project's beta (β). The **risk-free rate of return (k_{RF})** is the rate of return that investors demand from a project that contains no risk. Risk-averse managers and owners will always demand at least this rate of return from any investment project.

The required rate of return on the overall market minus the risk-free rate ($k_M - k_{RF}$) represents the additional return demanded by investors for taking on the risk of investing in the market itself. The term is sometimes called the **market risk premium.** In the CAPM, the term for the market risk premium, ($k_M - k_{RF}$), can be viewed as the additional return over the risk-free rate that investors demand from an "average stock" or an "average-risk" investment project. The S & P 500 stock market index is often used as a proxy for the market.

As discussed earlier, a project's beta (β) represents a project's degree of risk relative to the overall stock market. In the CAPM, when the beta term is multiplied by the market risk premium term, ($k_M - k_{RF}$), the result is the additional return over the risk-free rate that investors demand from that individual project. Beta is the relevant risk measure according to the CAPM. High-risk (high-beta) projects have high required rates of return, and low-risk (low-beta) projects have low required rates of return.

Table 7-4 shows three examples of how the CAPM is used to determine the appropriate required rate of return for projects of different degrees of risk.

As we can see in Table 7-4, Project High-Risk, with its beta of 1.5, has a required rate of return that is twice that of Project Low-Risk, with its beta of 0.5. After all,

---

[6]Some major league baseball teams are losing money and others make a great deal. Television revenues differ greatly from team to team, as do ticket sales and salary expenses.
[7]See William Sharpe, "Capital Asset Prices: A Theory of Market Equilibrium," *Journal of Finance* (September 1964); John Lintner, "The Valuation of Risk Assets and the Selection of Risky Investments in Stock Portfolios and Capital Budgets," *Review of Economics and Statistics* (February 1965); and Jan Mossin, "Equilibrium in a Capital Asset Market," *Econometrica* (October 1966).

TABLE 7-4

**Using the CAPM to
Calculate Required Rates
of Return for Investment
Projects**

Given:

The risk-free rate, k_{RF} = 4%
The required rate of return on the market, k_M = 12%

Project Low-Risk's beta = 0.5
Project Average-Risk's beta = 1.0
Project High-Risk's beta = 1.5

Required rates of return on the project's per the CAPM:

$$\text{Project Low-Risk:} \quad k_p = .04 + (.12 - .04) \times 0.5$$
$$= .04 + .04$$
$$= .08, \text{or } 8\%$$

$$\text{Project Average-Risk:} \quad k_p = .04 + (.12 - .04) \times 1.0$$
$$= .04 + .08$$
$$= .12, \text{or } 12\%$$

$$\text{Project High-Risk:} \quad k_p = .04 + (.12 - .04) \times 1.5$$
$$= .04 + .12$$
$$= .16, \text{or } 16\%$$

Given that the risk-free rate of return is 4 percent and the required rate of return on the market is 12 percent, the CAPM indicates the appropriate required rate of return for a low-risk investment project with a beta of .5 is 8 percent. The appropriate required rate of return for an average-risk project is the same as that for the market, 12 percent, and the appropriate rate for a high-risk project with a beta of 1.5 is 16 percent.

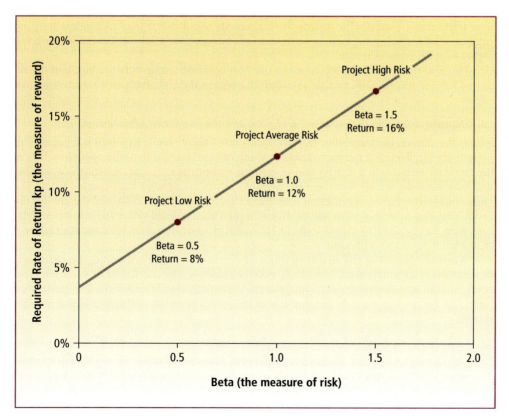

Figure 7-7 **CAPM and the
Risk–Return Relationship**

*This graph illustrates
the increasing return
required for increasing
risk as indicated by the
CAPM beta. This graphi-
cal depiction of the
risk/return relationship
according to the CAPM
is called the "security
market line (SML)."*

shouldn't we ask for a higher rate of return if the risk is higher? Note also that Project Average-Risk, which has the same beta as the market, 1.0, also has the same required rate of return as the market (12 percent). The risk–return relationship for these three projects is shown in Figure 7-7 (page 157).

Remember that the beta term in the CAPM reflects only the nondiversifiable risk of an asset, not its diversifiable risk. Diversifiable risk is irrelevant because the diversity of each investor's portfolio essentially eliminates (or should eliminate) that risk. (After all, most investors are well-diversified. They will not demand extra return for adding a security to their portfolios that contains diversifiable risk.) The return that well-diversified investors demand when they buy a security, as measured by the CAPM and beta, relates to the degree of nondiversifiable risk in the security.

What's Next

In this chapter we examined the risk–return relationship, types of risk, risk measurements, risk-reduction techniques, and the CAPM. In the next chapter, we will discuss the importance of, and how to adjust for the time value of money.

Summary

1. Define risk, risk aversion, and the risk/return relationship.

In everything you do, or don't do, there is a chance that something will happen that you didn't count on. Risk is the potential for unexpected events to occur.

Given two financial alternatives that are equal except for their degree of risk, most people will choose the less risky alternative because they are risk averse. Risk aversion is a common trait among almost all investors. Most investors avoid risk if they can, unless they are compensated for accepting risk. In an investment context, the additional compensation is a higher expected rate of return.

The risk–return relationship refers to the positive relationship between risk and the required rate of return. Due to risk aversion, the higher the risk, the more return investors expect.

2. Measure risk using the standard deviation and the coefficient of variation.

Risk is the chance, or probability, that outcomes other than what is expected will occur. This probability is reflected in the narrowness or width of the distribution of the possible values of the financial variable. In a distribution of variable values, the standard deviation is a number that indicates how widely dispersed the possible values are around the expected value. The more widely dispersed a distribution is, the larger the standard deviation, and the greater the probability that an actual value will be different than the expected value. The standard deviation, then, can be used to measure the likelihood that some outcome, substantially different than what is expected, will occur.

When the degree of risk in distributions of different sizes are compared, the coefficient of variation is a statistic used to measure *relative* riskiness. The coefficient of variation measures the standard deviation's percentage of the expected value. It relates the standard deviation to its mean to give a risk measure that is independent of the magnitude of the possible returns.

3. Identify the types of risk that business firms encounter.

Business risk is the risk that a company's operating income will differ from what is expected. The more volatile a company's operating income, the more business risk the firm contains. Business risk is a result of sales volatility, which translates into operating income volatility.

Business risk is increased by the presence of fixed costs, which magnify the effect on operating income of changes in sales.

Financial risk occurs when companies borrow money and incur interest charges that show up as fixed expenses on their income statements. Fixed interest charges act on a firm's net income the same way fixed operating expenses acted on operating income—they increase volatility. The additional volatility of a firm's net income caused by the presence of fixed interest expense is called financial risk.

Portfolio risk is the chance that investors won't get the return they expect from a portfolio. Portfolio risk can be measured by the standard deviation of possible returns of a portfolio. It is affected by the correlation of returns of the assets making up the portfolio. The less correlated these returns are, the more gains on some assets offset losses on others, resulting in a reduction of the portfolio's risk. This phenomenon is known as the *diversification effect*. Nondiversifiable risk is risk that remains in a portfolio after all diversification benefits have been achieved. Nondiversifiable risk is measured by a term called beta (β). The market has a beta of 1.0. Portfolios with betas greater than 1.0 contain more nondiversifiable risk than the market, and portfolios with betas less than 1.0 contain less nondiversifiable risk than the market.

4. Explain methods of risk reduction.

Firms can reduce the degree of risk by taking steps to reduce the volatility of sales or their fixed costs. Firms also obtain insurance policies to protect against many risks, and diversify their asset portfolios to reduce the risk of income loss.

5. Describe how firms compensate for assuming risk.

Firms almost always demand a higher rate of return to compensate for assuming risk. The more risky a project, the higher the return firms demand.

6. Explain how the Capital Asset Pricing Model (CAPM) relates risk and return.

When investors adjust their required rates of return to compensate for risk, the question arises as to how much return is appropriate for a given degree of risk. The Capital Asset Pricing Model (CAPM) is a model that measures the required rate of return for an investment or project, given its degree of nondiversifiable risk as measured by beta (β).

Equations Introduced in This Chapter

Equation 7-1. The Expected Value, or Mean (μ) of a Probability Distribution:

$$\mu = \Sigma\,(V \times P)$$

where: μ = the expected value, or mean
  V = the possible value for some variable
  P = the probability of the value V occurring

Equation 7-2. The Standard Deviation:

$$\sigma = \sqrt{\Sigma\,P(V - \mu)^2}$$

where: σ = the standard deviation
  V = the value the variable can take
  P = the probability of the value V occurring
  μ = the expected value

Equation 7-3. The Coefficient of Variation of a Probability Distribution:

$$\text{Coefficient of Variation} = \frac{\text{Standard Deviation}}{\text{Mean}}$$

Equation 7-4. The Expected Rate of Return, $E(R_p)$, Comprised of Two Assets, a and b:

$$E(R_p) = (w_a \times E(R_a)) + (w_b \times E(R_b))$$

where: w_a = the weight, or percentage of the new combined portfolio invested in Asset a
$E(R_a)$ = the expected return of Asset a
w_b = the weight, or percentage of the new combined portfolio invested in Asset b
$E(R_b)$ = the expected return of Asset b

Equation 7-5. The Standard Deviation of a Two-Asset Portfolio:

$$\sigma_p = \sqrt{w_a^2 \sigma_a^2 + w_b^2 \sigma_b^2 + 2w_a w_b r_{a,b} \sigma_a \sigma_b}$$

where: σ_p = the standard deviation of the combined portfolio containing Assets a and b
w_a = the weight of Asset a in the portfolio
σ_a = the standard deviation of the returns of Asset a
$r_{a,b}$ = the correlation coefficient of the cash flows of Asset a and Asset b
w_b = the weight of Asset b in the portfolio
σ_b = the standard deviation of the returns of Asset b

Equation 7-6. The Capital Asset Pricing Model (CAPM):

$$k_p = k_{RF} + (k_M - k_{RF}) \times \beta$$

where: k_p = the required rate of return appropriate for the investment project
k_{RF} = the risk free rate of return
k_M = the required rate of return on the overall market
β = the project's Beta

Self-Test

ST-1. For Bryan Corporation, the mean of the distribution of next year's possible sales is $5 million. The standard deviation of this distribution is $400,000. Calculate the coefficient of variation (CV) for this distribution of possible sales.

ST-2. Investors in Hoeven Industries common stock have a .2 probability of earning a return of 4 percent, a .6 probability of earning a return of 10 percent, and a .2 probability of earning a return of 20 percent. What is the mean of this probability distribution (the expected rate of return)?

ST-3. What is the standard deviation for the Hoeven Industries common stock return probability distribution described in ST-2?

ST-4. The standard deviation of the possible returns of Boris Company common stock is .08, while the standard deviation of possible returns of Natasha Company common stock is .12. Calculate the standard deviation of a portfolio comprised of 40 percent Boris Company stock and 60 percent Natasha Company stock. The correlation coefficient of the returns of Boris Company stock relative to the returns of Natasha Company stock is −.2.

ST-5. The mean of the normal probability distribution of possible returns of Gidney and Cloyd Corporation common stock is 18 percent. The standard deviation is 3 percent. What is the range of possible values that you would be 95 percent sure would capture the return that will actually be earned on this stock?

ST-6. Dobie's Bagle Corporation common stock has a beta of 1.2. The market risk premium is 6 percent and the risk free rate is 4 percent. What is the required rate of return on this stock according to the CAPM?

ST-7. Using the information provided in ST-6, what is the required rate of return on the common stock of Zack's Salt Corporation. This stock has a beta of .4.

ST-8. A portfolio of three stocks has an expected value of 14 percent. Stock A has an expected return of 6 percent and a weight of .25 in the portfolio. Stock B has an expected return of 10 percent and a weight of .5 in the portfolio. Stock C is the third stock in this portfolio. What is the expected rate of return of Stock C?

Review Questions

1. What is risk aversion? If common stockholders are risk averse, how do you explain the fact that they often invest in very risky companies?
2. Explain the risk–return relationship.
3. Why is the coefficient of variation often a better risk measure when comparing different projects than the standard deviation?
4. What is the difference between business risk and financial risk?
5. Why does the riskiness of portfolios have to be looked at differently than the riskiness of individual assets?
6. What happens to the riskiness of a portfolio if assets with very low correlations (even negative correlations) are combined?
7. What does it mean when we say that the correlation coefficient for two variables is −1? What does it mean if this value were zero? What does it mean if it were +1?
8. What is nondiversifiable risk? How is it measured?
9. Compare diversifiable and nondiversifiable risk. Which do you think is more important to financial managers in business firms?
10. How do risk-averse investors compensate for risk when they take on investment projects?
11. Given that risk-averse investors demand more return for taking on more risk when they invest, how much more return is appropriate for, say, a share of common stock, than is appropriate for a Treasury bill?
12. Discuss risk from the perspective of the Capital Asset Pricing Model (CAPM).

Build Your Communication Skills

CS-1. Go to the library, use business magazines, computer databases, the Internet, or other sources that have financial information about businesses. (See chapter 5 for a list of specific resources.) Find three companies and compare their approaches to risk. Do the firms take a conservative or aggressive approach? Write a one- to two-page report, citing specific evidence of the risk-taking approach of each of the three companies you researched.

CS-2. Research three to five specific mutual funds. Then form small groups of four to six. Discuss whether the mutual funds each group member researched will help investors diversify the risk of their portfolio. Are some mutual funds better than others for an investor seeking good diversification? Prepare a list of mutual funds the group would select to diversify its risk and explain your choices. Present your recommendations to the class.

Problems

7-1. Manager Paul Smith believes an investment project will have the following yearly cash flows with the associated probabilities throughout its life of five years. Calculate the standard deviation and coefficient of variation of the cash flows.

Standard Deviation and Coefficient of Variation

Cash Flows($)	Probability of Occurrence
$10,000	0.05
13,000	0.10
16,000	0.20
19,000	0.30
22,000	0.20
25,000	0.10
28,000	0.05

Measuring Risk

7-2. Milk-U, an agricultural consulting firm, has developed the following income statement forecast:

Milk-U Income Forecast (in 000's)

	Probability of Occurrence				
	2%	8%	80%	8%	2%
Sales	$500	$700	$1,200	$1,700	$1,900
Variable Expenses	250	350	600	850	950
Fixed Op. Expenses	250	250	250	250	250
Operating Income	0	100	350	600	700

a. Calculate the expected value of Milk-U's operating income.
b. Calculate the standard deviation of Milk-U's operating income.
c. Calculate the coefficient of variation of Milk-U's operating income.
d. Recalculate the expected value, standard deviation, and coefficient of variation of Milk-U's operating income if the company's sales forecast changed as follows:

	Probability of Occurrence				
	10%	15%	50%	15%	10%
Sales	$500	$700	$1,200	$1,700	$1,900

e. Comment on how Milk-U's degree of business risk changed as a result of the new sales forecast in d) above.

Measuring Risk

7-3. As a new loan officer in the Bulwark Bank, you are comparing the financial riskiness of two firms. Selected information from *proforma* statements for each firm follows.

Equity Eddie's Company
Net Income Forecast (in 000's)

	Probability of Occurrence				
	5%	10%	70%	10%	5%
Operating Income	$100	$200	$400	$600	$700
Interest Expense	0	0	0	0	0
Before-Tax Income	100	200	400	600	700
Taxes (28%)	28	56	112	168	196
Net Income	72	144	388	432	504

ST-7. Using the information provided in ST-6, what is the required rate of return on the common stock of Zack's Salt Corporation. This stock has a beta of .4.

ST-8. A portfolio of three stocks has an expected value of 14 percent. Stock A has an expected return of 6 percent and a weight of .25 in the portfolio. Stock B has an expected return of 10 percent and a weight of .5 in the portfolio. Stock C is the third stock in this portfolio. What is the expected rate of return of Stock C?

Review Questions

1. What is risk aversion? If common stockholders are risk averse, how do you explain the fact that they often invest in very risky companies?
2. Explain the risk–return relationship.
3. Why is the coefficient of variation often a better risk measure when comparing different projects than the standard deviation?
4. What is the difference between business risk and financial risk?
5. Why does the riskiness of portfolios have to be looked at differently than the riskiness of individual assets?
6. What happens to the riskiness of a portfolio if assets with very low correlations (even negative correlations) are combined?
7. What does it mean when we say that the correlation coefficient for two variables is −1? What does it mean if this value were zero? What does it mean if it were +1?
8. What is nondiversifiable risk? How is it measured?
9. Compare diversifiable and nondiversifiable risk. Which do you think is more important to financial managers in business firms?
10. How do risk-averse investors compensate for risk when they take on investment projects?
11. Given that risk-averse investors demand more return for taking on more risk when they invest, how much more return is appropriate for, say, a share of common stock, than is appropriate for a Treasury bill?
12. Discuss risk from the perspective of the Capital Asset Pricing Model (CAPM).

Build Your Communication Skills

CS-1. Go to the library, use business magazines, computer databases, the Internet, or other sources that have financial information about businesses. (See chapter 5 for a list of specific resources.) Find three companies and compare their approaches to risk. Do the firms take a conservative or aggressive approach? Write a one- to two-page report, citing specific evidence of the risk-taking approach of each of the three companies you researched.

CS-2. Research three to five specific mutual funds. Then form small groups of four to six. Discuss whether the mutual funds each group member researched will help investors diversify the risk of their portfolio. Are some mutual funds better than others for an investor seeking good diversification? Prepare a list of mutual funds the group would select to diversify its risk and explain your choices. Present your recommendations to the class.

Problems

7-1. Manager Paul Smith believes an investment project will have the following yearly cash flows with the associated probabilities throughout its life of five years. Calculate the standard deviation and coefficient of variation of the cash flows.

Standard Deviation and Coefficient of Variation

Cash Flows($)	Probability of Occurrence
$10,000	0.05
13,000	0.10
16,000	0.20
19,000	0.30
22,000	0.20
25,000	0.10
28,000	0.05

Measuring Risk

7-2. Milk-U, an agricultural consulting firm, has developed the following income statement forecast:

Milk-U Income Forecast (in 000's)

	Probability of Occurrence				
	2%	8%	80%	8%	2%
Sales	$500	$700	$1,200	$1,700	$1,900
Variable Expenses	250	350	600	850	950
Fixed Op. Expenses	250	250	250	250	250
Operating Income	0	100	350	600	700

a. Calculate the expected value of Milk-U's operating income.
b. Calculate the standard deviation of Milk-U's operating income.
c. Calculate the coefficient of variation of Milk-U's operating income.
d. Recalculate the expected value, standard deviation, and coefficient of variation of Milk-U's operating income if the company's sales forecast changed as follows:

	Probability of Occurrence				
	10%	15%	50%	15%	10%
Sales	$500	$700	$1,200	$1,700	$1,900

e. Comment on how Milk-U's degree of business risk changed as a result of the new sales forecast in d) above.

Measuring Risk

7-3. As a new loan officer in the Bulwark Bank, you are comparing the financial riskiness of two firms. Selected information from *proforma* statements for each firm follows.

Equity Eddie's Company
Net Income Forecast (in 000's)

	Probability of Occurrence				
	5%	10%	70%	10%	5%
Operating Income	$100	$200	$400	$600	$700
Interest Expense	0	0	0	0	0
Before-Tax Income	100	200	400	600	700
Taxes (28%)	28	56	112	168	196
Net Income	72	144	388	432	504

ST-7. Using the information provided in ST-6, what is the required rate of return on the common stock of Zack's Salt Corporation. This stock has a beta of .4.

ST-8. A portfolio of three stocks has an expected value of 14 percent. Stock A has an expected return of 6 percent and a weight of .25 in the portfolio. Stock B has an expected return of 10 percent and a weight of .5 in the portfolio. Stock C is the third stock in this portfolio. What is the expected rate of return of Stock C?

Review Questions

1. What is risk aversion? If common stockholders are risk averse, how do you explain the fact that they often invest in very risky companies?
2. Explain the risk–return relationship.
3. Why is the coefficient of variation often a better risk measure when comparing different projects than the standard deviation?
4. What is the difference between business risk and financial risk?
5. Why does the riskiness of portfolios have to be looked at differently than the riskiness of individual assets?
6. What happens to the riskiness of a portfolio if assets with very low correlations (even negative correlations) are combined?
7. What does it mean when we say that the correlation coefficient for two variables is −1? What does it mean if this value were zero? What does it mean if it were +1?
8. What is nondiversifiable risk? How is it measured?
9. Compare diversifiable and nondiversifiable risk. Which do you think is more important to financial managers in business firms?
10. How do risk-averse investors compensate for risk when they take on investment projects?
11. Given that risk-averse investors demand more return for taking on more risk when they invest, how much more return is appropriate for, say, a share of common stock, than is appropriate for a Treasury bill?
12. Discuss risk from the perspective of the Capital Asset Pricing Model (CAPM).

Build Your Communication Skills

CS-1. Go to the library, use business magazines, computer databases, the Internet, or other sources that have financial information about businesses. (See chapter 5 for a list of specific resources.) Find three companies and compare their approaches to risk. Do the firms take a conservative or aggressive approach? Write a one- to two-page report, citing specific evidence of the risk-taking approach of each of the three companies you researched.

CS-2. Research three to five specific mutual funds. Then form small groups of four to six. Discuss whether the mutual funds each group member researched will help investors diversify the risk of their portfolio. Are some mutual funds better than others for an investor seeking good diversification? Prepare a list of mutual funds the group would select to diversify its risk and explain your choices. Present your recommendations to the class.

Problems

7-1. Manager Paul Smith believes an investment project will have the following yearly cash flows with the associated probabilities throughout its life of five years. Calculate the standard deviation and coefficient of variation of the cash flows.

Standard Deviation and Coefficient of Variation

Cash Flows($)	Probability of Occurrence
$10,000	0.05
13,000	0.10
16,000	0.20
19,000	0.30
22,000	0.20
25,000	0.10
28,000	0.05

Measuring Risk

7-2. Milk-U, an agricultural consulting firm, has developed the following income statement forecast:

Milk-U Income Forecast (in 000's)

	Probability of Occurrence				
	2%	8%	80%	8%	2%
Sales	$500	$700	$1,200	$1,700	$1,900
Variable Expenses	250	350	600	850	950
Fixed Op. Expenses	250	250	250	250	250
Operating Income	0	100	350	600	700

a. Calculate the expected value of Milk-U's operating income.
b. Calculate the standard deviation of Milk-U's operating income.
c. Calculate the coefficient of variation of Milk-U's operating income.
d. Recalculate the expected value, standard deviation, and coefficient of variation of Milk-U's operating income if the company's sales forecast changed as follows:

	Probability of Occurrence				
	10%	15%	50%	15%	10%
Sales	$500	$700	$1,200	$1,700	$1,900

e. Comment on how Milk-U's degree of business risk changed as a result of the new sales forecast in d) above.

Measuring Risk

7-3. As a new loan officer in the Bulwark Bank, you are comparing the financial riskiness of two firms. Selected information from *proforma* statements for each firm follows.

Equity Eddie's Company
Net Income Forecast (in 000's)

	Probability of Occurrence				
	5%	10%	70%	10%	5%
Operating Income	$100	$200	$400	$600	$700
Interest Expense	0	0	0	0	0
Before-Tax Income	100	200	400	600	700
Taxes (28%)	28	56	112	168	196
Net Income	72	144	388	432	504

Barry Borrower's Company
Net Income Forecast (in 000's)

	Probability of Occurrence				
	5%	10%	70%	10%	5%
Operating Income	$110	$220	$440	$660	$770
Interest Expense	40	40	40	40	40
Before-Tax Income	70	180	400	620	730
Taxes (28%)	19.6	50.4	112	173.6	204.4
Net Income	50.4	129.6	288	446.4	525.6

a. Calculate the expected value of Equity Eddie's and Barry Borrower's net income.
b. Calculate the standard deviation of Equity Eddie's and Barry Borrower's net income.
c. Calculate the coefficient of variation of Equity Eddie's and Barry Borrower's net income.
d. Compare Equity Eddie's and Barry Borrower's degree of financial risk.

7-4. George Taylor, owner of a toy manufacturing company, is considering the addition of a new product line. Marketing research shows that gorilla action figures will be the next fad for the six- to ten-year-old age group. This new product line of gorilla-like action figures and their high-tech vehicles will be called Go-Rilla. George estimates that the most likely yearly incremental cash flow will be $26,000. There is some uncertainty about this value because George's company has never before made a product similar to the Go-Rilla. He has estimated the potential cash flows for the new product line along with their associated probabilities of occurrence. His estimates follow.

Standard Deviation and Coefficient of Variation

Go-Rilla Project

Cash Flows	Probability of Occurrence
$20,000	1%
$22,000	12%
$24,000	23%
$26,000	28%
$28,000	23%
$30,000	12%
$32,000	1%

a. Calculate the standard deviation of the estimated cash flows.
b. Calculate the coefficient of variation.
c. If George's other product lines have an average coefficient of variation of 12%, what can you say about the risk of the Go-Rilla Project relative to the average risk of the other product lines?

7-5. Assume that a company has an existing portfolio A with an expected return of 9 percent and a standard deviation of 3 percent. The company is considering adding an asset B to its portfolio. Asset B's expected return is 12 percent with a standard deviation of 4 percent. Also assume that the amount invested in A is $700,000 and the amount to be invested in B is $200,000. If the degree of correlation between returns from portfolio A and project B is zero, calculate:

Portfolio Risk

a. the standard deviation of the new combined portfolio and compare it with that of the existing portfolio.
b. the coefficient of variation of the new combined portfolio and compare it with that of the existing portfolio.

	Challenge Problem

Challenge Problem

7-6. A firm has an existing portfolio of projects with an expected return of 11 percent a year. The standard deviation of these returns is 4 percent. The existing portfolio's value is $820,000. As financial manager, you are considering the addition of a new project, PROJ1. PROJ1's expected return is 13 percent with a standard deviation of 5 percent. The initial cash outlay for PROJ1 is expected to be $194,000.

    a. Calculate the coefficient of variation for the existing portfolio.
    b. Calculate the coefficient of variation for PROJ1.
    c. If PROJ1 is added to the existing portfolio, calculate the weight (proportion) of the existing portfolio in the combined portfolio.
    d. Calculate the weight (proportion) of PROJ1 in the combined portfolio.
    e. Assume the correlation coefficient of the cash flows of the existing portfolio and PROJ1 is zero. Calculate the standard deviation of the combined portfolio. Is the standard deviation of the combined portfolio higher or lower than the standard deviation of the existing portfolio?
    f. Calculate the coefficient of variation of the combined portfolio.
    g. If PROJ1 is added to the existing portfolio, will the firm's risk increase or decrease?

CAPM

7-7. Assume the risk-free rate is 5 percent, the expected rate of return on the market is 15%, and the beta of your firm is 1.2. Given these conditions, what is the required rate of return on your company's stock per the Capital Asset Pricing Model?

Challenge Problem

7-8. Your firm has a beta of 1.5 and you are considering an investment project with a beta of 0.8. Answer the following questions assuming that short-term Treasury bills are currently yielding 5 percent and the expected return on the market is 15 percent.

    a. What is the appropriate required rate of return for your company per the Capital Asset Pricing Model?
    b. What is the appropriate required rate of return for the investment project per the Capital Asset Pricing Model?
    c. If your firm invests 20 percent of it's assets in the new investment project what will be the beta of your firm after the project is adopted? (Hint: compute the weighted average beta of the firm with the new asset using Equation 7-4).

The following problems (7-9 to 7-13) relate to the expected business of Power Software Company (PSC) in the year 1998 (000's of dollars):

Power Software Company Forecasts

	Probability of Occurrence						
	2%	8%	20%	40%	20%	8%	2%
Sales	$800	$1000	$1,400	$2,000	$2,600	$3000	$3200

Measuring Risk

7-9. Calculate the expected value, standard deviation, and coefficient of variation of sales revenue of PSC.

Business Risk

7-10. Assume that PSC has no fixed expense but has a variable expense which is 60 percent of sales as follows:

Power Software Company Forecasts

	Probability of Occurrence						
	2%	8%	20%	40%	20%	8%	2%
Sales	$800	$1,000	$1,400	$2,000	$2,600	$3,000	$3,200
Variable Expense	480	600	840	1,200	1,560	1,800	1,920

Calculate PSC's business risk (coefficient of variation of operating income).

7-11. Now assume that PSC has a fixed operating expense of $400,000, in addition to the variable expense of 60 percent of sales, shown as follows:

Business Risk

Power Software Company Forecasts

				Probability of Occurrence			
	2%	8%	20%	40%	20%	8%	2%
Sales	$800	$1000	$1,400	$2,000	$2,600	$3000	$3200
Variable Expense	480	600	840	1,200	1560	1800	1920
Fixed Op. Expense	400	400	400	400	400	400	400

Recalculate PSC's business risk (coefficient of variation of operating income). How does this figure compare with the business risk calculated with variable cost only?

7-12. Assume that PSC has a fixed interest expense of $60,000 on borrowed funds. Also assume that the applicable tax rate is 30 percent. What is the expected value, standard deviation and coefficient of variation of PSC's net income? What is PSC's financial risk?

Various Statistics and Financial Risk

7-13. To reduce the various risks, PSC is planning to take suitable steps to reduce volatility of operating and net income. It has projected that fixed expenses and interest expenses can be reduced. The revised figures follow:

Business and Financial Risk

Power Software Company Forecasts

				Probability of Occurrence			
	1%	6%	13%	60%	13%	6%	1%
Sales	$800	$1,000	$1,400	$2,000	$2,600	$3,000	$3,200
Variable Expense	480	600	840	1,200	1,560	1,800	1,920
Fixed Op. Expense	250	250	250	250	250	250	250
Interest Expense	40	40	40	40	40	40	40

Recalculate PSC's business and financial risks and compare these figures with those calculated in problems 7-11 and 7-12.

Answers to Self-Test

ST-1. $CV = \sigma \div \mu = \$400,000 \div \$5,000,000 = .08 = 8\%$

ST-2. $\mu = (.2 \times .04) + (.6 \times .10) + (.2 \times .20) = .108 = 10.8\%$

ST-3. $\sigma = \{[.2 \times (.04 - .108)^2] + [.6 \times (.10 - .108)^2] + [.2 \times (.20 - .108)^2]\}^{.5}$
$= [(.2 \times .004624) + (.6 \times .000064) + (.2 \times .008464)]^{.5}$
$= .002656^{.5} = .0515 = 5.15\%$

ST-4. $\sigma_p = [(.4^2 \times .08^2) + (.6^2 + .12^2) + (2 \times .4 \times .6 \times -(.2) \times .08 \times .12)]^{.5}$
$= [(.16 \times .0064) + (.36 \times .0144) + (-.0009216)]^{.5}$
$= .0052864^{.5} = .0727 = 7.27\%$

ST-5. $.18 + (2 \times .03) = .24 = 24\%$
$.18 - (2 \times .03) = .12 = 12\%$
∴ We are 95% confident that the actual return will be between 12% and 24%.

ST-6. $k_s = .04 + (.06 \times 1.2) = .112 = 11.2\%$

ST-7. $k = .04 + (.06 \times .4) = .064 = 6.4\%$

ST-8. WT of Stock C must be .25 for the total of the weights to equal 1
$.14 = (.06 \times .25) + (.10 \times .5) + [E(R_C) \times .25]$
$.14 = .065 + [E(R_C) \times .25]$
$.075 = E(R_C) \times .25$
$E(R_C) = .30 = 30\%$

chapter 8

The Time Value of Money

Time is money.

Benjamin Franklin

Give Me $6 Million Now and I'll Pay You Back Later!

Who wouldn't want to have $6 million dollars in hand right now? It's worth a lot more than $6 million down the line.

Certainly, Joseph J. Grano, Jr., President of Paine Webber, Inc., couldn't turn down that offer. Despite his strong managerial skills and business acumen, Mr. Grano had $9 million in losses due to risky personal investments. Those investments performed so poorly that Paine Webber CEO Donald Marron advised Grano to declare personal bankruptcy. Mr. Grano did not take the advice, claiming that he wanted to honor his debt obligations, rather than discharge them through bankruptcy proceedings.

To help Mr. Grano cover his investment losses, Paine Webber's compensation committee approved a 5-year loan of $6 million. The loan has a below-market interest rate of 3.85 percent—but *Paine Webber is*

paying the loan interest. In essence, Mr. Grano received an interest-free loan.

This is quite a perk. Once we consider the time value of money, receiving $6 million today and having 5 years to pay back that amount, with-

Joseph J. Grano

Chapter Objectives

After reading this chapter, you should be able to:

1. Explain the time value of money and its importance in the business world.

2. Calculate the future value and present value of a single amount.

3. Find the future and present values of an annuity.

4. Solve time value of money problems with uneven cashflows.

5. Solve for the interest rate, number or amount of payments, or the number of periods in a future or present value problem.

out any interest, is quite a deal. Mr. Grano could earn over 2.8 million in interest if he invested this money at an 8 percent annual interest rate.

The time value of money. It's an important concept. Especially when you become involved in risky deals like Mr. Grano did. ✳

Source: "Joe Grano Could Use a Little Financial Advice," *Business Week,* (December 18, 1995): 74; Junius Ellis, "Why Pros Are Counting on Paine Webber to Double Their Money in 18 Months," *Money* (July 1995): 31–32.

CHAPTER OVERVIEW

A dollar in hand today is worth more than a promise of a dollar tomorrow. This is one of the basic principles of financial decision making. As the PaineWebber example shows, time value analysis is a crucial part of financial decisions. It helps answer questions about how much money an investment will make over time and how much a firm must invest now to earn an expected payoff later.

In this chapter we will investigate why money has time value, as well as learn how to calculate the *future value* of cash invested today and the *present value* of cash to be received in the future. We will also discuss the present and future values of an *annuity*—a series of equal cash payments at regular time intervals. Finally, we will examine special time value of money problems, such as how to find the rate of return on an investment and how to deal with a series of uneven cash payments.

WHY MONEY HAS TIME VALUE

We discussed the real rate of interest and interest rate determinants in chapter 2, on pages 29–32.

The **time value of money** means that money you hold in your hand today is worth more than money you expect to receive in the future. Similarly, money you must pay out today is a greater burden than the same amount paid in the future.

In chapter 2 we learned that interest rates are positive in part because people prefer to consume now rather than later. Positive interest rates indicate, then, that money has time value. When one person lets another borrow money, the first person requires compensation in exchange for reducing current consumption. The person who borrows the money is willing to pay to increase current consumption. The cost paid by the borrower to the lender for reducing consumption, known as an *opportunity cost,* is the real rate of interest.

The real rate of interest reflects compensation for the **pure time value of money.** The real rate of interest does not include interest charged for expected inflation or the risk factors discussed in chapter 2. Recall from the interest rate discussion in chapter 2 that many factors—including the pure time value of money, inflation default risk, liquidity risk, and maturity risk—determine market interest rates.

The required rate of return on an investment reflects the pure time value of money, an adjustment for expected inflation, and any risk premiums present.

MEASURING THE TIME VALUE OF MONEY

Financial managers adjust for the time value of money by calculating the *future value* and the *present value*. Future value and present value are mirror images of each other. **Future value** is the value of a starting amount at a future point in time, given the rate of growth per period and the number of periods until that future time. How much will $1,000 invested today at a 5 percent interest rate grow to in fifteen years? **Present value** is the value of a future amount today, assuming a specific required interest rate for a number of periods until that future amount is realized. How much should we pay today to obtain a promised payment of $20,000 in fifteen years if investing money today would yield a 10 percent rate of return per year?

The Future Value of a Single Amount

To calculate the future value of a single amount, we must first understand how money grows over time. Once money is invested, it earns an interest rate that compensates for the time value of money and, as we learned in chapter 2, for default risk, inflation, and other factors. Often, the interest earned on investments is **compound interest**—interest earned on interest *and* on the original principal. In contrast, *simple interest* is interest earned only on the original principal.

To illustrate compound interest, assume the financial manager of SaveCom decided to invest $100 of the firm's excess cash in an account that earns an annual interest rate of 5 percent. In year 1 SaveCom will earn $5 in interest, calculated as follows:

$$
\begin{aligned}
\text{Balance at the end of one year} &= \text{Principal} + \text{Interest} \\
&= \$100 + (100 \times .05) \\
&= \$100 \times (1 + .05) \\
&= \$100 \times 1.05 \\
&= \$105
\end{aligned}
$$

The total amount in the account at the end of year 1, then, is $105.

But look what happens in years 2 and 3. In year 2 SaveCom will earn 5 percent of *$105*. The $105 is the original principal of $100 *plus* the first year's interest—so the interest earned in year 2 is $5.25, rather that $5.00. The end of year 2 balance is $110.25—$100 in original principal and $10.25 in interest. In year 3 SaveCom will earn 5 percent of $110.25, or $5.51, for an ending balance of $115.76, shown as follows:

	BEG. BAL.	$\times$	**(1 + INTEREST RATE)**	**= END. BAL.**	**INTEREST**
Year 1	$100.00	$\times$	1.05	= $105.00	$5.00
Year 2	$105.00	$\times$	1.05	= $110.25	$5.25
Year 3	$110.25	$\times$	1.05	= $115.76	$5.51

In our example SaveCom earned $5 in interest in year 1, $5.25 in interest in year 2 ($110.25 − $105.00), and $5.51 in year 3 ($115.76 − $110.25) because of the compounding effect. If the SaveCom deposit earned interest only on the original principal, rather than on the principal and interest, the balance in the account at the end of year 3 would be $115 ($100 + ($5 × 3) = $115). In our case the compounding effect accounts for an extra $.76 ($115.76 − $115.00 = .76).

The simplest way to find the balance at the end of year 3 is to multiply the original principal by 1 plus the interest rate per period, 1 + k, raised to the power of the

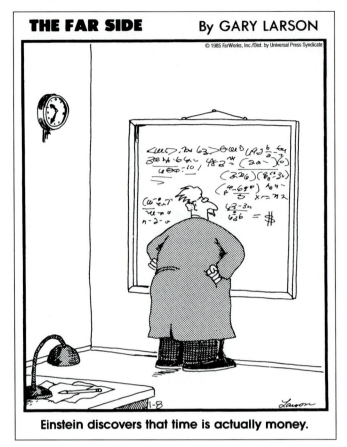

THE FAR SIDE By GARY LARSON

© 1985 FarWorks, Inc./Dist. by Universal Press Syndicate

Einstein discovers that time is actually money.

number of compounding periods, n.[1] Here's the formula for finding the future value—or ending balance—given the original principal, interest rate per period, and number of compounding periods:

Future Value for a Single Amount
Algebraic Method

$$FV = PV \times (1 + k)^n \tag{8-1a}$$

where: FV = Future Value, the ending amount
PV = Present Value, the starting amount, or original principal
k = Rate of interest per period (expressed as a decimal)
n = Number of time periods

In our SaveCom example, PV is the original deposit of $100, k is 5 percent, and n is 3. To solve for the ending balance, or FV, we apply Equation 8-1a as follows:

$$FV = PV \times (1 + k)^n = \$100 \times (1.05)^3 = \$100 \times 1.1576 = \$115.76$$

---

[1]The compounding periods are usually years, but not always. As you will see later in the chapter, compounding periods can be months, weeks, days, or any specified period of time.

We may also solve for future value using a financial table. Financial tables are a compilation of values, known as interest factors, that represent a term, $(1 + k)^n$ in this case, in time value of money formulas. Table I in the inside cover of the book is developed by calculating $(1 + k)^n$ for many combinations of k and n.

Table I is the **future value interest factor (FVIF)** table. The formula for future value using the FVIF table follows:

Future Value Formula for a Single Amount
Table Method

$$FV = PV \times (FVIF_{k,n}) \qquad (8\text{-}1b)$$

where: FV = Future Value, the ending amount
         PV = Present Value, the starting amount
         $FVIF_{k,n}$ = Future Value Interest Factor given interest rate, k, and number
            of periods, n, from Table I

In our SaveCom example, in which $100 is deposited in an account at 5 percent interest for three years, the ending balance, or FV, according to Equation 8-1b, is as follows:

$$FV = PV \times (FVIF_{5\%,\,3})$$
$$= \$100 \times 1.1576$$
$$= \$115.76$$

To solve for FV using a financial calculator, we enter the numbers for PV, n, and k (k is depicted as I/Y on the TI BAII PLUS calculator; on other calculators it may be symbolized by i or I), and ask the calculator to compute FV. The keystrokes follow[2]:

▶ **Take Note**

Because future value interest factors are rounded to four decimal places in Table I, you may get a slightly different solution compared to a problem solved by the algebraic method.

TI BAII PLUS FINANCIAL CALCULATOR SOLUTION

Step 1: First press [2nd] [CLR TVM] . This clears all the time value of money keys of all previously calculated or entered values.

Step 2: Press [2nd] [P/Y] 1 [ENTER] , [2nd] [QUIT] . This sets the calculator to the mode where one payment per year is expected, which is the assumption for the problems in this chapter.

Step 3: Input values for principal (PV), interest rate (k or I/Y on the calculator), and number of periods (n).

100 [+/−] [PV]   5 [I/Y]   3 [N]   [CPT] [FV]   Answer: 115.76

In the SaveCom example, we input −100 for the present value (PV), 3 for number of periods (N), and 5 for the interest rate per year (I/Y). Then we ask the calculator to compute the future value, FV. The result is $115.76. Our TI BAII PLUS is set to display two decimal places. You may choose a greater or lesser number if you wish.

---

[2]We will be using the keystroke patterns for the TI BAII PLUS financial calculator throughout this book. The separate reference card provided with this text gives keystroke sequences for other popular financial calculators.

We have learned three ways to calculate the future value of a single amount: the algebraic method, the financial table method, and the financial calculator method. In the next section, we see how future values are related to changes in the interest rate, k, and the number of time periods, n.

The Sensitivity of Future Values to Changes in Interest Rates or the Number of Compounding Periods

Future value has a positive relationship with the interest rate, k, and with the number of periods, n. That is, as the interest rate increases, future value increases. Similarly, as the number of periods increases, so does future value. In contrast, future value decreases with decreases in k and n values.

It is important to understand the sensitivity of future value to k and n because increases are exponential, as shown by the $(1 + k)^n$ term in the future value formula. Consider this: A business that invests $10,000 in a savings account at 5 percent for twenty years will have a future value of $26,532.98. If the interest rate is 8 percent for the same twenty years, the future value of the investment is $46,609.57. We see that the future value of the investment increases as k increases.

Now let's say that the business deposits $10,000 for ten years at a 5 percent annual interest rate. The future value of that sum is $16,288.95. Another business deposits $10,000 for twenty years at the same 5 percent annual interest rate. The future value of that $10,000 investment is $26,532.98. Just as with the interest rate, the higher the number of periods, the higher the future value. Figure 8-1 shows how different values of k and n affect the future value of $1.

Figure 8-1 **Future Value of $1.00**

Figure 8-1 shows the future value interest factor (the future value of $1) for various combinations of k and n.

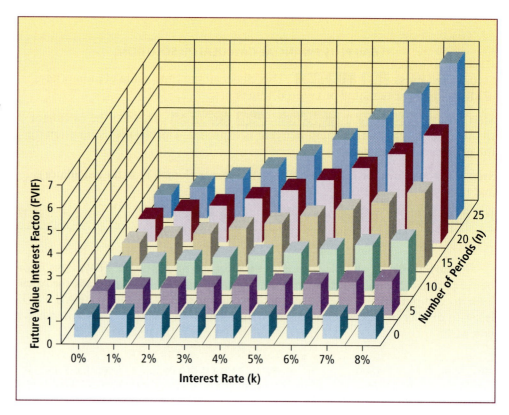

Figure 8-1 shows how future value increases at an increasing rate with increases in k and n values, illustrating that compound interest causes exponential growth.[3]

THE PRESENT VALUE OF A SINGLE AMOUNT

Present value is today's dollar value of a specific future amount. With a bond, for instance, the issuer promises the investor future cash payments at specified points in time. With an investment in new plant or equipment, certain cash receipts are expected. When we calculate the present value of a future promised or expected cash payment, we discount it (mark it down in value) because it is worth *less* if it is to be received later rather than now. Similarly, future cash outflows are less burdensome than present cash outflows of the same amount. Future cash outflows are similarly discounted (made less negative). In present value analysis, then, the interest rate used in this discounting process is known as the **discount rate.** The discount rate is the required rate of return on an investment. It reflects the lost opportunity to spend or invest now (the opportunity cost) and the various risks assumed because we must wait for the funds.

Discounting is the inverse of compounding. Compound interest causes the value of a beginning amount to increase at an increasing rate. Discounting causes the present value of a future amount to decrease at an increasing rate.

To demonstrate, imagine the SaveCom financial manager needed to know how much to invest *now* to generate $115.76 in three years, given an interest rate of 5 percent. The calculation would look like this:

$$FV = PV \times (1 + k)^n$$
$$\$115.76 = PV \times 1.05^3$$
$$\$115.76 = PV \times 1.157625$$
$$PV = \$100.00$$

To solve present value problems, we modify the future value for a single amount equation by multiplying both sides by $1/(1 + k)^n$ to isolate PV on one side of the equal sign. The present value formula for a single amount follows:

The Present Value of a Single Amount Formula
Algebraic Method

$$PV = FV \times \frac{1}{(1 + k)^n} \tag{8-2a}$$

where: PV = Present Value, the starting amount
FV = Future Value, the ending amount
k = Discount rate of interest per period (expressed as a decimal)
n = Number of time periods

---

[3]We have depicted the changes in k in one-step increments, while the n values change in five-step increments. This is to help you to see the change in FVIF more dramatically. To see a true picture of exponential growth, examine the change in FVIF as k changes. The five-step increments in n, of course, make the change in the FVIF along the n axis appear greater than they would be if one-step changes had been used for n also.

Applying this formula to the SaveCom example, in which its financial manager wanted to know how much the firm should pay today to receive $115.76 at the end of three years, assuming a 5 percent discount rate starting today, the following is the present value of the investment:

$$PV = FV \times \frac{1}{(1 + k)^n}$$

$$= \$115.76 \times \frac{1}{(1 + .05)^3}$$

$$= \$115.76 \times .86384$$

$$= \$100$$

SaveCom should be willing to pay $100 today to receive $115.76 three years from now at a 5 percent discount rate.

To solve for PV, we may also use the Present Value Interest Factor Table in Table II on the inside cover of the book. A **present value interest factor,** or PVIF, is calculated and shown in Table II. It equals $1/(1 + k)^n$ for given combinations of k and n. The table method formula, Equation 8-2b, follows:

Present Value Formula for a Single Amount
Table Method

$$PV = FV \times (PVIF_{k,n}) \tag{8-2b}$$

where: PV = Present Value
FV = Future Value
$PVIF_{k,n}$ = Present Value Interest Factor given discount rate, k, and number of periods, n, from Table II.

In our example, SaveCom's financial manager wanted to solve for the amount that must be invested today at a 5 percent interest rate to accumulate $115.76 within three years. Applying the present value table formula, we find the following solution:

$$PV = FV \times (PVIF_{5\%,3})$$

$$= \$115.76 \times .8638 \text{ (from the PVIF table)}$$

$$= \$99.99 \text{ (slightly less than \$100 due to the rounding to four places}$$
$$\text{in the table).}$$

The present value of $115.76, discounted back three years at a 5 percent discount rate, is $100.

To solve for present value using our financial calculator, enter the numbers for future value, FV, the number of periods, n, and the interest rate, k—symbolized as I/Y on the calculator—then hit the CPT (compute) and PV (present value) keys. The sequence is shown below:

TI BAII PLUS FINANCIAL CALCULATOR SOLUTION

Step 1: Press `2nd` `CLR TVM` to clear previous values.

Step 2: Press `2nd` `P/Y` 1 `ENTER` , `2nd` `QUIT` to ensure the calculator is in the mode for annual interest payments.

Step 3: Input the values for future value, the interest rate, and number of periods, and compute PV.

115.76 `FV`   5 `I/Y`   3 `N`   `CPT` `PV`   Answer: −100.00

The financial calculator result is displayed as a negative number to show that the present value sum is a cash outflow—that is, that sum will have to be invested to earn $115.76 in three years at a 5 percent annual interest rate.

We have examined how to find present value using the algebraic, table, and financial calculator methods. Next, we see how present value analysis is affected by the discount rate, k, and the number of compounding periods, n.

The Sensitivity of Present Values to Changes in k and n

In contrast to future value, present value is inversely related to k and n values. In other words, present value moves in the opposite direction of k and n. If k increases, present value decreases; if k decreases, present value increases. If n increases, present value decreases; if n decreases, present value increases.

Figure 8-2 shows how the present value of $1 varies with changes in values for k and n.

Figure 8-2 not only shows that the relationship of k and n to present value interest factor is inverse, it also shows that changes in k and n result in exponential changes in present value.[4] The exponential changes result because the opportunity cost associated with discounting is a lost opportunity to earn compound interest (an exponential function).

---

[4]Note again here that n values change in five-step increments, while k values change in one-step increments.

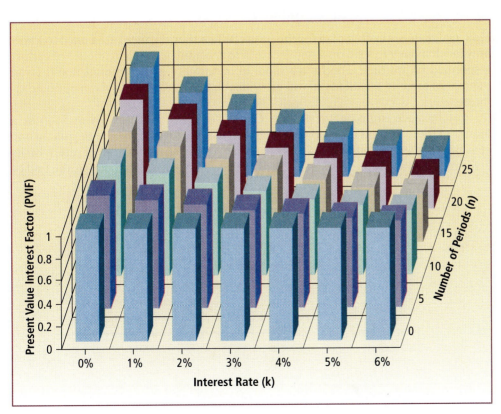

Figure 8-2 **Present Value of $1.00**

Figure 8-2 shows the present value interest factor (the present value of $1) for various combinations of k and n.

In this section we have learned how to find the future value and the present value of a single amount. Next, we will examine how to find the future value and present value of several amounts.

Working with Annuities

Financial managers often need to assess a series of cash flows rather than just one. One common type of cash flow series is the **annuity**—a series of equal cashflows, spaced evenly over time.

Professional athletes often sign contracts that provide annuities for them after they retire, in addition to the signing bonus and regular salary they may receive during their playing years. Consumers can purchase annuities from insurance companies as a means of providing retirement income. The investor pays the insurance company a lump sum now in order to receive future payments of equal size at regularly spaced time intervals (usually monthly). Another example of an annuity is the interest on a bond. The interest payments are usually equal dollar amounts paid either annually or semiannually during the life of the bond.

Annuities are a significant part of many financial problems. You should learn to recognize annuities and determine their value, future or present. In this section we will explain how to calculate the future value and present value of annuities where cash flows occur at the end of the specified time periods. Annuities where the cash flows occur at the end of each of the specified time periods are known as *ordinary annuities*.

Future Value of an Ordinary Annuity

Financial managers often plan for the future. When they do, they often need to know how much money to save on a regular basis to accumulate a given amount of cash at a specified future time. The future value of an annuity is the amount that a given number of annuity payments, n, will grow to at a future date, for a given periodic interest rate, k.

For instance, suppose the Save'N'Grow Company plans to invest $500 in a money market account at the end of each year for the next four years, beginning one year from today. The business expects to earn a 5 percent annual rate of return on its investment. How much money will Save'N'Grow have in the account at the end of

Figure 8-3 Save'N'Grow Annuity Timeline

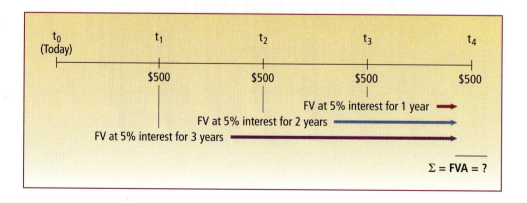

five years? The problem is illustrated in the following timeline, Figure 8-3. The t values in the timeline represent the end of each time period. Thus t_1 is the end of the first year, t_2 is the end of the second year, and so on. The symbol t_0 is *now,* the present point in time.

Since the $500 payments are each single amounts, we can solve this problem one step at a time. Looking at Figure 8-4, we see that the first step is to calculate the future value of t_1, t_2, t_3, and t_4 using the future value formula for a single amount. The next step is to add the four values together. The sum of those values is the annuity's future value.

The sum of the future values of the four single amounts is the annuity's future value, $2,155.05. However, the step-by-step process illustrated in Figure 8-4 is time consuming even in this simple example. Calculating the future value of a twenty- or thirty-year annuity, such as would be the case with many bonds, would take an enormous amount of time. Instead, we can calculate the future value of an annuity easily by using the following formula:

Future Value of an Annuity Formula
Algebraic Method

$$FVA = PMT \times \left[\frac{(1+k)^n - 1}{k} \right]$$

(8-3a)

where: FVA = Future Value of an Annuity
PMT = Amount of each annuity payment
k = Interest rate per time period
n = Number of annuity payments

The bracketed term in Equation 8-3a is the result of adding the corresponding $(1 + k)^n$ values from the future value of a single amount formulas, Equation 8-1a and 8-1b, for each of the individual annuity payments. This is the same as the sum of the FVIF values from Table I for each individual annuity payment. For example, the

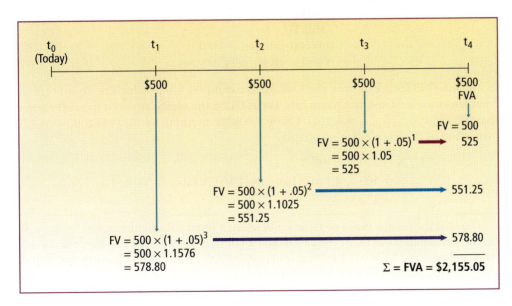

Figure 8-4 **Future Value of the Save'N'Grow Annuity**

sum of the individual future value interest factors for each of the $500 payments in our example is as follows:

$$1.1576 \ (n = 3)$$
$$1.1025 \ (n = 2)$$
$$1.0500 \ (n = 1)$$
$$\underline{1.0000} \ (n = 0)$$
$$4.3101$$

Using Equation 8-3a in our Save'N'Grow example, we solve for the future value of the annuity at 5 percent interest (k = 5%) with four $500 end-of-year payments (n = 4 and PMT = $500), as follows:

$$FVA = 500 \times \left[\frac{(1 + .05)^4 - 1}{.05} \right]$$
$$= 500 \times 4.3101$$
$$= \$2,155.05$$

Notice that 4.3101 is also the number we found by summing the values for the FVIF terms for the future value of a single amount computations. For a $500 annuity with a 5 percent interest rate and four annuity payments, we see that the future value of the SaveN Grow annuity is $2,155.05.

To find the future value of an annuity with the table method, we must find the **future value interest factor for an annuity** (FVIFA), found in Table III on the inside cover of the text. The $FVIFA_{k,n}$ is the value of $[(1 + k)^n - 1] \div k$ for different combinations of k and n.

Future Value of an Annuity Formula
Table Method

$FVA = PMT \times FVIFA_{k,n}$ (8-3b)

where: FVA = Future Value of an Annuity
         PMT = Amount of each annuity payment
  $FVIFA_{k,n}$ = Future Value Interest Factor for an Annuity from
                Table III
          k = Interest rate per period
          n = Number of annuity payments

In our Save'N'Grow example, then, we need to find the FVIFA for a discount rate of 5 percent with four annuity payments. Table III on the inside cover of the text shows that the $FVIFA_{k=5\%, n=4}$ is 4.3101. Using the table method, we find the following future value of the Save'N'Grow annuity:

$$FVA = 500 \times FVIFA_{5\%, 4}$$
$$= 500 \times 4.3101 \ \text{(from the FVIFA table in Table III)}$$
$$= \$2,155.05$$

To find the future value of an annuity using a financial calculator, key in the values for the annuity payment (PMT), n, and k (remember that the notation for the interest rate on the TI BAII PLUS calculator is I/Y, not k). Then compute the future value of the annuity (FV on the calculator). For a series of four $500 end-of-year (ordinary annuity) payments where n = 4 and k = 5 percent, the computation is as follows:

TI BAII PLUS FINANCIAL CALCULATOR SOLUTION

Step 1: Press `2nd` `CLR TVM` to clear previous values

Step 2: Press `2nd` `P/Y` 1 `ENTER` , `2nd` `BGN` `2nd` `SET` `2nd` `SET` repeat `2nd` `SET` until END shows in the display `2nd` `QUIT` to set the annual interest rate mode and to set the annuity payment to end of period mode

Step 3: Input the values and compute.

0 `PV`   5 `I/Y`   4 `N`   500 `+/−` `PMT`   `CPT` `FV`   Answer: 2,155.06

In the financial calculator inputs, note that the payment is keyed in as a negative number to indicate that the payments are cash outflows—the payments flow out from the company into an investment.

The Present Value of an Ordinary Annuity

Because annuity payments are often promised (as with interest on a bond investment) or expected (as with cash inflows from an investment in new plant or equipment), it is important to know how much these investments are worth to us today. For example, assume that the financial manager of Buy4Later, Inc., learns of an annuity that promises to make four annual payments of $500, beginning one year from today. How much should the company be willing to pay to obtain that annuity? The answer is the present value of the annuity.

Since an annuity is nothing more than a series of single amounts, we could calculate the present value of an annuity with the present value formula for a single amount and sum the totals, but that would be a cumbersome process. Imagine calculating the present value of a fifty-year annuity! We would have to find the present value for each of the fifty annuity payments and total them.

Fortunately, we can calculate the present value of an annuity in one step with the following formula:

The Present Value of an Annuity Formula
Algebraic Method

$$PVA = PMT \times \left[\frac{1 - \dfrac{1}{(1 + k)^n}}{k} \right]$$

(8-4a)

where: PVA = Present Value of an Annuity
PMT = Amount of each annuity payment
k = Discount rate per period
n = Number of annuity payments

> **Take Note**
>
> *Note that slight differences occur between the table method, algebraic method, and calculator solution. This is because our financial tables round interest factors to four decimal places, while the other methods generally use many more significant figures for greater accuracy.*

Using our example of a four-year ordinary annuity with payments of $500 per year and a 5 percent discount rate, we solve for the present value of the annuity as follows:

$$PVA = 500 \times \left[\frac{1 - \dfrac{1}{(1 + .05)^4}}{.05} \right]$$

$$= 500 \times 3.54595$$

$$= \$1,772.97$$

The present value of the four-year ordinary annuity with equal yearly payments of $500 at a 5 percent discount rate is 1,772.97.

We can also use the financial table for the **present value interest factor for an annuity (PVIFA)** to solve present value of annuity problems. The PVIFA table is found in Table IV on the inside cover of the text. The formula for the table method follows:

The Present Value of an Annuity Formula
Table Method

$$PVA = PMT \times PVIFA_{k,n}$$

(8-4b)

where: PVA = Present Value of an Annuity
PMT = Amount of each annuity payment
$PVIFA_{k,n}$ = Present Value Interest Factor for an Annuity from Table IV
k = Discount rate per period
n = Number of annuity payments

Applying Equation 8-4b, we find that the present value of the four-year annuity with $500 equal payments and a 5 percent discount rate is as follows:

$$PVA = 500 \times PVIFA_{5\%,4} = 500 \times 3.5460 = \$1,773.00^5$$

We may also solve for the present value of an annuity with a financial calculator. Simply key in the values for the payment, PMT, number of payment periods, n, and the interest rate, k—symbolized by "I/Y" on the TI BAII PLUS calculator—and ask the calculator to compute PVA (PV on the calculator). For the series of four $500 payments where n = 4 and k = 5% the computation follows:

TI BAII PLUS FINANCIAL CALCULATOR SOLUTION

Step 1: Press `2nd` `CLR TVM` to clear previous values.

Step 2: Press `2nd` `P/Y` 1 `ENTER` , `2nd` `BGN` `2nd` `SET` , repeat `2nd` `SET` until END shows in the display `2nd` `QUIT` to set to the annual interest rate mode and to set the annuity payment to end of period mode.

Step 3: Input the values and compute.

5 `I/Y`   4 `N`   500 `PMT`   `CPT` `PV`   Answer: −1,772.97

---

[5] The $.03 difference between the algebraic result and the table formula solution is due to differences in rounding.

When a Million Isn't a Million. Taking a Chance on the Time Value of Money

You've won the lottery: $1 million. Congratulations! You're rich. No, wait a minute—maybe not.

"I wish they would stop *calling* us millionaires," whispers Cindy, who doesn't want to give out her last name. You see, Cindy, a recent lottery winner has faced an awful truth. The time value of money.

In fact, most lottery winners wish the news media would tell the truth about those "millions." Those huge prizes that the media report are usually doled out over twenty years (twenty-five in Colorado). The annual check for a million-dollar winner is $50,000—before taxes. They also take any student loans you haven't paid out of the check.

Michael Ondrish, a "millionaire" winner who thought he'd won a real, lump-sum million in 1982, tried suing the Arizona lottery for fraud and deception because lottery officials never mentioned the drawn-out payment scheme. He lost his case and received a good lesson in the time value of money.

A million dollars paid out over twenty years is an annuity. Like any other million-dollar annuity, it actually costs about $450,000 to buy because that is its present value. Depending on interest rates, taxes, and inflation, the value of the yearly check dwindles over time. Again, it's what financial experts call the time value of money. In fact, investors willing to buy those annuities from winners who need cash offer about forty cents on the dollar.

But you won't see the time value of money in any lottery commercial. "You Could Win An Annuity Spread Over Twenty Years" just doesn't have the same appeal as "You've Won A Million." But look on the bright side. When you win the lottery, you'll know the truth. Especially after reading this chapter.

Questions to Consider

▶ Do you think it is ethical to advertise the lottery without explaining that the winnings are an annuity? Explain.

▶ Is it ethical to fail to disclose that the jackpot winnings are the future value of the jackpot, not the present value?

▶ Why do you think that Michael Ondrish lost his case against the Arizona lottery?

Source: Lois Gould "Ticket To Trouble," *New York Times Magazine* (April 23, 1995): 39

The financial calculator present value result is displayed as a negative number to signal that the present value sum is a cash outflow—that is, $1,772.97 will have to be invested to earn a 5 percent annual rate of return on the four future annual annuity payments of $500 each to be received.

Future and Present Values of Annuities Due

Sometimes we must deal with annuities where the annuity payments occur at the *beginning* of each period. These are known as annuities due, in contrast to *ordinary* annuities where the payments occurred at the end of each period, as described in the preceding section.

Annuities due are more likely to occur when doing future value of annuity (FVA) problems than when doing present value of annuity (PVA) problems. Today, for instance, you may start a retirement program, investing regular equal amounts each month or year. Calculating the amount you would accumulate when you reach retirement age would be a future value of an annuity due problem. Evaluating the present value of a promised or expected series of annuity payments that began today would be a present value of an annuity due problem. This is less common, since car and mortgage payments almost always start at the end of the first period, making them ordinary annuities.

Whenever you run into an FVA or a PVA of an annuity due problem, the adjustment needed is the same in both cases. Use the FVA or PVA of an ordinary annuity formula shown earlier, then multiply your answer by $(1 + k)$. We multiply the FVA or PVA formula by $(1 + k)$ because annuities due have annuity payments earning interest one period sooner. So, higher FVA and PVA values result with an annuity due. The first payment occurs sooner in the case of a future value of an annuity due. In present value of annuity due problems, each annuity payment occurs one period sooner, so the payments are discounted less severely.

In our Save'N'Grow example, the future value of a $500 ordinary annuity, with $k = 5\%$ and $n = 4$, was $2,155.06. If the $500 payments occurred at the *beginning* of each period instead of at the end, we would multiply $2,155.06 by 1.05 $(1 + k = 1 + .05)$. The product, $2,262.81, is the future value of the annuity due. In our earlier Buy4Later, Inc., example, we found that the present value of a $500 ordinary annuity, with $k = 5\%$ and $n = 4$, was $1,772.97. If the $500 payments occurred at the *beginning* of each period instead of at the end, we would multiply $1,772.97 by 1.05 $(1 + k = 1 + .05)$ and find that the present value of Buy4Later's annuity due is $1,861.62.

The financial calculator solutions for these annuity due problems are shown next.

Future Value of a Four-Year, $500 Annuity Due, k = 5%

TI BAII PLUS FINANCIAL CALCULATOR SOLUTION

Step 1: Press 2nd CLR TVM to clear previous values.

Step 2: Press 2nd P/Y 1 ENTER , 2nd BGN , 2nd SET , Repeat the 2nd SET command until the display shows BGN, 2nd QUIT to set to the annual interest rate mode and to set the annuity payment to beginning of period mode.

Step 3: Input the values for the annuity due and compute.

5 I/Y   4 N   500 PMT   CPT FV   Answer: −2,262,82

Present Value of a Four-Year, $500 Annuity Due, k = 5%

TI BAII PLUS FINANCIAL CALCULATOR SOLUTION

Step 1: Press 2nd CLR TVM

Step 2: Press 2nd P/Y 1 ENTER , 2nd BGN , 2nd SET . Repeat the 2nd SET command until the display shows BGN 2nd QUIT to set to the annual interest rate mode and to set the annuity payment to beginning of period mode.

Step 3: Input the values for the annuity due and compute.

5 I/Y   4 N   500 PMT   CPT PV   Answer: −1,861.62

In this section we discussed ordinary annuities and annuities due and learned how to compute the present and future values of the annuities. Next, we will learn what a perpetuity is and how to solve for its present value.

Perpetuities

An annuity that goes on forever is called a perpetual annuity or a **perpetuity.** Perpetuities contain an infinite number of annuity payments. An example of a perpetuity is the dividends typically paid on a preferred stock issue.

The future value of perpetuities cannot be calculated, but the present value can be. We start with the present value of an annuity formula, Equation 8-3a.

$$PVA = PMT \times \left[\frac{1 - \frac{1}{(1 + k)^n}}{k} \right]$$

Now imagine what happens in the equation as the number of payments (n) gets larger and larger. The $(1+k)^n$ term will get larger and larger. And as it does, it will cause the $1/(1+k)^n$ fraction to become smaller and smaller. As n approaches infinity, the $(1+k)^n$ term becomes infinitely large, and the $1/(1+k)^n$ term approaches zero. The entire formula reduces to the following equation:

Present Value of a Perpetuity Formula

$$PVP = PMT \times \left[\frac{1 - 0}{k} \right] \qquad (8\text{-}5)$$

or

$$PVP = PMT \times \left(\frac{1}{k} \right)$$

where: PVP = Present value of a perpetuity.
         k = Discount rate

Neither the table method nor the financial calculator can solve for the present value of a perpetuity. This is because the PVIFA table does not contain values for infinity and the financial calculator does not have an infinity key.

Suppose you had the opportunity to buy a share of preferred stock that pays $70 per year forever. If your required rate of return is 8 percent, what is the present value of the promised dividends to you? In other words, given your required rate of return, how much should you be willing to pay for the preferred stock? The answer, found by applying Equation 8-5, follows:

$$PVP = PMT \times \left(\frac{1}{k} \right) = \$70 \times \left(\frac{1}{.08} \right) = \$875$$

The present value of our preferred stock with a k of 8 percent and a payment of $70 per year forever is $875.

Present Value of an Investment with Uneven Cash Flows

Unlike annuities that have equal payments over time, many investments have payments that are unequal over time. That is, some investments have payments that vary over time. When the periodic payments vary, we say that the cash flow streams

TABLE 8-1

**The Present Value
of an Uneven Series
of Cashflows**

t_0	\$7,000,000	$\$7,000,000 \times \dfrac{1}{1.08^0} = \$7,000,000$
t_1	\$2,000,000	$\$2,000,000 \times \dfrac{1}{1.08^1} = \$1,851,851,85$
t_2	\$4,000,000	$\$4,000,000 \times \dfrac{1}{1.08^2} = \$3,429,355.28$
t_3	\$6,000,000	$\$6,000,000 \times \dfrac{1}{1.08^3} = \$4,762,993.45$
t_4	\$6,000,000	$\$6,000,000 \times \dfrac{1}{1.08^4} = \$4,410,179.12$
		Sum of the PVs = \$21,454,379.70

are uneven. For instance, a professional athlete may sign a contract that provides for an immediate \$7 million signing bonus, followed by a salary of \$2 million in year 1, \$4 million in year 2, then \$6 million in years 3 and 4. What is the present value of the promised payments that total \$25 million? Assume a discount rate of 8 percent. The present value calculations are shown in Table 8-1.

As we see from Table 8-1, we calculate the present value of an uneven series of cash flows by finding the present value of a single amount for each series and sum the totals.

We can also use a financial calculator to find the present value of this uneven series of cash flows. The worksheet mode of the TI BAII PLUS calculator is especially helpful in solving problems with uneven cash flows. The C display shows each cash payment following CF_0, the initial cash flow. The F display key indicates the frequency of that payment. The keystrokes follow.

TI BAII PLUS FINANCIAL CALCULATOR PV SOLUTION
Uneven Series of Cashflows

KEYSTROKES	DISPLAY
CF	CF_0 = old contents
2nd CLR Work	CF_0 = 0.00
7000000 ENTER	7,000,000.00
↓ 2000000 ENTER	C01 = 2,000,000.00
↓	F01 = 1.00
↓ 4000000 ENTER	C02 = 4,000,000.00
↓	F02 = 1.00
↓ 6000000 ENTER	C03 = 6,000,000.00
↓ 2 ENTER	F03 = 2.00
NPV	I = 0.00
8 ENTER	I = 8.00
↓ CPT	NPV = 21,454,379.70

Take Note

We used the NPV (net present value) key on our calculator to solve this problem. NPV will be discussed in chapter 10.

We see from the calculator keystrokes that we are solving for the present value of a single amount for each payment in the series except for the last two payments, which are the same. The value of F03, the frequency of the third cash flow after the initial cash flow, was 2 instead of 1 because the $6 million payment occurred twice in the series (in years 3 and 4).

We have seen how to calculate the future value and present value of annuities, the present value of a perpetuity, and the present value of an investment with uneven cash flows. Now we turn to time value of money problems where we solve for k, n, or the annuity payment.

SPECIAL TIME VALUE OF MONEY PROBLEMS

Financial managers often face time value of money problems even when they know both the present value and the future value of an investment. In those cases financial managers may be asked to find out what return an investment made—that is, what the interest rate is on the investment. Still other times financial managers must find either the number of payment periods, or the amount of an annuity payment. In the next section, we will learn how to solve for k and n. We will also learn how to find the annuity payment (PMT).

Finding the Interest Rate

Financial managers frequently have to solve for the interest rate, k, when firms make a long-term investment. The method of solving for k depends on whether the investment is a single amount or an annuity.

Finding k of a Single Amount Investment   Financial managers may need to determine how much periodic return an investment generated over time. For example, imagine that you are head of the finance department of GrabLand, Inc. Say that GrabLand purchased a house on prime land twenty years ago for $40,000. Recently, GrabLand sold the property for $106,131. What average annual rate of return did the firm earn on its twenty-year investment?

First, the future value—or ending amount—of the property is $106,131. The present value—the starting amount—is $40,000. The number of periods, n, is twenty. Armed with those facts, you solve this problem using the future value of a single amount formula as follows:

$$FV = PV \times (FVIF_{k, n})$$
$$\$106,131 = \$40,000 \times (FVIF_{k=?, n=20})$$
$$\$106,131 \div \$40,000 = 2.6533 = (FVIF_{k=?, n=20})$$

Now find the FVIF value in Table I, shown in part on page 186. The whole table is on the inside cover. You know n = 20, so find the n = 20 row on the left hand side of the table. You also know that the FVIF value is 2.6533, so move across the n = 20 row until you find (or come close to) the value 2.6533. You find the 2.6533 value in the k = 5% column. You discover, then, that GrabLand's property investment had an interest rate of 5 percent.

Future Value Interest Factors, Compounded at k Percent for n Periods, Part of Table I

NUMBER OF PERIODS, n	INTEREST RATE, k										
	0%	1%	2%	3%	4%	5%	6%	7%	8%	9%	10%
18	1.0000	1.1961	1.4282	1.7024	2.0258	2.4066	2.8543	3.3799	3.9960	4.7171	5.5599
19	1.0000	1.2081	1.4568	1.7535	2.1068	2.5270	3.0256	3.6165	4.3157	5.1417	6.1159
20	1.0000	1.2202	1.4859	1.8061	2.1911	2.6533	3.2071	3.8697	4.6610	5.6044	6.7275
25	1.0000	1.2824	1.6406	2.0938	2.6658	3.3864	4.2919	5.4274	6.8485	8.6231	10.8347

Solving for k using the FVIF table works well when the interest rate is a whole number, but it does not work well when the interest rate is not a whole number. To solve for the interest rate, k, we rewrite the future value of a single amount formula, Equation 8-1a, to solve for k:

Solve for the Rate of Return, k

$$k = \left(\frac{FV}{PV}\right)^{\frac{1}{n}} - 1 \qquad (8\text{-}6)$$

Let's use Equation 8-6 to find the average annual rate of return on GrabLand's house investment. Recall that the company bought it twenty years ago for $40,000 and sold it recently for $106,131. We solve for k applying Equation 8-6 as follows:

$$k = \left(\frac{FV}{PV}\right)^{\frac{1}{n}} - 1 = \left(\frac{\$106,131}{\$40,000}\right)^{\frac{1}{20}} - 1 = 2.653275^{.05} - 1 = 1.05 - 1$$
$$= .05 \text{ or } 5\%$$

Equation 8-6 will find any interest rate given a starting value, PV, an ending value, FV, and a number of compounding periods, n.

To solve for k with a financial calculator, key in all the other variables and ask the calculator to compute k (depicted as I/Y on your calculator). For GrabLand's house-buying example, the calculator solution follows:

TI BAII PLUS FINANCIAL CALCULATOR SOLUTION

Step 1: Press [2nd] [CLR TVM]

Step 2: Press [2nd] [P/Y] 1 [ENTER] , [2nd] [QUIT]

Step 3: Input the values and compute.

40000 [+/−] [PV]   106131 [FV]   20 [N]   [CPT] [I/Y]   Answer: 5.00

Remember when using the financial calculator to solve for the interest rate, you must enter cash outflows as a negative number. In our example, the $40,000 PV is entered as a negative number because GrabLand spent that amount to invest in the house.

Finding k for a PVA Problem   Financial managers may need to find the interest rate for a PVA problem when they know the starting amount (PVA), n, and the annuity payment (PMT), but they do not know the interest rate, k. For example, suppose GrabLand wanted a fifteen-year, $100,000 amortized loan from a bank. An **amortized loan** is a loan that is paid off in equal amounts that include principal as well as interest.[6] GrabLand's payments will be $12,405.89 per year for fifteen years. What interest rate is the bank charging on this loan?

To solve for k when the known values are PVA (the $100,000 loan proceeds), n (15), and PMT (the loan payments $12,405.89), we start with the present value of an annuity formula, Equation 8-3b, as follows:

Present Value of an Annuity Formula
Table Method

$$PVA = PMT \times (PVIFA_{k,n}) \qquad (8\text{-}3b)$$

$$\$100{,}000 = \$12{,}405.89 \times (PVIFA_{k\,=\,?,\,n\,=\,15})$$

$$8.0607 = (PVIFA_{k\,=\,?,\,n\,=\,15})$$

Now refer to the PVIFA values in Table IV, shown in part below. You know n = 15, so find the n = 15 row on the left hand side of the table. You have also determined that the PVIFA value is 8.0607 ($100,000/$12,405 = 8.0607), so move across the n = 15 row until you find (or come close to) the value of 8.0607. In our example, the location on the table where n=15 and the PVIFA is 8.0607, is in the k = 9% column, so the interest rate on GrabLand's loan is 9 percent.

Present Value Interest Factors for an Annuity, Discounted at k Percent for n Periods, Part of Table IV

NO. OF ANN. PMTS., n	DISCOUNT RATE, k									
	0%	1%	2%	3%	4%	5%	6%	7%	8%	9%	10%
13	13.0000	12.1337	11.3484	10.6350	9.9856	9.3936	8.8527	8.3577	7.9038	7.4869	7.1034
14	14.0000	13.0037	12.1062	11.2961	10.5631	9.8986	9.2950	8.7455	8.2442	7.7862	7.3667
15	15.0000	13.8651	12.8493	11.9379	11.1184	10.3797	9.7122	9.1079	8.5595	8.0607	7.6061
16	16.0000	14.7179	13.5777	12.5611	11.6523	10.8378	10.1059	9.4466	8.8514	8.3126	7.8237

To solve this problem with a financial calculator, key in all the variables but k, and ask the calculator to compute k (depicted as I/Y on the TI calculator) as follows:

TI BAII PLUS FINANCIAL CALCULATOR SOLUTION

Step 1: Press 2nd   CLR TVM .

Step 2: Press 2nd   P/Y 1 ENTER , 2nd   BGN   2nd   SET , repeat 2nd   SET until END shows in the display 2nd   QUIT .

Step 3: Input the values and compute.

100000 PV   15 N   12405.89 +/−   PMT   CPT   I/Y   Answer: 9.00

---

[6]Amortize comes from the Latin word *mortalis,* which means "death". You will kill off the entire loan after making the scheduled payments.

In this example the PMT was entered as a negative number to indicate that the loan payments are cash outflows, flowing away from the firm. The missing interest rate value was 9 percent, the interest rate on the loan.

Finding the Number of Periods

Suppose you found an investment that offered you a return of 6 percent per year. How long would it take you to double your money? In this problem you are looking for n, the number of compounding periods it will take for a starting amount, PV, to double in size (FV = 2 × PV).

To find n in our example, start with the formula for the future value of a single amount and solve for n as follows:

$$FV = PV \times (FVIF_{k, n})$$
$$2 \times PV = PV \times (FVIF_{k = 6\%, n = ?})$$
$$2.0 = (FVIF_{k = 6\%, n = ?})$$

Now refer to the FVIF values, shown below in part of Table I. You know k = 6%, so scan across the top row to find the k = 6% column. Knowing that the FVIF value is 2.0, move down the k = 6% column until you find (or come close to) the value 2.0. Note that it occurs in the row where n = 12. Therefore n in this problem, and the number of periods it would take for the value of an investment to double at 6 percent interest per period, is 12.

Future Value Interest Factors, Compounded at k Percent for n Periods, Part of Table I

NUMBER OF PERIODS, N	INTEREST RATE, k										
	0%	1%	2%	3%	4%	5%	6%	7%	8%	9%	10%
11	1.0000	1.1157	1.2434	1.3842	1.5395	1.7103	1.8983	2.1049	2.3316	2.5804	2.8531
12	1.0000	1.1268	1.2682	1.4258	1.6010	1.7959	2.0122	2.2522	2.5182	2.8127	3.1384
13	1.0000	1.1381	1.2936	1.4685	1.6651	1.8856	2.1329	2.4098	2.7196	3.0658	3.4523
14	1.0000	1.1495	1.3195	1.5126	1.7317	1.9799	2.2609	2.5785	2.9372	3.3417	3.7975

This problem can also be solved on a financial calculator quite quickly. Just key in all the known variables (PV, FV, and I/Y) and ask the calculator to compute n.

TI BAII PLUS FINANCIAL CALCULATOR SOLUTION

Step 1: Press [2nd] [CLR TVM]

Step 2: Press [2nd] [P/Y] 1 [ENTER] , [2nd] [QUIT]

Step 3: Input the values and compute.

1 [+/−] [PV]   2 [FV]   6 [I/Y]   [CPT] [N]   Answer: 12.00

In our example n = 12 when $1 is paid out and $2 received with a rate of interest of 6%. That is, it takes twelve years to double your money at a 6 percent annual rate of interest.

Solving for the Payment

Lenders and financial managers frequently have to determine how much each payment—or installment—will need to be to repay an amortized loan. Suppose you are a business owner and you want to buy an office building for your company that costs $200,000. You have $50,000 for a down payment and the bank will loan you the $150,000 balance at a 6 percent annual interest rate. How much will the annual payments be if you obtain a ten-year amortized loan?

As we saw earlier, an amortized loan is repaid in equal payments over time. The period of time may vary. Let's assume in our example that your payments will occur annually, so that at the end of the ten-year period you will have paid off all interest and principal on the loan.

Because the payments are regular and equal in amount, this is an annuity problem. The present value of the annuity (PVA) is the $150,000 loan amount, the annual interest rate (k) is 6 percent, and n is ten years. The payment amount (PMT) is the only unknown value.

Since all the variables but PMT are known, the problem can be solved by solving for PMT in the present value of an annuity formula as follows:

$$\text{Present Value of an Annuity}$$
$$\text{Algebraic Method}$$

$$PVA = PMT \times \left[\frac{1 - \frac{1}{(1 + k)^n}}{k} \right] \tag{8-4a}$$

$$\$150,000 = PMT \times \left[\frac{1 - \frac{1}{(1.06)^{10}}}{.06} \right]$$

$$\$150,000 = PMT \times 7.36009$$

$$\frac{\$150,000}{7.36009} = PMT$$

$$\$20,380.19 = PMT$$

We see, then, that the payment for an annuity with a 6 percent interest rate, an n of ten, and a present value of $150,000 is $20,380.19.

We can also solve for PMT using the table formula as follows:

$$\text{Present Value of an Annuity Formula}$$
$$\text{Table Method}$$

$$PVA = PMT \times (PVIFA_{k, n}) \tag{8-4b}$$

$$\$150,000 = PMT \times (PVIFA_{6\%, 10 \text{ years}})$$

$$\$150,000 = PMT \times 7.3601 \text{ (Look-up PVIFA, Table IV)}$$

$$\frac{\$150,000}{7.3601} = PMT$$

$$\$20,380.16 = PMT$$

The table formula shows that the payment for a loan with the present value of $150,000 at an annual interest rate of 6 percent and an n of 10 is $20,380.16.

With the financial calculator, simply key in all the variables but PMT and have the calculator compute PMT as follows:

TI BAII PLUS FINANCIAL CALCULATOR SOLUTION

Step 1: Press `2nd` `CLR TVM` to clear previous values.

Step 2: Press `2nd` `P/Y` 1 `ENTER` , `2nd` `BGN` , `2nd` `SET` , repeat the `2nd` `SET` command until the display shows `END` `2nd` `QUIT` to set to the annual interest rate mode and to set the annuity payment to end of period mode.

Step 3: Input the values and compute the payment.

150000 `PV`   6 `I/Y`   10 `N`   `CPT` `PMT`   Answer: −20,380.19

The financial calculator will display the payment, $20,380.19, as a negative number because it is a cash outflow.

As each payment is made on an amortized loan, the interest due for that period is paid, along with a repayment of some of the principal that must also be "killed off." After the last payment is made, all the interest and principal on the loan has been paid. This step-by-step payment of the interest and principal payments owed is often shown in an *amortization table*. The amortization table for a four-year 10 percent annual interest rate loan of $1,000 with annual payments follows in Table 8-2. The annual payment of $315.47 is computed with our financial calculator.

TI BAII PLUS FINANCIAL CALCULATOR SOLUTION

Step 1: Press `2nd` `CLR TVM` .

Step 2: `2nd` `P/Y` 1 `ENTER` , `2nd` `BGN` , `2nd` `SET` , repeat the `2nd` `SET` command until the display shows `END` `2nd` `QUIT` to set to the annual interest rate mode and to set the annuity payment to end of period mode.

Step 3: Input all known values and compute the payment.

1000 `PV`   10 `I/Y`   4 `N`   `CPT` `PMT`   Answer: −315.47

We see from Table 8-2 how the $1,000 loan and interest is "killed off" a little each year until the balance at the end of year 4 is zero, with more interest paid early and more principal paid late.

We have seen how to solve for k, n, and PMT. Next, we will see how to solve time value of money problems where interest is compounded more than once per year.

	COL. 1 Beginning Balance	COL. 2 Total Payment	COL. 3 COL. 1 × .10 Payment of Interest	COL. 4 COL. 2 − COL .3 Payment of Principal	COL. 5 COL. 1 − COL. 4 Ending Balance
YR1	$1,000.00	$315.47	$100.00	$215.47	$784.53
YR2	$784.53	$315.47	$78.45	$237.02	$547.51
YR3	$547.51	$315.47	$54.75	$260.72	$286.79
YR4	$286.79	$315.47	$28.68	$286.72	$0.00

COMPOUNDING MORE THAN ONCE PER YEAR

So far in this chapter, we have assumed that interest is compounded *annually*. However, there is nothing magical about annual compounding. Many investments pay interest that is compounded semiannually, quarterly, or even daily. Most banks, savings and loan associations, and credit unions, for example, compound interest on their deposits more frequently than annually.

Suppose you deposited $100 in a savings account that paid 12 percent interest, compounded *annually*. After one year you would have $112 in your account ($112 = $100 × 1.12^1).

Now, however, let's assume the bank used *semiannual* compounding. With semiannual compounding you would receive half a year's interest (6 percent) after six months. In the second half of the year, you would earn interest both on the interest earned in the first six months *and* on the original principal. The total interest earned during the year on a $100 investment at 12 percent annual interest would be:

$\quad$ $ 6.00 (interest for the first 6 months)

$+$ $ .36 (interest on the $6 interest during the second 6 months[7])

$\underline{+ \ \$ \ 6.00}$ (interest on the principal during the second six months)

$= $12.36 total interest in year 1

At the end of the year, you will have a balance of $112.36 if the interest is compounded semiannually, compared to $112.00 with annual compounding—a difference of $.36.

Here's how to find answers to problems in which the compounding period is less than a year: Apply the relevant present value or future value equation, but adjust k and n so they reflect the actual compounding periods.

To demonstrate, let's look at our example of a $100 deposit in a savings account at 12 percent for one year with semiannual compounded interest. Because we want to find out what the future value of a single amount will be, we use that formula to solve for the future value of the account after one year. Next, we divide the *annual* interest rate, 12 percent, by two, because interest will be compounded twice each year. Then, we multiply the number of *years* n (one in our case) by two because with semiannual interest there are two compounding periods in a year. The calculation follows:

---

[7]The $.36 was calculated by multiplying $6 by half of 12%. $6.00 × .06 = $.36

$$FV = PV \times (1 + k/2)^{n \times 2}$$
$$= \$100 \times (1 + .12/2)^{1 \times 2}$$
$$= \$100 \times (1 + .06)^2$$
$$= \$100 \times 1.1236$$
$$= \$112.36$$

The future value of $100 after one year, earning 12 percent annual interest compounded semiannually, is $112.36.

To use the table method for finding the future value of a single amount, find the $FVIF_{k,n}$ in Table I on the inside of the text cover. Then, divide the k by 2 and multiply the n by 2 as follows:

$$FV = PV \times (FVIF_{k/2,\, n \times 2})$$
$$= \$100 \times (FVIF_{12\%/2,\, 1 \times 2 \text{ periods}})$$
$$= \$100 \times (FVIF_{6\%,\, 2 \text{ periods}})$$
$$= \$100 \times 1.1236$$
$$= \$112.36$$

To solve the problem using a financial calculator, divide the k (represented as I/Y on the TI BAII PLUS calculator) by 2 and multiply the n by 2. Next, key in the variables as follows:

TI BAII PLUS FINANCIAL CALCULATOR SOLUTION

Step 1: Press [2nd] [CLR TVM] .

Step 2: Press [2nd] [P/Y] 1 [ENTER] , [2nd] [QUIT]

Step 3: Input the values and compute.

100 [+/−] [PV]   6 [I/Y]   2 [N]   [CPT] [FV]   Answer: 112.36

The future value of $100 invested for 2 periods at 6% per period is $112.36.[8]

Other compounding rates, such as quarterly or monthly rates, can be found by modifying the applicable formula to adjust for the compounding periods. With a quarterly compounding period, then, annual k should be divided by four and annual n multiplied by four. For monthly compounding, annual k should be divided by twelve and annual n multiplied by twelve. Similar adjustments could be made for other compounding periods.

Annuity Compounding Periods Many annuity problems also involve compounding or discounting periods of less than a year. For instance, suppose you want to buy a car that costs $20,000. You have $5,000 for a down payment and plan to finance the remaining $15,000 at 6 percent annual interest for four years. What would your *monthly* loan payments be?

---

[8]Note that we "lied" to our TI BAII PLUS calculator. It asks us for the interest rate per year (I/Y). We gave it the semiannual interest rate of 6 percent, not the annual interest rate of 12 percent. Similarly, n was expressed as the number of semiannual periods, two in one year. As long as we are consistent in expressing the k and n values according to the number of compounding or discounting periods per year, the calculator will give us the correct answer.

First, change the stated annual rate of interest, 6 percent, to a monthly rate by dividing by twelve (6% / 12 = 1/2% or .005) Second, multiply the four-year period by twelve to obtain the number of months involved (4 × 12 = 48 months). Now solve for the annuity payment size using the annuity formula.

In our case, we apply the present value of an annuity formula as follows:

Present Value of an Annuity Algebraic Method

$$PVA = PMT \times \left[\frac{1 - \frac{1}{(1 + k)^n}}{k} \right] \qquad (8\text{-}3a)$$

$$\$15,000 = PMT \times \left[\frac{1 - \frac{1}{(1.005)^{48}}}{.005} \right]$$

$$\$15,000 = PMT \times 42.5803$$

$$\frac{\$15,000}{42.5803} = PMT$$

$$\$352.28 = PMT$$

The monthly payment on a $15,000 car loan with a 6 percent annual interest rate (.5 percent per month) for four years (forty-eight months) is $352.28.

Solving this problem with the PVIFA table in Table IV inside the back cover of the text would be difficult because the .5 percent interest rate is not listed in the PVIFA table. If the PVIFA were listed, we would apply the table formula, make the adjustments to reflect the monthly interest rate and the number of periods, and solve for the present value of the annuity.

On a financial calculator, we would first adjust the k and n to reflect the same time period—monthly, in our case—and then input the adjusted variables to solve the problem as follows:

TI BAII PLUS FINANCIAL CALCULATOR SOLUTION

Step 1: Press `2nd` `CLR TVM`

Step 2: Press `2nd` `P/Y` 1 `ENTER` , `2nd` `BGN` , `2nd` `SET` , repeat the `2nd` `SET` command until the display shows END `2nd` `QUIT` , to set to the annual interest rate mode and to set the annuity payment to end of period mode.

Step 3: Input the values and compute.

15000 `PV` .5 `I/Y` 48 `N` `CPT` `PMT` Answer: −352.28

Note that once again we have lied to our TI BAII PLUS financial calculator. The interest rate we entered was not the 6 percent rate per year but rather the .5 percent rate per month. We entered not the number of years, four, but rather the number of months, forty-eight. Because we were consistent in entering the k and n values in monthly terms, the calculator gave us the correct monthly payment of −352.28 (an outflow of $352.28 per month).

Continuous Compounding The effect of increasing the number of compounding periods per year is to increase the future value of the investment. The more frequently interest is compounded, the greater the future value. The smallest compounding period is used when we do **continuous compounding**—compounding that occurs every tiny unit of time (the smallest unit of time imaginable).

Recall our $100 deposit in an account at 12 percent for one year with annual compounding. At the end of year 1, our balance was $112. With semiannual compounding, the amount increased to $112.36.

When continuous compounding is involved, we cannot divide k by infinity and multiply n by infinity. Instead, we use the term e, which you may remember from your math class. We define e as follows:

$$e = \lim_{h \to \infty} \left[1 + \frac{1}{h} \right]^h \approx 2.71828$$

The value of e is the natural antilog of 1 and is approximately equal to 2.71828. This number is one of those like pi (approximately equal to 3.14159), which we can never express exactly, but can approximate. Using e, the formula for finding the future value of a given amount of money, PV, invested at annual rate, k, for n years, with continuous compounding, is as follows:

Future Value with Continuous Compounding

$$FV = PV \times e^{(k \times n)} \tag{8-7}$$

where k and n are expressed in annual terms

Applying Equation 8-7 to our example of a $100 deposit at 12 percent annual interest with continuous compounding, at the end of one year we would have the following balance:

$$FV = \$100 \times 2.71828^{\,(.12 \times 1)}$$
$$= \$112.75$$

The future value of $100, earning 12 percent annual interest compounded continuously, is $112.75.

As this section demonstrates, the compounding frequency can impact the value of an investment. Investors, then, should look carefully at the frequency of compounding. Is it annual, semiannual, quarterly, daily, or continuous? Other things being equal, the more frequently interest is compounded, the more interest the investment will earn.

WHAT'S NEXT

In this chapter we investigated the importance of the time value of money in financial decisions, and learned how to calculate present and future values for a single amount, for ordinary annuities, and for annuities due. We also learned how to solve special time value of money problems, such as finding the interest rate or the number of periods.

The skills acquired in this chapter will be applied in later chapters, as we evaluate proposed projects, bonds, and preferred and common stock. They will also be used when we estimate the rate of return expected by suppliers of capital. In the next chapter, we will turn to bond and stock valuation.

Summary

1. *Explain the time value of money and its importance in the business world.*

Money grows over time when it earns interest. Money expected or promised in the future is worth less than the same amount of money in hand today. This is because we lose the opportunity to earn interest when we have to wait to receive money. Similarly, money we owe is less burdensome if it is to be paid in the future rather than now. These concepts are at the heart of investment and valuation decisions of a firm.

2. *Calculate the future value and present value of a single amount.*

To calculate the future value and the present value of a single dollar amount, we may use the algebraic, table, or calculator methods. Future value and present value are mirror images of each other. They are compounding and discounting, respectively. With future value, increases in k and n result in an exponential increase in future value. Increases in k and n result in an exponential decrease in present value.

3. *Find the future and present values of an annuity.*

Annuities are a series of equal cash flows. An annuity that has payments that occur at the end of each period is an ordinary annuity. An annuity that has payments that occur at the beginning of each period is an annuity due. A perpetuity is a perpetual annuity.

To find the future and present values of an ordinary annuity, we may use the algebraic, table, or financial calculator method. To find the future and present values of an annuity due, multiply the applicable formula by (1 + k) to reflect the earlier payment.

4. *Solve time value of money problems with uneven cashflows.*

To solve time value of money problems with uneven cash flows, we find the value of each payment (each single amount) in the cash flow series and total each single amount. Sometimes the series has several cash flows of the same amount. If so, calculate the present value of those cash flows as an annuity, and add the total to the sum of the present values of the single amounts to find the total present value of the uneven cash flow series.

5. *Solve special time value of money problems, such as finding the interest rate, number or amount of payments, or number of periods in a future or present value problem.*

To solve special time value of money problems, we use the present value and future value equations, and solve for the missing variable, such as the loan payment, k, or n. We may also solve for the present and future value of single amounts or annuities where the interest rate, payments, and number of time periods are expressed in terms other than a year. The more often interest is compounded, the larger the future value.

Equations Introduced in This Chapter

Equation 8-1a. Future Value of a Single Amount—Algebraic Method:

$$FV = PV \times (1 + k)^n$$

where: FV = Future Value, the ending amount
PV = Present Value, the starting amount, or original principal
k = Rate of interest per period (expressed as a decimal)
n = Number of time periods

Equation 8-1b. Future Value of a Single Amount—Table Method:

$$FV = PV \times (FVIF_{k,n})$$

where: FV = Future Value, the ending amount
PV = Present Value, the starting amount
$FVIF_{k,n}$ = Future Value Interest Factor given interest rate, k, and number of periods, n, from Table I

Equation 8-2a. Present Value of a Single Amount—Algebraic Method:

$$PV = FV \times \frac{1}{(1 + k)^n}$$

where: PV = Present Value, the starting amount
FV = Future Value, the ending amount
k = Discount rate of interest per period (expressed as a decimal)
n = Number of time periods

Equation 8-2b. Present Value of a Single Amount—Table Approach:

$$PV = FV \times (PVIF_{k,n})$$

where: PV = Present Value
FV = Future Value
$PVIF_{k,n}$ = Present Value Interest Factor given interest rate, k, and number of periods, n, from Table II

Equation 8-3a. Future Value of an Annuity—Algebraic Method:

$$FVA = PMT \times \left[\frac{(1 + k)^n - 1}{k} \right]$$

where: FVA = Future Value of an Annuity
PMT = Amount of each annuity payment
k = Interest rate per time period
n = Number of annuity payments

Equation 8-3b. Future Value of an Annuity—Table Approach:

$$FVA = PMT \times FVIFA_{k,n}$$

where: FVA = Future Value of an Annuity
PMT = Amount of each annuity payment
$FVIFA_{k,n}$ = Future Value Interest Factor for an Annuity from Table III
k = Interest rate per period
n = Number of annuity payments

Equation 8-4a. Present Value of an Annuity—Algebraic Method:

$$PVA = PMT \times \left[\frac{1 - \dfrac{1}{(1 + k)^n}}{k} \right]$$

where: PVA = Present Value of an Annuity
PMT = Amount of each annuity payment
k = Discount rate per period
n = Number of annuity payments

Equation 8-4b. Present Value of an Annuity—Table Method:

$$PVA = PMT \times PVIFA_{k,n}$$

where: PVA = Present Value of an Annuity
PMT = Amount of each annuity payment
$PVIFA_{k,n}$ = Present Value Interest Factor for an Annuity from Table IV
k = Discount rate per time period
n = Number of annuity payments

Equation 8-5. Present Value of a Perpetuity:

$$PVP = PMT \times \left(\frac{1}{k}\right)$$

where: PVP = Present value of a perpetuity
PMT = Amount of each of the perpetual annuity payments
k = Discount rate

Equation 8-6. Rate of Return:

$$k = \left(\frac{FV}{PV}\right)^{\frac{1}{n}} - 1$$

where: k = Rate of return
FV = Future Value
PV = Present Value
n = Number of compounding periods

Equation 8-7. Future Value with Continuous Compounding:

$$FV = PV \times e^{(k \times n)}$$

where: FV = Future Value
PV = Present Value
e = Natural antilog of 1
k = Stated annual interest rate
n = Number of years

Self-Test

ST-1. Jed is investing $5,000 into an eight-year certificate of deposit (CD) that pays 6 percent annual interest with annual compounding. How much will he have when the CD matures?

ST-2. How much money would Jed have at maturity if he put his $5,000 into an eight-year CD that pays 6 percent annual interest compounded monthly?

ST-3. Heidi's grandmother died and provided in her will that Heidi will receive $100,000 from a trust when Heidi turns twenty-one years of age, ten years from now. If the appropriate discount rate is 8 percent, what is the present value of this $100,000 to Heidi?

ST-4. Zack wants to buy a new Ford Mustang automobile. He will need to borrow $20,000 to go with his down payment in order to afford this car. If car loans are available at a 6 percent annual interest rate, what would Zack's monthly payment be on a four-year loan?

ST-5. Bridget invested $5,000 in a growth mutual fund and in ten years her investment had grown to $15,529.24. What annual rate of return did Bridget earn over this ten-year period?

Review Questions

1. What is the time value of money?
2. Why does money have time value?
3. What is compound interest? Compare compound interest to discounting.
4. How is present value affected by a change in the discount rate?
5. What is an annuity?
6. Suppose you are planning to make regular contributions in equal payments to an investment fund for your retirement. Which formula would you use to figure out how much your investments will be worth at retirement time, given an assumed rate of return on your investments?
7. How does continuous compounding benefit an investor?
8. If you are doing PVA and FVA problems, what difference does it make if the annuities are "ordinary annuities" or "annuities due"?
9. Which formula would you use to solve for the payment required for a car loan if you know the interest rate, length of the loan, and the borrowed amount? Explain.

Build Your Communication Skills

CS-1. Obtain information from four different financial institutions about the terms of their basic savings accounts. Compare the interest rates paid and the frequency of the compounding. For each account, how much money would you have in ten years if you deposited $100 today? Write a 1–2 page report of your findings.

CS-2. Interview a mortgage lender in your community. Write a brief report about the mortgage terms. Include in your discussion comments about what interest rate is charged on different types of loans, why rates differ, what fees are charged in addition to the interest and principal that mortgagees must pay to this lender, and describe the advantages and disadvantages of some of the loans offered.

Problems

Future Value

8-1. What is the future value of $10,000 to be received five years from now if you earn 6 percent annual interest?

Future Value

8-2. Calculate the future value of $50,000 twenty years from now if the annual interest rate is:

    a. 0 percent
    b. 5 percent
    c. 10 percent
    d. 20 percent

Present Value

8-3. What is the present value of $20,000 to be received ten years from now using a 12 percent annual discount rate?

Present Value

8-4. Calculate the present value of $60,000 to be received twenty years from now at an annual discount rate of:

    a. 0 percent
    b. 5 percent
    c. 10 percent
    d. 20 percent

8-5. What is the present value of a $500 ten-year annual ordinary annuity at a 7 percent annual discount rate?

Present Value of an Annuity

8-6. Calculate the present value of a $5,000 thirty-year annual ordinary annuity at an annual discount rate of:

Present Value of an Annuity

    a. 0 percent
    b. 10 percent
    c. 20 percent
    d. 50 percent

8-7. What is the future value of a five-year annual ordinary annuity of $500, using a 9 percent interest rate?

Future Value of an Annuity

8-8. Calculate the future value of a twelve-year, $6,000 annual ordinary annuity, using a discount rate of:

Future Value of an Annuity

    a. 0 percent
    b. 2 percent
    c. 10 percent
    d. 20 percent

8-9. You invested $50,000, and ten years later the value of your investment has grown to $185,361. What is your compounded annual rate of return over this period?

Solving for k

8-10. You invested $1,000 five years ago, and the value of your investment has *fallen* to $773.78. What is your compounded annual rate of return over this period?

Solving for k

8-11. What is the present value of a $50 annual perpetual annuity using a discount rate of 8 percent.

Present Value of a Perpetuity

8-12. What is the future value of $10, earning 8 percent annual interest, 200 years later?

Future Value

8-13. Indicate the number of periods (n) and the interest rate per period (k) for each of the following:

Different Compounding Frequencies

    a. 10 years, 8 percent annual interest rate, compounded annually.
    b. 10 years, 8 percent annual interest rate, compounded semi-annually.
    c. 10 years, 8 percent annual interest rate, compounded quarterly.
    d. 10 years, 8 percent annual interest rate, compounded monthly.
    e. 10 years, 8 percent annual interest rate, compounded daily.

8-14. If you deposit $6,000 into your savings account today, what will your balance be after five years assuming the following independent scenarios?

Future Value

    a. 10 percent annual interest, compounded annually.
    b. 10 percent annual interest, compounded semi-annually.
    c. 10 percent annual interest, compounded monthly.
    d. 10 percent annual interest, compounded daily.
    e. 10 percent annual interest, compounded continuously.

8-15. What is the amount you have to invest today at 7 percent annual interest to be able to receive $10,000 after

Present Value

    a. five years?
    b. ten years?
    c. twenty years?

8-16. How much money would Ruby Carter need to deposit in her savings account at Great Western Bank today in order to have $16,850.58 in her account after five years? Assume she

Future Value

makes no other deposits or withdrawals and the bank guarantees an 11 percent annual interest rate, compounded annually.

Future Value

8-17. If you invest $13,000 today, how much will you receive after

a. seven years at a 5 percent annual interest rate?
b. ten years at a 7 percent annual interest rate?

Solving for k

8-18. The property you purchased twelve years ago for $40,000 is now worth $200,000. What is the compounded annual rate of return you have earned on this investment?

Solving for n

8-19. Amy Jolly deposited $1,000 in a savings account. The annual interest rate is 10 percent, compounded semiannually. How many years will it take for her money to grow to $2,653.30?

Present Value of an Annuity

8-20. Beginning a year from now, Bernardo O'Reilly will receive $10,000 a year from his pension fund. There will be fifteen of these annual payments. What is the present value of these payments if a 6 percent annual interest rate is applied as the discount rate?

Future Value of an Annuity

8-21. If you invest $ 2,000 per year for the next ten years at an 8 percent annual interest rate, beginning one year from today compounded annually, how much are you going to have at the end of the tenth year?

8-22. It is the beginning of the quarter and you intend to invest $300 into your retirement fund at the end of every quarter for the next thirty years. You are promised an annual interest rate of 8 percent, compounded quarterly.

Challenge Problem
Future Value of an Annuity

a. How much will you have after thirty years upon your retirement?
b. How long will your money last if you start withdrawing $6,000 at the end of every quarter after your retirement?

Solve for the Payment

8-23. A $10,000 loan obtained today is to be repaid in equal annual installments over the next seven years starting at the end of this year. If the annual interest rate is 10 percent, compounded annually, how much is to be paid each year?

Present Value of a Perpetuity

8-24. Allie Fox is moving to Central America. Before he packs up his wife and son he purchases an annuity that guarantees payments of $10,000 a year in perpetuity. How much did he pay if the annual interest rate is 12 percent?

Future Value

8-25. Matt and Christina Drayton deposited $500 into a savings account the day their daughter, Joey, was born. Their intention was to use this money to help pay for Joey's wedding expenses when and if she decided to get married. The account pays 5 percent annual interest with continuous compounding. Upon her return from a graduation trip to Hawaii, Joey surprises her parents with the sudden announcement of her planned marriage to John Prentice. The couple set the wedding date to coincide with Joey's twenty-third birthday. How much money will be in Joey's account on her wedding day?

Future Value

8-26. To finance your college education your bank has agreed to lend you $5,000 on January 1, 1998, and $5,000 on the first day of each year for the next three years. The annual interest rate of 10 percent is compounded yearly. You plan to graduate on December 31, 2001. What will be the amount you will owe the bank on that date?

Solving for the Payment

8-27. You plan to repay the loan in Problem 8-26 in ten equal installments beginning at the beginning of each year starting in the year 2002. What amount will you have to pay each year?

Solving for k

8-28. Joanne and Walter borrow $14,568.50 for a new car before they move to Stepford, Connecticut. They are required to repay the amortized loan with four annual payments of $5000 each. What is the interest rate on their loan?

8-29. Norman Bates is planning for his eventual retirement from the motel business. He plans to make quarterly deposits of $1,000 into an IRA starting three months from today. The guaranteed annual interest rate is 8 percent, compounded quarterly. He plans to retire in fifteen years.

Future Value of an Annuity Challenge Problem

  a. How much money will be in his retirement account when he retires?
  b. Norman also supports his mother. At Norman's retirement party, Mother tells him they will need $2,000 each month in order to pay for their living expenses. Using the interest rate above and the total account balance from part a, for how many years will Norman keep Mother happy by withdrawing $6,000 at the end of each quarter? It is very important that Norman keep Mother happy.

Challenge Problem

8-30. Jack Torrance comes to you for financial advice. He hired the Redrum Weed-N-Whack Lawn Service to trim the hedges in his garden. Because of the large size of the project (the shrubs were really out of control), Redrum has given Jack a choice of four different payment options. Which of the four options below would you recommend that Jack choose? Why?

  Option 1. Pay $5,650 cash immediately.
  Option 2. Pay $6,750 cash in one lump sum two years from now.
  Option 3. Pay $800 at the end of each quarter for two years.
  Option 4. Pay $1,000 immediately plus $5,250 in one lump sum two years from now. Jack tells you he can earn 8 percent interest, compounded quarterly, on his money. You have no reason to question his assumption.

Solving for the Payment

8-31. Sarah has $30,000 for a down payment on a house and wants to borrow $120,000 from a mortgage banker to purchase a $150,000 house. The mortgage loan is to be repaid in monthly installments over a thirty-year period. The annual interest rate is 9 percent. How much will Sarah's monthly mortgage payments be?

Solving for Payment

8-32. Slick has his heart set on a new Miata sportscar. He will need to borrow $18,000 to get the car he wants. The bank will loan Slick the $18,000 at an annual interest rate of 6 percent.

Solving for Payment

  a. How much would Slick's monthly car payments be for a four-year loan?
  b. How much would Slick's monthly car payments be if he obtains a six-year loan at the same interest rate?

Comprehensive problem

8-33. On January 1, 1997, you won a jackpot in a Lottery. The amount you received in hand after deduction of taxes is $1 million. A part of this fortune you are planning to spend on an exotic round-the-world trip right after your graduation in three years on December 31, 1999. The rest you are planning to invest in your retirement fund which you will keep untouched until you retire after thirty years in December 31, 2027. The investment in the retirement fund will consist of an investment in stocks with an average after-tax return of 7 percent and a savings account earning an after-tax interest of 4 percent both compounded annually. To achieve adequate security you plan to invest at least 40 percent of the initial investment in the savings account. From January 1, 2002, onward, you are going to add $5,000 per year at the beginning of each year for next fifteen years (2017) and then $10,000 per year at the beginning of each year for the subsequent ten years (2027) in the retirement fund savings account. Your psychic friend has predicted that you are going to live twenty-five years after retirement, and you do believe him—considering whatever he has predicted so far did ultimately come true. All the stock investments are assumed to be transferred to the savings account immediately after your retirement. After your retirement, you would like to withdraw $300,000 per year at the beginning of each year, starting January 1, 2028, for the next twenty-five years till the year 2052—at the end of which you think you are going to die. At that point in time, you would like to leave $3 million in a trust fund to award a scholarship each year from the interest earnings of the fund. With the above objectives in view, how much will you be able to set aside on January 1, 1997, for your world trip before you commit the rest of the funds to long-term retirement fund investments? Assuming you keep this amount in a NOW account earning 2 percent per year compounded annually, what would be the amount available for spending when you actually take the trip?

Answers to Self-Test

ST-1. $FV = \$5{,}000 \times 1.06^8 = \$7{,}969.24 = $ Jed's balance when the eight-year CD matures

ST-2. $FV = \$5{,}000 \times (1 + .06/12)^{12 \times 8}$
$= \$5{,}000 \times 1.005^{96} = \$8{,}070.71$
$= $ Jed's balance in 8 years with monthly compounding

ST-3. $PV = \$100{,}000 \times 1/1.08^{10} = \$46{,}319.35$
$= $ the present value of Heidi's $100,000

ST-4. $\$20{,}000 = PMT \times [1-(1/1.005^{48})]/.005$
$\$20{,}000 = PMT \times 42.5803$
$PMT = \$469.70 = $ Zach's car loan payment

ST-5. $\$5{,}000 \times FVIF_{k=?,\,n=10} = \$15{,}529.24$
$FVIF_{k=?,\,n=10} = 3.1058 \therefore k = 12\% = $ Bridget's annual rate of return on the mutual fund

chapter 9

Bond and Stock Valuation

Nowadays we know the price of everything and the value of nothing.

Oscar Wilde

Valuation Is Both Art and Science

Frank Martin wanted to sell stock in his company. Frank runs Physician Dispensing Systems (PDS), a company that allows doctors to bypass the local pharmacy and dispense drugs in their offices. After many attempts, Frank learned that predicting how much investors would be willing to pay for stock in his company was tough.

Those who invest in securities use all types of techniques to value the stocks they purchase. They try to estimate which stocks have the most potential for gain, assess risk factors, pore over financial data such as the price-to-earnings ratio per share, and examine industry trends. As a stock issuer, Frank learned that arriving at a precise value for PDS stock was darned near impossible.

Frank decided to figure out how much his company was worth first. That seemed easy enough. He looked at the value of health-care companies that were similar to his and discovered that many health-care companies were valued at 20 times their net earnings. So, he reasoned, if PDS earned $1 million, he should be able to raise $20 million in long-term funds by selling stock to investors.

Chapter Objectives

After reading this chapter, you should be able to:

1. Explain the importance of bond and stock valuation.

2. Discuss the concept of securities valuation.

3. Compute the market value and the yield to maturity of a bond.

4. Calculate the market value and expected yield of preferred stock.

5. Compute the market value and expected yield of common stock.

Frank discovered, however, that people weren't willing to rely on the price-to-earnings ratio for PDS stock. Why? Investors look at risk factors, especially with a new company. Frank weighed the risk factors and reasoned that he could raise $10 million in his stock issue. Well, no. Because, for a new company's stock offering to be successful, the company must be undervalued. So, even if investors thought his company was worth $10 million, they would only be willing to invest $7 million.

John D. Higgins, senior vice president of Royce Investment Group, Inc., advises that when it comes to valuing stock in certain companies, you can't expect scientific precision. He says, "With early-stage companies, you often run up against the limits of what an investor will do." ※

Sources: Michael Brush, "The Eight Best S&P 500 Stocks to Buy Now," *Money Magazine* (December 1995): 141; David Evanson, "For What It's Worth," *Entrepreneur Magazine* (May 1995).

Chapter Overview

In this chapter we will discuss how to value bonds and shares of stock in a dynamic marketplace. First, we will investigate the importance of valuation and introduce a general model that analysts and investors use to value securities. Then, we will show how to adapt the model to bonds, preferred stock, and common stock. For common stock, we'll explore additional valuation techniques.

The Importance of Bond and Stock Valuation

As chapter 1 explained, the primary financial goal of financial managers is to maximize the market value of their firm. It follows, then, that financial managers need to assess the market value of their bonds and stock to gauge progress.

Accurate bond and stock valuation is also a concern when a corporation such as Physician Dispensing Systems contemplates selling securities to raise long-term funds. Issuers want to raise the most money possible from selling securities. Issuers lose money if they undervalue their stock or bonds. Likewise, would-be purchasers are concerned about securities' value because they don't want to pay more than the securities are worth.

A General Valuation Model

The value of a security depends on its future earning power. To value a security, then, we consider three factors that affect future earnings:

- size of cash flows
- timing of cash flows
- risk

In chapter 7 we examined how risk factors affect an investor's required rate of return. In chapter 8 we learned that time value of money calculations can determine an investment's value, given the size and timing of the cash flows.

Financial managers and investors determine the value of a security by finding the present value of the security's future cash flows. We can calculate a bond's value by taking the sum of the present values of each of future cash flows from the bond's interest and principal payments. We can calculate a stock's value by taking the sum of the present values of future dividend cash flow payments.

Analysts and investors use a general valuation model to calculate the present value of future cash flows of a security. This model, the **discounted cash flow model (DCF),** is a basic valuation model for a security that is expected to generate cash payments, such as dividends or interest and principal. The DCF equation is shown in Equation 9-1:

The Discounted Cash Flow Valuation Model

$$V_0 = \frac{CF_1}{(1 + k)^1} + \frac{CF_2}{(1 + k)^2} + \frac{CF_3}{(1 + k)^3} \cdots + \cdots \frac{CF_n}{(1 + k)^n} \qquad (9\text{-}1)$$

where:
V_0 = Present value of the anticipated cash flows from the security, its current value

$CF_{1, 2, 3, \text{ and } n}$ = Cash flows expected to be received one, two, three, and so on up to n periods in the future

k = Discount rate, the required rate of return

The discounted cash flow model, Equation 9-1, is derived from the present value equations in chapter 8, pages 172–175.

The DCF model values a security by calculating the sum of the present values of all expected future cash flows. Each cash flow is discounted back the appropriate number of periods according to its expected timing and required rate of return.

The discount rate in Equation 9-1 is the investor's required rate of return, which is a function of the risk of the investment. Recall from chapter 7 that the riskier the security, the higher the required rate of return.

The discounted cash flow model is easy to use if we know the cash flows and discount rate. For example, suppose you were considering purchasing a security that entitled you to receive payments of $100 in one year, another $100 in two years, and $1,000 in three years. If your required rate of return for securities of this type were 20 percent, then we would calculate the value of the security as follows:

$$V_0 = \frac{\$100}{(1 + .20)^1} + \frac{\$100}{(1 + .20)^2} + \frac{\$1,000}{(1 + .20)^3}$$

$$= \$83.3333 + \$69.4444 + \$578.7037$$

$$= \$731.48$$

The total of the security's three future cash flows at a 20 percent required rate of return yields a present value of $731.48.

In the sections that follow, we'll adapt the discounted cash flow valuation model to apply to bonds and stocks.

BOND VALUATION

Remember from chapter 2 that a bond's cash flows are determined by the bond's coupon interest payments, face value, and maturity.

Because coupon interest payments occur at regular intervals throughout the life of the bond, those payments are an annuity. Instead of using several terms representing the individual cash flows from the future coupon interest payments (CF_1, CF_2, and so on), we adapt Equation 9-1 by using one term to show the annuity. The remaining term represents the future cash flow of the bond's face value,

We discussed bonds and bond terminology in chapter 2, pages 25–28.

or principal, that is paid at maturity. Equation 9-2 shows the adapted valuation model:

The Bond Valuation Formula (Algebraic Version)

$$V_B = INT \times \left[\frac{1 - \frac{1}{(1 + k_d)^n}}{k_d} \right] + \frac{M}{(1 + k_d)^n} \tag{9-2}$$

where: V_B = Current market value of the bond
INT = Dollar amount of each periodic interest payment
n = Number of times the interest payment is received (which is also the number of periods until maturity)
M = Principal payment received at maturity
k_d = Required rate of return per period on the bond debt instrument

The table version of the bond valuation model is shown in Equation 9-3, as follows:

The Bond Valuation Formula (Table Version)

$$V_B = (INT \times PVIFA_{k, n}) + (M \times PVIF_{k, n}) \tag{9-3}$$

where: $PVIFA_{k, n}$ = Present Value Interest Factor for an Annuity from Table IV
$PVIF_{k, n}$ = Present Value Interest Factor for a single amount from Table II

To use a calculator to solve for the value of a bond, enter the dollar value of the interest payment as [PMT], the face value payment at maturity as [FV], the number of payments as "n," and the required rate of return, k_d depicted as [I/Y] on the TI BAII Plus calculator. Then compute the present value of the bond's cash flows.

Now let's apply the bond valuation model. Suppose Microsoft Corporation issues a 6 percent coupon interest rate bond with a maturity of ten years. The face value of the bond, payable at maturity, is $1,000.

First, we calculate the dollar amount of the coupon interest payments. At a 6 percent coupon interest rate, each payment is $.06 \times \$1,000 = \$60$.

Next, we need to choose a required rate of return, k_d. Remember that k_d is the required rate of return that is appropriate for the bond based on its risk, maturity, marketability, and tax treatment. Let's assume that 8 percent is the rate of return the market determines to be appropriate.

Now we have all the factors we need to solve for the value of Microsoft Corporation's bond. We know that k_d is 8 percent, n is 10, the coupon interest payment is $60 per year, and the face value payment at maturity is $1,000. Using Equation 9-2, we calculate the bond's value as follows:

$$V_B = \$60 \times \left[\frac{1 - \frac{1}{(1 + .08)^{10}}}{.08} \right] + \frac{\$1,000}{(1 + .08)^{10}}$$

$$= (\$60 \times 6.7100814) + \left(\frac{\$1,000}{2.158925} \right)$$

$$= \$402.604884 + \$463.1935$$

$$= \$865.80$$

Take Note

The determinants of nominal interest rates, or required rates of return, include the real rate of interest, the inflation premium, the default risk premium, the liquidity premium, and the maturity premium. Each person evaluating a bond will select an appropriate required rate of return, k_d, for the bond based on these determinants.

Notice that the value of Microsoft Corporation's bond is the sum of the present values of the ten annual $60 coupon interest payments plus the present value of the one-time $1,000 face value to be paid ten years from now, given a required rate of return of 8 percent.

To find the Microsoft bond's value using present value tables, recall that the bond has a face value of $1,000, a coupon interest payment of $60, a required rate of return of 8 percent, and an n value of 10. We apply Equation 9-3 as shown:

$$V_B = (\$60 \times \text{PVIFA}_{8\%, \, 10 \, \text{yrs}}) + (\$1,000 \times \text{PVIF}_{8\%, \, 10 \, \text{yrs}})$$
$$= (\$60 \times 6.7101) + (\$1,000 \times .4632)$$
$$= \$402.606 + \$463.200$$
$$= \$865.81$$

We see that the sum of the present value of the coupon interest annuity, $402.606, plus the present value of the principal, $463.200, results in a bond value of $865.81.

Here's how to find the bond's value using the TI BAII PLUS financial calculator. Enter the $60 coupon interest payment as PMT, the one-time principal payment of $1,000 as FV, the ten years until maturity as n (N on the TI BAII PLUS), and the 8 percent required rate of return—depicted as I/Y on the TI BAII Plus. As demonstrated in Chapter 8 calculator solutions, clear the time value of money TVM registers before entering the new data. Skip steps 2 and 3 if you know your calculator is set to one payment per year and is also set for end of period payment mode.

TI BAII PLUS FINANCIAL CALCULATOR SOLUTION

Step 1: Press `2nd` `CLR TVM` to clear previous values.

Step 2: Press `2nd` `P/Y` 1 `ENTER` , `2nd` `BGN` `2nd` `SET` , repeat `2nd` `SET` until END shows in the display `2nd` `QUIT` to set to the annual interest rate mode and to set the annuity payment to end of period mode.

Step 3: Input the values and compute.

1000 `FV`   8 `I/Y`   10 `N`   60 `PMT`   `CPT` `PV`   Answer: −865.80

The $865.80 is negative because it is a cash outflow—the amount an investor would pay to buy the bond today.

We have shown how to value bonds with annual coupon interest payments in this section. Next, we show how to value bonds with semi-annual coupon interest payments.

Semi-Annual Coupon Interest Payments

In the hypothetical bond valuation examples for Microsoft Corporation, we assumed the coupon interest was paid annually. However, most bonds issued in the United States pay interest semiannually (twice per year). With semiannual interest payments, we must adjust the bond valuation model accordingly. If the Microsoft bond paid interest twice per year, the adjustments would look like this:

To see how to adjust table and calculator solutions for semiannual interest, review chapter 8, pages 191–193.

	ANNUAL BASIS	SEMI-ANNUAL BASIS
Coupon Interest Payments	$60	÷ 2 = $30 per six-month period
Maturity	10 yrs	× 2 = 20 six-month periods
Required Rate of Return	8%	÷ 2 = 4%

These values can now be used in Equation 9-2, Equation 9-3, or a financial calculator, in the normal manner. For example, if Microsoft's 6 percent coupon, ten-year bond paid interest semiannually, its present value per Equation 9-2 would be:

$$V_B = \$30 \times \left[\frac{1 - \frac{1}{(1 + .04)^{20}}}{.04} \right] + \frac{\$1000}{(1 + .04)^{20}}$$

$$= (\$30 \times 13.590326) + \left(\frac{\$1,000}{2.191123} \right)$$

$$= \$407.709780 + \$456.3870$$

$$= \$864.10$$

The value of our Microsoft bond with semiannual interest and a 4 percent per semiannual discount rate is $864.10. This compares to a value of $865.80 for the same bond if it pays annual interest and has an 8 percent annual discount rate. Note that a required rate of return of 4% per semiannual period is not the same as 8% per year. The difference in the frequency of discounting gives a slightly different answer.

The Yield to Maturity of a Bond

Most investors want to know how much return they will earn on a bond to gauge whether the bond meets their expectations. That way, investors can tell whether they should add the bond to their investment portfolio. As a result, investors often calculate a bond's yield to maturity before they buy a bond. **Yield to maturity (YTM)** represents the average rate of return on a bond if all promised interest and principal payments are made on time and if the interest payments are reinvested at the YTM rate given the price paid for the bond.

Calculating a Bond's Yield to Maturity
To calculate a bond's YTM, we apply the bond valuation model. However, we apply it differently than we did when solving for a bond's present value (price) because we solve for k_d, the equivalent of YTM.

To compute a bond's YTM, we must know the values of all variables except k_d. We take the market price of the bond, P_B, as the value of a bond, V_B, examining financial sources such as the *Wall Street Journal* for current bond prices.

Once you have all variables except k_d, solving for k_d algebraically is exceedingly difficult because that term appears three times in the valuation equation. Instead, we use the trial-and-error method. In other words, we guess a value for k_d and solve for V_B using that value. When we find a k_d value that results in a bond value that matches the published bond price, P_0, we know that the k_d value is the correct YTM. The YTM is the return that bond investors require to purchase the bond.[1]

Here's an illustration of the trial-and-error method for finding YTM. Suppose that the *Wall Street Journal* reported that the Microsoft bond in our earlier example is currently selling for $929.76. What is the bond's YTM if purchased at this price?

Recall the annual coupon interest payments for the Microsoft bond were $60 each, the bond had a ten-year maturity, and a face value of $1,000. Applying the bond valuation model, we solve for the k_d that produces a bond value of $929.76.

$$\$929.76 = \$60 \times \left[\frac{1 - \dfrac{1}{(1 + k_d)^{10}}}{k_d} \right] + \frac{1,000}{(1 + k_d)^{10}}$$

Although we can try any k_d value, remember that when k was 8 percent, the bond's calculated value, V_B, was $865.80. Bond prices and yields vary inversely—the higher the YTM, the lower the bond price; and the lower the YTM, the higher the bond price. The bond's current market price of $929.76 is higher than $865.80, so we know the YTM must be less than 8 percent. If you pay more than $865.80 to buy the bond, your return will be less than 8 percent.

Because we know that YTM and bond prices are inversely related, let's try 6 percent in our bond valuation model, Equation 9-2. We find that a k_d value of 6 percent results in the following bond value:

$$\begin{aligned} V_B &= \$60 \times \left[\frac{1 - \dfrac{1}{(1 + .06)^{10}}}{.06} \right] + \frac{\$1,000}{(1 + .06)^{10}} \\ &= (\$60 \times 7.36009) + \left(\frac{\$1,000}{1.79085} \right) \\ &= \$441.605400 + \$558.3941 \\ &= \$1,000.00 \end{aligned}$$

At a k_d of 6 percent, the bond's value is $1,000 instead of $929.76. We'll need to try again. Our second guess should be higher than 6 percent because at $k_d = 6\%$ the bond's calculated value is lower than the market price. Let's try 7 percent. At a k_d of 7 percent, the bond's value is as follows:

$$\begin{aligned} V_B &= \$60 \times \left[\frac{1 - \dfrac{1}{(1 + .07)^{10}}}{.07} \right] + \frac{\$1,000}{(1 + .07)^{10}} \\ &= (\$60 \times 7.02358) + \left(\frac{\$1,000}{1.96715} \right) \\ &= \$421.414800 + \$508.3496 \\ &= \$929.76 \end{aligned}$$

With a k_d of 7 percent, the bond's value equals the current market price of $929.76. We conclude that the bond's YTM is 7 percent.[2]

---

[1]In chapter 12 this required rate of return is called the firm's cost of debt capital, which we adjust for taxes. In this chapter, however, our main focus is finding the value of different types of securities, so k_d is referred to as the investor's required rate of return.
[2]We were lucky to find the bond's exact YTM in only two guesses. Often the trial-and-error method requires four or five guesses.

To use the table method to find the YTM of Microsoft's 6 percent coupon rate, ten-year bond at a price of $929.76, use Equation 9-3 as follows:

First guess: $k_d = 6\%$:

$$V_B = (\$60 \times PVIFA_{6\%, 10\ periods}) + (\$1,000 \times PVIF_{6\%, 10\ periods})$$
$$= (\$60 \times 7.3601) + (\$1,000 \times .5584)$$
$$= (\$441.606 + \$558.40$$
$$= \$1,000.01$$

$1,000.01 is too high. We must guess again. Let's try $k_d = 7\%$, as follows:

$$V_B = (\$60 \times PVIFA_{7\%, 10\ periods}) + (\$1,000 \times PVIF_{7\%, 10\ periods})$$
$$= (\$60 \times 7.0236) + (\$1,000 \times .5083)$$
$$= \$421.416 + \$508.30$$
$$= \$929.72$$

Close enough (to $929.76). The bond's YTM is about 7 percent.

Finding a bond's YTM with a financial calculator avoids the trial-and-error method. Simply plug in the values on the calculator and solve for k_d, as shown:

TI BAII PLUS FINANCIAL CALCULATOR SOLUTION

Step 1: Press `2nd` `CLR TVM` to clear previous values.

Step 2: Press `2nd` `P/Y` 1 `ENTER` , `2nd` `BGN` `2nd` `SET` , repeat `2nd` `SET` until END shows in the display `2nd` `QUIT` to set to the annual interest rate mode and to set the annuity payment to end of period mode.

Step 3: Input the values and compute.

929.76 `+/−` `PV`   1000 `FV`   10 `N`   60 `PMT`   `CPT` `I/Y` Ans: 7.00

Using the financial calculator, we find that the YTM of the Microsoft $1,000 face value ten-year bond with a coupon rate of 6 percent and a market price of $929.76 is 7 percent.

The Relationship between Bond YTM and Price

A bond's market price depends on its yield to maturity. When a bond has a YTM greater than its coupon rate, it sells at a *discount* from its face value. When the YTM is equal to the coupon rate, the market price equals the face value. When the YTM is less than the coupon rate, the bond sells at a *premium* over face value.

For instance, in our initial calculations of the Microsoft bond, we found that the present value of its future cash flows was $865.80. That price was lower than the bond's $1,000 face value. Because its market price was lower than its face value, the bond sold at a discount (from its face value). A bond will sell at a discount because buyers and sellers have agreed that the appropriate rate of return for the bond should be higher than the bond's coupon interest rate. With the Microsoft bond, investors required an 8 percent rate of return, but the fixed coupon interest rate was only 6 percent. To compensate for a coupon interest rate that is lower than the required rate, investors would be unwilling to pay the $1,000 face value. Instead, they would only be willing to pay $865.80 to buy the bond.

Now recall the trial-and-error calculations for the YTM of the Microsoft 6 percent coupon rate bond in the previous section. We found that when the YTM was 6 percent, the bond's price was $1,000. This was no coincidence. When the YTM is equal to the coupon interest rate—that is, when the bond is selling at *par*—the bond's price is equal to its face value.

Suppose next that the would-be buyers and sellers of Microsoft Corporation's bond agree that the appropriate yield to maturity for the bond is 4 percent instead of 6 percent. The coupon rate and the face value remain the same, at 6 percent and $1,000, respectively. Using Equation 9-2, the bond's value calculations follow:

$$V_B = \$60 \times \left[\frac{1 - \frac{1}{(1 + .04)^{10}}}{.04} \right] + \frac{\$1,000}{(1 + .04)^{10}}$$

$$= (\$60 \times 8.110896) + \left(\frac{\$1,000}{1.48024} \right)$$

$$= \$486.6538 + \$675.5642$$

$$= \$1,162.22$$

The change from a 6 percent to a 4 percent yield to maturity results in a market value of $1,162.22. That market value for the bond is higher than the $1,000 face value. Because the market price is higher than the bond's face value in our case, the bond sells at a *premium*. Why? Investors pay more to receive "extra" interest because the coupon rate paid is higher than the yield to maturity demanded.

In our example, the calculations show that investors were willing to pay $1,162.22 for a bond with a face value of $1,000 because the coupon interest was 2 percent points higher than the expected rate of return.

Figure 9-1 shows the relationship between YTM and the price of a bond.

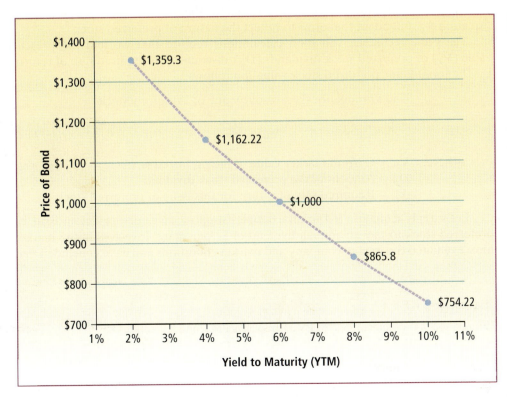

Figure 9-1 **Bond YTM Versus Bond Price**

Figure 9-1 shows the inverse relationship between the price and the YTM for a $1,000 face value, ten year, 6% coupon interest rate bond that pays annual interest.

The inverse relationship between bond price and YTM is important to bond traders. Why? Because if market YTM interest rates rise, bond prices fall. Conversely, if market YTM interest rates fall, bond prices rise. The suggestion that the Fed might raise interest rates is enough to send the bond market reeling as bond traders unload their holdings.

In this section we examined bond valuation for bonds that pay annual and semiannual interest. We also investigated how to find a bond's yield to maturity, and the relationship between a bond's YTM and its price. We turn next to preferred and common stock valuation.

PREFERRED STOCK VALUATION

To value preferred stock, we adapt the discounted cash flow valuation formula, Equation 9-1, to reflect the characteristics of preferred stock. First, recall that the value of any security is the present value of its future cash payments. Second, review characteristics of preferred stock. Preferred stock has no maturity date, so it has no maturity value. Its future cash payments are dividend payments that are paid to preferred stockholders at regular time intervals for as long as they (or their heirs) own the stock. Cash payments from preferred stock dividends are scheduled to continue forever. To value preferred stock, then, we must adapt the discounted cash flow model to reflect that preferred stock dividends are a perpetuity.

We discussed the present value of a perpetuity in chapter 8, page 183.

Finding the Present Value of Preferred Stock Dividends

To calculate the value of preferred stock, we need to find the present value of its future cash flows—which are a perpetuity. In chapter 8 we learned how to find the present value of a perpetuity. We use the formula for the present value of a perpetuity, Equation 8-5, but adapt the terms to reflect the nature of preferred stock.[3]

The preferred stock valuation calculations require that we find the present value (V_P) of preferred stock dividends (D_p), discounted at required rate of return, k_p. The formula for preferred stock valuation follows:

The Formula for the Present Value of Preferred Stock

$$V_P = \frac{D_p}{k_p} \tag{9-4}$$

where: V_P = Current market value of the preferred stock
D_p = Amount of the preferred stock dividend
k_p = Required rate of return for this issue of preferred stock

Let's apply Equation 9-4 to an example. Suppose investors expect an issue of preferred stock to pay an annual dividend of $2 per share. Investors in the market have evaluated the issuing company and market conditions and have concluded that

---

[3]Equation 8-5 is $PV = \dfrac{PMT}{k}$.

In Equation 9-4, V_P substitutes for PV, D_p replaces PMT, and k_p replaces k.

10 percent is a fair rate of return on this investment. The present value of one share of this preferred stock, assuming a 10 percent required rate of return follows:

$$V_P = \left(\frac{\$2}{.10} \right)$$
$$= \$20$$

We find that for investors whose required rate of return (k_p) is 10 percent, the value of each share of this issue of preferred stock is $20.

The Yield on Preferred Stock

The yield on preferred stock represents the annual rate of return that investors would realize if they bought the preferred stock for the current market price and then received the promised preferred dividend payments.

Like bond investors, preferred stock investors want to know the percent yield they can expect if they buy shares of preferred stock at the current market price. That way, investors can compare the yield with the minimum they require to decide whether to invest in the preferred stock.

Fortunately, calculating the yield on preferred stock is considerably easier than calculating the YTM for a bond. To calculate the yield we rearrange Equation 9-4 so that we solve for k_p. We are not solving for the value of the preferred stock, V_P, but rather are taking the market price of the preferred stock, P_p, as a given and solving for k_p as follows:

With bonds, an investor's annual percent return on investment is called the yield to maturity, or YTM. With preferred and common stocks, an investor's percent return on investment is simply called the yield because preferred and common stock don't have a maturity date.

Formula for the Yield on Preferred Stock

$$k_p = \frac{D_p}{P_P} \qquad (9\text{-}5)$$

where: D_p = Amount of the preferred stock dividend
P_P = Current market price of the preferred stock
k_p = Yield on investment that an investor can expect if the shares are purchased at the current market price P_P and if the preferred dividend D_p is paid forever

To illustrate how to find the yield using Equation 9-5, suppose Sure-Thing Corporation's preferred stock is selling for $24 per share today and the dividend is $2 a share. Now assume you are a potential buyer of Sure-Thing's preferred stock, so you want to find the expected annual percent yield on your investment. You know that the current market value of the stock, P_p, is $24, and the stock dividend, D_p, is $2. Applying Equation 9-5, you calculate the yield as follows:

$$k_p = \frac{D_p}{P_P}$$
$$= \frac{\$2}{\$24}$$
$$= .12, \text{ or } 12\%$$

You find that the yield for Sure-Thing's preferred stock is 12 percent. If your minimum required rate of return is less than or equal to 12 percent, you would invest in the Sure-Thing preferred stock. If your required rate of return is greater than 12 percent, you would look for another preferred stock that had a yield of over 12 percent.

Chapter 9   *Bond and Stock Valuation*   **213**

COMMON STOCK VALUATION

The valuation of common stock is somewhat different than the valuation of bonds and preferred stock. Common stock valuation is complicated by the fact that common stock dividends are difficult to predict compared to the interest and principal payments on a bond, or dividends on preferred stock. Indeed, corporations may pay common stock dividends irregularly, or not pay dividends at all.

Analysts use many different approaches to common stock valuation. The most widely accepted models assume that the business is a going concern—that is, it has more value from its future earning potential than the sum of its assets less the sum of its liabilities. For this reason, financial analysts rarely use valuation methods that rely on balance sheet values.

Going concern valuation methods are typically more reliable because the cash flows associated with potential earnings of a firm are usually worth more than the firm's book or liquidation value. To illustrate, assume you were valuing a popular restaurant that is packed every night with customers who appreciate the excellent cuisine, service, and decor. The eatery's physical assets—the furniture, tableware, decorations, and kitchen equipment—are probably worth much less than the value that comes from its potential earnings and related cash flows. Thus, the going concern value of the restaurant would be a more accurate valuation measure in this instance.

Occasionally, balance sheet valuation methods are appropriate because a company is "worth more dead than alive." For example, a mining company whose mines are entirely depleted of minerals could have valuable digging, drilling, or moving equipment. The assets cannot yield any future returns for this business—there is nothing of value to mine—so their book or liquidation values are probably worth more than the firm's future earning power.

In the sections that follow, we examine the most popular going concern and balance sheet common stock valuation models.

Common Stock Going Concern Valuation Models

As with bonds and preferred stock, we value common stock by estimating the present value of the expected future cash flows from the common stock. Those future cash flows are the expected future dividends and the expected price of the stock when the stock is sold.

The discounted cash flow valuation model, Equation 9-1, adapted for common stock is shown in Equation 9-6:

The DCF Valuation Model Applied to Common Stock

$$P_0 = \frac{D_1}{(1 + k_s)^1} + \frac{D_2}{(1 + k_s)^2} + \frac{D_3}{(1 + k_s)^3} \cdots + \cdots \frac{P_n}{(1 + k_s)^n} \qquad (9\text{-}6)$$

where: P_0 = Present value of the expected dividends, the current price of the common stock

D_1, D_2, D_3, etc. = Common stock dividends expected to be received at the end of periods 1, 2, 3, and so on until the stock is sold

P_n = Anticipated selling price of the stock in n periods

k_s = Required rate of return on this common stock investment

In practice, however, using Equation 9-6 to value common stock is problematic because an estimate of the future selling price of a share of stock is often speculative. This severely limits the usefulness of the model.

Instead, some analysts use models that are a variation of Equation 9-6, but do not rely on an estimate of a stock's future selling price. We turn to those models next.

The Constant Growth Dividend Model   Common stock dividends can grow at different rates. The two growth patterns we examine here are no growth, and constant growth. In Appendix 9A, we discuss one additional common stock growth pattern: supernormal growth.

The constant dividend growth model assumes common stock dividends will be paid regularly and grow at a constant rate. The constant growth dividend model (also known as the Gordon Growth model because financial economist Myron Gordon helped develop and popularize it) is shown in Equation 9-7:

The Constant Growth Dividend Valuation Model

$$P_0 = \frac{D_1}{k_s - g} \qquad (9\text{-}7)$$

where: P_0 = Current price of the common stock

D_1 = Dollar amount of the common stock dividend expected 1 period from now

k_s = Required rate of return per period on this common stock investment

g = Expected constant growth rate per period of the company's common stock dividends

Equation 9-7 is easy to use if the stock grows at a constant rate. For example, assume your required rate of return (k_s) for Wendy's common stock is 10 percent. Suppose your research leads you to believe that Wendy's Corporation will pay a \$.25 dividend next year (D_1), and for every year after the dividend will grow at a constant rate (g) of 8 percent a year. Using Equation 9-7, we calculate the present value of Wendy's common stock dividends as follows:

$$P_0 = \frac{\$.25}{.10 - .08}$$
$$= \frac{\$.25}{.02}$$
$$= \$12.50$$

We find that with a common stock dividend in one year of \$.25, a constant growth rate of 8 percent, and a required rate of return of 10 percent, the value of the common stock is \$12.50.

In a no-growth situation, g, in the denominator of Equation 9-7 becomes zero. To value stocks that have no-growth, then, we adapt the general model, as shown in the next section.

No Growth Dividend Model   When common stock dividends are not expected to grow, the cash flow patterns are similar to those of preferred stock—the stockholder receives the same dividend every year. To find the value of common stock that has no-growth dividends, we simply alter the notation of Equation 9-5, the formula for preferred stock valuation, as follows:

No-Growth Common Stock Dividend Valuation Formula

$$P_0 = \frac{D_s}{k_s}$$ (9-8)

where: P_0 = Current price of the common stock
D_s = Amount of the common stock dividend, a constant amount
k_s = Required rate of return per period on this common stock investment

We see that Equation 9-8 is like Equation 9-7, except that g equals zero. Since zero is subtracted from k_s, the "−g" is dropped in Equation 9-8.

As an example of a no–growth stock valuation, let's say that the common stock annual dividend was \$2, and investors' required rate of return was 10 percent. The value (price) of the common stock, according to Equation 9-8, follows:

$$P_0 = \left(\frac{\$2}{.10}\right)$$
$$= \$20$$

We find that if market investors' required rate of return (k_s) were 10 percent, the market price of each share of this common stock would be \$20.

The P/E Model Many investment analysts use the price-to-earnings, or P/E, ratio to value common stock. As we discussed in chapter 6, the P/E ratio, defined as follows, is the price per share of a common stock divided by the company's earnings per share:

The P/E Ratio

$$P/E \text{ ratio} = \frac{Price\ per\ share}{Earnings\ per\ share}$$

The P/E ratio indicates how much investors are willing to pay for each dollar of a stock's earnings. So, a P/E ratio of 20 means that investors are willing to pay \$20 for \$1 of a stock's earnings. A high P/E ratio indicates that investors believe the stock's earnings will increase, or that the risk of the stock is low, or both.

Financial analysts often use a P/E model to estimate common stock value for businesses that are not public. First, analysts compare the P/E ratios of similar companies within an industry to determine an appropriate P/E ratio for companies in that industry. Second, analysts calculate an appropriate stock price for firms in the industry by multiplying each firm's earnings per share (EPS) by the industry average P/E ratio. The P/E model formula, Equation 9-9, follows:

The P/E Model

Appropriate Stock Price = Industry P/E Ratio × EPS (9-9)

To illustrate how to apply the P/E model, let's value the common stock of the Zumwalt Corporation. Suppose that Zumwalt Corporation has current earnings per share of \$2 and, given the risk and growth prospects of the firm, the analyst has determined that the company's common stock should sell for fifteen times current earnings. Applying the P/E model, we calculate the following price for Zumwalt Corporation's common stock:

$$\text{Appropriate Stock Price} = \text{Industry P/E Ratio} \times \text{EPS}$$
$$= 15 \times \$2$$
$$= \$30$$

Our P/E model calculations show that $30 per share is the appropriate price for common stock that has a $2 earnings per share and an industry P/E ratio of 15. The industry P/E ratio would be adjusted up or down according to the individual firm's growth prospects and risk relative to the industry norm.

Balance Sheet Valuation Approaches

Some valuation approaches view the firm as if it were about to cease operations immediately. These rely on the balance sheet value of the firm's assets, less liabilities, to value the firm. Such valuation approaches are *balance sheet valuation approaches*. We discuss two valuation methods that start with the balance sheet: book value and liquidation value.

Book Value   One of the simplest ways to value a firm's common stock is to subtract the value of the firm's liabilities, and preferred stock, if any, as recorded on the balance sheet, from the value of its assets. The result is the **book value** or **net worth** of a company's common stock. To find the book value per share of common stock, divide the company's book value by the number of outstanding common stock shares. The solution follows:

Book Value per Share

$$\text{Book Value per Share} = \frac{(\text{Total Assets} - \text{Total Liabilities})}{\text{Number of Shares Outstanding}} \qquad (9\text{-}10)$$

The book value approach has severe limitations. The asset values recorded on a firm's balance sheet usually reflect what the current owners originally paid for the assets, not the current value of the assets. Due to these and other limitations, the book value is rarely used.

Liquidation Value   The liquidation value and book value valuation methods are similar, except that the liquidation method uses the market values of the assets and liabilities, not book values, as in Equation 9-10. The market values of the assets are the amounts the assets would earn on the open market if they were sold (or liquidated). The market values of the liabilities are the amounts of money it would take to pay off the liabilities.

The **liquidation value** is the amount each common stockholder would receive if the firm closed, sold all assets and paid all liabilities and preferred stock, and distributed the net proceeds to the common stockholders. To calculate the liquidation value per share, divide the liquidation value by the number of common shares outstanding.

Although more reliable than book value, liquidation value is a worst-case valuation assessment. A company's common stock should be worth at least the amount generated per share at liquidation. Because liquidation value does not consider the earnings and cash flows the firm will generate in the future, it may provide misleading results for companies that have significant future earning potential.

Deciding Which Stock Valuation Approach to Use

To choose between valuation approaches, determine first whether the business has a significant going concern value. The value of a company is whichever is greater, the going concern or the liquidation value. Owners will either continue operating a company or liquidate it, depending on the alternative that generates the greater value for them.

The Yield on Common Stock

We calculate the yield for common stock by rearranging the terms in Equation 9-7, to arrive at the constant growth dividend model, as shown in Equation 9-11:

Formula for the Yield on Common Stock

$$k_s = \frac{D_1}{P_0} + g \qquad (9\text{-}11)$$

where: D_1 = Amount of the common stock dividend anticipated in one period
P_0 = Current market price of the common stock
g = Expected constant growth rate of dividends per period
k_s = Expected rate of return per period on this common stock investment

Equation 9-10 is also called the formula for an investor's total rate of return from common stock. The stock's **dividend yield** is the term D_1/P_0.

To demonstrate how Equation 9-11 works, suppose you found that the price of General Motors common stock today was $52 per share. Then suppose you believe that General Motors will pay a common stock dividend next year of $4.80 a share, and the dividend will grow each year at a constant annual rate of 4 percent. If you buy one share of General Motors common stock at the listed price of $52, your expected annual percent yield on your investment will be:

$$k_s = \frac{D_1}{P_0} + g$$

$$= \frac{\$4.80}{\$52} + .04$$

$$= .0923 + .04$$

$$= .1123, \text{ or } 11.23\%$$

If your minimum required rate of return for General Motors common stock, considering its risk, were less than 11.23 percent, you would proceed with the purchase. Otherwise you would look for another stock that had an expected return appropriate for its level of risk.

WHAT'S NEXT

In this chapter we investigated valuation methods for bonds, preferred stock, and common stock. The valuation methods applied risk and return, and time value of money techniques learned in chapters 7 and 8, respectively. In the next chapter, we will explore capital budgeting techniques.

Summary

1. Explain the importance of bond and stock valuation.

When corporations contemplate selling securities in the open market to raise long-term funds, they do not want to undervalue the securities because they want to raise the most money possible. Likewise, would-be purchasers of securities use valuation methods to avoid paying more than the securities are worth.

2. Discuss the concept of securities valuation.

To value any security, we apply risk and return and time value of money techniques. In sum, the value of a security is the present value of the security's future cash flows. Bond cash flows are the periodic interest payments and the principal at maturity. Stock cash flows come from the future earnings that the assets produce for the firm, usually leading to cash dividend payments.

To value securities, investors and financial managers use a general valuation model to calculate the present value of the future cash flows of the security. That model incorporates risk and return and time value of money concepts.

3. Compute the market value and the yield to maturity of a bond.

The market value of a bond is the sum of the present values of the coupon interest payments plus the present value of the face value to be paid at maturity, given a market's required rate of return.

The yield to maturity of a bond (YTM) is the average annual rate of return that investors realize if they buy a bond for a certain price, receive the promised interest payments and principal on time, and reinvest the interest payments at the YTM rate.

A bond's market price and its YTM vary inversely. That is, when the YTM rises, the market price falls, and vice versa. When a bond has a YTM greater than its coupon rate, it sells at a discount to its face value. When the YTM is equal to the coupon rate, the market price equals the face value. When the YTM is less than the coupon rate, the bond sells at a premium over face value.

4. Compute the market value and expected yield of preferred stock.

The market value of preferred stock is the present value of the stream of preferred stock dividends, discounted at the market's required rate of return for that investment. Because the dividend cash flow stream is a perpetuity, we adapt the present value of a perpetuity formula, Equation 8-5, to value preferred stock.

The yield on preferred stock represents the annual rate of return that investors realize if they buy the stock for the current market price and then receive the promised dividend payments on time.

5. Compute the market value and expected yield of common stock.

The market value of common stock is estimated in a number of ways, including (1) finding the present value of all the future dividends the stock is expected to pay, discounted at the market's required rate of return for that stock; (2) finding the price implied, given the level of earnings per share and the appropriate P/E ratio; (3) estimating the value based on the book value of the firm's assets as recorded on the balance sheet; and (4) estimating the value of the firm's assets if they were liquidated on the open market and all claims on the firm were paid off.

The dividend growth model and the P/E valuation approaches assume the firm will be a going concern. That is, the model values the future cash flows that a firm's assets are expected to produce. The book value and liquidation value approaches concentrate on the current value of the firm's assets and liabilities without regard to future earning potential. The book value method is less reliable than the liquidation method because the book value typically uses the original asset and liability accounting values whereas the liquidation method uses market values.

The yield on common stock is the percent return on investment investors can expect if they purchase the stock at the prevailing market price and receive the expected cash flows.

Equations Introduced in This Chapter

Equation 9-1. The Discounted Cash Flow Valuation Model:

$$V_0 = \frac{CF_1}{(1 + k)^1} + \frac{CF_2}{(1 + k)^2} + \frac{CF^3}{(1 + k)^3} \cdots + \frac{CF_n}{(1 + k)^n}$$

where: V_0 = Present value of the anticipated cash flows from the security, its current value

where: $CF_{1, 2, 3, \text{ and } n}$ = Cash flows expected to be received one, two, three, and so on up to n periods in the future

k = Discount rate, the required rate of return

Equation 9-2. The Bond Valuation Formula (Algebraic version):

$$V_B = INT \times \left[\frac{1 - \dfrac{1}{(1 + k_d)^n}}{k_d} \right] + \frac{M}{(1 + k_d)^n}$$

where: V_B = Current market value of the bond

INT = Dollar amount of each periodic interest payment

n = Number of times the interest payment is received (which is also the number of periods until maturity)

M = Principal payment received at maturity

k_d = Required rate of return per period on the bond debt instrument

Equation 9-3. The Bond Valuation Formula (Table version):

$$V_B = (INT \times PVIFA_{k, n}) + (M \times PVIF_{k, n})$$

where: $PVIFA_{k, n}$ = Present Value Interest Factor for an Annuity from Table IV

$PVIF_{k, n}$ = Present Value Interest Factor for a single amount from Table II

Equation 9-4. The Formula for the Present Value of Preferred Stock:

$$V_p = \frac{D_p}{k_p}$$

where: V_p = Current market value of the preferred stock

D_p = Amount of the preferred stock dividend

k_p = Required rate of return for this issue of preferred stock

Equation 9-5. Formula for the Yield on Preferred Stock:

$$k_p = \frac{D_p}{P_P}$$

where: k_p = Yield on investment that an investor can anticipate if the shares are purchased at the current market price P_P and if the preferred dividend D_p is paid forever

D_p = Amount of the preferred stock dividend

P_P = Current market price of the preferred stock

Equation 9-6. The DCF Valuation Model Applied to Common Stock:

$$P_0 = \frac{D_1}{(1 + k_s)^1} + \frac{D_2}{(1 + k_s)^2} + \frac{D_3}{(1 + k_s)^3} \cdots + \frac{P_n}{(1 + k_s)^n}$$

where: P_0 = Present value of the expected dividends, the current price of the common stock

$D_1, D_2, D_3,$ = Common stock dividends expected to be received at the end of periods 1, 2, 3, and so on until the stock is sold

P_n = Anticipated selling price of the stock in n periods

k_s = Required rate of return on the common stock investment

Equation 9-7. The Constant Growth Version of the Dividend Valuation Model:

$$P_0 = \frac{D_1}{k_s - g}$$

where: P_0 = Current price of the common stock

D_1 = Dollar amount of the common stock dividend expected 1 period from now

k_s = Required rate of return per period on this common stock investment

g = Expected constant growth rate per period of the company's common stock dividends

Equation 9-8. No-Growth Common Stock Dividend Valuation Formula:

$$P_0 = \frac{D_s}{k_s}$$

where: P_0 = Current price of the common stock

D_s = Amount of the common stock dividend, a constant amount

k_s = Required rate of return on this common stock investment

Equation 9-9. The P/E Model for Valuing Common Stock:

$$\text{Appropriate Stock Price} = \text{Industry P/E Ratio} \times \text{EPS}$$

Equation 9-10. The Book Value per Share of Common Stock:

$$\text{Book Value per Share} = \frac{(\text{Total Assets} - \text{Total Liabilities})}{\text{Number of Shares Outstanding}}$$

Equation 9-11. The Yield, or Total Return, on Common Stock:

$$k_s = \frac{D_1}{P_0} + g$$

where: D_1 = Amount of the common stock dividend anticipated in one period

P_0 = Current market price of the common stock

g = Expected constant growth rate of dividends per period

k_s = Expected rate of return per period on this common stock investment

Self-Test

ST-1. The Chrysler Corporation has issued a 10.95 percent annual coupon rate bond that matures Dec. 31, 2017. If the required rate of return on bonds of similar risk and maturity is 9 percent, and assuming the time now is Jan. 1, 1997, what is the current value of Chrysler's bond?

ST-2. Chrysler's 10.95 percent coupon rate, 2017 bond is currently selling for $1,115. At this price what is the yield to maturity of the bond? Assume the time is Jan. 1, 1997.

ST-3. McDonald's is offering preferred stock that pays a dividend of $1.93 a share. The dividend is expected to continue indefinitely. If your required rate of return for McDonald's preferred stock is 8 percent what is the value of the stock?

ST-4. Quaker Oats Corporation's next annual dividend is expected to be $1.14 a share. Dividends have been growing at a rate of 6 percent a year and you expect this rate to continue indefinitely. If your required rate of return for this stock is 9 percent, what is the maximum price you should be willing to pay for it?

ST-5. Goodyear Corporation stock is currently selling for $38. The company's next annual dividend is expected to be $1.00 a share. Dividends have been growing at a rate of 5 percent a year and you expect this rate to continue indefinitely. If you buy Goodyear at the current price what will be your yield, or total return?

Review Questions

1. Describe the general pattern of cash flows from a bond with a positive coupon rate.
2. How does the market determine the fair value of a bond?
3. What is the relationship between a bond's market price and its promised yield to maturity? Explain.
4. All other things held constant, how would the market price of a bond be affected if coupon interest payments were made semiannually instead of annually?
5. What is the usual pattern of cash flows for a share of preferred stock? How does the market determine the value of a share of preferred stock, given these promised cash flows?
6. Name two patterns of cash flows for a share of common stock. How does the market determine the value of the most common cash flow pattern for common stock?
7. Define the P/E valuation method. Under what circumstances should a stock be valued using this method?
8. Compare and contrast the book value and liquidation value per share for common stock. Is one method more reliable? Explain.

Build Your Communication Skills

CS-1. Check the current price of Texas Instruments Corporation stock or a stock of your choice in the financial press. Then research financial information from last year predicting how Texas Instruments stock (or the stock you chose) would fare and analyze what valuation methods the analysts used. Next, compare the current price with the analysts' price predictions. Prepare a brief oral report that you present to the class discussing your assessment of the analysts' stock valuation.

CS-2. Choose a stock in the financial press. Check its current price. Then estimate the value of the stock using the dividend growth model, Equation 9-7. Compare the value of the stock with its current price and prepare a short memo in which you explain why the two figures might differ.

Problems

Bond Valuation

9-1. Martin Brody is considering the purchase of a $1,000 Amity Island Municipal Bond. The city is raising funds for a much needed advertising campaign to promote its East Coast resort community. The stated coupon rate is 8 percent, paid annually. The bond will mature in 10 years. The yield-to-maturity for similar bonds in the market is 10 percent.

a. How much will the annual interest payments be?

b. What is the market price of the bond today?

c. Is the interest received on a municipal bond generally tax-free?

9-2. Assume MGM Studios is offering a corporate bond with a face value of $1,000 and an annual coupon rate of 14 percent. The maturity period is fifteen years. The interest is to be paid annually. The annual yield to maturity for similar bonds in the market is currently 10 percent.

Bond Valuation

a. What is the amount of interest to be paid annually for each bond?

b. What is the value of this $1,000 bond today?

c. What would be the present value of the interest and principal paid to holders of one of their bonds if the interest payments were made semiannually, instead of annually?

9-3. After a major earthquake, the San Francisco Opera Company is offering zero coupon bonds to fund the needed structural repairs to their historic building. Blackie Norton is considering the purchase of several of these bonds. The bonds have a face value of $2,000 and are scheduled to mature in ten years. Similar bonds in the market have an annual yield to maturity of 12 percent. If Mr. Norton purchases three of these bonds today, how much money will he receive ten years from today at maturity?

Bond Valuation

9-4. Two best friends, Thelma and Louise, are making long-range plans for a road trip vacation to Mexico. They will embark on this adventure in five years, and want to invest during the five-year period to earn money for the trip. They decide to purchase a $1,000 Grand Canyon Oil Company bond with an annual coupon rate of 10 percent with interest to be paid semiannually. The bond will mature in five years. The yield to maturity of similar bonds is 8 percent. How much should they be willing to pay for the bond if they purchase it today?

Bonds with Semiannual Interest Payments

9-5. Sea Tiger Submarines, Inc., is offering $1,000 par value bonds for sale. The bonds will mature ten years from today. The annual coupon interest rate is 12 percent, with payments to be made annually. James Hobson just purchased one bond at the current market price of $1,265.

a. Will the yield to maturity of this bond be greater than or less than the coupon interest rate? Answer this part without doing any calculations.

YTM

b. To the nearest whole percent, what is the yield to maturity of Mr. Hobson's bond? You'll need to crunch some numbers for this part.

YTM

c. What would the yield to maturity have to be to make the market price of the bond equal to the face value? No number crunching is needed to answer.

Pricing

9-6. A corporate bond has a face value of $1,000 and an annual coupon interest rate of 12 percent. Interest is paid annually. Of the original twenty years to maturity, only ten years of the life of the bond remain. The current market price of the bond is $945. To the nearest whole percent, what is the yield to maturity of the bond today?

YTM

9-7. The new King Kong Corporation will offer their preferred stock for sale in the very near future. These shares will have a guaranteed annual dividend of $10 per share. As you research the market, you find that similar preferred stock has an expected rate of return of 12 percent. If this preferred stock could be purchased today, what price per share would you expect to pay for it?

Preferred Stock Valuation

9-8. Lucky Jackson knows that one share of Grand Prix Enterprises preferred stock sells for $20 per share on the open market. From its annual reports, he sees that Grand Prix pays an annual dividend of $1.75 per share on this preferred stock. What is the market's required rate of return on Grand Prix's stock?

Preferred Stock k

9-9. Ludwig Shipping Corporation is planning to sell preferred stock that will pay an annual dividend of $6 per share. The current expected rate of return from similar preferred stock issues is 13 percent.

    a. What price per share would you expect to have to pay to purchase this stock?

    b. If the stock is actually selling for $50 per share, what is the market's required rate of return for this stock?

9-10. China S. Construction, Inc. is in the business of building nuclear power plants in the Eastern United States. Jack Godell and the rest of the board members of the firm have just approved a $4 per share dividend on the corporation's common stock. Because the quality of some of their recent projects is under attack by investigative television reporters, the expected constant dividend growth rate is only estimated to be 1 percent. The required rate of return for similar stocks in this industry is 16 percent.

    a. What is the present value of the expected dividends from one share of China S. Construction's common stock?

    b. What is the stock's dividend yield (D_1/P_0)?

9-11. The current listed price per share of a certain common stock is $15. The cash dividend expected from this corporation in one year is $2 per share. All market research indicates that the expected constant growth rate in dividends will be 4 percent per year in future years. What is the rate of return on this investment that an investor can expect if shares are purchased at the current listed price?

9-12. Golden Manufacturing Company is expected to pay a dividend of $8 per share of common stock in one year. The dollar amount of the dividends is expected to grow at a constant 3 percent per year in future years. The required rate of return from shares of similar common stock in the present environment is 14%.

    a. What would you expect the current market price of a share of Golden common stock to be?

    b. Assuming the cash dividend amount and the growth rate are accurate, what is the annual rate of return on your investment in Golden common stock if you purchased shares at the stock's actual listed price of $65 per share?

9-13. Jack and Frank Baker know their piano renditions of lounge songs have limited appeal on the night club circuit, so they work part-time as investment consultants. They are researching relatively unknown corporations, one of which is Susie Diamond Enterprises. To get a quick idea of the value of SDE's common stock, they have taken the following numbers from the most recent financial statements.

Total Assets	$675,000
Total Liabilities	$120,000
250,000 shares of common stock issued	
100,000 shares of common stock outstanding	

    a. What is the book value (net worth) of Susie Diamond Enterprises?

    b. What is the book value per share?

9-14. The most recent Balance Sheet of Free Enterprise, Inc. is given below.

Free Enterprise, Inc.
Balance Sheet
December 31, 1996
(Thousands of dollars)

Assets		Liabilities + Equity	
Cash	$ 4,000	Accounts Payable	$ 4,400
Accounts Receivable	10,000	Notes Payable	4,000
Inventory	13,000	Accrued Expenses	5,000
Prepaid Expenses	400	Total Current Liabilities	13,400
Total Current Assets	27,400	Bonds Payable	6,000
Fixed Assets	11,000	Common Equity	19,000
Total Assets	$38,400	Total Liabilities + Equity	$38,400

a. What was Free Enterprise's book value (net worth) at the beginning of 1997?

b. If the company had 750,000 shares of common stock authorized and 500,000 shares outstanding, what was the book value per share of common stock at the beginning of 1997?

c. Net income of Free Enterprise, Inc., was $5,610,000 in 1996. Calculate the earnings per share of Free Enterprise's common stock.

d. The P/E Ratio for a typical company in Free Enterprise, Inc.'s industry is estimated to be 6. Using the EPS from part c) above, calculate the price of one share of common stock at the beginning of 1997 assuming that Free Enterprise commands a P/E ratio value equal to that of an average company in its industry.

e. What would you infer about the company's total assets shown on the balance sheet when comparing this calculated stock price with the company's book value per share?

f. Calculate the liquidation value of Free Enterprise's common stock assuming the market value of the total assets is $50 million and the market value of total liabilities is $20 million, as estimated by your analyst.

9-15. Lucky Jackson is trying to choose from among the best of the three investment alternatives recommended to him by his full-service investment broker. The alternatives are:

a. The corporate bond of Star Mining Company has a face value of $1,000 and an annual coupon interest rate of 13 percent. The bond is selling in the market at $1,147.58. Of the original twenty years to maturity, only sixteen years of the life of the bond remain.

b. The preferred stock of Supernova Minerals Company has a par value of $100 per share and it offers an annual dividend of $14 per share. The market price of the stock is $140 per share.

c. The common stock of White Dwarf Ores Company sells in the market at $300 per share. The company paid a dividend of $39 per share yesterday. The company is expected to grow at 3 percent per annum in the future.

Which of the three alternatives should Lucky choose? Remember the priority of claims for bondholders, preferred stockholders, and common stockholders from chapters 1 and 4.

Answers to Self-Test

ST-1. The present value of Chrysler's 10.95% 2017 bond can be found using Equation 9-2:

$$V_B = INT \times \left[\frac{1 - \dfrac{1}{(1 + k_d)^n}}{k_d} \right] + \frac{M}{(1 + k_d)^n}$$

Face Value is $1,000
The coupon interest payment is 10.95% of $1,000, or $109.50
n is $2017 - 1996 = 21$
$k_d = 9\%$

$$V_B = \$109.50 \times \left[\frac{1 - \dfrac{1}{(1 + .09)^{21}}}{.09} \right] + \frac{\$1,000}{(1 + .09)^{21}}$$

$$= (\$109.50 \times 9.29224) + \left(\frac{\$1,000}{6.108801} \right)$$

$$= \$1017.50 + \$163.70$$

$$= \$1,181.20$$

So the present value of the bond is $1,181.20

ST-2. The bond's YTM is found by trial and error. We know that the bond has a price of $1,115, face value of $1,000, coupon interest payment is $109.50 (10.95% of $1,000), and matures in twenty-one years ($2017 - 1996 = 21$). Now we can find that value of k_d that produces a P_b of $1,115. Use Equation 9-2 and solve for P_B.

First try, k = 9%:

$$V_B = \$109.50 \times \left[\frac{1 - \dfrac{1}{(1 + .09)^{21}}}{.09} \right] + \frac{\$1,000}{(1 + .09)^{21}}$$

$$= (\$109.50 \times 9.29224) + \left(\frac{\$1,000}{6.108801} \right)$$

$$= \$1017.50 + \$163.70$$

$$= \$1,181.20 > 1,115$$

$1,181.20 is too high. Try again using a higher yield (remember, bond prices and yields vary inversely).

Second try at $k_d = 10\%$:

$$V_B = \$109.50 \times \left[\frac{1 - \dfrac{1}{(1 + .10)^{21}}}{.10} \right] + \frac{\$1,000}{(1 + .10)^{21}}$$

$$= (\$109.50 \times 8.64869) + \left(\frac{\$1,000}{7.40025} \right)$$

$$= \$947.03 + \$135.13$$

$$= \$1,082.60 < 1,115$$

$1,082.16 is too low. Try again using a lower yield.

Third try, at $k_d = 9.65\%$:

$$V_B = \$109.50 \times \left[\frac{1 - \dfrac{1}{(1 + .0965)^{21}}}{.0965} \right] + \frac{\$1,000}{(1 + .0965)^{21}}$$

$$= (\$109.50 \times 8.86545) + \left(\frac{\$1,000}{6.92120} \right)$$

$$= \$970.77 + \$144.48$$

$$= \$1,115.25$$

At $k_d = 9.65\%$ the calculated value of P_B is within $.25 of the current market price. We conclude the bond's YTM is 9.65%.[4]

ST-3. Equation 9-5 is used to find the value of preferred stock as follows:

$$V_P = \frac{D_P}{k_P} \tag{9-5}$$

D_p is $1.93 and k_p is 8%

$$V_P = \frac{\$1.93}{.08}$$

$$= \$24.125, \text{ or } \$24\tfrac{1}{8}$$

(Stock prices are usually quoted in eighths.)

ST-4. The maximum price you are willing to pay for Quaker Oats is what it is worth to you, or its value. Since the characteristics of the stock fit the constant dividend growth model, use Equation 9-7 to compute the value.

$$P_0 = \frac{D_1}{k_s - g} \tag{9-7}$$

D_1 is $1.14, k_e is 9%, and g is 6%

Given these conditions, the value of Quaker Oats stock is:

$$P_0 = \frac{\$1.14}{.09 - .06}$$

$$= \frac{\$1.14}{.03}$$

$$= \$38$$

ST-5. The yield on common stock can be found using Equation 9-10:

$$k_s = \frac{D_1}{P_0} + g \tag{9-10}$$

D_1 is $1.00, P_0 is $38, and g is 5%. Given these conditions, the yield on Goodyear common stock is as follows:

$$k_s = \frac{\$1.00}{\$38} + .05$$

$$= .0263 + .05$$

$$= .0763, \text{ or } 7.63\%$$

---

[4]The exact YTM, found using a financial calculator, is 9.652590645 percent.

APPENDIX 9A

Common Stock Valuation: Supernormal Growth

In addition to the constant growth and no–growth common stock dividend cash flow patterns that we discussed in the chapter, some companies have very high growth rates, known as supernormal growth of the cash flows. Valuing the common stock of such companies presents a special problem since high growth rates cannot be sustained indefinitely. A young high technology firm, such as Netscape, for instance, may be able to grow at a 40 percent rate per year for a few years, but that growth must slow down because it is not sustainable given the population and productivity growth rates. In fact, if the firm's growth rate did not slow down, its sales would surpass the gross domestic product of the entire nation over time. Why? The company has a 40 percent growth rate that will compound annually, whereas the gross domestic product may grow at a 4 percent compounded average annual growth rate.

The constant dividend growth model for common stock, Equation 9-6, then, must be adjusted for those cases where a company's dividend grows at a supernormal rate that will not be sustained over time. We do this by dividing the projected dividend cash flow stream of the common stock into two parts: the initial supernormal growth period and the next period where normal and sustainable growth is expected. We then calculate the present value of the dividends during the fast-growth time period first. Then we solve for the present value of the dividends during the constant growth period that are a perpetuity. The sum of these two present values determines the current value of the stock.

To illustrate, suppose Supergrowth Corporation is expected to pay an annual dividend of $2 per share one year from now, and that this dividend will grow at a 30 percent annual rate during each of the following 4 years (taking us to the end of year 5). After this supernormal growth period, the dividend will grow at a sustainable 5 percent rate each year beyond year 5. The cash flows are shown in Figure 9A-1.

The valuation of a share of Supergrowth Corporation's common stock is described in the following three steps.

Step 1. Add the present values of the dividends during the supernormal growth period. Assume that the required rate of return, k_s, is 14 percent.

$$
\begin{aligned}
\$2.00 \times 1/1.14 &= \$\ 1.75 \\
\$2.60 \times 1/1.14^2 &= \$\ 2.00 \\
\$3.38 \times 1/1.14^3 &= \$\ 2.28 \\
\$4.39 \times 1/1.14^4 &= \$\ 2.60 \\
\$5.71 \times 1/1.14^5 &= \underline{\$\ 2.97} \\
\Sigma &= \$11.60
\end{aligned}
$$

Step 2. Calculate the sum of the present values of the dividends during the normal growth period, from t_6 through infinity in this case. To do this, pretend for a moment that t_6 is t_0. The present value of the dividend growing at the constant rate of 5 percent to perpetuity could be computed using Equation 9-7.

$$
P_0 = \frac{D_1}{k_s - g}
$$

Figure 9A-1 Timeline of Supergrowth Common Stock Dividend with Initial Supernormal Growth

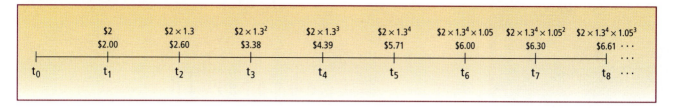

Substituting our values we would have:

$$P_0 = \frac{\$6.00}{.14 - .05} = \$66.67$$

Since the $6.00 dividend actually occurs at t_6 instead of t_1, the $66.67 figure is not a t_0 value, but rather a t_5 value.

It therefore needs to be discounted back 5 years at our required rate of return of 14 percent. This gives us $\$66.67 \times 1/1.14^5 = \$34.63$. The result of $34.63 is the present value of the dividends from the end of year 6 through infinity.

Step 3. Finally we add the present values of the dividends from the supernormal growth period and the normal growth period. In our example we add $11.60 + $34.63 = $46.23. The sum of $46.23 is the market price of Supergrowth Corporation's common stock, given the projected dividends and the 14 percent required rate of return on those dividends.

chapter 10

Capital Budgeting Decision Methods

Everything is worth what its purchaser will pay for it.

Publilius Syrus

Chapter Objectives

After reading this chapter, you should be able to:

1. Explain the capital budgeting process.

2. Calculate the payback period, net present value, and internal rate of return for a proposed capital budgeting project.

3. Describe capital rationing and how firms decide which projects to select.

4. Measure the risk of a capital budgeting project.

5. Explain risk-adjusted discount rates.

To Accept or Not to Accept, That Was the Question

In September 1995 the PanAmSat Corporation announced that it planned to spend $800 million to expand its network of communications satellites. PanAmSat, the world's first private company to provide global satellite services, wanted to expand its network of satellites to open up new video, voice, and data transmissions capacity between North, South, and Central America.

Financial analysts at the PanAmSat Corporation had to determine whether the proposed expansion project made financial sense for the firm. Since the project was a major risk—the company's future was at stake—the financial analysts could not just recommend that the firm spend $800 million willy-nilly. Analysts decided to accept the project based on objective financial decision methods, concluding that, despite the risks, the project's returns would justify the $800 million initial investment.

The result of the firm's decision? The firm's earnings increased 163 per- cent, primarily due to the expansion project. ✺

Source: *The Wall St. Journal* (October 12, 1995): A7; " PanAmSat Experiences 163% In- crease in Revenues," Retrieved from Internet at http://www.panamsat.com (July18, 1996).

Chapter Overview

In this chapter we'll look at the decision methods analysts use to approve invest- ment projects and how they account for a project's risk. Investment projects such as the PanAmSat expansion project fuel a firm's success, so effective project selection often determines a firm's value. The decision methods for choosing investment pro- jects, then, are some of the most important tools financial managers use.

We begin this chapter by looking at the capital budgeting process and three capi- tal budgeting decision methods: *the payback method, the net present value method,* and the *internal rate of return method.* Then we discuss how to select projects when firms limit their budget for capital projects, a practice called *capital rationing.* Finally, we look at how firms measure and compensate for the risk of capital budgeting projects.

The Capital Budgeting Process

All businesses budget for capital projects—an airline that considers purchasing new planes, a production studio that decides to buy new film cameras, or a pharmaceuti- cal company that invests in researching and developing a new drug. **Capital budget- ing** is the process of evaluating proposed large, long-term investment projects. The projects may be the purchase of fixed assets, investments in research and develop- ment, advertising, or intellectual property. For instance, Microsoft's development of *Windows '95* software was a capital budgeting project.

Long-term projects may tie up cash resources, time, and additional assets. They can also affect a firm's performance for years to come. As a result, careful capital budgeting is vital to ensure that the proposed investment will add value to the firm.

Before we discuss the specific decision methods for selecting investment pro- jects, we briefly examine capital budgeting basics: capital budgeting decision prac- tices, types of capital budgeting projects, the cash flows associated with such projects, and the stages of the capital budgeting process.

Decision Practices

Financial managers apply two decision practices when selecting capital budgeting projects: *accept/reject* and *ranking.* The accept/reject decision focuses on the ques- tion of whether the proposed project would add value to the firm or earn a rate of return that is acceptable to the company. The ranking decision practice ranks com- peting projects in order of desirability in order to choose the best one.

The accept/reject decision practice determines whether a project is acceptable in light of the firm's financial objectives. That is, if a project meets the firm's basic risk and return requirements, it will be accepted. If not, it will be rejected.

Ranking compares projects to a standard measure and orders the projects based on how well they meet the measure. If, for instance, the standard is how quickly the project pays off the initial investment, then the project that pays off the investment most rapidly would be ranked first. The project that paid off most slowly would be ranked last.

Types of Projects

Firms invest in two categories of projects: independent projects and mutually exclusive projects. **Independent projects** do not compete with each other. A firm may accept none, some, or all from among a group of independent projects. Say, for example, that a firm is able to raise funds for all worthwhile projects it identifies. The firm is considering two new projects—a new telephone system and a warehouse. The telephone system and the warehouse would be independent projects. Accepting one does not preclude accepting the other.

In contrast, **mutually exclusive projects** compete against each other. The best project from among a group of acceptable mutually exclusive projects is selected. For example, if a company needed only one copier, a proposal to buy a Xerox™ copier and a second proposal to buy a Toshiba™ copier would indicate that these two projects are mutually exclusive.

Capital Budgeting Cash Flows

Although decision makers examine accounting information such as sales and expenses, capital budgeting decision makers base their decisions on relevant cash flows associated with a project. The relevant cash flows are **incremental cash flows—** cash flows that will occur if an investment is undertaken, but won't occur if it isn't.

For example, imagine that you are an animator who helps to create children's films. Your firm is considering whether to buy a computer to help you design your characters more quickly. The computer would enable you to create two characters in the time it now takes you to draw one, thereby increasing your productivity.

The incremental cash flows associated with the animation project are (1) the initial investment in the computer and (2) the *additional* cash the firm receives because you will double your animation output for the life of the computer. These cash flows will occur if the new computer is purchased, and will not occur if it is not purchased. These are the cash flows, then, that affect the capital budgeting decision.

Estimating cash flows, the subject of chapter 11, is a major component of capital budgeting decisions, as we see in the next section.

Stages in the Capital Budgeting Process

The capital budgeting process has four major stages:

1. finding projects
2. estimating the incremental cash flows associated with projects
3. evaluating and selecting projects
4. implementing and monitoring projects

This chapter focuses on stage 3—how to evaluate and choose investment projects. We assume that the firm has found projects in which to invest and has estimated the projects' cash flows effectively.

CAPITAL BUDGETING DECISION METHODS

The three formal capital budgeting decision methods we as going to examine are the *payback, net present value,* and *internal rate of return.* Let's begin with the payback method.

The Payback Method

One of the simplest capital budgeting decision methods is the payback method. To use it, analysts find a project's **payback period**—the number of time periods it will take before the cash inflows of a proposed project equal the amount of the initial project investment (a cash outflow). In the PanAmSat example discussed at the beginning of this chapter, the analysts would determine how many years it would take to recoup the initial $800 million investment.

How to Calculate the Payback Period To calculate the payback period, simply add up a project's positive cash flows, one period at a time, until the sum equals the amount of the project's initial investment. That number of time periods is the payback period.

To illustrate, imagine that you work for a firm called the AddVenture Corporation. AddVenture is considering two investment proposals, Projects X and Y. The initial investment for both projects is $5,000. The finance department estimates that the projects will generate the following cash flows:

Cash Flows

	FOR INITIAL INVESTMENT	END OF YEAR 1	END OF YEAR 2	END OF YEAR 3	END OF YEAR 4
Project X	−$5,000	$2,000	$3,000	$500	$0
Project Y	−$5,000	$2,000	$2,000	$1,000	$2,000

By analyzing the cash flows, we see that Project X has a payback period of two years because the project's initial investment of $5,000 (a cash flow of −$5,000) will

Source: DILBERT © 1996 United Feature Syndicate, Inc. Reprinted by Permission.

be recouped (offsetting positive cash flows) at the end of year 2. In comparison, Project Y has a payback of three years.

Payback Method Decision Rule   To apply the payback decision method, firms must first decide what payback time period is acceptable for long-term projects. In our case, if the firm sets two years as its required payback period, it will accept Project X but reject Project Y. If, however, the firm allows a three-year payback period, then both projects would be accepted if they were independent.

Problems with the Payback Method   The payback method is used in practice because of its simplicity. But it does not consider cash flows that occur after the payback period. For example, suppose Project Y's cash flows were $10 million instead of $2,000 in year 4. It wouldn't make any difference. Project Y would still be rejected under the payback method if the company's policy were to demand a payback of no more than two years. Failing to look beyond the payback period can lead to poor business decisions, as shown.

Another deficiency of the payback method is that it does not consider the time value of money. For instance, compare the cash flows of Projects A and B:

| | **Cash Flows** | | |
	FOR INITIAL INVESTMENT	**END OF YEAR 1**	**END OF YEAR 2**
Project A	−$5,000	$3,000	$2,000
Project B	−$5,000	$2,000	$3,000

Assuming the required payback period is two years, we see that both projects are equally preferable—they both pay back the initial investment in two years. However, time value of money analysis indicates that if both projects are equally risky, then Project A is better than Project B because the firm will get more money sooner. Nevertheless, timing of cash flows makes no difference in the payback computation.

Because the payback method does not factor in the time value of money, nor the cash flows after the payback period, its usefulness is limited. Although it does provide a rough measure of a project's liquidity and can help to supplement other techniques, financial managers should not rely on it as a primary decision method.

The Net Present Value (NPV) Method

The project selection method that is most consistent with the goal of owner wealth maximization is the net present value method. The **net present value (NPV)** of a capital budgeting project is *the dollar amount of change in the value of the firm as a result of undertaking the project*. The change in firm value may be positive, negative, or zero, depending on the NPV value.

If a project has an NPV of zero, it means that the firm's overall value will not change if the new project is adopted. Why? Because the new project is expected to generate exactly the firm's required rate of return—no more and no less. A positive NPV means that the firm's value will increase if the project is adopted because the new project's estimated return exceeds the firm's required rate of return. Conversely, a negative NPV means the firm's value will decrease if the new project is adopted, because the new project's estimated return is less than what the firm requires.

Calculating NPV To calculate the net present value of a proposed project, we add the present value of a project's projected cash flows and then subtract the amount of the initial investment.[1] The result is a dollar figure that represents the change in the firm's value if the project is undertaken.

Formula for Net Present Value (NPV), Algebraic Version   (10-1a)

$$NPV = \left(\frac{CF_1}{(1+k)^1}\right) + \left(\frac{CF_2}{(1+k)^2}\right) \cdots + \left(\frac{CF_n}{(1+k)^n}\right) - \text{Initial Investment}$$

where: CF = Cash flow at the indicated times
k = Discount rate, or required rate of return for the project
n = Life of the project measured in the number of time periods

To use financial tables to solve present value problems, write the NPV formula as follows:

The Formula for NPV, Table Version   (10-1b)

$$NPV = CF_1(PVIF_{k,1}) + CF_2(PVIF_{k,2}) \cdots + CF_n(PVIF_{k,n}) - \text{Initial Investment}$$

where: PVIF = Present Value Interest Factor
k = Discount rate, or required rate of return for the project
n = Life of the project measured in the number of time periods

To use the TI BAII Plus financial calculator to solve for NPV, switch the calculator to the spreadsheet mode, enter the cash flow values in sequence, then the discount rate, depicted as I on the TI BAII Plus calculator, then compute the NPV.

For simplicity, we use only the algebraic equation and the financial calculator to calculate NPV. If you prefer using financial tables, simply replace Equation 10-1a with Equation 10-1b.[2]

To show how to calculate NPV, let's solve for the NPVs of our two earlier projects, Projects X and Y. First, note the following cash flows of Projects X and Y:

Cash Flows

	FOR INITIAL INVESTMENT	END OF YEAR 1	END OF YEAR 2	END OF YEAR 3	END OF YEAR 4
Project X	−$5,000	$2,000	$3,000	$500	$0
Project Y	−$5,000	$2,000	$2,000	$1,000	$2,000

Assume the required rate of return for Projects X and Y is 10 percent. Now we have all the data we need to solve for the NPV of Projects X and Y.

---

[1] We use many of the time value of money techniques learned in chapter 8 to calculate NPV.
[2] If the future cash flows are an annuity, Equations 10-1a and 10-1b can be modified to take advantage of the present value of annuity formulas discussed in chapter 8, Equations 8-4a and 8-4b.

Applying Equation 10-1a and assuming a discount rate of 10 percent, the NPV of Project X follows:

$$NPV_x = \left(\frac{\$2,000}{(1+.10)^1}\right) + \left(\frac{\$3,000}{(1+.10)^2}\right) + \left(\frac{\$500}{(1+.10)^3}\right) - \$5,000$$

$$= \frac{\$2,000}{1.1} + \frac{\$3,000}{1.21} + \frac{\$500}{1.331} - \$5,000$$

$$= \$1,818.1818 + \$2,479.3388 + \$375.6574 - \$5,000$$

$$= -\$326.82$$

We may also find Project X's NPV with the financial calculator at a 10 percent discount rate as follows:

TI BAI I PLUS FINANCIAL CALCULATOR SOLUTIONS
Project X NPV

KEYSTROKES	DISPLAY
CF	CF_0 = old contents
2nd CLR Work	$CF_0 = 0.00$
5000 +/− ENTER	$CF_0 = -5,000.00$
↓ 2000 ENTER	$C01 = 2,000.00$
↓	$F01 = 1.00$
↓ 3000 ENTER	$C02 = 3,000.00$
↓	$F02 = 1.00$
↓ 500 ENTER	$C03 = 500.00$
↓	$F03 = 1.00$
NPV	$I = 0.00$
10 ENTER	$I = 10.00$
↓ CPT	$NPV = -326.82$

The calculations above show that at a 10 percent discount rate, an initial cash outlay of $5,000 and cash inflows of $2,000, $3,000 and $500 at the end of years one, two, and three, the NPV for Project X is −326.82.

To find the NPV of Project Y, we apply Equation 10-1a as follows:

$$NPV_y = \left(\frac{\$2,000}{(1+.10)^1}\right) + \left(\frac{\$2,000}{(1+.10)^2}\right) + \left(\frac{\$1,000}{(1+.10)^3}\right) + \left(\frac{\$2,000}{(1+.10)^4}\right) - \$5,000$$

$$= \frac{\$2,000}{1.1} + \frac{\$2,000}{1.21} + \frac{\$1,000}{1.331} + \frac{\$2,000}{1.4641} - \$5,000$$

$$= \$1,818.1818 + \$1,652.8926 + \$751.3148 + \$1,366.0269 - \$5,000$$

$$= \$588.42$$

Using the financial calculator, we solve for Project Y's NPV at a 10 percent discount rate as follows:

TI BAI I PLUS FINANCIAL CALCULATOR SOLUTIONS
Project Y NPV

KEYSTROKES	DISPLAY
CF	CF_0 = old contents
2nd CLR Work	$CF_0 = 0.00$
5000 +/− ENTER	$CF_0 = -5,000.00$
↓ 2000 ENTER	$C01 = 2,000.00$
↓ 2 ENTER	$F01 = 2.00$
↓ 1000 ENTER	$C02 = 1,000.00$
↓	$F02 = 1.00$
↓ 2000 ENTER	$C03 = 2,000$
↓	$F03 = 1.00$
NPV	$I = 0.00$
10 ENTER	$I = 10.00$
↓ CPT	$NPV = 588.42$

Our calculations show that with a required rate of return of 10 percent, an initial cash outlay of $5,000, and positive cash flows in years 1 through 4 of $2,000, $2,000, $1,000 and $2,000, respectively, the NPV for Project Y is $588.41. If we compare Project X's NPV of −326.82 to Project Y's NPV of $588.42, we see that Project Y would add value to the business and Project X would decrease the firm's value.

NPV Decision Rules NPV is used in two ways: (1) to determine if independent projects should be accepted or rejected (the accept/reject decision); and (2) to compare acceptable mutually exclusive projects (the ranking decision). The rules for these two decisions are:

- NPV Accept/Reject Decision—A firm should accept all independent projects having NPVs greater than or equal to zero. Projects with positive NPVs will add to the value of the firm if adopted. Projects with NPVs of zero will not alter the firm's value, but (just) meet the firm's requirements. Projects with NPVs less than zero should be rejected because they will reduce the firm's value if adopted. Applying this decision rule, Project X would be rejected and Project Y would be accepted.
- NPV Ranking Decision—The mutually exclusive project with the highest positive NPV should be ranked first, the next highest should be ranked second, and so on. Under this decision rule, if the two projects in our previous example were mutually exclusive, Project Y would be ranked first and Project X second. (Not only is Project X second in rank here, but it is unacceptable because it has a negative NPV.)

We discussed the inverse relationship between k and present value (PV) in chapter 8, page 175.

The NPV Profile   The k value is the cost of funds used for the project. It is the discount rate used in the NPV calculation because the cost of funds for a given project is that project's required rate of return. The relationship between the NPV of a project and k is inverse—the higher the k, the lower the NPV and the lower the k, the higher the NPV.[3]

Since a project's NPV varies inversely with k, financial managers need to know how much the value of NPV will change in response to a change in k. If k is incorrectly specified, what appears to be a positive NPV could in fact be a negative NPV and vice versa—a negative NPV could turn out to be positive. Mutually exclusive project rankings could also change if an incorrect k value is used in the NPV computations.[4]

To see how sensitive a project's NPV value is to changes in k, analysts often create an NPV profile. The **NPV profile** is a graph that shows how a project's NPV changes when different discount rate values are used in the NPV computation.

Building an NPV profile is straightforward. First, the NPV of the project is calculated at a number of different discount rates. Then, the results are plotted on the graph, with k values on one axis and the resulting NPV values on the other. If more than one project is included on the graph, the process is repeated for each project until all are depicted. To illustrate, we will build an NPV profile of Projects X and Y. We will plot Project X and then Project Y on the graph.

To begin, we first calculate the NPV of Project X with a number of different discount rates. The different k values may be chosen arbitrarily. For our purposes, let's use 0 percent, 5 percent, 10 percent, 15 percent, and 20 percent. The results of Project X's NPV calculations follow:

DISCOUNT RATE	PROJECT X NPV
0%	$500.00
5%	$57.77
10%	−$326.82
15%	−$663.68
20%	−$960.65

Take Note

The NPV profile line is curved, not straight. The curve is steepest at low discount rates and gets more shallow at higher rates. This shape occurs because discounting is the inverse of the exponential compounding phenomenon, as described in chapter 8.

Now Project X's NPV values may be plotted on the NPV Profile graph. Figure 10-1 shows the results.

When the data points are connected in Figure 10-1, we see how the NPV of Project X varies with the discount rate changes. The graph shows that with a k of about 5.7 percent, the value of the project's NPV is zero. At that discount rate, then, Project X would provide the firm's required rate of return, no more and no less.

Next, we add Project Y to the NPV Profile graph. We calculate the NPV of Project Y at a number of different discount rates, 0 percent, 5 percent, 10 percent, 15 percent, and 20 percent. The results follow:

---

[3]We are assuming here that the project is a typical one, meaning that it has an initial negative cash flow, the initial investment, followed by all positive cash flows. It is possible that if a project has negative cash flows in the future the relationship between NPV and k might not be inverse.

[4]The estimation of the cost of funds used for capital budgeting projects is covered in chapter 13.

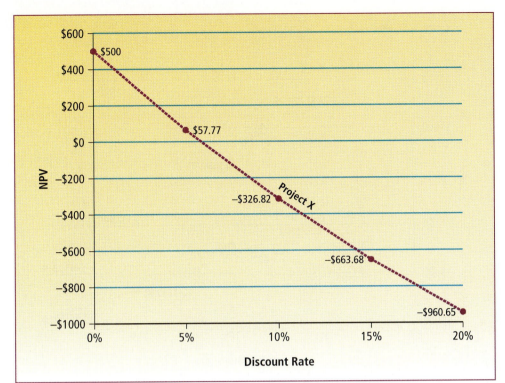

Figure 10-1 NPV Profile of Project X

The NPV profile shows how the NPV of Project X varies inversely with the discount rate, k. Project X's NPV is highest ($500) when the discount rate is zero. Its NPV is lowest (−$960.65) when the discount rate is 20 percent.

DISCOUNT RATE	PROJECT Y NPV
0%	$2,000.00
5%	$1,228.06
10%	$588.42
15%	$52.44
20%	−$401.23

Figure 10-2 shows these NPV values plotted on the NPV profile graph.

Notice in Figure 10-2 that Project Y's NPV profile falls off more steeply than Project X's. This indicates that Project Y is more sensitive to changes in the discount rate than is Project X. Project X's NPV becomes negative, and thus the project unacceptable, when the discount rate rises above about 6 percent. Project Y's NPV becomes negative, and thus the project unacceptable, when the discount rate rises above about 16 percent.

Problems with the NPV Method Although the NPV method ensures that a firm will choose projects that add value to a firm, it suffers from two practical problems. First, it is difficult to explain NPV to people who are not formally trained in finance. Few nonfinance people understand phrases such as "the present value of future cash flows" or "the change in a firm's value given its required rate of return." As a result, many financial managers have difficulty using NPV analysis persuasively.

A second problem is that the NPV method results are in dollars, not percentages. Many owners and managers prefer to work with percentages because percentages can be easily compared to other alternatives—Project 1 has a 10 percent rate of

Figure 10-2 **NPV Profile of Projects X and Y**

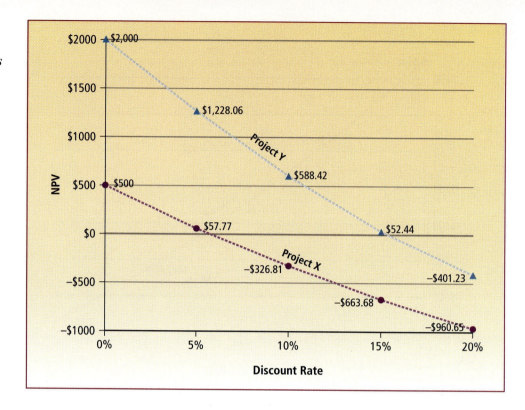

This NPV profile shows how the NPVs of two capital budgeting projects, Projects X and Y, vary inversely with the discount rate, k.

return compared to Project 2's 12 percent return rate. The next method we discuss, the internal rate of return, provides results in percentages.

The Internal Rate of Return (IRR) Method

The **internal rate of return (IRR)** is the estimated rate of return for a proposed project, given the project's incremental cash flows. Just like the NPV method, the IRR method considers all cash flows for a project and adjusts for the time value of money. However, the IRR results are expressed as a percentage, not a dollar figure.

When capital budgeting decisions are made using the IRR method, the IRR of the proposed project is compared to the rate of return management requires for the project. The required rate of return is often referred to as the **hurdle rate.** If the project's IRR is greater than or equal to the hurdle rate (jumps over the hurdle), the project is accepted.

The IRR calculation is the same trial-and-error procedure we used to find a bond's yield to maturity in chapter 9, pages 208–210.

Calculating Internal Rate of Return: Trial-and-Error Method If the present value of a project's incremental cash flows were computed using management's required rate of return as the discount rate, and the result exactly equaled the cost of the project, then the NPV of the project would be zero. When NPV equals zero, the required rate of return, or discount rate used in the NPV calculation, is the projected rate of return, IRR. To calculate IRR, then, we reorder the terms in Equation 10-1a to solve for a discount rate, k, that results in an NPV of zero.

The formula for finding IRR, Equation 10-2, follows:

Formula for IRR (10-2)

$$NPV = 0 = \left(\frac{CF_1}{(1 + k)^1}\right) + \left(\frac{CF_2}{(1 + k)^2}\right) \cdot \cdot \cdot + \left(\frac{CF_n}{(1 + k)^n}\right) - \text{Initial Investment}$$

To find the IRR of a project using Equation 10-2, fill in the cash flows, the n values, and the initial investment figure. Then choose different values for k (all the other values are known) until the result equals zero. The IRR is the k value that causes the left-hand side of the equation, the NPV, to equal zero.

To illustrate the process, let's calculate the internal rate of return for Project X. Recall that the cash flows associated with Project X were as follows:

Cash Flows

	For Initial Investment	Year 1	Year 2	Year 3	Year 4
Project X	−$5,000	$2,000	$3,000	$500	$0

First, we insert Project X's cash flows and the times they occur into Equation 10-2.

$$0 = \left(\frac{\$2,000}{(1 + k)^1}\right) + \left(\frac{\$3,000}{(1 + k)^2}\right) + \left(\frac{\$500}{(1 + k)^3}\right) - \$5,000$$

Next, we try various discount rates until we find the value of k that results in an NPV of zero. Let's begin with a discount rate of 5 percent.

$$0 = \left(\frac{\$2,000}{(1 + .05)^1}\right) + \left(\frac{\$3,000}{(1 + .05)^2}\right) + \left(\frac{\$500}{(1 + .05)^3}\right) - \$5,000$$

$$= \left(\frac{\$2,000}{1.05}\right) + \left(\frac{\$3,000}{1.1025}\right) + \left(\frac{\$500}{1.157625}\right) - \$5,000$$

$$= \$1,904.76 + \$2,721.09 + \$431.92 - \$5,000$$

$$= \$57.77$$

This is close, but not quite zero. Let's try a second time, using a discount rate of 6 percent.

$$0 = \left(\frac{\$2,000}{(1 + .06)^1}\right) + \left(\frac{\$3,000}{(1 + .06)^2}\right) + \left(\frac{\$500}{(1 + .06)^3}\right) - \$5,000$$

$$= \left(\frac{\$2,000}{1.06}\right) + \left(\frac{\$3,000}{1.1236}\right) + \left(\frac{\$500}{1.191016}\right) - \$5,000$$

$$= \$1,886.79 + \$2,669.99 + \$419.81 - \$5,000$$

$$= -\$23.41$$

This is close enough for our purposes. We conclude the IRR for Project X is slightly less than 6 percent.

Although calculating IRR by trial and error is time-consuming, the guesses do not have to be made entirely in the dark. Remember that the discount rate and NPV are inversely related. When an IRR guess is too high, the resulting NPV value will be too low. When an IRR guess is too low, the NPV will be too high.

Calculating Internal Rate of Return: Financial Calculator Finding solutions to IRR problems with a financial calculator is simple. After clearing previous values, enter the initial cash outlay and other cash flows and compute the IRR value.

> ◄ **Take Note**
>
> *We could estimate the IRR more accurately through more trial and error. However, carrying the IRR computation to several decimal points may give a false sense of accuracy, as in the case where the cash flows estimates are in error.*

The TI BAII PLUS financial calculator keystrokes for finding the IRR for Project X are shown next.

TI BAI I PLUS FINANCIAL CALCULATOR SOLUTION
IRR

KEYSTROKES	DISPLAY
CF	CF_0 = old contents
2nd CLR Work	CF_0 = 0.00
5000 +/− ENTER	−5,000.00
↓ 2000 ENTER	C01 = 2,000.00
↓	F01 = 1.00
↓ 3000 ENTER	C02 = 3,000.00
↓	F02 = 1.00
↓ 500 ENTER	C03 = 500.00
↓	F03 = 1.00
IRR	IRR = 0.00
CPT	IRR = 5.71

Take Note

If you are using a financial calculator other than the TI BAII PLUS, the calculator procedure will be similar but the keystrokes will differ. Be sure to check your calculator's instruction manual.

We see that with an initial cash outflow of $5,000, and Project X's estimated cash inflows in years 1 through 3, the IRR is 5.71 percent.

IRR and the NPV Profile   Notice in Figure 10-2 that the point where Project X's NPV profile crosses the zero line is, in fact, the IRR (5.71 percent). This is no accident. When the required rate of return, or discount rate, equals the expected rate of return, IRR, then NPV equals zero. Project Y's NPV profile crosses the zero line just below 16 percent. If you use your financial calculator, you will find that the Project Y IRR is 15.54 percent. If an NPV profile graph is available, you can always find a project's IRR by locating the point where a project's NPV profile crosses the zero line.

IRR Decision Rule   When evaluating proposed projects with the IRR method, those that have IRRs equal to or greater than the required rate of return (hurdle rate) set by management are accepted, and those projects with IRRs that are less than the required rate of return are rejected. Acceptable, mutually exclusive projects are ranked from highest to lowest IRR.

Benefits of the IRR Method   The IRR method for selecting capital budgeting projects is popular among financial practitioners for three primary reasons:

1. IRR focuses on all cash flows associated with the project.
2. IRR adjusts for the time value of money.
3. IRR describes projects in terms of the *rate* of return they earn, which makes it easy to compare them to other investments and the firm's hurdle rate.

Problems with the IRR Method The IRR method has several problems, however. First, since the IRR is a percentage number, it does not show how much the value of the firm will change if the project is selected. If a project is quite small, for instance, it may have a high IRR, but a small effect on the value of the firm. (Consider a project that requires a $10 investment and returns $100 a year later. The project's IRR is 900 percent, but the effect on the value of the firm if the project is adopted is negligible.)

If the primary goal for the firm is to maximize its value, then knowing the *rate* of return of a project is not the primary concern. What is most important is the *amount* by which the firm's value will change if the project is adopted, which is measured by NPV.

To drive this point home, ask yourself whether you would rather earn a 100 percent rate of return on $5 ($5) or a 50 percent rate of return on $1,000 ($500). As you can see, it is not the rate of return that is important, but the dollar value. Why? Dollars, not percentages, comprise a firm's cash flows. NPV tells financial analysts how much value will be created. IRR does not.

A second problem with the IRR method is that, in rare cases, a project may have more than one IRR, or no IRR. This is shown in detail in Appendix 10A.

The IRR can be a useful tool in evaluating capital budgeting projects. As with any tool, however, knowing its limitations will enhance decision making.

Conflicting Rankings between the NPV and IRR Methods

As long as proposed capital budgeting projects are independent, both the NPV and IRR methods will produce the same accept/reject indication. That is, a project that has a positive NPV will also have an IRR that is greater than the discount rate. As a result, the project will be acceptable based on both the NPV and IRR values. However, when mutually exclusive projects are considered and ranked, a conflict occasionally arises. For instance, one project may have a higher NPV than another project, but a lower IRR.

To illustrate how conflicts between NPV and IRR can occur, imagine that the AddVenture Company owns a piece of land that can be used in different ways. On the one hand, this land has minerals beneath it that could be mined, so AddVenture could invest in mining equipment and reap the benefits of retrieving and selling the minerals. On the other hand, the land has perfect soil conditions for growing grapes that could be used to make wine, so the company could use it to support a vineyard.

Clearly, these two uses are mutually exclusive. The mine cannot be dug if there is a vineyard, and the vineyard cannot be planted if the mine is dug. The acceptance of one of the projects means that the other must be rejected.

Now let's suppose that AddVenture's finance department has estimated the cash flows associated with each use of the land. The estimates are presented next:

TIME	CASH FLOWS FOR THE MINING PROJECT	CASH FLOWS FOR THE VINEYARD PROJECT
t_0	($736,369)	($736,369)
t_1	$500,000	$0
t_2	$300,000	$0
t_3	$100,000	$0
t_4	$20,000	$50,000
t_5	$5,000	$200,000
t_6	$5,000	$500,000
t_7	$5,000	$500,000
t_8	$5,000	$500,000

Note that although the initial outlays for the two projects are the same, the incremental cash flows associated with the projects differ in amount and timing. The Mining Project generates its greatest positive cash flows early in the life of the project, while the Vineyard Project generates its greatest positive cash flows later. The differences in the projects' cash flow timing has a considerable effect on the NPV and IRR for each venture.

Assume AddVenture's required rate of return for long-term projects is 10 percent. The NPV and IRR results for each project given its cash flows are summarized as follows:

	NPV	IRR
Mining Project	$65,727.39	16.05%
Vineyard Project	$194,035.65	14.00%

These figures were obtained with our TI BAII PLUS calculator, as shown on page 245.

The NPV and IRR results show that the Vineyard Project has a higher NPV than the Mining Project ($194,035.65 versus $65,727.39), but the Mining Project has a higher IRR than the Vineyard Project (16.05% versus 14.00%). AddVenture is faced with a conflict between NPV and IRR results. Because the projects are mutually exclusive, the firm can only accept one.

In cases of conflict among mutually exclusive projects, the one with the highest NPV should be chosen because NPV indicates the dollar amount of value that will be added to the firm if the project is undertaken. In our example, then, AddVenture should choose the Vineyard Project (the one with the higher NPV) if its primary financial goal is to maximize firm value.

In this section we looked at three capital budgeting decision methods: the payback method, net present value, and the internal rate of return. We also investigated how to resolve conflicts between NPV and IRR decision methods. Next, we turn to a discussion of capital rationing.

CAPITAL RATIONING

Our discussion so far has shown that all independent projects with NPVs greater than or equal to zero should be accepted. All such projects that are adopted will add value to the firm. To act consistently with the goal of shareholder wealth maximization, then, it seems that if a firm locates $200 billion worth of positive NPV projects, it should accept all the projects. In practice, however, many firms place dollar limits on the total amount of capital budgeting projects they will undertake. They may wish to limit spending on new projects to keep a ceiling on business size. This practice of setting dollar limits on capital budgeting projects is known as **capital rationing.**

If capital rationing is imposed, then financial managers should seek the combination of projects that maximizes the value of the firm within the capital budget limit. For example, suppose a firm called BeLimited does not want its capital budget to exceed $200,000. Seven project proposals, Proposals A–G, are available, as shown in Table 10-1.

Note that all the projects in Table 10-1 have positive net present values, so they are all acceptable. However, BeLimited cannot adopt them all as that would require the expenditure of more than $200,000, its self-imposed capital budget limit.

TI BAII PLUS FINANCIAL CALCULATOR SOLUTIONS
IRR and NPV Solutions

THE MINING PROJECT		THE VINEYARD PROJECT	
KEYSTROKES	DISPLAY	KEYSTROKES	DISPLAY
CF	CF_0 = old contents	CF	CF_0 = old contents
2nd CLR Work	CF_0 = 0.00	2nd CLR Work	CF_0 = 0.00
736369 +/− ENTER	−736,369.00	736369 +/− ENTER	−736.369.00
↓ 500000 ENTER	C01 = 500,000.00	↓ 0 ENTER	C01 = 0.00
↓	F01 = 1.00	↓ 3 ENTER	F01 = 3.00
↓ 300000 ENTER	C02 = 300,000.00	↓ 50000 ENTER	C02 = 50,000.00
↓	F02 = 1.00	↓	F02 = 1.00
↓ 100000 ENTER	C03 = 100,000.00	↓ 200000 ENTER	C03 = 200,000.00
↓	F03 = 1.00	↓	F03 = 1.00
↓ 20000 ENTER	CO4 = 20,000.00	↓ 500000 ENTER	CO4 = 500,000.00
↓	FO4 = 1.00	↓ 3 ENTER	FO4 = 3
↓ 5000 ENTER	C05 = 5,000	NPV	I = 0.00
↓ 4 ENTER	F05 = 4.00	10 ENTER	I = 10.00
		↓ CPT	NPV = 194,035.65
NPV	I = 0.00	IRR	IRR = 0.00
10 ENTER	I = 10.00	CPT	IRR = 14.00
↓	NPV = 0.00		
CPT	NPV = 65,727.39		
IRR	IRR = 0.00		
CPT	IRR = 16.05		

TABLE 10-1

BeLimited Project Proposals

PROJECT	INITIAL CASH OUTLAY	NET PRESENT VALUE
A	$20,000	$8,000
B	$50,000	$7,200
C	$40,000	$6,500
D	$60,000	$5,100
E	$50,000	$4,200
F	$30,000	$3,800
G	$30,000	$2,000

Under capital rationing, BeLimited must choose the combination of acceptable Projects A through G that produces the highest total NPV without exceeding its capital budget limit of $200,000.

Jim Bruner, Former Maricopa County Supervisor, State of Arizona

Jim Bruner

Jim Bruner is a former Scottsdale City Council member and Maricopa County Supervisor for the state of Arizona. Currently, he is Executive Vice President for First Interstate Bank. During his tenure in public life, Jim voted for and against many long-term projects. In fact, Jim cast a key vote in favor of using a sales tax to help finance a domed stadium for the Arizona Diamondbacks baseball team.

Q. *What factors are considered when making a capital budgeting decision for a private versus a public project?*

In the private sector, corporations try to assess how much value—in dollars—a project will add to the firm. The goal is, of course, to maximize the wealth of the stockholders. In public ventures, measuring value becomes more complicated because value is often intangible. Members of the community are owners and stakeholders in the city, county, or state. Quantifying how much value a project will add to a community is difficult because an increase in job growth, national recognition, or public spirit can add value, but it's hard to put an exact price tag on those intangible items.

Q: *How do government workers make capital budgeting decisions in a public/private venture?*

A: Quite honestly, it depends on the project. Let me explain how we made a decision about building a golf course for the Tournament Players Club in Scottsdale as one example. The annual Phoenix Open, sanctioned by the Professional Golf Association tour, was looking for a larger golf course for its tournament. I was serving on the Scottsdale City Council when we decided to build a golf course for the tournament in a partnership between Scottsdale and the private sector, the PGA tour. During the other fifty-one weeks of the year, the course would be open to the general public for its enjoyment. Thus, the city of Scottsdale agreed to build the golf course and the PGA tour, a for-profit entity, agreed to operate the golf course, pro shop, restaurant, and so on. Scottsdale, as owner of the course, rents the golf course to the PGA and receives a percent of all receipts from all the course and retail activities. The estimates of the future receipts were our expected cash flows, and the cost of building the course was the city's initial investment. We calculated that Scottsdale would earn millions of dollars in excess of cost of building the golf course, so the two 18-hole courses and the tournament would clearly add value to the city of Scottsdale.

But we recognized that there was more to the capital budgeting equation than future cash flows from the tournament receipts. Although we couldn't estimate it with precise certainty, we knew that the tournament would increase the Scottsdale tourist industry, add new jobs, and increase the quality of life. A city is more than streets, sewers, lights, and fire and police departments. Having two eighteen-hole golf courses benefits a community by providing open space and entertainment.

Q. *How did the Maricopa County Board of Supervisors do capital budgeting analysis before building a stadium for the Arizona Diamondbacks?*

If you look at building a baseball stadium as a corporation might—what is the project's NPV for the state of Arizona—the estimates of cash flows are tough to make. The County of Maricopa instituted a tax (¼ of 1 percent for three years) to raise the initial cash outlay of $238 million for the stadium. In effect, the owners of the stadium—the public—voted to accept the project.

Had the county taken that $238 million raised to build the stadium and put it in a savings account, the county would have received more direct revenue at less risk than it will receive from the stadium. But the total economic impact through increased sales tax, property tax, employment, and so on, far exceed the direct revenues from the rent.

Q. *What future cash flows can the county expect from the Diamondbacks Stadium project?*

We receive an annual guaranteed revenue, even if nobody attends games. If, however, the team is successful, the taxpayers will benefit. As attendance increases, the stadium rent increases above the guaranteed revenue rate.

Maricopa County will also receive a percentage of the revenues from the skyboxes, the luxury suites. In addition, the County will receive a one-third percentage of the naming rights for the stadium. If a corporation wants its name on the stadium, the County gets one-third of the fee that corporation pays to display its name.

The Board of Supervisors estimated that its direct cash flows would be a $3.5 million annuity for the thirty years of the lease. Analyzing the amount and timing of those cash flows, and the $238 million initial investment, there's no way to justify accepting the project if direct revenue were the only means of the economic impact.

But we also looked at intangibles, such as the synergism created from having a stadium downtown, what it will do for economic development, for hotels, and for public spirit. We also knew that the stadium would generate at least 2,500 jobs during construction and believed it would generate many more jobs once the team began playing.

And because of the special tax, which stops once the stadium is complete, we will have enough money before the first pitch is thrown to ensure that the stadium is debt free and an ongoing asset to the community for years to come.

Source: Interview with Jim Bruner.

Under capital rationing, BeLimited's managers try different combinations of projects seeking the combination that gives the highest NPV without exceeding the $200,000 limit. For example, the combination of Projects B, C, E, F, and G costs $200,000 and yields a total NPV of $23,700. A better combination is that of Projects A, B, C, D, and F, which costs $200,000 and has a total NPV of $30,600. In fact, this combination has the highest total NPV, given the $200,000 capital budget limit (try a few other combinations to see for yourself), so that combination is the one BeLimited should choose.

In this section, we explored capital rationing. In the following section, we will examine how risk affects capital budgeting decisions.

RISK AND CAPITAL BUDGETING

Suppose you are a financial manager for AddVenture Corporation. You are considering two capital budgeting projects, Project X (discussed throughout the chapter) and Project X2. Both projects have identical future cash flow values and timing, and both have the same NPV, if discounted at the same rate, k, and the same IRR. The two projects appear equally desirable.

Now suppose you discover that Project X's incremental cash flows are absolutely certain, but Project X2's incremental cash flows, which have the same expected value, are highly uncertain. These cash flows could be higher or lower than forecast. In other words, Project X is a sure thing and Project X2 appears to be quite risky. As a risk-averse person, you would prefer Project X over Project X2.

Financial managers are not indifferent to risk. Indeed, the riskier a project, the less desirable it is to the firm. To incorporate risk into the NPV and IRR evaluation techniques, we use the standard deviation and coefficient of variation (CV) measures discussed in chapter 7. We begin by examining how to measure the risk of a capital budgeting project. Then we explain how to include the risk measurement in the NPV and IRR evaluation.

The assumption that most investors are risk averse is explained in chapter 7, pages 137–138.

Measuring Risk in Capital Budgeting

Financial managers may measure three types of risk in the capital budgeting process. The first type is *project-specific risk,* or the risk of a specific new project. The second type is *firm risk,* which is the impact of adding a new project to the existing projects of the firm. The third is *market (or beta) risk,* which is the effect of a new project on the stockholders' nondiversifiable risk.

In this chapter we focus on measuring firm risk. To measure firm risk, we compare the coefficient of variation (CV) of the firm's portfolio before and after a project is adopted. The before-and-after difference between the two CVs serves as the project's risk measure from a firm perspective. If the CAPM approach (discussed in chapter 7) is preferred, a financial manager could estimate the risk of a project by calculating the project's beta instead of the change in firm risk.

Take Note

The CV is often chosen as the risk measure because the CV reflects the expected return per unit of risk. Using only the standard deviation makes it more difficult to tell whether the risk is high or low.

We discussed the expected value formula, Equation 7-1, and the standard deviation formula, Equation 7-2, on page 140.

Computing Changes in the Coefficient of Variation   Let's reconsider our earlier example, Project X. Recall that the IRR of Project X was 5.71 percent. Now suppose that after careful analysis, we determine this IRR is actually the most likely value from a range of possible values, each with some probability of occurrence. We find the expected value and standard deviation of Project X's IRR distribution using Equations 7-1 and 7-2, respectively. We find that the expected value of the IRR distribution is 5.71 percent and the standard deviation is 2.89 percent.

To see how adding Project X to the firm's existing portfolio changes the portfolio's coefficient of variation (CV), we follow a five-step procedure.

1. Find the CV of the Existing Portfolio.   Suppose the expected rate of return and standard deviation of possible returns of AddVenture's existing portfolio are 6 percent and 2 percent, respectively. Given this information, calculate the CV of the firm's existing portfolio using Equation 7-3:

$$CV = \frac{\text{Standard Deviation}}{\text{Mean, or expected value}} \qquad (7\text{-}3)$$

$$= \frac{.02}{.06}$$

$$= .3333, \text{ or } 33.33\%$$

2. Find the Expected Rate of Return of the New Portfolio (the Existing Portfolio Plus the Proposed Project).   Assume that the investment in Project X represents 10 percent of the value of the portfolio. In other words, the new portfolio after adding Project X will consist of 10 percent Project X and 90 percent of the rest of the firm's assets. With these figures, solve for the expected rate of return of the new portfolio using Equation 7-4. In the calculations, Asset a represents Project X and Asset b represents the firm's existing portfolio.

$$E(R_p) = (w_a \times E(R_a)) + (w_b \times E(R_b))$$

$$= (.10 \times .0571) + (.90 \times .06)$$

$$= .00571 + .05400$$

$$= .05971, \text{ or } 5.971\%$$

3. Find the Standard Deviation of the New Portfolio (the Existing Portfolio Plus the Proposed Project).   Calculate the standard deviation of the new portfolio using Equation 7-5. Assume the degree of correlation (r) between project X (Asset a) and the firm's existing portfolio (Asset b) is zero. Put another way, there is no relationship between the returns from Project X and the returns from the firm's existing portfolio.

$$\sigma_p = \sqrt{w_a^2\sigma_a^2 + w_b^2\sigma_b^2 + 2w_aw_br_{ab}\sigma_a\sigma_b}$$ (7-5)

$$= \sqrt{(.10^2)(.0289^2) + (.90^2)(.02^2) + (2)(.10)(.90)(0.0)(.0578)}$$

$$= \sqrt{(.01)(.000835) + (.81)(.0004) + 0}$$

$$= \sqrt{.00000835 + .000324}$$

$$= \sqrt{.000332352}$$

$$= .0182, \text{ or } 1.82\%$$

4. Find the CV of the New Portfolio (the Existing Portfolio Plus the Proposed Project). To solve for the CV of the new portfolio with Project X included, we use Equation 7-3, as follows:

$$CV = \frac{\text{Standard Deviation}}{\text{Mean, or expected value}}$$ (7-3)

$$= \frac{.0182}{.05971}$$

$$= .3048, \text{ or } 30.48\%$$

5. Compare the CV of the Portfolio with and without the Proposed Project. To evaluate the effect of Project X on the risk of the AddVenture portfolio, we compare the CV of the old portfolio (without Project X) to the CV of the new portfolio (with Project X). The coefficients follow:

CV OF THE PORTFOLIO WITHOUT PROJECT X	CV OF THE PORTFOLIO WITH PROJECT X	CHANGE IN CV
33.33%	30.48%	− 2.85

The CV of the firm's portfolio dropped from 33.3 percent to 30.48 percent with the addition of Project X. This 2.85 percentage point decrease in CV is the measure of risk in Project X from the firm's perspective.

Adjusting for Risk

Most business owners and financial managers are risk averse, so they want the capital budgeting process to reflect risk concerns. Next, we discuss how to adjust for risk in the capital budgeting process—risk-adjusted discount rates.

Risk Adjusted Discount Rates (RADRs) One way to factor risk into the capital budgeting process is to adjust the rate of return demanded for high- and low-risk projects. **Risk-adjusted discount rates (RADRs),** then, are discount rates that differ according to their effect on a firm's risk. The higher the risk, the higher the RADR and the lower the risk, the lower the RADR. A project with a normal risk level would have a RADR equal to the actual discount rate.

To find the risk-adjusted discount rate for a capital budgeting project, we first prepare a risk adjustment table like the one in Table 10-2. We assume in Table 10-2 that the coefficient of variation, CV, is the risk measure to be adjusted for. The CV is based on the probability distribution of the IRR values.

Adjusting required rates of return to compensate for the presence of risk was discussed in chapter 7, pages 155–158.

TABLE 10-2

Risk Adjustment Table

IF ADOPTION OF THE PROPOSED CAPITAL BUDGETING PROJECT WOULD CHANGE THE CV OF THE FIRM'S PORTFOLIO IRR BY THE FOLLOWING AMOUNT:	THEN ASSIGN THE PROJECT TO THE FOLLOWING RISK CATEGORY:	AND ADJUST THE DISCOUNT RATE FOR THE PROJECT AS FOLLOWS:
More than a 1% point increase	High Risk	+2%
Between a 1% point decrease and a 1% point increase	Average Risk	0
More than a 1% point decrease	Low Risk	−2%

Table 10-2 shows how the discount rates for capital budgeting projects might be adjusted for varying degrees of risk. The discount rate of a project that decreased the CV of the firm's portfolio of assets by 2.5 percent point, for example, would be classified as a low-risk project. That project would be evaluated using a discount rate two percentage points lower than that used on average projects.

This has the effect of making Project X a more desirable project. That is, financial managers would calculate the project's NPV using an average discount rate that is two percentage points lower, which would increase the project's NPV. If the firm uses the IRR method, financial managers would compare the project's IRR to a hurdle rate two percentage points lower than average, which would make it more likely that the firm would adopt the project.

RADRs are an important part of the capital budgeting process because they incorporate the risk–return relationship. All other things being equal, the more a project increases risk, the less likely it is that a firm will accept the project; the more a project decreases risk, the more likely it is that a firm will accept the project.

WHAT'S NEXT

In this chapter we explored the capital budgeting process and decision methods. We examined three capital budgeting techniques—the payback method, net present value, and internal rate of return. We also discussed capital rationing and how to measure and adjust for risk when making capital budgeting decisions.

In the next chapter, we'll investigate how to estimate incremental cash flows in capital budgeting.

Summary

1. Explain the capital budgeting process.

Capital budgeting is the process of evaluating proposed investment projects. Capital budgeting projects may be independent—the projects do not compete with each other—or mutually exclusive—accepting one project precludes the acceptance of the other(s) in that group.

Financial managers apply two decision practices when selecting capital budgeting projects: *accept/reject* decisions and *ranking* decisions. The accept/reject decision is the determination of which independent projects are acceptable in light of the firm's financial objectives.

Ranking is a process of comparing projects to a standard measure, and ordering the mutually exclusive projects based on how well they meet the measure. The capital budgeting process is concerned only with incremental cash flows; that is, those cash flows that will occur if an investment is undertaken, but won't occur if it isn't.

2. Calculate the payback period, net present value, and internal rate of return for a proposed capital budgeting project.

The payback period is defined as the number of time periods it will take before the cash inflows from a proposed capital budgeting project will equal the amount of the initial investment. To find a project's payback period, add all the project's positive cash flows, one period at a time, until the sum equals the amount of the initial cash outlay for the project. The number of time periods it takes to recoup the initial cash outlay is the payback period. A project is acceptable if it pays back the initial investment within a time frame set by firm management.

The net present value (NPV) of a proposed capital budgeting project is the dollar amount of the change in the value of the firm that will occur if the project is undertaken. To calculate NPV, total the present values of all the projected incremental cash flows associated with a project and subtract the amount of the initial cash outlay. A project with an NPV greater than or equal to zero is acceptable. An NPV profile—a graph that shows a project's NPV at many different discount rates (required rates of return)—shows how sensitive a project's NPV is to changes in the discount rate.

The internal rate of return (IRR) is the projected percent rate of return that a proposed project will earn, given its incremental cash flows and required initial cash outlay. To calculate IRR, find the discount rate that makes the project's NPV equal to zero. That rate of return is the IRR. A project is acceptable if its IRR is greater than or equal to the firm's required rate of return (the hurdle rate).

3. Describe capital rationing and how firms decide which projects to select.

The practice of placing dollar limits on the total size of the capital budget is called capital rationing. Under capital rationing the firm will select the combination of projects that yields the highest NPV without exceeding the capital budget limit.

4. Measure the risk of a capital budgeting project.

To measure the risk of a capital budgeting project, we determine how the project would affect the risk of the firm's existing asset portfolio. We compare the coefficient of variation of expected returns of the firm's asset portfolio with the proposed project and without it. The difference between the two coefficients of variation is the measure of the risk of the capital budgeting project.

5. Explain risk-adjusted discount rates.

To compensate for the degree of risk in capital budgeting, firms may adjust the discount rate for each project according to risk. The more risk is increased, the higher the discount rate. The more risk is decreased, the lower the discount rate. Rates adjusted for the risk of projects are called risk-adjusted discount rates (RADRs).

Equations Introduced in This Chapter

Equation 10-1a. NPV Formula, Algebraic Version:

$$NPV = \left(\frac{CF_1}{(1+k)^1}\right) + \left(\frac{CF_2}{(1+k)^2}\right) \ldots + \left(\frac{CF_n}{(1+k)^n}\right) - \text{Initial Investment}$$

where: CF = Cash flow at the indicated times
k = Discount rate, or required rate of return for the project
n = Life of the project measured in the number of time periods

Equation 10-1b. NPV Formula, Table Version:

$$NPV = CF_1(PVIF_{k,1}) + CF_2(PVIF_{k,2}) + \ldots CF_n(PVIF_{k,n}) - \text{Initial Investment}$$

$$\text{where:} \quad PVIF = \text{Present Value Interest Factor}$$

Equation 10-2. Formula for IRR Using Equation 10-1a:

$$NPV = 0 = \left(\frac{CF_1}{(1+k)^1}\right) + \left(\frac{CF_2}{(1+k)^2}\right) \ldots + \left(\frac{CF_n}{(1+k)^n}\right) - \text{Initial Investment}$$

$$\text{where: } k = \text{the IRR value}$$

Fill in cash flows (CFs) and periods (n). Then choose values for k by trial and error until the NPV equals zero. The value of k that causes the NPV to equal zero is the IRR.

Self-Test

ST-1. What is the NPV of the following project?

Initial Investment:	$50,000
Net cash flow at the end of year 1:	$20,000
Net cash flow at the end of year 2:	$40,000
Discount rate:	11%

ST-2. What is the IRR of the project in ST-1?

ST-3. You've been assigned to evaluate a project for your firm that requires an initial investment of $200,000, is expected to last for ten years, and is expected to produce after-tax net cash flows of $44,503 per year. If your firm's required rate of return is 14 percent, should the project be accepted?

ST-4. What is the IRR of the project in ST-3?

ST-5. Assume you have decided to reinvest your portfolio in zero-coupon bonds. You like zero-coupon bonds because they pay off a known amount, $1,000 at maturity, and involve no other cash flows other than the purchase price. Assume your required rate of return is 12 percent. If you buy some ten-year zero coupon bonds for $400 each today, will the bonds meet your return requirements? (Hint: Compute the IRR of the investment given the cash flows involved.)

ST-6. Joe the cut-rate bond dealer has offered to sell you some zero-coupon bonds for $300. (Remember, zero-coupon bonds pay off $1,000 at maturity and involve no other cash flows other than the purchase price.) If the bonds mature in ten years and your required rate of return for cut-rate bonds is 20 percent what is the NPV of Joe's deal?

Review Questions

1. How do we calculate the payback period for a proposed capital budgeting project? What are the main criticisms of the payback method?
2. How does the net present value relate to the value of the firm?
3. What are the advantages and disadvantages of the internal rate of return method?
4. Provide three examples of mutually exclusive projects.
5. What is the decision rule for accepting or rejecting proposed projects when using net present value?

6. What is the decision rule for accepting or rejecting proposed projects when using internal rate of return?

7. What is capital rationing? Should a firm practice capital rationing? Why?

8. Explain how to resolve a "ranking conflict" between the net present value and the internal rate of return. Why should the conflict be resolved as you explained?

9. Explain how to measure the firm risk of a capital budgeting project.

10. Why is the coefficient of variation a better risk measure to use than the standard deviation when evaluating the risk of capital budgeting projects?

11. Explain why we measure a project's risk as the change in the CV.

12. Explain how using a risk-adjusted discount rate improves capital budgeting decision making compared to using a single discount rate for all projects?

Build Your Communication Skills

CS-1. Arrange to have a person who has no training in finance visit the class on the next day after the Net Present Value (NPV) evaluation method has been covered. Before the visitor arrives, choose two teams who will brief the visitor on the results of their evaluation of a capital budgeting project. The visitor will play the role of the CEO of the firm. The CEO must choose one capital budgeting project for the firm to undertake. The CEO will choose the project based on the recommendations of Team A and Team B.

Now have each team describe the following projects:

	Team A	Team B
	Solar Energy Satellite (a plan to beam energy down from orbit)	Fresh Water Extraction Project (a plan to extract drinking water from the sea)
Initial Investment	$40 million	$40 million
NPV	$10 million	$8 million
IRR	12%	18%

After the projects have been described, have the CEO ask each team for its recommendation as to which project to adopt. The CEO may also listen to input from the class at large.

When the debate is complete, have the CEO select one of the projects (based on the class's recommendations). Then critique the class's recommendations.

CS-2. Divide the class into groups of two members each. Have each pair prepare a written description (closed book) of how to measure the risk of a capital budgeting project. When the explanations are complete, select a volunteer from each group to present their findings to the class.

Problems

10-1. Three separate projects each have an initial cash outlay of $10,000. The cash flows for Peter's Project is $4,000 per year for three years. The cash flow for Paul's Project is $2,000 in years 1 and 3, and $8,000 in year 2. Mary's Project has a cash flow of $10,000 in year 1, followed by $1,000 each year for years 2 and 3.

    a. Use the payback method to calculate how many years it will take for each project to recoup the initial investment.

    b. Which project would you consider most liquid?

10-2. The Bedford Falls Bridge Building Company is considering the purchase of a new crane. George Bailey, the new manager has had some past management experience while he

Payback

NPV and IRR

was the Chief Financial Officer of the local savings and loan. The cost of the crane is $17,291.42 and the expected incremental cash flows are $5,000 at the end of year 1, $8,000 at the end of year 2, and $10,000 at the end of year 3.

    a. Calculate the net present value if the required rate of return is 12 percent.
    b. Calculate the internal rate of return.
    c. Should Mr. Bailey purchase this crane?

NPV

10-3. Lin McAdam and Lola Manners, managers of the Winchester Company, do not practice capital rationing. They have three independent projects they are evaluating for inclusion in this year's capital budget. One is for a new machine to make rifle stocks. The second is for a new forklift to use in the warehouse. The third project involves the purchase of automated packaging equipment. The Winchester Company's required rate of return is 13 percent. The initial investment (a negative cash flow) and the expected positive net cash flows for years 1 through 4 for each project follow:

	Expected Net Cash Flow		
Year	Rifle Stock Machine	Forklift	Packaging Equipment
0	$(9,000)	$(12,000)	$(18,200)
1	2,000	5,000	0
2	5,000	4,000	5,000
3	1,000	6,000	10,000
4	4,000	2,000	12,000

    a. Calculate the net present value for each project.
    b. Which project(s) should be undertaken? Why?

NPV and IRR

10-4. The Trask Family Lettuce Farm is located in the fertile Salinas Valley of California. Adam Trask, the head of the family, makes all the financial decisions that affect the farm. Because of an extended drought, the family needs more water per acre than what the existing irrigation system can supply. The quantity and quality of lettuce produced is expected to increase when more water is supplied. Cal and Aron, Adam's sons, have devised two different solutions to their problem. Cal suggests improvements to the existing system. Aron is in favor of a completely new system. The negative cash flow associated with the initial investment and expected positive net cash flows for years 1 through 7 for each project follow. Adam has no other alternatives and will choose one of the two projects. The Trask Family Lettuce Farm has a required rate of return of 12 percent for these projects.

	Expected Net Cash Flow	
Year	Cal's Project	Aron's Project
0	$(100,000)	$(300,000)
1	22,611	63,655
2	22,611	63,655
3	22,611	63,655
4	22,611	63,655
5	22,611	63,655
6	22,611	63,655
7	22,611	63,655

    a. Calculate the net present value for each project.
    b. Calculate the internal rate of return for each project.
    c. Which project should Adam choose? Why?
    d. Is there a conflict between the decisions indicated by the NPVs and the IRRs?

10-5. Dave Hirsh publishes his own manuscripts and is unsure which of two new printers he should purchase. He is a novelist living in Parkman, Illinois. Having slept through most of his Finance 300 course in college, he is unfamiliar with cash flow analysis. He enlists the help of the finance professor at the local university, Dr. Gwen French, to assist him. Together they estimate the following expected initial investment (a negative cash flow) and net positive cash flows for years 1 through 3 for each machine. Dave only needs one printer and estimates it will be worthless after three years of heavy use. Dave's required rate of return for this project is 10 percent.

Payback, NPV, and IRR

Expected Net Cash Flow

Year	Printer 1	Printer 2
0	$(2000)	$(2500)
1	900	1500
2	1100	1300
3	1300	800

a. Calculate the payback period for each printer.
b. Calculate the net present value for each printer.
c. Calculate the internal rate of return for each printer.
d. Which printer do you think Dr. French will recommend? Why?
e. Suppose Dave's required rate of return was 16 percent. Does the decision about which printer to purchase change?

10-6. Project A has an initial investment of $11,000 and it generates positive cash flows of $4,000 each year for the next six years. Project B has an initial investment of $17,000 and it generates positive cash flows of $4,500 each year also for the next six years. Assume the discount rate, or required rate of return, is 13 percent.

Independent and Mutually Exclusive Projects

a. Calculate the net present value of each project. If Project A and Project B are mutually exclusive, which one(s) would you select?
b. Assume Projects A and B are independent. Based on NPV, which one(s) would you select?
c. Calculate the internal rate of return for each project.
d. Using IRR for your decision, which project would you select if Project A and Project B are mutually exclusive? Would your answer change if these two projects were independent instead of mutually exclusive?
e. Project C was added to the potential capital budget list at the last minute as a mutually exclusive alternative to Project B. It has an initial cash outlay of $17,000 and it generates its only positive cash flow of $37,500 in the sixth year. Years 1 through 5 have $0 cash flow. Calculate Project C's NPV. Which alternative, Project B or C, would you choose?
f. Now calculate the IRR of Project C and compare it to Project B's IRR. Based solely on the IRRs, which project would you select?
g. Since Projects B and C are mutually exclusive, would you recommend that Project B or Project C be added to the capital budget for this year? Explain your choice.

10-7. Joanne Crale is an independent petroleum geologist. She is taking advantage of every opportunity to lease the mineral rights of land she thinks lies over oil reserves. She thinks there are many reservoirs with oil reserves left behind by major corporations when they plugged and abandoned fields in the 1960s. Ms. Crale knows that with today's technology, production can be sustained at much lower reservoir pressures than was possible in the 1960s. She would like to lease the mineral rights from George Hansen and Ed McNeil, the landowners. Her net cost for this current oil venture is $5 million. This includes costs for the initial leasing and the three planned development wells. The expected positive net cash flows for the project are $1.85 million each year for four years. On depletion, she anticipates a negative

NPV and IRR

cash flow of $250,000 in year 5 because of reclamation and disposal costs. Because of the risks involved in petroleum exploration, Ms. Crale's required rate of return is 16 percent.

a. Calculate the net present value for Ms. Crale's project.
b. Calculate the internal rate of return for this project.
c. Would you recommend the project?

Challenge Problem

10-8. The product development managers at World Series Innovations are about to recommend their final capital budget for next year. They have a self-imposed budget limit of $100,000. Five independent projects are being considered. Vernon Simpson, the Chief Scientist and CEO, has minimal financial analysis experience and relies on his managers to recommend the projects that will increase the value of the firm by the greatest amount. Given the following summary of the five projects, which ones should the managers recommend?

Projects	Initial Cash Outlay	Net Present Value
Chalk Line Machine	(10,000)	4000
Gel Padded Glove	(25,000)	3600
Insect Repellent	(35,000)	3250
Titanium Bat	(40,000)	2500
Recycled Base Covers	(20,000)	2100

Various Capital Budgeting Issues

10-9. A project you are considering has an initial investment of $5,669.62. It has positive net cash flows of $2,200 each year for three years. Your required rate of return is 12 percent.

a. Calculate the net present value of this project.
b. Would you undertake this project if you had the cash available?
c. What would the discount rate have to be before this project's NPV would be positive? Construct an NPV profile with discount rates of 0 percent, 5 percent, and 10 percent to answer this question.
d. What other method might you use to determine at what discount rate the net present value would become greater than 0?

Expected IRR

10-10. The internal rate of return (IRR) of a capital investment Project B is expected to have the following values with the associated probabilities for an economic life of five years. Calculate the expected value, standard deviation and coefficient of variation of the IRR distribution.

IRR	Probability of Occurrence
0%	0.05
1%	0.10
3%	0.20
6%	0.30
9%	0.20
11%	0.10
12%	0.05

Capital Budgeting Risk

10-11. Four capital investment alternatives have the following expected IRRs and standard deviations respectively.

Project	Expected IRR	Standard Deviation
A	14%	2%
B	16%	6%
C	11%	5%
D	14%	4%

If the firm's existing portfolio of assets has an expected IRR of 13 percent with a standard deviation of 3 percent, identify the lowest and the highest risk projects in the list above. You may assume the correlation coefficient of returns from each project relative to the existing portfolio is .50 and the investment in each project would constitute 20 percent of the firm's total portfolio.

10-12. Assume that a company has an existing portfolio A, with an expected IRR of 10 percent and standard deviation of 2 percent. The company is considering adding a Project B, with expected IRR of 11 percent and standard deviation of 3 percent, to its portfolio. Also assume that the amount invested in Portfolio A is $700,000 and the amount to be invested in Project B is $200,000.

Portfolio Risk

  a. If the degree of correlation between returns from Portfolio A and Project B is .90 (r = +.9), calculate:
    1. the coefficient of variation of portfolio A
    2. the expected IRR of the new combined portfolio
    3. the standard deviation of the new combined portfolio
    4. the coefficient of variation of the new combined portfolio.
  b. What is the change in the coefficient of variation as a result of adopting project B?
  c. Assume the firm classifies projects as high risk if they raise the coefficient of variation of the portfolio 2 percent or more, as low risk if they lower the coefficient of variation of the portfolio 2 percent or more, and as average risk if they change the coefficient of variation of the portfolio by less than 2 percent in either direction. In what risk classification would project B be?
  d. The required rate of return for average risk projects for the company in this problem is 13 percent. The company policy is to adjust the required rate of return downward by 3 percent for low-risk projects and raise it 3 percent for high-risk projects (average risk projects are evaluated at the average required rate of return). The expected cash flows from Project B are as follows:

Coefficient of Variation
Risk in Capital Budgeting

RADRs

CF of Initial Investment	($200,000)
end of year 1	55,000
end of year 2	55,000
end of year 3	55,000
end of year 4	100,000

Calculate the NPV of Project B when its cash flows are discounted at:

  1. the average required rate of return
  2. the high-risk discount rate
  3. the low-risk discount rate

10-13. Dorothy Gale is thinking of purchasing a Kansas amusement park, Glinda's Gulch. She already owns at least one park in each of the surrounding states and wants to expand her operations into Kansas. She estimates the IRR from the project may be one of a number of values, each with a certain probability of occurrence. Her estimated IRR values and the probability of their occurrence are shown below.

Risk in Capital Budgeting

Glinda's Gulch

Possible IRR Value	Probability
2%	.125
5%	.20
9%	.35
13%	.20
16%	.125

Now Dorothy wants to estimate the risk of the project. Assume she has asked you to do the following for her:

a. Calculate the mean, or expected IRR of the project.
b. Calculate the standard deviation of the possible IRRs
c. Assume the expected IRR of Dorothy's existing portfolio of parks is 8 percent, with a standard deviation of 2 percent. Calculate the coefficient of variation of Dorothy's existing portfolio.
d. Calculate the expected IRR of Dorothy's portfolio if the Glinda's Gulch project is adopted. For this calculation assume that Dorothy's new portfolio will consist of 80 percent existing parks and 20 percent new Glinda's Gulch.
e. Again assuming that Dorothy's new portfolio will consist of 80 percent existing parks and 20 percent new Glinda's Gulch, calculate the standard deviation of Dorothy's portfolio if the Glinda's Gulch project is added. Since Glinda's Gulch is identical to Dorothy's other parks, she estimates the returns from Glinda's Gulch and her existing portfolio are perfectly positively correlated (r = +1.0).
f. Calculate the coefficient of variation of Dorothy's new portfolio with Glinda's Gulch.
g. Compare the coefficient of variation of Dorothy's existing portfolio with and without the Glinda's Gulch project. How does the addition of Glinda's Gulch affect the riskiness of the portfolio?

Risk in Capital Budgeting

10-14. Four capital investment alternatives have the following expected IRRs and standard deviations.

Project	Expected IRR	Standard Deviation
A	18%	9%
B	15%	5%
C	11%	3%
D	8%	1%

The firm's existing portfolio of projects has an expected IRR of 12 percent and a standard deviation of 4 percent.

a. Calculate the coefficient of variation of the existing portfolio.
b. Calculate the coefficient of variation of the portfolio if the firm invests 10 percent of its assets in Project A. You may assume that there is no correlation between the returns from Project A and the returns from the existing portfolio (r = 0). (Note: In order to calculate the coefficient of variation, you must first calculate the expected IRR and standard deviation of the portfolio with Project A included.)
c. Using the same procedure as in b, and given the same assumptions, calculate the coefficient of variation of the portfolio if it includes, in turn, projects B, C, and D.
d. Which project has the highest risk? Which has the lowest risk?

Firm Risk

10-15. A firm has an existing portfolio of projects with a mean, or expected IRR of 15 percent. The standard deviation of this estimate is 5 percent. The existing portfolio is worth $820,000. The addition of a new project, PROJ1, is being considered. PROJ1's expected IRR is 18 percent with a standard deviation of 9 percent. The initial investment for PROJ1 is expected to be $194,000. The returns from PROJ1 and the existing portfolio are perfectly positively correlated (r = +1.0).

a. Calculate the coefficient of variation for the existing portfolio.
b. If PROJ1 is added to the existing portfolio, calculate the weight (proportion) of the existing portfolio in the combined portfolio.
c. Calculate the weight (proportion) of PROJ1 in the combined portfolio.
d. Calculate the standard deviation of the combined portfolio. Is the standard deviation of the combined portfolio higher or lower than the standard deviation of the existing portfolio?

e. Calculate the coefficient of variation of the combined portfolio.

f. If PROJ1 is added to the existing portfolio, will the firm's risk increase or decrease?

10-16. VOTD Pharmaceuticals is considering the mass production of a new sleeping pill. Neely O'Hara, VOTD's financial analyst, has gathered all the available information from the finance, production, advertising and marketing departments and has estimated that the yearly net incremental cash flows will be $298,500. She estimates the initial investment for this project will be $2 million. The pills are expected to be marketable for ten years and Neely does not expect that any of the investment costs will be recouped at the end of the ten-year period. VOTD's required rate of return for average risk projects is 8 percent. Two percent is added to the required rate of return for high-risk projects.

Risk in Capital Budgeting

a. Calculate the net present value of the project if VOTD management considers it to be average risk.

b. A lot of uncertainty is associated with the potential competition of new drugs that VOTD's competitors might introduce. Because of this uncertainty, VOTD management has changed the classification of this project to high risk. Calculate the net present value at the risk adjusted discount rate.

c. Assuming the risk classification does not change again, should this project be adopted?

d. What will the yearly net incremental cash flow have to be in order to have a positive NPV when using the high-risk discount rate?

10-17. Aluminum Building Products Company (ABPC) is considering investing in either of the two mutually exclusive projects described below:

Comprehensive Problem

Project 1. Buying a new set of roll-forming tools for their existing roll-forming line to introduce a new cladding product. After its introduction the product will need to be promoted. This means that cash inflows from additional production will start some time after and will gradually pick up in subsequent periods.

Project 2. Modifying their existing roll-forming line to increase productivity of their available range of cladding products. Cash inflows from additional production will start immediately and will reduce over time as the products move through their life-cycle.

Sarah Brown, project manager of ABPC, has requested that you do the necessary financial analysis and give your opinion as to which project ABPC should select. The projects have the following net cash flow estimates:

Year	Project 1	Project 2
0	($200,000)	($200,000)
1	0	90,000
2	0	70,000
3	20,000	50,000
4	30,000	30,000
5	40,000	10,000
6	60,000	10,000
7	90,000	10,000
8	100,000	10,000

Both the above projects have the same economic life of eight years and average risk characteristics. ABPC's weighted average cost of capital or hurdle rate is 7.2 percent.

a. Which project would you recommend Ms. Brown accept to maximize value of the firm? (Hint: Calculate and compare NPVs of both the projects)

b. What are the IRRs of each project? Which project should be chosen using IRR as the selection criterion?

c. Draw the NPV profiles of both the projects. What is the approximate discount rate at which both the projects would have the same NPV? What is that NPV?

d. Does the selection remain unaffected for i) WACC > 5.4 percent; ii) WACC > 8.81 percent; and iii) WACC > 14.39 percent?

e. Further market survey research indicates that both the projects have lower than average risk and hence the risk adjusted discount rate should be 5 percent. What happens to the ranking of the projects using NPV and IRR as the selection criteria? Explain the conflict in ranking, if any.

f. Answer the questions a), d), and e), assuming the projects are independent of each other.

Answers to Self-Test

ST-1. The NPV of the project can be found using equation 10-1a as follows:

$$\text{NPV} = \left(\frac{\$20,000}{(1 + .11)^1}\right) + \left(\frac{\$40,000}{(1 + .11)^2}\right) - \$50,000$$

$$= \left(\frac{\$20,000}{1.11}\right) + \left(\frac{\$40,000}{1.2321}\right) - \$50,000$$

$$= \$18,018 + \$32,465 - \$50,000$$

$$= \$483$$

ST-2. To find the IRR, we solve for the k value that results in an NPV of zero in the NPV formula (equation 10-1a) by trial and error:

Try using k = 11%:

$$0 = \left(\frac{\$20,000}{(1 + .11)^1}\right) + \left(\frac{\$40,000}{(1 + .11)^2}\right) - \$50,000$$

$$= \left(\frac{\$20,000}{1.11}\right) + \left(\frac{\$40,000}{1.2321}\right) - \$50,000$$

$$= \$18,018 + \$32,465 - \$50,000$$

$$= \$483$$

The result does not equal zero. Try again using a slightly higher discount rate:

Second try using k = 11.65%

$$0 = \left(\frac{\$20,000}{(1 + .1165)^1}\right) + \left(\frac{\$40,000}{(1 + .1165)^2}\right) - \$50,000$$

$$= \left(\frac{\$20,000}{1.1165}\right) + \left(\frac{\$40,000}{1.24657225}\right) - \$50,000$$

$$= \$17,913 + \$32,088 - \$50,000$$

$$= \$1$$

Close enough. The IRR of the project is almost exactly 11.65%

ST-3. The NPV of the project must be calculated to see if it is greater or less than zero. Since the project in this problem is an annuity, its NPV can be found most easily using a modified version of Equation 10-1b as follows:

$$\text{NPV} = \text{PMT}(\text{PVIFA}_{k,n}) - \text{Initial Investment}$$

We include this problem (and some others that follow) to show you that Equations 10-1a and 10-1b can be modified to take advantage of the present value of an annuity formulas covered in chapter 8, Equations 8-4a and 8-4b. The problem could also be solved using the basic forms of Equations 10-1a and 10-1b, but would take longer.

In this problem the initial investment is $200,000, the annuity payment is $44,503, the discount rate k is 14 percent and the number of periods n is 10.

$$\text{NPV} = \$44,503(\text{PVIFA}_{14\%,\,10}) - \$200,000$$
$$= \$44,503(5.2161) - \$200,000$$
$$= \$232,132 - \$200,000$$
$$= \$32,132$$

Since the NPV is positive the project should be accepted.

ST-4. The IRR is found by setting the NPV formula to zero and solving for the IRR rate, k. In this case, there are no multiple cash flows so the equation can be solved algebraically. For convenience we use Equation 10-1b modified for an annuity:

$$0 = \$44,503(\text{PVIFA}_{k\%,\,10}) - \$200,000$$
$$\$200,000 = \$44,503(\text{PVIFA}_{k\%,\,10})$$
$$\frac{\$200,000}{\$44,503} = \text{PVIFA}_{k\%,\,10}$$
$$4.49408 = \text{PVIFA}_{k\%,\,10}$$

Finding the PVIFA in Table IV inside the book cover, we see that 4.4941 (there are only four decimal places in the table) occurs in the year 10 row in the 18 percent column. Therefore the IRR of the project is 18 percent.

ST-5. There are only two cash flows in this problem, a $400 investment at time 0 and the $1,000 payoff at the end of year 10. To find the IRR, we set the NPV formula to zero, fill in the two cash flows and periods, and solve for the IRR rate k that makes the right-hand side of the equation equal zero. Equation 10-1b is more convenient to use in this case:

$$0 = \$1,000(\text{PVIF}_{k\%,\,10}) - \$400$$
$$\$400 = \$1,000(\text{PVIF}_{k\%,\,10})$$
$$\frac{\$400}{\$1,000} = \text{PVIF}_{k\%,\,10}$$
$$.4000 = \text{PVIF}_{k\%,\,10}$$

If we find the PVIF in Table II inside the book cover, we see that .4000 occurs in the year 10 row between the 9 percent and 10 percent columns. Therefore, the IRR of the project is between 9 percent and 10 percent. (The exact value of the IRR is 9.596 percent). Since your required rate of return in this problem was 12 percent, the bonds would NOT meet your requirements.

ST-6. Solve for the NPV using Equation 10-1a or b. Equation 10-1a would be the most convenient version for this problem. The cash flows are a $300 investment at time-0 and a $1,000 future value (FV) in 10 years. The discount rate is 20 percent.

$$\text{NPV} = \left(\frac{\$1,000}{(1 + .20)^{10}}\right) - \$300$$
$$= \left(\frac{\$1,000}{6.191736}\right) - \$300$$
$$= \$161.51 - \$300$$
$$= -\$138.49$$

Appendix 10A

Wrinkles in Capital Budgeting

In this appendix we discuss three situations that change the capital budgeting decision process. First, we examine *non-simple projects*, projects that have a negative initial cash flow, in addition to one or more negative future cash flows. Next, we explore projects that have multiple IRRs. Finally, we discuss how to compare mutually exclusive projects with unequal project lives.

Non-Simple Projects

Most capital budgeting projects start with a negative cash flow—the initial investment—at t_0 followed by positive future cash flows. Such projects are called **simple projects**. **Non-simple projects** are projects that have one or more negative future cash flows after the initial investment.

To illustrate a non-simple project, consider Project N, the expected cash flows for a nuclear power plant project. The initial investment of $500 million is a negative cash flow at t_0, followed by positive cash flows of $25 million per year for thirty years as electric power is generated and sold. At the end of the useful life of the project, the storage of nuclear fuel and the shutdown safety procedures require cash outlays of $100 million at the end of year 31. The timeline depicted in Figure 10A-1 shows the cash flow pattern:

Figure 10A-1 Cash Flow Time Line for Project N (in millions)

With a 20 percent discount rate, an initial investment of −$500 million, a thirty-year annuity of $25 million, and a shutdown cash outlay of −$100 million in year 31, the NPV of Project N follows (in millions):

The $25 million annual payment for thirty years constitutes an annuity, so we were able to adapt Equation 10-1a by using the present value of annuity formula, Equation 8-4a.

$$\text{NPV}_n = -\$500\left(\frac{1}{(1 + .20)^0}\right) + \$25\left[\frac{1 - \frac{1}{(1 + .20)^{30}}}{.20}\right] - \$100\left(\frac{1}{(1 + .20)^{31}}\right)$$

$$= (-\$500 \times 1) + (\$25 \times 4.97894) - (\$100 \times .0035106)$$

$$= -\$500 + \$124.47341 - \$.35106$$

$$= -\$375.87765$$

We find that at a discount rate of 20 percent, Project N has a negative net present value of −375.878, so the firm considering Project N should reject it.

MULTIPLE IRRs

Some projects may have more than one internal rate of return. That is, a project may have several different discount rates that result in a net present value of zero.

Here is an example. Suppose Project Q requires an initial cash outlay of $160,000 and is expected to generate a positive cash flow of $1,000,000 in year one. In year two, the project will require an additional cash *outlay* in the amount of $1 million. The cash flows for Project Q are shown on the following time line:

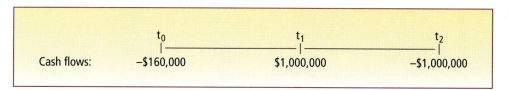

Figure 10A-2 Cash Flow Timeline for Project Q

We find the IRR of Project Q by using the trial and error procedure, Equation 10-2. When k = 25%, the NPV is zero.

$$0 = \left(\frac{\$1,000,000}{(1+.25)^1}\right) - \left(\frac{\$1,000,000}{(1+.25)^2}\right) - \$160,000$$
$$= \$800,000 - \$640,000 - \$160,000$$
$$= \$0$$

Since 25 percent causes the NPV of Project Q to be zero, the IRR of the project must be 25 percent. But wait! If we had tried k = 400%, the IRR calculation would look like this:

$$0 = \left(\frac{\$1,000,000}{(1+4.00)^1}\right) - \left(\frac{\$1,000,000}{(1+4.00)^2}\right) - \$160,000$$
$$= \$200,000 - \$40,000 - \$160,000$$
$$= \$0$$

Since 400 percent results in an NPV of zero, 400 percent must also be the IRR of the Project Q. Figure 10A-3 shows the net present value profile for Project Q. By examining this graph we see how 25 percent and 400 percent both make the net present value equal to zero.

As the graph shows, Project Q's net present value profile crosses the horizontal axis (has a zero value) in two different places, at discount rates of 25 percent and 400 percent.

Project Q had two IRRs because the project's cash flows changed from negative to positive (at t_1) and then from positive to negative at (t_2). It turns out that a non-simple project may have (but does not have to have) as many IRRs as there are sign changes. In this case, two sign changes resulted in two internal rates of return.

Whenever we have two or more IRRs for a project, the IRR method is not a useful decision-making tool. Remember the IRR accept/reject decision rule: Firms should accept projects with IRRs higher than the discount rate, and reject projects

Figure 10A-3 Net Present Value Profile Project Q

The net present value profile for Project Q crosses the zero line twice, showing that two IRRs are possible.

with IRRs lower than the discount rate. With more than one discount rate, decision makers will not know which IRR to use for the accept/reject decision. In projects that have multiple IRRs, then, switch to the NPV method.

Mutually Exclusive Projects with Unequal Project Lives

When mutually exclusive projects have different expected useful lives, selecting among the projects requires more than comparing the projects' NPVs. To illustrate, suppose you are a business manager considering a new business telephone system. One is the Cheap Talk System, which requires an initial cash outlay of $10,000 and is expected to last three years. The other is the Rolles Voice System, which requires an initial cash outlay of $50,000 and is expected to last twelve years. The Cheap Talk System is expected to generate positive cash flows of $5,800 per year for each of its three years of life. The Rolles Voice System is expected to generate positive cash flows of $8,000 per year for each of its twelve years of life. The cash flows associated with each project are summarized in Figure 10A-4.

To decide which project to choose, we first compute and compare their NPVs. Assume the firm's required rate of return is 10 percent. We solve for the NPVs as follows:

1. NPV of Cheap Talk.

$$\text{NPV}_{CT} = \$5,800 \left[\frac{1 - \dfrac{1}{(1 + .10)^3}}{.10} \right] - \$10,000$$

$$= \$5,800(2.48685) - \$10,000$$

$$= \$14,424 - \$10,000$$

$$= \$4,424$$

2. NPV of Rolles Voice.

$$NPV_{Rolles} = \$8,000 \left[\frac{1 - \dfrac{1}{(1 + .10)^{12}}}{.10} \right] - \$50,000$$

$$= \$8,000(6.81369) - \$50,000$$

$$= \$54,510 - \$50,000$$

$$= \$4,510$$

We find that Project Cheap Talk has an NPV of $4,424, compared to Project Rolles' NPV of $4,510. We might conclude based on this information that the Rolles Voice System should be selected over the Cheap Talk system because it has the higher NPV. However, before making that decision, we must assess how Project Cheap Talk's NPV would change if its useful life were twelve years, not three years.

Comparing Projects with Unequal Lives

Two possible methods that allow financial managers to compare projects with unequal lives are the replacement chain approach and the equivalent annual annuity (EAA) approach.

The Replacement Chain Approach The *replacement chain* approach assumes each of the mutually exclusive projects can be replicated, until a common time period has passed in which the projects can be compared. The NPVs for the series of replicated projects are then compared to the project with the longer life. An example illustrates this process. Project Cheap Talk could be repeated four times in the same time span as the twelve-year Rolles Voice project. If a business replicated project Cheap Talk four times, the cash flows would look like this:

> **Take Note**
>
> *Note that the unequal lives problem is only an issue when the projects under consideration are mutually exclusive. If the projects were independent, we would adopt all projects that had NPVs greater than or equal to zero, no matter what the lives of the projects.*

The NPV of this series of cash flows, assuming the discount rate is 10 percent, is (in thousands) $12,121. Each cash flow, be it positive or negative, is discounted back the appropriate number of years to get the NPV of the four consecutive investments in the Cheap Talk systems.

The NPV of $12,121 for Cheap Talk System is the sum of the NPVs of the four repeated Cheap Talk projects, such that the project series would have a life of twelve years, the same life as the Rolles Voice System Project. We are now comparing apples to apples. Cheap Talk's replacement chain NPV is $12,121, while the NPV of Project Rolles Voice is $4,510 over the same twelve year period. If a firm invested in project Cheap Talk four successive times, it would create more value than investing in one project Rolles Voice.

The Equivalent Annual Annuity (EAA)   The equivalent annual annuity (EAA) approach converts the NPVs of the mutually exclusive projects into their equivalent annuity values. The *equivalent annual annuity* is the amount of the annuity payment that would give the same present value as the actual future cash flows for that project. The EAA approach assumes that you could repeat the mutually exclusive projects indefinitely as each project came to the end of its life.

The equivalent annuity value (EAA) is calculated by dividing the NPV of a project by the present value interest factor for an annuity (PVIFA) that applies to the project's life span.

Formula for an Equivalent Annual Annuity (EAA)   (10A-1)

$$EAA = \frac{NPV}{PVIFA_{k,\,n}}$$

where: k = Discount rate used to calculate the NPV
n = Life span of the project

The NPVs of Cheap Talk ($4,424) and Rolles Voice ($4,510) were calculated earlier, assuming a required rate of return of 10 percent. With the project's NPV and the discount rate, we calculate each project's EAA, per Equation 10A-1, as follows:

1. EAA of Project Cheap Talk

$$EAA_{CT} = \frac{\$4,424}{2.48685}$$
$$= \$1778.96$$

2. EAA of Project Rolles

$$EEA_{Rolles} = \frac{\$4,510}{6.81369}$$
$$= \$661.90$$

The EAA approach decision rule calls for choosing whichever mutually exclusive project has the highest EAA. Our calculations show that Project Cheap Talk has an EAA of $1778.96 and Project Rolles Voice System has an EAA of $661.90. Because Project Cheap Talk's EAA is higher than Project Rolles', Project Cheap Talk should be chosen.

Both the replacement chain and the EAA approach assume that mutually exclusive projects can be replicated. If the projects can be replicated, then either the replacement chain or the equivalent annuity methods should be used because they lead to the same correct decision. Note in our case that the EAA method results in the same project selection (Project Cheap Talk) as the replacement chain method. If the projects cannot be replicated, then the normal NPVs should be used as the basis for the capital budgeting decision.

Equations Introduced in This Appendix

Equation 10A-1. The Formula for an Equivalent Annual Annuity:

$$EAA = \frac{NPV}{PVIFA_{k,n}}$$

where: k = Discount rate used to calculate the NPV
n = Life span of the project

chapter 11

Estimating Incremental Cash Flows

Never underestimate the value of cold cash.

Gregory Nunn

Chapter Objectives

After reading this chapter, you should be able to:

1. Explain the difference between incremental cash flows and sunk costs.

2. Identify types of incremental cash flows in a capital budgeting project.

3. Explain why cash flows associated with project financing are not included in the capital budgeting analysis.

Reinventing the Wheel at Cragar

Cragar Wheels is famed worldwide for their upscale wheel designs. When they introduce a new product line, they literally reinvent the wheel, so the cost of designing a new wheel does not come cheaply.

Michael Hartzmark, CEO of Cragar Wheels, has a Ph.D. in economics and watches the cash flow associated with the design and production of new wheels closely. Determining which costs are directly related to designing and producing a wheel can be tricky.

For instance, in one of their newest wheel designs, Hartzmark estimates a cost of $3,000 for the design of the new wheel. Then Hartzmark estimates the cost of new tooling to manufacture the wheel is about $10,000 to $15,000. Also, this new design requires a special spoke, a spe-

cial technique, and tools to attach the wheel to the hub. The technique and tools cost an additional $3,000 to $4,000.

What costs are not directly related to the new wheel development and production? "The selling costs are not included in the cash flow estimate because we have a wide variety of wheels we're selling," says Hartzmark. "We don't have specific sales costs for that particular wheel."

Testing costs are not included either. "We have to test to see how strong every wheel is. Our customers don't want to buy a new Cragar wheel, install it, and watch the wheel collapse under the weight of their car," explains Hartzmark. Because Cragar tests a wide variety of wheels, these costs (much like the sales costs) are not considered relevant to the cash flow estimate of the new wheel project. �

Source: Interview with Michael Hartzmark, CEO of Cragar Wheels (March 26, 1996).

Chapter Overview

In chapter 10 we applied capital budgeting decision methods, taking the cash flow estimates as a given. In this chapter, we see how financial managers determine which cash flows are incremental and therefore relevant to a capital budgeting decision. We define incremental cash flows and distinguish incremental cash flows from sunk costs. We also examine how financial managers estimate incremental initial investment cash flows and incremental operating cash flows in the capital budgeting decision. Finally, we explore how the financing cash flows of a capital budgeting project are factored into the capital budgeting decision.

Incremental Cash Flows

The capital budgeting process focuses on cash flows, not accounting profits. Recall from our discussion in chapter 1, it is cash flow that changes the value of a firm. Cash outflows reduce the value of the firm, whereas cash inflows increase the value of the firm.

We discussed the importance of cash in chapter 1, pages 7 and 8.

In capital budgeting **incremental cash flows** are the positive and negative cash flows directly associated with a project. They occur if a firm accepts a project, but do not occur if the project is rejected.

For instance, suppose that the chief financial officer of Photon Manufacturing, Mr. Sulu, is analyzing the cash flows associated with a proposed project. He finds that the CEO hired a consultant to assess the proposed project's environmental effects. The consultant will be paid $50,000 for the work. Although the $50,000 fee is related to the project, it is not an incremental cash flow because the money must be paid whether the project is accepted or rejected. Therefore the fee should not be included as a relevant cash flow of the expansion project decision. Cash flows that have already occurred, or will occur whether a project is accepted or rejected, are **sunk costs.**

Financial managers carefully screen out irrelevant cash flows, such as sunk costs, from the capital budgeting decision process. If they include irrelevant cash flows in their capital budgeting decision, then their calculations of a project's payback period, net present value (NPV), or internal rate of return (IRR) will be distorted and inaccurate. The calculations may be so distorted that they lead to an incorrect decision about a capital budgeting project.

Source: *DILBERT* © 1996 United Feature Syndicate, Inc. Reprinted by Permission.

TYPES OF INCREMENTAL CASH FLOWS

To accurately assess the value of a capital budgeting project, financial managers must identify and estimate many types of incremental cash flows. The three main types of incremental cash flows are *initial investment cash flows, operating cash flows,* and *shutdown cash flows.* We examine these three types of incremental cash flows in the sections that follow.

Initial Investment Cash Flows

Generally, financial managers begin their incremental cash flow estimates by assessing the costs of the initial investment. The negative cash flow associated with the initial investment occurs only if the project is accepted. Initial investment cash flows include the purchase price of the asset or materials to produce the asset, the installation and delivery costs, and the additional investment in net working capital.

Purchase Price, Installation, and Delivery Financial managers usually obtain quotes on the purchase price and installation and delivery costs from suppliers. These figures, then, can usually be estimated with a high degree of accuracy.

We defined net working capital in chapter 4, page 65.

Changes in Net Working Capital Aside from the set-up costs and purchase price of a proposed capital budgeting project, a company may have to invest in changes in net working capital. As explained in chapter 4, net working capital is defined as current assets (working capital) minus current liabilities. If a proposed capital budgeting project will cause a positive change in net working capital (the most likely scenario), the cash outlay needed to finance this must be included in the cash flow estimates.

A capital budgeting project may affect working capital. Recall that working capital consists of cash, accounts receivable and inventory, along with other current assets, if any. Companies invest in these assets in much the same way they invest in plant and equipment. Accepting a new project often triggers an increase in cash, accounts receivable, and inventory investments. Working capital investments tie up cash the same way that investment in a new piece of equipment does.

CURRENT ASSET CHANGES	CURRENT LIABILITY CHANGES
$5,000 increase in Cash	$8,000 increase in Accounts Payable
$7,000 increase in Receivables	$2,000 increase in Accruals
$15,000 increase in Inventory	
Total Current Asset Changes: $27,000	Total Current Liability Changes: $10,000
Increase in Net Working Capital (NWC): $27,000 − $10,000 = $17,000	
Incremental Cash Flow Due to the Increase in NWC = −$17,000	

A company's current liabilities—such as accounts payable, accrued wages, and accrued taxes—may also be affected if a firm accepts a capital budgeting project. For example, if a plant is expanded, the company may place larger orders with suppliers to accommodate the increased production. The increase in orders is likely to lead to an increase in accounts payable.

Increases in current liabilities create cash inflows. It is unlikely that current liabilities will increase sufficiently to finance all the needed current asset buildup. This is the reason that an investment in net working capital is almost always required.

Table 11-1 shows an example of the incremental changes in net working capital that might occur with a proposed capital budgeting project for the McGuffin Company.

As Table 11-1 indicates, the McGuffin Company project has an estimated increase of $27,000 in current assets and a $10,000 increase in current liabilities, resulting in a $17,000 change in net working capital. That is, the firm will have to spend $17,000 to increase its net working capital by this amount—a negative cash flow.

Figure 11-1 (page 272) depicts graphically the $17,000 change in the McGuffin Company's net working capital if the new project is accepted.

Once financial managers estimate the initial investment incremental cash flows, they analyze the operating cash flows of a capital budgeting project. We turn to those cash flows next.

Operating Cash Flows

Operating cash flows are those cash flows that the project generates after it is in operation. For example, cash flows that follow a change in sales or expenses are operating cash flows. Those operating cash flows incremental to the project under consideration are the ones relevant to our capital budgeting analysis. Incremental operating cash flows also include: tax changes, including those due to changes in depreciation expense; opportunity costs; and externalities.

Taxes The change in taxes that will occur if a project is accepted is part of the incremental cash flow analysis. Tax effects are considered because a tax increase is equivalent to a negative cash flow, and a tax decrease is equivalent to a positive cash flow. In a capital budgeting decision, then, financial managers must examine whether and how much tax the firm will pay on additional income that the proposed project generates during a given period. They must also see whether and how much taxes will decrease if the project increases the firm's periodic operating expenses (such as payments for labor and materials), thereby creating additional tax deductions.

Figure 11-1 shows the $17,000 increase in net working capital. The McGuffin company must raise an additional $17,000 in funds if it accepts the new project.

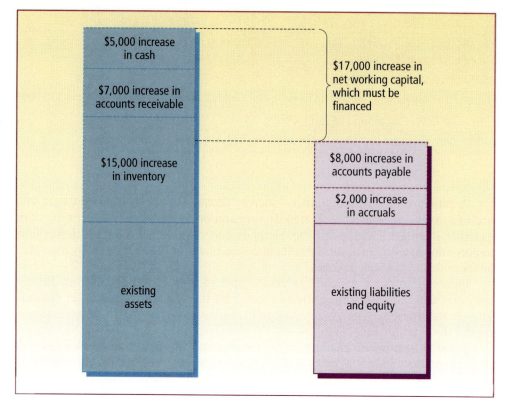

Depreciation and Taxes Financial managers estimate changes in depreciation expense as part of the incremental cash flow analysis because increases in depreciation expense may increase a firm's cash flow. How? Depreciation expense is deductible for tax purposes. The greater the depreciation expense deduction, the less tax a firm must pay, and the less cash it must give to the IRS. Financial managers estimate the amount of depreciation expense a capital budgeting project will have, therefore, to see how much the firm's taxable income and taxes owed will decrease.

Incremental depreciation expense is the change in depreciation expense that results from accepting a proposed capital budgeting project. Incremental depreciation expense affects the change in taxes attributable to a capital budgeting project.

To illustrate how incremental depreciation expense changes taxes due, recall how we converted after-tax net profits into operating cash inflows in chapter 4. We added all noncash charges (including depreciation) that were deducted as expenses on the firm's income statement to net profits after taxes. Once the tax effects of a project's depreciation expense are calculated, we add this incremental depreciation expense back to the project's net profits after taxes.

We discussed converting after-tax net profits into operating cash flows in chapter 4, page 61.

The following example demonstrates how to estimate the incremental depreciation expense of a capital budgeting project. Suppose your firm is considering a project that is expected to earn $100,000 in cash sales in year 1. Suppose that, in addition to the sales increase, the project is expected to increase cash operating expenses by $50,000 and new depreciation expense will be $10,000. Assume your firm's marginal tax rate is 40 percent. First, compute the net operating cash flows from the project for this year, as shown in Table 11-2.

Compare line three and line seven in Table 11-2. Note that once we used the new project incremental depreciation expense of $10,000 to make the tax change

New Project Sales (cash inflow)	$100,000
New Project Cash Operating Expenses (cash outflow)	− 50,000
New Project Depreciation Expense (noncash expense)	− 10,000
Net New Project Taxable Income	40,000
Taxes on New Project Income (40%)(cash outflow)	− 16,000
Net New Project After Tax Income	24,000
Plus Depreciation Expense (added back)	+ 10,000
Net Incremental Cash Flow	$ 34,000

TABLE 11-2

Net Operating Cash Flows for New Project

calculations, we added the $10,000 depreciation expense back to the new project's after-tax net income to calculate the year's incremental operating cash flow for this year from the new project. The incremental depreciation expense affected cash flow only because of its effect on taxes.

Opportunity Costs   Sometimes accepting a capital budgeting project precludes other opportunities for the firm. For instance, if an industrial mixer, already owned by a toy company, is used to make a new product called Slime #4, then that mixer will not be available to make the Slime #2 currently produced in that mixer. The foregone benefits of the alternative not chosen are opportunity costs.

Opportunity costs are incremental cash flows that financial managers consider in a capital budgeting decision. In our example, the opportunity cost comes from the lost use of the industrial mixer for other products our firm makes. If our cash flows decrease by $30,000 due to the decrease in sales of Slime #2 that we can no longer make, then this $30,000 is the opportunity cost of choosing to produce the new product, Slime #4.

Externalities   In estimating incremental operating cash flows, financial managers consider the effect a capital budgeting project might have on cash flows related to other parts of the business. **Externalities** are the positive or negative effects on existing projects if a new capital budgeting project is accepted.

For instance, suppose that a tennis ball manufacturer decides to start making tennis racquets but does not want to hire any more managers. The current managers may become overworked because the expansion project requires manager time and oversight. This is a negative externality. Existing projects suffer due to manager inattention, but it is difficult to measure the size of those incremental costs.

On the other hand, the new racquet project may give the company more visibility than it had before and increase sales of its existing tennis ball business, thereby leading to an increase in cash flows. Because these cash flows from the increased tennis ball sales are incremental to the tennis racquet project under consideration, they should be considered in the capital budgeting analysis. This is a positive externality. Here again, however, the costs associated with the positive externalities are likely to be difficult to measure.

If the impact of externalities can be measured, they should be incorporated in the capital budgeting analysis. If the cost of externalities cannot be measured precisely—as is likely the case—most firms use a subjective analysis of externalities before making a project's final accept or reject decision. For example, if the net present value of a project is only slightly greater than zero, company officials may reject the project if they believe significant unmeasured negative externalities are present.

After estimating the operating cash flows, financial managers then estimate the shutdown cash flows of a proposed capital budgeting project. We examine these costs next.

Cash Flows at the End of a Project's Life

Financial managers estimate the shutdown cash flows that are expected to occur at the end of the useful life of a proposed capital budgeting project. Shutdown cash flows may include those from the project's salvage value, the reduction of net working capital, and taxes tied to the sale of the used asset.

Project Salvage Value   If a project is expected to have a positive salvage value at the end of its useful life, there will be a positive incremental cash flow at that time. However, this salvage value incremental cash flow must be adjusted for tax effects.

Four possible tax scenarios may occur when the used asset is sold, depending on the asset's sale price (These are summarized in Table 11-3). First, the asset may be sold for more than its purchase price. In this instance, the difference between the purchase and the sale price is taxed at the capital gains tax rate. (The *capital gain* is the portion of the sale price that exceeds the purchase price.) In addition, the purchase price minus depreciation book value is taxed at the ordinary income rate.

Second, the asset may be sold for less than the purchase price but for more than its depreciation book value. The amount that the sales price exceeds the depreciation book value is ordinary income, so it is taxed at the ordinary income tax rate.

Third, the asset may be sold for its depreciation book value. In that case the asset sale has no tax effects.

Fourth, the asset may be sold for less than its depreciation book value. The amount the depreciation book value exceeds the sales price is an ordinary loss. The firm's tax liability is reduced by the amount of the loss, times the ordinary income tax rate.

Incremental Cash Flows of an Expansion Project

To practice capital budgeting cash flow estimation, let's examine a proposed expansion project. An expansion project is one in which the company adds a project and does not replace an existing one. Photon Manufacturing makes torpedoes. It is considering a project to install $3 million worth of new machine tools in its main plant. The new tools are expected to last for five years. Photon operations management

TABLE 11-3 Tax Effects of the Sale of an Asset at the End of Its Useful Life

TYPE OF SALE	TAX EFFECT
The asset is sold for more than its purchase price.	This difference is taxed at the capital gains rate. In addition, the purchase price minus the depreciation book value is ordinary income and is taxed at the ordinary income rate.
The asset is sold for less than its purchase price but for more than its depreciation book value.	The sales price minus the depreciation book value is ordinary income and is taxed at the ordinary income tax rate.
The asset is sold for its depreciation book value.	There is no tax effect.
The asset is sold for less than its depreciation book value.	The depreciation book value minus the sales price is an ordinary loss and reduces the firm's tax liability by that amount times the ordinary income tax rate.

FINANCIAL MANAGEMENT AND YOU

The Incremental Costs of Studying Abroad

Imagine that you want to study international finance at the Universität Heidelberg in Germany during the next academic year. Your college has an exchange agreement with Heidelberg that guarantees tuition and housing at your in-state resident rate. To decide whether to spend the academic year studying abroad instead of at home, you draw up a list of costs in U.S. dollars. Here is what you find:

1. Cost of travel to and from Heidelberg	$ 1,100.00
2. Cost of student lodging and tuition for academic year	4,985.00
3. Cost of books and other supplies	600.00
4. Cost of food ($450 per month for nine months)	4,050.00
5. Cost of summer travel in Europe (including food, supplies, rail passes, and student hostel charges)	2,000.00
	$12,735.00

At first glance the opportunity appears too expensive to consider. Now that you have read this chapter, however, you realize you need to screen out irrelevant costs, and consider opportunity costs and externalities. Your new list looks like this:

1. Cost of travel to and from Heidelberg	$1,100.00
2. Cost of tuition and lodging in Heidelberg minus cost of lodging and tuition in U.S.	0.00
3. Cost of books and other supplies ($600) minus cost of same in U.S. ($500)	100.00
4. Cost of food abroad for academic year ($4,050) minus cost of same in U.S. ($3,150 with cafeteria pass)	900.00
5. Cost of summer travel in Europe ($2,000) minus cost of summer room/board/travel in U.S. ($1,200)	800.00
6. Opportunity cost of no summer job abroad (U.S. summer job income of $1,200 minus $0 income abroad)	1,200.00
	$4,100.00

You estimate that your relevant costs are $4,100 for the year. Although you can't measure them exactly, you know the study abroad has positive externalities—it will further your career plans. Can you afford to accept this opportunity?

Source: Air travel, rail passes, and lodging price information retrieved from Saber® Database (March 30, 1996).

and marketing experts estimate that during that five years the tools will result in a sales increase of $800,000 per year.

The Photon Manufacturing CEO has asked Mr. Sulu, the company CFO, to identify all incremental cash flows associated with the project, and to calculate the project's net present value (NPV) and internal rate of return (IRR). Based on the incremental cash flow analysis and Sulu's recommendation, the company will make an accept or reject decision about the project.

Sulu's first step is to identify the relevant (incremental) cash flows associated with the project. He begins with the initial investment in the project, then looks at the operating cash flows, and finally the shutdown cash flows.

The cash flows that will occur as soon as the project is implemented (at t_0) make up the project's initial investment. The initial investment includes the cash outflows for the purchase price, installation, delivery, and increase in net working capital.

Sulu knows that its tool supplier gave Photon a bid of $3 million to cover the cost of the new tools, including set-up and delivery. Photon inventory and account-

TABLE 11-4

Cost of Tools & Setup	$3,000,000
+ Investment in Additional NWC	110,000
= Total Initial Cash Outlay	$3,110,000

ing specialists estimate that if the tools are purchased, inventory will need to increase by $40,000, accounts receivable by $90,000, and the needed increase in cash will be $10,000. This is a $140,000 increase in current assets (working capital).

Also, Photon experts estimate that if the tools are purchased, accounts payable will increase by $20,000 as larger orders are placed with suppliers, and accruals (wages and taxes) will increase by $10,000—a $30,000 increase in current liabilities. Subtracting the increases in current liabilities from the increases in current assets ($140,000 − $30,000) results in a $110,000 increase in net working capital associated with the expansion project.

Sulu concludes after extensive research that he has found all the initial investment incremental cash flows. Those cash flows are summarized in Table 11-4.

Now Sulu examines the operating cash flows, those cash flows expected to occur from operations during the five year period after the project is implemented (at t_1 through t_5). The Photon expansion project operating cash flows reflect changes in sales, operating expenses, and depreciation tax effects. We assume these cash flows occur at the end of each year.

Sulu learns from the vice president of sales that cash sales are expected to increase by $800,000 per year because the new tools will increase manufacturing capacity. If purchased, the tools will be used to perform maintenance on other equipment at Photon, so operating expenses (other than depreciation) are expected to decrease by $100,000 per year.

Depreciation is a noncash expense, but remember: Sulu must use depreciation to compute the change in income tax that Photon must pay. After taxes are computed, Sulu then will add back the change in depreciation in the operating cash flow analysis.

To calculate depreciation expense, Sulu looks at MACRS depreciation rules and finds that the new manufacturing tools are in the three-year asset class. According to the MACRS rules, 33.3 percent of the new tools' $3 million cost will be charged to depreciation expense in the tools' first year of service, 44.5 percent in the second year, 14.8 percent in the third year, and 7.4 percent in the fourth year.

Now Sulu summarizes the incremental operating cash flows for the Photon capital budgeting project in Table 11-5.

Sulu is not quite through yet. He must include in his analysis additional shutdown cash flows that occur at t_5, the end of the project's life.

Photon company experts estimate that the actual economic life of the tools will be five years, after which time the tools should have a salvage value of $800,000. Under MACRS depreciation rules, assets are depreciated to zero at the end of their class life, so at t_5 the book value of the new tools is zero. Therefore, if the tools are

We listed MACRS depreciation rules in chapter 4, Table 4-1, page 70.[1]

---

[1]Depreciation expenses for the tools are spread over four years instead of three because the MACRS depreciation rules apply a half-year convention—all assets are assumed to be purchased and sold halfway through the first and last years, respectively. If an asset with a three-year life is assumed to be purchased halfway through year 1 then the three years will be complete halfway through year 4.

TABLE 11-5 Photon Manufacturing Expansion Project Incremental Operating Cash Flows, Years 1–5

	t_1	t_2	t_3	t_4	t_5
+ Change in Sales	+ 800,000	800,000	800,000	800,000	800,000
+ Reduction in Non-depreciation Operating Expenses	+ 100,000	100,000	100,000	100,000	100,000
− Depreciation Expense	− 999,000	1,335,000	444,000	222,000	0
= Change in Operating Income	= (99,000)	(435,000)	456,000	678,000	900,000
− Tax on New Income (See Note below)	− (39,600)	(174,000)	182,400	271,200	360,000
= Change in Earnings after Taxes	= (59,400)	(261,000)	273,600	406,800	540,000
+ Add Back Depreciation Expense	+ 999,000	1,335,000	444,000	222,000	0
= Net Incremental Operating Cash Flow	= 939,600	1,074,000	717,600	628,800	540,000

Note: Taxes at t_1 and t_2 are negative amounts, which means earnings after taxes on the lines above for those years is *increased* by the amount of the taxes saved. Operating losses in year 1 (−$99,000) and in year 2 (−$435,000) cause a decrease in the taxes Photon owes during years 1 and 2 of $39,600 and $174,000, respectively.

sold at the end of year 5 for their salvage value of $800,000, Photon Manufacturing will realize a taxable gain on the sale of the tools of $800,000 ($800,000 − 0 = $800,000). The income tax on the gain at Photon's marginal tax rate of 40 percent will be 800,000 × .40 = $320,000.

The net amount of cash that Photon will receive from the sale of the tools is the salvage value minus the tax paid:

$800,000	Salvage Value
− 320,000	Taxes Paid
$480,000	Net Proceeds

The net proceeds from the tool sale in year 5, then, are $480,000.

Finally, if the new tools are sold at t_5, Sulu concludes (based on sales department information) that Photon's sales will return to the level they were before the new tools were installed. Consequently, there will be no further need for the additional investment in net working capital that was made at t_0. When the $110,000 investment in net working capital is recaptured,[2] that amount is recovered in the form of a positive cash flow.

The additional incremental cash flows from the sale of the tools and the change in net working capital are summarized in Table 11-6.

Tables 11-4, 11-5, and 11-6 contain all the incremental cash flows associated with Photon Manufacturing's proposed expansion project. Sulu's next step is to summarize the total incremental net cash flows occurring at each point in time in one table. Table 11-7 shows the results.

---

[2]Current assets, in the amount by which they exceed current liabilities, are sold and not replaced since they are no longer needed.

TABLE 11-6

Photon Manufacturing Expansion Project Additional Incremental Operating Cash Flows at t_5

Salvage Value	800,000
− Taxes on Salvage Value	− 320,000
= Net Cash Inflow from Sale of Tools	+ 480,000
+ Cash From Reduction in NWC	+ 110,000
= Total Additional Cash Flows at t_5	= 590,000

TABLE 11-7 Photon Manufacturing Expansion Project Summary of Incremental Cash Flows

	t_0	t_1	t_2	t_3	t_4	t_5
For Purchase and Setup	(3,000,000)					
For additional NWC	(110,000)					
From Operating Cash Flows		939,600	1,074,000	717,600	628,800	540,000
From Salvage Value less Taxes						480,000
From Reducing NWC						110,000
Net Incremental Cash Flows	(3,110,000)	939,600	1,074,000	717,600	628,800	1,130,000

In chapter 10 we discussed the NPV and IRR techniques on pages 234–244.

Table 11-7 contains the "bottom line" net incremental operating cash flows associated with Photon's proposed expansion project. The initial investment at t_0 is −3,110,000. The operating cash flows from t_1 to t_5 total $4,490,000. The sum of all the incremental positive and negative cash flows for the project is $1,380,000.

Now Sulu is ready to compute the NPV and IRR of the expansion project based on the procedures described in chapter 10.

Assuming that Photon's discount rate is 10 percent, Sulu computes the NPV of the project using Equation 10-1 as follows[3]:

	t_0	t_1	t_2	t_3	t_4	t_5
Net Incremental Cash Flows	(3,110,000)	939,600	1,074,000	717,600	628,800	1,130,000
PV of Cash Flows	$\dfrac{(3,110,000)}{(1+.10)^0}$	$\dfrac{939,600}{(1+.10)^1}$	$\dfrac{1,074,000}{(1+.10)^2}$	$\dfrac{717,600}{(1+.10)^3}$	$\dfrac{628,800}{(1+.10)^4}$	$\dfrac{1,130,000}{(1+.10)^5}$
	= (3,110,000)	= 854,182	= 887,603	= 539,144	= 429,479	= 701,641

---

[3]The NPV Formula, Equation 10-1a, follows:

$$NPV = \left(\frac{CF_1}{(1+k)^1}\right) + \left(\frac{CF_2}{(1+k)^2}\right) \ldots + \left(\frac{CF_n}{(1+k)^n}\right) - \text{Initial Investment}$$

$$NPV = (3,110,000) + 854,182 + 887,603 + 539,144 + 429,479 + 701,641$$
$$= \$302,049$$

Assuming a discount rate of 10 percent, the NPV of the project is $302,049.

Next, Sulu uses the trial-and-error method described in chapter 10 to find the IRR of the project.[4] He finds the IRR, the discount rate that makes the NPV equal to zero, is 13.78 percent.

$$NPV_P = 0 = \frac{-3,110,000}{(1+k)^0} + \frac{939,600}{(1+k)^1} + \frac{1,074,000}{(1+k)^2} + \frac{717,600}{(1+k)^3} + \frac{628,800}{(1+k)^4} + \frac{1,130,000}{(1+k)^5}$$

$$k = .1378 \therefore IRR = .1378 = 13.78\%$$

To solve for the NPV and IRR of this project with the TI BAII PLUS financial calculator, first switch to the calculator's spreadsheet mode. Then enter the cash flows, keystrokes, and compute as follows:

TI BAI I PLUS FINANCIAL CALCULATOR SOLUTION
IRR and NPV

KEYSTROKES	DISPLAY
CF	CF_0 = old contents
2nd CLR Work	CF_0 = 0.00
3110000 +/− ENTER	−3,110,000.00
↓ 939600 ENTER	C01 = 939,600.00
↓	F01 = 1.00
↓ 1074000 ENTER	C02 = 1,074,000.00
↓	F02 = 1.00
↓ 717600 ENTER	C03 = 717,600.00
↓	F03 = 1.00
↓ 628800 ENTER	C04 = 628,800.00
↓	F04 = 1.00
↓ 1130000 ENTER	C05 = 1,130,000.00
↓	F05 = 1.00
IRR	IRR = 0.00
CPT	IRR = 13.78
NPV	I = 0.00
10 ENTER	I = 10.00
↓ CPT	NPV = 302,048.58

---

[4] The formula for finding a project's IRR, Equation 10-2, is:

$$0 = \left(\frac{CF_1}{(1+k)^1}\right) + \left(\frac{CF_2}{(1+k)^2}\right) \ldots + \left(\frac{CF_n}{(1+k)^n}\right) - \text{Initial Investment}$$

Since the project's NPV of $302,049 is positive, and the IRR of 13.78 percent exceeds the required rate of return of 10 percent, Sulu will recommend that Photon proceed with the expansion project.

In this discussion we examined how a firm determines the incremental costs of an expansion project, and the project's NPV and IRR. We turn next to replacement projects and their incremental costs.

An Asset Replacement Decision

Often a company considers replacing existing equipment with new equipment. A replacement decision is a capital budgeting decision to purchase a new asset and replace and retire an old asset, or to keep the old asset. Financial managers identify the *differences* between the company's cash flows with the old asset versus the company's cash flows if the new asset is purchased and the old asset retired. As illustrated in Figure 11-2, these differences are the incremental cash flows of the proposed new project.

As part of an asset replacement decision, financial managers must often estimate the tax changes associated with disposing of the old asset. Table 11-3 described the four tax effects that can occur when an asset is sold. Table 11-8 shows a case of an old asset (that will be replaced) that sells at a price above its depreciation book value but below its purchase price. The sales price of the old asset is $80,000 and it has been depreciated over the years in the amount of $30,000. Its original depreciation basis was $90,000.

The cash received from the sale of the old asset, $72,000 as shown in Table 11-8, would be netted against any cash outflows associated with the proposed new investment. After calculating the cash received from the old asset sale, the capital budgeting analysis is the same as the expansion project discussed earlier.

Figure 11-2 **Comparing Cash Flows: Replacing an Asset versus Keeping the Old**

Figure 11-2 illustrates how firms compare the difference between the cash flows of replacing an old asset with a new one or keeping the old asset. The scenario that generates the most cash flow will be the one the firm chooses.

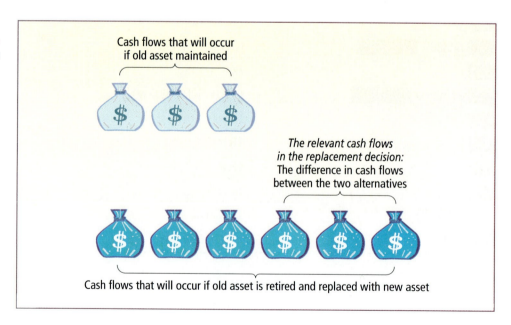

Cash flows that will occur if old asset maintained

The relevant cash flows in the replacement decision: The difference in cash flows between the two alternatives

Cash flows that will occur if old asset is retired and replaced with new asset

Cash from Sale of Old Asset		$80,000
Book Value of Old Asset:		
Original Depreciation Basis	$90,000	
− Accumulated Depreciation	30,000	
= Book Value		60,000
Sales Price − Book Value = Taxable Gain (loss)		20,000
Tax on Gain (Loss):		
$20,000 Gain (Loss) × 40% Marginal Tax Rate		8,000
Net Cash Flow from Sale of Old Asset:		
Total Cash Received − Tax on Gain (Loss)		$80,000
		− 8,000
		$72,000

FINANCING CASH FLOWS

Suppose a company planned to borrow or to sell new common stock to raise part or all of the funds needed for a proposed capital budgeting project. The company would receive a cash inflow on receipt of the loan or the sale of new common stock. Conversely, the company must pay the interest and principal payments on the loan or may make dividend payments to stockholders. **Financing cash flows** are the cash outflows that occur as creditors are paid interest and principal and stockholders are paid dividends.

If a capital budgeting project is rejected, financing cash flows will not occur, so they are relevant cash flows in the capital budgeting decision. However, as we will see in chapter 12, financing costs are factored into the discount rate (required rate of return) in the NPV calculation. Those costs are also included in the hurdle rate of the IRR decision rule. Therefore, to avoid double counting, we do not include financing costs in our operating incremental cash flow estimates when we make capi-

Figure 11-3 The Cash Flow Estimation Process

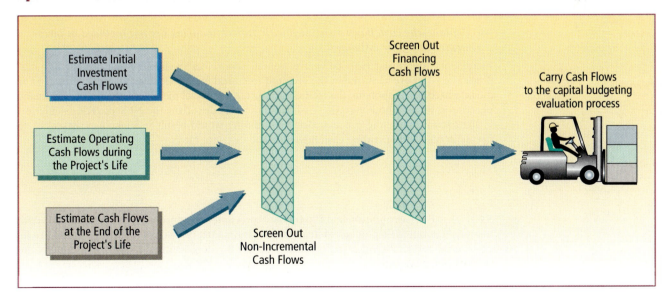

tal budgeting decisions. If we did include financing costs as part of the incremental operating cash flows, then the NPV or IRR analysis would be distorted. That distortion could lead in turn to a poor capital budgeting decision.

Figure 11-3 (page 281) summarizes the cash-flow estimation process and its role in capital budgeting.

What's Next

In this chapter, we learned how financial managers estimate incremental cash flows as part of the capital budgeting process. We described the difference between sunk costs and incremental cash flows. We also discussed various types of incremental cash flows. In chapter 12 we examine the cost of capital.

Summary

1. Explain the difference between incremental cash flows and sunk costs.

Incremental cash flows are the cash flows that will occur if a capital budgeting project is accepted. They will not occur if the investment is rejected. Sunk costs are costs that will occur whether a project is accepted or rejected. Financial managers must screen out sunk costs from the capital budgeting analysis to prevent distortion in cash flow estimates. Any distortion in these estimates will, in turn, lead to inaccurate NPV or IRR values and could result in poor capital budgeting decisions.

2. Identify types of incremental cash flows in a capital budgeting project.

Financial managers must examine three main types of cash flows to estimate the incremental cash flows of a proposed capital budgeting project. First, they must assess the cost of the initial investment: the purchase price, the installation and delivery costs, and any change in net working capital. Then, the financial manager must analyze incremental operating cash flows. These may include tax changes due to changes in sales and depreciation expense, opportunity costs, and externalities. Finally, a financial manager must examine the project shut down cash flows, such as those cash flows from the project's salvage value, from the reduction of net working capital, and tax–related cash flows from the sale of the used asset.

3. Explain why cash flows associated with project financing are not included in incremental cash flow estimates.

Incremental operating cash flows are treated separately from incremental financing cash flows. The latter are captured in the discount rate used in the NPV calculation and in the hurdle rate used when applying the IRR decision rule. Financial managers do not include financing costs as incremental operating cash flows to avoid distorting the NPV or IRR calculations in the capital budgeting process. Double counting would result if financing costs were reflected in both the operating cash flows and the discount rate.

Self-Test

ST-1. Fat Tire Corporation had $20,000 in depreciation expense last year. Assume its federal marginal tax rate is 36 percent while its state marginal tax rate is 4 percent. How much are the firm's taxes reduced (and cash flow increased) by the depreciation deduction on federal and state income tax returns?

ST-2. Skinny Ski Corporation had net income in 1996 of $2 million and depreciation expense of $400,000. What was the firm's operating cash flow for the year?

ST-3. Powder Hound Ski Company bought a new helicopter for $1.5 million. The company paid an aviation consultant $20,000 to advise them on the need for a new helicopter. The decision as to whether to buy the fifth chopper hasn't been made yet. If it is purchased, what is the total initial cash outlay that will be used in the NPV calculation?

ST-4. Rich Folks Ski Area is considering the replacement of one of its older ski lifts. By replacing the lift, Rich Folks expects sales revenues to increase by $500,000 per year. Maintenance expenses are expected to decrease by $75,000 per year if the new lift is purchased. Depreciation expense would be $100,000 per year (straight-line). The old lift has been fully depreciated. The firm's marginal tax rate is 38 percent. What would the firm's incremental annual operating cash flows be if the new lift is purchased?

ST-5. Snorkel Ski Company is considering the replacement of its aerial tram. Sales are expected to increase by $900,000 per year and depreciation expense is also expected to rise by $300,000 per year. The marginal tax rate is 32 percent. The purchase will be financed with a $900,000 bond issue carrying a 10 percent annual interest rate. What are the annual incremental operating cash flows if this project is accepted?

Review Questions

1. Why do we focus on cash flows instead of profits when evaluating proposed capital budgeting projects?
2. What is a sunk cost? Is it relevant when evaluating a proposed capital budgeting project? Explain.
3. How do we estimate expected incremental cash flows for a proposed capital budgeting project?
4. What role does depreciation play in estimating incremental cash flows?
5. How and why does working capital affect the incremental cash flow estimation for a proposed large capital budgeting project? Explain.
6. How do opportunity costs affect the capital budgeting decision–making process?
7. How are financing costs generally incorporated into the capital budgeting analysis process?

Build Your Communication Skills

CS-1. Pick a company and obtain a copy of its recent income statement, balance sheet, and statement of cash flows. Compare its profit and cash flow for the period covered by the income statement. Use the statement of cash flows to describe where the firm's cash came from and where it went during that period. Examine the balance sheet to assess the cash position of the firm at that point in time. Submit a written report that analyzes the firm's cash position.

CS-2. Stock market analysts often compare a firm's reported quarterly earnings and its expected quarterly earnings. Quarterly earnings that come in below expectations often mean a drop in the stock price while better than expected earnings usually mean a stock price increase. Is this consistent with the view that cash flows and not accounting profits are the source of firm value? Divide into small groups, and discuss these issues with the group members for fifteen minutes. Select a spokesperson to present the group's key points to the class.

Problems

11-1. An asset falling under MACRS five-years class was purchased three years ago for $200,000 (its original depreciation basis). Calculate the cash flows if the asset is sold now at

a. $40,000
b. $80,000

Assume the applicable tax rate is 40 percent.

11-2. Harry Callahan is evaluating the purchase of new trenching equipment for Scorpio Enterprises. For now, he is only figuring the incremental operating cash flow from the proposed project for the first year. Harry estimates that the firm's sales of earth-moving services will increase by $10,000 in year 1. Using the new equipment will add an additional $3,000 to their operating expenses. Interest expense will increase by $100 because the machine will be partly financed by a loan from the bank. The additional depreciation expense for the new machine will be $2,000. The Scorpio Enterprises' marginal tax rate is 35 percent.

a. Calculate the change in operating income (EBIT) for year 1.
b. Calculate the cash outflow for taxes associated with this new income.
c. What is the net new after-tax income (change in earnings after taxes)?
d. Calculate the net incremental operating cash flow from this project for year 1.
e. Are there any expenses listed that you did not use when estimating the net incremental cash flow? Explain.

11-3. Travis Bickle, a financial analyst at Rhodes Manufacturing Corporation, is trying to analyze the feasibility of purchasing a new piece of equipment that falls under the MACRS five-year class. The initial investment, including the cost of equipment and its start-up, would be $400,000. Over the next six years, the following earnings before depreciation and taxes will be generated from using this equipment:

End of Year	Cash Flow($)
1	120,000
2	90,000
3	70,000
4	70,000
5	70,000
6	70,000

Rhodes' discount rate is 13 percent and the company is in the 40 percent tax bracket. Should Travis recommend acceptance of the project?

11-4. Assume the same cash flows, initial investment, MACRS class, discount rate and income tax rate as given in problem 11-3. Now, assume that the resale value of the equipment at the end of six years will be $50,000. Calculate the NPV and recommend whether the project should be accepted.

11-5. George Kaplan is considering adding a new crop-dusting plane to his fleet at North Corn Corner, Inc. The new plane will cost $85,000. He anticipates spending an additional $20,000 immediately after the purchase to modify it for crop-dusting. Kaplan plans to use the plane for five years and then sell it. He estimates that the salvage value will be $20,000. With the addition of the new plane, George estimates revenue in the first year will increase by 10 percent over last year. Revenue last year was $125,000. Other first-year expenses are also expected to increase. Operating expenses will increase by $20,000 and depreciation expense will increase by $10,500. Kaplan's marginal tax rate is 40 percent.

a. For capital budgeting purposes, what is the net cost of the plane? Or, stated another way, what is the initial net cash flow?

b. Calculate the net incremental operating cash flow for year 1.

c. In which year would the salvage value affect the net cash flow calculations?

11-6. The management of the local cotton mill is evaluating the replacement of low-wage workers by automated machines. If this project is adopted, production and sales are expected to increase significantly: Norma Rae, the mill's financial analyst, expects cash will have to increase by $8,000 and the accounts receivable increase by $10,000 in response to the increase in sales volume. Because of the higher level of production, inventory will have to increase by $12,000 with an associated $6,000 increase in accounts payable. Accrued taxes and wages, even with the decrease in the number of laborers, are estimated to increase by $2,500.

Changes in Net Working Capital

a. Calculate the change in net working capital if the automation project is adopted.

b. Is this change in NWC a cash inflow or outflow?

c. Given the limited information about the duration of the project, in what year should this change affect the net incremental cash flow calculations?

11-7. Sunstone, Inc. has entrusted financial analyst Flower Belle Lee with the evaluation of a project that involves buying a new asset at a cost of $90,000. The asset falls under MACRS three-year class and will generate the following income stream:

Cash Flows and Capital Budgeting

End of Year	1	2	3	4
Cash Flow($)	50,000	30,000	20,000	20,000

The asset has a resale value of $10,000 at the end of the fourth year. Sunstone's discount rate is 11 percent. The company has an income tax rate of 30 percent. Should Flower recommend purchase of the asset?

11-8. Moonstone, Inc., a competitor of Sunstone, Inc. in problem 11-7, is considering purchasing a similar equipment with the same cash flows, initial investment, MACRS class, and resale value. Moonstone's discount rate is 10 percent and its income tax rate is 40 percent. However, Moonstone is considering the new asset to replace an existing asset with a book value of $20,000 and a resale value of $10,000. What would be the NPV of the replacement project?

Replacement Decision and Cash Flows

11-9. You have just joined Moonstone, Inc., as its new financial analyst. You have learned that accepting the project described in problem 11-8 will require an increase of $10,000 in current assets and will increase current liabilities by $5,000. What would be the new NPV of the project?

Changes in Net Working Capital

11-10. You have been hired by Drs. Venkman, Stantz, and Spenler to help them with net present value analysis for a replacement project. These three New York City parapsychologists need to replace their existing supernatural beings detector with the new, upgraded model. They have calculated all the necessary figures but were unsure about how to account for the sale of their old machine. The original depreciation basis of the old machine was $20,000 and the accumulated depreciation was $12,000 at the date of the sale. They can sell the old machine for $18,000 cash. Assume the tax rate for their company is 30 pecent.

Challenge Problem

a. What is the book value of the old machine?

b. What is the taxable gain (loss) on the sale of the old equipment?

c. Calculate the tax on the gain (loss).

d. What is the net cash flow from the sale of the old equipment? Is this a cash inflow or outflow?

e. Assume the new equipment costs $40,000 and they do not expect a change in net working capital. Calculate the incremental cash flow for t_0.

f. Assume they could only sell the old equipment for $6,000 cash. Recalculate parts b) through e).

11-11. Mitch and Lydia Brenner own a small factory located in Bodega Bay, California. They manufacture rubber snakes used to scare birds away from houses, gardens, and play-

Cash Flows and Capital Budgeting

grounds. The recent and unexplained increase in the bird population in Northern California has significantly increased the demand for the Brenners' products. To take advantage of this marketing opportunity, they plan to add a new molding machine that will double the output of their existing facility. The cost of the new machine is $20,000. The machine set-up fee is $2,000. With this purchase, current assets must increase by $5,000 and current liabilities will increase by $3,000. The economic life of the new machine is four years and it falls under the MACRS three-year depreciation schedule. The machine is expected to be obsolete at the end of the fourth year and have no salvage value.

The Brenners anticipate recouping 100 percent of the additional investment in net working capital at the end of year 4. Sales are expected to increase by $20,000 each year in years 1 and 2. By year 3, the Brenners expect sales to be mostly from repeat customers purchasing replacements instead of sales to new customers. Therefore the increase in sales for years 3 and 4 is estimated to only be $10,000 in each year. The increase in operating expenses is estimated to be 20 percent of the annual change in sales. Assume the marginal tax rate is 40 percent.

a. Calculate the initial net incremental cash flow.
b. Calculate the net incremental operating cash flows for years 1 through 4. Round all calculations to the nearest whole dollar. Use Table 5-2 to calculate the depreciation expense.
c. Assume the Brenners' discount rate is 14 percent. Calculate the net present value of this project. Would you recommend the Brenners add this new machine to their factory?

Cash Flows and Capital Budgeting

11-12. The RHPS Corporation specializes in the custom design, cutting, and polishing of stone raw materials to make ornate building facings. These stone facings are commonly used in the restoration of older mansions and estates. Janet Weiss and Brad Majors, managers of the firm, are evaluating the addition of a new stone cutting machine to their plant. The machine's cost to RHPS is $150,000. Installation and calibration costs will be $7500. They do not anticipate an increase in sales but the reduction in the operating expenses is estimated to be $50,000 annually. The machine falls under the MACRS three-year depreciation schedule. The machine is expected to be obsolete after five years. At the end of five years, Weiss and Majors expect the cash received (less applicable capital gains taxes) from the sale of the obsolete machine to offset the shutdown and dismantling costs. The RHPS cost of capital is 10 percent and the marginal tax rate is 35 percent.

a. Calculate the net present value for the addition of this new machine. Round all calculations to the nearest whole dollar.
b. Would you recommend that Weiss and Majors go forward with this project?

Comprehensive Problem

11-13. The Chemical Company of Baytown purchased new processing equipment for $40,000 on December 31, 1994. The equipment had an expected life of four years and was classified in the MACRS three-year class. Due to changes in environmental regulations, the operating cost of this equipment has increased. The company is considering replacing this equipment with a more efficient process line at the end of 1996. The salvage value of the old equipment is estimated to be $4,000. The marginal tax rate is 40 percent.

a. Calculate the cash flow from the sale of this equipment. Assume the sale occurred at the end of 1996. Use Table 4-1 (page 70) to calculate the depreciation.
b. The new process line has a higher capacity than the old one and is expected to boost sales. As a result, the cash requirement will increase by $1000, accounts receivable by $5,000, and inventory by $10,000. It will also increase accounts payable by $6,000 and accrued expenses by $3,000. Calculate the incremental cash flow due to the change in the net working capital.
c. The new equipment will cost $180,000, including installation and start-up costs. Calculate the net cash outflow in 1996 if the new process line is installed and is ready to operate by the end of 1996.

d. Beginning in January of 1997, this new equipment is expected to generate additional sales of $60,000 each year for the next four years. It will have an economic life of four years and will fall under the MACRS three-year classification. Being more efficient, the new equipment will reduce yearly operating expenses by $6,000. Calculate the net incremental operating cash flows for the years 1997 through 2000. Assume the marginal tax rate will remain at 40 percent. Round calculations to the nearest whole dollar.

e. At the end of its economic life, the new process line is expected to be sold for $20,000. The cost of capital for the company is 6 percent. Calculate the net present value and the internal rate of return (only if you have a financial calculator) for this project. Round calculations to the nearest whole dollar. Recommend whether the replacement project should be adopted or rejected. (Hint: Preparation of a summary of incremental cash flows similar to Table 11-5 may be helpful).

f. Draw an NPV profile for the project.

Answers to Self-Test

ST-1. $20,000 × (.36 + .04)
= $20,000 × .40 = $8,000 tax savings

ST-2. $2,000,000 + $400,000 = $2,400,000 operating cash flow

ST-3. $1,500,000 total initial cash outlay (The $20,000 for the consultant is a sunk cost.)

ST-4. ($500,000 − $75,000 − $100,000) × (1 − .38)
= $325,000 × .62 = $201,500 incremental net income
$201,500 + $100,000 depreciation expense
= $301,500 incremental operating cash flow

ST-5. ($900,000 − $300,000) × (1 − .32)
= $600,000 × .68 = $408,000 incremental net income
$408,000 + $300,000 depreciation expense
= $708,000 incremental operating cash flow
(The finance costs are not part of operating cash flows. They will be reflected in the required rate of return.)

chapter 12

The Cost of Capital

There's no such thing as a free lunch.

Milton Friedman

Chapter Objectives

After reading this chapter, you should be able to:

1. Describe the sources of capital and how firms raise capital.

2. Estimate the cost of capital for each financing source.

3. Estimate the weighted average cost of capital.

4. Use the marginal cost of capital (MCC) schedule to make capital budgeting decisions.

5. Explain the importance of the marginal cost of capital (MCC) schedule in financial decision making.

Raising Capital for an Indoor Soccer Stadium: You Have to Pay for Your Kicks

Four years ago, two University of Nebraska students, Andrew and Glen Ferguson, started a company, Thunder Sports, Inc., to bring indoor soccer to their hometown of Lincoln, Nebraska. To succeed they had to overcome several obstacles. First, they were young business people—nineteen and twenty-three, respectively. Second, soccer is not easy to market. And third, they had to find someone to lend them $100,000 to bankroll their company.

For two years the brothers pursued banks, private investors, and even the Small Business Administration. They were unsuccessful because they didn't have assets and weren't experienced in business. They finally decided to hire someone to raise the money for them. They found a financial "headhunter" who promised to bring them investors.

But there was a cost to this new source of capital. First, the financial headhunter charged a commission of 5 percent of all the money he raised. Second, the investor that the headhunter found to provide the $100,000 in capital demanded a 25 percent share of Thunder Sports, Inc., as the cost of the capital—a high price, indeed.

As of 1996, Thunder Sports, Inc., had its fourth successful soccer season. Unlike their first attempts, however, raising capital had become easier because of their track record. For instance, the Fergusons are trying to restructure the capital of their company by buying out their original investor and reselling his 25 percent equity stake for further capital. Also, they've raised the $1.5 million they need to build a bigger, better, indoor multisports complex.

How did they raise the money? "We're older, and we have a successful track record now," says Glen. "We're part of the network we need to raise money." ✺

Sources: Gianna Jacobson, "Raise Money Now," *Success Magazine* (November 1995); Interview with Glen Ferguson, April 10, 1996.

CHAPTER OVERVIEW

In capital budgeting decisions, financial managers must analyze many factors to determine whether a project will add value to a firm, including estimated incremental cash flows, the timing of those cash flows, risk, and the project's required rate of return.

One of the key components of the capital budgeting decision is the cost of capital. **Capital** is the term for funds that firms use. Businesses, such as Thunder Sports, Inc., raise capital from creditors and owners. All capital raised has a cost because the suppliers of capital demand compensation for the funds provided.

In this chapter we examine the cost of different types of capital. We see how to estimate the cost of capital from a particular source, as well as the overall cost of capital for a firm. We also see how estimating a firm's cost of capital affects a firm's financing and investment decisions.

THE COST OF CAPITAL

To properly evaluate potential investments, firms must know how much their capital costs. Without a measure of the cost of capital, for example, a firm might invest in a new project with an expected return of 10 percent, even though the capital used for the investment costs 15 percent. If a firm's capital costs 15 percent, then the firm must seek investments that return at least that much. It is vital, then, that managers know how much their firm's capital costs *before* committing to investments.

Suppliers and users of capital use cost estimates before making short- or long-term financial decisions. As we saw in chapter 9, investors determine their required rate of return, k, to value either a bond or stock before they invest. That required rate of return, k, for each type of security issued is the cost of capital for that source. Overall, the cost of capital is the compensation investors demand of firms that use their funds, adjusted for taxes and transaction costs in certain cases, as we will explain later in this chapter.

In chapter 10 we saw that firms determine their discount rate, k, to solve for a project's NPV or use k as the IRR hurdle rate before deciding whether to accept a capital budgeting project. The discount rate or hurdle rate, k, is the firm's cost of cap-

Source: *DILBERT © 1996 United Feature Syndicate, Inc. Reprinted by Permission.*

ital for that project. Investors supply capital, so they require a return, and firms use capital, so they must pay suppliers of capital for the use of those funds.

Sources of Capital

A firm's capital is supplied by its creditors and owners. Firms raise capital by borrowing it (issuing bonds to investors or promissory notes to banks), or by issuing preferred or common stock. The overall cost of a firm's capital depends on the return demanded by each of these suppliers of capital.

To determine a firm's overall cost of capital, the first step is to determine the cost of capital from each supplier. The cost of capital from a particular source, such as bondholders or common stockholders, is known as the **component cost of capital.**

In the following sections, we estimate the cost of debt capital, k_d; the cost of capital raised through a preferred stock issue, k_p; and the cost of equity capital supplied by common stockholders, k_s for internal equity and k_n for external equity.

The Cost of Debt

When a firm borrows money at a stated rate of interest, determining the cost of debt, k_d, is relatively straightforward. As shown in Figure 12-1, the lender's cost of capital is the required rate of return on either a company's new bonds or a promissory note. The firm's **cost of debt** when it borrows money by issuing bonds is the interest rate demanded by the bond investors. When borrowing money from an individual or financial institution, the interest rate on the loan is the firm's cost of debt.

The After-Tax Cost of Debt (AT k_d)
The **after-tax cost of debt, AT k_d,** is the cost to the company of obtaining debt funds. Because the interest paid on bonds or banks loans is a tax-deductible expense for a business, a firm's AT k_d is less than the required rate of return of the suppliers of debt capital. For example, suppose Ellis Industries borrowed $100,000 for one year at 10 percent interest compounded an-

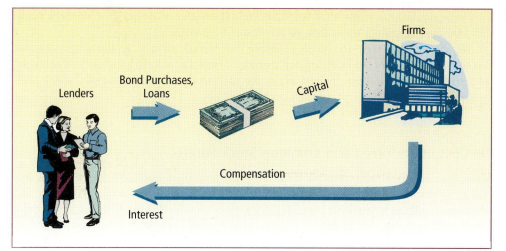

Figure 12-1 The Flow of Debt Capital from Investors to Firms

Figure 12-1 shows how debt investors supply capital to and receive interest from the firm.

nually. The interest rate on the loan is 10 percent, so Ellis must pay the lender $10,000 in interest each year the loan is outstanding (10 percent of $100,000). However, look at what happens when Ellis takes its taxes for the year into account:

	BEFORE MAKING LOAN	AFTER MAKING LOAN
Operating Income	$50,000	$50,000
Interest Expense	0	10,000
Before-Tax Income	50,000	40,000
Income Tax (40% rate)	20,000	16,000
Net After-Tax Income	30,000	24,000

The $10,000 interest charge caused a $6,000 decrease in Ellis's net after-tax income ($30,000 − $24,000 = $6,000). Assuming a tax rate of 40 percent, we see that the true cost of the loan is only $6,000 (6 percent), not $10,000 (10 percent).

The following formula converts k_d into AT k_d, the true after-tax cost of borrowing:

Formula for the After Tax Cost of Debt

$$AT\ k_d = k_d\ (1 - T) \tag{12-1}$$

where: k_d = the before-tax cost of debt
T = the firm's marginal tax rate[1]

To solve for AT k_d in our Ellis Industries example, recall that Ellis's before-tax cost of debt is 10 percent and its marginal tax rate is 40 percent. The after-tax cost of debt, according to Equation 12-1, follows:

$$AT\ k_d = .10\ (1 - .40)$$
$$= .10 \times .60$$
$$= .06,\ \text{or}\ 6\%$$

---

[1]The tax rate used here should reflect the firm's total combined federal, state, and/or local income tax rate.

Our calculations show that for Ellis Industries the after-tax cost of debt on a $100,000 loan at a 10 percent rate of interest is 6 percent.

We have seen that the cost of using borrowed money is the interest rate charged by the lender. In addition, we discussed how the tax deductibility of interest lowers the firm's true cost of debt. Next, we turn to the cost of preferred stock and common stock equity.

The Cost of Preferred and Common Stock Funds

When corporations raise capital by issuing preferred or common stock, these investors expect a return on their investments. If that return is not realized, investors will sell their stock, driving the stock price down. Although the claim of preferred and common stockholders may not be contractual, as it is for bondholders, there is a cost nonetheless. To calculate the cost of using preferred and common stockholders' money, then, the firm must estimate the rate of return that these investors demand. Figure 12-2 shows how firms raise capital from, and compensate, equity investors.

The Cost of Preferred Stock (k_p) The **cost of preferred stock (k_p)** is investors' required rate of return on a company's new preferred stock. To calculate k_p, the firm's managers must estimate the rate of return that preferred stockholders will demand. When investors buy preferred stock, they are normally doing so to obtain the stream of constant preferred stock dividends associated with the preferred stock issue. Their return on investment, therefore, can normally be measured by dividing the amount of the firm's expected preferred stock dividend by the price of the shares. Equation 12-2 shows how to estimate the cost of preferred stock:

Formula for the Cost of Preferred Stock, k_p

$$k_p = \frac{D_p}{P_p}$$

(12-2)

Figure 12-2 **The Flow of Capital from Equity Investors to Firms**

Figure 12-2 shows how equity investors supply capital to the firm and receive dividends from it.

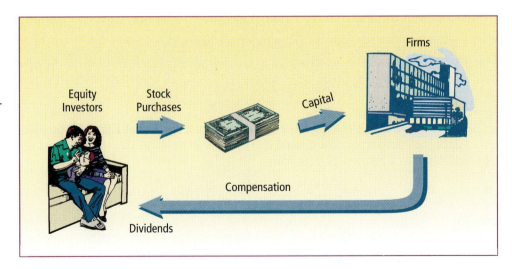

where: k_p = the cost of the preferred stock issue; the expected return
          D_p = the amount of the expected preferred stock dividend
          P_p = the current price of the preferred stock

The cost of using the company's preferred stock is k_p. The value of k_p, the expected return from the preferred stock issue, is the minimum return the firm's managers must earn when they use the money supplied by preferred stockholders. If they cannot earn this return, the preferred stockholders will sell their shares, causing the preferred stock's price to fall. This means the firm must issue more shares of the stock than before the stock price fell to raise the same amount of funds.

Suppose Ellis Industries issued preferred stock that has been paying annual dividends of $2.50 and is expected to continue to do so indefinitely. The current price of Ellis's preferred stock is $20 a share. According to Equation 12-2, the cost of Ellis's preferred stock is as follows:

$$k_p = \frac{\$2.50}{\$20}$$
$$= .125, \text{ or } 12.5\%$$

We see that Ellis Industries' cost of preferred stock, assuming that stock pays dividends of $2.50 per year and has a market price of $20, is 12.5 percent.

The cost of preferred stock, k_p, is higher than the before-tax cost of debt, k_d, because a company's bondholders and bankers have a prior claim on the earnings of the firm and on its assets in the event of a liquidation. Preferred stockholders, as a result, take a greater risk than bondholders or bankers and demand a correspondingly greater rate of return.

The Cost of Internal Common Equity (k_s)

The **cost of internal common equity** (**k_s**) is the required rate of return on funds supplied by existing common stockholders. The cost of equity depends on the rate of return the common stockholders demand for holding the company's common stock. Calculating k_s is tougher than calculating k_p because common stockholders do not receive a constant stream of dividends. Instead, investors own the firm, including the corporate earnings left over after other claimants on the firm have been paid. Neither creditors nor preferred stockholders have a claim on these residual earnings. Corporations may either retain the residual earnings, or return them in the form of common stock dividends. Retained earnings have a cost, however. The cost of retained earnings, another name for the cost of internal equity, is the rate of return that the company must earn to justify retaining the earnings instead of paying them as dividends. These are internally generated (within the firm) equity funds.

As noted, common stock dividend payments change from year to year or may not be paid at all. Ultimately, however, dividends are the only payments a corporation makes to its common stockholders. The corporation may pay regular dividends, or it may pay a liquidation dividend some time in the future. For companies that pay regular dividends that grow at a constant rate, the constant dividend growth model, introduced in chapter 9, may be used to estimate the cost of equity. For companies that do not pay regular dividends, or when the market approach to risk is more appropriate, the CAPM may be used to estimate the cost of equity.

Take Note

There is no tax adjustment in the cost of preferred stock calculation. Unlike interest payments on debt, firms may not deduct preferred stock dividends on their tax returns. The dividends are paid out of after-tax profits.

We discussed the constant dividend growth model in chapter 9, page 215.

Using the Dividend Growth Model to Estimate k_s.   Recall the dividend growth model introduced in chapter 9:

$$P_0 = \frac{D_1}{k_s - g}$$

where: P_0 = the current price of the common stock
D_1 = the dollar amount of the common stock dividend expected one period from now
k_s = Required rate of return per period on this common stock investment
g = Expected constant growth rate per period of the company's common stock dividends[2]

Rearranging the terms in the dividend growth model to solve for k_s, we rewrite the formula as follows:

We can now solve for k_s, assuming we know the values of the terms P_0, D_1, and g.

Formula for the Cost of Common Stock Equity

$$k_s = \frac{D_1}{P_0} + g \tag{12-3}$$

The term D_1 / P_0 in Equation 12-3 represents the stock's *dividend yield,* and the g term represents dividend growth rate from year to year.

To apply Equation 12-3, suppose that Ellis Industries' common stock is selling for $40 a share. Next year's common stock dividend is expected to be $4.20, and the dividend is expected to grow at a rate of 5 percent per year indefinitely. Given these conditions, Equation 12-3 tells us that the expected rate of return on Ellis's common stock is as follows:

$$k_s = \frac{\$4.20}{\$40} + .05$$

$$= .105 + .05$$

$$= .155, \text{ or } 15.5\%$$

At a stock share price of $40, a dividend of $4.20, and an expected dividend growth rate of 5 percent, the expected return from Ellis's common stock is 15.5 percent. The expected return of 15.5 percent is the minimum return the firm's managers must earn when they use money supplied by common stockholders. If they cannot achieve this return, common stockholders will sell their shares, causing the stock's price to fall. This will make it necessary to sell more shares to raise the desired amount of funds. The cost of using money supplied by the company's common stockholders, then, is 15.5 percent. Since dividends paid are not tax deductible to the corporation, there is no tax adjustment to the k_s calculation.

The CAPM Approach to Estimating k_s.   A firm may pay dividends that grow at a changing rate, pay no dividends at all, or the managers of the firm may believe that market risk is the relevant risk. In such cases the firm may choose to use the capital asset pricing model (CAPM) to calculate the rate of return that investors require for

---

[2]This is the *constant growth version* of the dividend growth model. It assumes that the company's dividends grow at the same rate indefinitely.

holding common stock. The CAPM solves for the rate of return that investors demand for holding a company's common stock according to the degree of nondiversifiable risk[3] present in the stock. The CAPM formula, Equation 12-4, follows:

CAPM Formula for the Cost of Common Stock Equity

$$k_s = k_{RF} + (k_M - k_{RF}) \times \beta \qquad (12\text{-}4)$$

where: k_s = the required rate of return from the company's common stock equity
k_{RF} = the risk-free rate of return
k_M = the expected rate of return on the overall stock market
β = the beta of the company's common stock, a measure of the amount of nondiversifiable risk

We discussed the CAPM in chapter 7, pages 156–158.

Suppose Ellis Industries has a beta of 1.39, the risk-free rate as measured by the rate on short-term U.S. Treasury bills is 3 percent, and the expected rate of return on the overall stock market is 12 percent. Given those market conditions, according to Equation 12-4, the required rate of return for Ellis's common stock is as follows:

$$
\begin{aligned}
k_s &= .03 + (.12 - .03) \times 1.39 \\
&= .03 + (.09 \times 1.39) \\
&= .03 + .1251 \\
&= .1551, \text{ or about } 15.5\%
\end{aligned}
$$

According to the CAPM, we see that the cost of using money supplied by Ellis's common stockholders is about 15.5 percent, given a company beta of 1.39, a risk-free rate of 3 percent, and an expected market rate of return of 12 percent.

Deciding How to Estimate k_s.   Should you use the dividend growth model, Equation 12-3, or the CAPM, Equation 12-4, to estimate a firm's cost of common equity? The choice depends on the firm's dividend policy, available data, and management's view of risk. As a financial manager, if you were confident that your firm's dividends would grow at a fairly constant rate in the future, you could apply the dividend growth model to calculate k_s. If your firm's growth rate were erratic or difficult to determine, you might use the CAPM instead, assuming that you agreed with the CAPM's underlying hypothesis that common stockholders hold well-diversified portfolios and that nondiversifiable risk is what is priced in the market. Where possible, practitioners apply both models and use their business judgment to reconcile differences between the two outcomes.

The Cost of Equity from New Common Stock (k_n)   The cost incurred by a company when new common stock is sold is the **cost of equity from new common stock (k_n).** In the preceding section, we discussed the cost of using funds supplied by the firm's existing stockholders. Capital from existing stockholders is internal equity capital. That is, the firm already has these funds. In contrast, capital from issuing new stock is external equity capital. The firm is trying to raise new funds from outside sources.

New stock is sometimes issued to finance a capital budgeting project. The cost of this capital is not only stockholders' expected return on their investment, but also the costs incurred to issue new securities. The cost to issue new securities, known as **flotation costs,** include investment bankers' fees and commissions, and attorneys'

---

[3]According to the CAPM, common stockholders hold well-diversified portfolios, so the only relevant risk measure is nondiversifiable (market) risk.

fees. Flotation costs make the cost of using funds supplied by new stockholders slightly higher than using retained earnings supplied by the existing stockholders.

To estimate the cost of using funds supplied by new stockholders, we use a variation of the dividend growth model that includes flotation costs:

Formula for the Cost of New Common Stock

$$k_n = \frac{D_1}{P_0 - F} + g \qquad (12\text{-}5)$$

where: k_n = the cost of new common stock equity
        P_0 = the price of one share of the common stock
        D_1 = the amount of the common stock dividend expected to be paid in one year
        F = the flotation cost per share
        g = the expected constant growth rate of the company's common stock dividends

Equation 12-5 shows mathematically how the cost of new common stock, k_n, is greater than the cost of existing common stock equity, k_s. By subtracting flotation costs, F, from the common stock price in the denominator, the k_n term becomes larger.

Let's look at the cost of new common stock for Ellis Industries. Suppose again that Ellis Industries' anticipated dividend next year is $4.20 a share, its growth rate is 5 percent a year, and its existing common stock is selling for $40 a share. New shares of stock can be sold to the public for the same price. But to do so Ellis must pay its investment bankers 5 percent of the stock's selling price, or $2 per share. Given these conditions, we use Equation 12-5 to calculate the cost of Ellis Industries' new common equity as follows:

$$k_n = \frac{\$4.20}{\$40 - \$2} + .05$$

$$= .1105 + .05$$

$$= .1605, \text{ or } 16.05\%$$

Because of $2 flotation costs, Ellis Industries only keeps $38 of the $40 per share paid by investors. As a result, the cost of new common stock is higher than the cost of existing equity—16.05 percent compared to 15.5 percent.

If the cost of new common equity is higher than the cost of internal common equity, the cost of preferred stock, and the cost of debt, why use it? Sometimes corporations have no choice. Take Duramed Pharmaceuticals. Duramed issued new stock to raise $25 million to invest in a promising project to develop a new generic version of a drug used to fight osteoporosis and the effects of menopause. In addition, Duramed needed new funds to pay $7 million it owed to Provident Bancorp. If Duramed did not repay Provident within a month, the interest rate would leap from 10.75 percent to 36.5 percent. With further delays, that rate could increase to 53.6 percent. Facing skyrocketing interest rates, Duramed had to raise capital through a new stock issue.[4]

Also, if the amount of debt a firm has incurred continues to increase, and internal equity funds have run out, it may be necessary to issue new common stock to

---

[4]Floyd Norris, "Duramed Pharmaceuticals Faces Some Harsh Terms to Raise Cash," *The New York Times* (November 16, 1995): D10.

bring the weight of debt and equity on the balance sheet into line. This capital structure issue is discussed in chapter 13.

We have examined the sources of capital and the cost of each capital source. Next, we investigate how to measure the firm's overall cost of capital.

The Weighted Average Cost of Capital (WACC)

To estimate a firm's overall cost of capital, the firm must first estimate the cost for each component source of capital. The component sources include the after-tax cost of debt, AT k_d; the cost of preferred stock, k_p; and the cost of common stock equity, k_s, and the cost of new common stock equity, k_n. In the following section, we first discuss all component sources except k_n, which we discuss separately.

To illustrate the first step in estimating a firm's overall cost of capital, let's review Ellis Industries' component costs of capital. From our previous calculations, we know the following costs of capital:

$$AT\ k_d = 6\%$$
$$k_p = 12.5\%$$
$$k_s = 15.5\%$$

The next step in finding a firm's overall cost of capital is assessing the firm's *capital structure*. In practice, the assets of most firms are financed with a mixture of debt, preferred stock, and common equity. The mixture of capital used to finance a firm's assets is the **capital structure** of the firm. To analyze the capital structure of a business, we must find the percentage of each type of capital source.

To illustrate how to assess a firm's capital structure, assume that Ellis Industries finances its assets through a mixture of capital sources, as shown on its balance sheet:

Total Assets:	$1,000,000
Long- & Short-Term Debt:	$400,000
Preferred Stock:	100,000
Common Equity:	500,000
Total Liabilities & Equity:	$1,000,000

In percentage terms, then, the mixture of capital used to finance Ellis's $1 million worth of assets is as follows:

Debt:	400,000 / 1,000,000 = .40, or 40%
Preferred Stock:	100,000 / 1,000,000 = .10, or 10%
Common Equity:	500,000 / 1,000,000 = .50, or 50%

Our calculations show that Ellis Industries' capital structure consists of 40 percent debt, 10 percent preferred stock, and 50 percent common equity. If Ellis Industries thinks that this mixture is optimal and wants to maintain it, then it will finance new capital budgeting projects with a mixture of 40 percent debt, 10 percent preferred stock, and 50 percent common equity.[5] This mixture might not be used for each and every project. But in the long run, the firm is likely to seek this capital structure if it is believed to be optimal.

The final step in estimating a firm's overall cost of capital is to find the weighted average of the costs of each individual financing source. The **weighted average cost of capital (k_a or WACC)** is the mean of all component costs of capital, weighted according to the percentage of each component in the firm's optimal capital structure. We find the WACC by multiplying the individual source's cost of capital times its percentage of the firm's capital structure, then adding these results. For Ellis Industries, the weighted average of the financing sources follows:

$$(.40 \times AT\ k_d) + (.10 \times k_p) + (.50 \times k_s)$$
$$= (.40 \times .06) + (.10 \times .125) + (.50 \times .155)$$
$$= .024 + .0125 + .0775$$
$$= .114, \text{ or } 11.4\%$$

Ellis Industries' weighted average cost of capital is 11.4 percent. The general formula for any firm's WACC is shown in Equation 12-6:

Formula for the Weighted Average Cost of Capital (WACC)

$$k_a = (WT_d \times AT\ k_d) + (WT_p \times k_p) + (WT_s \times k_s) \tag{12-6}$$

where: k_a = the weighted average cost of capital (WACC)

WT_d = the weight, or proportion, of debt used to finance the firm's assets

$AT\ k_d$ = the after-tax cost of debt

WT_p = the weight, or proportion of preferred stock being used to finance the firm's assets

k_p = the cost of preferred stock

WT_s = the weight, or proportion of common equity being used to finance the firm's assets

k_s = the cost of common equity

A firm must earn a return equal to the weighted average cost of capital (WACC) to pay suppliers of capital the return they expect. In the case of Ellis Industries, for instance, its average risk capital budgeting projects must earn a return of 11.4 percent to pay its capital suppliers the return they expect.

To illustrate how earning the WACC ensures that all capital suppliers will be paid their required cost of capital, let's return to our example. Suppose Ellis Industries undertakes a plant expansion program that costs $1 million and earns an annual return of 11.4 percent, equal to Ellis's WACC. Capital for the project is supplied as follows:

- 40 percent of the $1 million, or $400,000, is supplied by lenders expecting a return equal to before-tax k_d, 10 percent.
- 10 percent of the $1 million, or $100,000, is supplied by preferred investors expecting a return equal to k_p, 12.5 percent.
- 50 percent of the $1 million, or $500,000, is supplied by common stockholders expecting a return equal to k_s, 15.5 percent.

---

[5]Ideally, the percentage of each component in the capital structure would be measured on the basis of market values instead of accounting values. For the sake of simplicity, we use accounting values here, as do many real-world companies.

If the project does in fact produce the expected 11.4 percent return, will all these suppliers of capital receive the return they expect? The computations that follow show how Ellis will pay its capital suppliers:

First-year return from the project:	$1,000,000 × .114 = $114,000
Interest @ 10 percent paid to the bondholders:	$400,000 × .10 = $40,000
Less tax savings on interest expense:	$40,000 × firm's tax rate of 40% = $16,000
Net interest cost to the firm:	$40,000 − $16,000 = $24,000
Amount remaining to repay other sources of capital:	$114,000 − $24,000 = $90,000
Preferred dividend paid to preferred stockholders:	$100,000 × .125 = $12,500
Amount remaining for common stockholders:	$90,000 − $12,500 = $77,500
Amount returned to common stockholders:	$500,000 × .155 = $77,500

Summary:	
Return realized by lenders	10.0 percent
Return realized by preferred stock investors	12.5 percent
Return realized by common stockholders	15.5 percent

We see that Ellis was able to pay all its capital suppliers by earning an overall return of 11.4 percent, its WACC.

In the long run, companies generally try to maintain an optimal mixture of capital from different sources. In the short run, however, one project may be financed entirely from one source. However, even if a particular project is financed entirely from one source, the WACC should still be used as the required rate of return for an average risk project. Say, for instance, such a project is entirely financed with debt, a relatively cheap source of capital. The cost of debt should not be used as that project's cost of capital. Why? Because the firm's risk would increase with the increase in debt, and the costs of all sources of capital would increase.

The Marginal Cost of Capital (MCC)

A firm's weighted average cost of capital will change if one component cost of capital changes. Often, a change in WACC occurs when a firm raises a large amount of capital. For example, lenders may increase the interest rate they charge, k_d, if they think the firm's debt load will be too heavy. Or, a firm's cost of equity may increase when new stock is issued after new retained earnings run out. This is because of the flotation costs incurred when new stock is issued.

Firms, then, must consider how increasing component costs of capital affect the WACC. The weighted average cost of the next dollar of capital to be raised is the **marginal cost of capital (MCC).** To find the MCC, financial managers must: (1) assess at what point a firm's cost of debt or equity will change the firm's WACC; (2) estimate how much the change will be; and (3) calculate the cost of capital up to and after the points of change.

Interview with Fred Higgins: Minit Mart Foods, Inc., CEO

Fred Higgins

Fred Higgins was a law student when he launched his first Minit Mart. He owned six stores by the time he was out of law school. Now his company owns over a hundred Minit Marts spread throughout Kentucky. Fred realized the importance of raising capital and assessing its cost as he built his Minit Mart empire.

Q. Tell us about your first experience in trying to raise capital.

When I was in law school trying to build my first Minit Mart, I had convinced the people who owned the land to build, and then lease, the building back to me. I was convinced the site had a great location because of its heavy traffic count and apartments nearby. And it was a great location; it's still making money today.

However, I needed capital to buy inventory, so I went to a bank. I explained the whole scenario to the banker. Then the banker asked what assets I had. I said, "Me." The banker threw me out of his office. I was lucky, though. I was finally able to obtain financing with the help of my father, who knew another banker.

If someone is starting in business, he or she needs credibility. The first time I talked with a banker, I had no credibility, no track record. The banker didn't know me from a hole in the ground. Today when I walk into the bank, the bankers can accurately judge the risk of loaning money to me because they can look at my past experience.

Q. How do you raise debt capital now?

Aside from bank loans, I sometimes use insurance companies for long-term debt financing, particularly when I want to buy some real estate. But as a small business, it's tough to have insurance companies work with you. It costs them the same to loan millions of dollars as it does $100,000. They'd rather make a big loan and be done with it. Again, I was lucky because I knew people who could provide introductions to insurance company lenders.

Q. Why is it important to measure your capital costs?

At Minit Mart, we want our projects to generate a positive return. We need to be able to estimate how much the cost of our capital is to be sure that our investments earn a certain amount of dollars, after all the costs, including capital, have been deducted. There are a lot of projects out there, and if we can't get our desired rate of return with one, we will bypass it and move onto the next one.

Q. What outside factors affect your cost of capital?

So many outside factors can increase your cost of debt capital. A few years ago, Circle K went bankrupt, and Seven-Eleven and several other convenience store chains were not performing as well as they had been. The financial markets became very leery of our industry. And that raised the cost of debt capital.

Another time our cost of capital increased due to the Environmental Protection Agency. The EPA started closely scrutinizing businesses that sold gas for potential environmental violations. Minit Marts sell gas, so because of the EPA's new scrutiny, banks either wouldn't loan to us or demanded a higher interest rate.

Source: Interview with Fred Higgins (November 14, 1995).

The Firm's MCC Schedule

The marginal cost of the *first* dollar of capital a firm raises is the same as the firm's basic WACC. However, as the firm raises more capital, a point is reached at which the marginal cost of capital changes. Why? Because one of the component sources of capital changes. This point is the *break point* in the firm's MCC schedule. Capital above the break point can only be raised at a higher cost.

Finding the Break Points in the MCC Schedule To find break points in the MCC schedule, financial managers determine what limits, if any, there are on the firm's ability to raise funds from a given source at a given cost. Suppose that Ellis Industries' financial managers, after consulting with bankers, determined that the firm can borrow up to $300,000 at an interest rate of 10 percent, but any money borrowed above that amount will cost 12 percent. To calculate Ellis Industries' after-tax cost of debt, assume the firm's tax rate is 40 percent. We apply Equation 12-1 as follows:

$$AT\,k_d = k_d\,(1 - T) \qquad\qquad (12\text{-}1)$$
$$AT\,k_d = .10 \times (1 - .40)$$
$$= .06,\text{ or } 6.0\%$$

We see that at an interest rate of 10 percent, and a tax rate of 40 percent, that Ellis's after-tax cost of debt is 6 percent. However, if Ellis Industries borrows more than $300,000, then its interest rate increases to 12 percent. At a tax rate of 40 percent and interest rate of 12 percent, the firm's after-tax k_d for amounts borrowed over $300,000 is:

$$AT\,k_d\,(\text{over } \$300,000 \text{ borrowed}) = .12 \times (1 - .40)$$
$$= .072,\text{ or } 7.2\%$$

Since Ellis's AT k_d increases when it borrows more than $300,000, its MCC will also increase when it borrows more than $300,000. (We'll see how much it increases in the next section.) The financial managers at Ellis Industries want to know how much total capital they can raise before the debt portion reaches $300,000, causing an increase in the AT k_d and the MCC.

Ellis Industries' marginal cost of capital break point is not $300,000 because the firm's capital structure is 40 percent debt, 10 percent preferred stock, and 50 percent common stock. At $300,000, then, only 40 percent of that capital is debt. Instead, the financial managers of Ellis Industries must figure out at what point the firm will use $300,000 of debt capital.

To find a firm's marginal cost of capital break point, we use Equation 12-7:

Formula for the MCC Break Point

$$BP = \frac{\text{limit}}{\text{proportion of total}} \qquad\qquad (12\text{-}7)$$

where: BP = the capital budget size at which the MCC changes (break point)

limit = the point at which the cost of the source of capital changes

proportion of total = the percentage of this source of capital in the firm's capital structure

In our Ellis Industries example, we know that the firm has a $300,000 debt limit before its after-tax cost of debt will increase, and that debt is 40 percent of the firm's capital structure. Applying Equation 12-7 to our Ellis example, we see that its debt break point is the following:

$$BP_d = \frac{\$300,000}{.40}$$
$$= \$750,000$$

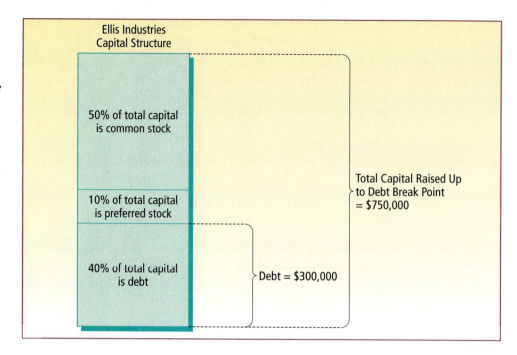

Figure 12-3 Ellis Industries Debt Break Point

Figure 12-3 shows how Ellis Industries can raise up to $750,000 of total capital before the $300,000 of lower-cost debt is exhausted.

Ellis Industries Capital Structure

50% of total capital is common stock

10% of total capital is preferred stock

40% of total capital is debt

Debt = $300,000

Total Capital Raised Up to Debt Break Point = $750,000

We find that Ellis Industries' break point is $750,000. By applying Equation 12-7, Ellis's financial managers know that they may raise up to $750,000 in capital before their borrowing costs rise from 6 percent to 7.2 percent. Any capital raised over $750,000 will reflect the higher cost of borrowing, as shown in Figure 12-3.

Notice we used subscript $_d$ with BP in Equation 12-7. That was to identify the break point as a *debt break point*. There could be other debt break points for Ellis Industries. If, for instance, the company's lenders set additional limits on the company's borrowing, the debt break points would be denoted as BP_{d1}, BP_{d2}, and so on. For our example, let's assume that Ellis's bankers will lend the firm an unlimited amount of money over $300,000 at 7.2 percent so there are no further debt break points.

The Equity Break Point. The equity break point is the point at which the marginal cost of capital changes because the cost of equity changes. Equity costs may change because firms exhaust the supply of funds from the firm's existing common stockholders—that is, they exhaust additions to retained earnings. After firms exhaust their supply of internal equity that has a capital cost of k_s, they will have to raise additional equity funds by issuing new stock that has a higher cost, k_n. This additional equity is external equity capital. The marginal cost of capital increases accordingly.

Let's illustrate how the marginal cost of capital increases because of changes in the cost of equity. We'll assume that Ellis Industries expects to realize $600,000 in income this year after it pays preferred stockholders their dividends. The $600,000 in earnings belong to the common stockholders. The firm may either pay dividends, or retain the earnings. Let's assume Ellis retains the $600,000. The finite supply of capital from the existing common stockholders is the $600,000 addition to retained earnings. To find the equity break point, then, Ellis's managers must know at what point the firm will exhaust the common equity capital of $600,000, assuming existing common stock equity is 50 percent of the firm's capital budget. Figure 12-4 graphically depicts the Ellis equity break point analysis.

Figure 12-4 **Ellis Industries Equity Break Point**

Figure 12-4 shows how Ellis Industries can raise up to $1,200,000 of total capital before the $600,000 of lower-cost internal equity is exhausted.

Inside figure:

Ellis Industries Capital Structure

50% of total capital is common stock

Common Stock = $600,000

10% of total capital is preferred stock

Total Capital Raised Up to Equity Break Point = $1,200,000

40% of total capital is debt

To find the equity break point, we apply Equation 12-7, the marginal cost of capital break point formula. We know that the existing common stock capital limit is $600,000, and that common equity finances 50 percent of the total capital budget. Using Equation 12-7, we solve for the equity break point, BP_e, as follows:

$$BP_e = \frac{\$600,000}{.50}$$
$$= \$1,200,000$$

Our calculations show that the Ellis equity break point is $1,200,000. If the capital budget exceeds $1,200,000, the portion financed with common equity will exceed $600,000. At that point, Ellis will need to issue new common stock to raise the additional capital. The new common stock's cost, k_n, will be greater than the cost of internal common equity, k_s, so the marginal cost of capital, MCC, will rise when the capital budget exceeds $1,200,000 as shown in Figure 12-4.

Calculating the Amount the MCC Changes   To calculate MCC changes, we must first identify the break points. In our Ellis Industries example, we identified two break points at which the firm's MCC will change:

Debt Break Point, BP_d = $ 750,000

Equity Break Point, BP_e = $1,200,000

The next step in the MCC analysis is to estimate how much the change in MCC will be for varying amounts of funds raised.

The MCC Up to the First Break Point.   Since the marginal cost of capital, MCC, is simply the weighted average cost of the next dollar of capital to be raised, we can use the WACC formula, Equation 12-6, to calculate the MCC as well.

We assume that Ellis Industries wants to maintain its current capital structure of 40 percent debt, 10 percent preferred stock, and 50 percent common equity. We assume further that its after-tax cost of debt, AT k_d, is 6 percent, its cost of preferred stock, k_p, is 12.5 percent, and its cost of internal common equity, k_s, is 15.5 percent. With these values, we use Equation 12-6 to find the Ellis MCC for capital raised up to the first break point, BP_d, as follows:

$$\text{MCC up to } BP_d \ (\$750,000) = (.40 \times AT \ k_d) + (.10 \times k_p) + (.50 \times k_s)$$
$$= (.40 \times .06) + (.10 \times .125) + (.50 + .155)$$
$$= .024 + .0125 + .0775$$
$$= .114, \text{ or } 11.4\%$$

We see from our calculations that up to the first break point, the Ellis MCC is 11.4 percent—the WACC we calculated earlier. We know, however, that the Ellis lenders will raise the interest rate to 10 percent if the firm raises more than $750,000, at which point the AT k_d increases from 6 percent to 7.2 percent. So between the first break point, BP_d, and the second break point, BP_e, the MCC is:

$$\begin{array}{l} \text{MCC between } BP_d \ (\$750,000) \\ \text{and } BP_e \ (1,200,000) \end{array} = (.40 \times AT \ k_d) + (.10 \times k_p) + (.50 \times k_s)$$
$$= (.40 \times .072) + (.10 \times .125) + (.50 + .155)$$
$$= .0288 + .0125 + .0775$$
$$= .1188, \text{ or } 11.88\%$$

Our calculations show that the MCC between the first and second break point, $750,000 and $1,200,000, is 11.88 percent.

At the second break point, BP_e, we know from our earlier Ellis discussion that k_s of 15.5 percent changes to k_n that has a value of 16.05 percent. Applying Equation 12-6, the MCC for amounts raised over $1,200,000 follows:

$$\text{MCC over } BP_e \ (\$1,200,000) = (.40 \times ATk_d) + (.10 \times k_p) + (.50 \times k_n)$$
$$= (.40 \times .072) + (.10 \times .125) + (.50 + .1605)$$
$$= .0288 + .0125 + .08025$$
$$= .1216, \text{ or } 12.16\%$$

We find that the Ellis MCC with a capital budget exceeding $1,200,000, is 12.16 percent. A graph of Ellis Industries' marginal cost of capital is shown in Figure 12-5. Now that we have learned to estimate the MCC for a firm, we examine how MCC estimates affect capital budgeting decisions.

The MCC Schedule and Capital Budgeting Decisions

Firms use the MCC schedule to identify which new capital budgeting projects should be selected for further consideration and which should be rejected. For example, Ellis Industries has identified the following projects for possible adoption:

Project	Initial Investment Required	Project's IRR
A	$500,000	18.00%
B	$300,000	14.00%
C	$200,000	12.05%
D	$300,000	11.50%
E	$200,000	9.00%

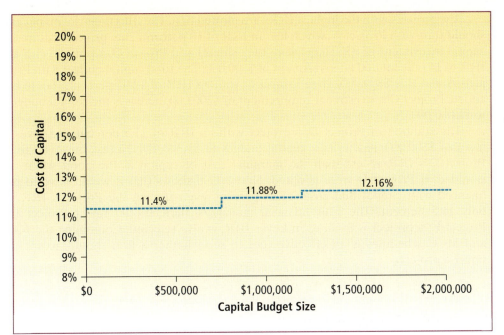

Figure 12-5 **Ellis Industries Marginal Cost of Capital Schedule**

Figure 12-5 shows the marginal cost of capital (MCC) schedule that reflects the cost of debt and cost of equity break points.

The projects are ranked from highest to lowest IRR. The list of proposed capital budgeting projects ranked by IRR is the firm's *investment opportunity schedule (IOS)*. To determine which proposed projects will be accepted, the Ellis financial managers determine which projects have IRRs that exceed their respective costs of capital. To compare the projects' IRRs to the firm's cost of capital, the financial managers plot the investment opportunity schedule (IOS) on the same graph as the MCC. Figure 12-6 shows this technique.

Take Note

Remember that in chapter 10 we learned that capital budgeting projects whose IRRs exceed the cost of capital are acceptable.

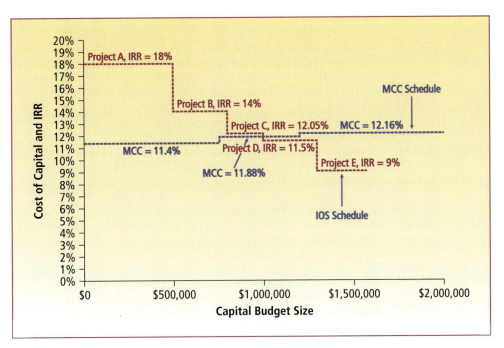

Figure 12-6 **Ellis Industries MCC and IOS Schedules**

Figure 12-6 shows the MCC and IOS schedules. Those projects on the IOS schedule above the MCC schedule are accepted.

The projects with the highest IRRs are plotted first. The Ellis financial managers should start with Project A, which has an IRR of 18 percent. That project requires a capital investment of $500,000. Next, they should add Project B, a project with an IRR of 14 percent and an investment of $300,000. The total capital budget with Projects A and B is $800,000. Then Project C, with an IRR of 12.05 percent, should be added. Project C's investment requirement of $200,000 increases the capital budget to $1,000,000.

The addition of Project D, a project with an IRR of 11.5 percent and investment of $300,000, results in a capital budget to $1,300,000. Notice, however, that Project D's IRR is less than the marginal cost of capital at the point where it is added. If Project D were adopted, Figure 12-6 shows that it would have to be financed with capital that costs 11.88 percent, even though the Project's IRR is only 11.5 percent. The Ellis financial managers, then, should reject Project D. Project E, a project with an even lower IRR, is also rejected. Combining the IOS and MCC schedules is an effective tool to see whether a firm should accept or reject a project.

The Optimal Capital Budget

When we integrate the investment opportunity schedule and the marginal cost of capital schedule, as shown in Figure 12-6, we see that Ellis Industries' optimal capital budget is $1 million, consisting of projects A, B, and C. The **optimal capital budget** is the list of all accepted projects and the total amount of initial cash outlays for these projects. All projects on the IOS schedule that are above the MCC schedule are accepted; the rest are rejected.

Table 12-1 summarizes the seven steps to calculate the optimal capital budget.

TABLE 12-1

Determining the Optimal Capital Budget

STEPS	ACTIONS
Step 1	Calculate the costs of the firm's sources of capital, AT k_d, k_p, k_s, and k_n. Record any borrowing limits and the resulting changes in AT k_d with those limits.
Step 2	Calculate the break points in the capital budget size at which the MCC will change. There will always be an equity break point, BP_e, and there may be one or more debt break points, BP_{d1}, BP_{d2}, and so on.
Step 3	Calculate the MCC up to, between, and above all the break points. The MCC increases at each break point. Record the MCC values before and after each break point.
Step 4	Plot the MCC values on a graph with the capital budget size on the X axis and cost of capital/IRR on the Y axis.
Step 5	Identify the firm's potential investment projects. Record each investment project's initial investment requirement and IRR. Make an investment opportunity schedule (IOS) by lining up the projects from highest IRR to lowest.
Step 6	Plot the IOS on the same graph with the MCC.
Step 7	Note the point where the IOS and MCC schedules cross. Projects on the IOS line above the MCC line should be accepted, and those below the MCC line rejected.

The Importance of MCC to Capital Budgeting Decisions

Analyzing the combined IOS and MCC schedule allows financial managers to examine many projects at once, rather than each project in isolation. This way they choose the best projects.

To demonstrate how important the MCC schedule is to capital budgeting decisions, look at Figure 12-6 again. Notice that Project D is rejected because it is below the MCC line. The graph shows us that if Project D is accepted, it will have to be financed in part with capital costing 11.88 percent and in part with capital costing 12.16 percent. Since Project D's IRR is only 11.5 percent, it's a poor investment. However, this statement is only true because Projects A, B, and C were already considered *before* Project D. Together Projects A, B, and C require $1 million of capital investment. Given that $1 million has already been spent for Projects A, B, and C, the $300,000 required for Project D can only be raised at a cost of 11.88 percent (the first $200,000) and 12.16 percent (the last $100,000).

If Project D were considered by itself, as if it were Ellis Industries' only capital budgeting project, then the $300,000 investment the project requires could have been raised at the company's initial WACC of 11.4 percent. Since the Project's IRR of 11.5 percent exceeds that WACC rate by .1 percent, the project looks like a good investment. But because its IRR was lower than Project's A, B, and C, Project D is not a good investment, given the changes in Ellis's cost of capital due to the MCC break points.

This example illustrates the importance of using a firm's marginal cost of capital (MCC) and not the firm's initial weighted average cost of capital (WACC) to evaluate investments. If all investment projects are treated in isolation, and evaluated using the firm's initial WACC, then some of them may be overvalued. The discrepancy will become apparent when the firm tries to raise the entire amount of capital to support the complete capital budget and finds that the cost of the last dollar raised exceeds the IRR of the last project adopted.

What's Next

In this chapter we learned how to calculate a firm's individual component costs of capital and how to calculate its weighted average cost of capital and its marginal cost of capital. In chapter 13 we discuss how a firm should structure its sources of capital.

Summary

1. Describe the sources of capital and how firms raise capital.

Firms raise debt capital from lenders or bondholders. They also raise funds from preferred stockholders, from current stockholders, and from investors who buy newly issued shares of common stock. All suppliers of capital expect a rate of return proportionate to the risk they take. To ensure a supply of capital to meet their capital budgeting needs, firms must pay that return to capital suppliers. To compensate creditors, firms must pay the interest and principal on loans. For bondholders, firms must pay the market required interest rate. For preferred stockholders, the dividend payments serve as compensation for investors. To compensate common stock investors, firms pay dividends or reinvest the stockholders' earnings.

2. Estimate the cost of capital for each financing source.

To find a firm's overall cost of capital, a firm must first estimate how much each source of capital costs. The after-tax cost of debt, AT k_d, is the market's required rate of return on the firm's debt, adjusted for the tax savings realized when interest payments are deducted from taxable income. The before-tax cost of debt, k_d, is multiplied by one minus the tax rate $(1 - T)$ to arrive at the firm's after-tax cost of debt.

The cost of preferred stock, k_p, is the investor's required rate of return on that security. The cost of common stock equity, k_s, is the opportunity cost of new retained earnings, the required rate of return on the firm's common stock. The cost of new common stock, k_n, (external equity) is the required rate of return on the firm's common stock, adjusted for the flotation costs incurred when new common stock is sold in the market.

3. Estimate the weighted average cost of capital.

The weighted average cost of capital, k_a or WACC, is the overall average cost of funds considering each of the component capital costs and the weight of each of those components in the firm's capital structure. To estimate WACC, we multiply the individual source's cost of capital times its percentage of the firm's capital structure, and then add the results.

4. Use the marginal cost of capital schedule (MCC) to make capital budgeting decisions.

A firm's weighted average cost of capital changes as the cost of debt or equity increases as more capital is raised. Financial managers calculate the break points in the capital budget size at which the MCC will change. There will always be an equity break point, BP_e, and there may be one or more debt break points, BP_{d1}, BP_{d2}, and so on. Financial managers then calculates the MCC up to, between, and above all the break points, and plots the MCC values on a graph showing how the cost of capital changes as capital budget size changes.

Financial managers create an investment opportunity schedule (IOS) by ranking all potential capital budgeting projects from the highest internal rate of return to the lowest, and then plotting the IOS on the same graph with the MCC. To increase the value of the firm, projects on the IOS line above the MCC line should be accepted and those below the MCC line rejected.

5. Explain the importance of the marginal cost of capital (MCC) schedule in financial decision making.

The marginal cost of capital schedule forces financial managers to match the project's rate of return with the cost of funds for that specific project. This marginal analysis prevents financial managers from estimating a project's value incorrectly because of faulty cost of capital estimates that fail to consider how a larger capital budget increases capital costs.

Equations Introduced in This Chapter

Equation 12-1. Formula for the After-Tax Cost of Debt (AT k_d):

$$AT\ k_d = k_d\ (1 - T)$$

where: k_d = the before-tax cost of debt
T = the firm's marginal tax rate

Equation 12-2. Formula for the Cost of Preferred Stock (k_p):

$$k_p = \frac{D_p}{P_p}$$

where: k_p = the cost of the preferred stock issue; the expected return
D_p = the amount of the expected preferred stock dividend
P_p = the current price of the preferred stock

Equation 12-3. Formula for the Cost of Common Stock Equity (k_s):

$$k_s = \frac{D_1}{P_0} + g$$

where: P_0 = the current price of the common stock
  D_1 = the amount of the common stock dividend expected one period from now
  g = the expected constant growth rate of the company's common stock dividends

Equation 12-4. CAPM Formula for the Cost of Common Equity (k_s):

$$k_s = k_{RF} + (k_M - k_{RF}) \times \beta$$

where: k_s = the required rate of return from the company's common stock equity
  k_{RF} = the risk-free rate of return
  k_M = the expected rate of return on the overall stock market
  β = the beta of the company's common stock, a measure of the amount of nondiversifiable risk

Equation 12-5. Formula for the Cost of New Common Equity (k_n):

$$k_n = \frac{D_1}{P_0 - F} + g$$

where: k_n = the cost of new common stock equity
  P_0 = the price of one share of common stock
  D_1 = the amount of the common stock dividend expected to be paid in one year
  F = the flotation cost per share
  g = the expected constant growth rate of the company's common stock dividends

Equation 12-6. Formula for the Weighted Average Cost of Capital, (WACC):

$$k_a = (WT_d \times AT\ k_d) + (WT_p \times k_p) + (WT_s \times k_s)$$

where: k_a = the weighted average cost of capital (WACC)
  WT_d = the weight, or proportion, of debt used to finance the firm's assets
  $AT\ k_d$ = the after-tax cost of debt
  WT_p = the weight, or proportion of preferred stock being used to finance the firm's assets
  k_p = the cost of preferred stock
  WT_s = the weight, or proportion of common equity being used to finance the firm's assets
  k_s = the cost of common equity

Equation 12-7. Formula for the Marginal Cost of Capital (MCC) Break Point:

$$BP = \frac{limit}{proportion\ of\ total}$$

where: BP = the capital budget size at which the MCC changes (break point)
  $limit$ = the point at which the cost of the source of capital changes
  proportion of total = the percentage of this source of capital in the firm's capital structure

Self-Test

ST-1. Jules' Security Company can issue new bonds with a market interest rate of 14 percent. Jules' marginal tax rate is 32 percent. Compute the after-tax cost of debt, AT k_d, for this company.

ST-2. Mr. White's company, The Problem Solvers, wants to issue new preferred stock. The market's required rate of return, considering the risk of this company, is 16 percent. The company's marginal tax rate is 38 percent. What is the cost of preferred stock, k_p?

ST-3. Vincent's Dance Studio Incorporated has a beta of 1.9. The risk-free rate of interest is 4 percent. The market portfolio has an expected rate of return of 10 percent. What is the cost of internal equity, k_s, for this company using the CAPM approach?

ST-4. Marsalis's Entertainment Corporation has an after-tax cost of debt of 8 percent, a cost of preferred stock of 12 percent, and a cost of equity of 16 percent. What is the weighted average cost of capital, k_a or WACC, for this company? The capital structure of Marsalis's company contains 20 percent debt, 10 percent preferred stock, and 70 percent equity.

ST-5. Quinten's Movie Company has been told by its investment banking firm that it could issue up to $8 million in bonds at an after-tax cost of debt of 10 percent. But after that, additional bonds would have a 12 percent after-tax cost. Quinten's company uses 40 percent debt and 60 percent equity for major projects. How much money could this company raise, maintaining its preferred capital structure, before the after-tax cost of debt would jump to 12 percent?

Review Questions

1. Which is lower for a given company: the cost of debt or the cost of equity? Explain. Ignore taxes in your answer.
2. When a company issues new securities, how do flotation costs affect the cost of raising that capital?
3. What does the "weight" refer to in the weighted average cost of capital?
4. How do tax considerations affect the cost of debt and the cost of equity?
5. If dividends paid to common stockholders are not legal obligations of a corporation, is the cost of equity zero? Explain your answer.
6. What is the investment opportunity schedule (IOS)? How does it help financial managers make business decisions?
7. What is a marginal cost of capital schedule (MCC)? Is the schedule always a horizontal line? Explain.
8. For a given IOS and MCC, how do financial managers decide which proposed capital budgeting projects to accept, and which to reject?

Build Your Communication Skills

CS-1. Prepare a brief paper in which you explain to the CEO of a fictional company why the cost of equity is greater than either the cost of debt or the cost of preferred stock. Be sure to explain why equity funds have a cost even though those costs are not reflected on the income statement. Finally, discuss why it is important for a firm to know its cost of capital.

CS-2. Write a short report that analyzes the role of the marginal cost of capital (MCC) schedule in making capital budgeting decisions. In your report, explain how the investment opportunity schedule (IOS) affects this decision-making process. Be sure to explain your rationale for choosing some proposed projects, while rejecting others.

Problems

Cost of Debt

12-1.

    a. What would be the after-tax cost of debt for a company with the following yields to maturity for its new bonds, if the applicable tax rate were 40 percent?
        (i) YTM = 7%
        (ii) YTM = 11%
        (iii) YTM = 13%
    b. How would the cost of debt change if the applicable tax rate were 34 percent?

12-2. Calculate the after-tax cost of debt for loans with the following effective annual interest rates and corporate tax rates.

Cost of Debt

   a. Interest rate, 10%; tax rate 0%.
   b. Interest rate, 10%; tax rate 22%.
   c. Interest rate, 10%; tax rate 34%.

12-3. What would be the cost of debt for the following companies given their yields to maturity (YTM) for new bonds and the applicable corporate tax rates?

Cost of Debt

Company	YTM	Tax Rate
A	8%	34%
B	11%	40%
C	14%	30%

12-4. Mary Lynn Eatenton is the Chief Financial Officer of Magnolia Steel, Inc. She has asked Trudy Jones, one of the financial analysts, to calculate the after-tax cost of debt based on different bond yield to maturity rates. Magnolia Steel's current tax rate is 34 percent, but increasing sales and profits will put them in the 40 percent tax bracket by the end of the year. Calculate the after-tax cost of debt figures that will be shown in Ms. Jones's report at each tax rate for the following YTM rates.

Cost of Debt

   a. Yield to Maturity, 8%.
   b. Yield to Maturity, 14%.
   c. Yield to Maturity, 16%.

12-5. A firm is issuing new bonds that pay 8 percent annual interest. The market required annual rate of return on these bonds is 13 percent. The firm has a tax rate of 40 percent.

Cost of Debt

   a. What is the before-tax cost of debt?
   b. What is the after-tax cost of debt?

12-6. A company can sell preferred stock for $26 per share and each share of stock is expected to pay a dividend of $2.

Cost of Preferred Stock

   a. What is the cost of preferred stock?
   b. If the flotation cost per share of stock is $0.75, what would be the revised estimate of the cost of capital from this source?

12-7. Leo Bloom, the treasurer of a manufacturing company, thinks that debt (YTM = 11%, tax rate = 40%) will be a cheaper option for acquiring funds compared to issuing new preferred stock. The company can sell preferred stock at $60 per share and pay a yearly preferred dividend of $8 per share. Is Leo correct?

Cost of Debt and of Preferred Stock

12-8. One-Eyed Jacks Corporation needs money to fund a new production line of playing cards. Rio Longworth, manager of the finance department, suggests they sell preferred stock for $50 per share. They expect to pay $6 per share annual dividends.

Cost of Preferred Stock

   a. What is the cost of the capital obtained from issuing this preferred stock?
   b. Mr. Longworth forgot about the need to account for the flotation costs associated with the preferred stock issue. What is the revised estimate of the cost of preferred stock if the flotation cost is $2.25 per share?

12-9. El Norte Industries will issue $100 par, 12 percent preferred stock. The market price for the stock is expected to be $89 per share. El Norte must pay flotation costs of 5 percent of the market price. What is El Norte's cost of preferred stock?

Cost of Preferred Stock

12-10.   Twister Corporation is expected to pay a dividend of $7 per share one year from now on its common stock which has a current market price of $143. Twister's dividends are expected to grow at 13 percent.

   a. Calculate the cost of the company's retained earnings.
   b. If the flotation cost per share of new common stock is $4, calculate the cost of issuing new common stock.

12-11.   Amy Jolly is the treasurer of her company. She expects the company will grow at 4 percent in the future, and debt securities (YTM = 14%, tax rate = 30%) will always be a cheaper option to finance the growth. The current market price per share of its common stock is $39 and the expected dividend in one year is $1.50 per share. Calculate the cost of the company's retained earnings and check if Amy's assumption is a correct one.

12-12.   Pedro Muzquiz and Tita de la Garza are the CEOs of a large bakery chain, Chocolates, Inc. The common stock sells on the NASDAQ with a current market price of $65 per share. A $7 dividend is planned for one year from now. Business has been good and they expect the dividend growth rate of 10 percent to continue.

   a. Calculate the cost of the corporation's retained earnings.
   b. At the beginning of the year, 1 million shares were authorized with 500,000 issued and outstanding. They plan to issue another 200,000 shares. Calculate the cost of capital of the new common stock if the flotation cost per share is $3. Do you expect the cost of new common equity (external) to be higher than the cost of the internal equity? Why?

12-13.   Margo Channing, the financial analyst for Eve's Broadway Production Company, has been asked by management to estimate a cost of equity for use in the analysis of a project under consideration. In the past, dividends declared and paid have been very sporadic. Because of this, Ms. Channing elects to use the CAPM approach to estimate the cost of equity. The rate on the short-term U.S. Treasury bills is 3 percent, and the expected rate of return on the overall stock market is 11 percent. Eve's Broadway Production Company has a beta of 1.6. What will Ms. Channing report as the cost of equity?

12-14.   African Queen River Tours, Inc., has capitalized on the renewed interest in riverboat travel. Charlie Allnut, the lone financial analyst, estimates the firm's earnings, dividends, and stock price will continue to grow at the historical 5 percent rate. AQRT's common stock is currently selling for $30 per share. The dividend just paid was $2. They pay dividends every year. The rate of return expected on the overall stock market is 12 percent.

   a. What is AQRT's cost of equity?
   b. If they issue new common stock today and pay flotation costs of $2 per share, what is the cost of new common equity?
   c. If AQRT has a risk-free rate of 3 percent and a beta of 1.4, what will be AQRT's cost of equity using the CAPM approach?

12-15.   Alvin C. York, the founder of York Corporation, thinks that the optimal capital structure of his company is 30 percent debt, 15 percent preferred stock, and the rest common equity. If the company is in the 40 percent tax bracket, what is its weighted average cost of capital given that:

   YTM of its debt is 10 percent.
   New preferred stock will have a face value of $30 and a dividend of $2 per share.
   Price of common stock is currently $100 per share and new stock can be issued at the same price. The expected dividend in one year is $4 per share and the growth rate is 6 percent.

   Assume flotation costs are zero.

12-16. A company has an optimal capital structure as given below:

Weighted Average Cost of Capital

Total Assets	= $600,000
Debt	= $300,000
Preferred Stock	= $100,000
Common Equity	= $200,000

What would be the minimum expected return from a new capital investment project to satisfy the suppliers of the capital? Assume the applicable tax rate to be 40 percent, YTM of its debt to be 11 percent, flotation cost per share of preferred stock to be $0.75, and flotation cost per share of common stock $4. The preferred stock and common stock are selling in the market for $26 and $143, respectively, and are expected to pay a dividend of $2 and $7, respectively in one year. The company's dividends are expected to grow at 13 percent per year. The firm would like to maintain the above optimal capital structure to finance the new project.

12-17. Great Expectations, a wedding and maternity clothing manufacturer, has a cost of equity of 16 percent, and a cost of preferred stock of 14 percent. Their before-tax cost of debt is 12 percent and their marginal tax rate is 40 percent. Assume that the most recent balance sheet, shown below, reflects the optimal capital structure. Calculate Great Expectations' after-tax weighted average cost of capital.

Weighted Average Cost of Capital

Great Expectations
Balance Sheet
December 31, 1996

Assets		Liabilities and Equity	
Cash	$ 50,000		
Accounts Receivable	90,000	Long-term Debt	$ 600,000
Inventories	300,000	Preferred Stock	250,000
Plant & Equip, net	810,000	Common Stock	400,000
Total Assets	$1,250,000	Total L. & E.	$1,250,000

12-18. Puppet Masters is considering a new capital investment project. The company has an optimal capital structure and plans to maintain it. The yield to maturity on Puppet Masters' debt is 11 percent and their tax rate is 40 percent. The market price of the new issue of preferred stock is $26 per share with an expected per share dividend of $2 at the end of this year. Flotation costs are set at $0.75 per share. The new issue of common stock has a current market price of $143 per share with an expected dividend in one year of $7. Flotation costs for issuing new common stock are $4 per share. Puppet Masters' dividends are growing at 13 percent per year, and this growth is expected to continue for the foreseeable future. Selected figures from last year's balance sheet are given below.

Weighted Average Cost of Capital

Total Assets	$600,000
Long-term Debt	300,000
Preferred Stock	100,000
Common Stock	200,000

Calculate the minimum expected return from the new capital investment project needed to satisfy the suppliers of the capital.

12-19. Fans By Fay Company has a capital structure of 60 percent debt and 40 percent common equity. The company expects to realize $200,000 in net income this year and will pay no dividends. The effective annual interest rate on their new borrowings increases by 3 percent for amounts over $500,000.

Marginal Cost of Capital Schedule

a. At what capital budget size will Fans By Fay's cost of equity increase? In other words, what is their equity break point?

b. At what capital budget size will their cost of debt increase (debt break point)?

Marginal Cost of Capital Schedule

12-20. Babe's Dog Obedience School, Inc., wants to maintain its current capital structure of 50 percent common equity, 10 percent preferred stock, and 40 percent debt. Their cost of common equity is 13 percent and the cost of preferred stock is 12 percent. The bank's effective annual interest rate is 11 percent for amounts borrowed that are less than or equal to $1 million, and 13 percent for amounts between $1 million and $2 million. If more than $2 million is borrowed, the effective annual interest rate charged is 15 percent. Babe's tax rate is 40 percent. The firm expects to realize $2,750,000 in net income this year after preferred dividends have been paid.

a. Calculate the marginal cost of capital if $900,000 is needed for an upcoming project.

b. Calculate the marginal cost of capital if $1,500,000 is needed for the project instead.

c. If a different project is adopted, and $2,005,000 is needed for it, what is the marginal cost of capital?

Comprehensive Problem

12-21. Stone Wood Products has a capital structure of 35 percent debt and 65 percent common equity. The managers consider this mix to be optimal and want to maintain it in the future. Net income for the coming year is expected to be $1.2 million dollars. Duke Mantee, the loan officer at the local bank, has set up the following schedule for Stone Wood Products' borrowings.

Loan Amount	Interest Rate
$0 to $750,000	10%
> $750,000	12%

The market price per share of Stone Wood Product's common stock is $50 per share. They have declared a $5 dividend to be paid in one year. The company's expected growth rate is 9 percent. The flotation costs for new common stock issued are set at 8% of the market price.

The managers are considering several investment opportunities for the upcoming year. They have asked the senior financial analyst, Gabrielle Maple, to recommend which of the following projects the firm should undertake. Because you are the newest member of her team and need the experience, she has passed this management request on to you.

Investment Opportunities		
Project	Initial Investment (in millions)	Rate of Return
A	$0.5	16%
B	1.6	12%
C	0.6	15%
D	1.5	18%

a. Calculate all of Stone Wood Products' component costs of capital (after-tax cost of debt, cost of equity, and cost of new equity).

b. Calculate all of the MCC break points.

c. Calculate all of the marginal cost of capital figures.

d. Make an investment opportunity schedule (IOS) by listing the projects from the highest to the lowest internal rates of return.

e. Plot the MCC values and the IOS values on the same graph.

f. Which projects will you recommend management adopt for the next year?

Answers to Self-Test

ST-1. $.14 \times (1 - .32) = .0952 = 9.52\%$ AT k_d

ST-2. 16% k_p The tax rate is irrelevant here since preferred stock dividends paid by a company are not tax deductible.

ST-3. $.04 + (.10 - .04) \times 1.9 = .154 = 15.4\%$ k_s

ST-4. $(.08 \times .2) + (.12 \times .10) + (.16 \times .70) = .14 = 14\%$ k_a

ST-5. The break point in the MCC schedule caused by the increase in the cost of debt, BP_d, after $8,000,000 is borrowed, equals $8,000,000 \div .40 = $20,000,000$.

chapter 13

Capital Structure Basics

The Lord forbid that I should be out of debt, as if, indeed, I could not be trusted.

Francois Rabelais

Chapter Objectives

After reading this chapter, you should be able to:

1. Find the breakeven level of sales for a firm.

2. Explain operating, financial, and combined leverage effects and the resulting risks.

3. Describe the risks and returns of a leveraged buyout.

4. Explain how changes in capital structure affect a firm's value.

A Popcorn Venture

Jason is a college student who wants to start his own business. Jason's business idea is to sell popcorn from a cart, just as he has seen in the downtown area of the city in which he lives. The downtown vendor sells about 500 bags of popcorn a day, and Jason thinks he might be able to do as well with a similar popcorn stand near the college in his town.

However, the wagon contains both a popcorn-making machine and a storage room for supplies, so it isn't cheap. Also, if Jason went into the business, he would need an expensive business operator's license from the city. The downtown vendor charges only $1 for a bag of pop-

corn, so Jason would have to sell a lot of popcorn to recoup the high price of the wagon and the license.

Is this a viable business idea or not? What are the risks and the potential returns of this business? Is this a better path than taking a McJob, as many of Jason's friends have done? In this chapter we'll look at some of these issues. ✺

Source: Jason's popcorn venture is based on actual events. The entrepreneur's name has been changed and approximate numbers have been used, since data about this private company are confidential.

CHAPTER OVERVIEW

In this chapter we investigate how fixed costs affect the volatility of a firm's operating and net income. We see how fixed operating costs create *operating leverage,* which magnifies the effect of sales changes on operating income. We also examine how fixed financial costs create *financial leverage,* which magnifies the effect of changes in operating income on net income. Then, we analyze the risk and return of leveraged buy outs (LBOs). Finally, we see how changes in a firm's capital structure affect the firm's overall value.

BREAKEVEN ANALYSIS AND LEVERAGE

Investments in projects may change a firm's fixed operating and financing costs, thereby affecting firm value. Fixed costs may affect firm value because of *leverage effects* and the resulting risk from those leverage effects.

To understand a firm's potential for risk and return, then, financial managers must understand two types of leverage effects: operating leverage and financial leverage.

Breakeven analysis is a key to understanding *operating leverage.* In breakeven analysis we examine fixed and variable operating costs. **Fixed costs** are those costs that do not vary with the company's level of production. **Variable costs** are those costs that change as the company's production levels change.

In breakeven analysis the **sales breakeven point** is the level of sales that a firm must reach to cover its operating costs. Put another way, it is the point where the operating income (earnings before interest and taxes) equals zero.

A company with high fixed operating costs must generate high sales revenue to reach the sales breakeven point. A company with low fixed operating costs requires relatively low sales revenue to reach its sales breakeven point.

We usually observe a high/low trade-off in breakeven analysis. Firms with high fixed operating costs tend to have low variable costs, and vice versa. A company that automates a factory, for instance, commits to significant fixed costs—the expensive equipment. But the company's variable labor costs are likely to be low at a highly automated plant that operates with relatively few employees. In contrast, a company that produces handmade pottery with little overhead, and hires hourly workers as needed, is likely to have low fixed costs but high variable costs.[1]

To demonstrate the high/low trade-off, we gather data for a sales breakeven chart for two firms. The first firm has high fixed and low variable costs. The second firm has low fixed and high variable costs.

We introduced the topic of leverage in chapter 7, pages 145–148.

We discussed operating income in chapter 4, page 61.

Constructing a Sales Breakeven Chart

A breakeven chart shows graphically how fixed costs, variable costs, and sales revenue interact. Analysts construct the chart by plotting sales revenue and costs at various unit sales levels on a graph. To illustrate, let's construct the breakeven chart for Jason's Popcorn wagon, featured in the opening of the chapter.

---

[1]Labor costs can be either fixed or variable. If workers are guaranteed pay for a certain minimum number of hours per week, as might be called for in a union contract, the labor costs associated with this minimum guaranteed pay would be fixed costs. The costs associated with hourly worker pay with no guaranteed minimum are variable.

TABLE 13-1

Jason's Relevant Figures
for Breakeven Analysis

Fixed Costs:	
Wagon (annual rental)	$8,000
City License (annual fee)	$4,000
Total	$12,000
Variable Costs per Unit:	
One Paper Bag	$0.020
Oil	$0.005
Salt	$0.003
Popcorn	$0.012
Total	$0.040
Sales Price per Unit:	$1.00

The first step in constructing the breakeven chart is to find the breakeven point for the business. Let's look at some of the numbers for Jason's business and calculate the level of sales Jason must achieve to breakeven. Recall that at the breakeven point, operating income equals zero. If sales are below the breakeven point, Jason suffers an operating loss. If sales are above the breakeven point, Jason enjoys an operating profit. (Interest and taxes, subtracted after finding operating income, will be discussed in the last section of the chapter.)

Jason wants to know that his business venture has the potential for a positive operating profit, so he is keenly interested in finding his breakeven point. To find this point, we need to know how many bags of popcorn he must sell before the sales revenue contributed by each bag sold just covers his fixed and variable operating costs. The relevant sales breakeven figures for Jason's proposed business are shown in Table 13-1.

The numbers in Table 13-1 show that Jason's fixed costs are high compared to his sales price of $1 per bag of popcorn. The fixed costs include the $8,000 annual rental fee for the wagon and the $4,000 annual license fee. Jason must pay these costs no matter how much popcorn he produces and sells.

In contrast to the high fixed operating costs, Jason's variable operating costs per unit are a tiny fraction of his sales price of $1 per unit. The bag, oil, salt, and popcorn that help produce one bag of popcorn cost a total of $0.04. Each bag of popcorn that is sold, then, contributes $0.96 to cover the fixed costs, variable costs, and ultimately profit of the business ($1.00 − $0.04 = $0.96). The sales price per unit minus the variable cost per unit, $.96 in this case, is the **contribution margin.**

From the numbers presented in Table 13-1, we can calculate the breakeven level of sales for Jason's business. We find the level of sales needed to reach the operating income breakeven point by applying the following formula:

The Breakeven Point in Unit Sales

$$Q_{b.e.} = \frac{FC}{p - vc} \tag{13-1}$$

where: $Q_{b.e.}$ = Quantity unit sales breakeven level
FC = Total fixed costs
p = Sales price per unit
vc = Variable cost per unit

For Jason's business, the total fixed costs are $12,000, the price per unit is $1, and the variable cost per unit is $.04. According to Equation 13-1, Jason's popcorn business has the following sales breakeven point:

$$Q_{b.e.} = \frac{\$12,000}{\$1.00 - \$.04}$$

$$= \frac{\$12,000}{\$.96}$$

$$= 12,500$$

We find that Jason's sales breakeven point with $12,000 in fixed costs, $.04 per unit in variable costs, and a $1 per bag sales price, is 12,500 units. At $1 per bag, this is $12,500 in sales to reach the breakeven point.

Now that we know Jason's sales breakeven point, we need revenue and cost information to construct the breakeven chart.

Revenue Data   At any given level of unit sales, Jason's total sales revenue can be found using Equation 13-2:

Total Revenue, TR

$$TR = p \times Q \tag{13-2}$$

where: p = Sales price per unit
Q = Unit sales (Quantity sold)

Table 13-2 shows how to calculate Jason's sales revenues at different sales levels. For instance, we see that if Jason sells 5,000 bags of popcorn at the price of $1 per bag, his total revenue will be 5,000 × $1.00 = $5,000. If Jason sells 10,000 bags, his total revenue will be $10,000.

Cost Data   By definition, Jason's fixed costs will remain $12,000, regardless of the level of unit sales. His variable costs, however, increase by $0.04 for each unit sold. Jason's total costs for any given level of unit sales can be found using Equation 13-3 as follows:

Total Costs, TC

$$TC = FC + (vc \times Q) \tag{13-3}$$

where: FC = Fixed costs
vc = Variable costs per unit
Q = Unit sales (Quantity sold)

Table 13-3 demonstrates how we use Equation 13-3 to calculate Jason's total costs for different sales levels. For instance, we see that if Jason sells 5,000 bags of popcorn at a variable cost of $0.04 per bag and fixed costs of $12,000, his total cost will be $12,200. At 10,000 bags, his total cost will be $12,400.

UNIT SALES (Q)	×	PRICE (P)	=	TOTAL REVENUE (TR)
0	×	$1	=	$0
5,000	×	$1	=	$5,000
10,000	×	$1	=	$10,000
15,000	×	$1	=	$15,000
20,000	×	$1	=	$20,000
25,000	×	$1	=	$25,000
30,000	×	$1	=	$30,000

TABLE 13-2

Sales Revenues at Different Unit Sales Levels

TABLE 13-3

Jason's Total Costs for
Different Sales Levels

FIXED COSTS (FC)	+	(VARIABLE COST/UNIT (VC)	×	UNIT SALES (Q))	=	TOTAL COST (TC)
$12,000	+	($.04	×	0)	=	$12,000
$12,000	+	($.04	×	5,000)	=	$12,200
$12,000	+	($.04	×	10,000)	=	$12,400
$12,000	+	($.04	×	15,000)	=	$12,600
$12,000	+	($.04	×	20,000)	=	$12,800
$12,000	+	($.04	×	25,000)	=	$13,000
$12,000	+	($.04	×	30,000)	=	$13,200

Plotting Data on the Breakeven Chart   Jason's breakeven chart is shown in Figure 13-1. The chart is constructed with unit sales (Q) on the horizontal axis and cost and revenue dollars on the vertical axis. Total revenues from Table 13-2 are shown on the TR line, and total costs from Table 13-3 are shown on the TC line.

We see from the chart that to breakeven, Jason has to sell $12,500 worth of popcorn at $1 per bag—a quantity of 12,500 bags.

Applying Breakeven Analysis

Twelve thousand five hundred bags of popcorn may seem like a lot of sales just to breakeven, but Jason has watched another vendor downtown who sells on average 500 bags of popcorn a day. Jason plans to sell for three months during the summer, four weeks a month, five days a week. He estimates that he could sell 30,000 bags of popcorn (500 bags × 3 months × 4 weeks × 5 days) during the summer. At this sales level, Jason expects $30,000 in gross sales revenue at $1 per bag and $16,800 in operating income [$30,000 total revenue − $12,000 fixed costs − ($30,000 × .04 variable costs) = $16,800 operating income]. Not a bad summer job income.

Figure 13-1   Breakeven Chart for Jason's Popcorn Wagon

Figure 13-1 shows the fixed costs, total costs, and total revenues of Jason's Popcorn Wagon at different levels of unit sales. The breakeven sales point, the intersection of the total costs and total revenues lines, is 12,500 units.

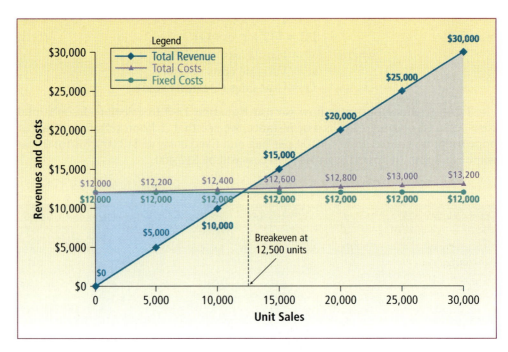

How is it possible to make so much money selling popcorn? Note how once Jason passes the breakeven point in sales, each additional $1 bag of popcorn he sells generates $0.96 of operating profit. The $0.04 in variable costs incurred in the production of that bag of popcorn represents a small part of the $1 in revenue generated. Operating profit rises rapidly as sales climb above the breakeven point of 12,500 units, as shown by Figure 13-1. Were Jason's sales potential not so promising, however, his risk of loss (negative operating income) would be high. The blue area of the graph in Figure 13-1 shows Jason's loss potential.

The breakeven chart allows Jason to see the different sales scenarios to understand his profit and loss potential. Because the total revenue line in Figure 13-1 is much steeper than the total cost line (because the sales price per unit is much greater than the variable cost per unit) the profit potential is great. Because of the high fixed costs, however, the loss potential is great, too. What happens depends on how much popcorn Jason can sell.

To illustrate what happens with a low breakeven business, let's construct a breakeven chart for Carey, another college student, who wants to sell hotplate mini-cookbooks (only five pages long) to college students.[2]

Because Carey plans to operate from her apartment and use her own recipes for the mini-cookbook, her only fixed cost would be a $1,000 printer's design fee. Her variable costs consist of her paper printing costs at $0.60 per unit. Carey plans to sell her cookbook for $1 per unit.

This is a low-risk business. The design fee is modest and there are no other fixed costs. The contribution margin is $0.40 ($1.00 sales price − $0.60 variable cost per unit). We can find Carey's breakeven point using Equation 13-1:

$$Q_{b.e.} = \frac{FC}{p - vc}$$
$$= \frac{\$1,000}{\$1.00 - \$.60}$$
$$= \frac{\$1,000}{\$.40}$$
$$= 2,500$$

We find that Carey's breakeven point is 2,500 units. Carey figures she can sell to friends in the dorm. Beyond that, however, the sales potential is uncertain. She may or may not reach the breakeven point.

To find Carey's breakeven point, we find her total revenue and total costs at different sales levels and plot them on a breakeven chart.

Note how small the loss potential is for Carey's business, as shown in the blue area in Figure 13-2, compared to Jason's loss potential, shown in the blue area in Figure 13-1. Carey's loss potential is small because her breakeven level of sales ($0 operating income) is 2,500 units, compared to Jason's 12,500 unit breakeven point. Even if she sold nothing, Carey would lose only the $1,000 in fixed costs that she had to pay (compared to Jason's $12,000). Table 13-4 shows the profit and loss potential for Jason and Carey.

---

[2]Believe it or not, Carey's business is also inspired by a true story. Oliver Stone would be proud.

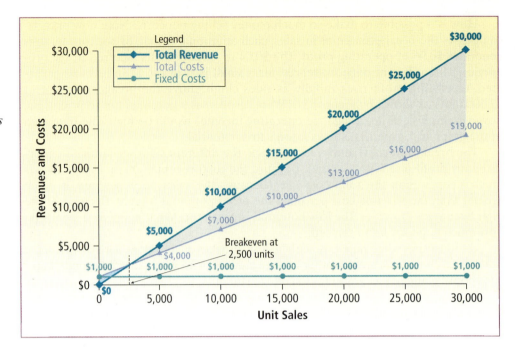

Figure 13-2 Breakeven Chart for Carey's Mini-Cookbooks

Figure 13-2 shows the fixed costs, total costs, and total revenues of Carey's Mini-Cookbooks at different levels of unit sales. The breakeven sales level of 2,500 units is the point where the total costs line crosses the total revenues line.

The risk of Jason's business is also evident when we look at sales of 15,000 units for each business. Jason has a profit of only $2,400, while Carey would earn a profit of $5,000; at 30,000 units sold, however, Jason earns a profit of $16,800 and Carey earns only $11,000, as shown in Table 13-4. Jason's profits are much more dependent on selling a large number of units than are Carey's.

Now compare the profit potential for the two proposed businesses. Jason has the potential to make much more profit (operating income) than Carey. At a sales level of 30,000, Table 13-4 shows Jason makes $16,800 while Carey would make only $11,000. Even though Jason's business has more risk—he stands to lose much more if sales don't go well—he has the potential for greater returns.

TABLE 13-4

Jason's and Carey's Profit and Loss Potential

UNITS PRODUCED AND SOLD	JASON			CAREY		
	$Total Costs	$Total Revenue	$Operating Income	$Total Costs	$Total Revenue	$Operating Income
0	12,000	0	−12,000	1,000	0	−1,000
5,000	12,200	5,000	−7,200	4,000	5,000	1,000
10,000	12,400	10,000	−2,400	7,000	10,000	3,000
15,000	12,600	15,000	2,400	10,000	15,000	5,000
20,000	12,800	20,000	7,200	13,000	20,000	7,000
25,000	13,000	25,000	12,000	16,000	25,000	9,000
30,000	13,200	30,000	16,800	19,000	30,000	11,000
35,000	13,400	35,000	21,600	22,000	35,000	13,000
40,000	13,600	40,000	26,400	25,000	40,000	15,000

Whether the high fixed cost and low variable cost per unit business (like Jason's) is better than the low fixed cost and high variable cost per unit business (like Carey's) depends on two factors: how many units you think you can sell, and how much tolerance you have for risk. High fixed costs and low variable costs per unit mean high profit potential and high loss potential, as in the case of Jason's proposed business. Conversely, low fixed costs and high variable costs per unit mean low profit potential and low loss potential, as in the case of Carey's proposed business.

Take Note

Long distance telephone and cable companies are examples of firms with high fixed costs and low variable costs per unit. A consulting firm would be an example of a firm with low fixed costs and high variable costs.

LEVERAGE

In physics the term *leverage* describes how a small force can be magnified to create a larger force. For example, a farmer wants to move a large boulder in a field. He wedges a long board (a lever) between the large boulder and a small rock (a fulcrum), which gives him enough leverage to push down on the end of the long board and easily move the boulder.

The power of leverage can also be harnessed in a financial setting. Its magnifying power can help or hurt a business. A firm that has leverage will earn or lose more than it would without leverage. In the sections that follow, we investigate operating and financial leverage and the risks associated with each type.

Operating Leverage

Operating leverage refers to the phenomenon whereby a small change in sales triggers a relatively large change in operating income (or earnings before interest and taxes, also known as EBIT). Operating leverage occurs because of fixed costs in the operations of the firm. A firm with fixed costs in the production process will see its EBIT rise by a larger percentage than sales when unit sales are increasing. If unit sales drop, however, the firm's EBIT will decrease by a greater percentage than does its sales.

Table 13-5 illustrates the operating leverage effect for a firm in which all production costs, a total of $5,000, are fixed. Observe how the presence of the fixed costs causes a 10 percent change in sales to produce a 20 percent change in operating income.

Calculating the Degree of Operating Leverage   The degree of operating leverage, or DOL, measures the magnitude of the operating leverage effect. The **degree of operating leverage** is the percent change in earnings before interest and taxes (% △ EBIT) divided by the percent change in sales (% △ Sales):

Degree of Operating Leverage (DOL)

$$DOL = \frac{\% \triangle EBIT}{\% \triangle SALES}$$

(13-4)

where: %△EBIT = Percent change in earnings before interest and taxes
%△SALES = Percent change in sales

	PERIOD 1	**PERIOD 2**	**PERCENT CHANGE**
Sales	$10,000	$11,000	10%
Fixed Costs	−5,000	−5,000	
Operating Income	$ 5,000	$ 6,000	20%

TABLE 13-5

The Operating Leverage Effect—Fixed Costs Only

According to Equation 13-4, the DOL for the firm in Table 13-5 is:

$$DOL = \frac{20\%}{10\%}$$
$$= 2.0$$

We see that, for a firm with a 10 percent change in sales and a 20 percent change in EBIT, the DOL is 2.0. A DOL greater than 1 shows that the firm has operating leverage. That is, when sales changes by some percentage, EBIT will change by a greater percentage.

The Effect of Fixed Costs on DOL   Table 13-6 shows the projected base-year and second-year income statement for Jason's Popcorn Wagon. The income statement allows us to analyze Jason's operating leverage. (Note that Table 13-6 divides the operating expenses into two categories, fixed and variable.) We see that sales and operating expenses are likely to change in the second and subsequent years. We also see the predicted impact on EBIT, given the sales forecast.

We see from Table 13-6 that Jason's percentage change in sales is 10 percent, and his percentage change in EBIT (or operating income) is 17.1 percent. We use Equation 13-4 to find Jason's DOL, as follows:

$$DOL = \frac{\%\triangle EBIT}{\%\triangle Sales}$$
$$= \frac{(19{,}680 - 16{,}800)/16{,}800}{(33{,}000 - 30{,}000)/30{,}000}$$
$$= \frac{.171}{.10}$$
$$= 1.71$$

Our DOL calculations indicate that if Jason's Popcorn Wagon business sales increase by 10 percent from the base year to the next year, EBIT will increase by 17.1 percent. This larger percent increase in EBIT is caused by the company's fixed operating costs. No matter how much popcorn Jason produces and sells, his wagon and license costs stay the same. The fixed costs cause the EBIT to increase faster than sales. If sales were to decrease, the fixed costs must still be paid. As a result, the fixed costs cause EBIT to drop by a greater percentage than sales.

The Alternate Method of Calculating DOL   Instead of using Equation 13-4, we may also find the degree of operating leverage (DOL) by using only numbers found in the base-year income statement. Subtract total variable costs from sales, divide that number by sales minus total variable costs minus fixed costs, and solve for DOL. The formula for the alternate method of finding DOL, Equation 13-5, follows:

TABLE 13-6

Jason's Popcorn Wagon Projected Income Statement (Fixed Costs are $12,000 and Variable Costs $0.04 per Unit)

	BASE YEAR	YEAR 2	
Sales	$30,000	$33,000	$\%\triangle = \dfrac{33{,}000 - 30{,}000}{30{,}000} = 10\%$
− VC	− 1,200	− 1,320	
− FC	− 12,000	− 12,000	
= EBIT	= $16,800	= $19,680	$\%\triangle = \dfrac{19{,}680 - 16{,}800}{16{,}800} = 17.1\%$

Degree of Operating Leverage, DOL (Alternate Formula)

$$DOL = \frac{Sales - VC}{Sales - VC - FC} \qquad (13\text{-}5)$$

where: VC = Total variable costs

FC = Total fixed costs

From Table 13-6 we know that in the base year, Jason's Popcorn Wagon is projected to have sales of $30,000, variable costs of $1,200, and fixed costs of $12,000. Using the alternate formula, we find that Jason has the following DOL:

$$
\begin{aligned}
DOL &= \frac{Sales - VC}{Sales - VC - FC} \\
&= \frac{30{,}000 - 1{,}200}{30{,}000 - 1{,}200 - 12{,}000} \\
&= \frac{28{,}800}{16{,}800} \\
&= 1.71
\end{aligned}
$$

We find a DOL of 1.71, just as we did with Equation 13-4. How did this happen? The alternate formula, Equation 13-5, uses only numbers from the base year income statement, whereas Equation 13-4 requires information from the base year and year 2.[3] Why use two different ways to calculate DOL when they both give the same answer? Because each method reveals different information about operating leverage.

The percent change version of the DOL formula, Equation 13-4, shows the effect of the leverage—sales change by a certain percentage, triggering a greater percentage change in operating income if the DOL is greater than 1. The percent change in operating income, then, is the product of the percent change in sales and this degree of operating leverage.

The alternate DOL formula, Equation 13-5, shows that fixed costs cause the leveraging effect. Whenever fixed costs are greater than zero, DOL is greater than one, indicating a leverage effect (the percent change in EBIT is greater than the percent change in sales). The larger the amount of fixed costs, then, the greater the leveraging effect.

Taken together, then, the two formulas demonstrate that leverage has the effect of triggering a greater percentage change in operating income when a percentage change in sales occurs and that fixed costs cause operating leverage. Equation 13-6 shows how a change in sales and DOL combine to determine the change in EBIT.

Change in EBIT

$$\%\triangle EBIT = \%\triangle SALES \times DOL \qquad (13\text{-}6)$$

where: %△SALES = Percent change in sales

DOL = Degree of operating leverage

The Risk of Operating Leverage   As we know from chapter 7, the risk associated with operating leverage is business risk. Recall that business risk refers to the volatility of operating income. The more uncertainty about what a company's operating income will be, the higher its business risk. Volatility of sales triggers business risk. The presence of fixed costs, shown by the amount of DOL, magnifies

We discussed business risk and how to measure it in chapter 7, pages 144–145.

[3]Equations 13-4 and 13-5 give the same numeric result when sales price per unit, fixed costs, and variable costs per unit are constant.

business risk. The total degree of business risk that a company faces is a function of both sales volatility and the degree of operating leverage.

Financial Leverage

Fluctuations in sales and the degree of operating leverage determine the fluctuations in operating income (also known as EBIT). Now let's turn our attention to financial leverage. **Financial leverage** is the additional volatility of net income caused by the presence of fixed-cost funds (such as fixed rate debt) in the firm's capital structure. Interest on fixed rate debt is a fixed cost because a firm must pay the same amount of interest, no matter what the firm's operating income.

Calculating the Degree of Financial Leverage (DFL) The **degree of financial leverage (DFL)** is the percent change in net income (% $\triangle$ NI) divided by the percent change in sales (% $\triangle$ EBIT). The formula for DFL follows:

Degree of Financial Leverage, DFL

$$DFL = \frac{\% \triangle NI}{\% \triangle EBIT}$$

(13-7)

where: %$\triangle$NI = Percent change in net income
%$\triangle$EBIT = Percent change in earnings before interest and taxes

If net income changes by a greater percentage than does EBIT, then the DFL will have a value greater than 1, and this indicates a financial leverage effect.

Table 13-7 shows the entire base-year income statement for Jason's Popcorn Wagon, and the projections for year 2. Notice that the lower portion of the income statements contains fixed interest expense, so we would expect the presence of financial leverage.

As shown in Table 13-7, the percent change in EBIT from the base year to year 2 is 17.1 percent, and the percent change in net income from the base year to year 2 is 18 percent. Jason's degree of financial leverage according to Equation 13-7 follows:

$$DFL = \frac{\% \triangle NI}{\% \triangle EBIT}$$
$$= \frac{.18}{.1714}$$
$$= 1.05$$

Our calculations show that Jason's Popcorn Wagon business has a degree of financial leverage of 1.05.

Another Method of Calculating Financial Leverage Just as with DOL, there are two ways to compute DFL. Instead of using Equation 13-7, the percent change in NI divided by the percent change in EBIT, we could instead calculate the DFL using only numbers found in the base-year income statement. By dividing EBIT by EBIT minus interest expense (I), we can find DFL. The equation looks like this:

Degree of Financial Leverage, DFL (Alternate Formula)

$$DFL = \frac{EBIT}{EBIT - I}$$

(13-8)

where: EBIT = Earnings before interest and taxes
I = Interest expense

TABLE 13-7

Jason's Income Statement—Base Year and Projected Year 2

	BASE YEAR	YEAR 2		
Sales	$30,000	$33,000	$\% \triangle = \dfrac{33,000 - 30,000}{30,000} = 10\%$	
− VC	− 1,200	− 1,320		
− FC	− 12,000	− 12,000		
= EBIT	= 16,800	= 19,680	$\% \triangle = \dfrac{19,680 - 16,800}{16,800} = 17.1\%$	
− I	− 800	− 800		
= EBT	= 16,000	= 18,880		
− Tax (15%)	− 2,400	− 2,832		
= NI	= 13,600	= 16,048	$\% \triangle = \dfrac{16,048 - 13,600}{13,600} = 18\%$	

The base-year income statement numbers in Table 13-7 show that Jason's EBIT is $16,800 and his interest expense is $800. To find the degree of financial leverage, we apply Equation 13-8 as follows:

$$\begin{aligned} DFL &= \frac{EBIT}{EBIT - I} \\ &= \frac{16,800}{16,800 - 800} \\ &= \frac{16,800}{16,000} \\ &= 1.05 \end{aligned}$$

Equation 13-8 yields the same DFL for Jason's business as Equation 13-7.[4] Both formulas are important because they give us different but equally important insights about financial leverage. Equation 13-7 shows the effect of financial leverage—net income (NI) will vary by a larger percentage than operating income (EBIT). Equation 13-8 pinpoints the source of financial leverage—fixed interest expense. The degree of financial leverage, DFL, will be greater than 1 if interest expense (I) is greater than zero. In sum, interest expense magnifies the volatility of NI as operating income changes.

How Interest Expense Affects Financial Leverage   To illustrate the financial leverage effect, suppose that to help start his business, Jason borrowed $10,000 from a bank at an annual interest rate of 8 percent. This 8 percent annual interest rate means that Jason will have to pay $800 ($10,000 × .08) in interest each year on the loan. The interest payments must be made, no matter how much operating income Jason's business generates. In addition to Jason's fixed operating costs, he also has fixed financial costs (the interest payments on the loan) of $800.

The fixed financial costs magnify the effect of a change in operating income on net income. For instance, even if Jason's business does well, the bank interest payments do not increase, even though he could afford to pay more. If Jason's business does poorly, however, he cannot force the bank to accept less interest simply because he cannot afford the payments.

---

[4]Equations 13-7 and 13-8 give the same DFL value only if the fixed financial costs (interest expense) and the tax rate are constant.

The Risk of Financial Leverage The presence of debt in a company's capital structure, and the accompanying interest cost, creates extra risk for a firm. As we know from chapter 7, the extra volatility in NI caused by fixed interest expense is financial risk. The financial risk of the firm compounds the effect of business risk and magnifies the volatility of net income. Just as fixed operating expenses increase the volatility of operating income and business risk, so too fixed financial expenses increase the volatility of NI and magnify financial risk. This is shown in Equation 13-9.

We discussed financial risk and how to measure it in chapter 7, pages 146–148.

Change in Net Income

$$\% \triangle NI = \% \triangle EBIT \times DFL \tag{13-9}$$

where: $\% \triangle EBIT$ = Percent change in earnings before interest and taxes
DFL = Degree of financial leverage

We explore the combined effect of operating and financial leverage next.

Combined Leverage

The combined effect of operating leverage and financial leverage is known as **combined leverage.** Combined leverage occurs when net income changes by a larger percentage than sales which occurs if there are any fixed operating or financial costs. The following combined leverage formula solves for the net income change due to sales changes that occur when fixed operating and financial costs are present.

The **degree of combined leverage (DCL)** is the percent change in net income (NI) divided by the percent change in sales, as shown in Equation 13-10:

Degree of Combined Leverage Formula, DCL

$$DCL = \frac{\% \triangle NI}{\% \triangle SALES} \tag{13-10}$$

where: $\% \triangle NI$ = Percent change in net income
$\% \triangle Sales$ = Percent change in sales

The alternate DCL formula follows:

Degree of Combined Leverage, DCL

$$DCL = \frac{Sales - VC}{Sales - VC - FC - I} \tag{13-11}$$

where: VC = Total variable costs
FC = Total fixed costs
I = Interest expense

We can also calculate the degree of combined leverage (DCL) a third way: multiplying the degree of operating leverage (DOL) by the degree of financial leverage (DFL). The third DCL formula is shown in Equation 13-12.

Degree of Combined Leverage, DCL

$$DCL = DOL \times DFL \tag{13-12}$$

where: DOL = Degree of operating leverage
DFL = Degree of financial leverage

Equation 13-13 shows the combined effect of DOL and DFL on net income (NI).

Change in Net Income

$$\%\triangle\, NI = \%\triangle\, Sales \times DOL \times DFL \qquad (13\text{-}13)$$

where: $\%\triangle$Sales = Percent change in sales
  DOL = Degree of operating leverage
  DFL = Degree of financial leverage

Equation 13-13 shows how the change in net income is determined by the change in sales and the compounding effects of operating and finanical leverage.

Fixed Costs and Combined Leverage Fixed operating costs create operating leverage, fixed financial costs create financial leverage, and these two types of leverage together form combined leverage. If fixed operating costs (FC) and fixed interest costs (I) were both zero, there would be no leverage effect. The percent change in net income (NI) would be the same as the percent change in sales. If either, or both, fixed operating costs and fixed financial costs exceed zero, a leverage effect will occur (DCL > 1).

Firms that have high operating leverage need to be careful about how much debt they pile onto their balance sheets, and the accompanying interest costs they incur, because of combined leverage effects. Remember that for Jason's Popcorn Wagon, the degree of operating leverage (DOL) was 1.71 and the degree of financial leverage was 1.05. The degree of combined leverage for Jason's business according to Equation 13-11 is 1.80 (1.71 × 1.05 = 1.80 rounded to two decimal places). Jason is quite confident that his sales will be high enough so that this high leverage will not be a problem. If the sales outlook were questionable, though, the combined leverage effect could magnify poor sales results.

Leverage is helpful when sales increase (positive percent changes). Magnifying this positive change benefits the firm. However, leverage is harmful when sales decrease because it magnifies the negative change. Because future sales for most companies are uncertain, most companies view leverage with mixed feelings.

LBOs

During the 1980s many publicly owned corporations were bought out by a small group of investors, sometimes including top management of the firm, using a large amount of borrowed money. Such a purchase is called a *leveraged buyout,* or LBO. The leverage referred to is financial leverage.

In an LBO, investment banking firms work to identify attractive target companies. These investment banking firms solicit investors to acquire the target. To take over the target, the purchasing group raises cash, mostly borrowed, to purchase the common stock shares from the general public. The stock purchase converts the publicly owned corporation to a privately owned one. The investment banking firm would collect fees for its advice and for underwriting the bond issue that helped raise the additional debt capital.

Because of the dramatic increase in financial leverage, some LBOs have worked out well for investors and others have been disasters. For instance, Kohlberg, Kravis, & Roberts (KKR) made a 50 percent annual rate of return on its $1.34 billion investment after the Beatrice Company LBO. In contrast, the 1986 $1.4 billion LBO of Revco Drug Stores didn't fare as well. Two years later the company filed for bank-

TABLE 13-8

	BEFORE THE BUYOUT (1988)	AFTER THE BUYOUT (1989)
Long-Term Debt	$4,975 million	$21,948 million
Total Equity	$5,819 million	$1,237 million
Debt to Equity ratio	85.5%	1,774%
Source: Value-Line Investment Survey		

ruptcy when it was unable to generate enough cash flow to pay the interest and principal due on its bonds.

When a company with a normal debt load goes through an LBO, investors holding the company's bonds issued before the LBO are often hurt. The surge in the company's debt results in more financial risk. With higher risk, the market requires a higher rate of return, so the bonds issued before the LBO will see their market interest rates rise—and their market prices fall—after the company announces an LBO.

To illustrate the effects on bondholders, consider the 1989 LBO of RJR/Nabisco. Table 13-8 shows how the holders of the RJR/Nabisco bonds suddenly had a claim on a much riskier company.

ETHICAL CONNECTIONS

Et Tu, Wilson?

William Wilson, a big player in Southern California politics and former U.S. ambassador to the Vatican, agreed to use his contacts to find potential companies for a company named Kelso & Co. to target as LBO candidates. There was nothing in writing, but Wilson expected a fee from Kelso if any of his suggestions resulted in an LBO. Kelso had been eyeing Jorgensen, a steel-distribution company, for years. Finally, it offered to buy Jorgensen. That offer placed Wilson in an awkward position because he was a member of Jorgensen's board of directors. As a member of that board, he was legally obligated to do the best he could for Jorgensen's shareholders. Yet he had a personal interest in seeing Jorgensen accept Kelso's bid—a potential conflict of interest.

Then the plot thickened. A rival offer was made by another company, Leonard, Green & Partners. At this point Wilson—who had a personal stake in Kelso prevailing—should have stepped aside or disclosed his Kelso ties. He didn't do that. Instead, he served on the special board committee that weighed both bids and recommended Kelso by a 3-to-1 vote.

Finally, just days after the deal was sealed, Kelso paid Wilson $750,000. An SEC investigation ensued, but resulted in a mild wrist slap: The SEC ordered Wilson not to fail to disclose important information in the future.

Questions to Consider

▶ Was Wilson really wrong in playing both sides of the fence? After all, the vote to accept the Kelso bid was 3-to-1.

▶ Should the SEC have pursued Wilson as vigorously as it would an insider trader? Do you think his status affected the investigation? Should it? Explain your answers.

▶ When, if at all, should Wilson have disclosed his potential conflict of interest? Explain.

Sources: Allan Sloan, "Director Makes a Civil Killing by Scouting Takeover of Brea Company," *Los Angeles Times* (July 11, 1993): D2; Allan Sloan, "Former Vatican Envoy's Tacky Role in a Budget Draws Only a Wrist Slap," *Washington Post* (July 13, 1993): D3.

The bondholders, led by Metropolitan Life Insurance Company, sued when the value of the bonds they held dropped precipitously after the firm announced its LBO. The lawsuit was settled out of court in 1991.

The risk of an LBO is large because of financial leverage effects. As the Beatrice and Revlon examples indicate, potential returns from an LBO may be large positive or negative values because of financial leverage effects. Bondholders may suddenly see the value of their bonds drop precipitously after an LBO announcement. In chapter 14 we discuss how bondholders can protect themselves against this risk.

Now that we have analyzed how fixed operating and financial costs can create leverage effects and risk, we will consider the optimal capital structure for a firm.

Capital Structure Theory

A central question in finance is how much debt and equity a firm should have in its capital structure. **Capital structure** is the mixture of sources of funds a firm uses (debt, preferred stock, common stock). The amount of operating leverage a company has is largely determined by the original equity investors who decide what kind of business to operate. The amount of financial leverage a company has, however, is much more controllable.

Every time a company borrows, it increases its financial leverage and financial risk. New equity financing decreases financial leverage and risk. Changes in financial leverage, we have seen, bring the potential for good and bad results. How then do financial managers decide on the right balance of debt and equity? Financial managers analyze many factors, including the tax effects of interest payments, and how the comparative costs of debt and equity affect firm value.

Tax Deductibility of Interest

Debt in a firm's capital structure can be beneficial. First, debt creates the potential for leveraged increases in net income (NI) when operating income (EBIT) is rising. Second, debt gives the company a tax deduction for the interest that is paid on the debt. In contrast to debt, an issue of common stock to raise equity funds results in no tax break. In short, interest paid on business debt is tax deductible, but dividends paid to common stockholders are not. The tax laws, therefore, give companies an incentive to use debt in their capital structures.

Although the tax deductibility of interest payments on debt is a benefit, debt has costs, too. We know that the financial risk of the firm increases as debt increases. As financial risk increases, including an increasing risk of bankruptcy, a company will incur costs to deal with this risk. For example, suppliers may refuse to extend trade credit to the company; and lawyers' fees may drain funds that could go to either bondholders or common stock investors.

Modigliani and Miller

How does a company balance the costs and benefits of debt? In 1958 Franco Modigliani and Merton Miller wrote a seminal paper that has influenced capital structure discussion ever since. Modigliani and Miller (known in economics and finance circles as M&M) concluded that when interest payments are tax deductible to a firm, a capital structure of all debt is optimal.

In reaching this conclusion, M&M assumed the following:

1. There were no transaction costs.
2. Purchasers of a company's bonds or common stock paid no income tax.
3. Corporations and investors can borrow at the same rate of interest.
4. Investors and management have the same information about the firm.
5. Debt the firm issues is riskless.
6. Operating income is not affected by the use of debt.

In such an environment, M&M showed that the tax benefits to the firm from issuing debt were so beneficial that the benefits allowed the company to increase its value by issuing more and more debt. Given the assumptions, a 100 percent debt capital structure is optimal.

The assumptions do not, of course, exist in the real world. Companies don't seek a 100 percent debt capital structure, suggesting that capital structure is not optimal. In the real world, capital structures vary widely.

Toward an Optimal Capital Structure

Firms seek to balance the costs and benefits of debt to reach an optimal mix that maximizes the value of the firm. Figure 13-3 shows the component costs and weighted cost of capital according to the view of most financial managers. Given the way suppliers of capital react in the real world, many financial managers believe this view is more realistic than the M&M model.

Figure 13-3 Cost of Capital and Capital Structure

Figure 13-3 shows the cost of debt, cost of equity, and weighted average cost of capital (WACC) for different capital structures. The WACC is minimized at point Z.

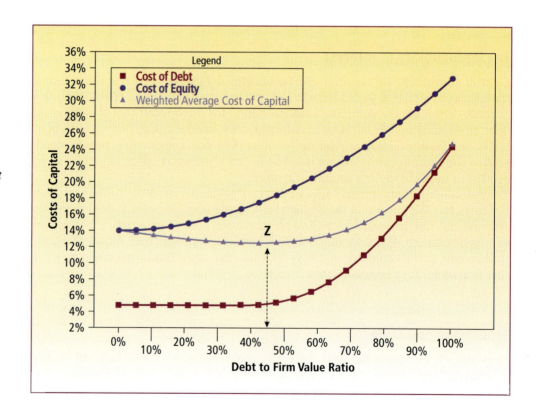

Figure 13-3 illustrates what many believe happens to the cost of debt, equity, and the weighted average cost of capital (WACC) as the capital structure of the firm changes. First, the graph shows that debt is cheaper than equity capital. Second, it shows that the weighted average cost of capital equals the cost of equity when the firm has no debt. Third, it shows that at point Z firms minimize the weighted average cost of capital, so at that point the capital structure maximizes the value of the firm. The cost advantage that debt has over equity dominates the increasing risk up to point Z. At this point the greater risk begins to dominate and causes the weighted average cost of capital to begin to turn upward.

We learned in chapter 12 how to estimate the costs of debt and equity and weighted average figures. Here we study how capital structure changes may affect the firm's cost of capital and its value.

To review how to estimate the costs of capital and the WACC, see chapter 12, pages 297–299.

The Lower Cost of Debt

Figure 13-3 shows that debt capital has a lower cost than equity capital. Debt is cheaper than equity for two reasons. As mentioned earlier, interest payments made by a firm are tax deductible and dividend payments made to common stockholders are not. Even without the tax break, debt funds are cheaper than equity funds. The required rate of return on a bond is lower than the required rate of return on common stock for a given company because debt is less risky than equity to investors. Debt is less risky because bondholders have a claim superior to that of common stockholders on the earnings and assets of the firm.

How Capital Costs Change as Debt Is Added

If we examine the WACC line in Figure 13-3, we see that the weighted average cost of capital equals the cost of equity when the firm has no debt. Then, as debt is added, the cost advantage (to the issuing company) of debt over equity makes the weighted average cost of capital decrease, up to a point, as more of the cheaper debt funds and less of the more expensive equity funds are used. The effect of adding debt to capital structure is shown in Figure 13-3 as we move along the horizontal axis from the origin.

The Effect of Risk

What causes the WACC to increase, as shown in Figure 13-3, beyond point Z? As the firm moves to a capital structure with higher debt (moves to the right along the horizontal axis of Figure 13-3), the risk of the firm increases. As financial risk rises with additional debt, the required return of both debt and equity investors increases. Notice that the cost of equity curve starts to climb sooner than does the cost of debt curve. This is because common stockholders get paid *after* bondholders.

As both the cost of debt and the cost of equity curves turn upward, the curve depicting the weighted average of the cost of debt and the cost of equity eventually turns upward, too. According to the capital structure view depicted in Figure 13-3, if a firm has less debt than the amount at Z, the WACC is higher than it needs to be. Likewise, if a firm has more debt than the amount at Z, the WACC is higher than it needs to be. Only at the capital structure at point Z do firms minimize the weighted average cost of capital. This is the capital structure, then, that maximizes the value of the firm.

Establishing the Optimal Capital Structure in Practice

In the real world, it is unlikely that financial managers can determine an exact point for Z where the WACC is minimized. Many financial managers try instead to estimate Z and set a capital structure close to it. Unfortunately, no formula can help estimate point Z. The optimal capital structure for a firm depends on the future prospects of that firm.

For example, say a company has a product in great demand that is protected by a patent with many years to expiration. The company will find that bond and common stock investors are comfortable with a large amount of debt. This firm's Z value will be high. But a firm in a competitive industry, with some quality control problems and soft demand for its product, is in a different position. It will find that bond and common stock investors get nervous (and demand higher returns) when the debt-to-total-value[5] ratio is above even a moderate level. This firm's Z value will be much lower than that of the first firm.

So the answer to the question, "What is the optimal capital structure for a firm?" is, "It depends." With no formula to use to estimate the firm's Z value, management examines the capital structure of similar companies and the future prospects of the firm. Financial managers must balance the costs and benefits of debt and use expertise and experience to develop the capital structure they deem optimal.

WHAT'S NEXT

In this chapter, we examined breakeven analysis, leverage effects, leveraged buyouts, and the effects of changes in a firm's capital structure. In chapter 14 we look at corporate bonds, preferred stock, and leasing.

SUMMARY

1. **Find the breakeven level of sales for a firm.**

The costs of operating a business can be categorized as fixed or variable. Operating costs that do not vary with the level of production are fixed; operating costs that do vary with the level of production are variable. High fixed costs are usually tied to low variable costs per unit, and low fixed costs are usually tied to high variable costs per unit.

The breakeven point is the level of sales that results in an operating income of zero. At sales levels above the breakeven point, a firm begins to make a profit. A company with high fixed operating costs must generate high sales revenue to cover its fixed costs (and its variable costs) before reaching the sales breakeven point. Conversely, a firm with low fixed operating costs will breakeven with a relatively low level of sales revenue.

2. **Explain operating, financial, and combined leverage effects and the resulting business and financial risks.**

Firms with high fixed costs have high operating leverage—that is, a small change in sales triggers a relatively large change in operating income. Firms with low fixed costs have less operating leverage. The effect of low operating leverage is that small changes in sales do not cause large changes in operating income.

Business risk refers to the volatility of a company's operating income. Business risk is triggered by sales volatility and magnified by fixed operating costs.

If a company uses fixed cost funds (such as fixed interest rate bonds) to raise capital, financial leverage results. With financial leverage, fixed interest costs cause net income to change by a greater percentage than a concurrent change in EBIT.

The presence of financial leverage creates financial risk for a firm—the risk that the firm will not be able to make its interest payments if operating income drops. Financial risk compounds the business risk already present.

The total effect of operating leverage and financial leverage is called combined leverage. The value of the degree of financial leverage is multiplied by the value of the degree of operating leverage to give the degree of combined leverage (DCL). The DCL gives the percent change in net income for a given percent change in sales.

---

[5]Total value here refers to the total market value of the firm's outstanding debt and equity.

3. Describe the risks and returns of a leveraged buyout.

LBOs, or leveraged buyouts, occur when publicly owned corporations are bought out by a small group of investors using mostly borrowed funds. The purchase is leveraged because the investors finance it with a large amount of borrowed money. Consequently, when a firm is purchased in an LBO, it is saddled with a large amount of debt in its capital structure, and a large amount of financial leverage and financial risk.

4. Explain how changes in capital structure affect a firm's value.

Capital structure theory deals with the mixture of debt, preferred stock, and equity a firm utilizes. Because interest on business loans is a tax-deductible expense, and because lenders demand a lower rate of return than do stockholders for a given company (because lending money is not as risky as owning shares), debt capital is cheaper than equity capital. However, the more a company borrows, the more it increases its financial leverage and financial risk. The additional risk causes lenders and stockholders to demand a higher rate of return. Financial managers use capital structure theory to help determine the mix of debt and equity at which the weighted average cost of capital is lowest.

Equations Introduced in This Chapter

Equation 13-1. The Breakeven Point in Unit Sales, $Q_{b.e.}$:

$$Q_{b.e.} = \frac{FC}{p - vc}$$

where: $Q_{b.e.}$ = Quantity unit sales breakeven level
FC = Total fixed costs
p = Sales price per unit
vc = Variable costs per unit

Equation 13-2. Total Revenue, TR:

$$TR = p \times Q$$

where: p = Sales price per unit
Q = Unit sales (Quantity sold)

Equation 13-3. Total Costs, TC:

$$TC = FC + (vc \times Q)$$

where: FC = Fixed costs
vc = Variable costs per unit
Q = Unit sales (Quantity sold)

Equation 13-4. Degree of Operating Leverage (DOL):

$$DOL = \frac{\% \triangle EBIT}{\% \triangle SALES}$$

where: $\% \triangle EBIT$ = Percent change in earnings before interest and taxes
$\% \triangle SALES$ = Percent change in sales

Equation 13-5. Degree of Operating Leverage (DOL) (alternate):

$$DOL = \frac{Sales - VC}{Sales - VC - FC}$$

where: VC = Total variable costs
FC = Total fixed costs

Equation 13-6. Change in EBIT:

$$\%\triangle EBIT = \%\triangle SALES \times DOL$$

where: $\%\triangle SALES$ = Percent change in sales
DOL = Degree of operating leverage

Equation 13-7. Degree of Financial leverage (DFL):

$$DFL = \frac{\%\triangle NI}{\%\triangle EBIT}$$

where: $\%\triangle NI$ = Percent change in net income
$\%\triangle EBIT$ = Percent change in earnings before interest and taxes

Equation 13-8. Degree of Financial Leverage (DFL) (alternate)

$$DFL = \frac{EBIT}{EBIT - I}$$

where: EBIT = Earnings before interest and taxes
I = Interest expense

Equation 13-9. The Change in Net Income

$$\%\triangle NI = \%\triangle EBIT \times DFL$$

where: $\%\triangle EBIT$ = Percent change in EBIT
DFL = Degree of financial leverage

Equation 13-10. Degree of Combined Leverage (DCL)

$$DCL: = \frac{\%\triangle NI}{\%\triangle Sales}$$

where: $\% NI$ = Percent change in net income
$\%\triangle SALES$ = Percent change in sales

Equation 13-11. Degree of Combined Leverage (DCL) (alternate 1):

$$DCL = \frac{Sales - VC}{Sales - VC - FC - I}$$

where: VC = Total variable Costs
FC = Total fixed Costs
I = Interest expense

Equation 13-12. Degree of Combined Leverage (DCL) (alternate 2):

$$DCL = DOL \times DFL$$

where: DOL = Degree of operating leverage
DFL = Degree of financial leverage

Equation 13-13. Change in Net Income (NI) as a Result of Combined Leverage:

$$\%\triangle NI = \%\triangle Sales \times DOL \times DFL$$

where: $\%\triangle Sales$ = Percent change in sales
DOL = Degree of operating leverage
DFL = Degree of financial leverage

Self-Test

ST-1. Mr. Marsalis's firm has fixed costs of $40,000, variable costs per unit of $4, and a selling price per unit of $9. What is Mr. Marsalis's breakeven level of sales (in units)?

ST-2. HAL's computer store has sales of $225,000, fixed costs of $40,000, and variable costs of $100,000. Calculate the degree of operating leverage (DOL) for this firm.

ST-3. HAL's computer store has operating income (EBIT) of $85,000 and interest expense of $10,000. Calculate the firm's degree of financial leverage (DFL).

ST-4. Kane Newspapers, Inc., has an after-tax cost of debt of 6 percent. The cost of equity is 14 percent. The firm believes that its optimal capital structure is 30 percent debt and 70 percent equity, and maintains its capital structure according to these weights. What is the weighted average cost of capital?

ST-5. Johnny Ringo's Western Shoppe expects its sales to increase by 20 percent next year. If this year's sales are $500,000, and the degree of operating leverage (DOL) is 1.4, what is the expected level of operating income (EBIT) for next year if this year's EBIT is $100,000?

ST-6. Marion Pardoo's Bookstore had a degree of operating leverage (DOL) of 1.6 and a degree of financial leverage (DFL) of 1.8. What is the company's degree of combined leverage (DCL)?

Review Questions

1. What is the operating leverage effect and what causes it? What are the potential benefits and negative consequences of high operating leverage?
2. Does high operating leverage always mean high business risk? Explain.
3. What is the financial leverage effect and what causes it? What are the potential benefits and negative consequences of high financial leverage?
4. Give two examples of types of companies likely to have high operating leverage. Find examples other than those cited in the chapter.
5. Give two examples of types of companies that would be best able to handle high debt levels.
6. What is an LBO? What are the risks for the equity investors and what are the potential rewards?
7. If an optimal capital structure exists, what are the reasons why too little debt is as undesirable as is too much debt?

Build Your Communication Skills

CS-1. Obtain balance sheet data from the library, the Internet, or some other source, and identify four companies having very high debt ratios and four having very low debt ratios. Write a one to two-page report describing the characteristics of the companies with high debt ratios and those with low debt ratios. Can you identify characteristics that seem to be common to the four high-debt firms? What are characteristics common to the four low-debt firms?

CS-2. Interview the owner of a small business in your community. Ask that person to describe the fixed operating costs and the variable costs of the business. Write a report, or give an oral presentation to your class on the nature of the business risk of this firm.

Problems

Breakeven Analysis

13-1. Technicians Guild manufactures molds for casting aluminum alloy test samples. Fixed costs amount to $20,000 per year. Variable costs for each unit manufactured is $16. Sales price per unit is $26.

    a. What is the contribution margin of the product?
    b. Calculate the breakeven point in unit sales and dollars.
    c. What is the operating profit (loss) if the company manufactures and sells
        (i) 1,500 units per year?
        (ii) 3,000 units per year?
    d. Plot a breakeven chart using the figures above.

Breakeven Analysis

13-2. Reliance Company, a competitor of Technicians Guild in problem 13-1, has a comparatively labor intensive process with old equipment. Fixed costs are $10,000 per year and variable costs are $22 per unit. Sales price is the same, $26 per unit.

    a. What is the contribution margin of the product?
    b. Calculate the breakeven point in unit sales and dollars.
    c. What is the operating profit (loss) if the company manufactures and sells
        (i) 1,500 units per year?
        (ii) 3,000 units per year?
    d. Plot a breakeven chart using the figures above.
    e. Comment on the profit and loss potential of Reliance Company compared to Technicians Guild.

Operating Leverage

13-3. Use the same data given in problem 13-1 (fixed cost = $20,000 per year, variable cost = $16 per unit, and sales price = $26 per unit) for Technicians Guild. The company sold 3,000 units in 1996 and expects to sell 3,300 units in 1997. Fixed costs, variable costs per unit, and sales price per unit are assumed to remain same in 1996 and 1997.

    a. Calculate the percentage change in operating income and compare it with the percentage change in sales.
    b. Comment on the operating leverage effect.
    c. Calculate the degree of operating leverage using
        (i) data for the years 1996 and 1997
        (ii) data for the year 1996 only
    d. Explain what the results obtained in (c) tell us.

Financial Leverage

13-4. Use the same data given in problems 13-1 and 13-3 (fixed cost = $20,000 per year, variable cost per unit = $16, sales price per unit = $26, 1996 sales = 3,000 units, and expected 1997 sales = 3,300 units) for Technicians Guild. Fixed costs, variable costs per unit, and sales price per unit are assumed to remain same in 1996 and 1997. The company has an interest expense of $2,000 per year. Applicable income tax rate is 30 percent.

    a. Calculate the percentage change in net income and compare it with the percentage change in operating income (EBIT).
    b. Comment on the financial leverage effect.
    c. Calculate the degree of financial leverage using
        (i) data for the years 1996 and 1997
        (ii) data for the year 1996 only
    d. Explain what the results obtained in (c) tell us about financial leverage.

Breakeven Analysis

13-5. Tony Manero owns a small company that refinishes and maintains the wood flooring of many discos in Brooklyn. Because of heavy use, his services are required at least quarterly by most of the clubs. Tony's annual fixed costs consist of depreciation expense for his van and polishing equipment, and other tools. These expenses were $9,000 this year. His variable costs include wood staining products, wax, and other miscellaneous supplies. Tony has been in this business since 1977 and accurately estimates his variable costs at $1.50 per square yard of dance floor. Tony charges a rate of $13 per square yard.

    a. How many square yards of dance floor will he need to work on this year to cover all of his expenses but leave him with zero operating income?

    b. What is this number called?

    c. Calculate the breakeven point in dollar sales.

    d. Tony has little competent competition in the Brooklyn area. What happens to the breakeven point in sales dollars if Tony increases his rate to $18 per square yard?

    e. At the $18 per square yard rate, what is Tony's operating income and net income if he completes work on 14,000 square yards this year. Assume his tax rate is 40 percent and he has a $25,000 loan outstanding on which he pays 12% interest annually.

13-6. Tom Rath's company manufactures and sells men's suits. His trademark gray flannel suits are popular on Wall Street and boardrooms throughout the East. Each suit sells for $650. Fixed costs are $200,000 and variable costs are $250 per suit.

Operating Leverage and Breakeven Analysis

    a. What is the firm's operating income on sales of 600 suits? On sales of 3,000 suits?

    b. What is Mr. Rath's degree of operating leverage (DOL) at a sales level of 600 suits? At a sales level of 3,000 suits?

    c. Calculate Mr. Rath's breakeven point in sales units and sales dollars.

    d. If the cost of the gray flannel material increases so that Mr. Rath's variable costs are now $350 per suit, what will be his new breakeven point in sales units and sales dollars?

    e. Considering the increase in variable costs, by how much will he need to increase the selling price per suit to reach the original operating income for sales of 3,000 suits calculated in part a)?

13-7. Three companies manufacture and sell identical products. They each sell 10,000 units annually at a price of $10 per unit. Assume Company A has $0 fixed costs and variable costs of $5 per unit. Company B has $10,000 in fixed costs and $4 in variable costs per unit. Company C has $40,000 fixed costs and $1 per unit variable costs.

Operating Leverage

    a. Calculate the operating income (EBIT) for each of the three companies.

    b. Before making any further calculations, rank the companies from highest to lowest by their relative degrees of operating leverage. Remember what you read about how fixed costs affect operating leverage.

13-8. Milan Peachbasket Corporation, a basketball hoop manufacturing firm in Hickory, Indiana, plans to branch out and begin producing basketballs in addition to basketball hoops. They have a choice of two different production methods for the basketballs. Method 1 will have variable costs of $6 per ball and fixed costs of $700,000 for the high-tech machinery, which requires little human supervision. Method 2 employs many people to hand-sew the basketballs. It has variable costs of $16.50 per ball, but fixed costs are estimated to only be $100,000. Regardless of which method CEO Norman Dale chooses, the basketballs will sell for $29 each. Marketing research indicates sales in the first year will be 50,000 balls. Sales volume is expected to increase to 60,000 in year 2.

Operating Leverage

    a. Calculate the sales revenue expected in years 1 and 2.

    b. Calculate the percentage change in sales revenue.

    c. Calculate the earnings before interest and taxes for each year for both production methods.

    d. Calculate the percentage change in EBIT for each method.

    e. Calculate the year one degree of operating leverage for each method, using your answers from parts b) and d) above.

    f. Calculate the degree of operating leverage again. This time use only revenue, fixed costs and variable costs from year 1 (your base year) for each production method.

g. Under which production method would EBIT be more adversely affected if the sales volume did not reach the expected levels?

h. What would drive this adverse effect on EBIT?

i. Recalculate the year 1 base year EBIT and the degree of operating leverage for both production methods if year 2 sales are expected to be only 53,000 units.

Financial Leverage

13-9. Three companies manufacture and sell identical products. They each have earnings before interest and taxes of $100,000. Assume Company A is an all-equity company and therefore has zero debt. Company B's capital structure is 10 percent debt and 90 percent equity. It makes annual interest payments of $2,000. Company C's capital structure is just the opposite of B. It has 90 percent debt and 10 percent equity. Company C has annual interest expense of $40,000. The tax rate for each of the three companies is 40%

a. Before making any calculations, rank the companies from highest to lowest by their relative degrees of financial leverage (DFL). Remember what you read about how debt and the interest expense which comes with it affects financial leverage.

b. Calculate the degree of financial leverage for each company. Was your answer to a) correct?

c. Calculate the net income for each company.

Financial Leverage

13-10. Michael Dorsey and Dorothy Michaels each own their own companies. They design and supply custom-made costumes for Broadway plays. The income statement from each company shows they each have earnings before interest and taxes of $50,000 this year. Mr. Dorsey has an outstanding loan for $70,000, on which he pays 13 percent interest annually. When she started her business, Ms. Michaels only needed to borrow $10,000. She is still paying 9 percent annual interest on the loan. Each company expects EBIT for next year to be $60,000. The tax rate for each is 40 percent and is not expected to change for next year.

a. Calculate the net income for each company for this year and next year.

b. Calculate the percentage change in net income for each company.

c. Calculate the percentage change in EBIT for each company.

d. Calculate this year's degree of financial leverage for each company using your answers from parts b) and c) above.

e. Calculate the degree of financial leverage for each company again. This time use only EBIT and interest expense for this year.

f. If earnings before interest and taxes do not reach the expected levels, in which company would net income be more adversely affected?

g. What would drive this adverse effect on net income?

h. Recalculate the degree of financial leverage and the net income expected for next year for both companies if EBIT only increases to $53,000.

Challenge Problem

13-11. Fanny Brice, owner of Funny Girl Comics, has sales revenue of $200,000, earnings before interest and taxes of $95,000, and net income of $30,000 this year. She is expecting sales to increase to $225,000 next year. The degree of operating leverage is 1.35 and the degree of financial leverage is relatively low at 1.09.

a. Calculate the percentage change in EBIT Ms. Brice can expect between this year and next year.

b. How much will EBIT be next year in dollars?

c. Calculate the percentage change in net income Ms. Brice can expect between this year and next year.

d. How much net income should Ms. Brice expect next year?

e. Calculate this year's degree of combined leverage (DCL).

f. Ms. Brice is considering a price increase. This would mean the percentage change in sales revenue between this year and next year would be 20 percent. If this is true, what net income (in dollars) can she expect for next year?

13-12. Clint Reno owns Real Cowboy, a western wear store that has current annual sales of $2,800,000 per year. The degree of operating leverage (DOL) is 1.4. EBIT is $600,000. Real Cowboy has $2 million in debt, on which it pays 10 percent annual interest. Calculate the degree of combined leverage for Real Cowboy.

Degree of Combined Leverage

13-13. Chad Gates owns Strings Attached, a store that sells guitars. The company has $5 million in current annual sales, fixed operating costs of $300,000 and $700,000 in variable operating costs, for a total EBT of $2.5 million. The firm has debt of $16,666,666.67, on which it pays 9 percent annual interest. The degree of combined leverage (DCL) for Strings Attached is 1.72.

DOL, DFL, and DCL Interactions

    a. Calculate the degree of operating leverage (DOL).
    b. What is the degree of financial leverage (DFL) for Strings Attached? Calculate your answer using the EBIT and interest expense figures and your knowledge of how DOL and DFL jointly determine DCL.
    c. If sales next year increase by 20 percent, what will be the percent change in net income?

13-14. Soccer International, Inc., produces and sells soccer balls. Partial information from the income statement for the years 1996 and 1997 is given below.

Comprehensive Problem

Soccer International, Inc.
Income Statement for the Year Ending December 31

	1996	1997
Sales Revenue	$560,000	616,000
Variable Costs	240,000	264,000
Fixed Costs	160,000	160,000
EBIT	—	—
Interest Expense	40,000	40,000
EBT	—	—
Income Taxes (30%)	—	—
Net Income	—	—

Soccer International sells each soccer ball for $14.

    a. Fill in the missing values in the income statements of 1996 and 1997.
    b. Calculate Soccer International's breakeven point in sales units 1996 and 1997.
    c. Calculate the breakeven point in dollar sales for 1996 and for 1997.
    d. How many soccer balls need to be sold to have an operating income of $200,000 in 1996?
    e. What is the operating profit (loss) if the company sells (i) 18,000 and (ii) 24,000 balls in 1996?
    f. Calculate the degree of operating leverage for the year 1996 and for 1997.
    g. If sales revenue is expected to increase by 10 percent in 1997, calculate the percentage increase in EBIT and the dollar amount of EBIT for 1997.
    h. Calculate the degree of financial leverage for the year 1996 and for 1997.
    i. Calculate the percentage change in net income and the dollar amount of net income expected in 1997.
    j. Calculate the degree of combined leverage for the year 1996 and for 1997.
    k. Assume Soccer International raises its selling price and that sales revenue increases to $650,000 in 1997. How much net income can be expected in 1997?

Answers to Self-Test

ST-1. Sales breakeven point (in units)
= $40,000 ÷ ($9.00 − $4.00) = 8,000 units

ST-2. Degree of operating leverage (DOL)
$= (\$225{,}000 - \$100{,}000) \div (\$225{,}000 - \$100{,}000 - \$40{,}000) = 1.47$

ST-3. Degree of financial leverage (DFL)
$= \$85{,}000 \div (\$85{,}000 - \$10{,}000) = 1.13$

ST-4. Weighted average cost of capital, k_a
$= (.3 \times 6\%) + (.7 \times 14\%) = 11.6\%$

ST-5. Next year's change in EBIT equals $20\% \times 1.4 \times$ this year's
EBIT $= \$100{,}000 \times 20\% \times 1.4$
$= \$100{,}000 \times 28\% = \$128{,}000$

ST-6. Degree of combined leverage (DCL) = DOL $\times$ DFL
$= 1.6 \times 1.8 = 2.88$

chapter 14

Corporate Bonds, Preferred Stock, and Leasing

The borrower is servant to the lender.

Proverbs 22:7

How Long Is Superlong?

When a company wants to borrow money from you, they offer you a bond. Then they pay you interest on the bond. How long would you be willing to let the company have your money at a fixed interest rate? Would you be willing to lend Coca Cola $20,000 at 6 percent interest for five years? How about twenty years?

Does half a century sound too long? Well, believe it or not, some companies are now offering hundred-year bonds! And investors are willing to buy them. For instance, investors scrambled to buy $500 million in hundred-year bonds from a subsidiary of the BellSouth corporation, a telecommunications company. They were also eager to buy hundred-year bonds from Columbia/HCA Healthcare Corporation that car-

ried a 7.5 percent coupon interest rate.

Of course, not all hundred-year bond offerings do well. When News

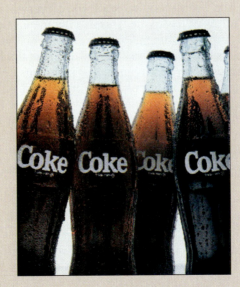

Chapter Objectives

After reading this chapter, you should be able to:

1. Describe the contract terms of a bond issue.

2. Distinguish the various types of bonds and describe their major characteristics.

3. Describe the key features of preferred stock.

4. Compare and contrast a genuine lease and a disguised purchase contract.

5. Explain why some leases must be shown on the balance sheet.

America, which publishes *TV Guide,* tried to offer hundred year bonds, investors were skeptical. Why? "This is a borderline-junk credit rating on a company in an industry that is changing dramatically," said Stephen Clark, a senior bond analyst at Technical Data. "Super-long debt is usually issued by companies known for their stability and the staying power of their products, like Coca Cola and Disneyland." ❄

Sources: Stephanie Storm, "A 'Supressing Debt' Offering Is Said to Draw Little Interest," *The New York Times* (November 30, 1995): C8; Zachary Schleps, "Balance Sheets That Get Well Soon," *Business Week,* (September 4, 1995).

CHAPTER OVERVIEW

In chapter 2 we examined the basic characteristics and terminology of corporate bonds. In chapter 9 we learned how to estimate the value of bonds. In this chapter we investigate how corporate bonds and preferred stock play a role in the financing decisions of a corporation. We also explore how leasing decisions affect a firm's finances.

To review bond information, see chapter 2, pages 25–28, and chapter 9, pages 206–211.

BOND BASICS

A **corporate bond** is a security that represents a promise by the issuing corporation to make certain payments to the owner of the bond, according to a certain schedule. The corporation that issues a bond is the debtor, and the investor who buys the bond is the creditor.

The **indenture** is the contract between the issuing corporation and the bond's purchaser. It spells out the various provisions of the bond issue, including the face value, coupon interest rate, interest payment dates, maturity date, and other details. The yield to maturity is not in the indenture, since it is market-determined and changes with market conditions. The major features of bond indentures are described in the next section.

The investment bankers who underwrite the new bond issue help the firm set the terms of that issue. This usually means obtaining a "rating" for the bonds from one or more of the major rating companies, such as Moody's and Standard & Poor's. Bond ratings shown in Table 14-1 reflect the likelihood that the issuer will make the promised interest and principal payments on time. Many institutional investors, the main purchasers of bonds, are prohibited, either by law or by client demands, from purchasing unrated bonds.

Bonds rated Baa3 or above by Moody's and BBB- or above by Standard & Poor's are called **investment grade bonds.** Bonds with lower than investment grade ratings (Ba1 or below by Moody's and BB+ or below by Standard & Poor's) are called **junk bonds.** We'll have more to say about junk bonds later in the chapter.

FEATURES OF BOND INDENTURES

In addition to the basic characteristics of the bond (interest, principal, maturity, and specific payment dates), the bond indenture specifies other features of the bond issue. These features include:

Table 14-1

Moody's and Standard & Poor's Bond Rating Categories

MOODY'S	STANDARD & POOR'S	REMARKS
Aaa	AAA	Best Quality
Aa1	AA+	
Aa2	AA	High Quality
Aa3	AA−	
A1	A+	
A2	A	Upper Medium Grade
A3	A−	
Baa1	BBB+	
Baa2	BBB	Medium Grade
Baa3	BBB−	
Ba1	BB+	
Ba2	BB	Speculative
Ba3	BB−	
B1	B+	
B2	B	Very Speculative
B3	B−	
Caa	CCC	
Ca	CC	Very, Very
C	C	Speculative
	D	In Default

- any security to be turned over to the bond's owner in the event the issuing corporation defaults
- the plan for paying off the bonds at maturity
- any provisions for paying off the bonds ahead of time
- any restrictions the issuing company places on itself to provide an extra measure of safety to the bondholder
- the name of an independent trustee to oversee the bond issue

Thus every feature of the bond issue is spelled out in the bond indenture.

Security

A person who buys a newly issued bond is, in effect, lending money to the issuing corporation for a specified period of time. Like creditors, bondholders are concerned about getting their money back. A provision in the loan agreement (the indenture) that provides security[1] to the lender in case of default will increase the bond's value, compared to a loan agreement without a security provision. The value is higher because the investor has an extra measure of protection. A bond that has a security provision in the indenture is a **secured bond.** A bond that does not pledge any specific asset(s) as security is a **debenture.** Debentures are backed only by the company's ability and willingness to pay.

---

[1]Chapter 2 used a different definition of security (a financial claim such as a stock or bond). Security has another definition, as used here. This definition is any asset (such as a piece of equipment, real estate, or a claim on future profits) that is promised to the investor in the event of a default.

Plans for Paying off the Bond Issue

Bonds are paid off, or retired, by a variety of means. Some of the more popular methods include *staggered maturities, sinking funds,* and *call provisions.*

Staggered Maturities   Some bond issues are packaged as a series of different bonds with different or staggered maturities. Every few years a portion of the bond issue matures and is paid off. Staggering maturities in this fashion allows the issuing company to retire the debt in an orderly fashion without facing a large one-time need for cash, as would be the case if the entire issue were to mature at once. **Serial payments** pay off bonds according to a staggered maturity schedule.

Sinking Funds   Although "sinking" is not an appealing word, sending your debt to the bottom of the ocean has its appeal. When a **sinking fund** provision is included in the bond's indenture, the issuing company makes regular contributions[2] to a fund that is used to buy back outstanding bonds. Putting aside a little money at a time in this fashion ensures that the amount needed to pay off the bonds will be available.

Call Provisions

Many corporate bonds have a provision in their indentures that allows the issuing corporation to pay off the bonds before the stated maturity date, at some stated price. This is known as a **call provision.** The price at which the bonds can be purchased before the scheduled maturity date is the *call price.*

Call provisions allow issuing corporations to refinance their debt if interest rates fall, just as homeowners refinance their mortgage loans when interest rates fall. For example, a company that issued bonds in 1988 with a 9 percent coupon interest rate would be making annual interest payments of 9 percent of $1,000, or $90 on each bond. Suppose that in 1999 the market rate of the company's bonds was 7 percent. If the bond indenture contained a call provision,[3] the company could issue 7 percent bonds in 1999 and use the proceeds from the issue to "call in" or pay off the 9 percent bonds. The company's new interest payments would be only 7 percent of $1,000, or $70, thus saving the company $20 on each bond each year.

When bonds are called, convention is that the call price the issuer must pay is generally more than the face value. This excess of the call price over the face value is known as the **call premium.** The call premium may be expressed as a dollar amount or as a percentage of par.

Figure 14-1 shows a notice in which the state of Hawaii called for all owners of its 5.625 percent 2003 bonds to send in their bonds for redemption at 100 percent ("the principal amount thereof" in the fine print). This is an unusual case, since the call premium is zero (the call price equals the par value). Note also that only the bonds with the listed serial numbers are being called in, not the entire issue. Call-

---

[2]These are called "contributions" in the same sense that the government refers to the money you pay into the Social Security system as contributions. You have no choice; you must pay. If a company fails to make its required contributions to a sinking fund as described in the indenture, the bond issue can be declared to be in default.

[3]If a bond issue is callable, there is usually a certain amount of time that must pass before the bonds can be called. This is known as a *deferred call provision.* The indenture specifies the call *date.* The issuer can call bonds in from investors on, or after, this call date.

Figure 14-1   State of Hawaii Notice of Bond Redemption

Figure 14-1 is an announcement by the state of Hawaii calling in part of a bond issue for the face value of the bonds.

Source: State of Hawaii Notice of Redemption, *The Wall Street Journal* (May 26, 1995): C5.

NOTICE OF REDEMPTION

State of Hawaii Airports System Revenue Bonds
Series 1971, 1972 and 1977

NOTICE IS HEREBY GIVEN that the State of Hawaii has duly called for redemption and will redeem prior to maturity, on July 1, 1995 (hereinafter referred to as the redemption date), pursuant to the provisions of Article V of the Certificate Of The Director Of Transportation Providing for the Issuance Of State Of Hawaii Airports System Revenue Bonds dated as of May 1, 1969 (the "Certificate") and upon the further terms and conditions as set forth in Section 6.01 of the Certificate and Section 3.02 of each Supplemental Certificate thereof as follows: the Fourth Supplemental Certificate Of The Director Of Transportation Providing For The Issuance Of State Of Hawaii Airports System Revenue Bonds, Series Of 1971, dated as of July 1, 1971 (the "Fourth Supplemental Certificate"); the Fifth Supplemental Certificate Of The Director Of Transportation Providing For The Issuance Of State Of Hawaii Airports System Revenue Bonds, Second Series of 1971, dated as of October 1, 1971 (the "Fifth Supplemental Certificate"); the Sixth Supplemental Certificate Of The Director Of Transportation Providing For The Issuance Of State Of Hawaii Airports System Revenue Bonds, Series Of 1972, dated as of October 1, 1972 (the "Sixth Supplemental Certificate"); the Tenth Supplemental Certificate Of The Director Of Transportation Providing for The Issuance Of State Of Hawaii Airports System Revenue Bonds, Series Of 1977, dated as of December 1, 1977 (the "Tenth Supplemental Certificate"), bonds of the Series of bonds the distinctive numbers which have been drawn by lot for such redemption as follows:

$930,000 Series of 1977, 5.625%, Due July 1, 2003 CUSIP 419794 EK4

Coupon Bonds each called in the amount of $5,000

1505	1910	2189	2235	2292	2411	2462	2499	2979	2985	3028	3190	3311	3321	3572	3582	3619	3863	3884	3957
1579	2160	2203	2236	2300	2412	2463	2500	2982	2986	3115	3192	3312	3389	3573	3617	3861	3882	3898	3958
1580	2161	2206	2290	2373	2426	2464	2581	2983	2987	3116	3193	3313	3432	3581	3618	3862	3883	3899	
1909	2162	2234	2291	2410	2427	2498	2582	2984	3027	3117	3194	3314	3486						

CHECK THE BONDS YOU HOLD AGAINST THE BOND NUMBERS OF THE VARIOUS BOND ISSUES LISTED ON THIS NOTICE TO DETERMINE IF YOU ARE AFFECTED BY THIS CALL FOR REDEMPTION. IF YOUR BOND IS NOT LISTED, PLEASE DISREGARD THIS NOTICE.

The Bonds specified above, or the specified portions thereof, as the case may be, are to be redeemed from moneys paid into or credited to the Sinking Fund Account, in the Airport Revenue Fund for the Redemption of such Bonds pursuant to priority item FOURTH Supplemental Certificate, the Fifth Supplemental Certificate, the Sixth Supplemental Certificate, and the Tenth Supplemental Certificate on July 1, 1995, the date on which they become due and payable, the redemption price equal to the principal amount thereof, together with an amount equal to accrued and unpaid interest to the date fixed for redemption.

On and after the redemption date, interest on said Bonds specified above, or the specified portions thereof to be redeemed, as the case may be, will cease to accrue and the coupons for interest becoming due after the redemption date shall be void. Upon presentation and surrender of such bonds with all coupons (in the case of Coupon Bonds) appertaining thereto maturing after the date fixed for redemption, payment will be made at the said redemption price at the principal office of Bankers Trust Company, Corporate Trust & Agency Group, 123 Washington Street, 1st Floor Window, New York, New York 10006 (or if by mail, P.O. Box 2579, Church Street Station, Attn: Bond Redemption Unit, New York, New York 10008), or at the office of the Director of Finance of the State of Hawaii, 250 South Hotel Street, 1st Floor, Room 104 (or if by mail, P.O. Box 150), Honolulu, Hawaii 96810-0150.

Coupons due July 1, 1995 should be detached and presented for payment in the usual manner.

In the case of any fully registered Bond to be redeemed in part only, on or after the redemption date, upon surrender of such Bond, a new Bond or Bonds in the principal amount equal to the unredeemed portion thereof will be issued.

All holders presenting bonds for redemption must submit a completed Department of the Treasury Internal Revenue Service Form W-9 with said Bonds. Failure to provide a completed Form W-9 will result in 31% backup withholding tax to holders pursuant to the Interest and Dividend Tax Compliance Act of 1983. Copies of Form W-9 may be obtained from the Internal Revenue Service or such other location as Internal Revenue Service Forms are generally available.

If you have any questions please call 1-800-879-BOND (800-879-2663) or call Bankers Trust at 1-800-735-7777.

Earl I. Anzai, *Director of Finance*
State of Hawaii

Dated: May 26, 1995

The CUSIP numbers set forth above are included solely for the convenience of Bondholders. The State of Hawaii shall not be responsible for the selection, accuracy or use of the CUSIP numbers, and no representation is made as to the correctness of the CUSIP numbers on the Bonds called for redemption or as indicated in this notice.

---

ing in part of a bond issue is one of many procedures that may be used in calling bonds.

Issuing new bonds to replace old bonds is known as a **refunding** operation. Remember, the option to call a bond is held by the issuing corporation. The owners of the bonds have no choice in the matter. If investors don't turn in their bonds when the bonds are called, they receive no further interest or principal payments.

A company approaches a bond refunding the same way it does any capital budgeting decision. The primary incremental cash inflows come from the interest savings realized when old high-interest debt is replaced with new low-interest debt. The primary incremental cash outflows are the call premium, if any, and the flotation costs associated with the new bond issue. All these variables must be adjusted for taxes and then evaluated by the firm. If the net present value of the incremental cash flows associated with the refunding is greater than or equal to zero, the refunding is done.

If the NPV is negative, the company allows the old bonds to remain outstanding. This is the same thing you do when deciding whether to refinance a mortgage loan on a home.

Occasionally, a corporation will refund a bond issue even though there are no significant interest savings to be had. If the outstanding bonds have indenture provisions that the issuing company now finds oppressive or too limiting, the old bonds could be called and new bonds issued without the offending features. Appendix 14A covers refunding in detail, and solves a sample refunding problem.

Restrictive Covenants

A company that seeks to raise debt capital by issuing new bonds often makes certain promises to would-be investors to convince them to buy the bonds being offered, or to make it possible to issue the bonds at a lower interest rate. These promises made by the issuer to the investor, to the benefit of the investor, are **restrictive covenants.** They represent something like a courtship. If the suitor does not give certain assurances as to the way the other party will be treated, there is little chance the relationship will blossom.

In a bond issuer–bond investor relationship, these assurances may include: limitations on future borrowings, restrictions on dividends, and minimum levels of working capital maintained.

Limitations on Future Borrowings
Investors who lend money to a corporation by buying its bonds expect that the corporation will not borrow excessively in the future. A company in too much debt may be unable to pay bond principal and interest payments on time. Bond investors would be worried if, after buying the bonds of a firm with a 20 percent debt-to-total-assets ratio, the company then issued $100 million of additional bonds, increasing that ratio to over 90 percent. The new debt would make the earlier issued bonds instantly more risky and lower their price in the market.

A restrictive covenant in which the corporation promises not to issue a large amount of future debt would protect the company's current bondholders from falling bond ratings and plunging market prices. A bond issue with this restriction in the indenture will have more value than a bond issue without this guarantee. As a result, the bonds could be issued at a lower coupon interest rate than bonds without the restriction in the indenture.

We explained the debt-to-total-assets ratio in chapter 5, page 88.

Restrictions on Dividends
An indenture may also include restrictions on the payment of common stock dividends if a firm's times interest earned ratio drops below a specified level. This restriction protects the bondholders against the risk of the common stockholders withdrawing value (cash for dividends that may be needed to make future interest payments) from the firm during difficult times. The bondholders are supposed to have priority over common stockholders. A bond issue with this sort of protection for investors can be issued at a lower interest rate than a bond issue without it.

Minimum Levels of Working Capital
Current assets can generally be quickly and easily converted to cash to pay bills. Having a good liquidity position protects all creditors, including bondholders. Minimum working capital guarantees in an

indenture provide an additional margin of protection for bondholders and therefore reduce the interest rate required on such bonds.

The Independent Trustee of the Bond Issue

Violations of any of the provisions included in the indenture could constitute a default. Therefore an independent **trustee** is named in the indenture to oversee the bond issue and to make sure all the provisions spelled out in the indenture are adhered to. The trustee is usually a commercial bank.

Most people think a default is a failure to make a scheduled interest or principal payment on time. Actually, this is only one possible type of default because the promise to pay interest and principal on their due dates is only part of the promise made by the bond issuer in the indenture. Failure to keep any of the substantive promises mentioned in the indenture constitutes a default.

Types of Bonds

Some of the more innovative new financial instruments have been developed in the bond market. Let's now look more closely at the many kinds of bonds, both traditional and new.

Secured Bonds

A secured bond is backed by specific assets pledged by the issuing corporation. In the event of a default, the investors in these secured bonds would have a claim on these assets.

Mortgage Bonds   A bond backed by real assets (not financial assets) is known as a **mortgage bond.** When you buy a house and finance the purchase with a mortgage loan, you are pledging your house (a real asset) as collateral for that loan. You are issuing a mortgage bond to the lender. That is what corporations do when they pledge real assets, such as airplanes and railroad cars, as collateral for the bonds issued to purchase those assets.

Different mortgage bonds can be issued that pledge the same real assets as collateral. Different classes of mortgage bonds signal the priority each investor has on the asset. An investor in a **first mortgage** bond has first claim on the proceeds from the sale of the pledged assets if there is a default. A later lender may be an investor in a **second mortgage** bond. In the event of default, the holder of the second mortgage receives proceeds from the sale of the pledged assets only after the first mortgage bond investors have received all payments due to them. Similarly, third mortgage bonds, fourth mortgage bonds, and so forth can be issued with correspondingly lower priorities.

Unsecured Bonds (Debentures)

A bond that is not backed by any collateral is called a debenture. A debenture is backed only by the ability and willingness of the issuing corporation to make the promised interest and principal payments as scheduled. If a debenture were to go into default, the bondholders would be unsecured creditors. They would only have a general claim on the issuing company, not a right to the firm's specific assets.

There may be different classes of debentures. Certain issues may have a higher priority for payment than do others. If bond issue A has priority for payment over bond issue B, according to their respective indentures, then bond issue A is said to be a **senior debenture** and bond issue B is said to be a **subordinated debenture.** A senior debenture has a prior claim to the earnings and liquidation proceeds from the general assets of the firm (those assets not specifically pledged as security for other bonds) relative to the claim of subordinated debenture investors.

Subordinated debentures have a lower priority claim on the firm's earnings and assets. Because subordinated debentures are riskier than senior debentures, investors demand and issuers pay higher interest rates on them. This higher interest rate is consistent with the risk–return relationship—the greater the risk of a security, the greater the required rate of return. Holders of first mortgage bonds assume less risk than holders of second mortgage bonds. Debenture holders have more risk than do secured bondholders, and subordinated debenture holders have more risk than senior debenture holders. Preferred stock investors take more risk than a bond investor, and common stock investors take more risk still for a given company. This risk hierarchy, reflecting the relative priority of claims, is shown in Figure 14-2.

Figure 14-2 **The Risk Hierarchy**

Figure 14-2 shows the different priorities of claims that creditors and investors have on a company in default. Mortgage bondholders are paid first, whereas common stockholders are paid last.

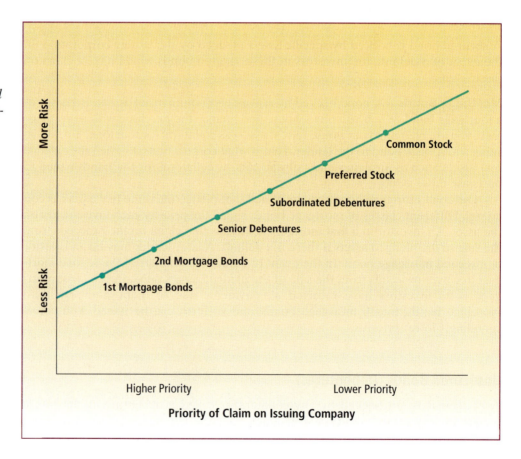

Convertible Bonds

One of the special types of bonds available is called a **convertible bond.** A convertible bond is a bond that may be converted, at the option of the bond's owner, into a certain amount of another security issued by the same company. In the vast majority of the cases, the other security is common stock.[4] This means that the investor who bought the convertible bond may send it back to the issuing company and "convert" it into a certain number of shares of that company's common stock.

Features of Convertible Bonds   Convertible bonds have a face value, coupon rate, interest payment frequency, and maturity spelled out in their indenture, as do regular nonconvertible bonds. The indenture also spells out the terms of conversion, if the investor chooses to exercise that option. If the bond's owner elects not to convert the bond, the owner continues to receive interest and principal payments as with any other bond.

The Conversion Ratio.   Each convertible bond has a conversion ratio. The **conversion ratio** is the number of shares of common stock that an investor would get if the convertible bond were converted. For example, California Microwave, Inc., issued a convertible $1,000 bond that matures in 2003, with a conversion ratio of 35.1648. That means the bond's owner can trade in the bond for 35.1648 shares of California Microwave common stock at any time.

The Conversion Value.   To find the conversion value of a bond, multiply the conversion ratio by the market price per share of the company's common stock, as shown in Equation 14-1:

Formula for the Conversion Value of a Convertible Bond

$$\text{conversion value} = \text{conversion ratio} \times \text{stock price} \tag{14-1}$$

The **conversion value** is the amount of money bond owners receive if they convert the bond to common stock and then sell the common stock. For example, if the California Microwave, Inc., stock were selling for $20, then the conversion value of the convertible bond described in Table 14-2 would be as follows:

$$\text{Conversion value} = \text{conversion ratio} \times \text{stock price}$$
$$= 35.1648 \times \$20.00$$
$$= \$703.30$$

Equation 14-1 shows us that at a rate of $20 per common stock share, the conversion value of the convertible bond is $703.30.

The Straight Bond Value.   If a convertible bond is not converted into stock, then it is worth at least the sum of the present values of its interest and principal payments.[5] The value coming from the interest and principal is called the convertible bond's **straight bond value.** The discount rate used to compute this straight bond value is the required rate of return for a nonconvertible bond having characteristics (risk, maturity, tax treatment, and liquidity) similar to the convertible bond.

---

[4]Some convertible bonds can be converted into a certain amount of preferred stock or some other security issued by the company.
[5]Equation 9-2 in chapter 9 gives the present value of a bond's interest and principal payments.

Table 14-2

California Microwave, Inc., Convertible Bond Characteristics

Maturity Date:	December 15, 2003
Face Value:	$1,000
Type of Interest:	Semiannual, paid on June 15 and December 15
Coupon Interest Rate:	5¼%
Conversion Ratio:	35.1648

Source: Prospectus, $50,000,000 California Microwave, Inc., 5¼% Convertible Subordinated Notes Due 2003, Bear, Stearing & Co. Inc., and Oppenheimer & Co., Inc., Underwriters

As shown in Table 14-2, the California Microwave Corporation's convertible bond has a coupon interest rate of 5¼ percent and a maturity date of December 15, 2003. The bond was issued in 1996. With a face value of $1,000, the annual interest payments will be $52.50 ($1,000 × .0525). Since interest is paid semiannually, actual interest payments of $26.25 ($52.50 ÷ 2) are made twice a year for fourteen semiannual periods (7 years × 2 semiannual periods per year.)[6] If the required rate of return on similar nonconvertible bonds is 8 percent annual interest (4 percent semiannually),[7] then according to Equation 9-2, the bond's straight bond value as of December 15, 1996, follows:

$$V_{Bond} = \$26.25 \times \left[\frac{1 - \dfrac{1}{(1.04)^{14}}}{.04} \right] + \$1,000 \times \frac{1}{(1.04)^{14}}$$

$$= \$26.25 \times 10.563123 + \$1,000 \times .577475$$

$$= \$277.281 + \$577.475$$

$$= \$854.76$$

We find that the present value of a seven-year, semiannual convertible bond with a face value of $1,000, and an 8 percent annual coupon interest rate is $854.76.

A rational investor may convert a bond if advantageous, but will not convert it if disadvantageous. A convertible bond, then, is always worth the conversion value or the straight bond value, whichever is greater.

Variable Rate Bonds

Although most corporate bonds pay a fixed rate of interest (the coupon interest rate is constant), some pay a variable rate. With a **variable rate bond,** the initial coupon rate is adjusted according to an established timetable and a market rate index. Figure 14-3 shows an ad for a variable rate bond issued by the Student Loan Marketing Association (Sallie Mae).

The interest rate on the SallieMae bond in Figure 14-3 is tied to ninety-one day Treasury bills. However, variable bond rates could be tied to any rate, such as a

---

[6]December 15, 2003, is seven years (fourteen semiannual periods) in the future from December 15, 1996.

[7]If 8 percent were the annual required market rate of return, then the corresponding semiannual required rate of return would be 3.923 percent ($1.03923^2 - 1 = .08$ or 8 percent) and not 4 percent. We will round this to 4 percent to simplify the calculation.

Figure 14-3

Announcement of SallieMae Bonds with Variable Rates

Figure 14-3 is an announcement of a variable rate bond issue offered by the Student Loan Marketing Association. The bond coupon interest rates will vary according to the rates for U.S. ninety-one-day Treasury Bills.

Source: Student Loan Marketing Association, May 9, 1995.

New Issue   May 9, 1995

SallieMae

Short Term Floating Rate Notes
$600,000,000

Dated May 11, 1995   Due November 9, 1995
Price 100%   Cusip #86387T EC8   Series 11-95

The interest rate of the Notes will be subject to weekly adjustment on the calendar day following each auction of 91-Day Treasury bills, and will be equal to 15 basis points above the "91-Day Treasury Bill Rate" (expressed on a bond equivalent basis). Interest on the Notes is paid at maturity and accrues from May 11, 1995. The Notes will be issued only in book-entry form.

These Notes are the obligations of the Student Loan Marketing Association, a federally chartered, stockholder-owned corporation, and are not obligations of or guaranteed by the United States. The Notes are legal for investment by savings banks, insurance companies, trustees and other fiduciaries under the law of many states.

This offering is made by the Student Loan Marketing Association with the assistance of a designated Selling Group of securities dealers.

Denise McGlone
Executive Vice President
and Chief Financial Officer

For more details, contact the Corporate Finance Department at 1-800-321-7179.

Student Loan Marketing Association
1050 Thomas Jefferson Street, N.W., Washington, D.C. 20007

This announcement appears as a matter of record only.

Treasury bond rate or the London Interbank Offer Rate (LIBOR). Bond issuers check this market rate on every adjustment date specified in the indenture and reset the coupon rate accordingly.

The variable rate protects investors from much of the interest rate risk inherent in fixed-rate bonds. Rising inflation hurts investors in fixed-rate bonds because the price of fixed-rate bonds falls as rising inflation increases an investor's required rate of return. In times of rising inflation, the price of a variable rate bond does not fall as much because the investor knows that a coupon rate adjustment will occur to adjust to new, higher interest rates. However, investors who buy bonds with fixed coupon interest rates will be better off when market interest rates are falling. A variable rate bond would have its coupon rate drop as market interest rates fell.

An issuing corporation can benefit from issuing variable rate bonds if market rates are historically high and a drop in rates is expected. Of course, high rates can rise even further, in which case the issuing company could lose money.

Putable Bonds

A **putable bond** is a bond that can be cashed in before maturity at the option of the bond's owner. This is like the callable bond described earlier in the chapter, except that the positions of the issuer and the bond's owner with respect to the option have been reversed. Investors may exercise the option to redeem their bonds early when it is in their best interest to do so. Investors usually redeem fixed rate bonds if interest rates have risen. The existing, lower-interest rate bond can be redeemed and the proceeds used to buy a new higher-interest rate bond.

Junk Bonds

Another type of bond that has become popular (and controversial) is the junk bond. Junk bonds, also known as *high yield bonds,* have a bond rating below investment grade. As shown earlier in this chapter, according to Moody's ratings, a Junk bond would have a rating of Ba1 or below; according to Standard and Poor's ratings, it would have a rating of BB+ or below. The name "junk" is perhaps unfairly applied, because these bonds are usually not trash; they are simply riskier than bonds having an investment grade. For instance, many bonds used to finance corporate takeovers have below investment grade ratings.

Some junk bonds start out with investment grade ratings, but then suffer a downgrade—the issuing company may have fallen on hard financial times, or may have gone through a major financial restructuring that increased the risk of the outstanding bonds. Such junk bonds are known as *fallen angels.* One example of a fallen angel is the January 1996 downgrade of K-Mart bonds to junk bond status because the company's financial health had deteriorated considerably.

RJR Nabisco bonds were also downgraded to junk bond status after a leveraged buyout (LBO). The bondholders sued RJR/Nabisco alleging that the company did not treat bondholders fairly or in good faith. It can be argued, however, that bondholders can reduce the risk of fallen angels by insisting on a protective provision in the indenture. Indeed, because of the RJR/Nabisco LBO and similar restructurings, bond investors have been reading their indentures more closely.

International Bonds

An **international bond** is a bond sold in countries other than where the corporate headquarters of the issuing company is located. The bonds may be denominated in the currency of the issuing company's country, or in the currency of the country in which the bonds are sold. Foreign corporations issue bonds in the United States, sometimes denominated in their home currencies and sometimes in U.S. dollars. In turn, U.S. corporations frequently issue bonds outside the United States. These bonds may be denominated in U.S. dollars or in some other currency.

Eurobonds are bonds denominated in the currency of the issuing company's home country, and sold in another country. For example, if General Motors issued a dollar-denominated bond in Italy it would be called a Eurobond. Similarly, if Ferrari, an Italian company, issued a lira-denominated bond

ETHICAL CONNECTIONS

Repealing a Subsidy Generates Trash Talk

What if you bought a municipal bond, thinking it was backed by the municipality or state that issued it, and then you found out that backing was not there?

That's exactly what happened to many investors in municipal bonds, thanks to Illinois. Illinois Governor Jim Edgar recently signed into law a bill that had been hotly contested by the mutual fund industry because it yanked away a subsidy shoring up the credit-worthiness of some $500 million in incinerator bonds.

Why? Struggling to contain their costs, some municipal officials felt investors got too good a deal on certain bonds. Governor Edgar signed legislation repealing a waste-incinerator subsidy that could have cost the state $4 billion over twenty years. That put into question the repayment on $500 million in bonds sold to finance three projects.

Governor Edgar signed the bill despite Wall Street's warning that Illinois could find it difficult to finance its activities after having pulled the rug out from under bondholders. Governor Edgar retorted by calling such talk "blackmail."

Even though bondholders are calling the repeal a double-cross, Governor Edgar also pointed out that investors should have been aware that the subsidies would be pulled. He noted that he had promised to repeal the law. Indeed, legislation for repeal had repeatedly been pushed in the state legislature. "Investors would have been fully aware," Governor Edgar said. "They took a chance and lost. They have only themselves to blame."

Meanwhile, the companies that are building the waste-incinerators are suing the State of Illinois for "an unconstitutional impairment of preexisting contracts." Now, instead of having the state help pay their way, the waste-incinerators are going to have to attract enough garbage at a disposal price of $40 to $45 a ton to survive.

All in all, it is a bond mess that some claim is as messy as the trash that will be burned at the new incinerators.

Questions to Consider

▶ Do you think the State of Illinois treated the bondholders fairly? What about taxpayers? The companies building the incinerators? Explain your answer.

▶ Should the buyers of the bonds be upset? After all, they were warned.

▶ Should Wall Street downgrade the rating of Illinois state bonds? Explain your answer.

Sources: Charles Gasparino and Jeff Bailey, "Muni Buyers Get a Scare About High-Yield Debt," *The Wall Street Journal* (March 15, 1996): C1; Judith Crown, "Tallying the Cost of Edgar's Subsidy Cut," *Crain's Chicago Business* (March 18, 1996).

---

in the United States, the bond would be called a Eurobond. If the Ferrari bond were denominated in dollars instead of lira, it would be referred to as a *Yankee bond.*

Take Note

Be careful not to confuse Eurobonds with Eurodollars. Eurodollars are dollar-denominated deposits in banks outside the U.S.

Super Long-Term Bonds

As the chapter opener mentioned, the Disney Corporation, BellSouth, and other corporations have issued bonds with a maturity of one hundred years. One hundred years is a much longer maturity than is typical among corporate bond issuers. Investors who purchase these bonds must have confidence in the future cash flow of these companies.

In this section we have described types of bonds. Next, we examine preferred stock, its characteristics, and those who purchase it.

PREFERRED STOCK

Preferred stock is so-called because owners of preferred stock have a priority claim over common stockholders to the earnings and assets of a corporation. That is, preferred stockholders receive their dividends before common stockholders do. Preferred stock is not issued by many corporations except in certain industries, such as public utilities.

The preferred stock dividend is usually fixed from year to year, so the potential return on investment for a preferred stockholder is not as high as it is for a common stockholder. Common stockholders are entitled to all residual income of the firm (which could be considerable).

Preferred stock is known as a hybrid security. It is a hybrid because it has both debt and equity characteristics. Preferred stock is like debt primarily because preferred stockholders do not have an ownership claim, nor do they have any claim on the residual income of the firm. It is also like equity because it has an infinite maturity and a lower priority claim against the firm than the bondholders have.

Preferred Stock Dividends

Issuers of preferred stock generally promise to pay a fixed dollar amount of dividends to the investor. This promise, however, does not result in bankruptcy if it is broken. Unlike failure to make a scheduled interest or principal payment to bondholders, failure to pay a scheduled dividend to preferred stockholders is not grounds for bankruptcy of the company that issued the preferred stock.

Occasionally, *participating preferred stock* is issued. This type of preferred stock offers the chance for investors to share the benefits of rising earnings with the common stockholders. This is quite rare, however.

Preferred stock can be either *cumulative* or *noncumulative* with respect to its dividends. With cumulative preferred stock, if a dividend is missed, it must be paid at a later date before dividends may resume to common stockholders. Seldom is any interest paid, however, to compensate preferred stockholders for the fact that when dividends are resumed, they are received later than when promised. Noncumulative preferred stock does not make up missed dividends. If the dividends are skipped, they are lost forever to the investors.

Preferred Stock Investors

Corporations can exclude 70 percent of the dividend income received on preferred stock issued by another corporation from their taxable income. As a result, corporations are the major investors in preferred stock. The tax exclusion is higher if the investor corporation owns more than 20 percent of the common stock of the other corporation.

Because of the favorable tax treatment corporations receive on this dividend income, they bid up the price on preferred stock, thus lowering the expected rate of return. The lower expected rate of return is the price they pay for receiving the preferential tax treatment. Individuals cannot exclude any dividend income on their personal tax returns and must pay taxes on all of it, so preferred stock is not often recommended by financial planners as a good investment for individuals.

LEASING

Debt is often incurred to acquire an asset. An alternative to borrowing and buying an asset is to lease the asset. A **lease** is an arrangement where one party that owns an asset contracts with another party to use that asset for a specified period of time, without conveying legal ownership of that asset. The party who owns the asset is known as the **lessor.** The party who uses the asset is the **lessee.** The lessee makes lease payments to the lessor for the right to use the asset for the specified time period.

A lease contract that is long-term and non-cancelable is very similar to a debt obligation, from the perspective of the lessee. Some contracts that look like genuine leases are not, according to federal tax laws. There are different types of lease contracts. These different types have different accounting treatments, which we turn to next.

Genuine Leases versus Fakes

When a business leases an asset, the entire amount of the lease payments made by the lessee to the lessor is tax deductible to the lessee. When bonds are issued, or a bank loan obtained, only the interest portion of the loan payment is tax deductible. This sometimes leads a company to enter into a contract that looks like a lease, to obtain the large tax deductions, but which is not in fact a lease. The IRS is ever vigilant in ferreting out these fake lease contracts and denying the associated deductions.

To illustrate, suppose you needed a new truck for your business. The purchase price of the truck you want is $40,000. If you buy the truck and depreciate it over five years (ignore the half-year convention), you would have tax-deductible depreciation expense of $8,000 per year for five years. What if instead of buying the truck for $40,000, you leased it from the truck dealer for $40,000 in up-front cash, followed by additional lease payments of $1 per year for four years and then an option to buy the truck at the end of five years for $10? The extra $14 paid, with the exercising of the purchase option, would be a drop in the bucket compared to the tax savings you would realize in year one from the $40,000 tax deduction for the "lease payments." Because money has time value, a $40,000 deduction in year 1 is much preferred to deductions of $8,000 per year for five years.

The above lease is a sham, a fake. What we have here is an installment purchase, disguised as a lease. In an audit, the IRS would deny the $40,000 year 1 "lease payment" and reclassify the deduction as a (much lower) depreciation expense. Your business would probably also be hit with interest charges and penalties.

The IRS standards for a genuine lease are as follows:

1. The remaining life of the asset at the end of the lease term must be the greater of 20 percent of the original useful life or one year.
2. The term of the lease must be thirty years or less.
3. The lease payments must provide the lessor with a reasonable rate of return.
4. Renewal options must contain terms consistent with the market value of the asset.
5. Purchase options must be for an amount close to the asset's fair market value at the time the option is exercised.
6. The property must not be limited use (custom made for only one firm's use) property.

You can see immediately that in our truck example, the purchase option specifies a price ($10) that is much lower than the fair market value of the truck in five years. The IRS would consider this "lease" to be a sham.

Operating and Financial (Capital) Leases

Once a lease passes the tests for being classified as a genuine lease, it must be further classified for accounting purposes as an *operating* or *financial (capital) lease*. An **operating lease** has a term substantially shorter than the useful life of the asset and is usually cancelable by the lessee. A **financial (capital) lease** is long-term and non-cancelable. The lessee uses up most of the economic value of the asset by the end of the lease's term with a financial lease.

If you went on a business trip and leased a car for the week to make your business calls, this would be an operating lease. This same car will be leased again to many other customers and in one week you will use up a small fraction of the car's economic value. Your company, which is paying your travel expenses, would deduct these lease payments as business expenses on the income statement.

If your company signed a ten-year, non-cancelable lease on a $20 million super-computer, this is likely to be a financial lease (also known as a capital lease). After ten years the supercomputer is likely to be obsolete. Your company would have used up most, if not all, its economic value by the end of the ten-year lease period. The lessor surely would demand lease payments high enough to recognize this fact and also to compensate for the time value of money that is paid over a ten-year period. The fact that the payments are spread out over time means that the lessor must be compensated for the cost of the asset and also for the delay in the receipt of the lease payments.

Accounting Treatment of Leases

Both operating and financial (capital) lease payments show up on the income statement. Assuming that the lease is genuine, payments made by the lessee to the lessor are shown on the income as tax-deductible business expenses for both types of leases. These are costs of doing business for the lessee.

Financial leases have another accounting impact, however, that operating leases do not. A financial lease also shows up on the company's balance sheet because it is functionally equivalent to buying the asset and financing the purchase with borrowed money. If the asset had been purchased and financed with debt, the asset and the liability associated with the debt would both show up on the balance sheet. Since a financial lease is functionally equivalent to a purchase financed with debt, the Financial Accounting Standards Board (FASB) has ruled that the accounting treatment should be similar.

Failure to make a bond payment can lead to bankruptcy, as can failure to make a contractual lease payment on a non-cancelable lease. The leased asset is shown in the asset section of the lessee's balance sheet, with a corresponding liability entry in the amount of the present value of all the lease payments owed to the lessor.

A lease is classified as a financial (capital) lease if it meets *any one* of the following four criteria:

1. Ownership of the asset is transferred to the lessee at the end of the lease's term.
2. There is an option for the lessee to buy the asset as a bargain purchase price at the end of the lease period.

3. The lease period is greater than or equal to 75 percent of the estimated useful life of the asset.
4. The present value of the lease payments equals 90 percent or more of the fair market value of the asset at the time the lease is originated, using the lower of the lessee's cost of debt or the lessor's rate of return on the lease as the discount rate.

Only if none of these four criteria applies is the lease considered an operating lease, with no balance sheet entry.

Lease or Buy?

Leasing is growing in popularity. Whether an asset should be leased or bought depends on the relative costs of the two alternatives. Leasing is most nearly comparable to a buy–borrow alternative. Since signing a debt contract is similar to signing a lease contract, comparisons are usually made between the lease option and the buy with borrowed funds option.

The alternative that has the lower present value of after-tax costs is usually chosen. The tax factor considered for the lease alternative would be the tax deductibility of the lease payments that would be made (assuming the lease is genuine and passes IRS muster). The tax factors for the buy with borrowed funds alternative would come primarily from two sources. One is the tax deduction that comes with the payment of interest on the borrowed funds. The other is the tax deduction that comes with the depreciation expense on the purchased asset.

Companies that are likely to see a clear advantage to leasing instead of buying are those that are losing money. Such companies, because they have negative taxable income, pay no taxes. The deductions for interest and depreciation expenses could not be used (subject to carry back and carry forward provisions of losses to earlier or later years). If the asset is leased instead from a profitable lessor, the lessor can take advantage of the interest and depreciation expense tax deductions and the lessee can negotiate a lease payment that is lower than it otherwise would be, so that these tax benefits are shared by the lessor and the lessee.

Many airlines are losing money. The next time you take a plane trip, look for a small sign just inside the passenger entrance of the plane. It may say that the airplane you are about to travel on is owned by a leasing company (the lessor) and leased by the airline (the lessee).

WHAT'S NEXT

In this chapter we learned about the basic characteristics of bonds and the different types of bonds available. We also examined preferred stock and leasing. In chapter 15 we will discuss common stock, how it is issued, and the nature of the equity claim of the common stockholders.

Summary

1. Describe the contract terms of a bond issue.

The indenture is the contract that spells out the terms of the bond issue. A call provision gives the issuer the option to buy back the bonds before the scheduled maturity date. A conversion provision gives the bondholder the option to exchange the bond for a given number of shares of stock. Restrictive covenants may include limits on future borrowings by the issuer, minimum working capital levels that must be maintained, and restrictions on dividends paid to common stockholders.

2. *Distinguish the various types of bonds and describe their major characteristics.*

All bonds are debt instruments that give the holder a liability claim on the issuer. A mortgage is a bond secured by real property. A debenture is an unsecured bond. A convertible bond is convertible, at the option of the bondholder, into a certain number of shares of common stock (sometimes preferred stock or another security).

A variable rate bond has a coupon interest rate that is not fixed, but is tied to a market interest rate indicator. A putable bond can be cashed in by the bondholder before maturity. Bonds that have below-grade investment ratings are junk bonds. An international bond, a bond sold in a country other than the country of the corporate headquarters of the issuing company, differs from a Eurobond. A Eurobond is a bond denominated in the currency of the issuing company's home country and sold in another country. A super long-term bond is one that matures in one hundred years.

3. *Describe the key features of preferred stock.*

Preferred stock is a hybrid security that has debt and equity characteristics. Preferred stockholders have a superior claim relative to the common stockholders to a firm's earnings and assets, and their dividend payments are usually fixed. Those traits resemble debt. In addition, preferred stock has an infinite maturity and lower priority claim to assets and earnings than bondholders. Because of the corporate tax exclusion of some preferred stock dividends from taxable income, corporations are much more likely to invest in stock than individuals.

4. *Compare and contrast a genuine lease and a disguised purchase contract.*

Because lease payments are entirely tax deductible, many attempt to disguise purchase contracts as genuine leases. A lease is an arrangement where the owner of an asset contracts to allow another party the use of the asset over time. In order for the lease to be genuine, the lessee (the party to whom the asset is leased) may not have an effective ownership of the asset. The IRS has six standards that a lease must meet to qualify for the lease tax deductions. Failure to comply with IRS rules will result in the less favorable tax treatment of a purchase contract.

5. *Explain why some leases must be shown on the balance sheet.*

Operating leases are usually short-term and cancelable. Financial (capital) leases are long-term and non-cancelable. Both operating and financial leases appear on the income statement of the lessee because they are tax-deductible business expenses. Because financial leases are functionally equivalent to a purchase financed with debt, FASB rules require that businesses treat them similarly for accounting purposes. Financial leases, therefore, appear on the balance sheet.

Equations Introduced in This Chapter

Equation 14-1. Conversion Value of a Convertible Bond:

$$\begin{matrix} \text{conversion} \\ \text{value} \end{matrix} = \begin{matrix} \text{conversion} \\ \text{ratio} \end{matrix} \times \begin{matrix} \text{stock} \\ \text{price} \end{matrix}$$

Self-Test

ST-1. Explain the features of a bond indenture.

ST-2. What is a callable bond?

ST-3. What is the straight bond value of a convertible bond?

ST-4. What is cumulative preferred stock?

ST-5. Which financial statement(s) would a financial lease affect? Why?

ST-6. What is the conversion value of a convertible bond having a current stock price of $15 and a conversion ratio of 20?

Review Questions

1. How does a mortgage bond compare to a debenture?
2. How does a sinking fund function in the retirement of an outstanding bond issue?
3. What are some examples of restrictive covenants that might be specified in a bond's indenture?
4. Define the following terms that relate to a convertible bond: conversion ratio, conversion value, and straight bond value.
5. If a convertible bond has a conversion ratio of 20, a face value of $1,000, a coupon rate of 8 percent, and the market price for the company's stock is $15 per share, what is the convertible bond's conversion value?
6. What is a callable bond? What is a putable bond? How do each of these features affect their respective market interest rates?

Build Your Communication Skills

CS-1. Select a corporate bond and research its indenture provisions. What must the issuer do and what must the issuer not do? Write a brief report of one to two pages on your findings.

CS-2. Does a bond issuer owe potential investors full disclosure of plans that might affect the value of the bonds, or is the issuer's duty to investors only what is explicitly stated in the indenture contract? Divide into small groups to debate this issue.

Problems

14-1. Sean Thornton has invested in a convertible bond issued by Cohan Enterprises. The conversion ratio is 20. The market price of Cohan common stock is $60 per share. The face value is $1,000. The coupon rate is 8% and the annual interest is paid until the maturity date ten years from now. Similar non-convertible bonds are yielding 12% (YTM) in the marketplace. Calculate the straight bond value of this bond.

Straight Bond Value

14-2. Use the same data given in problem 14-1. Now assume that interest is paid semiannually ($40 every six months). Calculate the straight bond value.

Straight Bond Value

14-3. Using the data in problem 14-1, calculate the conversion value of the Cohan Enterprises convertible bond.

Conversion Value

14-4. Two years ago a company issued $10 million in bonds with a face value of $1,000 and a maturity of ten years. The company is supposed to put aside $1 million in a sinking fund each year to pay off the bonds. Dolly Frisco, the finance manager of the company, has found out that the bonds are selling at $800 apiece in the open market now when a deposit to the sinking fund is due. How much would Dolly save by purchasing 1,000 of these bonds in the open market instead of calling them in at $1,000 each?

Sinking Fund

14-5. A company where Michael Kirby works as the vice president of finance, issued 20,000 bonds ten years back. The bonds had a face value of $1,000, annual coupon rate of 10 percent, and a maturity of twenty years. This year the market yield on the company's bond is 8 percent. The bonds are callable after five years at par. If Mr. Kirby decides in favor of exercising the call option, financing it through a refunding operation, what would be the annual savings in interest payments for the company? (Interest is paid annually.)

14-6. Use the same information given in problem 14-5. Now assume that the call premium is 5 percent and the bonds were called back today. J. B. Brooks purchased ten bonds when they were originally issued at $950 per bond. Calculate the realized rate of return for Brooks.

14-7. J. B. Brooks of problem 14-6 after getting her bonds called back by the original issuing company can now invest in a $1,000 par, 8 percent annual coupon rate, ten year maturity bond of equivalent risk selling at $950. (Interest is paid annually.)

    a. What is the overall return for Brooks over the twenty years assuming the bond is held till maturity?

    b. Compare the overall return with the return on the bond in problem 14-4 if they had not been called. Did Brooks welcome the recall?

14-8. Captain Nathan Brittles invested in a $1,000 par, twenty-year maturity, 9 percent annual coupon rate convertible bond with a conversion ratio of 20 issued by a company six years back. What is the conversion value of Captain Brittles' investment if the current market price for the company's common stock is $70 per share? (Interest is paid annually.)

14-9. Use the same information given in problem 14-8. If the current required rate of return on similar nonconvertible bond is 7 percent, What is the straight bond value for the bond? Should Captain Brittles convert the bond into common stock now?

14-10. Tom Dunston invested in a $1,000 par, ten-year maturity, 11 percent coupon rate convertible bond with a conversion ratio 30 issued by a company five years back. The current market price for the company's common stock is $30 per share? The current required rate of return on similar but nonconvertible bonds is 13 percent. Should Mr. Dunston consider converting the bond into common stock now?

14-11. Six years back Ruby Carter invested $1,000 in a $1,000 par, twenty-year maturity, 9 percent annual coupon rate putable bond which can be redeemed at $900 after five years. If the current required rate of return on similar bonds is 13 percent, should Ruby redeem the bond? What is the realized rate of return after redeeming? (Interest is paid annually.)

14-12. Five years back Diana Troy invested $1,000 in a $1,000 par, ten year maturity, 9 percent annual coupon rate putable bond which can be redeemed at $900 after five years. If the current required rate of return on similar bonds is 14 percent, should Diana redeem the bond? What is the realized rate of return after redeeming? If Diana reinvests the sum in a $1,000 par, five years to maturity, 13 percent annual coupon rate bond selling at $900 and holds it till maturity, what is her realized rate of return over the next five years? What is her realized rate of return over the entire 10 years?

14-13. Hot Box Insulators, a public company, initially issued investment grade, twenty-year maturity, 8% annual coupon rate bonds ten years back at $1,000 par. A group of investors bought all of Hot Box's common stock through a leveraged buyout which turned the bonds overnight into junk bonds. Similar junk bonds are currently yielding 25 percent in the market. Calculate the current price of the original bonds.

14-14. Profit Unlimited Company is in bankruptcy. The company has the following liability and equity claims:

1st Mortgage bonds	$5 million
2nd Mortgage bonds	5 million
Senior Debentures	10 million
Subordinated Debentures	4 million
Common Stock	10 million (par value)

Mortgaged assets have been sold for $7 million and other assets for $13 million. According to priority of claims determine the distribution of $20 million obtained from the sale proceeds.

Answers to Self-Test

ST-1. A bond indenture is the a contract that spells out the provisions of a bond issue. It always contains the face value, coupon rate, interest payment dates, and maturity date. It may also include: terms of security in the case of default, if any; the plan for paying off the bonds at maturity; provisions for paying off the bonds ahead of time; restrictive covenants to protect bondholders; and the trustee's name.

ST-2. A callable bond is a bond that can be paid off early by the issuer, at the issuer's option.

ST-3. The straight bond value of a convertible bond is the value a convertible bond would have without its conversion feature. It is the present value of the interest and principal using the required rate of return on a similar non-convertible bond as the discount rate.

ST-4. Cumulative preferred stock is preferred stock for which missed dividends must be made up (paid) by the issuing company before common stock dividends may be resumed.

ST-5. A financial (capital) lease would show up on both the income statement and the balance sheet. Lease payments are business expenses that belong on the income statement and FASB rules call for financial leases to be reflected on the balance sheet also.

ST-6. $15 market price of the stock x 20 conversion ratio = $300 conversion value of the convertible bond.

APPENDIX 14A

Bond Refunding

When a corporation issues a callable bond, it needs to decide when it is advantageous to exercise that call option. This generally occurs when interest rates drop significantly and the issuing company seeks to replace the old high-interest rate bonds and to issue new bonds at the lower interest rate. This process is known as bond refunding.

The decision whether to refund or not is a capital budgeting decision. There are cash outflows involved in the form of the call premium that are usually required when bonds are called, flotation costs incurred when new bonds are sold, and tax deductions lost when lower interest rate bonds replace higher interest rate bonds. The inflows come mainly from the interest savings (lower payouts of interest represent cash inflows) that come when high-interest rate debt is retired and replaced with lower-interest rate debt.

A SAMPLE BOND REFUNDING PROBLEM

Suppose the Mega-Chip Corporation has $50 million worth of bonds outstanding with an annual coupon interest rate of 10 percent. However, market interest rates have fallen to 8 percent since the bonds were issued five years ago. Accordingly, the Mega Chip Corporation would like to replace the old 10 percent bonds with a new issue of 8 percent bonds. In so doing, the firm could save 2 percent × $50 million = $1 million a year in interest payments. The original maturity of the 10% bonds was twenty years. The relevant financial data are summarized in Table 14A-1.

The Mega Chip Corporation will be issuing new bonds having the same maturity as the number of years remaining to maturity on the old bonds (fifteen years). The *call premium* on the old bonds is the amount specified in the original bond indenture that the company must pay the bond owners if the bonds are called. The call premium is expressed as a percentage of the bond's face value. Thus, in this case, Mega Chip will have to pay the old bondholders 5 percent, of $50 million, or $2.5 million in addition to the face value of the bonds, if it calls the bonds in.

The amount of the underwriting costs and the interest savings realized as a result of the refund are numbers that are essentially certain, so a very low discount rate is called for in this capital budgeting problem. The usual custom is to use the after tax cost of debt for the discount rate. In this case the number is 4.8 percent[1].

The calculations for this refunding capital budgeting problem are shown in Table 14A-2.

The cash outflows in Table 14A-2 are fairly straightforward. The 5 percent call premium on the old bonds and the 3 percent underwriting costs on the new bonds add up to a total outflow of $4 million.

The cash inflows are more complicated. There is an annual interest saving of $1 million per year for fifteen years. This amounts to $600,000 after taxes. The pre-

---

[1]This number was found using Equation 12-1. Mega-Chip's current before-tax cost of debt is 8 percent and its marginal tax rate is 40 percent. Per Equation 12-1 its after-tax cost of debt is:

$$\text{After-tax } k_d = \text{Before-tax } k_d \times (1 - \text{tax rate})$$
$$= .08 \times (1 - .40)$$
$$= .048, \text{ or } 4.8\%$$

Table 14A-1

Mega-Chip Bond Refunding Problem

Old Bond Issue:	$50,000,000; 10% Annual Interest Rate; Interest Paid Semi-Annually; 20 Years Original Maturity, 15 Years Remaining to Maturity
Call Premium on Old Bond:	5%
Underwriting Costs on Old Bonds When Issued 5 Years Ago:	2% of Amount Issued
New Bond Issue:	$50,000,000; 8% Annual Interest Rate; Interest Paid Semi-Annually; 15 Years to Maturity
Underwriting Costs on New Bonds:	3% of Amount Issued
Marginal Tax Rate:	40%
After Tax Cost of Debt:	AT k_d = 4.8%

Table 14A-2 **Mega-Chip Bond Refunding Calculations**

CASH OUTFLOWS	CALCULATIONS	INCREMENTAL CASH FLOWS
Call Premium Paid	$50,000,000 \times .05 =$	$2,500,000
New Bond Underwriting Costs	$50,000,000 \times .03 =$	$1,500,000
Total Outflows		$4,000,000

CASH INFLOWS		
Interest Savings	Interest on old bonds: $50,000,000 \times .10 = \$5,000,000$ Interest on new bonds: $50,000,000 \times .08 = \$4,000,000$ $\overline{}$ $1,000,000 Difference Each Year for 15 Years Less taxes on the additional income at 40%: $1,000,000 \times .40 = (\$400,000)$ $\quad$ Net Savings $= \$600,000$ per year Present value of the net savings for 15 years at 4.8%: $600,000 \times \left[\dfrac{1-\dfrac{1}{1.048^{15}}}{.048}\right] = \$600,000 \times 10.5214 =$	$6,312,840
Tax Savings on Call Premium Paid (the call premium is a tax-deductible expense amortized over the life of the bond issue)	$50,000,000 \times .05 \times .40 = \$1,000,000$ Amortized over 15 years = $\quad \$1,000,000/15$ years $= \$66,666.67$ per year Present Value of the savings for 15 years at 4.8%: $\qquad\qquad \$66,666.67 \times 10.5214 =$	$701,426.70
Tax Savings from Writing Off Balance of Old Bond Underwriting Costs	Unamortized Amount = $50,000,000 \times .02 \times (15/20)^a = \$750,000$ Current $\qquad\qquad\qquad\qquad\qquad\qquad$ Deduction PV of Unamortized Amount if Bond is not Called:[b] $(\$750,000 / 15) \times 10.5214 = \$526,070$ $\qquad$ Net Tax Savings = $\qquad \$750,000 - 526,070 =$	$223,930
Tax Savings from New Bond Underwriting Costs	$(\$50,000,000 \times .03) / 15 = \$100,000$ per year writeoff $\qquad$ Tax Savings = $\qquad \$100,000 \times .4 = \$40,000$ $\qquad$ PV of Tax Savings = $\qquad \$40,000 \times 10.5214 =$	$420,856
Total Inflows		$7,659,052.70
Net Present Value = $7,659,052.70 − $4,000,000 =		$3,659,052.70

[a]There are 5 of the original 20 years worth of underwriting costs on the old bonds that have been written off. This leaves 15 of the 20 years which is all written off immediately if the bonds are refunded.
[b]This is the PV of the tax savings you would have received anyhow, without the refunding. The difference if the incremental cash flow from the refunding associated with the underwriting costs on the old bonds that have not yet been written off.

sent value of these after tax annual savings is $6,312,840 using the after tax cost of debt of 4.8 percent as the discount rate. The tax savings on the call premium paid on the old bonds is $701,426.70. The tax deductions from the underwriting costs on the old bonds were amortized over the original twenty-year scheduled life of the bond. Thus, if the bonds are called now, the entire balance of the underwriting costs not yet claimed as a tax deduction will become immediately deductible.

The difference between the immediate tax savings from this deduction and the present value of the tax savings that would have been realized over the next fifteen years is the incremental cash inflow relating to these underwriting costs. That figure is shown to be $223,930 in this case. We see from our calculations, then, that the present value of the tax savings from the amortization of the underwriting costs on the new bonds is $420,856.

Netting out all the incremental cash outflows and inflows gives a net present value figure of $3,659,052.70. Since this NPV figure is greater than zero, Mega Chip will accept the project and proceed with the bond refunding.[2]

---

[2]This assumes that the management of Mega-Chip Corporation does not expect interest rates to fall further in the months to come. If they are confident in a forecast for even lower interest rates to come they may wait, expecting an even greater NPV in the near future.

chapter 15

Common Stock

Where your treasure is, there will your heart be also.

Matthew 6:21

To Issue Stock or Not to Issue Stock?

In the 125 years since it was founded, Green Point Savings bank of Flushing, Queens, New York, accumulated a giant pot of gold—retained earnings of $758 million. Under the arcane rules governing mutual savings banks like Green Point, the pot of gold is nominally owned by depositors. So how can the officers of the bank get hold of that pot of gold?

Simple. They announced that the bank would become a public corporation and issue stock in an initial public offering (IPO) worth $600 million to $800 million. The way the deal was structured, the bank's officers were to receive 30 percent of the bank shares. For example, Thomas Green, Green Point's chairperson, was to receive about $2 million in stock out-

right and options on $4 million more.

Yet, does a mutual savings bank that has millions in retained earnings need to convert to stock ownership at all? After an initial public offering, the public corporation has the option to issue more stock to raise capital or make acquisitions. But Green Point had plenty of cash to start with, and even more cash flowed in after the IPO. Top management, of course,

Chapter Objectives

After reading this chapter, you should be able to:

1. Describe the characteristics of common stock.

2. Explain the disadvantages and advantages of equity financing.

3. Explain the process of issuing new common stock.

4. Describe the features of rights and warrants.

could use the extra cash to buy back the stock issued in the IPO, increasing their control over the bank's operations. Who were the people who lost control at the moment of the IPO? Unless they became part of a majority shareholder group by paying for shares of stock, the former depositor–owners lost substantial control over the bank's operations.

Is all this legal? Yes. The state banking department ruled that the trustees of the bank were obligated to act "in a manner that is consistent with their roles as fiduciaries, although the banking department will not attempt to describe or define the scope of such fiduciary duties." ✻

Sources: Gautam Naik, "Green Point Parent's Shares Surge in IPO," *The Wall Street Journal* (January 31, 1994): B5; Saul Hansell, "A Fight for Green Point's Pot of Gold," *New York Times* (November 11, 1993): C1.

Chapter Overview

In this chapter we explore the characteristics and types of common stock, types of common stock owners, and the pros and cons of issuing stock to raise capital. Then, we investigate how firms issue common stock. Finally, we examine *rights* and *warrants*, and their risk and return features.

The Characteristics of Common Stock

We discussed common stock in chapter 2, pages 28–29.

As we learned in chapter 2, **common stock** is a security that represents an equity claim on a firm. Having an equity claim means that the one holding the security (the common stockholder) is an owner of the firm, has voting rights, and has a claim on the *residual income* of the firm. **Residual income** is income left over after other claimants of the firm have been paid. Residual income can be paid out in the form of a cash dividend to common stockholders, or it can be reinvested in the firm. Reinvesting this residual income increases the market value of the common stock due to the new assets acquired or liabilities reduced.

Corporations sometimes have different classes of stockholders. For example, a corporation's charter may provide for a certain class of stockholders to have greater voting rights than other classes. Or one class of stock may receive its dividends based on the performance of only a certain part of the company.

The Adolph Coors Brewing Company, for example, has two different classes of stock. Class A shares, owned by a trust for the benefit of Coors family members, have voting rights. Class B shares, available to the general public and traded on the NASDAQ stock market, have no voting rights. Separate voting and nonvoting classes of stock are often the case for public corporations, such as Coors, that started out as private family businesses and in which family members continue to actively manage the company. (There is no consistent standard, however, as to which designation, A or B, has the greater voting rights and which designation the lesser.)

Another special class of common stock is issued by General Motors. Its Class H common stock pays dividends tied to the performance of its subsidiary, Hughes Aircraft. General Motors bought Hughes Aircraft and created this special class of common stock as part of the financing arrangement of the purchase.

A relatively new special class of stock is sometimes created when a company that has long been in one line of business expands into a new, often riskier line. The company will then issue a new class of common stock that represents a claim only on the new business. This stock is called **target stock,** because its value is targeted toward specific (nontraditional) assets. In 1995, for example, U.S. West Communications Corporation (one of the Baby Bells spun off from the AT&T divestiture) issued target stock to finance its venture in the cellular, cable, and other nontelephone businesses. The idea is that a different kind of stockholder is likely to be attracted to the newer, nontraditional businesses than the stockholder interested in "plain old telephone service" (POTS).

All classes of stock have a value that is determined when that stock is traded from one investor to another at the various stock exchanges and in the over-the-counter market, as was described in chapter 2. The market takes into account the characteristics of a given class and values each class accordingly. Figure 15-1 shows a certificate of ownership for 288 shares of the common stock of Central Jersey Bancorp.

Common stockholders are paid dividends determined by the ability and willingness of the firm to pay. This dividend decision is made by the board of directors of the corporation. Residual income not paid out to the common stockholders in the

To review stock exchanges and over-the-counter exchanges, see chapter 2, page 228.

Figure 15-1 **Stock Certificate for 288 Shares of Central Jersey Bankcorp Common Stock**

form of dividends is reinvested in the firm. It benefits the common stockholders there as well (since they are the owners of the corporation).

All corporations issue stock reflecting the owners' claim. But some corporations are privately owned, while others are owned by members of the general public. The rules for private and public corporations differ, as we see next.

Stock Issued by Private Corporations

We discussed limited liability for corporate owners in chapter 1, pages 14–15.

Private corporations (also known as closely held corporations) are so called because their common stock is not traded openly in the marketplace. Private corporations do not report financial information to the government through the Securities and Exchange Commission. (Tax returns, of course, are filed with the IRS, but this information is confidential). Privately held corporations are usually small, and the stockholders are often actively involved in the management of the firm. The corporate form of organization is attractive to many small firms because the owners face only limited liability.

Stock Issued by Publicly Traded Corporations

To review the agency problem, see chapter 1, pages 10–11.

MCI. McDonald's. Motorola. These are just some samples of well-known publicly traded corporations. A **publicly traded corporation** is a corporation whose common stock can be bought by any interested party, and that must release audited financial statements to the public. It is typically run by a professional management team, which likely owns only a tiny fraction of the outstanding shares of common stock.

The professional management team that handles the operations of the firm reports to a group called the **board of directors.** The board of directors, in turn, is elected by the common stockholders to represent their interests. The board is an especially important body for large public corporations, where management typically owns such a tiny percentage of the firm. The agency problem discussed in chapter 1 described the conflict of interest that can occur when those who run a firm own very little of it. The common stockholders elect the board members, and the board members oversee the management of the company.

Source: DILBERT © 1996 United Feature Syndicate, Inc. Reprinted by Permission.

Chris Heller, Corporate Communications Consultant

Chris Heller

Chris Heller, a philosophy major in college, is a consultant specializing in corporate communications. Chris is a former assistant vice president at Aetna Life and Casualty and was responsible for all financial communications to investors and customers. These communications included annual reports, quarterly reports, and reports for financial analysts.

Q. How important is it for a professional communicator to understand financial information?

If you're going to be a practitioner in corporate public relations, especially in this day and age, you are inevitably going to have to communicate earning surprises, stock price changes, takeovers, divestitures, accounting charges, and bond rating declines—there are any number of financial transactions at the corporate level that you must be able to explain to stockholders.

You must understand financial concepts completely so you can interpret them in the company's official materials, be it a press release or an annual report. You must also be able to explain abstract financial concepts clearly to a reporter so he or she can describe them to the reader or listener in understandable and favorable terms.

Q. Can you share one of the toughest financial situations you had to explain?

Aetna was going through a tough time when it lost $2 billion in the commercial real estate market. That affected its ratings, which meant it went from a AAA− rated company to a AA− rated company. A rating decrease of this magnitude is a major problem for a financial services company because people lose trust in you. If customers start pulling their money out of the business—sell shares, cash in their bonds, and so forth—that could lead to serious liquidity problems.

My job was to explain to investors and customers what was happening, what wasn't happening, and what it meant, so they had a good grasp of the situation and how it affected their investments.

The challenge was to send information in a form that a variety of customers could understand. Aetna's customers ranged from a sophisticated 401K retirement plan sponsor representative to a school teacher or firefighter who was in a municipal plan for tax-deferred annuities. Aetna's debt and equity securities are also widely held and, therefore, most financial institutions watch the securities closely.

Aetna's real estate problems were covered in the press on a regular basis, in publications ranging from *US News Today* to *The Wall Street Journal.* We not only had to try to influence the content of these stories as they were being written, but we also had to give our customer service people the ability to explain the company's situation in a credible way to customers.

Q. Are the stockholders with whom you communicated changing?

Yes, there has been a major shift in the type of stockholders. With rare exceptions, the times when an individual stockholder has a majority of shares are over. Many individual stockholders now own their stock through a 401K retirement plan. Now, the majority of shares are owned by financial institutions, such as mutual funds.

Source: Interview with Chris Heller.

Members of the board of directors have a fiduciary responsibility to the common stockholders who elected them. **Fiduciary responsibility** is the legal duty to act in the best interests of the person that entrusted you with property or power. When stockholders elect board members to represent them, they entrust the board members with the management of their company. Those board members owe it to common stockholders to act in the common stockholders' interest. Stockholders may vote directly on some major issues, such as a proposal to merge or liquidate the company.

Institutional Ownership of Common Stock

Much of the common stock of publicly traded corporations is owned by **institutional investors**—financial institutions that invest in the securities of other companies. Money management firms handling pension fund money, bank trust departments, insurance companies, mutual funds, and the like, are major common stockholders. The link between ownership and control is likely to be a loose one in such cases because the individual shareholder is several layers away from the corporation. For instance, a worker may have a claim on a pension fund that is managed by a money management firm that has invested funds in another company's common stock.

In recent years many institutional investors have begun to take a more active role in overseeing the companies in which they own common stock. Institutional investors usually have substantial amounts of funds, so they can buy a large number of shares of stock and become major shareholders. As a result, they can exercise more control than widely dispersed individual investors. Fidelity Investments, for example, a large mutual fund company, has been seeking seats on the board of directors of companies in which Fidelity is a major shareholder.

In this section, we investigated common stock characteristics, including classes of stock for stock issued by private and public corporations. We also looked at institutional ownership of common stock. Next, we examine the voting rights of common stockholders.

VOTING RIGHTS OF COMMON STOCKHOLDERS

Common stockholders have power to vote according to the number of shares they own. The general rule is "one vote per share." A stockholder or stockholder group holding more than 50 percent of the voting shares has a *majority interest* in the firm. The stockholder or group of stockholders that owns enough voting shares to control the board and operations of the firm has a *controlling interest* in the firm. The stockholder or stockholder group gains control when it elects a majority of its supporters to the board of directors.

In practice, a group can gain control with much less than 50 percent of the voting shares. This can happen if the remaining voting shares are widely distributed among many thousands of stockholders (each of whom owns a tiny percentage of the outstanding voting shares) who do not act in concert with each other. Many firms are controlled by groups of common stockholders owning as little as 5 percent or 10 percent of the voting shares, sometimes less.

Proxies

In large publicly traded corporations, the typical shareholder is likely to be uninterested in the details of the company's operations. It is not worth going to the stockholders' meeting in another part of the country if you hold only a few hundred shares. Such stockholders will typically allow others to vote their shares for them by *proxy*. This means that another group—usually the management of the company, but sometimes a group opposing management—will vote the shares for the stockholder who has given his or her proxy.

To give permission to another to vote your shares, you sign a card sent out by the group seeking this permission. In contested votes, where several competing groups may solicit shareholder proxies, each group may send out a card of a different color.

Board of Directors Elections

Corporate elections typically use one of two different sets of voting rules to fill seats on the board of directors. These are *majority voting* and *cumulative voting* rules. Under majority voting rules, a given number of seats are to be filled in a given election. The number of voting shares held, plus proxy votes held, represents the number of votes a person may cast for a given candidate for each separate seat. If multiple seats are contested, the candidates for a given seat will compete against each other for that seat. The person receiving the greatest number of votes wins that seat. With majority voting, whoever controls the majority of the votes will get their candidates elected to every seat to be filled.

Under cumulative voting rules, all the candidates run against each other but do not run for a particular seat. If there are five seats to be filled in the election, the top five vote getters among all the candidates win those seats. Votes are cast—one vote per share times the number of seats being contested—for as many or as few candidates as they wish. This means that stockholders with shares and proxies for less than a majority of the number of voting shares can "accumulate" their votes by casting them all for only a few candidates (even casting all votes for one candidate).

Cumulative voting makes it more likely that those shareholders with less than a majority of the voting shares will get some representation on the board. With majority voting rules, where candidates run for specified seats, minority stockholders would get outvoted by the majority stockholders in each of these separate elections.

Suppose Burgerworld Corporation has a ten-member board, and terms for three of the ten members are expiring. The firm uses cumulative voting rules. Seven candidates are competing for the right to fill these three seats. There are 100,000 voting shares of common stock outstanding for Burgerworld. This means that 300,000 total votes will be cast (100,000 shares × 3 contested seats = 300,000 total votes).

The stockholders are divided into two camps of differing corporate management philosophy. The majority group controls 60 percent of the voting shares, while the minority group of common stockholders controls the other 40 percent. One of the seven candidates was nominated by the minority group. The minority stockholder group knows that with only 40 percent of the votes, they have no hope of winning two or three of the three seats contested. Does the minority group of stockholders have enough voting power to get their one candidate on the board?

The majority stockholders would like to get three of their people elected to the three seats available. If they want to succeed, they will have to spread their 180,000 votes (60 percent of 300,000) among their three favorite candidates. Spreading the votes evenly among their preferred candidates, each candidate supported by the majority group would receive 60,000 votes (180,000 ÷ 3 = 60,000). If the minority stockholders cast all their votes for their candidate, that person will receive 120,000 (300,000 total − 180,00 majority votes = 120,000 minority votes) votes and win a seat on the board.

The formula for determining the number of directors that a stockholder group could elect, given the number of voting shares they control, is shown next in Equation 15-1.

The Number of Directors That Can Be Elected Under Cumulative Voting Rules (15-1)

$$\text{NUM DIR} = \frac{(\text{SHARES CONTROLLED} - 1) \times (\text{TOT NUM DIR T.B.E.} + 1)}{\text{TOT NUM VOTING SHARES}}$$

where: NUM DIR = Number of directors that can be elected by a given group

SHARES CONTROLLED = The number of voting shares controlled by a given group

TOT NUM DIR T.B.E. = Total number of directors to be elected

TOT NUM VOTING SHARES = Total number of voting shares in the election

Using the number of shares owned by the minority stockholders described in our Burgerworld example (40,000 of 100,000 shares outstanding), we can calculate the number of directors that this minority group could elect. Recall that the number of directors to be elected is three. The calculations follow:

$$\text{NUM DIR} = \frac{(40{,}000 - 1) \times (3 + 1)}{100{,}000}$$

$$= 1.60$$

This group can elect one of their people to the board out of the three to be elected. Note that we rounded down to get the answer. Because people cannot be divided, the minority group can't elect .6 (60 percent) of a person to the board.

The formula for determining the number of shares needed by a given group to elect a given number of directors is shown next in Equation 15-2.

The Number of Shares Needed to Elect a Given Number of Directors Under Cumulative Voting Rules (15-2)

$$\text{NUM VOTING SHARES NEEDED} = \frac{\text{NUM DIR DESIRED} \times \text{TOT NUM VOTING SHARES}}{\text{TOT NUM DIR T.B.E.} + 1} + 1$$

where: NUM DIR DESIRED = Number of directors a given group of stockholders desires to elect

TOT NUM VOTING SHARES = Total number of voting shares in the election

TOT NUM DIR T.B.E. = Total number of directors to be elected in the election

For example, to calculate the number of voting shares needed to elect two of the three directors in the election described above, we could plug in the appropriate numbers into Equation 15-2. The calculation is shown next:

$$\text{NUM VOTING SHARES NEEDED} = \frac{2 \times 100{,}000}{3 + 1} + 1$$

$$= 50{,}001$$

We find that a group would need control of 50,001 voting shares to guarantee the election of two of the three directors in this election. This number is equivalent to 150,003 votes spread evenly between two director candidates. This would be

75,001.5 votes per candidate (50,001 voting shares × 3 total directors to be elected ÷ 2 directors sought to be elected). The other shareholders, holding 49,999 voting shares, would have the remaining 149,997 votes (49,999 voting shares × 3 total directors to be elected). If these 149,997 votes were divided between two candidates, that would be only 74,998.5 votes per candidate.

In this section, we reviewed the voting rights of common stockholders. We examine the advantages and disadvantages of equity financing next.

THE PROS AND CONS OF EQUITY FINANCING

Selling new common stock has advantages and disadvantages for a corporation. Some disadvantages include a dilution of power and earnings per share of existing stockholders, flotation costs, and possible unfavorable market perceptions about the firm's financial prospects. The advantages for a new stock issue include additional capital for the firm, lower risk, and the potential to borrow more in the future.

Disadvantages of Equity Financing

Selling new common stock is like taking in new partners (although we are referring to a corporation rather than to a partnership). When you sell new common stock, you must share the profits and the power with the new stockholders. When new common stock is issued, the ownership position of the existing common stockholders is diluted because the number of shares outstanding increases.

The dilution may result in a lower earnings per share for a profitable company. Losses, of course, would be shared, too, resulting in a less negative earnings per share figure for a money-losing company. The voting power of the existing common stockholders would also be diluted. Firms concerned with losing control through diluted voting power, then, often avoid raising funds through a stock issue.

Also, when new common stock is sold, flotation costs are incurred. As we discussed in chapter 12, **flotation costs** are fees paid to investment bankers, lawyers, and others when new securities are issued. The flotation costs associated with new common stock issues are normally much higher than those associated with debt.

We discussed flotation costs in chapter 12, pages 295–296.

Another reason why common stock issues are often a last resort for many corporations is because of signaling effects. **Signaling** is a message a firm sends, or investors infer, about a financial decision.

It is reasonable to suggest that the internal corporate managers have better insight about a firm's future business prospects than does the average outside investor. If we accept this proposition as true, then we would not expect a company to sell additional shares of common stock to the general public unless its managers know that the future prospects for the company are worse than is generally believed. How do we know this? Equity financing is expensive and often used as a last resort. The inference drawn by investors who agree with this view is that a corporation issuing new stock wants more "partners" with whom to share future bad times. A company that expected good times would attempt to preserve the benefits for the current owners alone. Instead of issuing new stock, then, the firm would issue more debt securities.

Management may issue new common stock even though the future financial prospects for the firm are bright. However, if the market believes otherwise, the price of the common stock will drop when the new common stock is issued.

Year	Long-Term Debt	Equity	% Long-Term Debt to Equity
1985	$102	$ 3,982	2.6%
1986	$110	$ 4,374	2.5%
1987	$ 88	$ 5,022	1.7%
1988	$ 61	$ 4,533	1.3%
1989	$474	$ 5,446	8.7%
1990	$139	$ 6,363	2.2%
1991	$188	$ 7,269	2.6%
1992	$425	$ 7,499	5.7%
1993	$667	$ 8,511	7.8%
1994	$547	$ 9,926	5.5%
1995	$545	$12,755	4.3%

Source: The Value-Line Investment Survey

Advantages of Equity Financing

Why would any corporation issue new stock? One big reason is that corporations do not pay interest (and are not legally obligated to pay any dividends) to common stockholders. Unlike interest payments on debt, dividends can be skipped without incurring legal penalties. Interest payments on debt reduce a firm's earnings, while dividend payments to stockholders do not.

Some firms choose equity financing because they do not like borrowing. Some business people view being "in debt" as undesirable. They avoid it if possible and pay off unavoidable debts as soon as possible. Companies whose managers and owners hold this view will tend to favor equity financing. The Hewlett-Packard Corporation is a classic example of a company that historically has avoided debt, as Table 15-1 illustrates.

A final reason why firms choose equity instead of debt financing is that the firm may have so much debt that borrowing more may be difficult or too expensive. Suppose, for example, that the "normal" ratio of debt to assets in your firm's industry is 20 percent, and your firm's debt-to-assets ratio is 40 percent. If this is the case, lenders may be reluctant to lend your firm any more money at an affordable interest rate; your firm might be forced to issue stock to raise funds. In this situation a new stock issue could bring the firm's debt ratios down to more normal industry levels. This would make it easier for the firm to borrow in the future.

In this section we described the pros and cons of a new stock issue. We turn to the process of issuing common stock next.

We discussed debt ratios in chapter 5, pages 87–88. We discussed debt levels in chapter 13, pages 326–329.

ISSUING COMMON STOCK

When a firm wishes to raise new equity capital, it must first decide whether to try to raise the capital from the firm's existing stockholders or whether to seek new investors. Private companies usually raise additional equity capital by selling new shares to existing common stockholders. This generally satisfies these stockholders because they continue to exercise complete control over the firm. However, when a large amount of equity capital must be raised, the existing stockholders may find that their only recourse is to sell shares of the firm's stock to the general public. A firm that sells its private shares of stock to the general public "goes public." The issuance of common stock to the public for the first time is known as an **initial public**

Figure 15-2 Announcement of Lucent Technologies Inc. Initial Public Offering

Source: Reprinted by permission of *The Wall Street Journal*, © 1996 Dow Jones & Company, Inc. All Rights Reserved Worldwide.

offering (IPO). Figure 15-2 is an announcement of Lucent Technologies IPO, the largest IPO in U.S. history.

Netscape, the company that makes the popular World Wide Web browser program for surfing the Internet, went public in late 1995. It was widely popular with investors, who bid its price up considerably from its issue price. The company's earnings at the time were quite limited, so investors were looking toward future profits they expected (and hoped) to see.[1]

Institutional investors are major buyers of new equity issues. Investment bankers who try to sell initial shares typically prefer to sell large blocks of shares to institutional investors as opposed to selling many small blocks of shares to individual investors. The institutional investors do well because a new issue is generally sold for 10 percent to 15 percent below value to ensure a favorable reception.[2]

The Function of Investment Bankers

When a corporation does decide to sell stock to the public, its first step is to contact an investment bank to handle the issue. Some of the names of investment banking firms that a corporation might contact would include: Merrill Lynch, Goldman Sachs, Morgan Stanley, and First Boston, to mention only a few.

Investment bankers handle all the details associated with pricing the stock and marketing it to the public. A potential investor in a new security must be given a **prospectus.** A prospectus is a disclosure document that describes the security and the issuing company. Investment bankers typically announce a new issue and the availability of the prospectus in a large boxed-in ad called a *tombstone ad*. It is so named because the large box with large print identifying the new issue looks like a

---

[1]Christopher Farrell, "The Boom in IPO Capitalism," *Business Week* (December 18, 1995): 68–72.
[2]*Ibid.*

This announcement is neither an offer to sell, nor a solicitation of an offer to buy, any of these securities. The offer is made only by the Prospectus.

May 17, 1996

2,300,000 Shares

Common Stock

Price $17.00 Per Share

Copies of the Prospectus may be obtained in any State from such of the undersigned as may legally offer these securities in compliance with the securities laws of such State.

Morgan Keegan & Company, Inc.   **Howard, Weil, Labouisse, Friedrichs**
Incorporated

CS First Boston	Dillon, Read & Co. Inc.	Lehman Brothers
Prudential Securities Incorporated		Salomon Brothers Inc

J. C. Bradford & Co.   Hanifen, Imhoff Inc.   Interstate/Johnson Lane   Johnson Rice & Company L.L.C.
Corporation

Petrie Parkman & Co.   Principal Financial Securities, Inc.   Rauscher Pierce Refsnes, Inc.

Raymond James & Associates, Inc.   The Robinson-Humphrey Company, Inc.

Simmons & Company   Stephens Inc.
International

tombstone. Figure 15-3 shows a tombstone ad for 2,300,000 shares of GeoScience Corporation common stock.

Underwriting versus Best Efforts   Investment bankers take on the job of marketing a firm's stock to the public on one of two bases: **underwriting** or **best efforts.** When an investment banker *underwrites* a stock issue it means the investment banker agrees to buy a certain number of shares from the issuing company at a certain price. Usually, a group of investment bankers will form a temporary alliance called a **syndicate** when underwriting a new security issue. The head of the investment banking syndicate is known as the **managing investment banker.** The managing investment banker has the primary responsibility for advising the security issuer. Extra fees are collected for this advice. It is up to the syndicate to sell the shares to the public at whatever price they can get. An underwriting poses the least risk to the firm whose stock is being issued. This is because the firm gets the stock issue proceeds from the investment bankers all at once, up front. However, since the investment bankers bear the risk that they might not be able to sell the firm's shares at the price they expect, they charge a rather substantial fee for underwriting.

A cheaper alternative to underwriting is called a *best efforts offering*. In this arrangement the investment banker agrees to use its "best efforts" to sell the issuing company's shares at the desired price, but it makes no firm promises to do so. If the shares can only be sold at a lower price than was expected, then the issuing firm must either issue more shares to make up the difference or be satisfied with lower proceeds from the stock issue. Not surprisingly, the fees investment bankers charge for marketing stock on a best efforts basis are considerably less than those they charge for underwriting.

Pricing New Issues of Stock

When new shares of stock in a company are to be sold to the public, someone must decide at what price to offer them for sale. This is not a significant problem when the company's shares are already publicly traded. The new shares are simply sold at the same price as the old shares, or perhaps a little lower.[3] However, if the company is going public, there is no previous market activity to establish what the shares are worth. In this situation the investment banker, in conjunction with the issuing company's managers, must put a price on the shares and hope that the market will agree that the price represents fair value. This is a daunting task indeed, and frequently investment bankers and firm managers miss the mark. Often an IPO stock will fluctuate wildly in price after it is issued. Table 15-2 shows four successful initial public offerings that involved stock price fluctuations after the IPO.

Netscape and Pixar were two of the hottest IPOs in late 1995 and Lucent Technologies and Yahoo Inc were hot IPOs in early 1996. Netscape and Yahoo attracted investors looking for Internet plays. Pixar made animation breakthroughs and Lucent Technologies was spun off from AT&T.

The figures in Table 15-2 show the differing fortunes of these four new public offering stocks.

Valuing the Stock of a Company That Is Not Publicly Traded   Before investment bankers offer a company's stock for sale to the public, they must have some idea of how the public will value the stock to predict the new issue market price. The trouble is, when a company's stock has not been sold to anyone before, it is perilously difficult to say how much it is worth.

Suppose you have been creating oil paintings for a few years and have become pretty good at it. One day the art club you belong to has a show, and one of your

---

[3]There is usually a little dilution (downward movement) in the price of a company's common stock when new shares are sold.

IPO DATE	STOCK	INITIAL PRICE	PRICE ON 4/30/96
8/95	Netscape	$28	$61
11/95	Pixar Animation	$22	$23½
4/96	Lucent Technologies	$27	$35⅛
4/96	Yahoo Inc.	$13	$29¾

TABLE 15-2

Four Recent Initial Public Offerings (IPOs)

paintings is included. When you deliver the painting to the gallery, you are asked what sale price you wish posted on the painting. Now you face the same question firms and investment bankers face. How much is the painting worth? How much can you get for it?

Naturally, you want to sell the painting for as high a price as possible but the potential buyers want to pay as low a price as possible. If you post too high an asking price, no one will buy your painting and you will leave empty handed. If you post too low a price, however, someone will snatch it up and may well resell it to someone else for a substantial profit. You can see that if you had previously sold a number of similar paintings in the past, you would have an idea of what to ask for this one. The first painting you try to sell is the one that presents the pricing problem.

In chapter 9 we presented some of the methods that companies and investment bankers use to estimate the market value of a company's stock. These methods include calculating the present value of expected cash flows, multiplying earnings per share by the appropriate P/E ratio, the book value approach, and the liquidation value approach.

To review stock valuation approaches, see chapter 9, pages 214–218.

Rights and Warrants

Rights and warrants are securities issued by a corporation that allow investors to buy new common stock. They originate in different ways and have somewhat different characteristics, as explained in the following sections.

Preemptive Rights

When some companies plan to issue new stock, they establish procedures to protect the ownership interest of the original stockholders. The existing stockholders are given securities that allow them to preempt other investors in the purchase of new shares. This security is called a preemptive right. A **preemptive right,** sometimes referred to simply as a *right,* gives the holder the option to buy additional shares of common stock at a specified price (the *subscription price*), until a given expiration date. Current stockholders who do not wish to exercise their rights can sell them in the open market.

The Number of Rights Required to Buy a New Share   Suppose that Right Stuff Corporation has 100,000 shares of common stock currently outstanding. An additional 20,000 shares of common stock are to be sold to existing shareholders by means of a rights offering. Since one right is sent out to existing shareholders for each share held, 100,000 rights must be sent out. There are five shares of common stock outstanding for each new share to be sold (100,000/20,000 = 5). Five rights are therefore needed, along with the payment of the subscription price, to purchase a new share of common stock through the rights offering.

The Value of a Right   We know that five rights are required to buy a new share of Right Stuff Corporation's common stock through the rights offering. To determine the value of each right, we must also know the subscription price and the market price of Right Stuff's common stock.

This information, along with our knowledge of the number of rights required to buy a new share, will allow us to estimate the value of one of these rights.[4]

Suppose that the current market price of Right Stuff Corporation's common stock is $65 and that the subscription price is set at $50. This means that you are saving $15 ($65 − $50 = $15) when you send in your five rights to receive one of the new shares (known as "exercising your rights"). This means that each right would be worth $3 ($15 ÷ 5 = $3) before dilution effects are considered.

The approximate value of a right can be determined by two formulas. The formula used depends on the status of the stock as it trades in the marketplace, relative to the timing of the issuance of the rights. Timing is the key to determining which approximation formula to use.

Rights are generally sent out several weeks after the announcement of the rights offering is made. This initial period is called the **rights-on** period, and the stock is said to *trade rights-on* during this time. This means that if the common stock is purchased during the rights-on period, the investor will receive the forthcoming rights.

At the opening of trading on the day following the rights-on period, the stock is said to be trading **ex-rights.** This means that the purchaser buys the stock without (ex is Latin for "without") receiving the entitlement to the preemptive rights if the purchase is on or after the ex-rights date.

Trading Rights-On.   If the stock is trading rights-on, then we calculate the approximate market value of the right as depicted in Equation 15-3:

Approximate Value of a Right, Stock Trading Rights-On

$$R = \frac{M_0 - S}{N + 1}$$

(15-3)

where: R = Approximate market value of a right
         M_0 = Market price of the common stock, selling rights-on
         S = Subscription price
         N = Number of rights needed to purchase one of the new shares of common stock.

We call R the approximate market value of the right because rights are securities that can be traded just like stock and bonds. Once the rights are sent to the existing common stockholders (those who bought the stock before it "went ex-rights"), the rights can be traded in the marketplace at the option of the owner. The actual market price of the right may be slightly different than shown in the formulas presented here because of the option characteristics of the rights, discussed later.

Table 15-3 shows the calculation of the approximate market value of a Right Stuff Corporation right. This is the value of the right as determined by the rights-on formula, Formula 15-3.

We see from the calculations in Table 15-3 that the market value of the Right Stuff right is $2.50, given a market price of common stock of $65, a subscription price of $50, and five rights required to purchase one new share.

---

[4]The actual pricing of a right is somewhat more complicated than what we are presenting here. A right is an option to buy the new stock at the specified subscription price. Option pricing is discussed in the following section on warrants. The rights valuation presented here should be considered an approximation only.

TABLE 15-3

**Right Valuation with
Stock Selling Rights-on**

M_0, Market Price of the Common Stock, Rights-on	$65
S, Subscription Price	$50
N, Number of Rights Required to Purchase One New Share	5
R, Approximate Market Price of One Right	$R = \dfrac{\$65 - 50}{5 + 1}$
	$= \dfrac{\$15}{6}$
	$= \$2.50$

Selling Ex-Rights.   To find the approximate value of the right when the stock is selling ex-rights, the ex-rights formula must be used. This formula is presented as follows in Equation 15-4:

Approximate Value of a Right, Stock Trading Ex-Rights

$$R = \frac{M_x - S}{N} \qquad (15\text{-}4)$$

where: R = Approximate market value of a right
  M_x = Market price of the common stock, selling ex-rights
  S = Subscription price
  N = Number of rights needed to purchase one of the new shares of common stock

When the common stock begins trading ex-rights, the entitlement to the forthcoming rights is lost. Thus the price of the common stock in the marketplace will drop by the value of the right now lost on the ex-rights date (other factors held constant).

Suppose Right Stuff Corporation common stock begins selling ex-rights today. When the opening bell rings on the exchange, the price of Right Stuff common stock will drop by the amount of the value of the right that has been lost. Holding other factors constant (no news overnight to otherwise affect the value of the common stock), the price of the common stock will drop by $2.50 from $65 to $62.50.

Table 15-4 shows the calculation of the approximate market value of the right when the common stock is selling ex-rights, using Formula 15-4.

When the common stock is selling ex-rights, Formula 15-4 gives the approximate market value of a right. The formula reflects the loss of the entitlement of the rights, $2.50 in our example.

TABLE 15-4

**Right Valuation with
Stock Selling Ex-Rights**

M_x, Market Price of the Common Stock, Ex-Rights	$62.50
S, Subscription Price	$50
N, Number of Rights Required to Purchase One New Share	5
R, Approximate Market Price of One Right	$R = \dfrac{\$62.50 - \$50}{5}$
	$= \dfrac{\$12.50}{5}$
	$= \$2.50$

Warrants

A **warrant** is a security that gives its owner the option to buy a certain number of shares of common stock from the issuing company, at a certain exercise price, until a specified expiration date. The corporation benefits from issuing warrants because the issue raises funds. It also creates the possibility of a future increase in the company's number of common stock shares. The investor values warrants because of the option to buy the company's stock.

Warrants are similar to rights except they are sold to investors instead of given away to existing shareholders. They typically have longer maturities than rights and are often issued with bonds as part of a security package.

Warrant Valuation   Warrants have value only until the expiration date, at which time they become worthless. Before a warrant expires, the value of a warrant depends on how the price of the common stock compares to the warrant's *exercise price*—the price the firm sets for exercising the right to buy common stock shares—and on other factors, described next.

To value warrants, investors must be able to find the exercise value. The exercise value is the amount saved by purchasing the common stock by exercising the warrant rather than buying the common stock directly in the open market. If there is no saving, the exercise value is zero.

The formula for calculating the exercise value of a warrant is described in Equation 15-5 as follows:

The Exercise Value of a Warrant

$$XV = (M - XP) \times \#$$ (15-5)

where: XV = Exercise value of a warrant
   M = Market price of the stock
   XP = Exercise price of a warrant
   $\#$ = Number of shares that may be purchased if the warrant is exercised

Suppose that the McGuffin Corporation warrant entitles the investor to purchase four shares of common stock, at an exercise price of $50/share, during the next three years. If the current common stock price is $60, the exercise value according to Equation 15-5 follows:

$$XV = (M - XP) \times \#$$
$$= (\$60 - \$50) \times 4$$
$$= \$40$$

Our calculations show that the exercise value is $40.

If the market price of the common stock price were $50 or less, the exercise value of the warrant would be zero. This is because you would have an option to buy the common stock at a price that is no better than the regular market price of the stock. You would have no reason to exercise the warrant, and a rational investor would not do so.

Note that the time remaining until the expiration of the warrant does not affect the exercise value. For the McGuffin Corporation warrants, the investor saves $10/share on four shares of common stock, creating an exercise value of $40.

As long as there is still time remaining until expiration, the actual market price of a warrant will be greater than the exercise value. The difference between the market price and the exercise value is called the warrant's time value. Warrants have time value because if the price of the common stock goes up, the exercise value increases with leverage and without limit (because of the fixed exercise price). If, on the other hand, the price of the common stock falls, the exercise value cannot dip below zero. Once the common stock price is at or below the exercise price, no further damage can be done to the exercise value.

The exercise value is zero if the common stock price is at or below the exercise value, but it can never be negative. Table 15-5 shows the exercise value for a McGuffin Corporation warrant for different possible stock values.

No matter how much below $50 the market price of the common stock goes, the exercise value stays at zero. As the stock value goes above $50, however, the exercise value increases at a much faster rate than the corresponding increase in the stock price. The difference between the potential benefit if the stock price increases (unlimited and leveraged) compared to the potential loss (limited) is what gives a warrant its time value.

Because of this time value, warrants are seldom exercised until they near maturity, even when the exercise value is high. This is because if a warrant is exercised, only the exercise value is realized. If the warrant is sold to another investor, the seller realizes the exercise value plus the time value. The time value approaches zero as the expiration date nears. A warrant approaching its expiration date, having a positive exercise value, would be exercised by the investor before the value goes to zero on the expiration date.

The greater the volatility of the stock price, and the greater the time to expiration, the greater the market value of the warrant. If the stock price is volatile, the stock price could easily increase. This would give the warrant owner the benefit of an even greater increase due to leverage. If the common stock price decreases, no more than the price paid can be lost. The more time left before expiration, the better the chance for a major stock price change, up or down. Again, the warrant value upside is substantial if the stock price moves up, and the downside potential limited if the stock price decreases. The asymmetry of the warrant's upside and downside potential gives the warrant greater value.

Option pricing has many applications in finance. We can apply the principles described here for warrant pricing to certain types of capital budgeting and even common stock valuation. What if a proposed capital budgeting project gives us an option to undertake future projects that are tied to the first? Common stock has unlimited upside price potential, coupled with limited downside risk, just like a warrant. These are issues you may explore further in other finance courses.

TABLE 15-5

McGuffin Corporation Warrant Exercise Value

MARKET PRICE OF COMMON STOCK	EXERCISE PRICE	NUMBER OF SHARES	EXERCISE VALUE
$100	$50	4	$200
$ 90	$50	4	$160
$ 80	$50	4	$120
$ 70	$50	4	$ 80
$ 60	$50	4	$ 40
$ 50	$50	4	$ 0
$ 40	$50	4	$ 0
$ 30	$50	4	$ 0
$ 20	$50	4	$ 0

What's Next

In this chapter we examined types and traits of common stock, and the advantages and disadvantages of issuing common stock. We also explored rights and warrants. In chapter 16 we will look at how a corporation determines the amount of cash dividends to pay, and the timing of those dividend payments.

Summary

1. Describe the characteristics of common stock.

Common stock is a security that represents an ownership claim on a corporation. The shareholders are entitled to the residual income of the firm, resulting in a high-risk position relative to other claimants and a relatively high return potential. Common stock may come in different classes with different voting rights or dividend payments.

The professional management team that handles the operations of the firm reports to the board of directors. The board of directors, in turn, is elected by the common stockholders to represent their interests. Because the stockholders have entrusted the board to represent their interests, board members have a fiduciary duty to act on stockholders' behalf. Stockholders usually vote according to the number of shares held. The two main types of voting rules are the majority voting rules, where candidates run for specific seats and the cumulative voting rules, where all the candidates run against each other but do not run for a particular seat.

2. Explain the disadvantages and advantages of equity financing.

Disadvantages of equity financing include the dilution of existing shareholder power and control, flotation costs incurred when new common stock is sold, and the negative signal investors often perceive (rightly or wrongly) when new common stock is sold. Equity financing has several advantages. It reduces the risk of a firm because common stockholders, as opposed to debtors, have no contractual entitlement to dividends. Equity financing can also increase the ability to borrow in the future.

3. Explain the process of issuing new common stock.

Once a firm decides that the benefits outweigh the cost of issuing stock, the firm almost always seeks the help of an investment banking firm. The investment banker usually underwrites the new issue, which means that it purchases the entire issue for resale to investors. Sometimes the investment banker will try to find investors for the new common stock without a guarantee to the issuing company that the stock will be sold. This arrangement is known as a best efforts offering.

4. Describe the features of rights and warrants.

Rights are securities given to existing common stockholders that allow them to purchase additional shares of stock at a price below market value. Corporations issue rights to safeguard the power and control of existing shareholders in the event of a new stock issue. Warrants are securities that give the holder the option to buy a certain number of shares of common stock of the issuing company at a certain price for a specified period of time. Warrants have high return potential because if the stock price increases, the value of the warrant increases at a much higher rate due to leverage. The downside risk of a warrant is limited, because the maximum loss potential is the price of the warrant. As a result of the high return and low risk potential, warrants have time value that is greatest when the stock price is volatile and the time to maturity is great.

Equations Introduced in This Chapter

Equation 15-1. The Number of Directors That Can Be Elected Under Cumulative Voting Rules:

$$\text{NUM DIR} = \frac{(\text{SHARES CONTROLLED} - 1) \times (\text{TOT NUM DIR T. B. E.} + 1}{\text{TOT NUM VOTING SHARES}}$$

where: NUM DIR = Number of directors that can be elected by a given group
SHARES CONTROLLED = The number of voting shares controlled by a given group
TOT NUM DIR T.B.E. = Total number of directors to be elected
TOT NUM VOTING SHARES = Total number of voting shares in the election

Equation 15-2. The Number of Shares Needed to Elect a Given Number of Directors Under Cumulative Voting Rules:

$$\begin{array}{c}\text{NUM VOTING} \\ \text{SHARES} \\ \text{NEEDED}\end{array} = \frac{\text{NUM DIR DESIRED} \times \text{TOT NUM VOTING SHARES}}{\text{TOT NUM DIR T. B. E.} + 1} + 1$$

where: NUM DIR DESIRED = Number of directors a given group of stockholders
desires to elect
TOT NUM VOTING SHARES = Total number of voting shares in the election
TOT NUM DIR T.B.E. = Total number of directors to be elected in the election

Equation 15-3. Approximate Value of a Right, Stock Trading Rights-On:

$$R = \frac{M_0 - S}{N + 1}$$

where: R = Approximate market value of a right
M_0 = Market price of the common stock, selling rights-on
S = Subscription price
N = Number of rights needed to purchase one of the new shares of
common stock

Equation 15-4. Approximate Value of a Right, Stock Trading Ex-Rights:

$$R = \frac{M_x - S}{N}$$

where: R = Approximate market value of a right
M_x = Market price of the common stock, selling ex-rights
S = Subscription price
N = Number of rights needed to purchase one of the new shares of
common stock

Equation 15-5. The Exercise Value of a Warrant:

$$XV = (M - XP) \times \#$$

where: XV = Exercise value of a warrant
M = Market price of the stock
XP = Exercise price of a warrant
# = Number of shares that may be purchased if the warrant is exercised

Self-Test

ST-1. What is residual income and who has a claim on it?

ST-2. Is a new common stock issue usually perceived as a good or bad signal by the market? Explain.

ST-3. What does it mean when a company's common stock is said to be trading ex-rights?

ST-4. If a company's common stock is selling at $80 per share and the exercise price is $60 per share, what would be the exercise value of a warrant that gives its holder the right to buy ten shares at the exercise price?

Review Questions

1. What are some of the government requirements imposed on a public corporation that are not imposed on a private, closely held corporation?
2. How are the members of the board of directors of a corporation chosen and to whom do these board members owe their primary allegiance?
3. What are the advantages and the disadvantages of a new stock issue?
4. What does an investment banker do when underwriting a new security issue for a corporation?
5. How does a preemptive right protect the interests of existing stockholders?
6. Explain why warrants are rarely exercised unless the time to maturity is small?
7. Under what circumstances is a warrant's value high? Explain.

Build Your Communication Skills

CS-1. Review a financial publication, such as *The Wall Street Journal,* for a tombstone advertisement. Contact one of the investment banking firms you see listed in a tombstone ad announcing a new issue. Request a prospectus for that new issue. Once you receive the prospectus, write a report describing its key elements and what those elements reveal about the new security and its issuer.

CS-2. Research a company that is having a contested stockholder vote. You will find notice of such a vote in business publications, such as *The Wall Street Journal.* Different groups will typically run their own advertisements soliciting proxies so that group can vote the shares of other stockholders. Analyze the positions of the opposing sides, break into small groups, and debate the direction the company should take on the issue in contention.

Problems

15-1. Frank Bullit owns 20,000 shares of common stock in QuickFix Company. The company has 1 million shares of common stock outstanding at a market value of $50 per share. What percent of the firm is owned by Frank?

    If the company issues 500,000 new shares at $50 per share to new stockholders, how does Frank's ownership change?

Ownership Claim

15-2. Angela Phinlay is considering buying some shares of common stock of an initial public offering by NewAge Communications Corporation. The privately held company is going

Valuation of IPO

public by issuing 5 million shares at $20 per share. Ms. Phinlay gathered the following information about NewAge:

Total Assets:	$200 million (historical cost)
Total Liabilities:	150 million (market value)
Estimated Liquidation Value:	250 million
Estimated Replacement Value of Assets:	400 million
Expected dividend in one year:	$2 per share
Expected dividend growth rate:	8%

The required rate of return for Ms. Phinlay from a share of common stock for this type of company is 13 percent.

Compare the selling price of the stock with its value as obtained from different valuation methods. Would you recommend that Ms. Phinlay buy the stock?

Term of Board Members

15-3. FourWheeler Corporation has nine board members. Three of these seats are up for election every three years. What is the length of the term served by each board member?

Cumulative Voting

15-4. The stockholders of Blue Sky, Inc., are divided into two camps of different corporate management philosophy. The majority group controls 65 percent and the minority group controls 35 percent of the voting shares. The total number of shares of common stock outstanding is 1 million. The total number of directors to be elected in the near future is four. What is the maximum number of directors the minority group can possibly elect, assuming that the company follows cumulative voting procedure?

Cumulative Voting

15-5. Gregory Miller owns 26,000 shares of Tri Star Corporation out of 200,000 shares of common stock outstanding. The board has seven members, and all seven seats are up for election now. Mr. Miller has long wanted to serve as a member of the board. Assuming that the company follows cumulative voting procedures, can Mr. Miller get himself elected to the board on the strength of his own votes?

Dissident Group and Cumulative Voting

15-6. The Rainbow Corporation had traditionally been a constant dollar dividend paying company, with the board enjoying the support of retired investors holding 65 percent of the voting shares. A dissident group of high-salaried young investors holding 30 percent of the voting shares prefer reinvestment of earnings to save personal taxes and hence wants to elect board members supportive of their cause. The company has 600,000 shares of common stock outstanding and the board has thirteen members—all to be reelected shortly.

    a. How many directors can the young stockholders elect under
      (i) cumulative voting rules
      (ii) majority voting rules
    b. What percentage of voting shares and/or proxies must the dissident group have to be able to elect seven out of the thirteen board members?

Rights Offering

15-7. XYZ Corporation has 500,000 shares of common stock currently outstanding. The company plans to sell 50,000 more shares of common stock to the existing shareholders through a rights offering. How many rights will it take to buy one share?

Value of Rights

15-8. A company with 2 million shares of common stock currently outstanding is planning to sell 500,000 new shares to its existing shareholders through a rights issue. Current market price of a share is $65, and the subscription price is $55. If the stock is selling rights-on, calculate the value of a right.

Value of Rights

15-9. Use the same information given in problem 15-8. Now calculate the value of a right if the stock were selling ex-rights.

15-10. Fillsulate Products, a manufacturer of refractory powders, is about to declare a rights issue. The subscription price is $65. Seven rights in addition to the subscription price are required to buy one new share of stock. Rights-on market price of the stock is $77. Calculate the value of one right. Also calculate the new stock price once it goes ex-rights.

Value of Rights

15-11. Johnny Rocco owns 700 shares of stock of East-West Tobacco Company, which is offering a rights issue to its existing shareholders. To buy one new share of stock, Johnny will need four rights plus $60. Rights-on market price of the stock is $72.

Rights Offering

- **a.** Calculate the value of a right.
- **b.** What is the maximum number of new shares Johnny can buy?
- **c.** How much would he have to spend if he decides to buy all the new stock he can?
- **d.** If he decides not to buy the new stock, how much would he able to sell his rights for?

15-12. Selena Rogers owns sixty shares of East Asia Shipping Company stock and has $750 in cash for investment. The company has offered a rights issue in which purchasing a new stock would require four rights plus $50 in cash. Current market value of the stock is $62.

Challenge Problem

- **a.** Calculate the value of a right, if the stock is selling ex-rights.
- **b.** Should Selena participate in the rights offering by buying as many shares as she can, or sell her rights and keep the shares she already owns at a diluted value?

15-13. The current market price of a share of common stock of SkyHigh, Inc., is $100. The company had issued warrants earlier to its new bond investors that gave the investors an option to buy five shares of common stock at an exercise price of $85. Calculate the exercise value of a warrant. What happens to the exercise value of the warrant if the stock price changes to:

Warrants

- **a.** $110?
- **b.** $80?

15-14. The current market price of Wilkerson, Inc.'s common stock is $40 per share. The company has 600,000 common shares outstanding. To finance its growing business, the company needs to raise $2 million. Due to its already high debt ratio, the only way to raise the funds is to sell new common stock. Alvin C. York, the vice president of finance of Wilkerson, has decided to go ahead with a rights issue but he is not sure at what price the existing shareholders would be willing to buy a share of new stock. Wilkerson's investment banker has suggested that an analysis based on a wide range of possible prices be carried out and the subscription prices agreed upon were $36, $33, $29, and $26 per share of new stock. Wilkerson's net income for the year is $1 million.

Comprehensive Problem

Based on the above information, Mr. York has asked you to carry out the following analysis:

- **a.** For each of the possible subscription prices, calculate the number of shares that would have to be issued and the number of rights required to buy one share of new stock.
- **b.** For each of the possible subscription prices, calculate the earnings per share immediately before and immediately after the rights offering.
- **c.** Guy Hamilton owns 10,000 shares of stock of Wilkerson. For each of the possible subscription prices, calculate the maximum number of new shares Guy would be able to buy. Under each of these cases, calculate Guy's total claim to earnings before and after the offering.

Answers to Self-Test

ST-1. Residual income is income that is left over after all claimants, except for common stockholders, have been paid. This left over income belongs to the common stockholders who receive this income in either the form of a dividend, or by having it reinvested in the corporation that they own.

ST-2. The market usually infers bad news when new common stock is issued. Investors ask themselves why the current owners would want to share their profits with new owners if management expected good news ahead. The market often infers (rightly or wrongly) that there must be bad news coming that the management of the firm wants to "share" with new stockholders. New stock issued is therefore usually perceived as a negative signal.

ST-3. A stock is selling ex-rights when the purchase of that stock no longer carries with it entitlement to the rights that are soon to be sent out to stockholders.

ST-4. ($80 stock price − $60 exercise price) × 10 shares purchased per warrant = $200 exercise value of the warrant

chapter 16

Dividend Policy

Finance is the art of passing currency from hand to hand until it finally disappears.

Robert W. Sarnoff

Who Gets the Money?

A company's dividend policy can soothe or irritate shareholders. For example, many people recognize Morton International by the little girl holding the umbrella on the blue salt box. Yet the current growth area of Morton's business is the production of automobile air bags. The air bag division's profits soared one year, giving Morton an influx of cash. During one of the worst winters in history, sales of road salt went through the roof and Morton was blessed with even more cash. The firm increased its dividend payment by 17 percent, making its stockholders very happy.

Yet not all companies share the wealth with shareholders, and this sometimes causes

shareholder unrest, often to the point of revolt.

In fact, Michael Price, an investor in Chase Manhattan Corporation, argued for a breakup of Chase because the firm had failed to pay sufficient dividends, despite pockets full of cash. Chase got the message, along with other financial institutions. Chase, Merrill Lynch, and Mellon Bank Corporation all raised their dividends to ease share-holder unrest.

When a company has extra cash on hand, shareholders often want a piece of it—or, at the very least, a darn good reason that explains why the company is not passing any of the cash back to them. ✳

Sources: Dave Kansas and Randall Smith, "How Much Cash a Firm Should Keep Is at Issue in Wake of Chrysler Bid," *The Wall Street Journal,* (April 20, 1995):A-1. Rick Green, "All for One: Every Analyst Says Buy," *Smart Money,* (March 1996): 26.

CHAPTER OVERVIEW

In this chapter we explore the importance of dividends, the factors that determine a firm's dividend policy, and leading dividend policy theories. We then examine how a firm makes dividend payments to shareholders. We finish by identifying alternatives to paying cash dividends.

DIVIDENDS

Dividends are the cash payments that corporations make to their common stock-holders. Dividends provide the return common stockholders receive from the firm for the equity capital they have supplied.[1] Even companies that do not currently pay dividends reinvest in the firm the earnings they generate. In this way they increase the ability of the firm to pay dividends in the future.

The board of directors decides what dividend policy best serves the common stockholders of the firm. Should a dividend be paid now, or should the earnings generated be reinvested for the future benefit of the common stockholders? If dividends are paid now, how much should be paid? These are some of the questions addressed in the following sections.

Although only corporations officially pay dividends to owners, sole proprietorships and partnerships also distribute profits to owners. Many of the same considerations examined in this chapter for corporate dividend policy can also be used to help make proper profit distribution decisions for these other forms of business organization.

WHY A DIVIDEND POLICY IS NECESSARY

Why does a company need a strategic policy relating to dividend payments? Why not just "wing it" each year (or quarter, or other span of time) and pay the dividend that "feels right" at that time? Because market participants (current and potential stockholders) generally do not like surprises. An erratic dividend policy means that those stockholders who liked the last dividend cannot be sure that the next one will be to their liking. This uncertainty can result in a drop in the company's stock price.

---

[1]You may wonder about this statement, since common stock investors can always receive a return by selling their stock. Remember, however, that when investors sell their stock they are paid by other investors, not by the corporation. Except when a corporation buys back its own stock (which is a form of dividend payment), the only cash corporations pay to investors is a dividend payment.

When stockholders do not get what they expect, they often show their displeasure by selling their stock. A well-planned policy, appropriate for the firm and its business strategy, can prevent unpleasant surprises for market participants and protect the stock price.

FACTORS AFFECTING DIVIDEND POLICY

Dividend policy is based on the company's need for funds, the firm's cash position, its future financial prospects, stockholder expectations, and contractual restrictions with which the firm may have to comply.

Need for Funds

Dividends paid to stockholders use funds that the firm could otherwise invest. To meet cash needs, then, firms short of cash may have to raise capital from expensive sources. However, because of the expense of equity funds, firms avoid raising equity capital to pay dividends—a distribution to equity investors—because of its high cost.

A company short of cash or with limited borrowing opportunities may decide to pay little or no dividends. Alternatively, there may be an abundance of cash and a dearth of good capital budgeting projects available. This could lead to very large dividend payments.

Management Expectations and Dividend Policy

If a firm's managers perceive the future as relatively bright, on the one hand, they may begin paying large dividends in anticipation of being able to keep them up during the good times ahead. On the other hand, if managers believe that bad times are coming, they may decide to build up the firm's cash reserves for safety instead of paying dividends.

Stockholders' Preferences

Reinvesting earnings internally, instead of paying dividends, would lead to higher stock prices and a greater percentage of the total return coming from capital gains. *Capital gains* are profits earned when the price of a capital asset, such as common stock, increases.

Common stockholders in high tax brackets may prefer to receive their return from the company in the form of capital gains instead of dividends. Some stockholders prefer capital gains because the federal income tax rate on capital gains is limited to 28 percent.[2] Returns in the form of dividends may be taxed at a stated rate as high as 39.6 percent. The effective tax rate on dividends, due to the phasing out of some deductions and exemptions for high-income taxpayers, may be even higher. If the stock is not sold, capital gains taxes can be postponed indefinitely. If, however, the stockholders are mainly retired people looking for current income from their investments, then they may prefer a high dividend payment policy.

---

[2]This was the maximum rate applied to capital gains as of 1996.

The board of directors should consider such stockholder preferences when establishing the firm's dividend policy.

Restrictions on Dividend Payments

A firm may have dividend payment restrictions in its existing bond indentures or loan agreements. For example, a company's loan contract with a bank may specify that the company's current ratio cannot drop below 2.0 during the life of the loan. Since payment of a cash dividend draws down the company's cash account, the current ratio may fall below the minimum level required.[3] In such a case, the size of a dividend may have to be cut or omitted. In addition, many states prohibit dividend payments if they would create negative retained earnings on the balance sheet. This restriction is a prohibition against "raiding the initial capital".

Figure 16-1 summarizes the factors that influence the dividend decision.

CASH VERSUS EARNINGS

Dividends are often discussed in relation to a firm's earnings. The dividend payout ratio is often cited as an indicator of the generosity (or lack thereof) of the firm's dividend policy. The dividend payout ratio is calculated by dividing the total dollar amount of dividends paid by net income, as seen in Equation 16-1.

Formula for Dividend Payout Ratio

$$\text{Dividend Payout Ratio} = \frac{\text{Dividends Paid}}{\text{Net Income}} \tag{16-1}$$

If Calvin Corporation, for example, earns a net income of $10,000 and pays $3,000 in dividends, then its dividend payout ratio would be as follows:

$$\text{Dividend Payout Ratio} = \frac{\$3,000}{\$10,000}$$
$$= .30, \text{ or } 30\%$$

We see from our calculations that Calvin Corporation has a dividend payment ratio of 30 percent, which tells us that the company does pay dividends.

A caution, however: By focusing on reported earnings and the dividend payout ratio, we ignore the key to paying dividends. That key is *cash*. When a company generates earnings, this usually results in cash flowing into the firm. The earnings and the cash flows do not necessarily occur at the same time, however. Table 16-1 illustrates these timing differences.

---

[3]Recall that the current ratio is found by dividing current assets (of which cash is a part) by current liabilities. Thus decreasing cash to pay a dividend will lower the ratio.

Table 16-1

Easy Credit Corporation Selected Financial Data for Current Year

Sales (all on credit payment due in next year)	$1,000,000
Total Expenses	400,000
Net Income	600,000
Cash received this year	$0

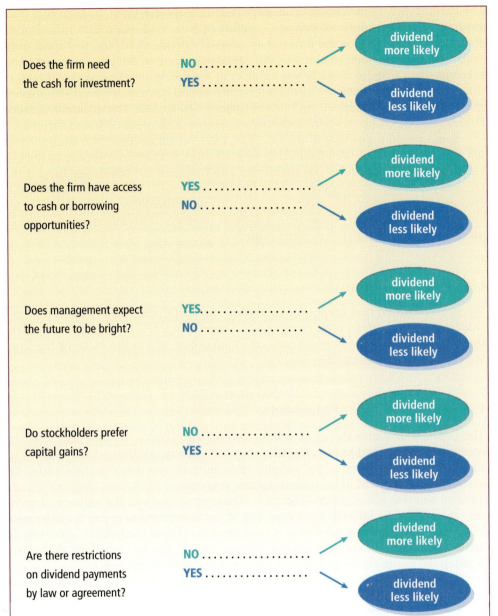

Figure 16-1 Dividend Decision Factors

This figure identifies key elements that make a dividend payment more or less likely.

Table 16-1 shows us that Easy Credit Corporation reported $600,000 of earnings this year but did not receive any cash. Unless cash was acquired from previous earnings, the firm could not pay dividends.

Even if the company reports negative earnings, it could pay dividends if it had, or could raise, enough cash to do so. If a company believed that a certain dividend payment were critical to the preservation of the firm's value, it might even choose to borrow so as to obtain the cash needed for the dividend payment. Corporate borrowing to obtain cash for a dividend payment happens occasionally, when the dividend payment expected by the common stockholders is believed to be crucial.

For instance, failure to make an expected dividend payment, in spite of a cash shortage, cost Consolidated Edison Company of New York (Con Ed) a third of its stock value. In 1974 Con Ed omitted its quarterly dividend for the first time since 1885. Con Ed's common stockholders included many retired people who counted on receiving their Con Ed dividends as a source of income. When the board of directors announced that the company would not pay its second quarter dividend, the price of the common stock dropped by one-third from $18 to $12. This incident demonstrates what can happen when stockholders receive unpleasant dividend surprises.

Some would argue that in the long run, the Con Ed decision was sound. After all, regulators later allowed Con Ed to raise its rates, perhaps in response to the crisis created by its failure to pay dividends. The rate increase ultimately helped the company and its stockholders, since profits increased due to the rate hikes. However, at least in the short run, the dividend omission was a disaster for stockholders—especially those who sold their holdings at greatly depressed prices after the dividend omission was announced.

Leading Dividend Theories

We've investigated how corporations consider many different factors when they decide what their dividend policies should be. Financial experts attempt to consolidate these factors into theories about how dividend policy affects the value of the firm. We turn to some of these theories next.

The Residual Theory of Dividends

The residual dividend theory is widely known. The theory hypothesizes that the amount of dividends should not be the focus of the company. Instead, the primary issue should be to determine the amount of earnings *retained* within the firm for investment. The amount of earnings retained, according to this view, depends on the number and size of acceptable capital budgeting projects and the amount of earnings available to finance the equity portion of the funds needed to pay for these projects. Any earnings left after these projects have been funded are paid out in dividends. Because dividends arise from "residual," or leftover earnings, the theory is called the *residual theory*. Table 16-2 shows how to apply this theory.

We see in Table 16-2 that Residual Corporation needs $10 million to finance its acceptable capital budgeting projects. It has earnings of $12 million. It needs equity funds in the amount of 70 percent of the $10 million needed or $7 million. This leaves residual earnings of $5 million for dividends.

If the earnings available had been $20 million instead of $12 million, then the dividend payment would have been $13 million ($20 million − $7 million).

Table 16-2

Residual Corporation— Applying the Residual Dividend Theory

Investment Needed for New Projects	$10,000,000
Optimal Capital Structure	30% Debt − 70% Equity
Equity Funds Needed	70% × $10,000,000 = $7,000,000
Earnings Available	$12,000,000
Residual Earnings	$12,000,000 − $7,000,000 = $5,000,000
Amount of Dividends to Be Paid	$5,000,000

However, if earnings available had been $6 million instead of $12 million, then no dividends would have been paid at all. In fact, $1 million in additional equity funding would need to be raised by issuing new common stock. The amount of dividends to be paid is an afterthought, according to this theory. The important decision is to determine the amount of earnings to retain.

The residual dividend theory focuses on the optimal use of earnings generated from the perspective of the firm itself. This may appeal to some, but it ignores stockholders' preferences about the regularity of and the amount of dividend payments. If a firm followed the residual theory, when earnings are large and the acceptable capital budgeting projects small and few, dividends would be large. Conversely, when earnings are small and many large, acceptable projects are waiting to be financed, there may be no dividends if the residual theory is applied. The dividend payments would be erratic and the amounts unpredictable.

The Clientele Dividend Theory

The **clientele dividend theory** is based on the view that investors are attracted to a particular company in part because of its dividend policy. For example, young investors just starting out may want their portfolios to grow in value from capital gains rather than from dividends, so they seek out companies that retain earnings instead of paying dividends. Stock prices tend to increase as earnings are retained, and the resulting capital gain is not taxed until the stock is sold. If it is sold, it is taxed at a maximum rate of 28 percent, which is lower than the maximum tax rate that applies to dividend income received.

Elderly investors, in contrast, may want to live off the income their portfolios provide. They would tend to seek out companies that pay high dividends rather than reinvesting for growth. According to the clientele dividend theory, each company therefore has its own clientele of investors who hold the stock, in part because of its dividend policy.

If the clientele theory is valid, then it doesn't much matter what a company's dividend policy is so long as it has one and sticks to it. If the policy is changed, the clientele that liked the old policy will probably sell their stock. A new clientele will buy the stock based on the firm's new policy. When a dividend policy change is contemplated, managers must ask whether the effect of the new clientele's buying will outweigh the effect of the old clientele's selling. The new clientele cannot be sure that the most recent dividend policy implemented will be repeated in the future.

The Signaling Dividend Theory

The **signaling dividend theory** is based on the premise that the management of a company knows more about the future financial prospects of the firm than do the stockholders. According to this theory, if a company declares a dividend larger than that anticipated by the market, this will be interpreted as a signal that the future financial prospects of the firm are brighter than expected. Investors presume that management would not have raised the dividend if it did not think that this higher dividend could be maintained. As a result of this signal of good times ahead, investors buy more stock, causing a jump in the stock price.

Conversely, if a company cuts its dividend, the market takes this as a signal that management expects poor earnings and does not believe that the current dividend can be maintained. In other words, a dividend cut signals bad times ahead for the business. The market price of the stock drops when the firm announces a lower dividend because investors sell their stock in anticipation of future financial trouble for the firm.

If a firm's managers believe in the signaling theory, they will always be wary of the message their dividend decision may send to investors. Even if the firm has some attractive investment opportunities that should be financed with retained earnings, management may turn them down if adopting them would prevent paying the expected dividend and send an unfavorable signal to the market.

The Bird-in-the-Hand Theory

The **bird-in-the-hand theory** claims that stockholders prefer to receive dividends instead of having earnings reinvested in the firm on their behalf. Although stockholders should expect to receive benefits in the form of higher future stock prices when earnings are retained and reinvested in their company, there is uncertainty as to whether the benefits will actually be realized. However, if the stockholders were to receive the earnings now, in the form of dividends, they could invest them now in whatever they desired. In other words, "A bird in the hand is worth two in the bush."

If the bird-in-the-hand theory is correct, then stocks of companies that pay relatively high dividends will be more popular—and therefore will have relatively higher stock prices—than are stocks of companies that reinvest their earnings.

Modigliani and Miller's Dividend Theory

Franco Modigliani and Merton Miller (commonly referred to as M&M) theorized in 1961 that dividend policy is irrelevant.[4] Given some simplifying assumptions, M&M showed how the value of a company is determined by the income produced from its assets, not by its dividend policy. According to the **M&M dividend theory,** the way a firm's income is distributed (in the form of future capital gains or current dividends) doesn't affect the overall value of the firm. Stockholders are indifferent as to whether they receive their return on their investment in the firm's stock from capital gains or dividends—so dividends don't matter.

M&M's arguments have been critiqued for decades. Most often, financial theorists who disagree with M&M maintain that M&M's assumptions are unrealistic. The validity of a theory, however, lies with its ability to stand up to tests of its predictions. The results of these tests are mixed, and modern financial theorists continue to argue as to what dividend policy a company should pursue.

THE MECHANICS OF PAYING DIVIDENDS

We've seen how the board of directors decides whether the firm will pay a dividend. Next, let's consider what happens when companies pay dividends and the timing of those payments.

---

[4]Merton Miller and Franco Modigliani, "Dividend Policy, Growth, and the Valuation of Shares," *Journal of Business* (October 1961): 411–33.

The board's decision to pay a dividend is called *declaring* a dividend. This occurs on the **declaration date.** At that date a liability, called **dividends payable,** is created on the firm's balance sheet.

Since the common stock of public corporations typically is traded every day in the marketplace, the board of directors must select a cutoff date, or **date of record,** to determine who will receive the dividend. At the end of business on this date, the company stockholder records are checked. All owners of the common stock at that time receive the forthcoming dividend.

When stock is traded on an exchange or in the over-the-counter market, it takes several days to process the paperwork necessary to record the change of ownership that occurs when the stock changes hands. On the date of record, then, the company's transfer agent will not yet know of stock trading that occurred in the days immediately preceding the date of record.

The **transfer agent** is the party, usually a commercial bank, that keeps the records of stockholder ownership for a corporation. The transfer agent pays dividends to the appropriate stockholders of record after the company has deposited the required money with the transfer agent.

Because it takes time for news of a stock trade to reach the transfer agent, the rules of trading dictate that four days before the date of record, common stock that has an upcoming dividend payment will begin to trade **ex-dividend.** (The prefix *ex* is a Latin word meaning "without.") Investors who buy the stock on or after the ex-dividend date will be buying it "without" entitlement to the forthcoming dividend. The four-day period gives exchange officials enough time to notify the transfer agent of the last batch of stock trades that occurred before the ex-dividend period. The extra time ensures that the stockholder records will be correct on the date of record.

A few weeks after the date of record, the checks are mailed out to the common stockholders. The date of mailing is called the **payment date.**

Figure 16-2 shows a time line for the dividend payment sequence.

Table 16-3 summarizes the dividend payment sequence for the Adolph Coors

Figure 16-2 **The Dividend Payment Time Line**

This figure shows the sequence of events for a dividend payment.

Dividend announced	February 16, 1995
Stock begins trading ex-dividend	February 24, 1995
Date of record	February 28, 1995
Payment date	March 15, 1995

Source: Retrieved via the Internet from SEC EDGAR database, maintained by the Securities & Exchange Commission.

Table 16-3

Adolph Coors Company First-Quarter 1995 Dividend Payment Sequence, $0.125 per Share

Dividend Reinvestment Records Can Avoid Tax Headaches

If you sign up for a dividend reinvestment plan, be sure to keep good tax records. The IRS treats the dividends reinvested in new shares of stock as though you had received the cash and used that cash to buy the shares. Here are some record-keeping tips to help you avoid tax headaches.

1. **Know how often your dividends are reinvested.** Most companies that pay dividends do so quarterly. This means that under a reinvestment plan, you will be buying new shares every quarter, including fractional shares.
2. **Know how each share is taxed.** When you sell your shares, you will have a capital gain in the amount of the sales price minus the basis for each share, including fractional shares. Over ten years you could have shares with forty different tax bases (ten years times four quarters per year), not including the basis of the original shares you bought. Keep track of each basis.
3. **Keep your records.** You should never throw away the records establishing the basis for your dividend reinvestment shares until you sell them (and not for several years after that in case you get audited). These records may be in your files for decades.

Company's first-quarter 1995 dividend. The table shows the sequence of events that led to the payment of a 1995 first quarter dividend of $0.125 per share.

Dividend Reinvestment Plans

Many corporations offer a **dividend reinvestment plan (DRIP),** under which stockholders reinvest their dividends rather than receive them in cash. DRIPs are popular because they allow stockholders to purchase additional shares of stock without incurring the commission costs that accompany regular stock purchases made through a stockbroker. The new shares, including fractional shares, are purchased at the price prevailing in the market at that time. The amount of the dividend paid and reinvested is still taxable income to the stockholder.

ALTERNATIVES TO CASH DIVIDENDS

Sometimes corporations want to give something to the stockholders even though there is insufficient cash available to pay a cash dividend. At other times corporations don't want to pay a cash dividend because they want to build up their cash position. Let's look at some of the options available for giving stockholders something without using precious cash.

Stock Dividends and Stock Splits

Instead of sending out checks to stockholders, the firm could issue additional shares. Many stockholders view the receipt of these extra shares as a positive event, similar to the receipt of a check. In the sections that follow we will question the validity of this widely held view.

New shares of common stock can be distributed to existing shareholders with no cash payment in two different ways: stock dividends and stock splits. Both increase the number of shares of common stock outstanding, and neither raises additional equity capital. There is an accounting difference between them, however. Let's examine these two alternatives to cash dividends next.

Stock Dividends   When a **stock dividend** is declared, the existing common stockholders receive new shares, proportionate to the number of shares currently held. This is usually expressed in terms of a percentage of the existing holdings, such as 5 percent, 10 percent, or 20 percent, but usually less than 25 percent. For example, if a 20 percent stock dividend were declared, one new share would be sent out to existing stockholders for every five currently owned. The following example illustrates how the process works and how the transaction would be accounted for on the firm's balance sheet.

Suppose that Bob and Bill own a chain of bed and breakfast lodges called BB Corporation. Now suppose the BB Corporation declares a 20 percent stock dividend so that each stockholder receives twenty new shares for every one hundred shares they hold. This will increase the total number of shares outstanding from 100,000 to 120,000. Assume that the market price of BB's stock at the time of this stock dividend is $16. The equity section of BB's balance sheet, before and after the 20 percent stock dividend, is shown in Table 16-4.

First, note in Table 16-4 that after the 20 percent stock dividend the common stock account changed from $100,000 to $120,000, an increase of 20 percent or $20,000. This change occurred because as of January 1, 1997, the firm had 20,000 more shares outstanding and each new share had the same $1 par value as the old shares (20,000 shares × $1 = $20,000). Next, note that the capital in excess of par account changed from $900,000 to $1,200,000, an increase of $300,000. This increase happened because the new shares were issued when the market price of the stock was $16, which is $15 in excess of the $1 par value. The $15 "in excess" figure is multiplied by the 20,000 additional shares to get the $300,000 increase in the capital in excess of par account ($15 × 20,000 shares = $300,000). The $20,000 increase in the common stock account and the $300,000 increase in the capital in excess of par account total $320,000.

Finally, note that the retained earnings account changed from $5 million to $4,680,000, a decrease of $320,000. This change reflects the transfer of $20,000 to the common stock account and $300,000 to the capital in excess of par account

Common Stock (100,000 shares, $1 par)	$100,000
Capital in Excess of Par	$900,000
Retained Earnings	$5,000,000
Total Common Stock Equity	$6,000,000

Common Stock (120,000 shares, $1 par)	$120,000
Capital in Excess of Par	$1,200,000
Retained Earnings	$4,680,000
Total Common Stock Equity	$6,000,000

Table 16-4

BB Corporation Capital Account as of December 31, 1996

BB Corporation Capital Account as of January 1, 1997 (after a 20% stock dividend)

THE FAMILY CIRCUS®   By Bil Keane

12-9
© 1991 Bil Keane, Inc.
Dist. by Cowles Synd., Inc.

"How come PJ got 4 sandwiches
and I only got 2?"

Source: Reprinted with special permission of King Features Syndicate.

($20,000 + $300,000 = $320,000). Retained earnings must decrease because the 20 percent stock dividend did not alter the firm's total equity capital.

Thus we see that a stock dividend is just an accounting transfer from retained earnings to the other capital accounts. The number of shares of common stock increased by 20,000 in this case, but the overall economic effect was zero. Neither profits nor cash flows changed, nor did the degree of risk in the firm. The firm's ownership "pie" was cut into more pieces, but the pie itself is the same size.

On receiving their new shares of stock in the mail, some stockholders may think they have received something of economic value since they have new stock certificates for which they did not pay. But who issued these new stock certificates? The corporation did. Who owns the corporation? The stockholders do. The stockholders gave themselves new shares of stock, but continue to hold the same percentage of the firm as they held before the stock dividend.

The price per share of common stock will drop because of the increase in the number of shares outstanding. The price decrease happens or the total market value of the common stock would increase (price per share × number of shares outstanding) while no economically significant event has occurred.

Adjustment of a Stock's Market Price after a Stock Dividend.   Investors in the stock market generally recognize that a stock dividend simply increases the number of shares of a firm, but it does not otherwise affect the total value of the firm. After a firm declares a stock dividend, then, the market price of the firm's stock will adjust accordingly. Table 16-5 illustrates the expected stock price adjustment for BB's Corporation.

	Number of Shares Outstanding	×	Price per Share	=	Total Value of the Firm's Stock
Before Stock Dividend	100,000	×	$16	=	$1,600,000
After Stock Dividend	120,000	×	?	=	$1,600,000

With the information from Table 16-5, we can find the new price of BB's stock is as follows:

New number of shares: 120,000

Total value of firm's stock: $1,600,000

Now let X = the new stock price. We solve for the new stock price as shown:

$$120,000 \, X = \$1,600,000$$
$$X = \$13.3333 \text{ (round to \$13.33)}$$

Here's the key to solving for the new stock price after a stock dividend: Remember that the total value of all the firm's stock remains the same as it was before the stock dividend. There may be a positive effect on the stock price due to expectations about the cash dividend. We explore this effect later in the chapter.

Stock Splits   When an increase of more than 25 percent in the number of shares of common stock outstanding is desired, a corporation generally declares a *stock split* instead of a stock dividend. The firm's motivation for declaring a stock split is generally different than that for a stock dividend. A stock dividend appears to give stockholders something in place of a cash dividend. A **stock split** is an attempt to bring the firm's stock price into what management perceives to be a more popular trading range.

Stock splits are usually expressed as ratios. A *4–1 (four-for-one) stock split,* for example, indicates that new shares are issued such that there are four shares after the split for every one share before the split. In a 3–2 split, there would be three shares after the split for every two outstanding before the split.

The accounting treatment for a stock split is simpler than for a stock dividend. Table 16-6 shows how the BB Corporation would account for a 4–1 stock split.

Note in Table 16-6 that only the common stock entry in the equity section of the balance sheet is affected by the stock split. The entry indicates that after the stock split, there are four times as many shares of common stock outstanding as before the split. It also indicates that the par value of each share is one-fourth the value it was

Table 16-6

BB Corp. Capital Account
as of Dec. 31, 1996 (before
a 4–1 stock split)

Common Stock (100,000 shares, $1 par)	$100,000
Capital in Excess of Par	$900,000
Retained Earnings	$5,000,000
Total Common Stock Equity	$6,000,000

BB's B&B Corp. Capital
Account as of Jan. 1, 1997
(after the 4–1 stock split)

Common Stock (400,000 shares, $.25 par)	$100,000
Capital in Excess of Par	$900,000
Retained Earnings	$5,000,000
Total Common Stock Equity	$6,000,000

	Number of Shares Outstanding	×	Price per Share	=	Total Value of the Firm's Stock
Before Stock Dividend	100,000	×	$16	=	$1,600,000
After Stock Dividend	400,000	×	$4	=	$1,600,000

before (100,000 shares × 4 = 400,000 shares and $1 par value ÷ 4 = $.25). The total dollar value of $100,000 remains the same. Capital in excess of par and retained earnings accounts are completely unaffected by a stock split.

Adjustment of a Stock's Market Price after a Stock Split. As with a stock dividend, investors in the stock market recognize that a stock split simply increases the number of shares of a firm, but does not otherwise affect the total value of the firm. Therefore the market price of the firm's stock will adjust accordingly following a stock split. Table 16-7 illustrates the stock price adjustment for the BB Corporation in response to the 4-1 stock split.

We see in Table 16-7 that just as with the stock dividend, no economically significant event has occurred. The common stock ownership "pie" has been cut into four times as many pieces as before, but the size of the pie is the same. As Table 16-7 shows, after the 4-1 split, each share will trade in the market at approximately one-fourth the price it commanded before the split.

Sometimes the cash dividend is increased at the same time as a stock split or a stock dividend. In our 4-1 stock split example, if the cash dividend per share is decreased by less than three-fourths, stockholder cash dividends received would increase. A $1 per share cash dividend, for instance, could be cut to $0.30 instead of the $0.25 value that would leave total cash dividends unchanged. The market sometimes anticipates such an increase in the cash dividend, leading to a possible increase in the total market value of the common stock.

The Rationale for Stock Splits. One of the most famous stock splits is the Berkshire Hathaway stock split of 1996. Before the split, Berkshire Hathaway shares were selling for $34,000 a share. Because the shares soared in value from $18 per share in 1965 to $34,000 in 1996, institutional investors began to offer—for a fee—thousand-dollar securities based on Berkshire stock. To halt others from making money off of the company's stock, Berkshire decided to offer some Baby Berkshire stock shares in a 30–1 stock split.[5]

Unlike Berkshire, which split some of its stock to prevent nonowners from dealing in Berkshire securities, many companies split stock to increase its value. Managers believe that as the market price per share of their common stock increases over time, it gets too expensive for some investors. Management perceives that a stock split will decrease the price per share, thereby increasing the number of potential investors who can afford to buy it. More potential investors might create additional buying pressure that results in an increase in stock price. This argument is less persuasive, however, as the percentage of stock ownership and trading activity by institutional investors (mutual funds, pension funds, insurance companies, and so on) continues to increase. These investors can afford to pay a very high price per

---

[5]Allan Sloan, "Stop Kicking Yourself," *Newsweek* (April 8, 1996): 47.

share. Managers, however, continue to use stock splits to adjust the stock price to a lower level to make it more affordable.

What's Next

In this chapter we looked at how firms make their dividend decisions. This chapter ends Part 3 on long-term financal management decisions. Part 4 focuses on short-term financial management decisions. In chapters 17–20 we will examine how firms manage the three primary current assets: cash, inventory, and accounts receivable.

Summary

1. Explain the importance of and identify the factors that influence the dividend decision.

Stock prices often change dramatically when a dividend change is announced, indicating that the market believes dividends affect value. The dividend decision, then, must be carefully planned and implemented. Factors that influence dividend decisions are a company's need for funds, its future financial prospects, stockholder preferences and expectations, and the firm's contractual obligations.

Although dividends are often discussed in the context of a firm's earnings, dividends are paid in cash. As a result, a firm's cash flow is a crucial factor affecting its dividend policy.

2. Compare the major dividend theories.

The major dividend theories that help guide dividend policy include the residual theory of dividends, the clientele theory, the signalling theory, the bird in the hand theory, and the Modigliani and Miller theory. The residual theory posits that the amount of dividends matter less than the amount of earnings retained. If a firm enacts a residual policy, its dividend payments are likely to be unpredictable and erratic.

The clientele dividend theory assumes that one of the key reasons investors are attracted to a particular company is its dividend policy. Under this theory, it doesn't matter what the dividend policy is so long as the firm sticks to it.

The signalling dividend theory is based on the premise that management knows more about the future finances of the firm than do stockholders, so dividends signal the firm's future prospects. A dividend decrease signals an expected downturn in earnings; a dividend increase signals a positive future is expected. Managers who believe the signalling theory will be conscious of the message their dividend decision may send to investors.

The bird in the hand theory assumes that stockholders prefer to receive dividends instead of having earnings reinvested in the firm on their behalf. If correct, stocks of companies that pay relatively high dividends will be more popular, and therefore will have relatively higher stock prices, than stocks of companies that reinvest their earnings. The Modigliani and Miller theory claims that earnings from assets, rather than dividend policy, affect firm value, so dividend policy is irrelevant.

3. Describe how firms make dividend payments.

Dividends are declared by the corporate board of directors. Stockholders on the date of record are entitled to the declared dividend. Investors who buy the stock before the ex-dividend date (four days before the date of record) will receive the dividend declared by the board. Investors who buy the stock on or after the ex-dividend date have bought the stock too late to get the dividend.

4. *Identify alternatives to paying cash dividends.*

Corporations often award stockholders stock dividends (additional shares of stock) and stock splits instead of cash dividends. Both stock splits and stock dividends increase the number of outstanding shares and decrease the price per share. Although neither of these actions is a real substitute for a cash dividend, many investors perceive these events as good news even though earnings do not increase nor does risk decrease.

Equations Introduced in This Chapter

Equation 16-1. The Dividend Payout Ratio:

$$\text{Dividend Payout Ratio} = \frac{\text{Dividends Paid}}{\text{Net Income}}$$

Self-Test

ST-1. A company pays $4 per share in dividends and has 100,000 shares outstanding. The company has net income of $1 million. Its market price per share of $100. What is its dividend payout ratio?

ST-2. Is the amount of the dividend to be paid the primary focus of the board of directors if the board is guided by the residual theory of dividends? Explain.

ST-3. Does a company following the clientele theory of dividends pay high or low dividends? Explain.

ST-4. When paying dividends what is the date of record?

ST-5. If a company has a $2 par value, what would be the accounting effect of a 4–1 stock split?

Review Questions

1. Explain the role of cash and of earnings when a corporation is deciding how much, if any, cash dividends to pay to common stockholders.
2. Are there any legal factors that could restrict a corporation in its attempt to pay cash dividends to common stockholders? Explain.
3. What are some of the factors that common stockholders consider when deciding how much, if any, cash dividends they desire from the corporation in which they have invested?
4. What is the Modigliani and Miller theory of dividends? Explain.
5. Do you believe an increased common stock cash dividend can send a signal to the common stockholders? If so, what signal might it send?
6. Explain the bird in the hand theory of cash dividends.
7. What is the effect of stock (not cash) dividends and stock splits on the market price of common stock? Why do corporations declare stock splits and stock dividends?

Build Your Communication Skills

CS-1. Find a company that has recently cut its dividend. Write a report on the market's reaction to this decision and the timing of that reaction. What are some possible explanations for this market reaction?

CS-2. Many people perceive a stock split as a very positive event. Find a company that has gone through a stock split. Write a short report on the market's reaction to the stock split around the time it was announced and at the time the split actually occurred. Were they different? Were they what you would expect? Explain.

Problems

16-1. After discussion with the board of directors of the company, Lionel Mandrake, founder and Chairman of Mandrake, Inc., decided to retain $600 million from its net income of $1 billion. Calculate the payout ratio.

Payout Ratio

16-2. The net income of Harold Bissonette Resorts, Inc. was $50 million this past year. The company decided to have a 40 percent payout ratio. How much was paid in dividends and how much was added to the retained earnings?

Payout Ratio

16-3. Hannah Brown International maintains a dividend policy with a constant payout ratio of 30 percent. In the last three years, the company had earnings as shown below:

Constant Payout Ratio and Retained Earnings

	Year 1	Year 2	Year 3
Net Income($ million)	30	20	25

What is the total addition to retained earnings over the last three years?

16-4. Use the same data given in problem 16-3. Now, if the company followed a constant dollar dividend policy and paid $10 million in dividends each year, compute the dividend payout ratios for each year and the total addition to retained earning over the last three years.

Constant Dollar Dividend Policy

16-5. Eliza Doolittle, the Chief Financial Officer of East West Communications Corporation, has identified $14 million worth of new capital projects which the company should invest in next year. The optimal capital structure for the company is 40 percent debt and 60 percent equity. If the expected earnings for this year is $10 million, what amount of dividend should she recommend according to residual theory?

Residual Theory of Dividend Policy

16-6. Use the same data give in problem 16-5. Now, what would be the amount of dividend that could be paid if East West's net income for this year was:

Residual Theory of Dividend Policy

a. $16 million
b. $6 million?

16-7. Jan Brady, Chief Accountant of Mulberry Silk Products, is trying to work out the feasibility of a 20 percent stock dividend. The equity section of the balance sheet follows:

Stock Dividend

	($ 000s)
Common Stock (2 million shares, $1 par)	2,000
Capital in excess of par	8,000
Retained Earnings	10,000
Total Common Equity	20,000

The current market price of the company's stock is $31 per share. Is it possible to pay 20 percent stock dividend? Is it possible to pay a 10 percent stock dividend? Explain.

16-8. Use the same data given in problem 16-7. After payment of a 10 percent stock dividend, what will be the expected market price of the stock? Also, show how the equity section of the balance sheet will change.

Stock Dividend

Stock Split

16-9. Wesley Crusher, Chief Accountant of Blue Sky Cruise Lines, is trying to figure out the effect of a 3–1 stock split. The equity section of the balance sheet follows:

	($ 000s)
Common Stock (3 million shares, $1.00 par)	3,000
Capital in excess of par	7,000
Retained Earnings	10,000
Total Common Equity	20,000

The current market price of the company's stock is $33 per share. If Blue Sky Cruise Lines decided to have a 3–1 stock split, how would the equity section change after the split? What would be the stock's market price?

Stock Split

16-10. Use the same information given in problem 16-9. If Blue Sky Cruise Lines' net income is $800,000, what is the earnings per share before and after the 3–1 stock split? Will there be any change in the price to earnings ratio before and after the stock split?

16-11. Sumner Outdoor Equipment Company has decided to go for a 5–1 stock split. The common shareholders received a dividend of $1.33 per share after the split.

   a. If the dollar amount of dividends paid after the split is same as that paid last year before the split, what was the dividend per share last year?
   b. If the dollar amount of dividends paid after the split is 10 percent higher than what was paid last year before the split, what was the dividend per share last year?

Challenge Problem

16-12. Market price of Linden Landscaping Company's stock is $30 the day before the stock goes ex-dividend. The earnings of the company are $10 million, and the company follows a dividend policy with constant payout ratio of 40 percent. There are 1 million shares of common stock outstanding. What would be the new ex-dividend price of the stock?

Long-term Dividend (Residual Theory)

16-13. In its strategic plan for the next five years, Springfield Manufacturing Company has projected the following net income and capital investments (Figures in $000s):

Year	Net Income	Investments
1998	1,000	800
1999	1,100	1,000
2000	1,200	2,000
2001	1,300	800
2002	1,400	1,000

The capital structure the company wishes to maintain is 40 percent debt and 60 percent equity. There are currently 500,000 shares of common stock outstanding.

If you own 500 shares of common stock, calculate the amounts you would receive in dividends over the next five years (1998 to 2002), assuming that the company uses the residual dividend theory each year to determine the dividend to be paid to its common stock holders.

Long-term Dividend (Residual Theory)

16-14. Use the same data given in problem 16-13. Now assume that the company plans to issue 100,000 new shares of common stock in the year 2000 at $6 per share ($1 per plus $5 capital in excess of per). What will be the dividend that you would receive in the years 2000, 2001, and 2002 assuming your common stock holding remains same at 500 shares?

Comprehensive Problem

16-15. The equity section of the balance sheet of Cafe Vienna is given next:

	($ 000s)
Common Stock (500,000 shares, $3 par)	1,500
Capital in excess of par	3,500
Retained Earnings	5,000
Total Common Equity	10,000

The company earned a net income of $3 million this year. Historically, the company has paid dividends with a constant payout ratio of 50 percent. The stock will sell at $47 after the ex-dividend date.

William Riker, the vice president of finance for Cafe Vienna, is considering all possible ways to increase the company's earning per share (EPS). One possibility he is weighing is to buy back some of the company's outstanding shares of common stock from the market using all its net income earned this year without paying any dividend to its common stockholders.

   a. Determine the repurchase price of the common stock.
   b. Calculate the number of shares that could be repurchased using this year's net income.
   c. Show the changes in the equity section of the balance sheet after the repurchase.
   d. If net income next year is expected to be $4 million, what would be the EPS next year with and without the repurchase?
   e. If you own 50 shares of the company's common stock, would you like the company's decision of buying back the stock instead of paying a dividend?

Answers to Self-Test

ST-1. Dividend Payout Ratio = dividends paid ÷ net income = ($4/share × 100,000 shares) ÷ $1,000,000 = $400,000 ÷ $1,000,000 = .40 = 40%

ST-2. No. According to the residual theory of dividends, the amount of earnings that should be retained is determined first and whatever amount is left over is paid out in dividends.

ST-3. A company following the clientele theory of dividends might have either high or low dividend payments. If the stockholders preferred high dividends, that is what would be paid. If they preferred low dividends, that would be the policy.

ST-4. The date of record is the date on which a company checks its stockholder records. Investors listed in the records on that date are entitled to receive the dividend that was recently declared.

ST-5. $2 original par value ÷ 4 (4 for 1 split) = $.50 new par value

**SHORT-TERM
FINANCIAL
MANAGEMENT
DECISIONS**

chapter 17

Working Capital Policy

Ready money is Aladdin's lamp.

Lord Byron

Chapter Objectives

After reading this chapter, you should be able to:

1. Explain the importance of managing working capital.

2. Discuss how the trade-off between liquidity and profitability affects a firm's current asset management policy.

3. Describe how a firm reaches an optimal level of current assets.

4. Discuss the effects of the three approaches to working capital financing policy.

Working Capital as an Endangered Species

It's one thing to have a thriving business; it's another to have cash on hand to pay those daily bills. Tom Buschman, owner and CEO of a $3 million manufacturer of parts for paper machinery, thought he had a lot of cash. So he decided to expand his production facilities. Whoops! That year his company computed its taxes at the last minute and discovered it owed the IRS $15,000. The company didn't have the cash because it had spent the money on the expansion. To make matters worse, its biggest customer had filed for bankruptcy.

"I was really scared. We didn't have a credit line. I didn't know how we'd pay off that tax bill." Buschman's company was saved by a strong flow of orders, but he learned a hard lesson about having enough working capital available to meet daily expenses and emergencies.

For Roxanne Coady, owner of a small bookstore, the problem was small items that were eating too deeply into her working capital, combined with low inventory turnover that kept her cash flow down. The store finally showed a profit when she cut back on such items as the $2,500 annual expense for shopping bags and increased inventory turnover by 50 percent.

Roxanne Coady and Tom Busch-man both learned a hard lesson: Working capital must be there when you need it. ✳

Sources: Jill Andresky Fraser, "The Tax-Wise Cash Monitor," *Entrepreneur Magazine* (January 1995): 75; Roxanne Coady, "The Cobbler's Shoes," *Inc. Magazine* (January 1996): 21; Brent Bowers, "This Store Is a Hit But Somehow Cash Flow Is Missing," *The Wall Street Journal* (April 13, 1993): B2.

Chapter Overview

In this chapter we examine *working capital policy*—the management of a firm's current assets and their financing. First, we'll see why firms manage working capital carefully, why they accumulate it, and how to classify current assets. We then investigate what determines a firm's working capital policy, and look at different types of policies.

Managing Working Capital

Working capital refers to a firm's current assets. By "current" we mean those assets that the firm expects to convert into cash within a year. Current assets include *cash*; *inventory*, which generates cash when the items are sold; and *accounts receivable*, which produces cash when customers pay off their credit accounts. Current assets are considered liquid because they can be transformed into cash in a relatively short time.

Net working capital is the firm's current assets minus current liabilities. Current liabilities are business obligations (that is, debts) that the firm plans to pay off or otherwise satisfy within a year. Examples include *accounts payable*—bills due soon—and *notes payable*—loans due to be paid in less than a year.

Table 17-1 shows the working capital and net working capital for the Green World Lawn Care Products Company, which manufactures lawn and gardening products and sells them to retailers.

In Table 17-1 we see that Green World has $13,000 in current assets (working capital), $11,000 in current liabilities, and $2,000 in net working capital ($13,000 − $11,000 = $2,000). Net working capital is important to firms. It represents the amount of current assets remaining if they were liquidated to pay the company's short-term debts.

Working capital policy is the firm's policy about its working capital level and how its working capital should be financed. For instance, a firm needs to make decisions about how much to keep in its cash account, what level of inventory to maintain, and how much to allow accounts receivable to build up. The firm must also decide whether to finance current assets with short-term funds, long-term funds, or

Cash	$ 2,000	Accounts Payable	$ 7,000
Accounts Receivable	1,000	Notes Payable	4,000
Inventory	10,000	Total Current Liabilities	11,000
Total Current Assets	13,000	Other Liabilities	7,000
Other Assets	32,000	Common Stock	27,000
Total Assets	$45,000	Total Liabilities & Equity	$45,000

TABLE 17-1

Green World Lawn Care Products Company Balance Sheet, as of December 31, 1996.

some mixture of the two. Together, the level and financing decisions make up the firm's working capital policy.

WHY BUSINESSES ACCUMULATE WORKING CAPITAL

Why do firms accumulate working capital, and why does its level vary over time? In this section we examine the answers to these two questions.

Fluctuating Current Assets

Many factors affect a firm's working capital policy. For instance, a service firm may require a different level of current assets than a manufacturing firm. Or, a business like Jason's Popcorn Wagon business (from chapter 13), which makes and sells popcorn during the summer months only, has different working capital needs than a firm that makes products year round.

To illustrate the principles of working capital policy, we focus on a manufacturing firm that has level production—that is, it produces the same amount of product every month, year round. However, its sales are seasonal—the firm sells more in certain time periods than in others. Many businesses are seasonal. (For instance, a swimwear manufacturer may sell many more swimsuits at the start of summer than it does in other months. A lawn care products manufacturer will probably have more sales at the start of the gardening season than it will in other months.)

If a business has level production but not level sales, inventory increases when production exceeds sales. Inventory then falls when sales exceed production. The firm's other current assets may fluctuate during the year as well. Accounts receivable,

Figure 17-1 **The Variation in Current Assets over Time for Green World Lawn Care Products**

Figure 17-1 shows how the current assets of a company tend to fluctuate over time, but never fall below a permanent level of current assets.

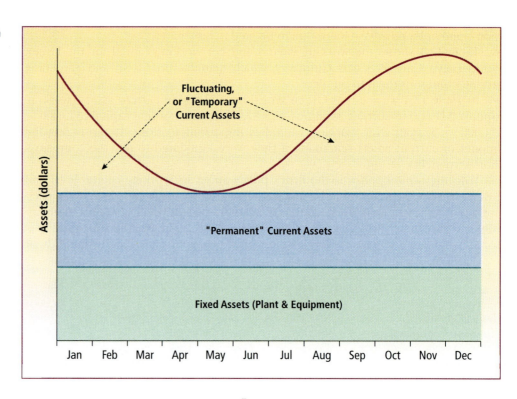

for example, will rise when new credit sales exceed customer payments, and will fall when customer payments exceed new credit sales. Cash will accumulate as sales revenues are collected and will decline when bills are paid. Thus, the current assets of the business will fluctuate over time.

Permanent and Temporary Current Assets

While the level of current assets in the firm may fluctuate, it rarely reaches zero. The firm will nearly always have some cash on hand, hold some inventory in stock, and be owed some amount of money. Current assets thus reach various temporary levels, but will rarely fall below some minimal permanent level. This effect is illustrated for the Green World Lawn Care Products Company in Figure 17-1 (page 412).

Figure 17-1 shows three categories of business assets that affect a firm's working capital policy:

1. **Temporary current assets** represent the level of inventory, cash, and accounts receivable that fluctuate seasonally.
2. **Permanent current assets** represent the base level of inventory, cash, and accounts receivable, which tends to be maintained.
3. **Fixed assets** represent the land, buildings, equipment, and other assets that would not normally be sold or otherwise disposed of for a long period of time.

Permanent current assets tend to build up on a firm's balance sheet year after year. Cash collections increase as the business grows, accounts receivable grow as the list of credit customers lengthens, inventory on hand rises as new facilities are opened, and so on. Figure 17-2 shows how the Green World Lawn Care Products' current assets might vary over several years.

◄ Take Note

The term "permanent current assets" may sound like an oxymoron (like "jumbo shrimp"), but it's not. A portion of a firm's current assets are likely to remain on a firm's balance sheet indefinitely.

Figure 17-2 **The Variation in Current Assets over Several Years for Green World Lawn Care Products**

Figure 17-2 shows how a typical firm's current assets tend to build up from year to year, while fluctuating within each year. The effect occurs because as firms grow, they accumulate more cash, accounts receivable, and inventory over time.

Fluctuating, or "Temporary" Current Assets

Assets (dollars)

"Permanent" Current Assets

Fixed Assets (Plant & Equipment)

Year 1   Year 2   Year 3

As Figure 17-2 shows, businesses have two tasks: First, they must contend with current assets that fluctuate through their business cycle. Second, they must manage permanent current asset growth due to long-term business growth over time. In the sections that follow, we discuss how firms do this.

Liquidity versus Profitability

Lenders would like a company to have a large excess of current assets over current liabilities. But the owners don't necessarily feel the same way. Think about it. Current assets—in the form of cash, accounts receivable, and inventory—do not earn the firm a very high return. Cash is usually held in a commercial bank checking account that pays no interest.[1] Accounts receivable earns no return because it represents money that customers owe to the firm that the firm doesn't have yet. Inventory earns no return until it's sold. (Inventory being held by the firm is just material sitting in a warehouse, earning nothing.) These assets have the advantage of being liquid, but holding them is not very profitable.

Now consider the company's noncurrent assets—its land, buildings, machinery, equipment, and long-term investments. These assets can earn a substantial return. The company's land, buildings, machinery, and equipment are used to turn raw material into products that can be sold for a profit. Long-term investments (such as investments in subsidiaries) generally produce greater returns than current assets. These noncurrent assets may be profitable, but they are usually not very liquid. Lenders are reluctant to let firms use them for collateral (protection in the event of a default) for short-term loans. Why? Because lenders will have to spend more time and expense to sell noncurrent assets if firms default on their loans and the lenders become the asset owners. As a result, lenders prefer that firms use liquid assets as loan collateral.

Firms, then, are faced with a trade-off in their working capital management policy. At one extreme they can seek liquidity, holding a lot of cash and other current assets in case cash is needed soon. At the other extreme they can seek profitability, holding a low level of current assets and investing primarily in long-term, high-return-producing assets.

In practice, no firm would actually choose either of these extreme positions. Instead, managers seek a balance between liquidity and profitability that reflects their desire for profit and their need for liquidity.

Establishing the Optimal Level of Current Assets

The search for a balance between liquidity and profitability serves as a general guide for financial managers looking for an optimal level of current assets. However, the level managers eventually achieve is actually a result of their efforts to maintain optimal levels of each of the *components* of the current asset group. In other words, a firm's optimal level of current assets is reached when the optimal level of cash, of inventory, and of accounts receivable[2] is achieved. Each asset

---

[1] Business checking accounts almost never pay interest.
[2] Along with any other current assets the firm possesses, of course. In this book we concentrate on these three major categories of current assets.

account is managed separately, and the combined results produce the actual level of current assets. Here's a description of the attempt to find the optimal level for each current asset account:

- *Cash:* Managers try to keep just enough cash on hand to conduct day-to-day business, while investing extra amounts in short-term marketable securities. We discuss cash in detail in chapter 18.
- *Inventory:* Managers seek the level that reduces lost sales due to lack of inventory, while at the same time holding down inventory costs. We discuss inventory management in chapter 19.
- *Accounts receivable:* Firms want to enhance sales but hold down bad debt and collection expenses through sound credit policies. We discuss credit policies in chapter 19.

Once financial managers set policies to attain the optimal level of current assets, they must turn their attention to the flip side of working capital management: managing current liabilities.

Managing Current Liabilities: Risk and Return

A firm's current asset fluctuations and any long-term build-up of current assets (its working capital) must, of course, be financed. The question facing financial managers is whether to obtain the financing from short–term borrowing, long–term borrowing, contributions from the owners (equity financing), or some mixture of all three.

As is so often the case, the choice of the firm's working capital financing blend depends on managers' desire for profit versus their degree of risk aversion. Short–term debt financing is generally less expensive than long-term debt and always less expensive than equity financing. Recall from chapter 2 that short-term interest rates are usually lower than long–term interest rates. Short–term loans, however, are more risky because a firm may not have enough cash to re-pay the loans (due to cash flow fluctuations) or interest rates may increase and increase the cost of short-term funds as loans are renewed. Long–term debt and/or equity financing is less risky from the firm's perspective because it puts repayment off (forever, in the case of stock) and locks in an interest rate for a long time period.

The balance between the risk and return of financing options depends on the firm, its financial managers, and its financing approaches. We discuss several financing approaches next.

In our discussion we assume that a firm has all available financing alternatives options. In practice, however, some firms may have limited financing options. For example small firms usually have limited access to long-term capital markets.

Three Working Capital Financing Approaches

The three primary working capital financing approaches are the *aggressive* approach, the *conservative* approach, and the *moderate* approach. A firm that takes an aggressive approach uses more short-term financing to finance current assets. Firm risk increases, due to the risk of fluctuating interest rates, but the potential for higher returns increases because of the generally low-cost financing. A firm that implements the conservative approach avoids short-term financing to reduce risk, but decreases the potential for maximum value creation because of the high cost of long-term debt and equity financing. The moderate approach tries to balance risk and return concerns.

The Aggressive Approach

We know that short-term interest rates are normally lower than long-term interest rates. We also know that borrowing short-term is riskier than borrowing long-term because the loan must be paid off or refinanced sooner rather than later.

The **aggressive working capital financing approach** involves the use of short-term debt to finance at least the firm's temporary assets, some or all of its permanent current assets, and possibly some of its long-term fixed assets. The aggressive approach is shown graphically in Figure 17-3.

If we compare current assets and current liabilities in Figure 17-3, we see that all the firm's temporary current assets and most of its permanent current assets are being financed with short-term debt (the current liabilities). As a result, the firm has very little *net* working capital. Depending on the nature of the firm's business, this small amount of net working capital can be risky. There isn't much cushion between the value of liquid assets and the amount of debt due in the short-term.

Firms may be more aggressive than the firm depicted in Figure 17-3. If the firm's managers financed *all* working capital from short-term debt, then current assets would equal current liabilities and the firm would have zero net working capital—no cushion at all. Managers may go even further and finance a portion of the firm's long-term assets (plant and equipment) with short-term debt, creating a *negative* net working capital. However, such an approach is *very* risky. (Think what would happen to a firm using that approach if short-term interest rates rose unexpectedly.)

What tempts financial managers to take the aggressive approach and use a relatively large amount of short-term debt for working capital financing? Usually lower interest rates tempt them. Managers will take a risk if the promise of return is high enough to justify it.

Figure 17-3 **The Aggressive Working Capital Financing Approach**

Figure 17-3 shows the firm's assets on the left, and liabilities and equity on the right. Subtracting current liabilities from current assets shows that the firm's working capital financing strategy is to finance nearly all current assets with current liabilities, resulting in a small amount of net working capital.

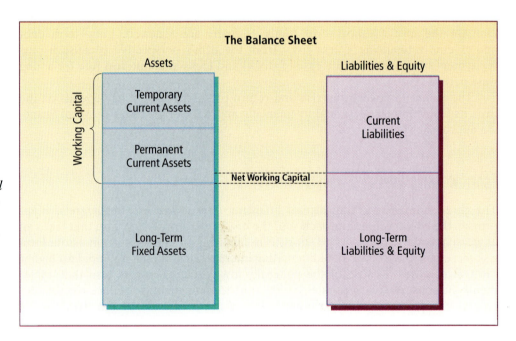

The Conservative Approach

Borrowing long-term is considered less risky than borrowing short-term. This is because the borrower has a longer time to use the loan proceeds before repayment is due. Furthermore, if interest rates should go up during the period of the loan, the long-term borrower has another advantage. The long-term borrower has locked in a fixed interest rate and may end up paying less total interest than the short-term borrower, who must renew the loan each time it comes due—at a new, higher interest rate. If market rates fall the long-term borrower can usually refinance.

The **conservative working capital financing approach** involves the use of long-term debt and equity to finance all long-term fixed assets and permanent current assets, in addition to some part of temporary current assets. The conservative approach is shown graphically in Figure 17-4.

Compare current assets to current liabilities in Figure 17-4. Note that all the firm's permanent current assets and most of its temporary current assets are being financed with long-term debt or equity. As a result, current assets exceed current liabilities by a wide margin and the firm has a large amount of *net* working capital. Having a large amount of net working capital is a relatively low-risk position because the firm has many assets that could be liquidated to satisfy short-term debts.

A financial manager who applies an ultra-conservative approach would use cash from the owners to finance all asset financing needs (high cash balance supported by equity), and incur no debt. By using only equity capital, the firm would also have the maximum amount of net working capital possible, since it would have no current liabilities.

The safety of the conservative approach has a cost. Long-term financing is generally more expensive than short-term financing. So relying on long-term debt and equity sources to finance working capital consumes funds that could otherwise be put to more productive use.

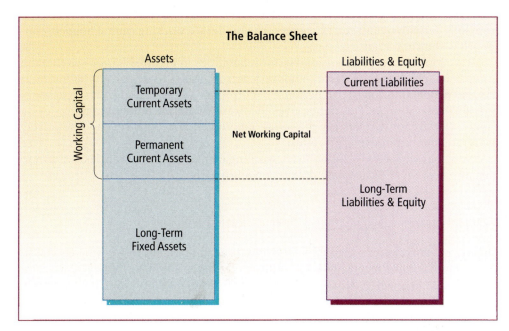

Figure 17-4 The Conservative Working Capital Financing Approach

The relative size of the current asset and current liability accounts in Figure 17-4 reveals the firm's working capital financing strategy. The figure shows that the firm is financing nearly all current assets with long-term liabilities and equity, resulting in a high level of net working capital.

Figure 17-5 **The Moderate Working Capital Financing Approach**

In Figure 17-5 we see that the firm's approach to working capital financing policy is to finance its permanent current assets with long-term debt and equity, and its temporary current assets with current liabilities. This results in a moderate level of net working capital.

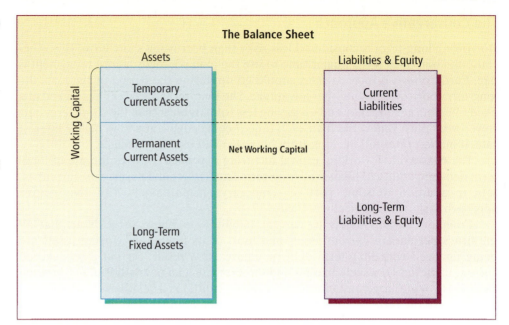

The Moderate Approach

An accounting concept known as *the matching principle* states that the cost of an asset should be recognized over the length of time that the asset provides revenue, or benefit, to the business.

The concept of the matching principle can be applied to define a moderate position between the aggressive and the conservative working capital financing approaches. According to the matching principle, temporary current assets that are only going to be on the balance sheet for a short time should be financed with short-term debt—that is, current liabilities. Permanent current assets and long-term fixed assets that are going to be on the balance sheet for a long time should be financed from long-term debt and equity sources. The **moderate working capital financing approach** is shown in Figure 17-5.

If we look at current assets and current liabilities in Figure 17-5, we see that the firm has matched its short-term temporary current assets to its current liabilities. It has also matched its long-term permanent current assets and fixed assets to its long-term financing sources. This policy gives the firm a moderate amount of net working capital. It calls for a relatively moderate amount of risk balanced by a relatively moderate amount of expected return.

Now that we have described three working capital financing policies, we turn to an analysis of the effect of such policies on a firm.

WORKING CAPITAL FINANCING AND FINANCIAL RATIOS

The use of *ratio analysis* highlights how the three approaches to working capital financing policy can affect the risk and return potential of a firm. In Table 17-2 we compare selected financial ratios for three different firms that differ only in the manner in which they finance their working capital. Firm A takes the aggressive approach, Firm C takes the conservative approach, and Firm M takes the moderate approach.

DATA AS OF THE END OF THE LAST FISCAL YEAR	FIRM A AGGRESSIVE	FIRM C CONSERVATIVE	FIRM M MODERATE
Temporary Current Assets	$ 200	$ 200	$ 200
Permanent Current Assets	$ 400	$ 400	$ 400
Fixed Assets	$ 600	$ 600	$ 600
Total Assets	$1,200	$1,200	$1,200
Current Liabilities	$ 300	$ 100	$ 200
Long-Term Debt	$ 300	$ 500	$ 400
Stockholders' Equity	$ 600	$ 600	$ 600
Total Liabilities & Equity	$1,200	$1,200	$1,200
Net Income for the Year	$ 126	$ 114	$ 120
Net Working Capital	$ 300	$ 500	$ 400
Current Ratio	2.0	6.0	3.0
Total Debt to Total Assets Ratio	50%	50%	50.0%
Return on Equity	21%	19%	20.0%

TABLE 17-3

The Three Approaches
to Working Capital
Financing Policy—Cost
and Risk Factors

	AGGRESSIVE	CONSERVATIVE	MODERATE
Cost	Low	High	In-Between
Risk	High	Low	In-Between

Notice in Table 17-2 that Firm A, which follows an aggressive financing approach, has the highest net income, smallest amount of net working capital, the lowest current ratio, and the highest return on stockholders' equity of any of the three firms. This is consistent with the relationship between risk and return (the more risk a firm takes, the more return it earns). There is no guarantee, of course, that net income will be positive.

Firm C, which follows the conservative financing approach, has the lowest net income, the largest amount of net working capital, the highest current ratio, and the lowest return on stockholders' equity of the three firms. This reflects its relatively lower risk and lower return potential.

Firm M, which follows the moderate approach of matching its short-term temporary current assets to its current liabilities is, of course, in a position between the other two.

Table 17-3 summarizes the cost and risk considerations of the aggressive, conservative, and moderate approaches to working capital financing.

In the real world, of course, each firm must decide on its balance of financing sources and its approach to working capital management based on its particular industry and the firm's risk and return strategy.

WHAT'S NEXT

In this chapter we examined the general working capital policy of a firm. In chapter 18 we will look at cash. Accounts receivable and inventory will follow in chapter 19. Chapter 20, short-term financing, will complete Part 5 of the text.

Interview with Michael Coleman, Vice President of Tek Soft

Michael Coleman

Michael Coleman, an engineering major in college, now serves as the executive vice president of Tek Soft, a leading international technical software developer for large companies. Before joining Tek Soft, Michael was a marketing manager for Doefer Engineering, a capital-intensive company that designed and built machines for industry. His comments show how working capital policies and working capital requirements for new, information-based companies differ greatly from the capital requirements of traditional manufacturers.

Q. *How important is managing working capital for a manufacturing company?*

Very important. In manufacturing, working capital is a huge factor because a substantial portion of your costs can be directly tied to working capital, especially inventory costs. If you only have a 10 percent profit margin, the management of working capital becomes a primary concern. If you mismanage it, your 10 percent profit margin can easily be erased by changing interest rates, paying off loans at the wrong time, or other basic working capital management problems. You can't even deliver a product to the client unless you have enough working capital. So you must manage it well.

For example, if you are building a new machine for a client and you receive payments in installments, those payments don't cover the money you used to build the machine. You have to pay a lot of money to buy raw materials—machine bases, metal, stainless steel, copper, and wire. Then the client company you're building the machine for sometimes holds off paying for as long as possible, so you don't receive cash quickly from the sale even though you've paid cash to build the machine.

So a manufacturer must watch payment schedules carefully to ensure that clients pay within a reasonable time limit, and must also watch how much to build in advance given the cost of the inventory items. The firm also has to be prepared for the cash from a sale coming later than the time of the actual sale. All these factors affect working capital management.

Q. *How important is managing working capital to a software development company?*

It's not as important as it is to a manufacturing company. In the software development business, the cost of our company's current assets is about $80,000 a year. We have about $7 million in retail sales a year.

We don't need to have huge capital investments in raw materials because disks and the paper for software manuals are relatively inexpensive. We are working mainly with people's ideas. So working capital levels are low because we take those ideas, a disk worth about 90 cents, a couple of manuals, and we sell them for $10,000 to $12,000 apiece.

Q. *Is it difficult to finance your current assets in the software business?*

Our financing options are limited. It's tough to finance our assets in the software development business because the only asset we really have is our source code—the unique way we put together the binary code to make our products. If we go to a bank and say, "We have a unique way of putting a binary code together, lend us money," the bank would probably say, "You're nuts. We can't verify that your source code has any value."

A machine builder, on the other hand, has assets that the bank can see. It has buildings, machine tools, inventory, work in progress, and a loyal customer base. These assets are easier for lenders to value than a software source code.

Source: Interview with Michael Coleman.

Summary

1. Explain the importance of managing working capital.

A firm's current assets—such as cash, inventory, and accounts receivable—are referred to as working capital. Managing the levels and financing of working capital effectively is necessary to keep the firm's costs and risk under control while maintaining a firm's returns and cash flow over the long-term.

Firms accumulate working capital because of fluctuations in sales, production, and cash or credit payments. For instance, cash accumulates as accounts are collected and declines when bills are paid. Inventory builds when production exceeds sales, and falls when sales exceed production. Accounts receivable rises as credit sales are made and falls when customers pay off their accounts. The combined effect of changes in each current asset account causes working capital to fluctuate. Furthermore, working capital will gradually build up over time unless the firm takes some concrete action to either reinvest the funds in long-term assets or distribute them to the firm's owners.

Temporary current assets represents the level of current assets that fluctuates, and permanent current assets represents the level of current assets a firm keeps regardless of periodic fluctuations.

2. Discuss how the trade-off between liquidity and profitability affects a firm's current asset management policy.

Current asset management involves a trade-off between the need for liquidity and the desire for profitability. The more current assets a firm holds, the more liquid the firm because the assets can be converted to cash relatively quickly. However, tying up funds to sustain a certain level of current assets prevents the funds from being invested in long-term, high-return producing assets.

3. Describe how a firm reaches an optimal level of current assets.

Firms reach an optimal level of current assets when the optimal level for each individual current asset account (mainly cash, inventory, and accounts receivable) is achieved. Separate techniques exist for managing each of the current asset accounts. The techniques for managing each current asset account are described in chapters 18 and 19.

4. Discuss the effects of the three approaches to working capital financing policy.

Short-term interest rates are usually lower than long-term interest rates, so financing working capital with short-term debt generally lowers the firm's financing costs. However, using short-term debt increases the risk that cash won't be available to pay the loans back, and that the firm may have to renew its loans at higher interest rates. Relying on long-term debt and/or equity sources to finance working capital decreases risk because firms repay such obligations in the long-term, and firms lock in an interest rate. A firm's return suffers, however, because long-term financing costs are normally higher than short-term costs.

The aggressive approach to working capital policy consists of financing all temporary current assets, and some or all long-term permanent current assets, and possibly a portion of fixed long-term assets with short-term debt. The conservative approach to working capital policy consists of financing all permanent current assets and some short-term temporary current assets with long-term debt and/or equity financing. The moderate approach consists of financing temporary current assets with short-term debt, and financing long-term permanent current assets with long-term debt and/or equity.

Self-Test

ST-1. Explain the liquidity–profitability tradeoff associated with working capital management.

ST-2. How is the optimal level of working capital established?

ST-3. Using the following financial data, draw a diagram showing the company's temporary current assets, permanent current assets, and long-term fixed assets during this last year.

Selected Financial Data for Past Fiscal Year (in thousands)

	Jan 1	Mar 31	Jun 30	Oct 31	Dec 31
Total Assets	$580	$480	$280	$400	$580
Fixed Assets	$100	$100	$100	$100	$100

ST-4. As of today a company has $100,000 of temporary current assets, $50,000 of permanent current assets, and $80,000 of long-term fixed assets. If the company follows the moderate approach to working capital financing, how much of its assets will be financed with short-term debt (current liabilities) and how much will be financed with long-term debt and/or equity as of today?

Review Questions

1. What is working capital?
2. What is the primary advantage to a corporation of investing some of its funds in working capital?
3. Can a corporation have too much working capital? Explain.
4. Explain how a firm determines the optimal level of current assets.
5. What are the risks associated with using a large amount of short-term financing for working capital?
6. What is the matching principle of working capital financing? What are the benefits of following this principle?
7. What are the advantages and disadvantages of the aggressive working capital financing approach?
8. What is the most conservative type of working capital financing plan a company could implement? Explain.

Build Your Communication Skills

CS-1. Research a business you find interesting. Prepare a short report outlining at least two ways that company could increase its liquidity. Consider both asset management and liability management.

CS-2. Choose any company for which you can locate balance sheet data for the last five years. Plot on a graph the company's total assets for each year and connect the data points with a line. Next, plot the company's net fixed assets for each year and connect the data points with a line. Finally, sketch a line that just touches the low points reached by the total asset line across the graph.

You should now have a graph similar to Figure 17-2. Label the appropriate areas of your graph as temporary current assets, permanent current assets, and fixed assets.

Refer to the company's latest balance sheet and note the amount of current liabilities and long-term debt and equity shown. Compare these amounts with the ending amount of current and fixed assets shown on your graph. The results will reveal the company's working capital financing policy. Explain your findings to the class.

Problems

17-1. Consider the following two companies:

Assessing Liquidity

	Company A	Company B
Cash	$1,000	$ 80
Accounts Receivable	400	880
Net Fixed Assets	1,500	1,620
	$2,900	$2,580
Accounts Payable	$ 900	$ 600
Long-Term Debt	800	1,100
Common Equity	1,200	880
	$2,900	$2,580

Which of the two firms is the most liquid? Why?

17-2. Capt. Louis Renault's Hikewell Outdoor Equipment Company has the following balance sheet accounts as of the end of last year.

Current Assets, Current Liabilities, and Net Working Capital

Cash	$ 30,000	Accounts Payable	$100,000
Accounts Receivable	15,000	Notes Payable	60,000
Inventory	130,000	Long-Term Debt	90,000
Fixed Assets	500,000	Common Equity	425,000
	$675,000		$675,000

a. What is the amount of the company's current assets, its working capital?
b. What is the amount of the company's current liabilities?
c. What is the amount of the company's net working capital?
d. What percentage of current assets is financed by current liabilities? Would you consider this an aggressive approach or a conservative approach?

17-3. Alexander Sebastian, the finance manager of Hikewell Outdoor Equipment Company of problem 17-2, thinks the way the company is financing its current assets is too risky. By the end of next year, he would like the *pro forma* balance sheet to look as shown below:

Conservative Working Capital Financing Approach

Cash	$ 30,000	Accounts Payable	$ 30,000
Accounts Receivable	15,000	Notes Payable	20,000
Inventory	130,000	Long-Term Debt	150,000
Fixed Assets	500,000	Common Equity	475,000
	$675,000		$675,000

a. What is the amount of the company's projected current assets, its working capital?
b. What is the amount of the company's projected current liabilities?
c. What is the amount of the company's projected net working capital?
d. What percentage of current assets is projected to be financed by current liabilities? Would you consider this an aggressive approach or a conservative approach?

17-4. Consider the following balance sheet for Lulu Belle's Killer Guard Dogs, Inc.:

Assessing Working Capital Policy

Assets		Liabilities & Equity	
Cash	$ 50	Accounts Payable	$ 80
Marketable Securities	0	Short-Term Debt	90
Accounts Receivable	40	Long-Term Debt	210
Inventories	70	Common Equity	310
Net Fixed Assets	530		$690
	$690		

a. How much working capital does Lulu Belle have?

b. How much net working capital does Lulu Belle have?

c. What working capital financing policy (aggressive, moderate, or conservative) is Lulu Belle following?

d. Explain what actions Lulu Belle could take to increase the company's liquidity.

Moderate Working Capital Financing Approach

17-5. Marian Pardoo, the chief financial officer of Envirosafe Chemical Company, believes in a moderate approach of financing following the matching principle. Some of the projected balance sheet accounts of the company for the end of next year follow:

	Current and Fixed Assets	Permanent Current Assets
Cash	$ 30,000	$15,000
Accounts Receivable	15,000	5,000
Inventory	130,000	80,000
Fixed Assets	500,000	
Total Assets	$675,000	

Liabilities	
Accounts Payable	$ 20,000
Short-Term Debt	?
Long-Term Debt	?
Common Equity	450,000
Total Liab. & Eq.	$675,000

How much should Marian finance by short-term debt and long-term debt to conform to the matching principle?

Aggressive Working Capital Financing Approach

17-6. Use the same data given in Problem 17-5. Marian's boss, Ann Lowell, is the Vice President of Finance of Envirosafe Chemical Company and she expects interest rates to decrease in the future and hence would like to follow a very aggressive policy using a large amount of short-term debt and a small amount of long-term debt. She would also like to decrease net working capital to $25,000. How much should Ann finance by short-term debt and how much by long-term debt to conform to her aggressive approach?

Different Working Capital Financing Approaches

17-7. Comparative data at the end of this past year for three firms following aggressive, moderate, and conservative approaches to working capital policy follow (in thousands of dollars):

	Aggressive	Moderate	Conservative
Temporary Current Assets	$ 75	$ 75	$ 75
Permanent Current Assets	100	100	100
Fixed Assets	500	500	500
Total Assets	675	675	675
Current Liabilities	160	75	50
Long-Term Debt	90	150	150
Stockholders' Equity	425	450	475
Net Income	70	70	70

Calculate, compare, and comment on the current ratios, total debt-to-asset ratios, and returns on equity of the three firms.

Challenge Problem

17-8. Greenplanet Recycling company is considering buying an additional facility at a cost of $500,000. The facility will have an economic life of five years. The company's financial officer, Karen Holmes, can finance the project by:

a. a five-year loan at an annual interest rate of 13 percent

b. a one-year loan rolled over each year for five years

Compare the total interest expenses for both the preceding alternatives under the following assumptions, and calculate the savings in the interest expenses by choosing one of two alternatives:

(i) the one-year loan has a constant interest rate of 11 percent per year over the next five years.

(ii) the one-year loan has an annual interest rate of 11 percent in the first two years, 14 percent in the third and fourth years, and 16 percent in the fifth year.

17-9. To analyze your company's working capital financing policy, you have gathered the following balance sheet data for the past twelve months (in thousands):

The Matching Principle

Date	Total Assets	Fixed Assets
Jan 31	$45	$14
Feb 28	46	14
Mar 31	34	14
Apr 30	48	14
May 31	40	14
Jun 30	30	14
Jul 31	28	14
Aug 31	39	14
Sep 30	45	14
Oct 31	39	14
Nov 30	52	14
Dec 31	50	14

Plot these data on a trendline graph. Indicate the amount of your firm's current liabilities each month if you follow the matching principle.

17-10. Milton Warden, the finance manager of WinHeart Gift Company, is analyzing past data on the firm's fixed assets, permanent current assets, and temporary current assets for each month over the last five years. The company maintains level production but its sales are seasonal. He found that the monthly level of the three types of assets over the last five years can be closely approximated by the following patterns (in thousands of dollars):

Comprehensive Problem

- Fixed assets: Remained constant at 39 each month over the last five years
- Permanent current assets: Were equal to 2 in January of Year 1 and had grown 0.16 per month each month over the last five years
- Temporary current assets: Followed the same pattern each year, starting at 0 in January, then each year it increased by 1 monthly until July and reduced by 1 monthly until it reached 0 again in January of the next year
  - **a.** Plot these data on a graph similar to the one shown in Figure 17-2.
  - **b.** Calculate and identify on the graph the level of temporary current assets, permanent current assets, and fixed assets in:
    - **(i)** the month of September of year 4
    - **(ii)** the month of August of year 5
  - **c.** Now calculate the levels of current liabilities and long-term debt in those months if the company followed:
    - **(i)** an aggressive working capital financing approach
    - **(ii)** a moderate working capital financing approach
    - **(iii)** a conservative working capital financing approach

Assume that the stockholders equity remained constant at 20 over those five years.

17-11. Buddy Love, a finance officer of Christmas Tree Ornaments and Gifts Company, is analyzing past data on the fixed assets, permanent current assets, and temporary current as-

Comprehensive Problem

sets of the company each month over the last several years. The company maintains level production but its sales peak at the end of the year. He found that the monthly level of the three types of assets over the last five years can be closely approximated by the following equations (in thousands of dollars):

- Fixed assets were equal to 55 and remained constant each month over the last five years.
- Permanent current assets were equal to 10 in January of year 1, and had grown 0.30 per month each month over the last five years.
- Temporary current assets = $m(m - 1)/4$, where m = 1, 2, . . ., 12 for Jan, Feb, . . ., Dec, respectively.
  a. Plot these data on a graph similar to the one shown in Figure 17-2.
  b. Calculate and identify on your graph the level of temporary current assets, permanent current assets, and fixed assets at the following times:
    (i) the month of September of year 2
    (ii) the month of October of year 4
    (iii) year 5's minimum and maximum levels of total assets and the months those levels occurred
  c. Now calculate the levels of current liabilities and long-term debt in the months described in part b of this problem if the company followed:
    (i) an aggressive working capital financing approach
    (ii) a moderate working capital financing approach
    (iii) a conservative working capital financing approach

Assume that the stockholders equity remained constant at 30 over those five years.

Answers to Self-Test

ST-1. Working capital (that is, current assets in the form of cash, accounts receivable, inventory, and so on) can normally be exchanged for cash, or liquidated, in a relatively short time. Therefore the more working capital a company maintains, the easier it is to raise cash quickly. However, maintaining working capital costs money and it ties up funds that could otherwise be used to invest in long-term income-producing assets, so that profits and returns suffer. For this reason, we say that managing working capital involves balancing liquidity and profitability.

ST-2. The optimal level of working capital is achieved when the optimal levels of each current asset account—cash, inventory, accounts receivable, and any others—are reached. Each current asset category is managed separately and the combined results produce the optimal level of current assets.

ST-3.

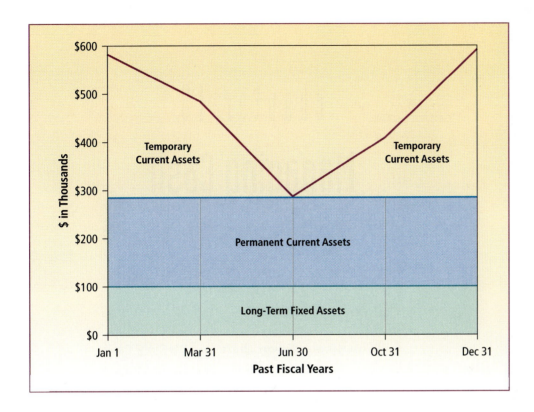

ST-4. Following the moderate approach, the company will finance its temporary current assets with short-term debt and the rest of its assets with long-term debt and equity. Therefore, as of today, the company will have on its balance sheet:

Current Liabilities	$100,000
Long-Term Debt & Equity	$130,000

chapter 18

Managing Cash

I've never been poor, but I've been broke.

Mike Todd

Chapter Objectives

After reading this chapter, you should be able to:

1. List the factors that affect a company's desired minimum cash balance.

2. List the factors that affect a company's maximum cash balance.

3. Apply the Miller–Orr model to establish a target optimal cash balance.

4. Prepare a cash budget.

5. Explain how firms manage their cash inflows and outflows to maximize value.

A Billion Here, a Billion There . . . It's Only Cash

What do you do with a lot of extra cash, especially if you're a big business? When Rockwell International had a few extra billion in cash, it bought Reliance Electric for $1.6 billion. When engine maker Briggs & Stratton had record earnings of $102 million and a strong cash balance, it shifted 2,000 jobs out of Milwaukee to lower wage sites in the southern United States. Said Chief Executive Frederick Stratton, "We have to think of the long-term competitiveness of the company." Recent profits enabled Northwest Airlines to build a cash pool of $1.6 billion, which it will use to pay off at least $600 million in debts.

Instead of buying assets, moving jobs, or paying off debt, other companies keep their cash.

Healthy profits allowed Ford to accumulate $9.2 billion. A cash account of $7.3 billion enticed Kirk Kerkorian to try to take over Chrysler. He claimed that Chrysler was carrying more cash than it needed, and proposed taking $5.5 billion out of the cash account to help pay for his $20 billion takeover bid.

Kerkorian wasn't too worried about taking the $5.5 billion out of Chrysler's pocket. He thought it could replenish its cash quickly. In fact, former Chrysler Chairman Lee Iacocca, a Kerkorian ally in the bid, stated that the company could handle a business downturn with as little as $2.5 billion in cash, with an equal amount from credit lines. Iacocca asked Chrysler's management, "What do you want all that cash for? You're not a bank." ❋

Sources: Neal Templin and Steven Lipin, "Sides in Chrysler Bid Differ on How Much a Rainy Day Costs," *The Wall Street Journal* (April 17, 1995): A3; Kevin Kelly, "The Problem Now: What to Do with All That Cash!" *Business Week* (December 5, 1994).

CHAPTER OVERVIEW

In this chapter we look at how firms manage cash. Cash flow management can differ greatly from firm to firm, as shown in the chapter opening. Here, we start by exploring factors that affect a company's optimal cash balance and learn how to estimate the optimal balance. Then, we examine how firms forecast their cash needs, develop a cash budget, and manage cash inflows and outflows.

CASH MANAGEMENT CONCEPTS

Whether they work in a large multinational corporation, such as Chrysler, or a small business, financial managers need to know how much cash to keep on hand. Cash management may sound simple. Shouldn't businesses accumulate as much cash as possible? It's not that easy. Recall from chapter 17 that cash earns no return for the business owners. In fact, a business that accumulated as much cash as possible and did not invest in any assets would fail because it would earn no return for the stockholders.[1] Cash, then, should not be obtained for its own sake. Rather, it should be considered the "grease" that enables the machinery of the firm to run. Cash management is the process of controlling how much of this grease is needed and where and when to apply it.

> **◄ Take Note**
>
> *In this chapter the term* **cash** *refers to dollar amounts in the firm's checking account at a commercial bank, and to coin and currency in the cash drawer. Interest is not generally paid on business checking accounts and, of course, coin and currency earn no interest when in the cash drawer.*

DETERMINING THE OPTIMAL CASH BALANCE

To determine how much cash a firm should keep on hand, financial managers must:

- Maintain enough in its cash account to make payments when needed (minimum balance).
- Keep just the needed amount in its cash account so that the firm can invest excess funds and earn returns (maximum balance).

Let's examine the factors that affect the minimum cash balance and the maximum cash balance.

---

[1]In fact, because there would be no investment in earning assets, such a business would never accumulate more cash than was originally contributed by the founders.

The Minimum Cash Balance

The size of a firm's minimum cash balance depends on three factors: (1) how quickly and cheaply a firm can raise cash when needed; (2) how accurately the firm's managers can predict when cash payment requirements will occur; and (3) how much precautionary cash the firm's managers want to safeguard against emergencies. The effect of these three factors on the minimum cash balance is shown in Figure 18-1.

We examine the three factors that affect a firm's minimum cash balance in the following sections.

Raising Cash Quickly When Needed   If a firm's managers could obtain cash instantly whenever they needed it, at zero cost, they wouldn't need to maintain any balance in the cash account at all. All the firm's funds could be invested in short-term income-producing securities as soon as received. In the real world, of course, neither firms nor anyone else can borrow or sell assets to raise all the cash they want any time, instantly, at zero cost. In practice, obtaining cash usually takes time and has a positive cost. Therefore businesses maintain at least some cash in their checking accounts.

The question is, how much cash is enough? The answer is, only experience will tell. The more difficult or expensive it is to get cash when needed, the more a firm needs to keep in its checking account. At most—if cash were very difficult to obtain because the firm had no liquid assets, or if short-term interest rates were very high— the firm would want to keep enough cash on hand to cover all foreseeable needs until the next time the firm expects to receive more cash.

Predicting Cash Needs   Cash flows can be volatile because of the business environment or the risk of the business. For instance, in a weak economy, people and firms pay bills more slowly. So even though sales may be strong, a firm may not have much cash. Also, in an economy with interest rate fluctuations or inflation, cash flow needs can vary suddenly because of economic factors. To protect against an uncertain business environment, firms may maintain extra cash to cover cash needs.

Similarly, the cash flows of a startup or high-risk business may vary because the company grows at uneven, often unpredictable rates. Managers, then, may have a

Figure 18-1 **Factors Affecting the Minimum Cash Balance**

Figure 18-1 shows the three factors that determine the minimum amount a firm will keep in its cash account.

The MINIMUM cash balance is affected by:

(1) Management's ability to raise cash quickly when needed

(2) Management's ability to forcast cash needs

(3) The amount maintained for emergencies

tough time estimating the firm's cash needs with certainty. Such firms often keep extra cash to act as a buffer against cash flow volatility.

How much extra cash a firm keeps in its coffers to protect against uncertainty depends on two factors: how difficult and expensive it is to raise cash when needed, and how volatile the firm's cash flow patterns are.

Coping with Emergencies   Most cash payments are expected and planned. But unforeseen emergencies may occur: storms, fires, strikes, riots, and outbreaks of disease. These emergencies can cause unexpected, sometimes large, drains on a firm's cash. Insurance can help, but there is no substitute for having cash ready when you need it. Managers, then, assess the likelihood of potential emergencies, and how quickly and easily cash can be obtained in case of an emergency. They adjust their cash balances accordingly. The more *risk averse* managers are, the more precautionary cash they keep on hand for emergencies.

The Maximum Cash Balance

Suppose that a firm's managers decide they wish to keep at least $20,000 in the firm's cash account. The next question is, how much should be allowed to accumulate in the cash account before the excess is withdrawn and invested in something that produces a return? If the balance in the cash account is $20,001, for example, should a dollar be withdrawn and invested? Should $30,000 be allowed to accumulate before any is withdrawn and invested? The answer depends on three factors: (1) the available investment opportunities, (2) the expected return from these opportunities, and (3) the transaction cost of withdrawing cash and making an investment. The factors that affect a firm's maximum cash balance are summarized in Figure 18-2.

We describe the three factors affecting the maximum cash balance in detail next.

Available Investment Opportunities   All businesses have at least a few (and some have many) alternative short-term income-producing investments in which they could invest their cash. These range from money market mutual funds and

We discussed types of short-term securities in chapter 2, pages 23–25.

Figure 18-2   **Factors Affecting the Maximum Cash Balance**

Figure 18-2 shows the three factors that affect a firm's maximum cash balance.

The MAXIMUM cash balance is affected by:

(1) Available investment opportunities

(2) Expected return from investment opportunities

(3) Transaction cost of making investments

CDs, to Eurodollars and commercial paper. The more opportunities a firm has, the sooner it will invest rather than allow cash to simply accumulate in the firm's checking account.

Expected Return on Investments The potential return on investments is just as important as the number of investments. If the expected return is relatively high, firms will be quick to invest excess cash. If the expected return is relatively low, however, firms might let more cash accumulate before investing.

Transaction Cost of Making Investments Investing has costs. For instance, when you deposit money in a savings account, someone must search for information about and arrange for the transfer of the funds to the savings account. The search and implementation efforts take time. And that time has a cost.

Monetary and other costs of transferring cash into an investment are **transaction costs**—the costs associated with the transaction. Managers are interested in transaction costs because if the potential income from an investment does not exceed the cost of making the investment, then the investment is not worthwhile. Transaction costs also affect the frequency of a firm's investments. If transaction costs are relatively low, the firm will invest often, and will let only a small amount of excess cash accumulate in the cash account. Conversely, if transaction costs are relatively high, the firm will make fewer investments, letting a larger amount of cash accumulate in the meantime.

In this section we have seen that firms determine some minimum and maximum amount to keep in their cash accounts. The minimum amount is based on how quickly and cheaply firms can raise cash when needed, how accurately cash needs can be predicted, and how much precautionary cash a firm keeps for emergencies. The maximum amount depends on available investment opportunities, the expected returns from the investments, and the transaction costs of withdrawing the cash and making the investment.

Determining the Optimal Cash Balance

Financial theorists have developed mathematical models to help firms find an optimal "target" cash balance, between the minimum and maximum limits, that balances liquidity and profitability concerns. In the following sections, we discuss one of these models, the Miller–Orr model.

The Miller–Orr Cash Management Model In 1966 Merton Miller and Daniel Orr developed a cash management model that solves for an optimal target cash balance about which the cash balance fluctuates until it reaches an upper or lower limit.[2] If the upper limit is reached, investment securities are bought, bringing the cash balance down to the target again. If the lower limit is reached, investment securities are sold, bringing the cash balance up to the target. Figure 18-3 shows the operation of the model.

---

[2]Merton Miller and Daniel Orr, "A Model of the Demand for Money by Firms," *Quarterly Journal of Economics* (August 1966): 413–35.

Figure 18-3 Cash Balances in a Typical Month Using the Miller–Orr Model

Figure 18-3 shows a firm's fluctuating cash flows, and its upper, lower, and optimal cash balances according to the Miller–Orr model.

The formula for the target cash balance Z shown in Figure 18-3 follows:

Miller–Orr Model
Formula for the Target Cash Balance

$$Z = \sqrt[3]{\frac{3 \times TC \times V}{4 \times r}} + L \qquad (18\text{-}1)$$

where: TC = the transaction cost of buying or selling short-term investment securities

V = the variance of net daily cash flows

r = the daily rate of return on short-term investment securities

L = the lower limit to be maintained in the cash account

Notice in Figure 18-3 that the target cash balance, Z, is one-third of the way between the lower limit, L, and the upper limit, H. The Miller–Orr formula for the upper limit, H, is as follows:

Miller–Orr Model
Formula for the Upper Limit for the Cash Account

$$H = 3Z - 2L \qquad (18\text{-}2)$$

In the Miller–Orr model, the lower limit, L, is set by management according to the minimum cash balance concerns discussed earlier.

To illustrate how the Miller–Orr model works, assume that short-term investment securities are yielding 4 percent per year, and that it costs the firm $30 each time it buys or sells investment securities. Now assume that the firm's cash inflows and outflows occur irregularly, and the variance of the daily net cash flows has been found to be $90,846. Management wants to keep at least $1,000 in the cash account for emergencies, so L = $1,000. Under these cir-

Karen Noble, Professional Golfer

Karen Noble

Karen Noble is a professional golfer and has been on the LPGA tour for five years. Her cash winnings have ranged from $20,000 one year to $115,000 another. With her income varying so greatly from year to year, Karen has taken several steps to ensure that she can forecast her cash needs and pay her expenses for a year of golf tournaments.

Q. How have you decreased the volatility of your cash flow?

Unlike many of the golfers on the LPGA tour, I have sponsors who advance me money at the beginning of the year. In exchange for the advance, I agree to repay my sponsors from my yearly winnings. That way, I know how much minimum cash I have for the year.

I also have one corporate sponsor that is a flat-out sponsorship. I don't have to pay them back. They pay me to advertise their company logo on my clothing and on my golf bag.

Q. How do you budget enough cash flow to cover the expenses of being on tour?

I construct my cash budget by first estimating my expenses. I start with the number of tournaments I'll play in for a year. I usually participate in twenty-five to thirty events. Once I've mapped out how many tournaments I plan to play in, I estimate how much it costs me to play in each tournament. Right now, tournament expenses range from $800 to $1,200 a week, so it averages out to about $1,000 a week. Once I have budgeted my expenses, I recruit sponsors, show them my estimated budget, and through them, I raise enough cash to cover the year's expenses.

Q. How do you estimate your cash flow?

Experience helps me estimate my cash needs. When I was just starting out, it was tough planning ahead. The biggest mistake I made was not realizing the amount of taxes I would have to pay. The year I won $115,000 I thought I could bank some of that for expenses down the road. But taxes took away the percentage I thought I could bank.

Now, after several years on the tour, I can gauge and budget for my cash needs. I have learned to minimize my expenses whenever possible. For instance, if I have to fly to a tournament, instead of drive, I try to use courtesy transportation instead of renting a car. And I don't necessarily stay in hotels. Often I can stay in private housing arranged by the tournament managers. Also, I don't always hire a caddy who tours with me. The average tour caddy costs between $400 and $450 a week. Instead, I might hire a local caddy who knows the golf course for about half the cost. One item I don't budget for is the cost of my golf equipment because the manufacturers provide it for free.

I then budget other large cash expenditures. Health insurance is one example. My computer upkeep and supplies are other examples. Without my laptop computer and printer, I can't keep track of my budget.

Q. What would be your ideal cash flow pattern?

To have a steady, reliable stream of cash. In my business, a complete corporate sponsorship provides that. A large company like AT&T signs you to a contract to represent them for a number of years. With a full sponsorship, I wouldn't have to spend the time and energy recruiting other sponsors each year or depend on the up-and-down earnings on the golf course.

Source: Interview with Karen Noble.

cumstances, the firm will have the following target cash balance, according to Equation 18-1:

$$Z = \sqrt[3]{\frac{3 \times 30 \times \$90,846}{4 \times (.04/365)}} + \$1,000$$

$$= \sqrt[3]{\frac{\$8,176,140}{.00043836}} + \$1,000$$

$$= \$2,652 + \$1,000$$

$$= \$3,652$$

With a 4 percent annual return (converted to a daily figure), a lower limit of $1,000, transaction costs of $30, and a variance of $90,846, we see that the firm's target cash balance, Z, is $3,652.

According to Equation 18-2, the firm's upper limit for the target cash balance will be:

$$H = (3 \times \$3,652) - (2 \times \$1,000)$$

$$= \$10,956 - \$2,000$$

$$= \$8,956.$$

According to the Miller–Orr model, then, the firm in this example will seek to maintain $3,652 in its cash account. If the cash balance increases to $8,956, the firm will buy $5,304 worth of investment securities to return the balance to $3,652. If the cash balance falls to $1,000, the firm will sell $2,652 worth of investment securities to raise the cash balance to $3,652. By finding the optimal cash balance, the firm seeks to accommodate its cash needs, given the volatility of cash inflows and outflows, and maximize its investment opportunities. We see, then, that the Miller–Orr model can help firms find their optimal cash balance.

Now that we have examined factors that affect a firm's minimum, maximum, and optimal cash balances, and described how a firm may find its target cash balance, we look at how a firm can forecast its cash needs next.

FORECASTING CASH NEEDS

Financial managers must frequently provide detailed estimates of their firm's future cash needs. The primary purpose of such estimates is to identify when excess cash will be available and when outside financing will be required to make up cash shortages.

Financial managers cannot base future cash estimates on *pro forma* income statements for the appropriate time period. Why? Because income and expenses are not always received and paid for in cash. Remember, if a firm is using an accrual-based accounting system, revenues and expenses may be recognized in one accounting period, but cash may not change hands until another period.

One technique for estimating true future cash needs is to develop a cash budget. A **cash budget** is a detailed budget plan that shows where cash is expected to come from and where it is expected to go during a given period of time.

The best way to learn about cash budgets is to practice creating one. In the following sections we will develop a cash budget for Bulldog Batteries that shows detailed cash flows from month to month throughout the upcoming year.

Developing a Cash Budget

The first step in developing a monthly cash budget is to identify sales revenue for each month of the period covered by the budget. Assume that it is the end of December 1997 and that Bulldog Batteries' 1998 sales are expected to occur as follows:

	SALES
Nov '97 (reference)	$ 13,441
Dec '97 (reference)	13,029
Jan '98	12,945
Feb '98	14,794
Mar '98	16,643
Apr '98	18,492
May '98	20,341
Jun '98	22,191
Jul '98	24,040
Aug '98	22,191
Sep '98	20,341
Oct '98	18,492
Nov '98	16,643
Dec '98	14,794
1998 Total	$221,907

Next, assume all of Bulldog's sales are on credit, so no cash is received immediately when a sale is made. Experience from past sales reveals that 30 percent of Bulldog's customers will pay off their accounts in the month of sale, 60 percent will pay off their accounts in the month following the sale, and the remaining 10 percent of the customers will pay off their accounts in the second month following the sale. Given this payment pattern, Bulldog's actual cash collections on sales throughout the year will follow the pattern shown in Table 18-1.

In Table 18-1 we computed January's cash collections as follows:

30% of January's 1998's sales:	$.30 \times \$12,945 = \$ 3,884$
+ 60% of December 1997's sales:	$.60 \times \$13,029 = 7,817$
+ 10% of November 1997's sales:	$.10 \times \$13,441 = 1,344$
= Total Collections in January 1998:	$\$13,045$

Take Note

If Bulldog's managers expected other cash receipts during 1998, they would add them to sales collections in the appropriate month to obtain the total cash inflows for each month, as shown in Table 18-1.

Collections for the other months are computed similarly.

The next step in developing the cash budget is to turn to cash outflows. Assume that Bulldog Batteries' cost of materials is 27 percent of sales. Bulldog manufactures batteries expected to be sold in February one month ahead of time in January, and orders all the materials it needs for January's production schedule one month ahead of time in December. This schedule repeats for each month of the year. Bulldog makes all its purchases on credit, and pays for them in cash during the month following the purchase. Therefore December's purchase orders will be paid for in January, and so on. The situation is summarized in Figure 18-4.

Table 18-1 Bulldog's Actual Cash Collections

	1997		1998											
	NOV	DEC	JAN	FEB	MAR	APR	MAY	JUN	JUL	AUG	SEP	OCT	NOV	DEC
Cash Inflows														
Sales (reference only; not a cash flow)	$13,441	$13,029	$12,945	$14,794	$16,643	$18,492	$20,341	$22,191	$24,040	$22,191	$20,341	$18,492	$16,643	$14,794
Cash collections on sales:														
30% in month of sale			$ 3,884	$ 4,438	$ 4,993	$ 5,548	$ 6,102	$ 6,657	$ 7,212	$ 6,657	$ 6,102	$ 5,548	$ 4,993	$ 4,438
60% in first month after sale			7,817	7,767	8,876	9,986	11,095	12,205	13,315	14,424	13,315	12,205	11,095	9,986
10% in second month after sale			1,344	1,303	1,295	1,479	1,664	1,849	2,034	2,219	2,404	2,219	2,034	1,849
Total collections			$13,045	$13,508	$15,164	$17,013	$18,862	$20,711	$22,561	$23,300	$21,821	$19,971	$18,122	$16,273
Other cash receipts			0	0	0	0	0	0	0	0	0	0	0	0
Total Cash Inflows			$13,045	$13,508	$15,164	$17,013	$18,862	$20,711	$22,561	$23,300	$21,821	$19,971	$18,122	$16,273

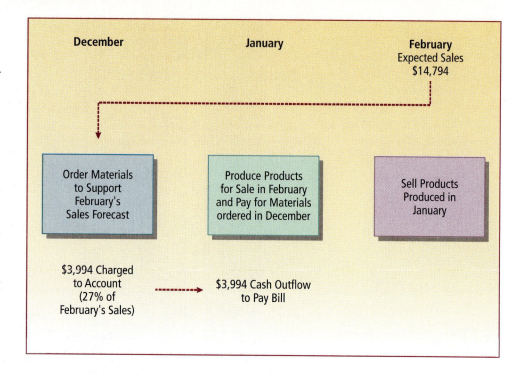

Figure 18-4 Timing for Bulldog Batteries' Cash Payments for Purchases

Figure 18-4 shows Bulldog Batteries' production and cash flow schedule

If Bulldog follows the production schedule illustrated in Figure 18-4 throughout 1998, its cash outflows for materials purchases will be as shown in Table 18-2. (Materials purchases for November and December of 1998 are based on sales forecasts for January and February 1999 of $14,342,000 and $14,794,000, respectively.)

For the sake of simplicity, assume Bulldog's remaining cash outflows are all direct expenses paid for in the month incurred as follows:

- Production expenses other than purchases are equal to purchases. (Bulldog's production costs are split evenly between materials cost and other production costs.)
- Sales and marketing expenses are 18.025 percent of sales each month.
- General and administrative expenses are $903,000 each month.
- Interest expense is expected to be $2,971 for the year. We assume that expense will be paid all at one time in December 1998.
- Bulldog's expected income tax bill for 1998 is $19,800. The bill will be paid in four installments in April, June, September, and December.
- Bulldog expects to declare four quarterly dividends of $6,098 in 1998. These will be paid in March, June, September, and December.

Bulldog's total cash outflows, including the expenses above and payments for materials purchases, are shown in Table 18-3.

After all the cash inflows and outflows for each month are accounted for (as we have done, see Tables 18-1, 18-2, and 18-3), the next step is to summarize the *net* gain (or loss) for each month in 1998. Table 18-4 contains the summary.

The final step in developing the cash budget is to summarize the effects of the monthly net cash flows on monthly cash balances and list any external financing required. The procedure for January 1998 is shown in Table 18-5. We assume a cash balance of $65,313 at the beginning of January, a desired target cash balance of $65,000, and short-term loans of $302 outstanding at the beginning of the month.

Table 18-2 Bulldog's Cash Outflows for Sales and Materials Purchased

| | 1997 | | 1998 | | | | | | | | | | | |
	Nov	Dec	Jan	Feb	Mar	Apr	May	Jun	Jul	Aug	Sep	Oct	Nov	Dec
Sales (reference only; not a cash flow)	$13,441	$13,029	$12,945	$14,794	$16,643	$18,492	$20,341	$22,191	$24,040	$22,191	$20,341	$18,492	$16,643	$14,794
Materials Purchases (27% of sales two months ahead—reference only, not a cash flow)		$3,994	$4,494	$4,993	$5,492	$5,992	$6,491	$5,992	$5,492	$4,993	$4,494	$3,994	$3,872	$3,994
Payments for materials purchases: 100% in month after purchase			$3,994	$4,494	$4,993	$5,492	$5,992	$6,491	$5,992	$5,492	$4,993	$4,494	$3,994	$3,872

Table 18-3 Bulldog's Total Cash Outflows

| | 1997 | 1998 | | | | | | | | | | | | |
	Dec	Jan	Feb	Mar	Apr	May	Jun	Jul	Aug	Sep	Oct	Nov	Dec
Cash Inflows													
Materials Purchases (reference only; not a cash flow)	$3,994	$4,494	$4,993	$5,492	$5,992	$6,491	$5,992	$5,492	$4,993	$4,494	$3,994	$3,872	$3,994
Payments for materials purchases: 100% in month after purchase		$3,994	$4,494	$4,993	$5,492	$5,992	$6,491	$5,992	$5,492	$4,993	$4,494	$3,994	$3,872
Other cash payments:													
Production costs other than purchases		3,994	4,494	4,993	5,492	5,992	6,491	5,992	5,492	4,993	4,494	3,994	3,872
Selling and marketing expenses		2,333	2,667	3,000	3,333	3,666	4,000	4,333	4,000	3,667	3,333	3,000	2,667
General and administrative expenses		903	903	903	903	903	903	903	903	903	903	903	903
Interest payments													2,971
Tax payments					4,995		4,995			4,995			4,995
Divided payments				6,098			6,098			6,098			6,098
Total Cash Outflows		$11,225	$12,557	$19,987	$20,215	$16,553	$28,978	$17,219	$15,887	$25,649	$13,223	$11,892	$25,378

Table 18-4 Bulldog's Cash Inflows and Outflows and Net Cash Flows

| | 1998 | | | | | | | | | | | |
	Jan	Feb	Mar	Apr	May	Jun	Jul	Aug	Sep	Oct	Nov	Dec
Total Cash Inflows	$13,045	$13,508	$15,164	$17,013	$18,862	$20,711	$22,561	$23,300	$21,821	$19,971	$18,122	$16,273
Total Cash Outflows	11,225	12,557	19,987	20,215	16,553	28,978	17,219	15,887	25,649	13,223	11,892	25,378
Net Cash Gain (Loss)	$ 1,820	$ 951	$(4,823)	$(3,203)	$ 2,309	$(8,267)	$ 5,341	$ 7,413	$(3,828)	$ 6,748	$ 6,230	$(9,105)

Table 18-5

Cash Flow and Financing Requirements Summary, January 1998

Cash Flow Summary:	
1. Cash balance at start of month	$65,313
2. Net cash gain (loss) during month	1,820
3. Cash balance at end of month before financing	67,133
4. Minimum cash balance desired	65,000
5. Surplus cash (deficit) (line 3 − line 4)	$ 2,133
External Financing Summary:	
6. External financing balance at start of month	$ 302
7. New financing required (negative amount on line 5)	0
8. Financing repayments (positive amount on line 5*)	302
9. External financing balance at end of month	0
10. Cash balance at end of month after financing (balance on line 3 + new financing on line 7 − repayments on line 8)	$66,831

*If the positive amount on line 5 exceeds the external financing balance on line 6 enter the external financing balance on line 6.

The procedure is repeated for February using January's cash balance at the end of the month after financing as the starting cash balance for February. Table 18-6 contains the twelve-month summary for Bulldog Batteries.

After filling out the cash budget through December 1998, Bulldog's managers can see that the firm will have surplus cash in January and February, but external financing will be needed in March, April, June, and September.

According to the budget, the loans can be fully paid off by October, and $66,598 will be in the cash account at the end of the year. Armed with this information, Bulldog's managers would approach their banker to establish a line of credit with a limit higher than $11,201—the largest anticipated loan balance.

For your convenience, Bulldog's complete cash budget for 1998 is shown in Table 18-7 (page 442).

We have described how to forecast a firm's short-term cash needs by constructing a cash budget. Next, we explore ways to manage a firm's short-term cash flow.

Take Note

Since the financing is only needed for a short time, it is typically obtained from a line of credit or short-term notes.

Managing the Cash Flowing in and out of the Firm

People who manage a firm's cash should focus on four objectives: 1) to increase the flow of cash into the business; 2) to decrease the flow of cash out of the business; 3) to receive cash as quickly as possible; and 4) to pay cash out as slowly as possible, without missing the due date. This gives you more time to put cash to work earning a return. These four objectives principles are displayed in Figure 18-5 (page 443).

In the sections that follow, we discuss ways to accomplish the four objectives of cash flow management.

Increasing Cash Inflows

There are really only two ways to increase the amount of cash flowing into a business during any given time period. First, the firm can do more of whatever it is that makes money—that is, a manufacturing business can sell more products or a service business can serve more people. Of course, when sales increase, costs increase too. Hopefully, however, the sales increase will be bigger than the cost increase. Second,

Table 18-6 Bulldog's Twelve-Month Summary of Cash Flow and Financing Requirements

							1998						
	DEC	JAN	FEB	MAR	APR	MAY	JUN	JUL	AUG	SEP	OCT	NOV	DEC
Cash Flow Summary:													
1. Cash balance at start of month		$65,313	$66,831	$67,782	$65,000	$65,000	$65,000	$65,000	$65,000	$66,554	$65,000	$69,473	$75,704
2. Net cash gain (loss) during month		1,820	951	(4,823)	(3,203)	2,309	(8,267)	5,341	7,413	(3,828)	6,748	6,230	(9,105)
3. Cash balance at end of month before financing (line 1 + line 2)		$67,133	$67,782	$62,959	$61,797	$67,309	$56,733	$70,341	$72,413	$62,725	$71,748	$75,704	$66,598
4. Minimum cash balance desired		65,000	65,000	65,000	65,000	65,000	65,000	65,000	65,000	65,000	65,000	65,000	65,000
5. Surplus cash (deficit) (Line 3 − line 4)		$ 2,133	$ 2,782	$(2,041)	$(3,203)	$ 2,309	$(8,267)	$ 5,341	$ 7,413	$(2,275)	$ 6,748	$10,704	$ 1,598
External Financing Summary:													
6. External financing balance at start of month		$ 302	$ 0	$ 0	$ 2,041	$ 5,243	$ 2,934	$11,201	$ 5,860	$ 0	$ 2,275	$ 0	$ 0
7. New financing required (negative amount from line 5)		0	0	2,041	3,203	0	8,267	0	0	2,275	0	0	0
8. Financing repayments (positive amount from line 5)		302	0	0	0	2,309	0	5,341	5,860	0	2,275	0	0
9. External financing balance at end of month	$302	0	0	2,041	5,243	2,934	11,201	5,860	0	2,275	0	0	0
10. Cash balance at end of month after financing (line 3 + line 7 − line 8)		$66,831	$67,782	$65,000	$65,000	$65,000	$65,000	$65,000	$66,554	$65,000	$69,473	$75,704	$66,598

	1997		1998											
	Nov	**Dec**	**Jan**	**Feb**	**Mar**	**Apr**	**May**	**Jun**	**Jul**	**Aug**	**Sep**	**Oct**	**Nov**	**Dec**
Cash Inflows:														
Sales (reference only; not a cash flow)	$13,441	$13,029	$12,945	$14,794	$16,643	$18,492	$20,341	$22,191	$24,040	$22,191	$20,341	$18,492	$16,643	$14,794
Cash collections on sales:														
30% in month of sale			$ 3,884	$ 4,438	$ 4,993	$ 5,548	$ 6,102	$ 6,657	$ 7,212	$ 6,657	$ 6,102	$ 5,548	$ 4,993	$ 4,438
60% in first month after sale			7,817	7,767	8,876	9,986	11,095	12,205	13,315	14,424	13,315	12,205	11,095	9,986
10% in second month after sale			1,344	1,303	1,295	1,479	1,664	1,849	2,034	2,219	2,404	2,219	2,034	1,849
Total collections			$13,045	$13,508	$15,164	$17,013	$18,862	$20,711	$22,561	$23,300	$21,821	$19,971	$18,122	$16,273
Other cash receipts			0	0	0	0	0	0	0	0	0	0	0	0
Total Cash Inflows			$13,045	$13,508	$15,164	$17,013	$18,862	$20,711	$22,561	$23,300	$21,821	$19,971	$18,122	$16,273
Cash Outflows:														
Materials Purchases (reference only; not a cash flow)		$ 3,994	$ 4,494	$ 4,993	$ 5,492	$ 5,992	$ 6,491	$ 5,992	$ 5,492	$ 4,993	$ 4,494	$ 3,994	$ 3,872	$ 3,994
Payments for materials purchases:														
100% in month after purchase			$ 3,994	$ 4,494	$ 4,993	$ 5,492	$ 5,992	$ 6,491	$ 5,992	$ 5,492	$ 4,993	$ 4,494	$ 3,994	$ 3,872
Other cash payments:														
Production costs other than purchases			3,994	4,494	4,993	5,492	5,992	6,491	5,992	5,492	4,993	4,494	3,994	3,872
Selling and marketing expenses			2,333	2,667	3,000	3,333	3,666	4,000	4,333	4,000	3,667	3,333	3,000	2,667
General and administrative expenses			903	903	903	903	903	903	903	903	903	903	903	903
Interest payments														2,971
Tax payments						4,995		4,995			4,995			4,995
Dividend payments					6,098			6,098			6,098			6,098
Total Cash Outflows			$11,225	$12,557	$19,987	$20,215	$16,553	$28,978	$17,219	$15,887	$25,649	$13,223	$11,892	$25,378
Net Cash Gain (Loss)			$ 1,820	$ 951	$(4,823)	$(3,203)	$ 2,309	$(8,267)	$ 5,341	$ 7,413	$(3,828)	$ 6,748	$ 6,230	$(9,105)
Cash Flow Summary:														
1. Cash balance at start of month			$65,313	$66,831	$67,782	$65,000	$65,000	$65,000	$65,000	$65,000	$66,554	$65,000	$69,473	$75,704
2. Net cash gain (loss) during month			1,820	951	(4,823)	(3,203)	2,309	(8,267)	5,341	7,413	(3,828)	6,748	6,230	(9,105)
3. Cash balance at end of month before financing (line 1 + line 2)			$67,133	$67,782	$62,959	$61,797	$67,309	$56,733	$70,341	$72,413	$62,725	$71,748	$75,704	$66,598
4. Minimum cash balance desired			65,000	65,000	65,000	65,000	65,000	65,000	65,000	65,000	65,000	65,000	65,000	65,000
5. Surplus cash (deficit) (line 3 – line 4)			$ 2,133	$ 2,782	$(2,041)	$(3,203)	$ 2,309	$(8,267)	$ 5,341	$ 7,413	$(2,275)	$ 6,748	$10,704	$ 1,598
External Financing Summary:														
6. External financing balance at start of month			$ 302	$ 0	$ 0	$ 2,041	$ 5,243	$ 2,934	$11,201	$ 5,860	$ 0	$ 2,275	$ 0	$ 0
7. New financing required (negative amount from line 5)			0	0	2,041	3,203	0	8,267	0	0	2,275	0	0	0
8. Financing repayments (positive amount from line 5)			302	0	0	0	2,309	0	5,341	5,860	0	2,275	0	0
9. External financing balance at end of month		$ 302	0	0	2,041	5,243	2,934	11,201	5,860	0	2,275	0	0	0
10. Cash balance at end of month after financing (line 3 + line 7 – line 8)			$66,831	$67,782	$65,000	$65,000	$65,000	$65,000	$65,000	$66,554	$65,000	$69,473	$75,704	$66,598

Table 18-7 Bulldog's Complete Cash Budget

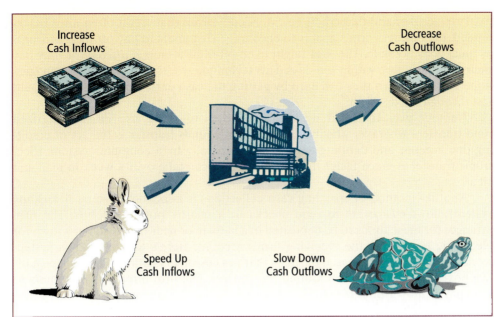

Figure 18-5 **Managing the Cash Flowing in and out of the Firm**

Figure 18-5 shows the four objectives of cash flow management.

firms can increase the return that the company's assets are earning—that is, firms can find ways to produce more money with the same amount of assets.

Decreasing Cash Outflows

Managers can also increase the *net* amount of cash flowing into their firms during any given time period by decreasing the amount of cash flowing out. How? By cutting costs.

Finding the proper balance between short-term and long-term considerations is a subject that business managers must grapple with every day. There are no easy answers.

A less obvious way to decrease cash outflows from the business is to decrease the *risk* of doing business. Risk in business equates to uncertainty, and a business that faces a lot of uncertainty must keep a lot of cash on hand to deal with unexpected events. If a firm could somehow reduce the degree of risk of doing business, the number of unexpected events would drop, and the amount needed in the cash account could be reduced.

Speeding up Cash Inflows

Most business managers would agree that, other things being equal, they would rather have cash earlier than later. This makes sense. The earlier a firm receives cash, the earlier it can put it to work earning a return. Accordingly, managers try to figure out how to speed the flow of cash into their firms.

Collecting funds from the firm's customers more quickly speeds cash inflow. The ideal situation, from a business firm's point of view, would be for all customers to pay for the products or services they buy immediately. However, the realities of the

Take Note

Be wary of cost-cutting measures that hurt the business in the long term. For example, a drug company might boost profits now by cutting research and development spending (an expense). But that action will rob the company of new products that would generate extra value later.

marketplace demand that credit be extended.[3] Given that credit often must be extended, the business firm's goal is to encourage customers to pay off their accounts as quickly as possible. The firm might even offer customers a *discount* if they pay their bills early, say, within ten days. This technique works and the firm's managers hope that the return they can earn by getting the cash early outweighs the amount lost through the discount.[4]

Another way to speed up cash inflows is to make use of computerized fund transfers wherever possible. An **electronic funds transfer** is the act of crediting one account and debiting another automatically by a computer system. Electronic transfer is much faster than checks, which can take over a week to mail and clear.

Another method of speeding cash collections is a lockbox system. A **lockbox** system allows customers to send checks to a nearby post office box. The firm arranges for these funds to be deposited in a bank in or near the customer's town for electronic transfer to the receiving firm's account. Here's how a lockbox system works. A San Francisco-based business that has customers nationwide rents post office boxes in major cities all around the country. The firm directs its customers to send payments for their bills to the post office box in the city nearest them. The firm arranges for a bank in each city to pick up the mail from the post office box at least once a day, and to deposit any payments received in the firm's account at the bank. From that point on, the funds are immediately available for the firm's use, either from the individual banks directly or by having the banks electronically transfer the funds to the firm's bank in San Francisco. By using the lockbox system, the firm can receive cash two to five days faster than if customers mailed all their payments to San Francisco.[5]

Slowing Down Cash Outflows

Just as speeding up the flow of cash into the firm gives managers more time to earn a return on the cash, so does slowing down the flow of cash out of the firm. Either way, the idea is to increase the amount of time that the firm has possession of the cash. One obvious way to slow down cash outflows is to delay paying bills as long as possible. However, the firm must take great care not to overstep the bounds of good sense and fair play in applying this principle. Imagine what would happen if a firm didn't pay its employees on time or delayed paying suppliers. Its business operations would suffer or it might not stay in business at all. Firms shouldn't pay bills that are due at the end of the month on the first of the month, but neither should they take unfair advantage of creditors by making late payments.

---

[3]A quick example illustrates why businesses must grant credit: Suppose two firms in town both sold office supplies. One will let you, a business owner, order supplies over the phone anytime you want, and they bill you once a month. The other demands that you go to the store and pay cash each time you want to buy supplies. How long do you think the second store will be able to stay in business?
[4]This subject is discussed more fully in chapter 19.
[5]Before implementing such a system, of course, the firm would have to evaluate whether the extra amount that could be earned on the funds collected two to five days early is greater than the cost of maintaining the lockbox system.

What's Next

This chapter examined how firms manage cash and the factors that determine how large a firm's cash balance will be. In chapter 19 we study another component of working capital management: accounts receivable and inventory management.

Summary

1. List the factors that affect a company's desired minimum cash balance.

Having a minimum balance ensures that enough money is maintained in the cash account to make payments when needed. The base level to be maintained is affected by: (1) how quickly and cheaply the firm can raise cash when needed; (2) how accurately the firm can predict cash needs; and (3) how much extra the firm wants to keep in the cash account for emergencies.

2. List the factors that affect a company's maximum cash balance.

Having a maximum balance ensures that firms limit the cash balance so that the firm invests and earns a return on as much cash as possible. The maximum amount to be maintained is affected by three factors: (1) available investment opportunities; (2) expected returns from these opportunities; and (3) the transaction costs of withdrawing the cash and making the investments.

3. Apply the Miller–Orr model to establish a target optimal cash balance.

The Miller-Orr model recognizes that a firm's cash balance might fluctuate up and down in an irregular fashion over time. The model solves for an optimal "target" cash balance about which the cash balance fluctuates until it reaches an upper or lower limit. If the upper limit is reached, short-term investment securities are bought, bringing the cash balance down to the target again. If the lower limit is reached, short-term investment securities are sold, bringing the cash balance up to the target.

4. Prepare a cash budget.

Managers use a cash budget to estimate detailed cash needs for future periods. Cash budgets are necessary because *pro forma* income statements and balance sheets do not indicate the actual flow of cash in and out of the firm. A monthly cash budget shows detailed cash flows from month to month throughout the year, and how much over or short the firm's cash account will be at the end of each month. By using a cash budget, managers can estimate when it will be necessary to obtain short-term loans from their bank.

5. Explain how firms manage their cash inflows and outflows to maximize value.

The four objectives of cash management are to increase the flow of cash into the business, to decrease the flow of cash out of the business, to receive cash more quickly, and to pay cash out more slowly.

Ways to increase the flow of cash into the firm include selling more products, serving more customers, and increasing the return earned by the firm's assets. Ways to reduce the flow of cash out of the business include cutting costs and decreasing the degree of risk in the business. Ways to speed up the flow of cash into the business include helping customers pay off their credit accounts more quickly and using electronic funds transfer or lockbox techniques. Ways to slow down the flow of cash out of the firm include taking advantage of credit terms whenever possible.

Equations Introduced in This Chapter

Equation 18-1. Formula for Miller–Orr Model Target Cash Balance:

$$Z = \sqrt[3]{\frac{3 \times TC \times V}{4 \times r}} + L$$

where: TC = the transaction cost of buying or selling short-term investment securities
V = the variance of net daily cash flows
r = the daily rate of return on short-term investment securities
L = the lower limit to be maintained in the cash account.

Equation 18-2. Formula for the Upper Limit in the Miller–Orr Model:

$$H = 3Z - 2L$$

Self Test

ST-1. Assume that short-term investment securities are yielding 5 percent, and it costs a firm $20 each time it buys or sells investment securities. The variance of the firm's daily net cash flows has been found to be $20,000. Management wants to keep at least $1,000 in the cash account for emergencies. Given these conditions, what is the firm's target cash balance?

ST-2. What is the maximum amount the firm in ST-1 above will let accumulate in its cash account before investing excess cash in marketable securities?

ST-3. Continuing with the firm in ST-1 and ST-2, how much will the firm invest in marketable securities if the upper limit in ST-2 is reached?

ST-4. Assume a company has $1,000 in its cash account at the beginning of a month and short-term loan balances of $3,500. If the company experiences a $14,000 net cash inflow during the month and its desired target cash balance is $3,000, how much of the outstanding loans can be paid off this month?

Review Questions

1. What are the primary reasons that companies hold cash?
2. Explain the factors affecting the choice of a minimum cash balance amount.
3. What are the negative consequences of a company holding too much cash?
4. Explain the factors affecting the choice of a maximum cash balance amount.
5. What is the difference between *pro forma* financial statements and a cash budget? Explain why *pro forma* financial statements are not used to forecast cash needs.
6. What are the benefits of "collecting early" and how do companies attempt to do this?
7. What are the benefits of "paying late" (but not too late) and how do companies attempt to do this?
8. Refer to the Bulldog battery company's cash budget in Table 18-7. Explain why the company would probably not issue $1 million worth of new common stock in January to avoid all short-term borrowing during the year.

Build Your Communication Skills

CS-1. Assume the company you work for has $10,000 in its cash account on January 1, 1998 and short-term loans outstanding in the amount of $15,000. Net cash flows for January, February, and March 1998 are forecasted to be +$2,000, −$5,000, and +$8,000, respectively. Prepare a report for your company's CEO showing any new borrowing required and any possible debt payoffs that may be made during the three month period. Your company's minimum desired cash balance is $5,000. (Hint: Use the format in Table 18-5.)

CS-2. Assume you work for an electric utility that serves several Western states and your boss is concerned that there is too much delay between the time the company's customers pay their bills and the time the cash is actually deposited in the corporation's cash account. Prepare a briefing for your boss outlining a method for streamlining cash collection procedures in such a way that the delay in making cash available is minimized.

Problems

18-1. Your company wants to have a minimum cash balance of $3,000 and an upper limit cash balance equal to $9,000. What would be your target cash balance?

Miller–Orr Model

18-2. Selena Rogers, the financial analyst of Keep-Fit Health Equipment Company, has a short-term investment yield of 3 percent and transaction cost of $40 per transaction. The cash inflows and outflows have traditionally been irregular with a variance of daily net cash flows equal to $39,000. Management of the company wants a minimum cash balance of $2,200. Calculate:

Miller–Orr Model

   a. the target cash balance
   b. the upper limit of cash balance.

18-3. Will Clark, the financial analyst of Get-Fit Health Equipment Company, a competitor of Keep-Fit of problem 18-2, has the same yield and transaction cost. However, the variance of daily net cash flows equal to $52,000. Management of the company wants a minimum cash balance of $3,900. Calculate:

Miller–Orr Model

   a. the target cash balance
   b. the upper limit of cash balance.

18-4. Marion Crane, a financial analyst of Lifelong Appliances Company, is trying to develop a cash budget for each month of the year 1998. The sales are expected to occur as follows:

Cash Inflow

Month	Sales
	(in thousand dollars)
Nov '97 (reference)	$131
Dec '97 (reference)	129
Jan '98	126
Feb '98	133
Mar '98	139
Apr '98	143
May '98	191
Jun '98	226
Jul '98	242
Aug '98	224
Sep '98	184
Oct '98	173
Nov '98	166
Dec '98	143
Jan '99 (reference)	136
Feb '99 (reference)	139

Assume all of Lifelong's sales are on credit, so no cash is received immediately when a sale is made. It is expected that 20 percent of Lifelong's customers will pay off their accounts in the month of sale, 70 percent will pay off their accounts in the month following the sale, and the remaining 10 percent of the customers will pay off their accounts in the second month following the sale. Given this payment pattern, help Marion in calculating Lifelong's actual monthly cash collections throughout the year 1998.

Cash Inflow

18-5. Use the same sales data given in problem 18-4. To improve the cash collections, Marion has decided to undertake stricter credit terms. With this change she expects that 40 percent of Lifelong's customers will pay off their accounts in the month of sale, 55 percent will pay off their accounts in the month following the sale, and the remaining 5 percent of the customers will pay off their accounts in the second month following the sale. Given this payment pattern, what would be Lifelong's actual monthly cash collections throughout the year 1998?

Challenge Problem

18-6. Use the same sales data given in problem 18-4. Assume that Lifelong's cost of materials is 30 percent of sales. Appliances that are expected to be sold in February will be manufactured one month ahead of time in January, and all the materials needed for January's production schedule will be ordered one month ahead of time in December. This schedule repeats for each month of the year. Lifelong makes all of its purchases on credit, and pays for them in cash during the month following the purchase. That is, December's purchase orders are paid for in January, and so on. Assume Lifelong's remaining cash outflows are all direct expenses paid for in the month incurred as follows:

- Production expenses other than purchases are equal to 80 percent of purchases
- Sales and marketing expenses are 19 percent of sales each month.
- General and administrative expenses are $11,000 each month.
- Interest expense is expected to be $31,000 for the year. Assume it will be paid all at once in December 1998.
- Lifelong's income tax bill for 1998 is expected to be $100,000. The bill will be paid in four equal installments in April, June, September, and December.
- Two semiannual dividends of $50,000 each are expected to be declared in 1998. These will be paid in June and December.

Calculate Lifelong's total cash outflows, including the expenses above and payments for materials purchases.

Cash Outflow

18-7. Use the same data given in problem 18-6, except for the payment schedule for materials purchased. Now assume that Lifelong pays for the material purchased in the following manner: Thirty percent is paid in cash in the month of purchase, and the remaining 70 percent is paid in cash during the month following the purchase. That is, 30 percent of December's purchase orders are paid for in December, and the balance of 70 percent is paid in January, and so on. With this change, calculate Lifelong's total cash outflows, including the expenses above and payments for materials purchases.

Comprehensive Problem

18-8. Rose Sayer, a financial analyst of Fit-and-Forget Fittings Company, is trying to develop a cash budget for each month of the year 1998. The sales are expected to occur as follows:

Month	Sales
	(in thousand dollars)
Nov '97 (reference)	$2266
Dec '97 (reference)	2230
Jan '98	2116
Feb '98	2300
Mar '98	2402
Apr '98	2420
May '98	3390
Jun '98	3909
Jul '98	4164
Aug '98	3933

Sep '98	3163
Oct '98	2912
Nov '98	2886
Dec '98	2424
Jan '99 (reference)	2353
Feb '99 (reference)	2442

Assume all of Fit-and-Forget's sales are on credit, so no cash is received immediately when a sale is made. It is expected that 30 percent of Fit-and-Forget's customers will pay off their accounts in the month of sale, 65 percent will pay off their accounts in the month following the sale, and the remaining 5 percent of the customers will pay off their accounts in the second month following the sale.

Assume that Fit-and-Forget's cost of materials is 20 percent of sales. Fit-and-Forget manufactures fittings expected to be sold in February one month ahead of time, in January. They order all the materials they need for January's production schedule one month ahead of time, in December. This schedule repeats for each month of the year. Fit-and-Forget makes all purchases on credit, and pays for the material purchased in the following manner: Twenty percent is paid in cash in the month of ordering, and the balance of 80 percent is paid in cash during the month following the purchase. That is, 20 percent of December's purchase orders are paid for in December, and the balance of 80 percent is paid in January, and so on. Assume Fit-and-Forget's remaining cash outflows are all direct expenses paid for in the month incurred as follows:

- Production expenses other than purchases are equal to 70 percent of purchases.
- Sales and marketing expenses are 16 percent of sales each month.
- General and administrative expenses are $180,000 each month.
- Interest expense is expected to be $500,000 for the year. Assume it will be paid all at once in December 1998.
- Fit-and-Forget's income tax bill for 1998 is expected to be $1,600,000. The bill will be paid in four equal installments in April, June, September, and December.
- Two semiannual dividends of $855,000 each are expected to be declared in 1998. These will be paid in June and December.

Assuming a cash balance of $1,133,000 at the beginning of January, a desired target cash balance of $1,110,000, and short-term loans of $50,000 outstanding at the beginning of the month, calculate total cash inflows, total cash outflows, net cash gain (loss), cash flow summary, and external financing (if any) summary in the same format as in Table 18-7.

Answers to Self-Test

ST-1. Per equation 18-1, the firm's target cash balance per the Miller–Orr model is:

$$Z = \sqrt[3]{\frac{3 \times 20 \times \$20,000}{4 \times (.05/365)}} + \$1,000$$

$$= \sqrt[3]{\frac{\$1,200,000}{.000547945}} + \$1,000$$

$$= \$1,299 + \$1,000$$

$$= \$2,299$$

ST-2. Per Equation 18-2, the upper limit will be:

$$H = (3 \times \$2,299) - (2 \times \$1,000)$$

$$= \$6,897 - \$2,000$$

$$= \$4,897$$

ST-3. If the upper limit is reached the firm will invest the amount necessary to bring the cash balance back down to the target balance level. This amount is:

$$\$4,897 - \$2,299 = \$2,598$$

ST-4. A summary of the company's cash flows and external financing is shown next:

1. Cash balance at start of month	$ 1,000
2. Net cash gain (loss) during month	14,000
3. Cash balance at end of month before financing	15,000
4. Minimum cash balance desired	3,000
5. Surplus cash (deficit) (line 3 − line 4)	12,000

External Financing Summary:

6. External financing balance at start of month	$ 3,500
7. New financing required (negative amount on line 5)	0
8. Financing repayments (the entire loan balance)	3,500
9. External financing balance at end of month	0
10. Cash balance at end of month after financing (balance on line 3 + new financing on line 7 − repayments on line 8)	$11,500

As shown on line 8 of the preceding summary, the company can pay off the entire $3,500 short-term loan balance this month.

chapter 19

Accounts Receivable and Inventory

Credit is a system whereby a person who can't pay gets another person who can't pay to guarantee that he can pay.

Charles Dickens

On-Demand Publishing Solves the Problem of Inventory Costs

Philip Theibert decided to start a small publishing business called Ascendix Publishing. With desktop publishing available, he thought it would be fairly easy. Typesetting and designing Ascendix's first book on the computer, *Kids Cook Microwave,* was easy. Then the hard decisions began. It was one thing to have a book on the computer screen. It was another to have it printed and marketed—especially on Ascendix's limited budget of $10,000.

Phil discovered that he could get the book printed for about $2 a book. Yet to get this low price, he had to commit to print 4,000 books. The cost of printing, then, would be $8,000. To complicate matters, he would have to store the books somewhere, plus pay tax on the books in inventory. This storage and tax would cost an additional $500.

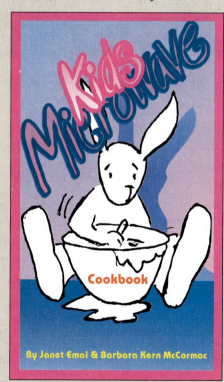

Chapter Objectives

After reading this chapter, you should be able to:

1. Describe how and why firms must manage accounts receivable and inventory as investments.

2. Compute the optimal levels of accounts receivable and inventory.

3. Describe alternative inventory management approaches.

4. Explain how firms make credit decisions and create collection policies.

Thus $8,500 of Ascendix's limited budget would be spent on production costs to produce an inventory of 4,000 books that required additional money to store. That only left $1,500 for a marketing campaign.

Obviously, production costs and inventory would eat too much of Ascendix's cash to market the book aggressively. Phil investigated further and found out that many books could be printed "on demand." The text of his book could be stored in a digital copy machine, then printed when orders came in. The cost of each book would be $3 compared to $2, but almost all of Phil's $10,000 budget could be spent on a direct marketing campaign to target potential buyers. Then, when the orders came in, the books could be printed and sent out.

This "just-in-time" printing helped Ascendix as it struggled to launch its first book and let Phil use the cash where it was more important—to get buyers for the book. The decision Ascendix faced, to carry inventory or not carry inventory, and the expenses associated with that decision, are the same problems big and small businesses across the nation face every day. ※

Source: Interview with Phil Theibert.

Source: From The Wall Street Journal —Permission, Cartoon Features Syndicate.

Chapter Overview

A key component of working capital policy is managing accounts receivable and inventory. In this chapter we see that accounts receivable and inventory are necessary investments that affect a firm's profitability and liquidity. Then, we investigate how financial managers determine the optimal level of these current assets. Finally, we examine inventory management techniques and collection policies.

Why Firms Accumulate Accounts Receivable and Inventory

As we saw in chapter 4, accounts receivable represent money that customers owe to the firm because they have purchased goods or services on credit. Accounts receivable, therefore, are assets that have value.[1] Nonetheless, anytime a firm accumulates accounts receivable, it suffers opportunity costs because it is unable to invest or otherwise use the money owed until customers pay. A firm may also incur a direct cost when it grants credit because some customers may not pay their bills at all. The ideal situation, from a firm's point of view, is to have customers pay cash at the time of the purchase.[2]

In the real world, of course, it's unrealistic to expect customers to always pay cash for products and services. Who would buy lumber from a firm that insisted that all its customers pay cash if other lumber companies offered credit? Like it or not, for most firms, granting credit is an essential business practice. The real question managers must answer is, how much credit should the firm grant and to whom? Offering more credit enhances sales but also increases costs. At some point the cost of granting credit outweighs the benefits. Financial managers must manage accounts receivable carefully to make sure this asset adds to, rather than detracts from, a firm's value.

The situation with inventory is similar. As Phil Theibert's experience from the chapter opener shows, inventory is costly to accumulate and maintain, so firms generally want to hold as few products in inventory as possible. For most firms, however, operating without any inventory is impractical—can you imagine a grocery store with no food on display? So almost all firms that sell products accumulate some inventory. Financial managers must find the best level of inventory. They do this by weighing the risk of losing sales due to unavailable products against the cost savings produced by reducing inventory.

Accounts receivable and inventory are investments because both tie up funds and have opportunity costs, but can add to the firm's value. Be careful not to be confused by the term "investment". Investment usually implies something desirable—a long-term venture specifically planned and implemented for profit. Instead, accounts receivable and inventory may be viewed as necessary evils. Most firms need accounts receivable and inventory to do business, but less is generally better. Managing accounts receivable and inventory, then, ought to be done with an eye toward reducing these assets to the lowest level possible consistent with the value maximization goal of the firm.

---

[1]In fact, firms sometimes sell their cutomers' "IOUs" to other businesses for cash. This process, known as *factoring* accounts receivable, is discussed later in this chapter.
[2]Individuals are the same way. For example, if you sell your bicycle to another student, which would you prefer: to be paid in cash at the time of sale, or to let the buyer pay you a little bit each month?

Table 19-1

Data as of December 31	FIRM A Sells Products for Cash and Holds No Inventory	FIRM B Sells Products for Credit and Accumulates Inventory
Cash	$ 100	$ 100
Accounts Receivable	0	200
Inventory	0	400
Fixed Assets	500	500
Total Assets	$ 600	$1,200
Current Liabilities	$ 50	$ 100
Long-Term Debt	200	400
Stockholders' Equity	350	700
Total Liabilities & Equity	$ 600	$1,200
Sales	$2,433	$2,433
Expenses	2,383	2,383
Net Income for the Year	$ 50	$ 50
Current Ratio	2.0	7.0
Quick Ratio	2.0	3.0
Return on Equity	14.3%	7.1%

How Accounts Receivable and Inventory Affect Profitability and Liquidity

Holding different levels of accounts receivable and inventory can affect a company's profitability and liquidity. To illustrate, consider Firms A and B in Table 19-1. Firm A sells all its products for cash and keeps no inventory. Firm B gives its customers thirty days to pay and maintains a large product inventory. Assuming every other factor is equal, including the firms' capital structure, Firm A can earn over twice the return on its stockholders' equity as Firm B simply by eliminating accounts receivable and inventory (and any associated current liabilities and long-term debt).

The comparison between Firms A and B in Table 19-1 illustrates the liquidity, profitability, and risk of each firm. Observe that although Firm A is more *profitable* than Firm B as measured by return on equity (14.3 percent versus 7.1 percent), it is much less *liquid,* as measured by the current ratio[3] (2.0 versus 7.0). If the managers of Firm A needed to raise more than $100,000 cash in a hurry, they would have no recourse but to seek outside financing or sell some of their fixed assets. The managers of Firm B, however, could collect cash from customers, draw down inventory, or both.

However, Firm B's business practice of accumulating inventory adds risk to the firm if the inventory is hard to liquidate. Some inventory may not be sold, or it may be sold for a low value. Note how when using the quick ratio[4] to compare firm liquidity, we see that Firm A's quick ratio is the same as its current ratio (2.0), but Firm B's quick ratio is 3.0 compared to its current ratio of 7.0. When using the quick ratio,

---

[3]The Current Ratio $= \dfrac{\text{Current Assets}}{\text{Current Liabilities}}$

[4]The Quick Ratio $= \dfrac{\text{Current Assets Less Inventory}}{\text{Current Liabilities}}$

then, we see that Firm A is less liquid than Firm B (2.0 versus 3.0), but how much less depends on the liquidity of the inventory.

Most firms accumulate some accounts receivable and inventory. Because these current assets can affect the profitability and liquidity of the firm, financial managers try to find the amounts of both assets that maximize firm value. In the following section, we examine how to find the optimal level of these current assets.

We discussed how to calculate return on equity, the current ratio, and quick ratio in chapter 5, pages 86–87.

Finding Optimal Levels of Accounts Receivable and Inventory

The conclusions drawn from Table 19-1 assumed that sales for both firms were $2,433,000. That may not be a reasonable assumption. Firm B may have greater sales than Firm A because it grants credit and has inventory immediately available for purchase. Depending on how well customers respond to Firm B's decision to grant credit and maintain inventory, the resulting increase in sales and net income might boost Firm B's return on equity beyond that of Firm A.

However, bad debts and inventory costs are likely to drive up Firm B's expenses, possibly causing its net income to fall. The net result could be a *decrease* in Firm B's return on equity.

Conflicting forces make it more difficult to assess the situation. For accounts receivable, the forces are sales that increase as more generous credit terms are offered *versus* costs that increase with collections, bad debts, and opportunity costs from foregone investments. For inventory, the conflicting forces are sales that increase as more products are made available *versus* storage costs that increase as more inventory is accumulated.

In the following sections, we discuss how to find a balance between these conflicting forces in order to determine the optimal levels of accounts receivable and inventory.

The Optimal Level of Accounts Receivable

To find the best level of accounts receivable, financial managers must review the firm's credit policies, any proposed changes in those policies, and the incremental cash flows of each proposed credit policy. We must then compute the net present value of each policy.

Credit Policy   A firm's credit terms and credit standards make up the firm's **credit policy.** Remember, accounts receivable are created by customers taking advantage of the firm's credit terms. These terms generally offer a discount to credit customers who pay off their accounts within a short time, and specify a maximum number of days that credit customers have to pay off the total amount of their accounts. An example of such terms is "2/10, n30." This means that credit customers will receive a 2 percent discount if they pay off their accounts within ten days of the invoice date, and the full net amount is due within thirty days if the discount is not taken.

For example, suppose you purchase $1,000 worth of camping supplies on credit July 1. If you pay the bill before July 11, you receive a 2 percent discount and the equipment will only cost you $980. If you pay the bill between July 11 and July 31, you'll owe the full amount—$1,000. The bill is past due if you don't pay it by July 31.

Some firms offer credit without a discount feature, simply giving their customers so many days to pay. An example would be "n90"—net 90, pay the invoice amount within ninety days.

Table 19-2

The Effects of Tightening Credit Policy

ACTION	EFFECT ON ACCOUNTS RECEIVABLE
Raise standards for granting credit	Fewer credit customers Fewer people owing money to the firm at any given time Accounts receivable goes down
Shorten net due period	Accounts paid off sooner Less money owed to the firm at any given time Accounts receivable goes down
Reduce discount percent	Fewer credit customers, *but* Some customers who previously took discount now do not Net effect on accounts receivable depends on whether the number of customers lost will be more than the number of those now foregoing the discount and paying the higher net amount
Shorten discount period	Same as above; some credit customers will leave, others will forego the discount and pay the higher net amount. Net effect on accounts receivable is indeterminate

Individual customers receive credit from the firm if they meet the firm's **credit standards** for character, payment history, and so on.[5] Taken together, the credit terms and credit standards comprise the firm's credit policy.

A firm that wishes to change its level of accounts receivable does so by changing its credit policy. *Relaxing* the credit policy—by adopting less stringent credit standards or extending the net due period—will tend to cause accounts receivable to increase. *Tightening* the credit policy—by adopting more stringent credit standards or shortening the net due period—will tend to cause accounts receivable to decrease. The discount percent or time period could also be changed. This may either increase or decrease accounts receivable, depending on the reaction of customers to competing influences. Table 19-2 summarizes the effects of tightening credit policy on accounts receivable.

Analyzing Accounts Receivable Levels

To decide what level of accounts receivable is best for the firm, we follow this three-step process:

1. Develop *pro forma* financial statements for each credit policy under consideration.
2. Use the *pro forma* financial statements to estimate the incremental cash flows of the proposed credit policy and compare them to the current policy cash flows.
3. Use the incremental cash flows and calculate the net present value (NPV) of each policy change proposal. Select the credit policy with the highest NPV.

To demonstrate how the three-step credit policy evaluation works, let's analyze a proposed credit policy for a fictional firm, Bulldog Batteries. Assume Bulldog Batteries currently offers credit terms of 2/10, n30, and Jackie Russell, the vice president for marketing, thinks the terms should be changed to 2/10, n40. Doing so, she says, will result in a 10 percent increase in sales, but only a small increase in bad debts. Should Bulldog make the change?

Take Note

In real life, the firm's credit policy may be limited by marketplace constraints. A new, small firm attempting to sell to large, well-established customers may have to offer credit terms that match those of competitors in the industry.

[5]We'll discuss credit standards more fully later in this chapter.

For the sake of simplicity, we make the following additional assumptions:

- Ms. Russell is correct that sales will increase by 10 percent if the new credit policy is implemented.
- Cost of goods sold and other operating expenses on the firm's income statement, and all current accounts on the balance sheet, will vary directly with sales. So, each of these accounts will increase by 10 percent with the change in credit policy.
- All of Bulldog's sales are made on credit.

Suppose further that Ms. Russell produced the following data on Bulldog's customers' historical payment patterns:

- 45 percent of Bulldog's customers take advantage of the discount and pay off their accounts in 10 days.
- 53 percent of Bulldog's customers forgo the discount, but pay off their accounts in 30 days.
- The remaining 2 percent of Bulldog's customers pay off their accounts in 100 days.[6]

Ms. Russell expects that under the new credit policy:

- 45 percent of Bulldog's customers will still take advantage of the discount and pay off their accounts in 10 days
- 52 percent of Bulldog's customers will forgo the discount and pay off their accounts in 40 days
- 3 percent of Bulldog's customers will pay off their accounts in 100 days.

With this information, we calculate the weighted average of the customers' payment periods (average collection period, or ACP) under the old and new credit policies. We weight the averages by multiplying the percentage of customers who pay times the number of days they take to pay for each scenario. Then we total each scenario result, as follows:

Under the old credit policy:

$$ACP = (.45 \times 10 \text{ days}) + (.53 \times 30 \text{ days}) + (.02 \times 100 \text{ days})$$
$$= 22.4 \text{ days}.$$

Under the new credit policy:

$$ACP = (.45 \times 10 \text{ days}) + (.52 \times 40 \text{ days}) + (.03 \times 100)$$
$$= 28.3 \text{ days}.$$

Based on Ms. Russell's information, we know that under the current credit policy, bad debt expenses are 2 percent of sales; under the new policy, they will climb to 3 percent of sales. Bulldog's CFO has informed us that any increases in current assets resulting from the policy change will be financed from short-term notes at an interest rate of 6 percent. The CFO also tells us that the firm's effective tax rate is 40 percent, and that the cost of capital is 10 percent. The long-term interest rate is 8 percent.

---

[6]In real life, many of these customers will never pay off their accounts, creating bad debts. Assume here, however, that they do pay off their accounts eventually. If we do not make that assumption, our mathematical average will include a certain percentage of customers taking an infinite amount of time to pay. As a result, we get an infinite average collection period (ACP), and that won't provide usable information.

1. Net Incremental Cash Outflow at Time Zero (t_0)	
External financing required from the projected balance sheet	$ 9,352
2. Incremental Cash Flows Occurring in the Future	
Incremental Cash Inflow:	
Increase in Sales	$20,173
Incremental Cash Outflows:	
Increase in Cost of Goods Sold	$10,728
Increase in Bad Debt Expenses	2,623
Increase in Other Operating Expenses	4,323
Increase in Interest Expense	2
Increase in Taxes	999
Total Incremental Cash Outflows:	$18,675
Net Incremental Cash Flows Occurring from Time t_1 through Infinity:	$ 1,498 per year

Step 1: Develop the *Pro Forma* Financial Statements   The first step is to develop the *pro forma* financial statements that reflect the effects of the proposed credit policy change. We begin by reviewing the firm's current income statement and balance sheet, and then we create new statements that incorporate the changes. The statements for Bulldog Batteries are shown in Figure 19-1. The left-hand column shows Bulldog's financial statements before the credit policy change, the middle column shows them after the change, and the right-hand column shows how the new figures were calculated, given our assumptions.

Step 2: Compute the Incremental Cash Flows   Now it's time to compute the incremental cash flows that occur as a result of the credit policy change. Table 19-3 contains these cash flows.

   Table 19-3 shows that Bulldog's initial investment cash flow is $9,352 and its net incremental cash flows from t_1 through infinity are $1,498 per year.

Step 3: Compute the NPV of the Credit Policy Change   Now that we have all the incremental cash flows, we can calculate the NPV of the proposed credit terms change. We learned in chapter 10 that NPV is calculated by summing the present value (PV) of all a project's projected cash flows and then subtracting the amount of the initial investment.[7] In our example, we have a net incremental cash outflow (the initial investment) that occurs at time t_0 of $9,354, followed by net incremental cash inflows occurring from time t_1 through infinity of $1,498 per year. The PV of the $1,498 per year from time t_1 through infinity can be found using the formula in chapter 8 for the present valve of a perpetuity:

$$PVP = PMT \times \left(\frac{1}{k}\right) \tag{8-5}$$

where: PMT = the cash flow per period
k = the required rate of return

---

[7]See Equation 10-1a in chapter 10.

Figure 19-1 Bulldog Batteries Financial Statements

Figure 19-1 shows the pro forma *financial statements for Bulldog Batteries with the current collection policy and with the proposed collection policy.*

INCOME STATEMENTS			
	With Old Credit Terms: 2/10, n30	With New Credit Terms: 2/10, n40	Remarks
Sales (all on credit)	$201,734	$221,907	10% increase assumed
Cost of Goods Sold	107,280	118,008	Increase in proportion with sales (10%)
Gross Profit	94,454	103,899	
Bad Debt Expenses	4,035	6,657	Old: 2% of sales New: 3% of sales
Other Operating Expenses	43,229	47,552	Increase in proportion with sales (10%)
Operating Income	47,190	49,690	
Interest Expense	1,221	1,223	Notes Payable × .06 + LTD × .08
Before-Tax Income	45,969	48,468	
Income Taxes (tax rate = 40%)	18,388	19,387	
Net Income	$ 27,581	$ 29,081	

BALANCE SHEETS, AS OF DECEMBER 31			
	With Old Credit Terms: 2/10, n30	With New Credit Terms: 2/10, n40	Remarks
Assets			
Current Assets:			
Cash & Marketable Sec'ties	$ 65,313	$ 71,844	Increase in proportion with sales (10%)
Accounts Receivable	12,380	17,205	See note 1
Inventory	21,453	23,598	Increase in proportion with sales (10%)
Total Current Assets	$ 99,146	$112,647	Increase in proportion with sales (10%)
Prop, Plant & Equipment, Net	92,983	92,983	No change
Total Assets	$192,129	$205,630	
Liabilities & Equity			
Current Liabilities:			
Accounts Payable	$ 26,186	$ 28,805	Increase in proportion with sales (10%)
Notes Payable	302	332	Increase in proportion with sales (10%)
Total Current Liabilities	$ 26,488	$ 29,137	
Long-Term Debt	15,034	15,034	No change
Total Liabilities	$ 41,522	$ 44,171	
Common Stock	35,000	35,000	No change
Capital in Excess of Par	32,100	32,100	No change
Retained Earnings	83,507	85,007	Old RE + 1,500 net income difference
Total Stockholders' Equity	$150,607	$152,107	
Total Liabilities & Equity	$192,129	$196,278	
Additional Funds Needed		$ 9,352	See notes 2 and 3
		$205,630	

Note 1: Accounts Receivable (AR) = Credit sales per day × ACP
Under the old credit policy: AR = ($201,734/365) × 22.4 = $12,380
Under the new credit policy: AR = ($221,907/365) × 28.3 = $17,205
Note 2: $9,352 is the amount of additional financing needed (AFN) to balance the balance sheet. It is the amount that must be obtained from outside sources to undertake the proposed credit policy change. Therefore $9,352 may be viewed as the net investment required at time zero for the project.
Note 3: If $9,352 is borrowed to make up for AFN, Bulldog will incur new interest charges. If included in the income statement, these will reduce the net income and retained earnings—throwing the balance sheet off balance again and changing the amount of AFN. If the problem is solved using an electronic spreadsheet, the financial statements can be recast several times until the additional interest expense becomes negligible. Here, however, we will use the original interest rate to simplify the calculations.

According to our assumptions, Bulldog Batteries' cost of capital is 10 percent. Applying Equation 8-5, we find the PV of an endless stream of payments of $1,499 discounted at 10 percent as follows:

$$PVP = PMT \times \left(\frac{1}{k}\right)$$

$$= \$1{,}498 \times \left(\frac{1}{.10}\right)$$

$$= \$14{,}980$$

We see that the present value of the $1,498 perpetuity with a 10 percent required rate of return is $14,980.

To complete the NPV calculation, we now need to subtract the $9,352 net cash outflow that occurs at time t_0—the initial investment—from the present value of the $14,980 perpetuity, as shown next:

$$NPV = \$14{,}980 - \$9{,}352$$

$$= \$5{,}628$$

We find that the net present value of the credit policy change is $5,628. Since the NPV is positive, the credit terms change proposal should be accepted. Doing so will increase the value of Bulldog Batteries by $5,628.[8]

Any credit policy change proposal can be evaluated using this framework. Managers may try any number of discount amounts, discount periods, and net due periods, until they discover that combination with the greatest NPV.

The Optimal Level of Inventory

Firms may be able to stimulate sales by maintaining more inventory, but they may drive up costs as well. The financial manager's task is to figure out what level of inventory produces the greatest benefit to the firm. Financial managers first estimate the costs that are associated with inventory.

The Costs of Maintaining Inventory
The two main costs associated with inventory are carrying costs and ordering costs. *Carrying costs* are those costs associated with keeping inventory on hand—warehouse rent, insurance, security expenses, utility bills, and so on. Carrying costs are generally expressed in dollars per unit per year.

Ordering costs are those costs incurred each time an order for inventory materials is placed—clerical expense, telephone calls, management time, and so on. Order-

---

[8]Given all the information presented so far, we could also calculate the internal rate of return (IRR) of the credit terms proposal. We simply solve the PV of a perpetuity formula for k, which represents the IRR:

$$k, \text{ or } IRR, = PMT/PVP$$
$$\text{In our example:} \quad IRR = \$1{,}498/\$9{,}352$$
$$= .1602, \text{ or } 16.02\%$$

Since 16.02 percent exceeds Bulldog's cost of capital of 10 percent, the credit terms change proposal should be accepted.

ing costs tend to be fixed no matter what the size of the order, so they are generally expressed in dollars per order.

Although you would think financial managers would like to minimize these two costs, it's not so easy. Carrying costs tend to rise as the level of inventory rises, but ordering costs tend to fall as inventory rises (because less ordering is necessary). Firms that minimize carrying costs by keeping no inventory have to order materials every time they want to produce an item, so they actually maximize ordering costs. Likewise, firms that minimize ordering costs by ordering all materials at once have sky-high carrying costs.

Complicating the situation is the possibility that a larger stock of inventory might increase sales. More inventory on display means more opportunities to catch the customer's eye, and more inventory on hand means fewer sales lost due to not having the correct size or model available. The fact that more inventory might translate into more sales means the lowest cost level of inventory might not be the optimal level of inventory. To find the optimal level, managers have to balance the costs and benefits of various inventory levels.

Analyzing Inventory Levels   To maximize the value created from the firm's investment in inventory, use a three-step process similar to the one used to find accounts receivable levels. First, generate . *pro forma* income statements and balance sheets for each proposed inventory level. Second, observe the incremental cash flows that occur with the change. Third, compute the NPV of the incremental cash flows. The following example illustrates the three-step process.

Dealin' Dan, the owner of Cream Puff Used Cars, wants to determine the optimal number of cars to display on his lot. Dan knows that increasing the number of cars on display will probably cause sales to increase, but would also increase his inventory carrying costs. Dan also knows that decreasing the number of cars on display will save him inventory costs, but might also cost him sales. As a result, Dan is not sure how a change in his planned average inventory level from thirty-two cars to forty-eight cars will affect the value of his firm.

We'll make the following assumptions about Cream Puff's financial condition:

1. Cream Puff's inventory ordering costs are $100 per order. (Each time Dealin' Dan takes action to obtain cars, whether from other dealers, or from trade-ins, he incurs $100 in processing costs.)
2. Inventory carrying costs are $500 per car per year.
3. Since Dealin' Dan does not expect to keep cars on the lot more than a few weeks, he finances all the firm's inventory with short-term debt. The short-term interest rate available to Cream Puff is 6 percent.
4. Cream Puff pays $5,000, on average, for each car it purchases for resale. The firm's average selling price per car is $6,000.
5. Cream Puff displays, on average, about thirty-two cars on its lot. Sales occur regularly throughout the year, and Dan expects to sell 200 cars this year.
6. Based on his business experience, Dan believes that the relationship between inventory and Cream Puff's car sales is direct, as shown in Figure 19-2. According to the graph, an increase in inventory from thirty-two to forty-eight cars should produce an increase in the number of cars sold per year from 200 to 232.

Figure 19-2 **Cream Puff Used Cars Inventory versus Number of Cars Sold**

Figure 19-2 shows the direct relationship between inventory and sales. As inventory increases, sales increase; as inventory decreases, sales decrease.

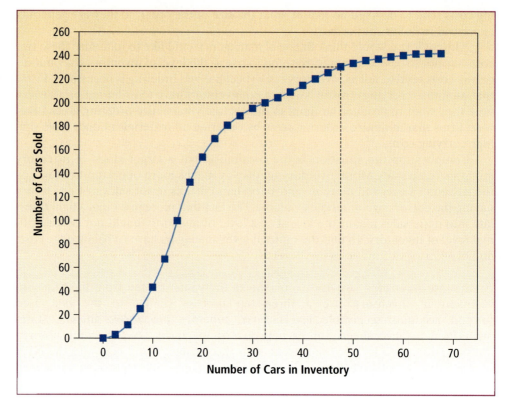

Dan uses the *economic order quantity* (EOQ) model to compute the number of cars to order from wholesale dealers when he replenishes his inventory.[9] According to the EOQ model, the optimal order size follows:

Formula for Economic Order Quantity Model

$$OQ = \sqrt{\frac{2 \times S \times OC}{CC}}$$

(19-1)

where: OQ = Order quantity
          S = Annual sales volume in units
        OC = Ordering costs, per order
        CC = Carrying costs, per unit per year.

We may use the model to see what order size Cream Puff should have. We know that sales are 200 cars per year, ordering costs are $100 per order, and the carrying costs are $500 per year. According to Equation 19-1, the ordering quantity for Cream Puff is as follows:

$$OQ = \sqrt{\frac{2 \times 200 \times 100}{500}}$$
$$= \sqrt{80}$$
$$= 8.94 \text{ (round to 9)}$$

---

[9]The EOQ model computes the inventory order size that, if certain other conditions are met, will minimize total inventory costs for the year. For a complete discussion of the model, refer to a production management text.

We find that the ordering quantity that minimizes inventory costs is nine cars per order. Cream Puff's sales occur regularly, so Dan orders nine replacement cars at even intervals throughout the year. The sales forecast calls for 200 cars to be sold this year, so the number of orders for replacement cars will be 200/9 = 22.22 (round to 22).[10] Each order for replacement cars costs $100, so Cream Puff's total ordering cost—assuming twenty-two orders are made—is $2,200.

Under the current inventory policy, Cream Puff's average inventory level is thirty-two cars. Carrying costs are $500 per car per year, so total carrying costs are 32 × $500 = $16,000. We sum the ordering and carrying costs to find the total inventory costs for Cream Puff. The total costs are $2,200 + $16,000 = $18,200.

We assume in our example that other operating expenses on Cream Puff's income statement and all current accounts on the balance sheet vary directly with sales, so each of these accounts will increase (or decrease) proportionally with sales. We also assume that the interest rate on short-term debt is 6 percent and the rate on long-term debt is 8 percent. Finally, assume that Cream Puff's effective tax rate is 40 percent, and the firm's cost of capital is 10 percent.

Now we're ready to apply the three-step process to determine the optimal level of inventory for Cream Puff Used Cars.

Step 1: Develop *Pro Forma* Financial Statements. Let's see how Dealin' Dan's proposed inventory change from thirty-two cars to forty-eight cars will affect the business. The left-hand column in Figure 19-3 shows Cream Puff's projected 1997 income statement and balance sheet. It also shows selected financial ratios, given our assumptions, current inventory policy of thirty-two cars, and the total inventory costs of $18,200. The right-hand column contains revised statements and ratios assuming average inventory is raised to forty-eight cars. The remarks column explains how the various numbers were computed.

If Dealin' Dan's assumptions are correct, increasing the number of cars on display at the Cream Puff used car lot to forty-eight will produce a $192,000 increase in sales (32 extra cars). Inventory costs and other expenses will increase too, of course, but only by a total of $186,534, so profits should rise by $5,466. On the surface it looks like Dan should go ahead with the inventory change, doesn't it? Perhaps, but let's see how the change will affect the value of Dan's firm by computing the incremental cash flows associated with the change and the NPV of those incremental cash flows.

Step 2: Compute the Incremental Cash Flows. Drawing the necessary information from the *pro forma* statements shown in Figure 19-3, Table 19-4 lists the incremental cash flows of changing the average inventory level from thirty-two cars to forty-eight cars.

We see in Table 19-4 that the initial investment cash flows of changing Dealin' Dan's inventory policy are $72,294. We also find that the net cash flows associated with changing the average inventory level are $5,466 per year.

Step 3: Compute the NPV of the Inventory Policy Change. We are ready now to calculate the NPV of the inventory policy change just as we did for accounts receivable. First, we compute the present value of the net cash inflows occurring from time

---

[10]Astute readers will note that after rounding, 22 × 9 = 198. So Dealin' Dan will not actually order the exact number of cars he expects to sell this year. However, this small discrepancy will not materially affect our analysis.

Figure 19-3   **Dealin' Dan's Cream Puff Used Cars Inventory Analysis**

Figure 19-3 shows the pro forma *financial statements with Cream Puff's current average inventory policy of thirty-two cars and with the new inventory policy of forty-eight cars.*

INCOME STATEMENTS			
	Current Inventory Policy	New Inventory Policy	Remarks
Sales	$1,200,000	$1,392,000	32 car increase × $6,000 each
Cost of Goods Sold	1,000,000	1,160,000	32 car increase × $5,000 each
Gross Profit	200,000	232,000	
Inventory Costs	18,200	26,300	See Note 1
Other Operating Expenses	85,000	98,600	16% increase (same as sales)
Operating Income	96,800	107,100	
Interest Expense	11,040	12,230	CL × .06 + LTD × .08
Before-Tax Income	$ 85,760	$ 94,870	
Income Taxes (tax rate = 40%)	34,304	37,948	
Net Income	$ 51,456	$ 56,922	

BALANCE SHEETS, AS OF DECEMBER 31			
	Current Inventory Policy	New Inventory Policy	Remarks
Assets			
Current Assets:			
Cash & Securities	$ 47,000	$ 54,520	Change in proportion with sales (16% increase)
Accounts Receivable	63,000	73,080	Change in proportion with sales (16% increase)
Inventory	160,000	240,000	16 car increase (48 − 32) × $5,000 each
Total Current Assets	$ 270,000	$ 367,600	
Prop, Plant & Equip, Net	72,000	72,000	No change
Total Assets	$ 342,000	$ 439,600	
Liabilities & Equity			
Current Liabilities:			
Accounts Payable	$ 50,000	$ 58,000	Change in proportion with sales (16% increase)
Notes Payable	74,000	85,840	Change in proportion with sales (16% increase)
Total Current Liabilities	$ 124,000	$ 143,840	
Long-Term Debt	45,000	45,000	No change
Total Liabilities	$ 169,000	$ 188,840	
Common Stock	35,000	35,000	No change
Capital in Excess of Par	34,000	34,000	No change
Retained Earnings	104,000	109,466	Old RE + 5,466 net income difference
Total Stockholders' Equity	$ 173,000	$ 178,466	
Total Liabilities & Equity	$ 342,000	$ 367,306	
Additional Funds Needed		72,294	To be obtained from external sources
		$ 439,600	

Note 1: The new total inventory costs were computed as follows:

$$\text{New Order Quantity per the EOQ} = \sqrt{\frac{2 \times 232 \times \$100}{500}}$$

$$= 9.63 \text{ (round to 10)}$$

Number of orders this year = 232/10 = 23.2 (round to 23)
New total ordering cost = 23 × $100 = $2,300
New average inventory level = 48
New total carrying cost = 48 × $500 = $24,000
New total inventory cost = $2,300 + $24,000 = $26,300 $8,100 increase

1. Incremental Cash Outflows at t_0	
Additional funds Needed from the Projected Balance Sheet	$ 72,294
2. Incremental Cash Flows Occurring in the Future	
Incremental Cash Inflows:	
Increase in Sales	$192,000
Incremental Cash Outflows:	
Increase in Cost of Goods Sold	$160,000
Increase in Inventory Costs	8,100
Increase in Other Operating Expenses	13,600
Increase in Interest Expense	1,190
Increase in Taxes	3,644
Total Incremental Cash Outflows:	$186,534
Net Incremental Cash Flows Occurring from Time t_1 through Infinity:	$ 5,466 per year

t_1 through infinity from Table 19-4 ($5,466 per year) using Equation 8-5, the formula for the present value of a perpetuity:

$$PVP = PMT \times \left(\frac{1}{k}\right)$$

$$= \$5,466 \times \left(\frac{1}{.10}\right)$$

$$= \$54,660$$

We find that the present value of the net cash flow perpetuity is $54,660.

Next, we subtract the present value of the net cash outflows at t_0 (the initial investment) to find the NPV of the inventory policy change. From Table 19-4 we see the net cash outflow that occurs at t_0 is $72,294. So, the NPV of Dealin' Dan's Cream Puff Used Cars inventory change proposal is as follows:

$$NPV = \$54,660 - \$72,294$$

$$= \$(17,634)$$

We find that the net present value of the inventory change proposal is $-\$17,634$. Since the NPV is negative, the inventory change proposal should be rejected. Accepting it would decrease the value of the Cream Puff Used Cars company by $17,634.[11]

In the preceding analysis, we used one possible inventory level and observed the effect on the value of the Cream Puff firm. By repeating this procedure a number of times, we could eventually find one inventory level, or a range of levels, at which the firm's value was maximized. We would then have found the true optimal level of inventory for the firm.

---

[11]The internal rate of return (IRR) of the inventory proposal is:

$$k, \text{ or IRR,} = PMT / PV \text{ (initial investment)}$$
$$IRR = 5,466 / 72,294$$
$$= .0756, \text{ or } 7.56\%$$

Since 7.56 percent is less than Dealin' Dan's cost of capital of 10 percent, the inventory change proposal should be rejected.

INVENTORY MANAGEMENT APPROACHES

Managing inventory is more than just determining the optimal level of items to keep on hand. Remember, the task is to hold down inventory costs without sacrificing sales too much. Techniques for doing this abound, but two approaches deserve special mention: the ABC classification system and the just-in-time (JIT) system.

The ABC Inventory Classification System

The **ABC system** of inventory classification is a tool used to lower inventory carrying costs. The system classifies inventory according to value. In many firms, inventory items may range in value from relatively expensive to relatively cheap. Generally, firms have fewer expensive items and more inexpensive items. In such a situation, it doesn't make sense to use one inventory control system to manage all inventory items, because the firm would waste a lot of time and effort monitoring the relatively cheap items. For example, imagine the inventory system of a bicycle store. Its inventory would probably include several custom-designed racing bicycles; standard ten-speed and mountain bikes; and cycling helmets, water bottles, and other cycling equipment. Wouldn't it waste time and effort to assign serial numbers to all items in inventory and keep them all locked up in glass cases?

Under the ABC system, firm managers classify the relatively few, very expensive items as group A, the larger number of less expensive items as group B, and the rest of the relatively cheap items as group C.[12] Then, different inventory control systems are designed for each group, appropriate for the value of that group. For example, the owner of a bicycle shop might assign custom-designed racing bikes to group A, less expensive standard bicycles to group B, and the rest of the inventory to group C. Then the owner could apply inventory control techniques appropriate for each group, as follows:

- *Group A:* Assign serial numbers to each item. Keep in secure storage. Check inventory daily. Keep fixed number on display, ordering replacements as each is sold.
- *Group B:* Assign serial numbers to each item. Keep in secure storage. Check inventory monthly. Manage levels of each type per the EOQ model.
- *Group C:* Check inventory annually. Reorder when visual checks of shelves indicate need.

This technique allows the bicycle store owner to concentrate his or her time and effort on those items that deserve it. Unnecessary carrying costs on the rest of the inventory items are thus avoided.

Just-in-Time Inventory Control (JIT)

The just-in-time inventory system (JIT), developed in Japan, is useful when storage space is limited and inventory carrying costs are high. As shown in the chapter opener, the system attempts to operate the firm on little or no inventory.

---

[12]Of course, the classifications are not limited to just A, B, and C. Depending on the firm's product lines, some companies might have D, E, and F as well. However, the guiding principle is the same.

Here is an example of how JIT works. A firm that makes kitchen cabinets needs wood, brass handles and knobs, screws, and varnish. All these items constitute the firm's raw materials inventory. On the one hand, the firm could order these raw materials once a month and keep them in storage areas until needed in the manufacturing process (incurring inventory carrying costs as a result). On the other hand, the firm might strike a deal with its raw materials suppliers to deliver just the number of items needed immediately upon request. The items would thus arrive just in time to be used. The firm would not need to store materials, and inventory carrying costs would be eliminated.[13]

In addition to lowering inventory carrying costs, just-in-time systems tend to force quality into the manufacturing process. Any defect in materials will force the entire production line to shut down until the firm can obtain replacement materials.

Carrying little or no inventory can have drawbacks, however. Suppliers that are late or produce poor quality products jeopardize the firm's customer relations. Little or no inventory means that the business does not have a buffer when a work slowdown occurs due to illness, natural disaster, or a labor dispute.

For instance, General Motors had an inventory system similar to JIT. When 3,000 workers at two brake plants in Dayton, Ohio, went on strike in early 1996, the ripple effects were staggering. Without the brake parts in inventory, workers at other GM plants could not complete car assembly, so eventually 177,775 GM workers were idled. The labor dispute virtually shut down GM's North American operations.[14]

Recall that the JIT inventory system was developed in Japan, where labor unions do not exist. Clearly, firms that employ organized labor should carefully consider the risks of JIT, as evidenced by the GM strike.

MAKING CREDIT DECISIONS

Earlier in this chapter, we said that individual customers receive credit from the firm if they meet the firm's credit standards. Credit standards are those requirements each individual customer must satisfy in order to receive credit from the firm. They are tests, in other words, of a person's creditworthiness.

Firms often base their credit standards on *the Five Cs of Credit:* character, capacity, capital, collateral, and conditions.

1. *Character:* the borrower's *willingness to pay.* Lenders evaluate character by looking at borrowers' past payment patterns. A good payment record in the past implies willingness to pay debts in the future.
2. *Capacity:* the borrower's *ability to pay,* as indicated by forecasts of future cash flows. The more confidence a lender has that a borrower is going to receive cash in the future, the more willing the lender will be to grant credit now.
3. *Capital:* how much wealth a borrower has to fall back on, in case the expected future cash flows with which the borrower plans to pay debts don't materialize.

---

[13]You can see that, in effect, the requirement to store materials (and the attendant carrying costs) are passed on to the suppliers. Presumably, the suppliers would adopt such systems as well, until a closely coordinated chain from original suppliers to final customers developed.

[14]Rebecca Blumenstein and Nichole Christian, "Parts Dispute to Remain Despite GM–UAW Accord," *The Wall Street Journal* (March 25, 1996): p A3; John Byrne, "Has Outsourcing Gone Too Far?" *Business Week* (April 1, 1996): p 26.

date if necessary to pay their debts.

4. *Collateral:* what the lender gets if capacity and capital fail, and the borrower defaults on a loan. Collateral is usually some form of tangible asset, such as the firm's inventory, buildings, manufacturing equipment, and so on that has been pledged as security by the borrower.

5. *Conditions:* the business conditions the borrower is expected to face. The more favorable business conditions appear to be for the borrower, the more willing lenders are to grant credit.

To evaluate potential credit customers (in terms of the Five Cs of Credit, or any other criteria), firms find some way to quantify how well the customers compare to the measurement criteria. Some firms use a method known as **credit scoring.** Credit scoring works by assigning points according to how well customers meet indicators of creditworthiness. For example, statisticians have determined that established businesses tend to pay their debts more faithfully than new businesses. So, a credit applicant might be awarded points for each year that the applicant's firm has been in business. A sample of a simplified credit score sheet is shown in Figure 19-4 for Wishful Thinking Company.

We cannot overemphasize the importance of investigating creditworthiness carefully before granting credit. Not doing so is a quick way to end up with lots of accounts receivable and no cash!

COLLECTION POLICIES TO HANDLE BAD DEBTS

Sometimes, despite precautions, a firm ends up with customers who don't pay their bills. You thought your firm did a good job of scoring customers. But now some of them are not paying their bills on time, and a few haven't paid at all. Now what?

Slow or no payment is bound to happen to any credit-granting business. Firms establish a **collection policy** to cope with the problem. For instance, what do you do if one of your long-time customers fails to pay a bill on the due date? Send it to a collection agency the next day? Ignore the situation and hope for the best? Send a reminder notice? Start charging interest? It helps to have a collection policy in place. That way, both the firm and its customers know what to expect once credit has been granted.

No one collection policy will be best for all firms and for all customers. The best policy depends on the business situation, the firm's tolerance for abuse, and the relationship it has with customers. However, most firms consider one or more of the following collection policies:

- *Send reminder letters.* Send one or more letters, each one becoming less friendly in tone. Certainly, the first letter should not sound threatening. (How often have you simply misplaced a bill and not realized it until you received a reminder notice?)

- *Make telephone calls.* If gentle reminders in the mail don't produce results, call the customer to see what the problem is. If there is a good reason why the customer hasn't paid the bill, you may choose to take no action or make accommodating arrangements. Make sure that any alternative payment plan is specific so that the firm can follow up early if the customer fails to pay again.

CRITERIA		SCORE
1. Length of time since missing a payment on any loan		_____
More than four years	4 points	
Three to four years	3 points	
Two to three years	2 points	
One to two years	1 point	
Less than one year	0 points	
2. Length of time in business		_____
More than four years	4 points	
Three to four years	3 points	
Two to three years	2 points	
One to two years	1 point	
Less than one year	0 points	
3. Net income		_____
More than $200,000	4 points	
$100,000 to $200,000	3 points	
$50,000 to $100,000	2 points	
$25,000 to $50,000	1 point	
Less than $25,000	0 points	
4. Net worth		_____
More than $1 million	4 points	
$500,000 to $1 million	3 points	
$100,000 to $500,000	2 points	
$50,000 to $100,000	1 point	
Less than $50,000	0 points	
5. Market value of tangible assets		_____
More than $1 million	4 points	
$500,000 to $1 million	3 points	
$100,000 to $500,000	2 points	
$50,000 to $100,000	1 point	
Less than $50,000	0 points	
6. Expected business growth rate in next five years		_____
More than 20 percent	4 points	
15 to 20 percent	3 points	
10 to 15 percent	2 points	
5 to 10 percent	1 point	
Less 5 percent	0 points	
	Total Score:	_____
	Approved for Credit if score = 12 or more	

Figure 19-4 Sample Items on a Credit Scoring Worksheet for Wishful Thinking Company

Figure 19-4 is an example of items on a credit scoring sheet to determine an applicant's creditworthiness. No attempt is made here to determine the amount of credit that may be extended.

- *Hire collection agencies.* When all efforts to collect are unsuccessful, you may want to turn to professional collection agencies. This action should be used sparingly for two reasons. First, it will probably cost the firm any future business from this customer. Second, the price of the collection agency service may be very high, often 50% of the uncollected debt.
- *Sue the customer.* Legal action is a last resort. A lawsuit is even more expensive than using a collection agency, so firms should determine whether the court action is worth the trouble. Remember the "lawyers first" rule: Lawyers almost always get paid first.

Joann K. Jones, CEO of Capital Electric Supply

Joann K. Jones

"I ain't gonna have no broad tell me what to do." These words from a hostile employee greeted Joann K. Jones after she took charge of her husband's company when he was diagnosed with Alzheimer's. Joann, whose previous years were spent taking care of the home front, had to become a CEO almost overnight. And she had to turn around Capital Electric Supply, a wholesale distributor, whose equity had dropped $2 million in two years, while sales had dropped by $8 million. Joann's efforts succeeded. One of the keys to the company's dramatic success was Joann's quick action in taking command of inventory and accounts receivable. Under Joann's guidance, Capital Electric's net income rose in four years from a $231,000 loss to a $300,000 profit.

Q. What is one basic premise everyone should understand about inventory?

Inventory costs money—lots of it. Inventory expenses include financing, storage, accounting, taxes, insurance, security, obsolescence, and shrinkage. Even if your inventory is just sitting on the shelf, you must cover those costs.

Q. What was Capital Electric's inventory level when you took over?

We had much too much inventory for our customers' demands. We also had too many items that moved slowly and held up our ability to collect money. For example, we kept five special electrical panels in stock, even though on average we only sold one a year. We had a great deal of money tied up in the other four. We also faced another problem. Our purchasing agent would buy the complete line that his favorite supplier sold, even though we had no demand for half the items.

Q. How did you correct your inventory problem?

First, we returned items to the vendor where possible to credit our account with that vendor. Doing so added more cash to the bottom line so we could pay our bills. Then we sold remaining excess inventory at heavily discounted rates. If we couldn't sell items, we donated them to charities. Once we got rid of items that didn't move quickly, we had the cash to stock quick-moving items. Now at least 60 percent of our inventory items move quickly—items like lock nuts, extension cords, light bulbs. These items are our bread and butter; they pay employees' salaries.

Because we are a relatively small company, we need to be smarter than our competitors. We have a strong relationship with our vendors and this allows us to obtain special items overnight, if needed. Those are items that our competitor has foolishly sitting on shelves collecting dust.

Q. How do you monitor your inventory and accounts receivable?

We take charge of our inventory with weekly "flash reports" that indicate gross sales, gross margin, administrative overhead, accounts receivable, and inventory turnover. These weekly reports are an important management tool. A business owner shouldn't wait until the middle of the following month to learn what happened this week or this month.

Q. How do you keep your accounts receivable at a low level?

Our accounts receivable are a goodwill gesture to our customers so they will come back more often. It's a way of extending credit to your customers for thirty days, so they can collect their money before they pay us. But we don't want to hold onto accounts receivable too long. Holding accounts receivable for too long affects our cash flow, which affects our ability to pay our bills. That's why we encourage our customers to pay early by offering them a 2 percent discount if they pay by the tenth of the following month.

Q. What do you view as the optimal level of accounts receivable and inventory?

Simply put, you want the right level of accounts receivable and inventory that not only satisfies your customers' needs, but that gives you a positive, timely cash flow.

Source: Interviews with Joann K. Jones.

- *Settle for a reduced amount.* A firm should keep in mind that trying too hard to collect from a customer may force the customer into bankruptcy. Once the client is in bankruptcy, the firm may not receive any money. In such a case, settling for a reduced amount, or a stretched-out payment schedule, may be the firm's best option.
- *Write off the bill as a loss.* In other words, forget it. This may be a firm's best alternative if the amount owed is relatively small or too costly to collect. Firms may have to write off all or part of the bill as a loss anyway, if efforts to collect are unsuccessful.
- *Sell accounts receivable to factors.* Selling accounts receivable to some other person or business is known as **factoring.** Businesses that make money by buying accounts receivable from other firms, at less than their face value, are called **factors.** Suppose your firm had one hundred customers who owed you a total of $10,000. Rather than wait for the customers to pay, you might sell the "IOUs" to a factor for $9,000 in cash. The factor discounts the accounts by an amount that both generates a return and compensates for the risk that some customers won't pay. Your firm no longer has to manage the accounts, plus it has cash to put to use elsewhere.

◀ **Take Note**

A firm that frequently writes off uncollected amounts needs to tighten its standards for granting credit.

When granting credit to customers, it is best to remember the old saying, "An ounce of prevention is worth a pound of cure." In other words, crafting credit standards that avoid frequent collections can save a firm time and money.

What's Next

In this chapter we have explored how and why firms manage inventory and accounts receivable. We have examined methods for finding the optimal levels of both categories of current assets and have explored additional management techniques. In chapter 20 we'll look at short-term financing.

Summary

1. Describe how and why firms must manage accounts receivable and inventory as investments.

Granting credit and maintaining inventory are necessary business practices. Offering more credit and increasing inventory enhance sales. However, both accounts receivable and inventory tie up cash and incur opportunity costs—the cost of not having funds that could generate returns. The financial manager's task is to balance (1) the risk of losing sales due to not granting credit or having products available, against (2) the savings produced by collecting cash immediately or maintaining inventory at a reduced level.

2. Compute the optimal levels of accounts receivable and inventory.

The optimal level of accounts receivable or inventory may be found by using a three-step process: (1) create *pro forma* financial statements for alternative credit or inventory policies; (2) use the *pro forma* data to estimate the incremental cash flows associated with the proposed changes; and (3) compute the net present value of each alternative. When this process is complete, managers compare the NPVs of each alternative to see which policy produces the most favorable effect on the value of the firm.

3. Describe alternative inventory management approaches.

Two popular inventory management approaches are the ABC and just-in-time (JIT) inventory systems. The ABC system classifies inventory items into categories according to their relative value. Management's time, money, and effort can then be directed to those inventory items in the proportions that they deserve.

The JIT inventory system calls for close coordination between manufacturers and suppliers to ensure that parts and materials used in the manufacturing process arrive just in time to be used. If the coordination is close enough, raw materials inventories at the manufacturing firm can be eliminated.

4. Explain how firms make credit decisions and create credit policies.

Firms evaluate the creditworthiness of their customers by applying the following Five Cs of Credit:

- *Character*—a borrower's willingness to pay.
- *Capacity*—a borrower's ability to pay.
- *Capital*—how much wealth a borrower has to fall back on, in case the expected future cash flows with which the borrower plans to pay debts don't materialize.
- *Collateral*—what the lender gets if capacity and capital fail, and the borrower defaults on a loan.
- *Conditions*—the business conditions a borrower is expected to face.

To evaluate potential credit customers, firms use a credit scoring procedure that assigns numerical values to the various indicators of creditworthiness.

A firm's collection policy includes the actions the firm plans to take in the event that credit customers don't pay their bills on time. Policy actions include reminder letters, telephone calls, use of collection agencies, court action, settling for partial payment, factoring the accounts, and writing off the bills as a loss.

Equations Introduced in This Chapter

Equation 19-1. The Economic Order Quantity for Inventory:

$$OQ = \sqrt{\frac{2 \times S \times OC}{CC}}$$

where: OQ = Order quantity
S = Annual sales volumes in units
OC = Ordering costs, per order
CC = Carrying costs, per unit per year

Self-Test

ST-1. Assume the Cash & Carry company is considering offering credit to its customers. Management estimates that if it does so, sales will increase 10 percent, expenses will increase 5 percent, accounts receivable will increase to $200,000, cash will decrease by $50,000, and current liabilities will increase to $300,000. No other accounts on the financial statements will be affected. Compute the company's return on equity (ROE) ratio and current ratio if it adopts the proposal. Base your calculations on Cash & Carry's latest financial statements shown next.

Selected Financial Data for Cash & Carry, Inc.
(in 000's)

	Prior to Granting Credit	After Granting Credit
Cash	$ 100	
Accounts Receivable	0	
Total Current Assets	$ 100	
Current Liabilities	$ 50	
Total Equity	$2,000	
Sales	$2,500	
Expenses	2,300	
Net Income for the Year	$ 200	

ST-2. Your firm sells inventory at an even rate throughout the year. Sales volume this year is expected to be 100,000 units. Inventory ordering costs are $30 per order and inventory carrying costs are $60 per unit per year. Given these conditions what is the most economical inventory order quantity (EOQ)?

ST-3. Refer again to the Dealin' Dan's Cream Puff Used Cars example in the text. Continue with the assumptions given and compute the NPV of raising the company's average inventory level of cars to sixty. Assume the inventory change would cause unit sales to increase to 240 per year.

ST-4. Your firm uses the credit scoring worksheet in Figure 19-4 to evaluate potential credit customers. If an applicant has never missed a loan payment, has been in business for two and a half years, has net income of $75,000, has a net worth of $90,000, has tangible assets worth $120,000, and has an expected business growth rate of 12 percent a year, will the applicant be granted credit?

Review Questions

1. Accounts receivable are sometimes not collected. Why do companies extend trade credit when they could insist on cash for all sales?
2. Inventory is sometimes thought of as a necessary evil. Explain.
3. What are the primary variables being balanced in the EOQ inventory model? Explain.
4. What are the benefits of the JIT inventory control system?
5. What are the primary requirements for a successful JIT inventory control system?
6. Can a company have a default rate on its accounts receivable that is too low? Explain.
7. How does accounts receivable factoring work? What are the benefits to the two parties involved? What are the risks?

Build Your Communication Skills

CS-1. The three-step process of evaluating the NPV of a proposed credit policy or inventory level change can intimidate some managers. Prepare an oral presentation to explain how to measure the value of the credit policy change analysis presented in this chapter. Lead a study group through the process.

CS-2. Evaluate the creditworthiness of a business in your local community using the credit scoring worksheet in Figure 19-4. To collect information, you may want to research local business publications, conduct interviews, or contact the local chamber of commerce. Prepare a brief written report of the results and include your credit scoring worksheet as an exhibit.

Problems

Accounts Receivable, ACP

19-1. FibreGlass Insulation Co. had an annual credit sales of $6,500,000 and an average collection period (ACP) of twenty-two days in 1997. What is the company's accounts receivable for the year? Assume 365 days in a year.

Accounts Receivable, ACP

19-2. If FibreGlass Insulation Co. of problem 19-1 is expected to have annual credit sales of $7,600,000 and an average collection period of twenty-six days in 1998, what would be the company's accounts receivables? Do you think that the company relaxed or tightened its credit policy in 1998, compared to its policy in 1997?

Accounts Receivable, ACP, Credit Policy

19-3. Goodwill Tools Company has credit terms of 2/15, n60. The historical payment patterns of its customers are as follows:

- 40 percent of customers pay in fifteen days
- 57 percent of customers pay in sixty days
- 3 percent of customers pay in one hundred days

Annual sales of tools is $200,000. Assume there are 365 days in a year.

a. Calculate the average collection period (ACP).
b. What is the accounts receivable (AR) assuming all goods are sold on credit?

Accounts Receivable, ACP, Credit Policy

19-4. If Goodwill Tools in problem 19-3 decides to adopt a more stringent credit terms of 2/10, n30, sales are expected to drop by 10 percent but the following improved payment pattern of its customers is expected:

- 40 percent of customers will pay in ten days
- 58 percent of customers will pay in thirty days
- 2 percent of customers will pay in one hundred days

Calculate the new average collection period (ACP) and accounts receivable (AR) assuming all goods are sold on credit.

Effect of Change of Credit Policy

19-5. Doris Walker, Vice President of Sales for East-West Trading, Inc., wants to change the firm's credit policy from 2/15, n40 to 2/15, n60, effective January 1, 1998. She is confident that the proposed relaxation will result in a 20 percent increase over the otherwise expected annual sales of $350,000 with the old policy. All sales are made on credit. The historical payment pattern under the present credit terms are as follows:

Under the old policy:

- 40 percent of the customers take advantage of the discount and pay in fifteen days.
- 58 percent of the customers forgo the discount and pay in 40 days.
- The remaining 2 percent pay in one hundred days.

Under the new credit policy, the payment pattern is expected to be as follows:

- 40 percent of the customers will take advantage of the discount and pay in fifteen days.
- 57 percent of the customers will forgo the discount and pay in forty days.
- The remaining 3 percent will pay in one hundred days.

Bad debt expenses are expected to rise from 2 percent to 3 percent with the change in credit policy. Assume (i) any increase in the current assets will be financed by short-term notes at an interest rate of 7 percent; (ii) long-term interest rate is 10 percent; (iii) income tax rate is 40 percent; (iv) cost of capital for East-West is 11 percent; (v) cost of goods sold is 80 percent of sales; (vi) other operating expenses is $10,000 under the old policy.

The *pro forma* balance sheet items of the company under the old policy would be as follows:

Cash & Securities	$ 15,000	Accounts Payable	$14,918
Inventory	50,000	Notes Payable	35,000
Plant & Equipment	120,000	Long-Term Debt	30,000
Common Stock	25,000	Capital in Excess of Par	60,000
Retained Earnings	50,000		

Also assume that the cost of goods sold and other operating expenses in the income statement and all current asset and current liability items vary directly with sales.

    a. Calculate average collection periods and accounts receivables under the old and the new policies.

    b. Develop *pro forma* income statements and balance sheets under the old and the new policies.

    c. Calculate the incremental cash flows for the year 1998 and the subsequent years.

    d. Advise Ms. Walker if she should adopt the new policy.

19-6. Use the same information given in problem 19-5 with the following changes. Ms. Walker asked Mr. Scott Hayward, the General Manager of Sales of East-West, to recheck the payment patterns and credit history of East-West's customers to be absolutely sure that the change in credit policy would indeed be beneficial to the company. A strict scrutiny by Mr. Hayward resulted in the following changes in expected payment pattern and bad debts: Under the old policy:

Effect of Change of Credit Policy

- 40 percent of the customers take advantage of the discount and pay in fifteen days.
- 58 percent of the customers forgo the discount and pay in forty days.
- The remaining 2 percent pay in one hundred days.

Under the new credit policy, the payment pattern is expected to be as follows:

- 30 percent of the customers will take advantage of the discount and pay in fifteen days.
- 60 percent of the customers will forgo the discount and pay in forty-five days.
- The remaining 10 percent will pay in one hundred days.

Bad debt expenses are expected to rise from 2 percent to 4 percent with the change in credit policy. Under this changed scenario, is adoption of the new credit policy advisable?

19-7. Tom Rath, the vice president of sales for A-Z Trading, Inc., wants to change the firm's credit policy from 3/10, n40 to 3/15, n30, effective January 1, 1998. He is confident that though the proposed tightening will result in a 10 percent decrease over the otherwise expected annual sales of $2 million with the old policy, it will increase profitability and value of the firm. All sales are made on credit. The historical payment pattern under the present credit terms are as follows:
Under the old policy:

Challenge Problem

- 30 percent of the customers take advantage of the discount and pay in ten days.
- 60 percent of the customers forgo the discount and pay in forty days.
- The remaining 10 percent pay in one hundred days.

Under the new credit policy, the payment pattern is expected to be as follows:

- 42 percent of the customers will take advantage of the discount and pay in fifteen days.
- 57 percent of the customers will forgo the discount and pay in forty days.
- The remaining 1 percent will pay in one hundred days.

Bad debt expenses are expected to decrease from 3 percent to 1 percent with the change in credit policy. Assume (i) any decrease in the current assets will be used to pay off short-term notes currently outstanding at an interest rate of 8 percent; (ii) long-term interest rate is 11 percent; (iii) income tax rate is 40 percent; (iv) cost of capital for A-Z is 13 percent; (v) cost of goods sold is 80 percent of sales; (vi) other operating expenses is $60,000 under the old policy.

The *pro forma* balance sheet items of the company under the old policy would be as follows:

Cash & Securities	$ 86,000	Accounts Payable	$ 85,000
Inventory	285,000	Notes Payable	200,000
Plant & Equipment	652,000	Long-Term Debt	171,000
Common Stock	143,000	Capital in Excess of Par	342,000
Retained Earnings	285,000		

Also assume that the cost of goods sold and other operating expenses in the income statement and all current account items in the balance sheet vary directly with sales.

   a. Calculate average collection periods and accounts receivable under the old and the new policies.
   b. Develop *pro forma* income statements and balance sheets under the old and the new policies.
   c. Calculate the incremental cash flows for the year 1998 and the subsequent years.
   d. Advise Mr. Rath if he should adopt the new policy.

Economic Order Quantity

19-8. Windhome and Drake Co., a dealer in building products, has the following costs associated with its business in 1997:

Ordering Cost	$250 per Order
Carrying Cost	$300 per Unit per Year
Annual Sales	500 Units

Calculate the EOQ and the number or orders placed per year.

Economic Order Quantity

19-9. Use the same data for problem 19-8 except that the carrying cost is expected to increase by 10 percent in 1998 due to increase in rentals of warehouse space. Recalculate the EOQ, number of orders placed per year, and total ordering cost for 1998.

Credit Scoring

19-10. Danny Fisher's firm uses the credit scoring sheet in Figure 19-4 to evaluate the creditworthiness of its customers. An applicant missed a loan payment three and a half years back, has been in business for six years, has a net income of $143,000, a net worth of $1.5 million, a market value of $550,000 in tangible assets, and a business growth rate of 14 percent. Would Danny approve credit to the applicant?

Effect of Change of Inventory Policy

19-11. Mr. Homer Smith is the Vice President of Sales for Sunrise Corporation, which buys and sells mobile homes. He is sure that increasing the number of homes on display will cause sales to increase. He thinks that an increase in inventory effective January 1, 1998, from the present level of sixty units to one hundred units will boost up sales from 350 units per year to 450 units per year. Assume ordering cost to be $200 per order, carrying cost to be $600 per unit per year, unit sales price to be $10,000, unit purchase price to be $8,000, and applicable income tax rate to be 40 percent. Also assume that any increase in the current assets will be financed by short-term notes at an interest rate of 7 percent, long-term interest rate to be 10 percent, cost of capital for Sunrise to be 11 percent, cost of goods sold to be 80 percent of sales, and other operating expenses to be $100,000 under the old policy. The *pro forma* balance sheet items of the company under the old policy would be as follows:

Cash & Securities	$ 55,000	Accounts Payable	$100,000
Accounts Receivable	105,000	Notes Payable	95,000
Plant & Equipment	100,000	Long-Term Debt	65,000
Common Stock	60,000	Capital in Excess of Par	220,000
Retained Earnings	200,000		

Also assume that the cost of goods sold and other operating expenses in the income statement and all current asset and current liability items vary directly with sales.

a. Calculate the EOQ, number of orders issued per year, and inventory cost.
b. Develop *pro forma* income statements and balance sheets under the old and the new policies.
c. Calculate the incremental cash flows for the year 1998 and the subsequent years.
d. Advise Ms. Walker if she should adopt the new policy.

19-12. Use the same information given in Problem 19-11 except that Ms. Judy Benjamin, the General Manager of Sales for Sunrise, thinks that increasing the inventory level from 60 to 90 will increase sales from 350 to 390 units per year. With other assumptions remaining the same as in problem 19-11, evaluate this change in the inventory policy.

Effect of Change of Inventory Policy

19-13. Ms. Terry McKay is the Vice President of Sales for Windermere Corporation, which sells hot air balloons. She is sure that increasing the number of balloons on display will cause sales to increase. She thinks that an increase in inventory effective January 1, 1998, from the present level will boost sales to higher levels in 1998 as shown:

Comprehensive Problem

	Inventory Level (Units)		Sales (Units)
Present		70	340
Future (1998)	(1)	80	375
	(2)	90	390
	(3)	100	400

Assume ordering costs are $160 per order, carrying costs are $400 per unit per year, unit sales price is $16,000, unit purchase price is $12,800, and applicable income tax rate is 40 percent. Also assume that any increase in the current assets will be financed by short-term notes at an interest rate of 7 percent, the long-term interest rate is 11 percent, cost of capital for Windermere is 13 percent, cost of goods sold is 80 percent of sales, and other operating expenses are $130,000 under the present policy. The *pro forma* balance sheet items of the company under the present policy would be as follows:

Cash & Securities	$ 65,000	Accounts Payable	$110,000
Accounts Receivable	114,000	Notes Payable	95,000
Plant & Equipment	113,000	Long-Term Debt	65,000
Common Stock	80,000	Capital in Excess of Par	320,000
Retained Earnings	853,000		

Also assume that the cost of goods sold and other operating expenses in the income statement and all current account items in the balance sheet vary directly with sales.

Find out for Ms. McKay what level of inventory maximizes value of the firm by doing the following, and comparing the net present values of the cash flows associated with each level of inventory:

a. Calculate the EOQ, number of orders issued per year, and inventory cost.
b. Develop *pro forma* income statements and balance sheets under the present and the future policies.
c. Calculate the incremental cash flows for the year 1998 and the subsequent years.
d. Advise Ms. McKay whether she should change the present inventory policy. If so, which inventory level should she adopt?

Answers to Self-Test

ST-1.

Selected Financial Data for Cash & Carry, Inc.
(in 000's)

	Prior to Granting Credit	After Granting Credit
Cash	$ 100	$ 50
Accounts Receivable	0	200
Total Current Assets	$ 100	$ 250
Current Liabilities	$ 50	$ 300
Total Equity	$2,000	$2,000
Sales	$2,500	$2,750
Expenses	2,300	2,415
Net Income for the Year	$ 200	$ 335
Current Ratio	$100/$50 = 2.0	$250/$300 = .833
Return on Equity	$200/$2,000 = .10	$335/$2,000 = .1675

ST-2. Per equation 19-1, the EOQ model:

$$OQ = \sqrt{\frac{2 \times 100{,}000 \times 30}{60}}$$

$$= \sqrt{100{,}000}$$

$$= 316.228 \text{ (round to 316)}$$

ST-3. Use the three-step process to compute the NPV of raising the average inventory to sixty cars:

- *Step 1:* Create *pro forma* financial statements for the new inventory policy:

Dealin' Dan's Cream Puff Used Cars Inventory Analysis

Income Statements

	Current Inventory Policy	New Inventory Policy	Remarks
Sales	$1,200,000	$1,440,000	Unit sales × price each, from assumptions
Cost of Goods Sold	1,000,000	1,200,000	Unit sales × cost each, from assumptions
Gross Profit	200,000	240,000	
Inventory Costs	18,200	32,400	See Note 1 below
Other Operating Expenses	85,000	102,000	Increase in proportion with sales
Operating Income	96,800	105,600	
Interest Expense	11,040	12,528	ST & LT Debt × Costs of Debt
Before-Tax Income	85,760	93,072	
Income Taxes (rate = 40%)	34,304	37,229	
Net Income	$ 51,456	$ 55,843	

Balance Sheets, as of December 31

	Current Inventory Policy	New Inventory Policy	Remarks
Assets			
Current Assets:			
Cash & Securities	$ 47,000	$ 56,400	Change in proportion with sales
Accounts Receivable	63,000	75,600	Change in proportion with sales
Inventory	160,000	300,000	Average inventory × cost each, from assumptions
Total Current Assets	270,000	432,000	
Prop, Plant & Equip, Net	72,000	72,000	No change
Total Assets	$ 342,000	$ 504,000	
Liabilities & Equity			
Current Liabilities:			
Accounts Payable	$ 50,000	$ 60,000	Change in proportion with sales
Notes Payable	74,000	88,800	Change in proportion with sales
Total Current Liabilities	124,000	148,800	
Long-Term Debt	45,000	45,000	No change
Total Liabilities	169,000	193,800	
Common Stock	35,000	35,000	No change
Capital in Excess of Par	34,000	34,000	No change
Retained Earnings	104,000	108,387	Old RE + net income change
Total Stockholders' Equity	173,000	177,387	
Total Liabilities & Equity	$ 342,000	$ 371,187	
Additional Funds Needed		132,813	Obtained from external sources
		$ 504,000	

Note 1: The new total inventory costs were computed as follows:

$$\text{New Order Quantity per the EOQ} = \sqrt{\frac{2 \times 240 \times \$100}{500}}$$
$$= 9.8 \text{ (round to 10)}$$

Number of orders this year   = 24/10 = 24
New total ordering cost   = 24 × $100 = $2,400
New average inventory level = 60
New total carrying cost   = 60 × $500 = $30,000
New total inventory cost   = $2,400 + $30,000 = $32,400

- *Step 2:* Compute the incremental cash flows:

**Incremental Cash Flows Associated with Changing
Cream Puff Used Cars Inventory Level from 32 Cars to 60 Cars**

1. Incremental Cash Outflows at Time Zero (t_0):

    Additional Funds Needed from the Projected
    Balance Sheet $132,813

2. Incremental Cash Flows Occurring in the Future

    Incremental Cash Inflows:

    Increase in Sales $240,000

    Incremental Cash Outflows:

    Increase in Cost of Goods Sold $200,000
    Increase in Inventory Costs   14,200
    Increase in Other Operating Expenses   17,000
    Increase in Interest Expense   1,488
    Increase in Taxes   2,925
        Total Incremental Cash Outflows: $235,613

    Net Incremental Cash Flows Occurring from Time
    t_1 through Infinity: $ 4,387 per year

- *Step 3:* Compute the NPV of the Inventory Policy Change

PV of the net cash inflows occurring from time t_1 through infinity ($4,387 per year) using Equation 8-5:

$$PVP = PMT \times \left(\frac{1}{k}\right)$$

$$= \$4,387 \times \left(\frac{1}{.10}\right)$$

$$= \$43,870$$

Subtract the PV of the net cash outflows at t_0 ($132,813) to obtain the NPV of the inventory policy change:

$$NPV = \$43,870 - \$132,813$$

$$= (\$88,943)$$

Since the NPV is negative, the inventory change proposal should be rejected.

ST-4. The applicant's completed credit scoring worksheet from Figure 19-4 is shown next.

Credit Scoring Worksheet
for _____(applicant)_____

Criteria		Score
1. Length of time since missing a payment on any loan		4
More than four years	4 points	
Three to four years	3 points	
Two to three years	2 points	
One to two years	1 point	
Less than one year	0 points	
2. Length of time in business		2
More than four years	4 points	
Three to four years	3 points	
Two to three years	2 points	
One to two years	1 point	
Less than one year	0 points	
3. Net income		2
More than $200,000	4 points	
$100,000 to $200,000	3 points	
$50,000 to $100,000	2 points	
$25,000 to $50,000	1 point	
Less than $25,000	0 points	
4. Net worth		1
More than $1 million	4 points	
$500,000 to $1 million	3 points	
$100,000 to $500,000	2 points	
$50,000 to $100,000	1 point	
Less than $50,000	0 points	
5. Market value of tangible assets		2
More than $1 million	4 points	
$500,000 to $1 million	3 points	
$100,000 to $500,000	2 points	
$50,000 to $100,000	1 point	
Less than $50,000	0 points	
6. Expected business growth rate in next five years		2
More than 20 percent	4 points	
15 to 20 percent	3 points	
10 to 15 percent	2 points	
5 to 10 percent	1 point	
Less 5 percent	0 points	
	Total Score:	13

Approved for Credit if score = 12 or more

Result for applicant: Approved

chapter 20

Short-Term Financing

If you would know the value of money try to borrow some.

Benjamin Franklin

Chapter Objectives

After reading this chapter, you should be able to:

1. Explain the need for short-term financing.

2. List the advantages and disadvantages of short-term financing.

3. Describe three types of short-term financing.

4. Compute the cost of trade credit and commercial paper.

5. Calculate the cost of a loan and explain how loan terms affect the effective interest rate.

6. Describe how accounts receivable and inventory can be used as collateral for short-term loans.

Why Use Credit Cards to Start a Business?

There are many ways to obtain short-term financing, ranging from unsecured bank loans to using accounts receivable or inventory as loan collateral. Research has shown, however, that women and minorities have lower qualification rates for short-term loans. According to Vickie Montgomery, a former banker, it's often tough for minorities and women to get short-term credit. In fact, American women start businesses at the rate of 1,600 a day, but they are three times as likely as men to use credit cards to launch or expand a business.

Women's organizations have conducted research that shows women frequently use credit cards to run businesses because they are routinely turned down by traditional avenues of short-term financing. "Using credit cards for short-term financing is frightening," says Sharon Hadary, executive director of the Business and Professional Women's Association. "It's the most expensive kind of credit. It puts women-owned businesses at great risk."

Minority business owners often have the same type of frustration when they apply for short-term financing. A recent survey, taken in Chicago, showed that only 32.1 percent of minority-owned firms were able to obtain short-term capital at a bank. Only 1.8 percent of minority business owners successfully received financial assistance from minority lending programs established at many banks and other lending institutions.

Most minority-owned companies are small businesses. Experts point to two main reasons why many minorities who own small businesses have difficulty obtaining short-term financing. One is the difficulty for some small companies to prepare a solid, well-documented financial proposal in the form banks generally require. Maria Medina, a second vice president at Northern Trust Bank, says, "Banks require a business plan, past records of tax returns, and some other documentation small business owners may not be in the habit of retaining." The second reason is there is sometimes a lack of awareness of the many alternative short-term financing sources.

And that is where this chapter can help you. It discusses the many sources of short-term financing available to businesses. ❁

Sources: Saara Behlim and Adolfo Mendez, "Cracks in the Infrastructure; Overall Minority Firms' Business Network is Weak," *Crain's Chicago Business* (October 18, 1993); Carolyn Brown, "High on Jobs, Low on Capital," *Black Enterprise* (July 1995): 31; Sandra Maltby, "Banks and the Woman Business Owner," *Vital Speeches of the Day* (January 1, 1996): 186–188.

CHAPTER OVERVIEW

The credit card is perhaps the best-known source of short-term financing. However, businesses use many other types of short-term financing to sustain their business operations. In this chapter we discuss the advantages and disadvantages of short-term financing, sources of that financing, and methods for calculating the cost of each source. We also show how loan terms can affect a loan's effective interest rate, and how accounts receivable and inventory can be used as short-term loan collateral.

Source: Reprinted by permission: Tribune Media Services.

The Need for Short-Term Financing

Businesses rely on short-term financing from external sources for two reasons. The first is growth—profits may simply not be high enough to keep up with the rate at which the company is buying new assets. Imagine a convenience store chain that wished to open one new store a month. If each new store cost $100,000, the company would have to be *very* profitable to be able to do this without obtaining external financing.

The second reason that businesses rely on external short-term financing is choice. Rather than waiting to save enough money from net profits to make their desired purchases, many firms would rather borrow the money at the outset and make their purchases on time. People make the same choices in their personal lives. For example, you could save a little money each month until you saved enough to buy a car with cash. This might take a long time, however, and in the meantime you would be without transportation. Alternatively, you could borrow the money to buy the car, and have it to drive around while you're paying off the loan. People—and businesses—often choose the latter alternative.

Clearly, the ability to obtain external financing is crucial for most businesses. Without it, most businesses could never even get started.

Short-Term Financing versus Long-Term Financing

We discussed the liquidity-profitability trade-off in chapter 17, page 414.

Two factors influence the duration of external financing that businesses seek. The first, of course, is availability. A firm may want to take out a ten-year loan to finance its inventory purchases, but may find no one willing to make such a loan. In general, businesses can usually find financing for short time periods. It is more difficult to find long-term financing.

The second factor influencing the length of time that firms finance for is the risk-return, or liquidity-profitability, trade-off discussed in chapter 17.

In the context of financing alternatives, here is how the trade-off works:

- *Short-term financing* is usually cheaper than long-term financing because short-term interest rates are normally lower than long-term interest rates.[1] Therefore the desire for profitability (return) pushes firms toward short-term financing.
- *Long-term financing* is regarded as less risky than short-term financing because the borrower locks in the agreed-on interest rate for a long period of time. No matter how interest rates change during the life of the loan, the borrower's interest costs are certain. Furthermore, the borrower does not have to incur the transaction costs of obtaining new financing every few months. So, the desire to avoid risk encourages firms to use long-term financing.

The length of time that firms finance for depends on whether they want "to eat well or to sleep well."[2] Returns generally increase as financing maturities grow shorter, but so does risk. Risk decreases as financing maturities grow longer, but so do returns. The blend of financing maturities that a firm selects reflects how "aggressive" or "conservative" the firm's managers are.

---

[1]Remember from chapter 2 that a normal yield curve is up sloping.
[2]The phrase is adapted from a remark by J. Kenfield Morley, who said, "In investing money, the amount of interest you want should depend on whether you want to eat well or sleep well."

Figure 20-1 **External Financing Source-Selection Process**

This flow chart illustrates the external financing source-selection process. A firm first determines the need for external financing, and then considers several factors before selecting the short-term financing sources.

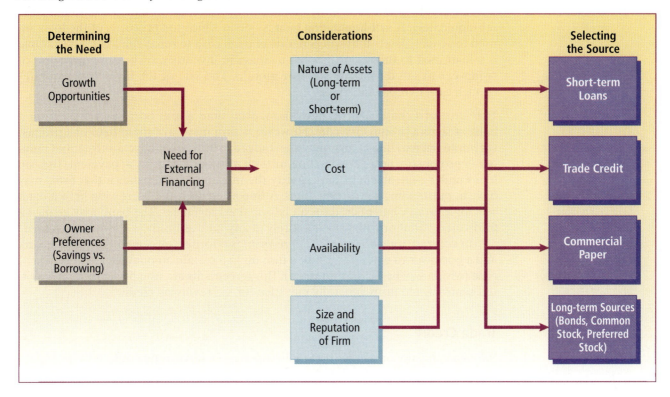

Figure 20-1 summarizes the factors that influence the sources of external financing. External financing can come from short-term or long-term sources. We discuss short-term financing sources next.

Short-Term Financing Alternatives

When most businesses need money for a short time—that is, for less than one year—they usually turn to two sources: short-term loans and trade credit (the process of delaying payments to suppliers). Large, well-established businesses may make use of a third financing source: commercial paper. In the sections that follow, we discuss the various aspects of obtaining money from these three sources.

Short-Term Loans from Banks and Other Institutions

Financial institutions offer businesses many types of short-term loans. No matter what the type of loan, however, the cost to a borrower is usually measured by the percent interest rate charged by the lender. The annual interest rate that reflects the dollars of interest paid divided by the dollars borrowed is the **effective interest rate.** Often, the effective interest rate differs from the interest rate advertised by the bank, which is known as the **stated interest rate.**

Two common types of short-term loans are the *self-liquidating loan* and the *line of credit*. We examine these loan alternatives next. No matter what type of loan a firm uses, the firm must sign a promissory note. A **promissory note** is the legal instrument that the borrower signs and is the evidence of the lender's claim on the borrower.

Self-Liquidating Loans Many of the short-term loans obtained from banks are self-liquidating. A **self-liquidating loan** is one in which the proceeds of the loan are used to acquire assets that will generate enough cash to repay the loan. An example is a loan used to finance a seasonal increase in inventory, such as the purchase of swimwear to sell during the summer months. The sale of the inventory generates enough cash to repay the loan.

The Line of Credit As we now know, each time a firm borrows money from a bank, it signs a promissory note. However, a firm may have more than one promissory note outstanding at any one time. Indeed, a firm could have a substantial number of promissory notes outstanding, all with overlapping terms of payment. To keep loans under control, banks may specify the maximum total balance that firms may have in outstanding short-term loans. A **line of credit** is the borrowing limit a bank sets for a firm. A line of credit is an informal arrangement. The bank may change a firm's credit limit or withdraw it entirely at any time as business conditions change.

In contrast, a *revolving credit agreement* is a formal agreement between a bank and a borrower to extend credit to a firm up to a certain amount for some period of time (which may be for several years). The agreements are usually set forth in a written contract, and firms generally pay a fee for the revolving credit.

Trade Credit

When a company purchases materials, supplies, or services on credit instead of paying cash, that frees up funds to be used elsewhere, just as if the funds had been borrowed from a bank. **Trade credit** is the act of obtaining funds by delaying payment to suppliers. The longer a company delays paying for purchases, the more trade credit the firm is said to be using.

Even though trade credit is obtained by simply delaying payment to suppliers, it is not always free. Next, we explain the cost of trade credit and how to compute that cost so it can be compared to the cost of a bank loan.

Computing the Cost of Trade Credit If a supplier charges a firm interest on credit balances, then computing the cost of trade credit is easy—simply read the interest rate charges on the supplier's account statements, much as we would read a credit card's interest charges.

Most wholesale suppliers, however, do not charge interest on credit balances. Instead, they simply give their customers so many days to pay, and offer them a discount on the amount of the purchase if they pay early. A typical example of such credit terms is 2/10, n30—if customers pay their bills within ten days of the invoice date they will receive a 2 percent discount; if not, the net amount of the bill is due within thirty days.[3] Figure 20-2 diagrams a purchaser's payment deadlines for a $100 purchase on credit terms of 2/10, n30.

We see from Figure 20-2 that if a firm takes the discount, it can obtain the use of $98 for up to ten days without any cost. In this case the trade credit the firm receives

---

[3]Credit terms of this type were introduced in chapter 19 from the point of view of the supplier granting the credit. Here, we discuss the terms from the purchaser's point of view.

Figure 20-2 **Payment Schedule with 2/10, n30 Credit Terms**

Figure 20-2 shows the purchaser's payment schedule for a $100 purchase from a supplier who offers 2/10, n30 credit terms.

is free. But suppose a firm doesn't take the discount? Look at Figure 20-2 again and think of the situation this way: Instead of paying $98 on the tenth day, the firm can pay $98 anytime during the next twenty days as long as it pays a "fee" of $2 for delaying payment. In essence, the firm is "borrowing" $98 for twenty days at a cost of $2. Assuming the firm pays its bill on day 30, we can compute the effective annual interest rate of the trade credit using the following equation:

Trade Credit Effective Annual Interest Rate Formula

$$k = \left(1 + \frac{\text{discount \%}}{100 - \text{discount \%}}\right)^{\left(\frac{365}{\text{days to pay} - \text{discount period}}\right)} - 1 \qquad (20\text{-}1)$$

where: k = the cost of trade credit expressed as an effective annual interest rate

discount % = the percent discount being offered

days to pay = the time between the day of the credit purchase and the day the firm must pay its bill

discount period = the number of days in the discount period

The 365 in the equation represents the number of days in a year. We also multiply the result, k, by 100 to express it as a percent.

In our example, the discount percentage is 2 percent, the total number of days to pay is thirty, and the number of days in the discount period is ten. We use Equation 20-1 to solve for k as follows:

$$k = \left(1 + \frac{2\%}{100 - 2\%}\right)^{\left(\frac{365}{30 - 10}\right)} - 1$$
$$= (1 + .020408)^{(18.25)} - 1$$
$$= (1.020408)^{(18.25)} - 1$$
$$= 1.4458 - 1$$
$$= .4458$$
$$\times 100 = 44.58\%$$

As the calculation shows, the firm's trade credit—the use of $98 for an additional twenty days—costs the firm an effective annual percent rate of interest of nearly 45 percent! Why would any reasonable financial manager pay such high rates? Most reasonable financial managers wouldn't, unless very unfavorable circumstances forced them to or they didn't realize they were doing it.

Instead, because bank loan rates are usually much lower than 45 percent, most reasonable financial managers would borrow $98 from the bank and use it to pay the supplier on the tenth day to take advantage of the discount. Twenty days later, the financial manager would repay the loan plus the interest charges, which would be considerably less than $2. Either way, a firm can obtain the use of $98 for twenty days, but borrowing from a bank is usually the much cheaper alternative.

We described commercial paper in chapter 2, page 25.

Commercial Paper

Firms can sell **commercial paper**—unsecured notes issued by large, very credit-worthy firms for up to 270 days—to obtain cash. Selling commercial paper is usually a cheaper alternative to getting a short-term loan from a bank. Remember that only large, credit-worthy corporations sell commercial paper because only they can attract investors who will lend them money for lower rates than banks charge for short-term loans.

Calculating the Cost of Commercial Paper   Commercial paper is quoted on a *discount basis*. So, to compare the percent cost of a commercial paper issue to the percent cost of a bank loan, we first convert the commercial paper **discount yield** to an effective annual interest rate. We use the following three-step process to find this rate.

1. Compute the discount from face value using Equation 20-2, the formula for the dollar amount of the discount on a commercial paper note:

Dollar Amount of the Discount on a Commercial Paper Note

$$D = \frac{DY \times Par \times DTG}{360} \tag{20-2}$$

where: D = the dollar amount of the discount
DY = the discount yield
Par = the face value of the commercial paper issue; the amount to be paid at maturity
DTG = the days to go until maturity

2. Compute the price of the commercial paper issue by subtracting the discount (D) from Par, as shown in Equation 20-3:

Price of a Commercial Paper Note

$$Price = Par - D \tag{20-3}$$

3. Compute the effective annual interest rate using the following formula, Equation 20-4:

Effective Annual Interest Rate of a Commercial Paper Note

$$\text{Effective Annual Interest Rate} = \left(\frac{Par}{price}\right)^{\left(\frac{365}{DTG}\right)} - 1 \tag{20-4}$$

To illustrate the three-step process, imagine you are a financial analyst at Texaco, Inc., and your commercial paper dealer[4] has informed you that she is willing to pay 3.3 percent discount yield for a $1 million issue of Texaco ninety-day commercial paper notes. What effective annual interest rate does the 3.3 percent discount yield equate to?

---

[4]Some firms sell commercial paper through dealers. Others, like General Motors Acceptance Corporation (GMAC), sell it directly to the public.

Step 1: Compute the discount using Equation 20-2.

$$D = \frac{DY \times Par \times DTG}{360}$$

$$= \frac{.033 \times \$1,000,000 \times 90}{360}$$

$$= \frac{\$2,970,000}{360}$$

$$= \$8,250$$

We see that with a 3.3 percent discount rate, $1 million face value, and ninety days to go until maturity, the dollar amount of the discount on the commercial paper note is $8,250.

Step 2: Compute the price using Equation 20-3.

$$\begin{aligned}
\text{Price} &= \text{Par} - D \\
&= \$1,000,000 - \$8,250 \\
&= \$991,750
\end{aligned}$$

Our calculations show that the price of the ninety-day commercial paper note with a face value of $1 million at a discount price of $8,250 is $991,750.

Step 3: Compute the effective annual interest rate using Equation 20-4.

$$\begin{aligned}
\text{Effective Annual Interest Rate} &= \left(\frac{\text{Par}}{\text{price}}\right)^{\left(\frac{365}{DTG}\right)} - 1 \\
&= \left(\frac{\$1,000,000}{\$991,750}\right)^{\left(\frac{365}{90}\right)} - 1 \\
&= (1.00832)^{4.056} - 1 \\
&= 1.0342 - 1 \\
&= .0342
\end{aligned}$$

$$.0342 \times 100 = 3.42\%$$

Applying Equation 20-4, we find that the effective annual interest rate of a $1 million, ninety-day commercial paper note with a price of $991,750 is 3.42 percent. Now, you can compare the 3.42 percent effective annual interest rate Texaco would pay for commercial paper to the various loan rates available, and choose the best deal.

In the next section, we examine the effect of loan terms on the effective interest rate.

How Loan Terms Affect the Effective Interest Rate of a Loan

The effective interest rate of a bank loan may not be the same as the stated interest rate advertised by the bank because of a lender's loan terms. In the following sections, we describe how to find the effective interest rate, and what terms affect the effective interest rate.

The Effective Interest Rate

Some loans have the same effective rate of interest as the stated rate of interest because the bank places no terms on the loan other than the amount of interest and the amount borrowed. In these cases finding the effective interest rate per period is straightforward. We divide the interest paid on the loan by the amount of money borrowed during the period of the loan (and afterwards multiply the result by 100 to obtain a percent). Equation 20-5 shows the effective interest rate formula:

Effective Interest Rate of a Loan

$$\text{Effective Interest Rate } k = \frac{\$ \text{ interest you pay}}{\$ \text{ you get to use}} \tag{20-5}$$

For example, suppose you borrow $10,000 from a bank for one year, and your promissory note specifies that you are to pay $1,000 in interest at the end of the year. We use Equation 20-5 to find the effective interest rate for the loan as follows:

$$k = \frac{\$1,000}{\$10,000}$$
$$= .10$$
$$\times 100 = 10\%$$

The calculations show that for a $10,000 loan with $1,000 in interest, the effective interest rate is 10 percent.

Effective interest rates are customarily expressed as annual rates. If a loan's maturity is for one year and there are no complicating factors, computing effective interest rates is quite simple, as we have just seen. Equation 20-5 gives the effective rate per period.

For many loans, however, things are not so simple. Lenders have a variety of terms and conditions that they apply to loans, and many of them affect the effective interest rate. Two of the more common loan terms, *discount loans* and *compensating balances,* are discussed next.

Discount Loans

Sometimes a lender's terms specify that interest is to be collected up front, at the time the loan is made, rather than at maturity. When this is the case, the loan is referred to as a **discount loan.** In a discount loan the amount the borrower actually receives is the principal amount borrowed minus the interest owed. So the amount the borrower may use is lower than if the loan were a standard loan with interest paid annually at year's end. As a result, the borrower's effective interest rate is higher than it would be for a standard loan.

Let's return to our earlier one-year, $10,000 loan example to see what happens if it were a discount loan. Instead of paying $1,000 in interest at the end of the year (the equivalent of an effective interest rate of 10 percent), the $1,000 in interest must be paid at the beginning of the year. According to Equation 20-5, the effective interest rate is as follows:

$$k = \frac{\$ \text{ interest you pay}}{\$ \text{ you get to use}}$$
$$= \frac{\$1,000}{\$10,000 - \$1,000}$$
$$= \frac{\$1,000}{\$9,000}$$
$$= .1111$$
$$\times 100 = 11.11\%$$

Note that by collecting the $1,000 interest on the loan at the start of the year, the effective rate of interest rose from 10 percent to 11.11 percent, solely because of the timing of the interest payment. The stated interest rate, then, is lower than the borrower's effective rate of interest.

Compensating Balances

Sometimes a lender's loan terms will specify that while a loan is outstanding the borrower must keep some minimum balance in a checking account at the lender's institution. The amount required is called a **compensating balance.** The lender would say that this minimum balance is its compensation for granting the borrower favorable loan terms (even though the terms may not be especially favorable). Since the borrower cannot allow the balance in the checking account to fall below the required minimum during the life of the loan, the borrower may not use these funds during the life of the loan. As a result, the borrower's effective interest rate is higher than it would be without a compensating balance requirement. This assumes that the borrower would not have kept the required compensating balance funds in the checking account if the loan were a standard loan.

Let's add a compensating balance requirement to our one-year, $10,000 loan with a year-end interest payment of $1,000. The stated rate of interest is 10 percent. Assume the bank requires a compensating balance of 12 percent of the amount borrowed in a checking account during the life of the loan. This compensating balance requirement would be referred to as a "12 percent compensating balance requirement". We quickly figure out that 12 percent of $10,000 is $1,200. Then we use Equation 20-5 to find the following effective interest rate:

$$k = \frac{\$ \text{ interest you pay}}{\$ \text{ you get to use}}$$
$$= \frac{\$1,000}{\$10,000 - \$1,200}$$
$$= \frac{\$1,000}{\$8,800}$$
$$= .1136$$
$$\times 100 = 11.36\%$$

	$ interest you pay / $ you get to use		
Simple Interest Rate	$\dfrac{\$ \text{ interest you pay}}{\$ \text{ you get to use}}$	$\dfrac{\$1,000}{\$10,000}$	= .10, or 10%
Discount Interest	$\dfrac{\$ \text{ interest you pay}}{\$ \text{ you get to use}}$	$\dfrac{\$1,000}{\$10,000 - \$1,000 = \$9,000}$	= .1111, or 11.11%
Compensating Balance (12%)	$\dfrac{\$ \text{ interest you pay}}{\$ \text{ you get to use}}$	$\dfrac{\$1,000}{\$10,000 - \$1,200 = \$8,800}$	= .1136, or 11.36%

Figure 20-3 **How Changing the Terms of a Loan Can Affect the Effective Interest Rate**

Figure 20-3 shows the impact of loan terms on the effective interest rate (the amount you pay to obtain the loan divided by the amount you get to use during the life of the loan).

We find that the effect of the bank's 12 percent compensating balance requirement is to raise the effective interest rate to the borrower by 1.36 percentage points. Instead of paying 10 percent, the borrower actually pays 11.36 percent. The effect of the compensating balance requirement is to increase the effective rate of interest, 11.36 percent, compared to the stated rate of interest of 10 percent.

Figure 20-3 (page 491) shows how changing the terms of a one year loan can affect the effective interest rate. The chart summarizes the effect of simple interest, discount interest, and compensating balances. Figure 20-3 demonstrates that loan terms such as discount interest and compensating balances reduce the amount the borrower gets to use, thus raising the effective interest rate.

Loan Maturities Shorter than One Year

Another term that affects the effective interest rate is a loan maturity that is less than one year. In such cases we modify Equation 20-5, to convert the effective interest rate of the loan that is for less than a year into an annual rate. We find the annual rate so that we can compare that rate with those from other lenders, almost all of which are expressed as annual rates. Annualizing the rates allows a comparison of apples to apples, rather than apples to oranges. An example demonstrates this point.

Suppose you are borrowing $10,000 for one *month* and paying $1,000 in interest at the end of the *month* (with no other conditions). The effective interest rate of this loan is 10 percent, according to Equation 20-5. However, remember that the rate is 10 percent *per month*. It would be inaccurate to say that the interest rate on this loan was the same as a 10 percent loan from another financial institution. Why? Because the 10 percent stated rate from the other institution is an annual rate and you are comparing it to a monthly rate. For one month, the other institution's stated rate would be 10%/12 = 0.83%, which is considerably less than the 10 percent monthly interest on your loan.

Annualizing Interest Rates We can modify Equation 20-5 so that it annualizes interest rates that are not paid yearly. The modified formula, Equation 20-6, follows:

Effective Annual Interest Rate

$$\text{Effective Annual Interest Rate} \quad k = \left(1 + \frac{\$ \text{ interest you pay}}{\$ \text{ you get to use}}\right)^{\left(\substack{\text{Loan periods} \\ \text{in a year}}\right)} - 1 \qquad (20\text{-}6)$$

We then multiply the result by 100 to find the percentage rate.

Now let's use Equation 20-6 to annualize the $10,000 loan with interest of $1,000 a month. Remember, the *monthly* interest rate for this loan is 10 percent, and there are twelve monthly loan periods in a year. The calculations follow:

$$k = \left(1 + \frac{\$1,000}{\$10,000}\right)^{(12)} - 1$$
$$= (1 + .10)^{(12)} - 1$$
$$= (1.10)^{(12)} - 1$$
$$= 3.1384 - 1$$
$$= 2.1384$$
$$\times 100 = 213.84\%$$

We find that the interest rate is over 213 percent. Surely there is a cheaper alternative at another bank. Suppose you find one whose *stated* annual interest rate for a $10,000 one-month loan is 12 percent. What's the *effective* annual interest rate for this loan? In order to apply Equation 20-6 to find out, we first compute the dollar amount of interest to be paid:

- The stated rate for one year, or twelve months, is 12 percent, so the rate for one month is 12/12 = 1 percent.[5]
- 1 percent of $10,000 is $10,000 × .01 = $100
- So, the amount of "dollars you pay" to get this loan is $100.

Since the loan is for one month, we know that there are twelve loan periods in a year. Now we're ready to plug these numbers into Equation 20-6 as shown next:

$$k = \left(1 + \frac{\$ \text{ interest you pay}}{\$ \text{ you get to use}}\right)^{\left(\substack{\text{Loan periods} \\ \text{in a year}}\right)} - 1$$

$$= \left(1 + \frac{\$100}{\$10,000}\right)^{(12)} - 1$$

$$= (1 + .01)^{(12)} - 1$$

$$= (1.01)^{(12)} - 1$$

$$= 1.1268 - 1$$

$$= .1268$$

$$\times 100 = 12.68\%$$

The effective annual rate, 12.68 percent, is a little higher than the bank's stated rate of 12 percent because of the compounding effect of adding "interest on interest" for twelve months.

We have seen how discount loans, compensating balances, and loans that have maturities less than a year affect the effective annual interest rate. Next, we walk through an example of a loan with more than one complicating term.

A Comprehensive Example

Let's consider a loan that includes all the complicating factors discussed in the preceding sections. Suppose you want to borrow $5,000 for one week, and the bank's terms are 8 percent interest, collected on a discount basis, with a 10 percent compensating balance. What is the effective annual interest rate of this loan?

Computing the Interest Cost in Dollars   The bank's stated rate of interest for one year, or 52 weeks, is 8 percent, so the rate for one week is 8/52 = 0.1538 percent.

$$0.1538 \text{ percent of } \$5,000 \text{ is } \$5,000 \times .001538 = \$7.69$$

So, the dollars in interest that you pay to obtain this loan are $7.69.

Computing the Net Amount Received   Because this is a discount loan, the interest will be collected up front. That means $7.69 will be deducted from the $5,000 loan.

The loan also has a 10 percent compensating balance requirement, so 10 percent of the $5,000, or $500, must remain in a checking account at the bank, denying you the use of it during the life of the loan.

---

[5]If the loan's term is one week, divide by 52. If it is one day, divide by 365, and so on.

The net amount of money that you will get to use during the life of the loan is $5,000 − $7.69 − $500 = $4,492.31.

Computing the Effective Annual Interest Rate   We use Equation 20-6, the formula for annualizing a loan with a term of interest payments less than a year, to find the effective annual interest rate for this loan. The calculations follow:

$$k = \left(1 + \frac{\$ \text{ interest you pay}}{\$ \text{ you get to use}}\right)^{\left(\begin{smallmatrix}\text{Loan periods}\\\text{in a year}\end{smallmatrix}\right)} - 1$$

$$= \left(1 + \frac{\$7.69}{\$4,492.31}\right)^{(52)} - 1$$

$$= (1 + .001712)^{(52)} - 1$$

$$= (1.001712)^{(52)} - 1$$

$$= 1.093 - 1$$

$$= .093$$

$$\times 100 = 9.3\%$$

We see that the effective annual interest rate for a one-week, $5,000 discounted loan with an interest rate of 8 percent, and a 10 percent compensating balance requirement is 9.3 percent. The effective rate of interest, 9.3 percent, is higher than the 8 percent stated rate of interest.

Computing the Amount to Borrow

In the preceding comprehensive example, you tried to borrow $5,000. Presumably that was the amount you needed to use for a week. But, as shown, if the bank collected $7.69 in interest up front, and made you keep $500 in a checking account during the term of the loan, you would only receive $4,492.31. Clearly, given the bank's terms, you will have to borrow some amount greater than $5,000 to end up with the $5,000 you need. So the question is, how much do you have to borrow to walk out of the bank with $5,000?

We solve this question algebraically. Let X = the amount to borrow. Now, because the loan is a discount loan, the bank will collect one week's worth of interest, or (.08/52) times X at the beginning of the week. Furthermore, 10 percent of X must remain in a checking account at the bank as a compensating balance. When these two amounts are subtracted from X, the remainder must equal $5,000. Here is the equation describing the situation:

$$X - \left(\frac{.08}{52}\right)X - .10X = \$5,000$$

We then solve for X as follows:

$$X - \left(\frac{.08}{52}\right)X - .10X = \$5,000$$

$$X - .001538X - .10X = \$5,000$$

$$.8985X = \$5,000$$

$$X = \$5,564.83$$

We find that if you borrow $5,564.83 for one week at 8 percent, discount interest, with a 10 percent compensating balance requirement, you will leave the bank with $5,000.[6]

We have examined how loan terms can affect the effective interest rate. Now we turn to types of collateral that are used to secure short-term loans.

COLLATERAL FOR SHORT-TERM LOANS

The promissory note that specifies the terms of the loan often includes the type of **collateral** used to secure the loan.

For secured short-term loans, lenders usually require that the assets pledged for collateral be short-term in nature also. Lenders require short-term assets because they are generally more liquid than long-term assets, and are easier to convert to cash if the borrower defaults on the loan. The major types of short-term assets used for short-term loan collateral are accounts receivable and inventory.

Loans for which collateral is required are called se-cured loans. If no collateral is required, the loan is unsecured.

Accounts Receivable as Collateral

Accounts receivable are assets with value because they represent money owed to a firm. Because of their value, a lender might be willing to accept the accounts as collateral for a loan. If so, the borrowing firm may *pledge* its accounts receivable. The pledge is a promise that the firm will turn over the accounts receivable collateral to the lender in the case of default.

Loan agreements that use accounts receivable as collateral usually specify that the firm is responsible for the amount of the accounts receivable even if the firm's credit customers fail to pay. In short, the borrowing firm still has to pay even if its customers don't.

Lenders try to safeguard against accounts receivable that fluctuate so much that the value of the account becomes less than the value of the loan. Accounts receivable fluctuate because some credit customers may send in payments on their outstanding accounts receivable, others may make new charges, and some may be late with payments. If accounts receivable are pledged as short-term loan collateral, lenders usually require a loan payment plan that prevents the value of the accounts from dropping below the value of the loans. For instance, a bank may require a borrower to send payments received on pledged accounts to the lender to apply against the loan balance. Sending payments as received decreases the balance of the loan as the value of accounts receivable decreases, thereby protecting the lender.

Inventory as Collateral

Like accounts receivable, inventory represents assets that have value, and so can be used as collateral for loans. The practice of using inventory as collateral for a short-term loan is called **inventory financing.**

A major problem with inventory financing is valuing the inventory. If a borrowing firm defaults on a loan secured by inventory, the lender wants to know that the

---

[6]In case you're wondering, the effective annual interest rate for this loan, per Equation 20-2, is 9.3 percent.

FINANCIAL MANAGEMENT AND YOU

Easy Come, Easy Go: The Cost of Credit

Many people use credit cards to take care of their short-term business and personal financial needs. Because credit cards are easy to obtain, this makes them an easy-to-tap source of capital. Just how easy is it to get a credit card? Just for fun, John Galbreath filled out a credit card application on which he stated that he was ninety-seven years old, had no income, no telephone, and no Social Security number. Plus, he wrote that he owed money to the Mafia. Back came a credit card.

Although it may be easy to get a credit card, it can be tough to find out how expensive that credit is. To help you assess the cost of the credit, start with these five items.

1. *The stated rate of interest:* Credit card interest rates vary. Compare interest rates before applying to make sure you select the lowest interest rate possible.
2. *The type of interest rate:* Some credit card companies may entice you with low interest rates, but those rates may not be fixed. Instead the rate may vary according to market rates, meaning that every quarter, or even every month, your interest rates may be adjusted upward or downward. Well over 60 percent of all cards in use have variable rates.
3. *When the rates change:* Variable-rate card issuers aren't legally required to tell customers of rate

changes. Often, the only way holders of variable-rate cards can tell if their rate has changed is to look at the monthly statement, see what the rate is, and then compare it with previous months.
4. *The rates that apply to every type of credit:* Many cards offer additional credit options to cardholders, including cash advances. However, card issuers often charge higher interest rates on the cash advances than on regular credit purchases.
5. *The annual fee:* To lure you to sign up for a card, credit card issuers often waive the annual fee for use of the credit card. The following year, though, issuers charge the fee without prior notification. The annual fee can range from $25 to $100, and is part of the cost of the credit.

The point? Read the fine print of the credit card terms to learn how much the credit will cost you. If it costs too much, you should consider other types of short-term loans.

Sources: "Give the Man Credit," *Forbes* (August 14, 1995): 19; Albert B. Crenshaw, "Variable Rate Credit Cards: How to Avoid a Bumpy Ride," *Washington Post* (October 21, 1994): H1.

inventory can compensate for the remaining loan balance. To illustrate how important valuing inventory is, suppose you were a banker that lent a firm $200,000 for six months. As collateral, the firm put up its entire inventory of Alien Angels dolls, based on characters in a soon-to-be-released major motion picture. Unfortunately, the movie was a bust. The firm was unable to repay its loan, and you as the banker have ended up with 10,000 dolls no one wants. It is small comfort to you now that the firm said the angels were worth $20 each when they were offered as collateral.

To compensate for the difficulties in valuing inventory, lenders usually lend only a fraction of the stated value of the inventory. If the inventory consists of fairly standard items that can be resold easily, like 2 × 4s, then the lender might be willing to lend up to 80 percent of the inventory's stated value. In contrast, if the inventory consists of perishable or specialized items, like the Alien Angels in our example, then the lender will only lend a small fraction of their value, or might not be willing to accept them as collateral at all.

Inventory depletion is an additional concern for lenders who allow borrowers to use inventory as short-term loan collateral. The borrowing firm can sell the pledged inventory and use the cash received for other purposes, leaving the lender with nothing if the borrower defaults. This can happen when the lender has only a general claim, or *blanket lien,* on the borrower's inventory in the event of a default. Therefore, when inventory is used as collateral for a loan, the lender will often insist on some procedures to safeguard its interests.

One procedure to safeguard the interests of the lender is for the borrower to issue trust receipts to the lender. A *trust receipt* is a legal document in which specifically identified assets, inventory in this case, are pledged as collateral for the loan. Automobiles, railroad cars, and airplanes are often financed this way. The lender can make surprise visits to the borrower's business, checking to be sure that the pledged assets are on hand as they should be. There is often a unique identification number (a car's VIN, vehicle identification number, for example) on these assets.

Another procedure to control pledged inventory is to use a *public warehouse* where the inventory cannot be removed and sold without permission of the lender. When the inventory is sold (with the lender's permission), the proceeds are sent to the lender and used to reduce the outstanding loan balance. While this arrangement gives the lender control, it is expensive for the borrowing firm. Usually, the borrowing firm must pay for the warehouse and seek the lender's permission each time it wants to sell some inventory.

We have seen that short-term secured loans generally have short-term liquid assets pledged as collateral, such as accounts receivable or inventory. Lenders often add loan terms to protect against problems such as fluctuating accounts receivable, and overvalued or depleted inventory.

What's Next

We discussed short-term financing in this chapter, the final chapter of Part 4 of the text. We turn next to Part 5, Finance in the Global Economy. In chapter 21, we discuss international finance.

Summary

1. Explain the need for short-term financing.

Firms rely on short-term financing from outside sources for two reasons:

- *Growth:* Profits may simply not be high enough to keep up with the rate at which they are buying new assets.
- *Choice:* Rather than save enough money to make desired purchases, many firms borrow money at the outset to make their purchases.

2. List the advantages and disadvantages of short-term financing.

Short-term financing is usually a cheaper option than long-term financing because of its generally lower interest rates. However, short-term financing is riskier than long-term financing because, unlike long-term financing, the loans come due soon, the lender may not be willing to renew financing on favorable terms, and short-term interest rates may rise unexpectedly.

3. Describe three types of short-term financing.

- *Loans from banks and other institutions:* When a bank or other institution agrees to loan money to a firm, the firm signs a promissory note that specifies the repayment terms. Two common types of short-term business loans are self-liquidating loans and a line of credit. A self-liquidating loan is a loan for an asset that will generate enough return to repay the loan balance. A line of credit is a maximum total balance that a bank sets for a firm's outstanding short-term loans.
- *Trade credit:* Trade credit is obtained by purchasing materials, supplies, or services on credit. By buying on credit, the firm has use of the funds during the time of the purchase until the account is paid.
- *Commercial paper:* Commercial paper consists of unsecured notes issued by large, credit-worthy corporations for periods up to 270 days.

4. Compute the cost of trade credit and commercial paper.

The cost of trade credit is calculated by dividing the amount of the discount offered by the supplier by the amount the buyer owes. The result is annualized for comparison with other financing sources.

The cost of commercial paper is quoted as a discount yield. To compare the percent cost of a commercial paper issue to the percent cost of a bank loan, the commercial paper's discount yield must be converted to an effective annual interest rate.

5. Calculate the cost of a loan and explain how loan terms affect the effective interest rate.

The cost of a loan is normally measured by dividing the amount paid to obtain the loan by the amount the borrower gets to use during the life of the loan. The result is converted to a percentage. The stated interest rate on a loan is not always the same as the loan's effective annual interest rate. If the lender collects interest up front (a discount interest loan) or requires the borrowing firm to keep a fraction of the loan in an account at the lending institution (a compensating balance), then the amount of money the borrower gets to use is reduced. As a result, the effective rate of interest the borrower is paying is increased.

6. Describe how accounts receivable and inventory can be used as collateral for short-term loans.

Short-term loans are often secured by short-term, liquid assets, such as accounts receivable and inventory. When accounts receivable are used for collateral, the borrower pledges to turn over its accounts receivable to the lender if the borrower defaults. When inventory is used for collateral, the borrowing firm often sets aside the inventory that has been identified for collateral in a separate warehouse. When the inventory is sold, the cash received is forwarded to the lender in payment for the loan.

Equations Introduced in This Chapter

Equation 20-1. Trade Credit Effective Annual Interest Rate Formula:

$$k = \left(1 + \frac{\text{discount \%}}{100 - \text{discount \%}}\right)^{\left(\frac{365}{\text{days to pay} - \text{discount period}}\right)} - 1$$

where: k = the cost of trade credit expressed as an effective annual interest rate
discount % = the percent discount being offered
days to pay = the time between the day the firm makes the credit purchase and the day it pays its bill
discount period = the number of days in the discount period

Equation 20-2. Dollar Amount of the Discount on a Commercial Paper Note:

$$D = \frac{DY \times Par \times DTG}{360}$$

where: D = the dollar amount of the discount
DY = the discount yield
Par = the face value of the commercial paper issue; the amount to be paid at maturity
DTG = the days to go until maturity

Equation 20-3. Price of a Commercial Paper Note:

$$Price = Par - D$$

where: Par = the face value of the note at maturity
D = the dollar amount of the discount

Equation 20-4. Effective Annual Interest Rate of a Commercial Paper Note:

$$\text{Effective Annual Interest Rate} = \left(\frac{Par}{price}\right)^{\left(\frac{365}{DTG}\right)} - 1$$

where: Par = the face value of the note at maturity
price = the price of the note when purchased
DTG = the number of days until the note matures

Equation 20-5. Effective Interest Rate of a Loan:

$$\text{Effective Interest Rate } k = \frac{\$ \text{ interest you pay}}{\$ \text{ you get to use}}$$

Equation 20-6. Effective Annual Interest Rate:

$$\text{Effective Annual Interest Rate } k = \left(1 + \frac{\$ \text{ interest you pay}}{\$ \text{ you get to use}}\right)^{\left(\text{Loan periods in a year}\right)} - 1$$

Self-Test

ST-1.   Your company's suppliers offer terms of 3/15, n40. What is the cost of foregoing the discount and delaying payment until the fortieth day?

ST-2.   A commercial paper dealer is willing to pay 4 percent discount yield for a $1 million issue of Pennzoil sixty-day commercial paper notes. What effective annual interest rate does the 4 percent discount yield equate to?

ST-3.   A bank is willing to lend your company $20,000 for 6 months at 8 percent interest, with a 10 percent compensating balance. What is the effective annual interest rate of this loan?

ST-4.   Using the loan terms from question ST-3, how much would your firm have to borrow in order to have $20,000 for use during the loan period?

Review Questions

1. Companies with rapidly growing levels of sales do not need to worry about raising funds from outside the firm. Do you agree or disagree with this statement? Explain.
2. Banks like to make short-term, self-liquidating loans to businesses. Why?
3. What are compensating balances and why do banks require them from some customers? Under what circumstances would banks be most likely to impose compensating balances?
4. What happens when a bank charges discount interest on a loan?
5. What is trustworthy collateral from the lenders' perspective? Explain whether accounts receivable and inventory are trustworthy collateral.
6. Trade credit is free credit. Do you agree or disagree with this statement? Explain.
7. What are the pros and cons of commercial paper relative to bank loans for a company seeking short-term financing?

Build Your Communication Skills

CS-1. Your firm's request for a $50,000 loan for one month has been approved. The bank's terms are 10 percent annual discount interest with a 10 percent compensating balance. Prepare a one-page report for the CEO of your firm explaining how the effective interest rate of this loan is calculated.

CS-2. Imagine you are a loan officer for a bank. One of the town's businesses has applied for a loan of $200,000 for six months. The company has offered to put up the building in which its manufacturing operations are located as collateral for the loan. Local real estate agents estimate the building is worth at least $220,000. Write a letter to the company explaining why your bank does not wish to accept the building as collateral. Propose two alternative assets that your bank would accept.

Problems

Simple and Discount Loans

20-1. Harold Hill is planning to borrow $20,000 for one year paying interest in the amount of $1,600 to a bank. Calculate the effective annual interest rate if the interest is paid:

    a. at the end of the year
    b. at the beginning of the year (discount loan)

Loans with Compensating Balance

20-2. Chad Gates is planning to borrow $40,000 for one year paying interest of $2,400 to a bank at the beginning of the year (discount loan). In addition, according to the terms of the loan, the bank requires Chad to keep 10 percent of the borrowed funds in a non-interest bearing checking account at the bank during the life of the loan. Calculate the effective annual interest rate.

Challenge Problem

20-3. Ralph Bellamy is considering borrowing $20,000 for a year from a bank that has offered the following alternatives:
    a. An interest payment of $1,800 at the end of the year
    b. An interest payment of 8 percent of $20,000 at the beginning of the year
    c. An interest payment of 7.5 percent of $20,000 at the end of the year in addition to a compensating balance requirement of 10 percent.
        (i) Which alternative is best for Ralph from the effective interest rate point of view?
        (ii) If Ralph needs the entire amount of $20,000 at the beginning of the year and chooses the terms under (c), how much should he borrow? How much interest would he have to pay at the end of the year?

20-4. If Joyce Heath borrows $14,000 for three months at an annual interest rate of 16 percent paid up-front with a compensating balance of 10 percent, compute the effective annual interest rate of the loan.

Loans with a Life of Less than a Year

20-5. You are planning to borrow $10,000 from a bank for two weeks. The bank's terms are 7 percent annual interest, collected on a discount basis, with a 10 percent compensating balance. Compute the effective annual interest rate of the loan.

Discount Loans with Compensating Balance for Less than a Year

20-6. Bud Baxter is planning a $1 million issue of commercial paper to finance increased sales from easing the credit policy. The commercial paper note has a sixty day maturity and 6 percent discount yield. Calculate:

Commercial Paper

    a. the dollar amount of the discount
    b. the price
    c. the effective annual interest rate for the issue

20-7. Carmen Velasco, an analyst at Smidgen Corporation, is trying to calculate the effective annual interest rate for a $2 million issue of Smidgen sixty-day commercial paper note. The commercial paper dealer is prepared to offer a 4 percent discount yield to the issue. Calculate the effective annual interest rate for Carmen.

Commercial Paper

20-8. Bathseba Everdene, the Sales Manager of Gordon's Bakery, Inc., wants to extend trade credit with terms of 2/15, n45 to your company to boost sales. Calculate the cost of foregoing the discount and paying on the forty-fifth day.

Trade Credit

20-9. Calculate the cost of foregoing the following trade credit discounts and paying on the last day allowed:

Trade Credit

    a. 3/10, n60
    b. 2/15, n30

Recalculate the costs assuming payments were made on the fortieth day in each of the above cases without any penalty. Compare your results.

20-10. To sustain its growth in sales, Monarch Machine Tools Company needs $100,000 in additional funds next year. The following alternatives for financing the growth are available:

Comparing Costs of Alternative Short-Term Financing

    a. Foregoing a discount available on trade credit with terms of 1/10, n45 and hence increasing its accounts payable,
    b. Obtaining a loan from a bank at 10 percent interest paid up front.

Calculate the cost of financing for each option and select the best source.

20-11. If the bank imposes an additional requirement of a 12 percent compensating balance on Monarch in problem 20-10 and the company could negotiate a more liberal credit terms of 1/15, n60 from its supplier, will there be any change in Monarch's choice of short-term financing?

Comparing Costs of Alternative Short-Term Financing

Answers to Self-Test

ST-1. The cost is found using Equation 20-1. The discount percent is 3 percent, the discount period is fifteen days, and payment is to be made on the fortieth day. The calculations follow:

$$k = \left(1 + \frac{3\%}{100 - 3\%}\right)^{\left(\frac{365}{40 - 15}\right)} - 1$$
$$= (1 + .0309278)^{(14.6)} - 1$$
$$= (1.0309278)^{(14.6)} - 1$$
$$= 1.56 - 1$$
$$= .56$$
$$\times 100 = 56\%$$

ST-2. Use the three-step process described in the text to find the effective annual interest rate as follows:

- *Step 1:* Compute the discount using Equation 20-2.

$$D = \frac{DY \times Par \times DTG}{360}$$

$$= \frac{.04 \times \$1,000,000 \times 60}{360}$$

$$= \frac{\$2,400,000}{360}$$

$$= \$6,667$$

- *Step 2:* Compute the price using Equation 20-3.

$$Price = Par - D$$

$$= \$1,000,000 - \$6,667$$

$$- \$993,333$$

- *Step 3:* Compute the effective annual interest rate using Equation 20-4.

$$\begin{array}{c}\text{Effective Annual} \\ \text{Interest Rate}\end{array} = \left(\frac{Par}{price}\right)^{\left(\frac{365}{DTG}\right)} - 1$$

$$= \left(\frac{\$1,000,000}{\$993,333}\right)^{\left(\frac{365}{60}\right)} - 1$$

$$= (1.00671)^{6.083} - 1$$

$$= 1.0415 - 1$$

$$= .0415$$

$$\times 100 = 4.15\%$$

ST-3. The amount your firm would pay in interest with the loan is:

$$.08/2 = .04 \text{ for six months}$$

$$.04 \times \$20,000 = \$800$$

The amount your firm would be able to use during the life of the loan is the principal less the compensating balance:

$$\$20,000 - (.10 \times \$20,000) = \$18,000$$

The loan is for six months, so we use Equation 20-6 to solve for the effective annual interest rate:

$$k = \left(1 + \frac{\$800}{\$18,000}\right)^{(2)} - 1$$

$$= (1 + .0444)^{(2)} - 1$$

$$= (1.0444)^{(2)} - 1$$

$$= 1.0908 - 1$$

$$= .0908$$

$$\times 100 = 9.08\%$$

ST-4. Let X = the amount to borrow.

$$X - .10X = \$20,000$$

$$.09X = \$20,000$$

$$X = \$22,222$$

chapter 21

International Finance

P
A
R
T
5

FINANCE IN THE GLOBAL ECONOMY

A man's feet must be planted in his country, but his eyes should survey the world.

George Santayana

Chapter Objectives

After reading this chapter, you should be able to:

1. Define a multinational corporation and explain its importance.

2. Demonstrate how the law of comparative advantage leads to international trade.

3. Describe exchange rates and their effects on firms.

4. Show how firms manage the risks of fluctuating exchange rates.

5. Discuss exchange rate theories.

6. Describe the political and cultural risks that affect MNCs.

7. Explain how international trade agreements affect international business.

Don't Count Your Yen Until the Deal's Hatched

International business is not only challenging, it can be scary. Indeed, agreeing to be paid in currencies that may lose value after the business contract is signed can lead to financial disaster. But the exchange rate changes can also lead to higher returns.

Lance Woeltjen, CEO of Virtual Reality Laboratories, Inc., licensed his software to a Japanese company. He had hopes of excellent returns, but was worried that he had made a big mistake. To control costs, the Japanese insisted on paying in their currency, the yen. The downside? If the dollar appreciated in value against the yen, Woeltjen's returns would be eaten up by the difference in the exchange rate. Woeltjen remembers "feeling a bit queasy. Up until then everything we'd done had been in dollars."

Woeltjen didn't spend much time thinking about the upside. That

would only happen if the dollar depreciated against the yen, giving Woeltjen yen that were worth more in dollars than he expected.

Luckily for the entrepreneur and his seventeen-person firm, that is exactly what happened. When pay-

Lance Woeltjen

ments under the contract started coming in, the dollar went down, the yen shot up and he made more return on the deal than he had anticipated. "We had a 34 percent profit jump based on that alone," says Woeltjen. "And all of a sudden, we're going to have a very fancy year that otherwise perhaps wouldn't have been."

In international finance, there is a variety of factors to consider, including the exchange rate. It can make or break your returns. ❉

Sources: Mark Hendricks, "Another Day, Another Dollar," *Entrepreneur* (October 1995): 150; James Hickman, "Red Stars Rising," *Inc. Magazine* (August 1995): 19.

CHAPTER OVERVIEW

This chapter addresses the financial issues that companies face when they maintain operations in or sell goods and services to, other countries. These issues include differences in currency, language, politics, and culture. We also explore the potential benefits and risks of doing business in other countries. We closely examine the risk of transacting business in either a domestic or foreign currency and how to manage that risk. Finally, we look at international trade agreements and their effect on business.

MULTINATIONAL CORPORATIONS

A **multinational corporation (MNC)** is a corporation that has operations in more than one country. Most large corporations conduct at least some of their business in countries other than the one they call home. In fact, it is getting difficult to accurately describe whether companies are U.S., German, or Japanese, in spite of what their names might suggest.[1] Table 21-1 shows the top-ten U.S.-based multinational corporations.

Financial Advantages of Foreign Operations

You may have read stories about McDonald's fast-food restaurants expanding into Russia and Japan, or Kentucky Fried Chicken opening a branch in the People's Republic of China. Coca-Cola and Pepsi-Cola executives count on the billion-dollar growth potential of their popular products in overseas markets. Boeing, once a leading supplier for U.S. firms, is now primarily an exporter. Companies are always looking for growth opportunities, and many of these opportunities are in other countries.

In addition to the potential demand for products and services, operating abroad can decrease production costs. Labor may be less costly in other countries. For instance, much of the production of clothing by companies based in the U.S. is done in other countries where lower wages are paid to workers.

Companies can often obtain political advantages by shifting some operations away from home. For example, Toyota, Honda, and Nissan of Japan, and the German company BMW, all produce some of their cars in the United States. This lessens

---

[1] A few years ago, the Volkswagen Rabbit, made by a German-based company, was the only car sold in the United States that was made in the United States, by U.S. workers, with all U.S.-made parts.

		REVENUE		
Rank	**Company**	**Foreign ($ mil)**	**Total ($ mil)**	**Foreign as % of Total**
1	Exxon	77,125	99,683	77.4
2	General Motors	44,041	154,951	28.4
3	Mobil	40,318[1]	59,621[1]	67.6
4	IBM	39,934	64,052	62.3
5	Ford Motor	38,075	128,439	29.6
6	Texaco[2]	24,760	44,306	55.9
7	Citicorp	19,703	31,650	62.3
8	Chevron[2]	16,533	38,516	42.9
9	Philip Morris Cos	16,329	53,776	30.4
10	Procter & Gamble	15,650[3]	30,296	51.7

[1]Includes other income
[2]Includes proportionate interest in unconsolidated subsidiaries or affiliates
[3]Estimate

Source: "Weak Dollar, Strong Results," *Forbes Magazine* (July 17, 1995): 274. Reprinted By Permission of FORBES *Magazine* © Forbes Inc., 1995.

Table 21-1 shows the ten largest U.S.-based MNCs, ranked by revenue of foreign subsidiaries.

the risk of the U.S. Congress passing laws that would restrict imports of, or increase the tax on, sales of these cars. U.S.-based firms often have the same import and tax reasons to open production plants in other countries.

Ethical Issues Facing Multinational Corporations

Using foreign labor may pose difficult ethical questions for U.S. companies. Are very poor people from other countries being exploited because they can be employed at lower wages than would be paid to American workers? Are overseas plants as safe

Source: CALVIN AND HOBBES © 1992, 1993 Watterson. Dist. by UNIVERSAL PRESS SYNDICATE. Reprinted with permission. All rights reserved.

as U.S. plants, where OSHA inspectors check up on employers?[2] Does a corporation have the moral responsibility to meet the same health and safety standards for its workers in other countries as it applies to its U.S. workers, even if not legally required to do so? Calvin Klein, Liz Claiborne, The Gap, and other garment industry companies that manufacture clothing outside of the United States to control labor costs, must balance the moral issues of human rights against their obligations to stockholders.

Another ethical issue arises when operations are moved to countries where environmental laws are less strict than the laws of the company's home country. Firms may lower costs by disposing of waste products or emitting pollutants in a potentially dangerous manner. Even though the laws of the other country may not have pollution control or disposal guidelines, should a business harm the environment or create a danger that could harm future generations? How should managers weigh the morality of business procedures against their fiduciary duty to the owners of the company's common stock to maximize value?

Unfortunately, there are no clear-cut answers to many of these questions. Certainly, worker exploitation and the destruction of the environment would be condoned by few people. But what if working conditions are only slightly less safe, or the environmental practices in that other country only slightly more offensive by the home country's standards? What if these slightly offensive environmental practices are commonplace and accepted in that other country? Where should we draw the line? Facing these questions, even when the answers are difficult to agree on, is an important first step in making ethical decisions.

COMPARATIVE ADVANTAGE

International trade creates significant financial benefits because not all countries can produce goods and services with the same degree of efficiency. The law of comparative advantage says that each country should concentrate on that which it does well.

For example, coffee does not grow well in the United States. If coffee drinkers in the United States had to depend on locally grown coffee for their entire supply, coffee would be scarce, of relatively poor quality, and extremely expensive. Coffee grows very well in Brazil, however. Brazilians can grow much more than they can consume themselves, and at a relatively low cost. It makes sense, then, that U.S. coffee drinkers should buy Brazilian coffee.

Brazil, in contrast, cannot easily make major motion pictures. If Brazilians could only watch movies made in Brazil, they wouldn't see very many. Filmmakers in the United States make many movies, most with sophisticated technology. Film companies can (and do) export films easily and cheaply to foreign countries like Brazil. It makes sense, then, for Brazilians to stick to growing coffee and to watch U.S. movies. Brazil has a comparative advantage over the United States with respect to coffee growing, while the United States has a comparative advantage over Brazil with respect to movie making. International trade makes it possible for U.S. citizens to enjoy high quality, affordable coffee, and for Brazilians to enjoy numerous, technologically advanced U.S. movies.[3]

---

[2]OSHA stands for Occupational Safety and Health Administration, a federal agency responsible for enforcing national laws intended to protect workers employed by U.S. companies.
[3]The quality of U.S.-produced movies is a subjective judgment; but it is clear from film company revenues that the world seems to enjoy watching them.

Figure 21-1 Exchange Rates Relative to the U.S. Dollar

Figure 21-1 shows various exchange rates relative to the U.S. dollar on May 7, 1996.
NOTE: *The letters on the horizontal axis of the graph on the left stand for months of the year, beginning with November. The letters on the horizontal axis of graph on the right stand for weekdays, excluding Saturday and Sunday.*

Source: Reprinted by permission of *The Wall Street Journal*, © 1996 Dow Jones & Company, Inc. All Rights Reserved Worldwide.

EXCHANGE RATES AND THEIR EFFECTS

Given that countries can benefit from trading with each other, how do they overcome the problem of having different units of currency? An **exchange rate** is an expression of the value of one country's currency in terms of another country's currency. It specifies how many units of one country's currency can be exchanged for one unit of the other country's currency. For example, the exchange rate between the U.S. dollar and the French franc might be five French francs per one U.S. dollar. The exchange rate between the U.S. dollar and the Japanese yen might be one hundred Japanese yen per one U.S. dollar.

Exchange rates can be expressed as the number of units of the foreign currency per one unit of domestic currency, as in the previous paragraph, or as the number of units of the domestic currency per one unit of the foreign currency. For example, if five French francs can be exchanged for one U.S. dollar, then one French franc is worth one-fifth of a U.S. dollar, or $0.20. The exchange rate can be expressed as five francs per dollar or two-tenths of a dollar per franc. The one exchange rate is the reciprocal of the other.

A sampling of actual exchange rates as of May 7, 1996, is shown in Figure 21-1. We see from Figure 21-1 that the exchange rate is expressed as how many U.S. dollars (the number of units of the domestic currency) per one unit of the foreign currency. That is, one British pound was worth a little more than one-and-a-half U.S. dollars on May 7, 1996.

Fluctuating Exchange Rates

Exchange rates fluctuate every day due to changing world conditions. Currency traders take advantage of these fluctuations by "buying" and "selling" currencies. This means they exchange a certain amount of one currency for a certain amount of another. The currency market is one of the largest financial markets in the world. Currency traders buy and sell the equivalent of over $1 trillion in an average trading day. The "price" of buying or selling a currency is its exchange rate. So, if a trader had wanted to sell U.S. dollars in exchange for British pounds on May 7, 1996, the trader would have paid 1.51 dollars for each pound.

If the value of one currency decreases relative to the value of another currency, the currency with the falling value is called a **weakening currency.** For example, if the exchange rate between the U.S. dollar and the French franc were to change from five French francs per dollar to four French francs per dollar, then the U.S. dollar has weakened relative to the French franc, and it now takes more dollars to buy a given number of French francs. At the same time, of course, the French franc is said to be a **strengthening currency** relative to the U.S. dollar because the exchange rate would have changed from $0.20 dollars per franc to $0.25 dollars per franc. A given number of French francs now buys more U.S. dollars.

When a country's currency weakens relative to the currencies of other countries, imported goods become more expensive for citizens of the country with the weakened currency. Say that one pound of French cheese costs five francs. If the exchange rate between francs and U.S. dollars is five francs per dollar, then one dollar (five francs) will buy a pound of French cheese. However, if the exchange rate changes from five French francs per dollar to four French francs per dollar, then the importer could no longer buy the pound of cheese with one dollar: The cheese costs five francs and the dollar is equivalent to four francs. Each franc is now worth one-quarter dollar, or $0.25, so the importer would need $0.25 × 5 = $1.25 to buy a pound of French cheese.

When the U.S. dollar weakens against the French franc, U.S. importers of French goods will require more dollars to purchase French goods that are sold in francs. Similarly, people in the United States will find that French goods and services are now more expensive in general. U.S. vacationers in France learn this lesson quickly.

Conversely, a weakened dollar relative to the French franc means that U.S. goods and services are less expensive for French citizens to buy. This is why French tourists tend to come to the United States in greater numbers when the dollar is weakening against the French franc, and why business improves for U.S. companies exporting goods to France. Generally, these same effects occur when the U.S. dollar weakens compared to any another country's currency.

What happens when the U.S. dollar strengthens against the currency of another country? Using our French franc example, if the dollar strengthens against the franc, more U.S. consumers would buy French cheese and other goods, and vacation in greater numbers in France. At the same time, French people would buy fewer U.S. goods and take fewer U.S. vacations.[4]

These changes in spending patterns usually occur whenever the exchange rate fluctuates. The relative attractiveness of one country's goods and services abroad fluctuates with the relative value of the currency changes.

Cross Rates

If we know the exchange rate between the currencies of Country A and Country B, and also between the currencies of Country A and Country C, then we can determine the exchange rate between the currencies of Country B and Country C. For example, if we know that one U.S. dollar is worth five French francs and that one U.S.

---

[4]In our running example, we assume that the domestic prices in the two countries stay the same.

dollar is worth one hundred Japanese yen, we can determine how many Japanese yen a person would receive in exchange for each French franc. An exchange rate of two currencies found by using a common third currency is known as a currency **cross rate.**

To calculate a currency cross rate, multiply the ratio of Currency A to Currency B exchange rate by the ratio of Currency B to Currency C exchange rate as shown in Equation 21-1.

Calculating Cross Rates

$$\frac{\text{Currency A}}{\text{Currency B}} \times \frac{\text{Currency B}}{\text{Currency C}} = \frac{\text{Currency A}}{\text{Currency C}} \tag{21-1}$$

The calculation of the Japanese yen to French franc cross rate using the cross rate formula in Equation 21-1 is shown next.

$$\frac{\text{Japanese Yen}}{\text{U.S. Dollar}} \times \frac{\text{U.S. Dollar}}{\text{French Franc}} = \frac{\text{Japanese Yen}}{\text{French Franc}}$$

Suppose one hundred Japanese yen are worth one dollar, as we said earlier. Then suppose one U.S. dollar is worth five French francs. Substituting these values into Equation 21-1 produces the following cross rate:

$$\frac{100 \text{ Japanese Yen}}{1 \text{ U.S. Dollar}} \times \frac{1 \text{ U.S. Dollar}}{5 \text{ French Francs}} = \frac{20 \text{ Japanese Yen}}{1 \text{ French Franc}}$$

We find that the U.S. dollar in the first term of the equation cancels out the U.S. dollar in the second term, leaving the yen-per-franc exchange rate, which in this case is 100 to 5, reduced to 20 to 1.

A sampling of currency cross rates is shown in Table 21-2.

Cross rates are a useful tool. Financial publications of many countries offer exchange rates relative to the domestic currency only. So, if you were on a business trip in Mexico but were managing a project for a U.S. firm that had a Japanese supplier, you might want to know the exchange rate between the dollar and yen but would only have information about the peso. The cross rate formula allows you to quickly calculate the dollar-to-yen exchange rate.

Table 21-2

Currency Cross Rates on May 7, 1996

Key Currency Cross Rates Late New York Trading May 7, 1996

	Dollar	Pound	SFranc	Guilder	Peso	Yen	Lira	D-Mark	FFranc	CdnDlr
Canada	1.3656	2.0627	1.0973	.80117	.18190	.01298	.00088	.89553	.26504	....
France	5.1524	7.7827	4.1401	3.0228	.68630	.04898	.00331	3.3788	....	3.7730
Germany	1.5249	2.3034	1.2253	.89463	.20312	.01450	.00098	....	.29596	1.1167
Italy	1557.0	2351.8	1251.1	913.46	207.39	14.80	....	1021.1	302.19	1140.2
Japan	105.2	158.9	84.532	61.719	14.013	....	.06757	68.988	20.418	77.036
Mexico	7.5075	11.34	6.0325	4.4045	....	.07136	.00482	4.9233	1.4571	5.4976
Netherlands	1.7045	2.5746	1.3696	....	.22704	.01620	.00109	1.1178	.33082	1.2482
Switzerland	1.2445	1.8798	....	.73013	.16577	.01183	.00080	.81612	.24154	.91132
U.K.	.66203	....	.53197	.38840	.08818	.00629	.00043	.43415	.12849	.48479
U.S.	....	1.5105	.80354	.58668	.13320	.00951	.00064	.65578	.19408	.73228

Source: Dow Jones Telerate Inc.

Source: Reprinted by permission of *The Wall Street Journal*, © 1996 Dow Jones & Company, Inc. All Rights Reserved Worldwide.

Table 21-2 shows the cross exchange rates for ten major currencies on May 7, 1996.

Exchange Rate Effects on MNCS

Fluctuating exchange rates present special risks and opportunities for multinational corporations. As the home currency of an MNC strengthens or weakens against currencies of other countries where the MNC has operations, the firm will feel a financial impact.

Suppose, for example, that McDonald's Corporation, a U.S.-based MNC, realized profits of 80 million deutsche marks from its operations in Germany during 1996. At some point, McDonald's Corporation is likely to convert its deutsche mark profits to U.S. dollars and bring the dollars to the United States. Converting foreign currency profits into domestic currency to send to the home country of the business is known as *repatriating* the profits. Why repatriate profits? McDonald's stockholders expect U.S. dollar dividends, not deutsche mark dividends.

To demonstrate how to report repatriated profits to shareholders, let's revisit the McDonald's example. Suppose the exchange rate were 1.4 deutsche marks per U.S. dollar at the start of the year. Also assume the exchange rate held steady throughout the year. When McDonald's repatriates its profits at year's end, it would report on the income statement 80 million/1.4 = 57.143 million in U.S. dollar profits from its German operations.

Now suppose the exchange rate did not hold steady during the year. Suppose instead that the exchange rate fell from 1.4 deutsche marks per dollar to 1.25 deutsche marks per dollar by year's end. Now when the profits are repatriated, they are worth 80 million/1.25 = 64 million U.S. dollars. Clearly, the weakening of the U.S. dollar during the year helped the McDonald's Corporation. Its U.S. dollar profits were nearly 7 million U.S. dollars higher ($64 million − $57.143 million) than they would have been had the dollar not weakened. The chapter opener profile of Lance Woeltjen also demonstrates how fluctuating currency can help when it's time to repatriate profits.

A weakening U.S. dollar has a positive effect on an MNC that repatriates its profits from the country whose currency is strengthening. However, if the U.S. dollar strengthens relative to the foreign currency, profits tumble. Going back to our McDonald's example, suppose that the U.S. dollar had strengthened relative to the German deutsche mark during the year. McDonald's U.S. dollar profits would have been lower after converting the deutsche marks to dollars and repatriating the profits back to the United States.

Exchange Rate Effects on Foreign Stock and Bond Investments

A corporation does not have to have actual business operations in another country to be affected by exchange rate fluctuations. If a company holds stocks or bonds denominated in the currencies of other countries, the fluctuations in the value of these currencies will affect the dollar value of the stocks and bonds. This applies to individual investors' holdings as well.

If Betsy Ross, a U.S. investor, held one hundred shares of Daimler Benz common stock valued at fourteen deutsche marks per share, a strengthening of the deutsche mark (weakening of the U.S. dollar) would help Betsy just as it helped McDonald's in our earlier example. If the exchange rate were, say, 1.4 deutsche marks per dollar, then Betsy's investment would be worth 14/1.4 = 10 U.S. dollars per share.

However, if the exchange rate went from 1.4 to 1.25 deutsche marks per dollar, the U.S. dollar value of Betsy's stock would increase from $10 per share to $11.20

(14 deutsche marks/1.25 = $11.20). Betsy experienced a gain of $1.20/$10 = .12, or 12 percent even though the stock's price on the German stock exchange did not change at all. Of course, if the dollar had strengthened, there would have been a negative financial impact on Betsy. A strengthening dollar is one of the risks of investing outside your home country.

Managing Risk

International operations provide special challenges and opportunities, but also special risks. Exchange rate risk can be hedged. Investors and MNCs often find diversification benefits when foreign investments are added to an all-domestic portfolio. Risk of foreign securities held by U.S. citizens, caused by fluctuating exchange rates, can be managed by purchasing foreign claims on foreign securities denominated in U.S. dollars.

Hedging

The risk that a multinational corporation faces due to fluctuating exchange rates is one that can be managed. *Forward contracts, futures contracts,* and *currency swaps* are all available to help an MNC hedge currency risk. A **hedge** is a financial agreement used to offset or guard against risk. A company may choose to hedge against adverse changes in interest rates, commodity prices, or currency exchange rates.

Forward contracts are contracts where one party agrees to buy, and the other party agrees to sell, a certain amount of an asset (a currency for example) at a specified price (exchange rate) at a specified future time. *Futures contracts* are similar except they are standardized contracts and can be traded on organized exchanges. *Swaps* are directly negotiated contracts, like forward contracts, in which each party agrees to swap payments at specified points in time according to a predetermined formula. For instance one party could pay U.S. dollars and the other Japanese yen, each according to the amounts called for in the swap contract. By agreeing to a forward, futures, or swap contract, an MNC can protect against a loss that will occur if the feared change in exchange rate occurs. The firm using these hedging instruments insulates itself from this risk.

Diversification Benefits of Foreign Investments

There are often significant diversification benefits to investing in a variety of countries, both for MNCs and for individual investors. Instead of putting all your money in one country, spreading your investment around several countries will often prove beneficial. If the economy or market is weak in one country, it may be stronger in another. If your money is spread around in several countries, the good news in one country will often cancel out the bad news from another.

The returns earned from investments in other countries often have low correlations with the returns earned from investments in the home country. Chapter 7 showed the risk-reducing potential of creating portfolios where the individual assets have returns with low correlations relative to each other. Figure 21-2 shows how

Figure 21-2 **Portfolio Risk as Diversification Changes**

Figure 21-2 shows the diversification effects for a sample domestic-only portfolio and a mixed (domestic and foreign) portfolio. The upper curve represents a domestic security only portfolio. The lower curve represents a portfolio containing both domestic and foreign securities.

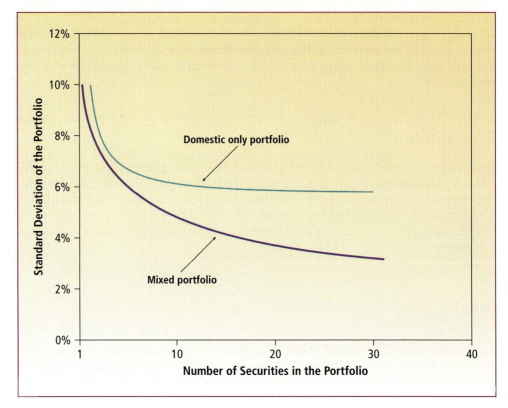

diversification benefits are greater with a portfolio that contains both domestic and foreign securities (average correlation of .4 in our example), rather than domestic securities alone (average correlation of .8 in our example).

If you review chapter 7, you will see specifically how the correlation between the returns of assets affects the risk of a portfolio. Because the correlation of returns between a U.S. stock and a foreign stock tends to be lower than between two U.S. stocks, international diversification is often an important risk-management tool.

Figure 21-2 shows how the diversification effects differ for a portfolio with U.S. stock only compared to one with U.S. and foreign stock. The sample domestic portfolio has an average correlation coefficient of returns of .8. The sample portfolio containing both domestic and foreign securities has an average correlation coefficient of returns of .4. The mixed portfolio has a lower correlation coefficient, so the risk of that portfolio is lower than that of the domestic only portfolio.

American Depository Receipts

The common stock of many major foreign companies is traded in the United States in a form that is denominated in U.S. dollars. Some examples include Nestle (Switzerland), Volvo (Sweden), and British Gas (United Kingdom).[5] Special trusts are created, and foreign stock is purchased and placed in these trusts. These trusts

---

[5]Sam Jaffe, "World-Class Investments," *SmartMoney* (February 1996): 88.

Interview with Don Burton, International Import–Export Institute

Don Burton is on the Board of Directors for the International Import–Export Institute, which certifies import–export professionals around the globe. Don brought a strong business background to the job. The President and CEO of Midland Cascade Corporation, Don has also developed export education programs for major universities. The International Import–Export Institute provides education and certification testing to import–export professionals in a variety of areas, ranging from finance and documentation to letters of credit and marketing.

Don Burton

Q. What risks do businesses face when they trade internationally?

There are a lot of different risks that people and businesses don't really think about when they start dealing in the international trade arena. In the United States, we take stability for granted, but many countries are economically and politically unstable. For instance, a firm may not get paid because a country might nationalize either the bank or company with which you were dealing. Once a bank or company has been nationalized, the firm usually has worthless contracts that the country won't recognize as a binding obligation.

Q. How safe are letters of credit?

When a business deals in international trade, accepting letters of credit creates a big risk. A letter of credit is an obligation on the part of a foreign bank to pay the firm. Sometimes the letters are forged or fake; the bank doesn't even exist. Nigeria is famous for invalid letters of credit. Companies present a letter of credit with names of banks that don't exist, trying to encourage U.S. firms to send goods. Once the goods are in Nigeria, the U.S. firm never gets paid.

Q. If a company is unsure about the buyer or their bank, how can a firm greatly reduce its trade credit risk?

The firm should get a confirmed letter of credit. This means that the company's local bank has confirmed the letter of credit. Even if the other company doesn't pay, the local bank will. The payment responsibility shifts from the foreign bank or company to the local bank. The bank charges only a small fee for this service.

Q. What are some of the risks of fluctuating exchange rates?

Exchange rates affect companies in many ways, but timing is a crucial factor. Let's say you ship some goods overseas. They go by boat. That means it may be twenty-eight to forty-five days before your customer receives the goods. That's often when the obligation to pay begins. If you have given the customer trade credit terms of thirty days net of receipt, that means that you may not get paid for up to seventy-five days after the day you ship the goods. If during this time the exchange rate drops—meaning the dollar strengthens if you're dealing in a foreign currency—you're at risk.

Q. Is there any way to avoid getting hurt by dropping exchange rates?

Agree to the exchange rate at the inception of the deal in a contract. Or buy insurance to guard against dropping exchange rates. Domestic banks and the federal government offer exchange rate insurance at fairly cheap rates. If the business transaction goes through the Export–Import Bank agency of the federal government, the government automatically insures a business for the current exchange rate.

Source: Interview with Don Burton.

then issue their own securities, called **American Depository Receipts (ADRs).** Many ADRs are traded on the New York Stock Exchange and the NASDAQ over-the-counter market.

In this section, we examined exchange rate risk management tools, the diversification benefits of foreign investments, and American depository receipts. We turn to exchange rate theories next.

EXCHANGE RATE THEORIES

To aid business decision makers, financial theorists try to explain exchange rate levels and fluctuations. Why is the current exchange rate between two currencies at the level it is? What causes that exchange rate to change? Among the most popular exchange rate theories are the *purchasing power parity theory,* the *international Fisher effect,* and the *interest rate parity theory.*

Purchasing Power Parity Theory

Economists have studied the question of how the financial market prices one country's currency in terms of another country's currency. One explanation, the *purchasing power parity (PPP) theory,* says that it is the relative prices in two countries that determine the exchange rate of their currencies. There are two versions of the PPP theory: the *absolute PPP* and the *relative PPP.*

The **absolute purchasing power parity theory** posits that exchange rates are determined by the differences in the prices of a given market basket of traded goods and services when there are no trade barriers. For instance, if a given basket of traded goods and services available in Japan and in the United States costs 80,000 yen in Japan and 1,000 dollars in the U.S., then the exchange rate should be 80 yen per dollar. The calculation follows:

$$\frac{¥80,000}{\$1,000} = 80 \text{ yen per dollar}$$

Another version of the theory is more realistically applicable in an economic world with transportation costs, tariffs, quotas, and other trade barriers. The **relative purchasing power parity theory** focuses on the *changes over time* in the relative prices of traded baskets of similar goods and services in the two countries. At any given time, the exchange rate between the two currencies is related to the rate of change in the prices of the similar market baskets. According to the relative PPP theory, as prices change in one country relative to those prices in another country for a traded basket of similar goods and services, the exchange rate will tend to change proportionately but in the opposite direction.

The rationale for this theory is that if one country experiences rising prices while its international trading partners do not, its exports will become less competitive. Similarly, imports will become more attractive because of their relatively lower prices. The exchange rate will change as citizens buy the currency of the country with falling prices and sell the currency of the country with rising prices.

Interview with Don Burton, International Import–Export Institute

Don Burton is on the Board of Directors for the International Import–Export Institute, which certifies import–export professionals around the globe. Don brought a strong business background to the job. The President and CEO of Midland Cascade Corporation, Don has also developed export education programs for major universities. The International Import–Export Institute provides education and certification testing to import–export professionals in a variety of areas, ranging from finance and documentation to letters of credit and marketing.

Don Burton

Q. *What risks do businesses face when they trade internationally?*

There are a lot of different risks that people and businesses don't really think about when they start dealing in the international trade arena. In the United States, we take stability for granted, but many countries are economically and politically unstable. For instance, a firm may not get paid because a country might nationalize either the bank or company with which you were dealing. Once a bank or company has been nationalized, the firm usually has worthless contracts that the country won't recognize as a binding obligation.

Q. *How safe are letters of credit?*

When a business deals in international trade, accepting letters of credit creates a big risk. A letter of credit is an obligation on the part of a foreign bank to pay the firm. Sometimes the letters are forged or fake; the bank doesn't even exist. Nigeria is famous for invalid letters of credit. Companies present a letter of credit with names of banks that don't exist, trying to encourage U.S. firms to send goods. Once the goods are in Nigeria, the U.S. firm never gets paid.

Q. *If a company is unsure about the buyer or their bank, how can a firm greatly reduce its trade credit risk?*

The firm should get a confirmed letter of credit. This means that the company's local bank has confirmed the letter of credit. Even if the other company doesn't pay, the local bank will. The payment responsibility shifts from the foreign bank or company to the local bank. The bank charges only a small fee for this service.

Q. *What are some of the risks of fluctuating exchange rates?*

Exchange rates affect companies in many ways, but timing is a crucial factor. Let's say you ship some goods overseas. They go by boat. That means it may be twenty-eight to forty-five days before your customer receives the goods. That's often when the obligation to pay begins. If you have given the customer trade credit terms of thirty days net of receipt, that means that you may not get paid for up to seventy-five days after the day you ship the goods. If during this time the exchange rate drops—meaning the dollar strengthens if you're dealing in a foreign currency—you're at risk.

Q. *Is there any way to avoid getting hurt by dropping exchange rates?*

Agree to the exchange rate at the inception of the deal in a contract. Or buy insurance to guard against dropping exchange rates. Domestic banks and the federal government offer exchange rate insurance at fairly cheap rates. If the business transaction goes through the Export–Import Bank agency of the federal government, the government automatically insures a business for the current exchange rate.

Source: Interview with Don Burton.

then issue their own securities, called **American Depository Receipts (ADRs).** Many ADRs are traded on the New York Stock Exchange and the NASDAQ over-the-counter market.

In this section, we examined exchange rate risk management tools, the diversification benefits of foreign investments, and American depository receipts. We turn to exchange rate theories next.

EXCHANGE RATE THEORIES

To aid business decision makers, financial theorists try to explain exchange rate levels and fluctuations. Why is the current exchange rate between two currencies at the level it is? What causes that exchange rate to change? Among the most popular exchange rate theories are the *purchasing power parity theory,* the *international Fisher effect,* and the *interest rate parity theory.*

Purchasing Power Parity Theory

Economists have studied the question of how the financial market prices one country's currency in terms of another country's currency. One explanation, the *purchasing power parity (PPP) theory,* says that it is the relative prices in two countries that determine the exchange rate of their currencies. There are two versions of the PPP theory: the *absolute PPP* and the *relative PPP.*

The **absolute purchasing power parity theory** posits that exchange rates are determined by the differences in the prices of a given market basket of traded goods and services when there are no trade barriers. For instance, if a given basket of traded goods and services available in Japan and in the United States costs 80,000 yen in Japan and 1,000 dollars in the U.S., then the exchange rate should be 80 yen per dollar. The calculation follows:

$$\frac{\yen 80{,}000}{\$1{,}000} = 80 \text{ yen per dollar}$$

Another version of the theory is more realistically applicable in an economic world with transportation costs, tariffs, quotas, and other trade barriers. The **relative purchasing power parity theory** focuses on the *changes over time* in the relative prices of traded baskets of similar goods and services in the two countries. At any given time, the exchange rate between the two currencies is related to the rate of change in the prices of the similar market baskets. According to the relative PPP theory, as prices change in one country relative to those prices in another country for a traded basket of similar goods and services, the exchange rate will tend to change proportionately but in the opposite direction.

The rationale for this theory is that if one country experiences rising prices while its international trading partners do not, its exports will become less competitive. Similarly, imports will become more attractive because of their relatively lower prices. The exchange rate will change as citizens buy the currency of the country with falling prices and sell the currency of the country with rising prices.

International Fisher Effect

Another theory used to explain currency exchange rates is the international Fisher effect, named for economist Irving Fisher. The *domestic Fisher effect* says simply that the nominal rate of interest equals the real rate plus the expected inflation rate. When this concept is used in an international setting, however, the **international Fisher effect** states that changes in the nominal interest rates for two countries will be offset by equal changes, in the opposite direction, in the exchange rate. The difference in nominal interest rates across countries reflects the difference in expected rates of inflation in those countries. According to Irving Fisher, the exchange rate would change by the same amount, but in the opposite direction, as the difference between the nominal interest rates of the two countries.

Changes in nominal interest rates are determined by changes in expected inflation, and exchange rates change for the same reason. The rationale is that investors must be compensated, or will offer compensation, to accommodate the expected change in the exchange rate.

Interest Rate Parity Theory

The **interest rate parity theory** says that the percentage difference between the exchange rate specified for future delivery (the **forward rate**), and for current delivery (the **spot rate**), equals the difference in the interest rates for equal maturity securities in the two countries.

If the difference between the spot and forward rates for two countries' currencies did not equal the difference between the interest rates on equal maturity securities in those countries, an *arbitrage* opportunity would exist. **Arbitrage** is the process whereby equivalent assets are bought in one place and simultaneously sold in another, making a risk-free profit. Arbitragers would buy in the spot market and sell in the forward market, or vice versa, depending on which was undervalued and which overvalued, until interest rate parity is achieved.

Other Factors Affecting Exchange Rates

Currency exchange rates fluctuate daily. Traders often buy and sell the dollar equivalent of $1 trillion per day, continually reevaluating how many units of one country's currency should be exchanged for a given number of units of another country's currency.

The purchasing power parity theory, the international Fisher effect, and interest rate parity theory focus on rational economic explanations for exchange rates. But, like any market, the foreign exchange market is affected by both real economic factors and psychological factors.

If a country is experiencing political trouble, for example, currency traders may fear that this will spill over to that country's economy. If investments in the foreign country are expected to suffer in the future because of the political turmoil, traders will dump that country's currency in the foreign exchange market. To liquidate investments in the troubled country, a firm must not only sell the investment, but also the foreign currency it receives through the sale of the security. Currencies from other countries, where the political climate is better, will be preferred. These other currencies can then be invested in countries where the political climate is more hospitable.

When the Soviet Union broke up in 1992, the German mark dropped precipitously in the foreign exchange market against other major currencies, particularly against the dollar. The reason given by most experts is that refugees from many of the states that had been part of the Soviet Union were fleeing their home countries and moving to Germany. (The German constitution established an open door policy for foreign refugees.) This influx of poor people into Germany was expected to strain the German economy as government money was spent to take care of them. The German mark went down accordingly, in anticipation of this drain.

The U.S. dollar often increases in value against other currencies on the foreign exchange market when there is a significant threatening world event. For instance, when Iraq invaded Kuwait in 1990, which subsequently led to the Persian Gulf War, the dollar soared against most other currencies in value. The U.S. dollar has become something of a "safe haven" for investors during difficult times.

The rationale seems to be that U.S. investments are safer because the United States has considerable military and economic power and secure location compared to countries with limited means to protect themselves from unfriendly neighbors. South Korea, for example, has a powerful economy that could crumble overnight if North Korea invaded. Similarly, Taiwan has a powerful economy that would be threatened if the People's Republic of China invaded.

Government Intervention in Foreign Exchange Markets

Sometimes the central banks of countries will enter the foreign exchange market in an attempt to influence exchange rates. If the Fed, for example, were unhappy with market conditions where the U.S. dollar was weakening against other currencies, it could buy U.S. dollars, using its holdings of other currencies such as German marks or British pounds, in an attempt to bid up (strengthen) the value of the dollar. Central banks of other countries can also buy or sell currencies in the foreign exchange market to further their own policy goals. Although the central banks of major countries have great market power, it is difficult to move a trillion-dollar-plus market when it doesn't want to be moved.

Sometimes central banks will act in concert with each other to pursue a common policy objective. The major economic powers of the world, known as the Group of Seven (G-7), have sometimes pursued a common effort to alter exchange rates. The Group of Seven countries are the United States, the United Kingdom, Germany, Japan, Canada, France, and Italy.

Psychological and political factors surely affect exchange rates. Like any other market, the foreign exchange market is influenced by logical and illogical factors alike, some of which are unidentifiable. The end result, however, is felt by multinational corporations and by individual consumers alike.

In this section we explored exchange rate theories that help decision makers understand exchange rate risks and fluctuations. In the next section, we address the main political and cultural risks that multinational corporations may confront.

POLITICAL AND CULTURAL RISKS FACING MNCs

MNCs must deal with political and cultural factors when engaging in international business. Awareness and sensitivity to these factors are crucial to successful international business activities.

Political Risk

Political risk is the risk that a country's government may take some action that would harm a foreign-owned company doing business in that country. For example, a foreign government might expropriate (take) the assets of the company for its own reasons. Expropriation of assets is an extreme example of political risk. Sometimes funds are blocked by the host country, making it impossible for an MNC to repatriate profits earned in the foreign country. For instance, the U.S. government froze the bank accounts of Iranian companies when tension developed after United States citizens were taken hostage by Iranian nationals in 1979.

Another political risk is the chance that special taxes could be imposed on profits made by foreign companies. An example of such a tax is the unitary tax imposed by many state governments in the United States. A **unitary tax** is a tax on a portion of the profits earned by non-U.S. companies.

Another political risk is the chance that a foreign government may impose a minimum number or minimum percentage of domestic workers that must be employed by foreign companies operating in that country. These workers may or may not have the same level of training and ability as the workers of the home country. In Bermuda, for instance, companies are not allowed to hire foreign workers unless they can demonstrate that they cannot obtain Bermudians for the job positions. If a Bermudian wants a job, then, he or she gets it even though there may be many more qualified foreigners willing to move to Bermuda to work.

Foreign governments may also impose a requirement for the use of a certain amount of raw materials or parts manufactured in the country where the foreign operation is located. Again, these materials and parts may or may not meet the standards of the home country.

These political risks must be weighed, along with other risks unique to international operations, against the special opportunities these international operations present.

Cultural Risk

When a company operates in another country, cultural issues often affect business. These differences include language barriers as well as differences in attitudes, values, and business protocol. Cultural risk is the risk that foreigners doing business in another country will fail to adapt to cultural differences, and this failure will affect the firm's success.

To offset cultural risk, companies that operate abroad often train their employees in cultural differences. A lack of awareness about differences in business practices could cause an unintentional insult or jeopardize a negotiation about a major project. For example, some hand gestures that have innocent connotations in one country are considered offensive or obscene in another country. What is called a bribe in one country may be considered a routine gratuity in another country.

Taking cultural risks can generate high returns. For example, take James Hickman, a U.S. entrepreneur who founded Rustel, a $10 million telephone company operating in Moscow after amassing a pile of rubles in the late 1980s by promoting American rock concerts. Rustel succeeded in large part because Hickman and his partner learned about the Russian culture and searched for employees who could both work with the Russian bureaucracy and act entrepreneurial. Finding such talented employees was tough, however.

Through trial and error, Hickman learned that the totalitarian regime in the former Soviet Union had created a work culture of secrecy and a lack of accountability. Few workers kept records of their business activities, and many dodged responsibility to avoid the risk of blame for failure. Because of the slow pace of the former Communist bureaucracy, few workers had a sense of urgency about deadlines. Project planners had no understanding of business in a market economy, so they did not value investments, estimate costs, or assess market potential. Fortunately, Hickman learned these cultural lessons quickly and was able to effectively hire and train employees. Otherwise, his business would not have succeeded.[6]

The risks of doing business in a foreign country are many: exchange rate fluctuations, and political and cultural risk. Yet the return potential is high. Recognizing the risk and potential return, governments have forged trade agreements to promote and regulate international business. We look at trade agreements next.

INTERNATIONAL TRADE AGREEMENTS

Groups of countries sometimes form alliances and agreements that both regulate and foster international trade. NAFTA, EU, and GATT are the major international agreements we discuss in this section. Read on to learn the details of this alphabet soup.

NAFTA

Canada, Mexico, and the United States signed an agreement in 1994 called the *North American Fair Trade Agreement (NAFTA)*. NAFTA breaks down some of the barriers to trade between these countries, such as tariffs and quotas.

Tariffs are taxes assessed by Country A on the goods of Country B that are sold in Country A. Mexico, for example, might impose a tariff on Canadian goods sold in Mexico. **Quotas** are quantity restrictions imposed by Country A on certain goods imported from Country B. Both are barriers to international trade. When Country A imposes tariffs and quotas on the goods of Country B, Country B is likely to impose tariffs and quotas on goods from Country A. This can lead to a trade war wherein each country increases the barriers imposed on the goods of the other. Trade wars can lead to economic decline of both countries.

NAFTA is, in effect, a pact to end such wars. It should increase business for all three countries as tariffs, quotas, and other trade barriers are eliminated. NAFTA is politically controversial, however, since its opponents believe that U.S. jobs will be

---

[6]James Hickman, "Red Stars Rising," *Inc. Magazine* (August 1995): 19–20.

lost as U.S.-based companies shift some operations to Mexico where labor costs tend to be lower. Proponents claim that jobs in exporting industries are likely to increase and create ripple effect benefits for the economies of all three countries.

GATT

The *General Agreement on Tariffs and Trade (GATT)* is a treaty that provides for ongoing discussions among participating nations to find ways to minimize international trade barriers. The Uruguay round of GATT talks established the World Trade Organization (WTO) on April 15, 1994. When one WTO country has a trade complaint against another, the WTO court can hear the complaint and impose economic sanctions if the accused country is found guilty. In 1995, the United States accused Japan of unfairly placing barriers to the sale of U.S. cellular phones, automobiles, and photographic film in Japan. Japan claimed that no such barriers existed. These are the types of disputes that the WTO adjudicates.

European Union

The *European Union (EU)* created a different type of association among the participating nations. The alliance was formed in late 1993 after the framework was negotiated by nations who signed the Maastricht Treaty, so-named because Maastricht is the city (in the Netherlands) where the EU leaders signed the treaty creating the integrated economic plan. The original country members of the EU are Belgium, Denmark, France, Germany, Greece, Great Britain, Ireland, Italy, Luxembourg, Netherlands, Portugal, and Spain. Most of the barriers to trade among these countries have been minimized.

The EU encourages joint business ventures and coordinated economic policies. All EU members now have a common passport. Further, each country recognizes professional and educational degrees of other member countries so that doctors, lawyers, and other licensed professionals can practice in any country within the EU.

Perhaps the most ambitious goal of the EU is to replace domestic currencies in use now (francs, marks, pounds, and so on) with a common currency, the **euro,** for all business transactions between EU members. To move member countries toward the goal of a common currency, the EU has a **European Currency Unit (ECU),** an index that represents the composite value of a basket of European currencies. Firms in member countries can now specify ECU values in business contracts.

EU members must carefully balance the costs of membership against the benefits. The union is designed to make member countries more integrated in business and trade matters, without wiping out their individual national identities. Historical animosity among some member countries can only be overcome if members believe that significant economic benefits will occur through cooperation.

Free Trade versus Fair Trade

"Free trade" and "fair trade" differ. *Free trade* suggests an unconditional lowering of trade barriers. *Fair trade* suggests lowering trade barriers only if the other country lowers its barriers, and perhaps only if the other country meets additional conditions. Examples of other conditions include meeting minimum wage, worker safety, human rights, or environmental standards.

NAFTA, GATT, and the EU are signs of an ever-increasing global economy. As the world moves into the twenty-first century, international business will become more significant for all countries. An understanding of the financial risks, potential returns, and basic rules of international business will hopefully lead to greater financial success.

Summary

1. Define a multinational corporation (MNC) and explain its importance.

A multinational corporation is a corporation that operates in more than one country. It is becoming increasingly difficult to accurately classify some corporations as U.S., Swedish, Canadian, and so forth, since many large corporations operate worldwide. International concerns are a vital concern for many U.S. businesses because of the potential market for products in countries throughout the world.

2. Demonstrate how the law of comparative advantage leads to international trade that benefits individuals and firms.

The law of comparative advantage says that countries (and individuals) should do that which they do best. Countries can export goods and services they produce well and import those goods and services that others develop better. By trading, both countries should see quality, quantity, or price benefits, or a combination of all three.

3. Describe exchange rates and their effects on businesses.

An exchange rate is an expression of the value of one country's currency relative to another country's currency. Fluctuating currency exchange rates affect the prices U.S. citizens pay for goods and services of other countries, and the prices that citizens of other countries pay for U.S. goods and services. When a country's currency weakens relative to the currencies of other countries, goods and services imported into that country become more expensive. That country's exported goods and services become cheaper to those countries that import them.

MNCs are also affected when their profits are earned in one country, then converted to the currency of the home country. Converting foreign currency profits into domestic currency to send to the home country of the business is known as *repatriating* the profits. If the U.S. dollar weakens relative to the foreign currency, the U.S. company's profits increase due to the change in exchange rates. However, if the dollar strengthens, profits decrease.

4. Show how firms manage the risks of fluctuating exchange rates.

Diversifying investments across several countries often reduces risk. Foreign securities can be bought in the United States by purchasing American Depository Receipts, which are U.S. dollar securities issued by a trust holding foreign currency denominated securities.

Firms can also manage risk through hedging—entering into a financial agreement that offsets or guards against risk. Three common types of hedging instruments are forward contracts, futures contracts, and swaps. Forward contracts are contracts where one party agrees to buy, and the other party agrees to sell, a certain amount of a currency at a specified exchange rate at a specified future time. Futures contracts are similar except they can be traded on organized exchanges. Swaps are negotiated contracts, like forward contracts, in which each party agrees to swap payments at specified points in time according to a predetermined formula.

5. Discuss exchange rate theories.

Currency exchange rates fluctuate for a variety of reasons. Among the most popular theories seeking to explain these changes are those that focus on relative prices in the two countries (purchasing power parity), relative interest rates (international Fisher effect), and the difference between spot and forward rates relative to the exchange rate (interest rate parity).

6. Describe the political and cultural risks that affect MNCs.

MNCs run the political risk of government trade restrictions, confiscation of assets by foreign governments, and even wars. Cultural risks include the risk of jeopardizing a deal or business due to insensitivity to differences in language, values, and attitudes. Training employees to recognize and respect cultural differences can reduce cultural risk.

7. Explain how major international trade agreements affect international business.

International agreements such as NAFTA, GATT, and the Maastricht Treaty that created the EU can bring down trade barriers and potentially create wide-ranging benefits. Opponents of these agreements claim, however, that they can result in job loss or harm a country's identity and economy.

Equations Introduced in This Chapter

Equation 21-1. Calculation of a Currency Cross Rate:

$$\frac{\text{Currency A}}{\text{Currency B}} \times \frac{\text{Currency B}}{\text{Currency C}} = \frac{\text{Currency A}}{\text{Currency C}}$$

Self-Test

ST-1. What is the law of comparative advantage?

ST-2. What is the rationale given for trade agreements such as the North American Free Trade Agreement (NAFTA)?

ST-3. If you can get 1.25 Canadian dollars for 1 U.S. dollar and 1 U.S. dollar gets you 5 French francs, how many French francs do you get for 1 Canadian dollar?

ST-4. What are American depository receipts (ADRs)?

Review Questions

1. What does it mean when the U.S. dollar weakens in the foreign exchange market?
2. What kinds of U.S. companies would benefit most from a stronger dollar in the foreign exchange market? Explain.
3. Under what circumstance would the U.S. dollar and the Italian lira be said to have achieved purchasing power parity?
4. What are some of the primary advantages when a corporation has operations in countries other than its home country? What are some of the risks?
5. What is GATT, and what is its goal?

Build Your Communication Skills

CS-1. Form two groups to debate the issue of free trade versus fair trade. Some questions to address in the discussion include: 1) Should a country allow other countries to sell goods to its citizens with few or no restrictions (free trade)? 2) Should opening markets to companies from other countries be conditional on those other countries showing reciprocating openness (fair trade)? 3) Who decides which countries are engaging in fair trading practices?

CS-2. Write a short report on the current state of exchange rates. Which currencies are strengthening in foreign exchange markets and which are weakening? Why? Incorporate what you learned in this chapter in your analysis. What are the implications for international trade that can be drawn from the direction of the change in exchange rate values you observe?

Problems

Calculating Exchange Rates

21-1. The New York foreign exchange selling rates on March 25, 1996, as reported in *The Wall Street Journal,* are shown next for a few selected currencies:

Country/(Currency)	U.S. $ Equivalent
Australia (Dollar)	.7739
Britain (Pound)	1.5220
Canada (Dollar)	.7340
France (Franc)	.1976
Germany (Mark)	.6764
India (Rupee)	.02928
Italy (Lira)	.0006410
Japan (Yen)	.009416
Mexico (Peso)	.1327
Netherlands (Guilder)	.6045
Singapore (Dollar)	.7108
Switzerland (Franc)	.8388
Thailand (Baht)	.03960
Turkey (Lira)	.00001427

Calculate the number of the following foreign currencies that can be bought with 1 million U.S. dollars.

a. British pounds   **e.** Mexican peso
b. Indian rupees   **f.** Turkish lira
c. Japanese yen   **g.** Swiss franc
d. Italian lira

Calculating Exchange Rates

21-2. Using the information given in problem 20-1, calculate the number of the following foreign currencies that can be bought with 1 million U.S. dollars.

a. Australian dollars   **e.** Dutch guilders
b. French francs   **f.** German marks
c. Singaporean dollars   **g.** Thai bahts
d. Italian lira

Calculating Exchange Rates

21-3. Using the information given in problem 21-1, calculate the number of U.S. dollars required to buy

a. 2 million Australian dollars
b. 1.6 million Singaporean dollars
c. 5 million French francs
d. 2.6 million Dutch guilders
e. 2 million German marks
f. 25 million Thai bahts

Cross Rates

21-4. If the Canadian dollar is selling at U.S. $ 0.73400 and the French franc at U.S. $0.19763, how many French francs are equal to one Canadian dollar?

21-5. If 943.0 Italian lira or 64.196 Japanese yen could be purchased with one Dutch guilder, how many Italian lira are equal to one Japanese yen?

Cross Rates

21-6. If one British pound is equivalent to 11.468 Mexican pesos or 1.8145 Swiss francs, how many Swiss francs can one purchase with 10 million Mexican pesos?

Cross Rates

21-7. If one British pound is equivalent to 1.8145 Swiss francs, and one Swiss franc can purchase 1.3876 Dutch guilders, how many Dutch guilders can one purchase with 1 million British pounds?

Cross Rates

21-8. If one British pound is equivalent to 1.8145 Swiss francs, and one Swiss franc can purchase 1.3876 Dutch guilders, and 1 Dutch guilder is worth 943 Italian lira, how many Italian lira can one purchase with 1 million British pounds?

Cross Rates

21-9. Assume that you invested $100,000 in a Japanese security a year back when the exchange rate was 100 yen per 1 U.S. dollar. However, the U.S. dollar depreciated against the yen throughout the year, and the current exchange rate is 85 yen per U.S. dollar. Calculate your percentage return on the investment due to this depreciation of the dollar.

Exchange Rate Effects

21-10. An Indian investor bought 1,000 shares of General Motors at $37 per share on January 1, 1996, when the exchange rate was 31 rupees per 1 U.S. dollar. At the end of the year, the U.S. dollar appreciated against the rupee and the present exchange rate is 32 rupees per 1 U.S. dollar. Calculate the yearly return on investment for the Indian investor assuming the stock price remained the same.

Challenge Problem

Answers to Self-Test

ST-1. The law of comparative advantage says that all will prosper when each party (or nation) does that at which it excels and then trades with others who do what they excel at.

ST-2. NAFTA is a trade agreement between the United States, Canada, and Mexico that eliminated major barriers so the countries could freely trade goods and services to the benefit of the citizens of all three countries. Whether this has occurred is a matter of interpretation.

ST-3.

$$\frac{5 \text{ FF}}{\$1.00 \text{ U.S.}} \times \frac{\$1.00 \text{ U.S.}}{1.25 \text{ CD}} = 4 \text{ FF per } 1.00 \text{ CD}$$

ST-4. American depository receipts (ADRs) are dollar-denominated securities traded in the U.S. that represent a claim on a special trust that is created to hold foreign stock.

GLOSSARY

ABC system An inventory system in which items are classified according to their value for inventory control purposes.

absolute purchasing power parity theory Theory that claims the current exchange rate is determined by the relative prices in two countries of a similar basket of traded goods and services.

actuaries People who use applied mathematics and statistics to predict claims on insurance companies and pension funds.

additional funds needed The additional external financing required to support asset growth when forecasted assets exceed forecasted liabilities and equity.

after-tax cost of debt (AT k_d) The after-tax cost to a company of obtaining debt funds.

agency costs Costs incurred to monitor agents to reduce the conflict of interest between agents and principals.

agency problem The possibility of conflict between the interests of a firm's managers and those of the firm's owners.

agent A person who has the implied or actual authority to act on behalf of another.

aggressive working capital financing approach The use of short-term funds to finance all temporary current assets, possibly all or some permanent current assets, and perhaps some fixed assets.

American Depository Receipts (ADRs) Securities denominated in U.S. dollars that represent a claim on foreign currency–denominated stocks held in a trust.

amortized loan A loan that is repaid in regularly spaced, equal installments, that cover all interest and principal owed.

annuitant A person who is entitled to receive annuity payments.

annuity A series of equal cash payments made at regular time intervals.

arbitrage The process whereby equivalent assets are bought in one place and simultaneously sold in another, making a risk-free profit.

average tax rate The amount of tax owed, divided by the amount of taxable income.

balance sheet The financial statement that shows an economic unit's assets, liabilities, and equity at a given point in time.

banker's acceptance A security that represents a promise by a bank to pay a certain amount of money, if the original note maker doesn't pay.

bearer The owner of a security.

best efforts basis An arrangement in which the investment banking firm tries its best to sell a firm's securities for the desired price, without guarantees. If the securities must be sold for a lower price, the issuer collects less money.

beta (β) The measure of nondiversifiable risk. The stock market has a beta of 1.0. Betas higher than 1.0 indicate more nondiversifiable risk than the market, and betas lower than 1.0 indicate less. Risk-free portfolios have betas of 0.0.

bird in the hand theory A theory that says that investors value a dollar of dividends more highly than a dollar of reinvested earnings because uncertainty is resolved.

board of directors A group of individuals elected by the common stockholders to oversee the management of the firm.

bond maturity date The date when a bond issuer makes the final payment promised.

bonds Securities that promise to pay the bearer a certain amount at a time in the future and may pay interest at regular intervals over the life of the security.

book value, net worth The total amount of common stockholder's equity on a company's balance sheet.

broker A person who brings buyers and sellers together.

business risk The uncertainty a company has due to fluctuations in its operating income.

call premium The premium the issuer pays to call in a bond before maturity. The excess of the call price over the face value.

call provision A bond indenture provision that allows the issuer to pay off a bond before the stated maturity date at a specified price.

capital Funds supplied to a firm.

Capital Asset Pricing Model (CAPM) A financial model that can be used to calculate the appropriate required rate of return for an investment project, given its degree of risk as measured by beta (β).

capital budget A document that shows planned expenditures for major asset acquisitions items, such as equipment or plant construction.

capital budgeting The process of evaluating proposed projects.

capital gains The profit made when an asset price is higher than the price paid.

capital market The market where long-term securities are traded.

capital rationing The process whereby management sets a limit on the amount of cash available for new capital budgeting projects.

capital structure The mixture of sources of capital that a firm uses (for example, debt, preferred stock, and common stock).

cash budget A detailed budget plan that shows the cash flows expected to occur during specific time periods.

chief financial officer The manager who directs and coordinates the financial activities of the firm.

clientele dividend theory The theory that says that a company should attempt to determine the dividend wants of its stockholders and maintain a consistent policy of paying stockholders what they want.

coefficient of variation The standard deviation divided by the mean. A measure of the degree of risk used to compare alternatives with possible returns of different magnitudes.

collateral Assets a borrower agrees to give to a lender if the borrower defaults on the terms of a loan.

collection policy The firm's plans for getting delinquent credit customers to pay their bills.

combined leverage The phenomenon whereby a change in sales causes net income to change by a larger percentage because of fixed operating and financial costs.

commercial paper A short-term, unsecured debt instrument issued by a large corporation or financial institution.

common stock A security that indicates ownership of a corporation.

compensating balance A specified amount that a lender requires a borrower to maintain in a non-interest paying account during the life of a loan.

component cost of capital The cost of raising funds from a particular source, such as bondholders or common stockholders.

compound interest Interest earned on interest in addition to interest earned on the original principal.

conservative working capital financing approach The use of long-term debt and equity to finance all long-term fixed assets and permanent current assets, in addition to some part of temporary current assets.

continuous compounding A process whereby interest is earned on interest every instant of time.

contribution margin Sales price per unit minus variable cost per unit.

controller The manager responsible for the financial and cost accounting activities of a firm.

conversion ratio The number of shares (usually of common stock) that the holder of a convertible bond would receive if he or she exercised the conversion option.

conversion value The value of the stock that would be received if the conversion option on a convertible bond were exercised.

convertible bond A bond that may be converted, at the option of the bond's owner, into a certain amount of a different type of security issued by the company.

corporate bond A security that represents a promise by the issuing corporation to make certain payments, according to a certain schedule, to the owner of the bond.

corporation A business chartered by the state, that is a separate legal entity having some of, but not all of, the rights and responsibilities of a natural person.

correlation The degree to which one variable is linearly related to another.

correlation coefficient The measurement of degree of correlation, represented by the letter r. Its values range from $+1.0$ (perfect positive correlation) to -1.0 (perfect negative correlation).

cost of debt (k_d) The lender's required rate of return on a company's new bonds or other instrument of indebtedness.

cost of equity from new common stock (k_n) The cost of external equity, including the costs incurred to issue new common stock.

cost of internal equity (k_s) The required rate of return on funds supplied by existing common stockholders through earnings retained.

cost of preferred stock (k_p) Investors' required rate of return on a company's new preferred stock.

coupon interest payments Periodic interest payments promised at the time of a bond's issuance.

credit policy Credit standards a firm has established and the credit terms it offers.

credit scoring A process by which candidates for credit are compared against indicators of creditworthiness and scored accordingly.

credit standards Requirements customers must meet in order to be granted credit.

credit unions Financial institutions owned by members who receive interest on shares purchased and who obtain loans.

cross rate An exchange rate determined by examining how each of two currencies is valued in terms of a common third currency.

cross-sectional analysis Comparing variables for different entities (such as ratio values for different companies) for the same point in time or time period.

current assets Liquid assets of an economic entity (e.g., cash, accounts receivable, inventory, etc.) usually converted into cash within one year.

current liabilities Liabilities that are coming due soon, usually within one year.

date of record The date on which stockholder records are checked for the purpose of determining who will receive the dividend that has been declared.

dealer A person who makes his or her living buying and selling assets.

debenture A bond that is unsecured.

declaration date The date on which the board of directors announces a dividend is to be paid.

default risk premium The extra interest lenders demand to compensate for assuming the risk that promised interest and principal payments may be made late or not at all.

deficit economic unit A government, business, or household unit with expenditures greater than its income.

degree of combined leverage (DCL) The percent change in net income divided by the percent change in sales.

degree of financial leverage (DFL) The percent change in net income divided by the percent change in operating income.

degree of operating leverage (DOL) The percent change in operating income divided by the percent change in sales.

depreciation basis The total value of an asset upon which depreciation expense will be calculated, a part at a time, over the life of the asset.

discount loan A loan with terms that call for the loan interest to be deducted from the loan proceeds at the time the loan is granted.

discount rate The interest rate used when calculating a present value representing the required rate of return.

discount yield The return realized by an investor who purchases a security for less than face value and redeems it at maturity for face value.

discounted cash flow (DCF) model A model that estimates the value of an asset by calculating the sum of the present values of all future cash flows.

diversification effect The effect of combining assets in a portfolio such that the fluctuations of the assets' returns tend to offset each other, reducing the overall volatility (risk) of the portfolio.

dividend payout ratio Dividends paid divided by net income.

dividend reinvestment plan An arrangement offered by some corporations where cash dividends are held by the company and used to purchase additional shares of stock for the investor.

dividend yield A stock's annual dividend divided by its current market price.

dividends Payments made to stockholders at the discretion of the board of directors of the corporation.

dividends payable The liability item on a firm's balance sheet that reflects the amount of dividends declared but not yet paid.

effective interest rate The annual interest rate that reflects the dollar interest paid divided by the dollar obtained for use.

electronic funds transfers The act of crediting one account and simultaneously debiting another by a computer.

equity multiplier The total assets to total common stockholders' equity ratio.

euro The common currency to be used by European Union countries.

Eurodollars Dollar-denominated deposits in banks located outside the United States.

European Currency Unit (ECU) An index reflecting the value of a market basket of currencies from European Union countries.

excess financing The amount of excess funding available for expected asset growth when forecasted liabilities and equity exceed forecasted assets.

exchange rate The number of units of one country's currency that is needed to purchase one unit of another country's currency.

ex-dividend A characteristic of common stock such that it is trading *without* entitlement to an upcoming dividend.

ex-rights A characteristic of common stock such that it is trading *without* the entitlement to an upcoming rights offering.

externalities Positive or negative effects that will occur to existing projects if a new capital budgeting project is accepted.

face value, or **par value,** or **principal** The amount the bond issuer promises to pay to the investor when the bond matures. The terms face value, par value, and principal are often used interchangeably.

factoring The practice of selling accounts receivable to another firm.

factors Firms that buy and administer another firm's accounts receivable.

Federal Reserve System The government sponsored entity that acts as the central bank of the United States, and that examines and regulates banks and other financial institutions.

fiduciary responsibility The legal requirement that those who are managing assets owned by someone else do so in a prudent manner and in accordance with the interests of the person(s) they represent.

financial (capital) lease A lease that is generally long-term and non-cancelable with the lessee using up most of the economic value of the asset by the end of the lease's term.

financial leverage The phenomenon whereby a change in operating income causes net income to change by a larger percentage because of the presence of fixed financial costs.

financial ratio A number that expresses the value of one financial variable relative to the value of another.

financial risk The additional volatility of a firm's net income caused by the presence of fixed financial costs.

financing cash flows Cash flows that occur as creditors are paid interest and principal and stockholders are paid dividends.

first mortgage A mortgage bond (a bond secured by real property) that gives the holder first claim on the real property pledged as security if there is a forclosure.

fixed assets Assets that would not normally be sold or otherwise disposed of for a long period of time.

fixed costs Costs that do not vary with the level of production.

flotation costs Fees that companies pay (to investment bankers and to others) when new securities are issued.

forward rate The exchange rate for future delivery.

future value The value money or another asset will have in the future.

future value interest factor for a single amount (FVIF) The $(1 + k)^n$ factor that is multiplied by the original value to solve for future value.

future value interest factor for an annuity (FVIFA) The factor, which when multiplied by an expected annuity, gives you the sum of the future values of the annuity stream:

$$\frac{(1 + k)^n - 1}{k}$$

going concern value That value which comes from the future earnings and cash flows that can be generated by a company if it continues to operate.

going out of business value That value that is that amount that would be left if all the assets were sold, the liabilities and preferred stock paid off, and the remainder distributed among the owners.

hedge A financial arrangement used to offset or protect against negative effects of something else, such as fluctuating exchange rates.

hurdle rate The minimum rate of return that management demands from a proposed project before that project will be accepted.

income statement A financial statement that presents the revenues, expenses, and income of a business over a specific time period.

incremental cash flows Cash flows that will occur only if an investment is undertaken.

incremental depreciation expense The change in depreciation expense that a company will incur if a proposed capital budgeting project is accepted.

indenture The contract between the issuing corporation and the bond's purchaser.

independent projects A group of projects such that any or all could be accepted.

industry comparison The process whereby financial ratios of a firm are compared to those of similar firms to see if the firm under scrutiny compares favorably or unfavorably with the norm.

inflation premium The extra interest that compensates lenders for the expected erosion of purchasing power of funds due to inflation over the life of the loan.

initial public offering (IPO) The process whereby a private corporation issues new common stock to the general public, thus becoming a publicly traded corporation.

institutional investors Financial institutions that invest in the securities of other companies.

interest The compensation lenders demand and borrowers pay when money is lent.

interest rate parity A theory that states that the difference between the exchange rate specified for future delivery, and that for current delivery, equals the difference in the interest rates for securities of the same maturity.

interest rate spread The rate a bank charges for loans minus the rate it pays for deposits.

intermediation The process by which funds are channeled from surplus to deficit economic units through a financial institution.

internal rate of return (IRR) The estimated rate of return for a proposed project, given the size of the project's incremental cash flows and their timing.

international bonds Bonds that are sold in countries other than where the issuer is domiciled.

international Fisher effect A theory developed by economist Irving Fisher that claims that changes in interest rates for two countries will be offset by equal changes, in the opposite direction, in the exchange rate.

inventory financing A type of financing that uses inventory as loan collateral.

investment banking firm A firm that helps issuers sell their securities and that provides other financial services.

investment grade bond Bonds rated Baa3 or above by Moody's bond rating agency and BBB- or above by Standard & Poor's.

JIT An inventory system in which inventory items needed are scheduled to be delivered "just in time" to be used as needed.

junk bond Bonds with lower than investment grade ratings.

lease A contract between an asset owner (lessor) and another party who uses that asset (lessee) that allows the use of the asset for a specified period of time, specifies payment terms, and does not convey legal ownership.

lessee The party in a lease contract who uses the asset.

lessor The party in a lease contract who owns the asset.

leverage effect The result of one factor causing another factor to be magnified, such as where debt magnifies the return stockholders earn on their invested funds over the return on assets.

liability insurance Insurance that pays obligations that may be incurred by the insured as a result of negligence, slander, malpractice, and similar actions.

line of credit An informal arrangement between a lender and borrower in which the lender sets a limit on the maximum amount of funds the borrower may use at any one time.

liquidation value The amount that would be received by the owners of a company that sold all its assets at market value, paid all its liabilities and preferred stock, and distributed what was left to the owners of the firm.

liquidity risk premium The extra interest lenders demand to compensate for holding a security that is not easy to sell at its fair value.

lockbox A way station (typically a post office box) at which customers may send payments to a firm.

MACRS, modified accelerated cost recovery system The depreciation rules established by the Tax Reform Act of 1986 that allow owners to take accelerated depreciation with greater deductions in earlier years than in later years.

managing investment banker The head of an investment banking underwriting syndicate.

marginal cost of capital (MCC) The weighted average cost of capital for the next dollar of funds raised.

marginal tax rate The tax rate applied to the next dollar of taxable income.

market efficiency The relative ease, speed, and cost of trading securities. In an efficient market, securities can be traded easily, quickly, and at low cost. In an inefficient market, one or more of these qualities is missing.

market risk premium The additional return above the risk-free rate demanded by investors for assuming the risk of investing in the market.

maturity date The date the bearer of a security is to be paid the principal, or face value, of a security.

maturity risk premium The extra (or sometimes lesser) interest that lenders demand on longer-term securities.

mixed ratio A financial ratio that includes variables from both the income statement and from the balance sheet.

moderate working capital financing approach An approach in which a firm finances temporary current assets with short-term funds and permanent current

assets and fixed assets with long-term funds.

Modigliani and Miller dividend theory A theory developed by financial theorists Franco Modigliani and Merton Miller that says the amount of dividends paid by a firm does not affect the firm's value.

money market The market where short-term securities are traded.

mortgage bond A bond secured by real property.

multinational corporation (MNC) A corporation that has operations in more than one country.

municipal bonds Bonds issued by a state, city, county, or other nonfederal government authority, including specially created municipal authorities such as a toll road or industrial development authority.

mutually exclusive projects A group of projects that compete against each other; only one of the mutually exlusive projects may be chosen.

mutuals Institutions (savings and loans or insurance companies for example) that are owned by their depositors or policy holders.

negotiable CDs A deposit security issued by financial institutions that comes in minimum denominations of $100,000 and can be traded in the money market.

net present value (NPV) The estimated change in the value of the firm that would occur if a project is accepted.

net working capital The amount of current assets minus the amount of current liabilities of an economic unit.

nominal interest rate The rate observed in the financial marketplace that includes the real rate of interest and various premiums.

nominal risk-free rate of interest The interest rate without any premiums for the uncertainties associated with lending.

nondiversifiable risk The portion of a portfolio's total risk that cannot be eliminated by diversifying. Factors shared to a greater or lesser degree by most assets in the market, such as inflation and interest rate risk, cause nondiversifiable risk.

non-simple project A project that has a negative initial cash flow, and also has one or more negative future cash flows.

NPV profile A graph that displays how a project's net present value changes as the discount rate, or required rate of return, changes.

open-market operations The buying and selling of U.S. Treasury securities or foreign currencies to achieve some economic objective.

operating lease A lease that has a term substantially shorter than the useful life of the asset and is usually cancelable by the lessee.

operating leverage The effect of fixed operating costs on operating income; because of fixed costs, any change in sales results in a larger percentage change in operating income.

opportunity cost The cost of foregoing the best alternative to make a competing choice.

optimal capital budget The list of all accepted projects and the total amount of their initial cash outlays.

over-the-counter market A network of dealers around the world who purchase securities and maintain inventories of securities for sale.

par value The stated value of a share of common stock.

partnership An unincorporated business owned by two or more people.

payback period The expected amount of time a capital budgeting project will take to generate cash flows that cover the project's initial cash outlay.

payment date The date the transfer agent sends out a company's dividend checks.

pension fund A financial institution that takes in funds for workers, invests those funds, and then provides for a retirement benefit.

permanent current assets The minimum level of current assets maintained.

perpetuity An annuity that has an infinite maturity.

portfolio A collection of assets that are managed as a group.

preemptive right A security given by some corporations to existing stockholders that gives them the right to buy new shares of common stock at a below-market price until a specified expiration date.

preferred stock A security issued by a corporation with a given dividend to be paid before any dividends are paid to holders of the firm's common stock.

present value Today's value of promised or expected future value.

present value interest factor for a single amount (PVIF) The $1/(1 + k)^n$ factor that is multiplied by a given future value, to solve for the present value.

present value interest factor for an annuity (PVIFA) The factor, which when multiplied by an expected annuity payment, gives you the present value of the annuity stream:

$$\frac{1 - \dfrac{1}{(1 + k)^n}}{k}$$

primary market The market where newly issued securities are sold to the public.

primary reserves Vault cash and deposits at the Fed that go toward meeting a bank's reserve requirements.

principal A person who authorizes an agent to act for him or her.

private corporation A corporation that does not offer its shares to the general public and that can keep its financial statements confidential.

pro forma financial statements Projected financial statements.

progressive tax rate structure A tax structure under which the tax rate increases as taxable income increases usually in a pattern of several steps.

promissory note A legal document the borrower signs indicating agreement to the terms of a loan.

proprietorship A business that is not incorporated and is owned by one person.

prospectus A disclosure document given to a potential investor when a new-security is issued.

publicly traded corporations Corporations that have common stock that can be bought in the marketplace by any interested party and that must release audited financial statements to the public.

pure time value of money The value demanded by an investor to compensate for the postponement of consumption.

putable bonds Bonds that can be redeemed before the scheduled maturity date, at the option of the bondholder.

quota A quantity limit imposed by one country on the amount of a given good that can be imported from another country.

real rate of interest The rate that the market offers to lenders to compensate for postponing consumption.

refunding Issuing new bonds to replace old bonds.

relative purchasing power parity theory A theory that states that as prices change in one country relative to those prices in another country, for a given traded basket of similar goods and services, the exchange rate will tend to change proportionately but in the opposite direction.

required reserve ratio The percentage of deposits that determines the amount of reserves a financial institution is required to hold.

residual income Income left over, and available to common stockholders, after all other claimants have been paid.

restrictive covenants Promises made by the issuer of a bond to the investor, to the benefit of the investor.

rights-on A characteristic of common stock such that it is trading *with* the entitlement to an upcoming right.

risk The potential for unexpected events to occur.

risk-adjusted discount rate (RADR) A required rate of return adjusted to compensate for the effect a project has on a firm's risk.

risk aversion A tendency to avoid risk that explains why most investors require a higher expected rate of return the more risk they assume.

risk-free rate of return The rate of return that investors demand in order to take on a project that contains no risk other than an inflation premium.

risk-return relationship The positive relationship between the risk of an investment and an investor's required rate of return.

sales breakeven point The level of sales that must be achieved such that operating income equals zero.

savings and loan associations (S&Ls) Financial institutions that take in deposits and make loans (primarily mortgage loans).

second mortgage A mortgage bond (a bond secured by real property) that gives the holder second claim (after the first mortgage bondholder) on the real property pledged as security.

secondary market The market where previously issued securities are traded from one investor to another.

secondary reserves Marketable securities that can be readily sold to obtain cash.

secured bond A bond backed by specific assets that the investor may claim if there is a default.

security A document that establishes the bearer's claim to receive funds in the future.

self-liquidating loan A loan that is used to acquire assets that generate enough cash to pay off the loan.

senior debenture An unsecured bond having a superior claim on the earnings and assets of the issuing firm relative to other debentures.

serial payments A mode of payment where the issuer pays off bonds according to a staggered maturity schedule.

signaling The message sent by managers, or inferred by investors, when a financial decision is made.

signaling dividend theory A theory that says that dividend payments often send a signal from the management of a firm to market participants.

simple project A project that has a negative initial cash flow, followed by positive cash flows only.

sinking fund A method for retiring bonds. The bond issuer makes regular contributions to a fund that the trustee uses to buy back outstanding bonds and retire them.

spot rate The exchange rate for current delivery.

stakeholder A party having an interest in a firm (for example, owners, workers, management, creditors, suppliers, customers, and the community as a whole).

standard deviation A statistic that indicates how widely dispersed actual or possible values are distributed around a mean.

stated interest rate The interest rate advertised by the lender. Depending on the terms of the loan, the stated rate may or may not be the same as the effective interest rate.

statement of retained earnings A financial statement that shows how the value of retained earnings changes from one point in time to another.

stock Certificates of ownership interest in a corporation.

stock dividend A firm sends out new shares of stock to existing stockholders and makes an accounting transfer from retained earnings to the common stock and capital in excess of par accounts of the balance sheet.

stock split A firm gives new shares of stock to existing shareholders; on the balance sheet, they decrease the par value of the common stock proportionately to the increase in the number of shares outstanding.

straight bond value The value a convertible bond would have if it did not offer the conversion option to the investor.

straight-line depreciation A depreciation rule that allows equal amounts of the cost of an asset to be allocated over the asset's life.

strengthening currency A currency that is now convertible into a larger number of units of another currency than previously.

Subchapter S corporation A small corporation whose income is taxed like a partnership.

subordinated debenture An unsecured bond having an inferior claim on the earnings and assets of the issuing firm relative to other debentures.

sunk costs A cost that must be borne whether a proposed capital budgeting project is accepted or rejected.

surplus economic unit A business, household, or government unit with income greater than its expenditures.

syndicate A temporary alliance of investment banking firms that is formed for the purpose of underwriting a new security issue.

target stock A class of common stock that represents a claim on a part of company.

tariff A tax imposed by one country on imports from another country.

temporary current assets That portion of current assets that fluctuates during the company's business cycle.

10-K reports An audited set of financial statements submitted annually by all public corporations to the Securities and Exchange Commission (SEC).

10-Q reports An unaudited set of financial statements submitted quarterly by all public corporations to the Securities and Exchange Commission (SEC).

time value of money The phenomenon whereby money is valued more highly the sooner it is received.

trade credit Funds obtained by delaying payment to suppliers.

transaction cost The cost of making a transaction, usually the cost associated with purchasing or selling a security.

transfer agent A party, usually a commercial bank, that keeps track of changes in stock ownership, collects cash from a company, and pays dividends to its stockholders.

treasurer The manager responsible for financial planning, fund raising, and allocation of money in a business.

Treasury bills Securities issued by the federal government in minimum denominations of $10,000 in maturities of three, six, or twelve months.

Treasury bonds and notes Securities issued by the federal government that make semi-annual coupon interest payments and pay the face value at maturity. Treasury notes come in maturities of one to ten years. Treasury bonds come in maturities of more than ten years.

trend analysis Where something (such as a financial ratio) is examined over time so as to discern any changes.

trustee The party that oversees a bond issue and makes sure all the provisions set forth in the indenture are carried out.

uncertainty The chance, or probability, that outcomes other than what is expected will occur.

underwriting The process by which investment banking firms purchase a new security issue in its entirety and resell it to investors. The risk of the new issue is transferred from the issuing company to the investment bankers.

unitary tax A tax assessed by a state on the earnings of a foreign corporation.

variable costs Costs that vary with the level of production.

variable rate bonds Bonds that have periodic changes in their coupon rates, usually tied to changes in market interest rates.

warrant A security that gives the holder the option to buy a certain number of shares of common stock of the issuing company, at a certain price, for a specified period of time.

weakening currency A currency that is now convertible into a smaller number of units of another currency than previously.

wealth Assets minus liabilities.

weighted average cost of capital (k_a) or (WACC) The average of all the component costs of capital, weighted according to the percentage of each component in the firm's optimal capital structure.

working capital Another name for the current assets on a firm's balance sheet.

yield to maturity (YTM) The investor's return on a bond, assuming that all promised interest and principal payments are made on time and the interest payments are reinvested at the YTM rate.

zero-coupon bonds Bonds that pay face value at maturity and that pay no coupon interest.

TABLE III
Future Value Interest Factors for an Annuity, FVIFA, Compounded at k Percent for n Periods: $FVIFA_{k,n} = \sum_{t=1}^{n}(1+k)^{n-t} = \dfrac{(1+k)^n - 1}{k}$ (for non-zero k)

Interest Rate, k

Number of Annuity Pmts., n	0%	1%	2%	3%	4%	5%	6%	7%	8%	9%	10%	12%	14%	16%	18%	20%	25%	30%	35%	40%	45%	50%
1	1.0000	1.0000	1.0000	1.0000	1.0000	1.0000	1.0000	1.0000	1.0000	1.0000	1.0000	1.0000	1.0000	1.0000	1.0000	1.0000	1.0000	1.0000	1.0000	1.0000	1.0000	1.0000
2	2.0000	2.0100	2.0200	2.0300	2.0400	2.0500	2.0600	2.0700	2.0800	2.0900	2.1000	2.1200	2.1400	2.1600	2.1800	2.2000	2.2500	2.3000	2.3500	2.4000	2.4500	2.5000
3	3.0000	3.0301	3.0604	3.0909	3.1216	3.1525	3.1836	3.2149	3.2464	3.2781	3.3100	3.3744	3.4396	3.5056	3.5724	3.6400	3.8125	3.9900	4.1725	4.3600	4.5525	4.7500
4	4.0000	4.0604	4.1216	4.1836	4.2465	4.3101	4.3746	4.4399	4.5061	4.5731	4.6410	4.7793	4.9211	5.0665	5.2154	5.3680	5.7656	6.1870	6.6329	7.1040	7.6011	8.1250
5	5.0000	5.1010	5.2040	5.3091	5.4163	5.5256	5.6371	5.7507	5.8666	5.9847	6.1051	6.3528	6.6101	6.8771	7.1542	7.4416	8.2070	9.0431	9.9544	10.9456	12.0216	13.1875
6	6.0000	6.1520	6.3081	6.4684	6.6330	6.8019	6.9753	7.1533	7.3359	7.5233	7.7156	8.1152	8.5355	8.9775	9.4420	9.9299	11.2588	12.7560	14.4384	16.3238	18.4314	20.7813
7	7.0000	7.2135	7.4343	7.6625	7.8983	8.1420	8.3938	8.6540	8.9228	9.2004	9.4872	10.0890	10.7305	11.4139	12.1415	12.9159	15.0735	17.5828	20.4919	23.8534	27.7255	32.1719
8	8.0000	8.2857	8.5830	8.8923	9.2142	9.5491	9.8975	10.2598	10.6366	11.0285	11.4359	12.2997	13.2328	14.2401	15.3270	16.4991	19.8419	23.8577	28.6640	34.3947	41.2019	49.2578
9	9.0000	9.3685	9.7546	10.1591	10.5828	11.0266	11.4913	11.9780	12.4876	13.0210	13.5795	14.7757	16.0853	17.5185	19.0859	20.7989	25.8023	32.0150	39.6964	49.1526	60.7428	74.8867
10	10.0000	10.4622	10.9497	11.4639	12.0061	12.5779	13.1808	13.8164	14.4866	15.1929	15.9374	17.5487	19.3373	21.3215	23.5213	25.9587	33.2529	42.6195	54.5902	69.8137	89.0771	113.330
11	11.0000	11.5668	12.1687	12.8078	13.4864	14.2068	14.9716	15.7836	16.6455	17.5603	18.5312	20.6546	23.0445	25.7329	28.7551	32.1504	42.5661	56.4053	74.6967	98.7391	130.162	170.995
12	12.0000	12.6825	13.4121	14.1920	15.0258	15.9171	16.8699	17.8885	18.9771	20.1407	21.3843	24.1331	27.2707	30.8502	34.9311	39.5805	54.2077	74.3270	101.841	139.235	189.735	257.493
13	13.0000	13.8093	14.6803	15.6178	16.6268	17.7130	18.8821	20.1406	21.4953	22.9534	24.5227	28.0291	32.0887	36.7862	42.2187	48.4966	68.7596	97.6250	138.485	195.929	276.115	387.239
14	14.0000	14.9474	15.9739	17.0863	18.2919	19.5986	21.0151	22.5505	24.2149	26.0192	27.9750	32.3926	37.5811	43.6720	50.8180	59.1959	86.9495	127.913	187.954	275.300	401.367	581.859
15	15.0000	16.0969	17.2934	18.5989	20.0236	21.5786	23.2760	25.1290	27.1521	29.3609	31.7725	37.2797	43.8424	51.6595	60.9653	72.0351	109.687	167.286	254.738	386.420	582.982	873.788
16	16.0000	17.2579	18.6393	20.1569	21.8245	23.6575	25.6725	27.8881	30.3243	33.0034	35.9497	42.7533	50.9804	60.9250	72.9390	87.4421	138.109	218.472	344.897	541.988	846.324	1311.68
17	17.0000	18.4304	20.0121	21.7616	23.6975	25.8404	28.2129	30.8402	33.7502	36.9737	40.5447	48.8837	59.1176	71.6730	87.0680	105.931	173.636	285.014	466.611	759.784	1228.17	1968.52
18	18.0000	19.6147	21.4123	23.4144	25.6454	28.1324	30.9057	33.9990	37.4502	41.3013	45.5992	55.7497	68.3941	84.1407	103.740	128.117	218.045	371.518	630.925	1064.70	1781.85	2953.78
19	19.0000	20.8109	22.8406	25.1169	27.6712	30.5390	33.7600	37.3790	41.4463	46.0185	51.1591	63.4397	78.9692	98.6032	123.414	154.740	273.556	483.973	852.748	1491.58	2584.68	4431.68
20	20.0000	22.0190	24.2974	26.8704	29.7781	33.0660	36.7856	40.9955	45.7620	51.1601	57.2750	72.0524	91.0249	115.380	146.628	186.688	342.945	630.165	1152.21	2089.21	3748.78	6648.51
25	25.0000	28.2432	32.0303	36.4593	41.6459	47.7271	54.8645	63.2490	73.1059	84.7009	98.3471	133.334	181.871	249.214	342.603	471.981	1054.79	2348.80	5176.50	11247.199	24040.7	50500.3
30	30.0000	34.7849	40.5681	47.5754	56.0849	66.4388	79.0582	94.4608	113.283	136.308	164.494	241.333	356.787	530.312	790.948	1181.88	3227.17	8729.99	23221.6	60501.1	154107	383500
35	35.0000	41.6603	49.9945	60.4621	73.6522	90.3203	111.435	138.237	172.317	215.711	271.024	431.663	693.573	1120.71	1816.65	2948.34	9836.76	32422.9	104136	325400	987794	2912217
40	40.0000	48.8864	60.4020	75.4013	95.0255	120.800	154.762	199.635	259.057	337.882	442.593	767.091	1342.03	2360.76	4163.21	7343.86	30088.7	120393	466960	1750092	6331512	22114663
45	45.0000	56.4811	71.8927	92.7199	121.029	159.700	212.744	285.749	386.506	525.859	718.905	1358.23	2590.56	4965.27	9531.58	18281.3	91831.5	447019	2093876	9412424	40583319	167933233
50	50.0000	64.4632	84.5794	112.797	152.667	209.348	290.336	406.529	573.770	815.084	1163.91	2400.02	4994.52	10435.6	21813.1	45497.2	280256	1659761	9389020	50622288	260128295	1275242998